THE AMERICANS
An Economic Record

THE
AMERICANS
An Economic Record

STANLEY LEBERGOTT
Wesleyan University

W. W. NORTON & COMPANY
New York   London

Published simultaneously in Canada by Stoddart Publishing, a subsidiary of General Publishing Company Ltd., Don Mills, Ontario.

PRINTED IN THE UNITED STATES OF AMERICA.

This book is composed in Janson. Composition by Publications Company. Manufacturing by The Maple-Vail Book Manufacturing Group. Book design by Nancy Dale Muldoon.

First Edition

ISBN 0-393-01823-7

ISBN 0-393-95311-4 (pbk.)

W.W. Norton & Company, Inc.
500 Fifth Avenue, New York, N.Y. 10110
W.W. Norton & Company, Ltd.
10 Coptic Street, London WC1A 1PU

2 3 4 5 6 7 8 9 0

FOR R—

"Etre avec les gens qu'on aime, cela suffit: revêr, leur parler, ne leur parler point, penser à eux, penser à des choses plus indifférentes, mais auprès d'eux, tout est égal."

He asserts that . . . the only proper subject of enquiry is "not how we got into this difficulty, but how we are to get out of it." In other words, we are . . . to consult our invention, and to reject our experience.
— EDMUND BURKE, Speech on American Taxation

The past gives us our vocabulary and fixes the limits of our imagination; we cannot get away from it. . . . [But] historic continuity with the past is not a duty, it is only a necessity.
— OLIVER WENDELL HOLMES. JR., *Learning and Science*

Nothing is more responsible for the good old days than a bad memory.
— FRANKLIN PIERCE ADAMS

Contents

Introduction   1

PART ONE. ORIGINS

1 Beginnings   7
2 The Destruction of the Indians   12
3 A New Nation   25
4 Colonialism   30
5 The American Revolution   39
6 Confederation and Constitution   48

PART TWO. 1783 1860

7 The Economic Problem, 1783–1860   59
8 Land Policy and Public Domain   74
9 Westward Ho   85
10 Transport   91
11 Finance and Investment   114
12 Manufacturing   124
13 The Tariff   139
14 Technology and Industrialization   162
15 Immigration   178
16 Population   191
17 Regional Growth   198
18 Slavery   210
19 The Hinge of Fate   226

PART THREE. 1860–1900

20 The Civil War   233
21 Reconstruction   249
22 The Land   268
23 The Railroads: After the War   277
24 Competition and Revolt   297
25 Oil   322
26 Immigration   337
27 Technology and Innovation   345
28 Urban Growth   357
29 Labor   366
30 Cycles and Depressions   388

PART FOUR: THE TWENTIETH CENTURY

31 The Transition   403
32 Conservation   410
33 The Technology of Dreams: The 1920s   431
34 Crash and Depression   444
35 The New Deal   453
36 War and Postwar Transition   466
37 The Greater Society   477

PART FIVE: PAST AND PRESENT

38 Effort and Return: The Content of Growth   489
39 Problems of the 1930s and Their Outcomes   494
40 Present and Past: The Costs of Growth   502

   Index   527

List of Figures

1.1 World Population Growth

5.1 Price Inflation, 1776–80

12.1 Tonnage in Foreign Trade and Number of
Factories Incorporated, Massachusetts, 1808–16

13.1 Tariffs versus Freight Costs, 1821–60

16.1 U.S. Fertility Rate

23.1 New York Central Railroad Rates, 1868–69

24.1 Value of Farms per Acre

29.1 Worker Earnings Compared to Net Product per
Person Employed, 1870–1940

30.1 Construction Business Cycle Changes Related to
Population Changes

32.1 Energy Utilization over the Long Run, 1830–1930

32.2 Percent of Homes Heating with Coal, 1940–80

33.1 Automobile Registration, 1929–39

40.1 Inflation: Yearly Percent Change in GNP Deflator, 1947–82

40.2 Fuel Imports

40.3 Life and Death: Long-Term Trends in U.S. Birth and Death
Rates per 1,000 Population, 1821–1979

List of Tables

2.1 Land Requirements by Indian Tribe
2.2 Annual Food and Acreage Requirements of European Immigrants, 1800
2.3 Land Requirements per Capita

3.1 Per Capita Product, 1975

4.1 British "Burden" on the Colonies, 1763–72
4.2 British "Contributions and Subsidies" to the Colonies, 1763–72
4.3 Tobacco Distribution Costs as Percent of Amsterdam Prices, 1720–72

5.1 Population Gains by Colonial Region

7.1 Annual Rate of Growth of U.S. National Product per Person, 1700–1967
7.2 Growth Rates of U.S. Gross National Product, 1800–1967
7.3 The Labor Force, 1800–1960
7.4 Trends in the Level of Living, 1800–79

8.1 Regional Migration Rates, 1800–1960

10.1 Federal Aid to Internal Improvements, 1802–60
10.2 Net Earnings and Costs of the Illinois Central Railroad, 1855–58
10.3 Pounds of Force Required to Move One Ton, 1800–60
10.4 Freight Speeds and Loads, 1800s
10.5 Passenger Speed, 1840
10.6 Travel Hours Required, New York to Albany, 1817–41

11.1 Stocks Issued by the States

12.1 New Factory Enterprises, 1800–30
12.2 American Cotton Textiles: The Forcing Period, 1802–20
12.3 Manufacturing Beginnings
12.4 Percent of U.S. Consumption Imported, 1810–44
12.5 Advancing Efficiency in Cotton Textiles, 1820–59
12.6 Factory Man-hours as Percent of Home Man-hours in the Nineteenth Century
12.7 Percent of U.S. Labor Force in Manufacturing and Agriculture, 1810–60

13.1 The Artificial Ocean, 1815–41
13.2 Number of Cotton and Iron Factories

13.3 Real Price Indices, 1820–60
13.4 Effective and Nominal Tariff Rates for Major Commodities and Activities, 1845
13.5 Tariff Impact on Cotton Income, 1824
B.1 Cost of Ship Construction and Tariff Duties, 1824
B.2 Shipbuilding Duties, 1845
B.3 Cotton Sheeting Duties, 1845
B.4 Cotton Print Duties, 1845

14.1 Cost of Producing Raw Cotton, 1850
14.2 Cotton Picking, 1800–1958
14.3 The Cotton Gin, 1788–1866
14.4 Cotton Bales

16.1 Women by Number of Births
16.2 Rural Fertility and Density
16.3 Women in the Labor Force, 1830–1979
16.4 U.S. Population
16.5 Children Under 5 Years of Age per 1,000 Females

17.1 U.S. Exports
17.2 U.S. Cotton Produced by Region
17.3 Barrels of Flour per Year from Two Regions
17.4 Major Farm Products, 1840–1979
17.5 Income per Farm Worker

18.1 Interest Rates Charged on Slave Sales in New Orleans, 1825–60

19.1 U.S. Population Distribution by Region

20.1 Number of Men Exempted from Confederate Draft, by Cause of Exemption

22.1 Improved Land
22.2 Land Investment Choices, 1870s

23.1 Miles of Railroad Built by Region
23.2 Freight Costs, 1860–80
23.3 Exports, 1850–80
23.4 Freight Rates
23.5 Railroad Costs
23.6 Share of Freight Carried by Transport Method

24.1 Technical Change on Farms, 1850–90
24.2 Farm Productivity Trends, 1800–1980
24.3 Farm Prices Received and Paid
24.4 Percent of Farm Mortgages Paying over 8 Percent Interest, 1890

25.1 Standard Oil Assets and Earnings
25.2 Petroleum Costs and Charges

26.1 Immigration to the United States by Place of Origin
26.2 Immigrants as Percentage of Workers in Selected Occupations
26.3 Average Earnings of Nonfarm Workers

26.4   Occupational Concentration in 1910

27.1   Travel Time from New York to London
27.2   Patents Issued per Decade
27.3   Engineers and Chemists in the Labor Force
27.4   Investment Cost Trends, 1860–1900
27.5   User Cost of Capital, 1860–1900
27.6   Expanding Markets for Electricity
27.7   Electricity Costs, 1880–1970

28.1   Public Facilities in 1902

29.1   Percent of Women in the Labor Force
29.2   U.S. Families Owning Specific Items by Year
29.3   Occupational Concentration Index, 1910–50
29.4   Nonfarm Employees, Annual Earnings, 1900–80
29.5   Union Membership, 1830–1980

30.1   Annual Growth Rates of Investment
30.2   Business Cycle Declines, 1860–1975
30.3   Business Cycle Changes

32.1   Conservation Investment
32.2   Waste Gas as a Percentage of Production
32.3   U.S. Bituminous Coal and Soot, 1869–1969

33.1   Percent of Households with Facilities, 1900–30
33.2   Employee Income and Unemployment, 1900–29
33.3   Productivity and Income Gains, 1889–1929
33.4   Consumer Debt and Purchases, 1899–1939
33.5   Farming and Automobile Industry Performance, 1909–29
33.6   The Stock Market: 1900 to the Crash of 1929

34.1   Deposits in Suspended Banks
34.2   Income Flows, 1929–32

35.1   Unemployment and Public Aid, 1933–40

36.1   Output and Demand, 1945–47
36.2   Economic Expansions and Contractions, 1854–1980

37.1   Farm Incomes, 1940–80
37.2   Distribution of Farm Price Support Payments, 1964

38.1   Homemakers' Time Use, 1900–75
38.2   Consumption Changes, 1900 to 1979

39.1   Unemployment as a Percent of the Labor Force, 1870–1980
39.2   Percent Distribution of Families—by Family Income, 1900–81
39.3   Tax Rates: 1970 Share of Income Taken by Taxes

40.1   Sources of Growth, 1909–81
40.2   Percent of Families (Husband-Wife) with Low Incomes, 1900–79
40.3   Percent in the Lower Tenth, 1910–70—Husband-Wife Families

40.4 Sons' Occupational Status in the 1970s as Compared to Fathers' Occupation
40.5 Oil Consumption
40.6 U.S. Petroleum Consumption
40.7 Lives Saved and Costs
40.8 Worker Fatalities, 1900–79
40.9 Deaths in 1967 Linked to Specified Factors
40.10 Health Expenditures and Death Rate, 1950–80

THE AMERICANS
An Economic Record

Introduction

CHURCHILL, the story goes, once commanded a waiter, "Remove this soup; it has no theme." If American economic history has a single theme it is that of choice. For three centuries immigration selected out the hardiest (and often the most astute) men and women in the world. Who else survived the slave ships from Africa? The long passage from the ghettos of Russia via the Baltic? A dangerous month in steerage from Galway or Palermo? Or the open boats from Cuba or Cambodia? Indeed, the Capitol might well have a plaque dedicated to tyrants from Robespierre and Napoleon to Alexander III, Hitler, and Stalin, as well as to the potato fungus in Ireland and to malaria in Sardinia. For they helped provide the human heritage of America, central to the nation's economic growth.

The immigrants (and their descendants) made their living by a wide variety of farming and production techniques. These techniques were winnowed no less rigorously than the people who used them. Inventions were similarly selected out, by an often bruising competitive process. Men fought to retain their emotional and financial investments. But at most they delayed change. They could not halt it. Such unending and unremitting choice between workers, land locations, and production processes created the new society.

This new society's workers and farmers reached higher real incomes than any other people on earth, achieving less inequality, shorter hours of work, a richer standard of living. Yet Lincoln's somber observation still applied: "We cannot escape history." The new economy was not created from virgin soil and purple mountain majesty. It was created by a set of humans, carrying their own personal histories. The competitive choice process limited the impact of moldering values and inherited attitudes. But it did not obliterate them. Much twentieth-century criticism of the United States somehow implies that its economic markets should have enabled it to operate outside its heritage, and even outside history. American society was expected to function without discrimination or discontent, unemployment or poverty, envy or resource consumption. Whether many nations ever did so is an open question. But it is clear that the United States could not have achieved these goals without a different heritage, a different set of humans, and perhaps a different polity and economy as well.

The present study focuses on central issues in U.S. development. Why were the Indians dispossessed so completely? How did U.S. capitalism stagger through more than thirty business depressions? Why did Congress dispose of two billion acres of the public domain so loosely? Why did Americans build machines and railroads that promptly obsolesced while Britons and Germans were building for the ages? Can the endless historic evidence that points to slavery as the center of the Civil War be reconciled with the judgment that slaveholding was not much more profitable than alternative investments, as econometricians contend? Cliometric work agrees with traditional history that merchants and sharecropping held down freedmen's incomes. But straightforward economic analysis raises questions. The cotton textile industry in the United States led the van of industrialization, as it did in many other nations. Why did equally ingenious machinery fail to compete successfully with such other home industries as baking and canning till half a century later? What conserved natural resources in the industrial century before the conservation movement, other than sloth and inaccessibility? Bank deposit insurance is now applauded by liberals and reactionaries alike for preventing loss and panic among small savers. Why was it not adopted before the 1930s? These are among the fascinating questions in American history for which reference to original sources, plus direct economic inquiry, yields new insights.

But there is a further reason for considering them. In their wisdom, the ancient Greeks saw Clio as the "Muse of Prophecy and History."[1] To guide every day's activity we must prophesy. But "we walk backward into the future."[2] Forecasters must look to the past; what other experience is there? Some analysts rely on models with dozens of behavioral equations. But they fit them to data from the past. All analysts choose decisive variables based on their view of the past, giving different weights to particular elements of supply and demand, to the class struggle, to human consciousness. As Sir George Savile wrote long ago, "The best qualification of a Prophet is to have a good memory."

History offers the raw materials for prophecy, but no easy conclusions. The future is not just the past run through again in different costumes. Who would simply rely on past data, even combined through a giant system of equations, to model how long inflation would last? Or how wealth differentials would narrow? Productivity would advance? A resource be exhausted? A powerful statesman once observed that we cannot make "a sound judgment of the facts" simply by looking at the "success or failure of undertakings." But

1. *The Greek Anthology*, III, Book IX, Ep. 505.
2. Paul Valery, "La politique de l'esprit," *Variete III* (1936):228.

he promptly added: "exact knowledge of the situation that provoked them" was essential to understand those outcomes.[3] Only on that premise can the past be prologue.

Historians often award gold stars, or black marks, to the persons and policies of the past. But we assume anyone interested in the complex course of the American economy will share Thoreau's view: "In reading a work on Agriculture, I skip the author's moral reflections, and the words 'Providence' and 'He' scattered along the page, to come at the profitable level of what he has to say."[4]

Much of the data, and Appendix material, used here was worked out in the superb conditions and company provided by the Center for Advanced Study in the Behavioral Sciences, in Stanford, with support from NSF Grant SES 8007179. The drafts of this volume have been meticulously typed into legibility thanks to the heroic skills of Joan Halberg at Wesleyan University and Deanna Dejanne at the Center for Advanced Study.

3. Prince von Metternich, quoted in John Morley, *The Life of William Ewart Gladstone* (1905)1:443.

4. Henry David Thoreau, *Journal* (April 1, 1841).

Part One
ORIGINS

Events have an unknown father; necessity is only their mother.

     —VALERY, *Regards sur le monde Actuel*

1

Beginnings

FOR 30 million centuries the land was without people. Then the glaciers retreated. Perhaps 150 centuries ago wave upon wave of Asian migrants surged across the Bering Strait from what is now Russia. These were the first Americans.[1] Those who eventually reached Latin America built high, bloody, and complex civilizations. Most, however, created simple economies in the colder, inhospitable domain of North America. Entering the northeast and central plains about 100 centuries ago, they attacked the primordial elephant population. Having exterminated the elephant, they shifted their diet largely to the bison.[2] Trade developed as they moved furs and obsidian, copper and textiles, from one part of the continent to another. Such interchanges helped create cultures and societies. Did these interchanges also yield a broad economy, or a rich standard of living? The answer can be surmised from a single fact: After centuries of tribal life in America, the real income of the typical Indian family did not exceed $1 a month, in addition to the food and shelter provided within the family.[3] This tiny figure hardly implies that the Indian hunters lived in misery. Women did nearly all the dull and wearying work, while the men hunted game, fished in well-stocked streams, drank early and rose late. The figure, however, does testify to the fact that the

---

 1. Arthur Jelinek, *"Hunting and Gathering," International Encyclopedia of the Social Sciences*, 7:16.

 2. Wendell Oswalt, *This Land Was Theirs* (1966), pp. 42, 401.

 3. Data in 30th Cong., 1st sess., S. D. 1, *Message of the President* (1847), pp. 848–50, imply an average income of $6 per Indian hunter on the Upper Missouri in 1847—earned chiefly by fur sales. Their money was spent largely for textiles, iron products, and muskets. The fall in the price of textiles and iron since then suggests that an annual figure of $12 (in 1983 prices) is on the high side.

passing centuries had not created a society committed to routine labor and the accumulation of more and more goods—that is, to economic growth. Per capita consumption by the Indians could hardly have been much less 50 centuries earlier. Hence, one common explanation of American economic growth is seen to be inadequate: Growth was not created by the enormous American supply of land, rich mineral reserves, and stimulating climate. A new outlook was requisite: a "taste for toil . . . and the telescopic appreciation of distant gain."[4] But the conquerors from Spain did not provide it.

"They filled the Contracion in Seville with money, and all the world with fame and desire."[5] So observed a seventeenth-century contemporary when the conquerors of Peru returned to Spain. The Spanish and Portugese search for sudden wealth had intensified after Columbus discovered the lake lying at the base of "the terrestrial Paradise."[6] (It was Columbus who declared that "gold is Treasure, and he who possesses it does whatever he wishes in this life, and succeeds in helping souls into Paradise."[7]) But by 1700 Spain had virtually ended its attempt at fortress settlement; gold was notably lacking in most of the areas it had seized and searched.

The society Spain developed in the West was no more committed to labor and the accumulation of goods than the Indian way that it brushed aside. One fur trapper caricatured its people as living "apparently unconscious in the paradise around them. They sleep and smoke and hum Castilian tunes while nature is inviting them to the noblest and richest reward of honorable toil."[8]

Finally, migrants arrived with a different perspective on "honorable toil," and on investment:

> The white man came, pale as the dawn, with a load of thought, with a slumbering intelligence, as a fire raked up . . . not guessing but calculating; strong in community, yielding obedience to authority; . . . of wonderful, wonderful, common sense; dull but capable, slow but persevering, severe but just, of little humor but genuine; a laboring man, despising game and sport, building a house that endures. . . . He buys the Indian's moccasins

---

4. "The restriction on population (among hunters and gatherers) is the lean season or the atypical year. . . Building by the hunters and the accumulation of gains was limited by maturation and technical knowledge, not by time." Sherwood Washburn and C. S. Lancaster, "The Evolution of Hunting," in Richard Lee and Irven DeVore, eds., Man the Hunter (1968), p. 303.

5. Quoted in James Lockhart, The Men of Cajamarca (1972), p. 55.

6. R. H. Major, ed., Select Letters of Christopher Columbus (1847), p. 137.

7. Carl Becker, Progress and Power (1949), p. 79.

8. Quoted in Herman Kroos, American Economic Development (1966), p. 52. But Humboldt saw the northern Mexicans as "busy night and day in honest work." Cf. Walker Wyman and Clifton Kroeber, The Frontier in Perspective (1957), p. 49.

and baskets, then buys his hunting ground . . . at length forgets where he is buried, and plows up his bones.[9]

The European expansion that eventually replaced the natives in North and South America, in Australia, was the work of two powerful forces: One was religion; the other was sex.

In May 1493 Pope Alexander VI drew a straight line across the map from the North Pole to the South. He then gave all America west of that line—north, south, and central—to Ferdinand and Isabella of Spain. He did so "of our own sole largess . . . and fullness of our apostolic power" so that the king and queen could "lead the peoples dwelling in those islands and countries to embrace the Christian religion." He excluded any land already "in the actual possession of any Christian king or prince" but included all heathen and unbelievers.[10] The present value of salvation was, of course, infinite. It was surely worth more to the pagans thus handed to Spain than their land could have been, or independence, or even freedom. Hence, neither the pope, giving, nor Ferdinand and Isabella, receiving, questioned the appropriateness of handing Spain entire nations—to conquer and to lead to grace.

The pope bestowed those heathen east of his demarcation line upon Portugal. Since Spain controlled Portugal from 1581 to 1640, it thereby possessed "most of the world." Its goal for the world was clear. "It can be said," wrote a Spanish commentator, "that the theme of Spanish history in both the 16th and 17th centuries was the catholicization of the world. The peninsula having been conquered for the faith, it remained to conquer the world for Christ."[11]

Coordinate with religion as a motive for European expansion overseas was sex. World population began its historic rise after the catastrophe of the Black Death at the end of the fourteenth century. In the next few centuries parents conceived millions of children without planning particularly for their worldly future (see Figure 1.1). As Bacon wrote:

> When a State grows to an Over-Power it is like a great Flood, that will be sure to overflow. . . . When the World hath . . . peoples who will not marry or generate unless they know they have the means to live . . . there is no Danger of Inundations of People. But when there be great Shoales of

9. Henry Thoreau, "Sunday," in *A Week on the Concord and Merrimack Rivers* (1849). How strangely different the new perspectives were. "We must exhort all Christians to gain all they can, and to save all they can—that is in effect to grow rich." By saving and giving "the more treasure they lay up in heaven." John Wesley, quoted in William Sweet, *Virginia Methodism, A History* (1955), p. 360.

10. Cf. his Bull *Inter Caetera*, reprinted in Frances Davenport, ed., *European Treaties Bearing Upon the History of the United States and Its Dependencies to 1648* (1917), p. 77.

11. Garcia Morente, quoted in Charles H. Carter, *The Secret Diplomacy of the Hapsburgs, 1598–1625* (1964), p. 39.

FIGURE 1.1
WORLD POPULATION GROWTH

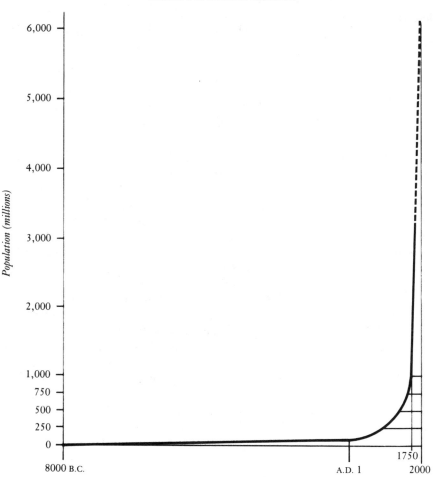

Source: John Durand, "The Modern Expansion of World Population," *Proceedings of the American Philosophical Society*, vol. III, no. 3 (June 22, 1967).

> People who go on to populate without foreseeing their Means of Life and Sustenance, it is inevitable that once in an Age or two, they discharge a Portion of their People upon other nations: Which the ancient Northern People were wont to do by Lot: casting Lots, what Part should stay at home, and what should seek their Fortunes.[12]

The accumulation of peoples by the eighteenth century, however, did not lead Europeans to cast lots designating who should emigrate. Such

12. Francis Bacon, "Of Vicissitude of Things," *Essays* (1625).

colonizing had ceased with the ancient Greeks and Romans. Instead, millions of poverty-stricken and restless failures left in an unplanned exodus. They followed a handful of earnest religious leaders and believers, entrepreneurs and gold seekers, who had shown the way. The attractions were clear. As Crèvecoeur wrote of America:

> The European does not find, as in Europe, a crowded society where every place is overstocked; he does not feel that . . . difficulty of beginning. . . . There is room for everybody, in America. Has he any particular talent, or industry? He exerts it in order to procure a livelihood, and it succeeds. . . . Is he a laborer, sober and industrious? He need not go many miles . . . before he will be hired, well fed . . . and paid four or five times more than he can get in Europe.[13]

This is not to suggest that such opportunities proved important to many Europeans. In no century did more than 1 percent of the European population move across the Atlantic. The United States in 1783 was a mere sideshow in world history, trivial not merely to the Melanesians and the Ashanti but to Europeans and Asians as well. Literate people who spoke of the "United States" were more likely to be referring to Holland than North America. The most ancient international organization in the world put Maryland, Alabama, and Mississippi in the Diocese of Baltimore, oblivious to the fact that the Diocese of Norfolk (i.e., Virginia), and of Charleston (i.e., South Carolina), came between them.[14] Queen Victoria, with the world's best-informed Foreign Office, was confident that bowie knives were "made entirely for Americans, who never move without one."[15] In time even royalty learned somewhat more of American character and conflicts. Meanwhile, the nation was taking the usual first step to nationhood—by displacing its predecessors.

---

13. [Hector St. John] de Crèvecoeur, *Letters from an American Farmer* (1782), Letter 3.

14. Thomas O'Gorman, *A History of the Roman Catholic Church in the United States* (1899), p. 301. O'Gorman comments: "Evidently the Irish bishops and the Propaganda were not well up in the geography of the United States."

15. Quoted in C.R. Fay, *Palace of Industry, 1851* (1951), p. 52.

> Ignorant how dear the knowledge of our corruptions will
> one day cost their repose, security and happiness, and
> how their ruin shall proceed from this commerce, which
> . . . is already well advanced [given their] desire for new
> fangled novelties.[1]
>
> —MONTAIGNE, *Essays*

2

The Destruction of the Indians

OF the two-hundred-odd nation states in the modern world, almost every one established its present system of central government long after its farming peoples had obliterated the hunters and fishers within its borders.[2] Most had been destroyed, or driven off, by superior technology[3] centuries before the Etruscans first entered the Roman marshes. "Ever since the origin of agriculture Neolithic peoples have been steadily expanding at the expense of the hunters."[4] Even the remembrance of those peoples vanished centuries before the ancient Princes of Vladimir first saw Moscow or Charlemagne ruled in Aachen. Of those millions of hunters and fishers, does a single epic of heroic resistance survive? Of the struggles when the present European and Asian peoples drove away their hunting and fishing predecessors is there record or count?

Late archaic life in America, however, ended in the sight of historians. We therefore know far more of its battles, sorrows, and choices than similar

1. Montaigne was writing about "cannibals" brought to sixteenth-century France, presumably from the New World.

2. "When the Indo-Germans migrated to Europe they expelled the aboriginal inhabitants by *force* and tilled the land, which was owned by the community," Friedrich Engels, *Anti-Duhring* (reprint ed. 1962), p. 480.

3. "Rudimentary iron technology, and knowledge of cereal agriculture [provided] the basis of [Bantu] success over earlier hunting, gathering and tenously agricultural peoples." Ronald Oliver, "Problems of Bantu Expansion," *Journal of African History* (1966), p. 367.

4. Richard B. Lee and Irven DeVore, eds., "Problems in the Study of Hunters and Gatherers," *Man the Hunter* (1968), p. 5.

experiences throughout Europe, Asia, and Africa. The Indian population of the Americas when Columbus arrived was largely wiped out in subsequent decades by disease and conflict under Spanish rule. (The 25 million people of Central Mexico in 1492 declined to less than 1 million by 1620.[5]) When Plymouth plantation began, in 1620, ministers viewed the scantiness of the Indian population around them as cogent testimony that the Lord had provided room for the immigrants.[6]

The new settlers faced hunting and fishing peoples with land requirements fully as great as their own European hunting ancestors' many thousands of years earlier.[7] But the land needs of the new immigrants were drastically smaller. That difference proved all-important in the resultant conflict, and the later growth of the United States.

How extensive were the land requirements of the American Indians? "In savage life, one hunter for every square mile is deemed by those people a full stock; when there are more, they say, it is time for our young men to go to war, or we shall starve."[8] Volney quoted an astute Indian chief:

> We must have a great deal of ground to live upon. A deer will serve us but a couple of days, and a single deer must have a great deal of ground to put him in good condition. If we kill two or three hundred a year, 'tis the same as to eat all the wood and grass of the land they live on, and that is a great deal.[9]

More precise measures of Indian land requirements can be determined by totaling the land cessions made by various tribes in treaty with the United States plus the acreage still claimed by them after the cessions (Table 2.1).

How do these land requirements contrast with those in Europe? From 1700 to 1840, when most Indians were displaced, the major migrant streams came from Ireland, Scotland, and England. They constituted the hard core of the frontier groups who fought the Indians—the Paxton boys in western Pennsylvania, the Regulators in North Carolina, the settlers who pioneered through the Cumberland Gap into Kentucky, Tennessee, and Georgia. To what size farms were they accustomed?

5. Sherburne Cook and Woodrow Borah, *Essays in Population History: Mexico and California* (1979), pp. 1, 100. Though authoritative, this estimate is extreme, according to some writers.

6. George E. Ellis, *The Puritan Age and Rule* (1888), p. 279: [William] *Bradford's History "of Plimoth Plantation"* (1898), p. 123. Squanto's people "being dead in ye late great mortalitie . . . about three years before ye coming of ye English, wherein thousands of them dyed."

7. Appendix A, this chapter.

8. Samuel Blodget, *Economica* (1806; reprint ed., 1964), p. 87.

9. C. F. Volney, *A View of the Soil and Climate of the United States of America* (1804), p. 384. "A white man gathers from a field, a few times bigger than this room, bread enough for a whole year," the chief added. Volney surmised that "a thousand acres a head, in a fruitful country, is a scanty allowance for Indian population."

TABLE 2.1
LAND REQUIREMENTS BY INDIAN TRIBE

	Tribal population, 1825 (000)	Acreage (000,000)		
		Ceded to 1820	Claimed in 1825	Total requirements
Chippewa, Ottawa, Wyandot, etc.	33	37	17	54
Sac, Fox, Kaskasias	6	19	5	24
Osage	5	58	3	61
Quapaw	1	31	—	31
Cherokee, Creek, Choctaw, Chickasaw	54	60	43	103

Source: Appendix B, this chapter.

When the Irish diet began to fix primarily on the potato, the acreage required fell rapidly.[10] An 1835 *Prize Essay on the Potato* indicated that one acre could grow the food for six persons, and it is this figure that a recent specialist accepted after surveying a morass of evidence.[11] To the potato consumption figure he added a daily average of one pint of milk per person to derive the typical diet.[12] Now, one acre yielded about 300 bushels of potatoes.[13] Hence, well under a half-acre per person more than accommodated the typical Irish consumer (in potatoes and in hay for the cow).

Scots farms averaged 5 arable acres in the highlands from which migration to the United States was heaviest.[14] A generous estimate of land requirements in Ireland and Scotland would therefore be two acres per capita. (Cantillon estimated 1.5 acres per adult male in eighteenth-century France.[15]) A half-acre allotment provided enough potatoes for an English family in the early 1840s.[16] Hence (after allowing for land to provide barley,

10. Near the end of the eighteenth century Sir John Sinclair estimated that in Ireland an acre of potatoes could feed nine persons. Blodget, *Economica*, p. 92.

11. K. H. Connell, *The Population of Ireland, 1750–1845* (1950), p. 123, cf. also pp. 122, 150. A daily consumption rate of 9 pounds per person was estimated.

12. A knowledgeable contemporary physician estimated similar consumption figures: 4.75 pounds of potatoes twice a day plus about 2.5 quarts of milk. B. Phillips, *Scrofula* (1846), p. 177.

13. William Cobbett, *Cottage Economy* (1833), p. 42, estimates 300 bushels of potatoes per acre (56 pounds per bushel) as compared with 32 bushels of wheat per acre. The same figure appears in A. Austin *Reports of Special Assistant Poor Law Commissioners on the Employment of Women and Children in Agriculture* (1843).

14. Malcolm Gray, *The Highland Economy, 1750–1850* (1957), pp. 24, 25, 251. Henry Hamilton, *An Economic History of Scotland* (1963), pp. 14–15. Hamilton implies that 20 to 60 acres was typical of the lowlands (p. 85).

15. Joseph Spengler, "Cantillon," *Journal of Political Economy* (August 1954), p. 289.

16. See Appendix C, this chapter.

hops, wheat, and animal feed), the requirements in England would also have come to less than 2 acres per capita.

What about these Europeans in America? The inroads against Indian culture were begun by the first settlers with their "few acres" planted. How much land did they use to establish themselves? In 1786 Benjamin Rush described the "first settler in the woods" as

> a man who has outlived credit or fortune in the cultivated parts of the state. He builds a log cabin, girdles some trees, feeds his cows on wild grass, plants a few acres, feeds his family with wild animals, and in his intercourse with the world, manifests all the arts which characterize the Indians of our country. [Above all he] revolts against the operation of laws. . . . The first settler is nearly related to an Indian in his manner. . . . It is to the third species of settlers only that it is proper to apply the term farmers.[17]

The European civilization that moved inland with Boone, for example, produced something like 21 bushels of corn per acre.[18] This yield can be matched against the corn required to feed the average immigrant (directly and as pork and whiskey) and his horse (Table 2.2).

TABLE 2.2
ANNUAL FOOD AND ACREAGE REQUIREMENTS
OF EUROPEAN IMMIGRANTS, 1800

| | Consumption | | |
Food	Per man	Per horse	Acreage
Pork	180 lbs		1.0
Corn meal	365 lbs		0.3
Hay		2 tons	} 0.5
Grain		50 bushels	

Source: Appendix E, F, this chapter.

The typical European immigrant therefore required about 2 acres to provide his food and whiskey, plus food for his horse.[19] The figure is not far distant from that for other peasant cultures (Table 2.3).

European settlers required fantastically less land than the largely hunting and fishing peoples with whom they came into conflict (Table 2.3). Even

17. L. M. Butterfield, ed., *Letters of Benjamin Rush* (1951), 1:400–02. Rush's description was written in 1786. An obvious parallel appears in Frederick Jackson Turner's description a century later.

18. See Appendix D, this chapter. Even after two centuries of further cultivation and erosion, Tennessee averaged 25 to 30 bushels per acre.

19. For this and the following data, see Appendix E, F, this chapter.

TABLE 2.3
LAND REQUIREMENTS PER CAPITA

Country	Acres
Europe, Mesolithic era	5,000
China, 1770	3 ½
Scotland, Ireland, England, 1750–1850	2
United States, 1750–1850	
European immigrants	2
United States, 1800–1825	
Chippewa, Ottawa	1,600
Cherokee, Creek	1,900
Sac, Fox, Kaskaskia	4,000
Osage	12,000

Source: Appendix F, this chapter.

ignoring the Osage claims, Indians required 1,000 to 2,000 times as much land for their near Mesolithic ways of life as did the European migrants. (In the 1950s the Cree Indians of Quebec required 260 square miles per hunter, i.e., per family.) Allowance for the new cities only added something like an additional one-tenth of an acre.[20] The newer European immigrants were, therefore, prepared to use land 1,000 times more economically than the descendants of earlier Asian immigrants.

The eventual conflict did not, of course, arise because the Indians' technology proved significantly inferior. The Indians farmed at least as efficiently as the first settlers—to whom, indeed, they taught basic farming.[21]

But an epochal transition occurred when a way of life requiring deer and buffalo steaks confronted one accepting pig and cattle meat.[22] Given their less land-intensive diet, the newer immigrants could buy up land at rates well above their value in the Indian way of life—yet still retain a wide margin for prospective capital gains.[23] Land used in the European style was worth far more to European immigrants in the seventeenth century and those centuries

20. Appendix G, H, this chapter.

21. Kroeber goes so far as to assert that Indians "derived nearly as many bushels from each acre of planting as we do today." He estimated 15 to 20 bushels for the Indians as compared with 25 to 30 bushels today. A. L. Kroeber, "Native American Population," *American Anthropologist* (January–March 1934), p. 8.

22. J. B. S. Haldane, *Heredity and Politics* (1938), p. 154, quotes Dr. Darre, the German minister of agriculture, to the effect that "the Nordic people . . . gives the pig the highest possible honour. . . . The Semites and the pig are faunal and thus physiological opposites."

23. The statement applies even to areas where a diet of grasshoppers, roots, berries, fish, etc., permitted higher Indian density.

yet to come. The prospect of enormous capital gains from land arose. Speculation should then have occurred to capture such possibilities. It did.

There were, of course, purchases by the European aristocracy. Lord Pulteney bought through agents. Mme. de Staël herself inspected the land (between affairs with internationally known lovers). Assorted counts and barons roved the country in search of select parcels. Yet by far the most important source of land speculation was the average American.

The typical American in the century from, say, 1763 to 1861 was a farmer, and, as such, a land speculator. New England and Mid Atlantic farms averaged from 100 to 150 acres. Massachusetts farms in 1807, according to the Massachusetts Society for Promoting Agriculture, averaged 100 acres.[24] Pennsylvania farms averaged 125 acres. Hence, investment (or speculation, if you will) beyond the immediate family needs of 2 acres per capita accounted for most of the value of typical farms.

The farmer–hunter conflict was put most cogently by de Tocqueville:

> In order to succeed in civilizing a people it is first necessary to settle them permanently, which cannot be done without inducing them to cultivate the soil. . . . Men who have once abandoned themselves to the restless and adventurous life of the hunter feel an insurmountable disgust for the constant and regular labor that tillage requires. We see this proved even in our own societies, but it is far more visible among races whose partiality for the chase is part of their national character. Independently of this general difficulty, there is another, which applies peculiarly to the Indians. They consider labor not merely an evil, but as a disgrace; so that their pride contends against civilization as obstinately as their indolence.[25]

Volney described the Indians' position:

> In all tribes there still exists a generation of old warriors who cannot forbear, when they see their countrymen using the hoe, from exclaiming against the degradation of ancient manners and asserting that the savages owe their decline to these innovations.[26]

Beyond the harsh conflict between Mesolithic and settled agricultural cultures another force was at work: the feeling among farming people that the land must be put to use. This bias is ancient and ubiquitous. In 58 A.D. the Romans fought the Ampsivarri because the latter claimed the right to occupy lands along the Rhine that the Romans owned but did not cultivate.[27] In 1780 Charles III issued a cedula asserting his intention to see "that the present

---

24. For this and following estimate, see Appendix J, this chapter.
25. Alexis de Tocqueville, *Democracy in America* (1948), 1:343.
26. Quoted in ibid.
27. Tacitus, XIII, 54 (Penguin edition, p. 300).

legitimate owners of idle lands [in Spanish America] make them yield their fruit, either by themselves, or by renting them out, or by selling them to others." In 1936 Colombia required "all privately owned lands that remained uncultivated for ten consecutive years" to revert to the public domain.[28] In nineteenth-century Saxony unworked mines were rented out by the state.[29] And a more recent study of the congested centers of Latin America and Asia by a U.N. housing expert not merely urged the virtues of land ownership but proposed that land be given to everyone who migrated to the cities.[30]

Earlier in America the same impulse was at work, even if the phrasing differed. "But what is the right of huntsman to the forest of a thousand miles, over which he has accidentally ranged in quest of prey?" John Quincy Adams, a descendant of English immigrants, asked. "Shall the liberal bounties of Providence . . . be monopolized by one of the ten thousand for which they were created?"[31] And in 1842 a German immigrant wrote:

> Here is the vast American continent, with rich, extensive territories appropriated or declared to be appropriated by certain governments, and by people who in many cases have made no use of the soil or any of its products. . . . If a whole district of land is not used by a nation . . . and if the nation has not been able to protect it as its own for a long time, it seems that the essential characteristics of property are really lost, and disimpropriation has taken place. The earth was given to mankind for use; and if it be left wholly unused, it fails to obtain its object. . . . While other territories are crowded and many over-peopled . . . no mere declaration "This belongs to us" can become a bar against the very destiny of so genial a soil.[32]

In 1845 an Irish immigrant declared:

> There is no such thing as title to the lands of the new world except that which actual possession gives. They belong to whoever will redeem them from the Indian and the desert, and subjugate them to the use of man. . . . Our manifest destiny is to overspread and possess the whole of the continent.[33]

28. Albert Hirschman, *Journeys Toward Progress* (1963), pp. 97, 111.

29. The rent was then turned over to the owner. Cf. John Morley, *Life of Cobden* (1881), p. 297.

30. Charles Abrams, *Man's Struggle for Shelter* (1964), p. 24. "A land policy that would have granted him a site, however small and humble, might have prevented a critical challenge to social and political equilibrium in the underdeveloped areas."

31. John Quincy Adams, *An Oration Delivered at Plymouth, December 22, 1802* (1802), p. 23.

32. Francis Lieber, *Essays on Property and Labour* (1842), pp. 142–50. He continued: "The question respecting Texas must be, perhaps, decided upon this ground: Was or was not the District of Coahuila and Texas unused and unappropriated for a long series of years by the government which claimed it. . . . This vast territory . . . might offer to millions upon millions happy and prosperous homes."

33. John L. O'Sullivan, *New York Morning News*, quoted in Ray Billington, *The Far Western Frontier* (1956), pp. 145, 149.

These remarks by leading members of the three major nationality groups that made up the United States—English, German, Irish—repeat a common theme. That belief was held in principle. It was certainly adopted in practice.

A mystical belief that the land must be farmed, combined with a distrust of those who sought to keep their land unfarmed, characterized American history. Scotch-Irish migrants (early in the eighteenth century) seized lands belonging to the Penns, the Proprietors of Pennsylvania. They declared it "against the laws of God and Nature that so much land should lie idle while so many Christians wanted it to labour on."[34] Minus the references to the Deity, and to religion, the view was repeated by Thomas Jefferson half a century later: "Whenever there is in any country uncultivated lands and unemployed poor, it is clear that the laws of property have been so far extended as to violate natural right. The earth is given as a common stock for man to labor and live on."[35]

But the birth rate among Europeans and Africans far exceeded that of the Indians. That fact guaranteed an endless supply of "unemployed poor" of European origin as immigrants to the United States. The doom of the Indian's land-intensive culture was projected, inevitable.

A final force made for conflict between Europeans and Indians: the method the United States used to pay its military. Nations from Rome to Florence to the Palatine states paid their soldiers by offering them opportunities to sack wealthy towns. They shared out the clothes, the ransoms, and the involuntary services provided by those conquered. But what underdeveloped country such as America could offer an equally attractive option? The American alternative was to promise soldiers a share of the land they conquered.

Virginia led the way. When "Colonel George Clark planned and executed the secret expedition by which the British posts were reduced, he was promised, if the enterprise succeeded, a liberal gratuity in lands in that country for the officers and soldiers who first marched thither with him."[36] In 1790 James O'Fallon, Agent General of the South Carolina Yazoo Company, recruited a battalion to fight near Natchez, promising infantry privates 200 acres of land for service up to eighteen months.[37]

34. J. Logan to the Penns, February 17, 1731, Logan Letterbooks (Historical Society of Pennsylvania). "Peaceable possession . . . of back waste vacant lands is a kind of right" held by "the poor." Cf. Richard Brown and Don Fehrenbacher, *Tradition, Conflict and Modernization* (1977), p. 78.

35. J. P. Boyd, *Papers of Thomas Jefferson* (1933), VIII, p. 19. Jefferson wrote this letter in 1785.

36. As the Virginia House of Delegates stated in 1781. Cf. *American State Papers: Public Lands*, 6:182.

37. Infantry lieutenants were promised 2,000 acres; the colonel-commandant, 6,000. Cf. *American State Papers: Indian Affairs*, 1:115–16.

Years later the founders of the would-be Republic of Texas sought to conquer Coahuila and Texas. Southerners cheered the volunteers forward but were reluctant to buy the new republic's bonds. (Such reluctance was terribly realistic: the Republic of Texas later refused to redeem its bonds.) They then financed the war by promising soldiers part of the land they themselves were to conquer.[38]

The Europeans "spread like oil on a blanket; we melt like snow before the sun. If things do not greatly change, the red men will disappear shortly."[39] So remarked a shrewd old Indian chief. Of course, the red men did not disappear—despite the millions of white, black, and yellow men who now live in the United States. There were as many Indians in 1960 as in 1783.[40] But the land was no longer "his land."

Given these overwhelming and persistent forces, the Indian way of life in North America inevitably came to an end. As Chief Justice Marshall declared in 1831 when the people of the Cherokee Nation sued to restrain the state of Georgia from driving them into exile:

> A people, once numerous, powerful and truly independent, . . . gradually sinking beneath our superior policy, our arts and our arms, have yielded their lands, by successive treaties, each of which contains a solemn guarantee of the residue, until they retain no more of their formerly extensive territory than is deemed necessary to their comfortable subsistence. To preserve this remnant, the present application is made. [If] courts were permitted to indulge their sympathies, a case better calculated to excite them, can scarcely be imagined.[41]

But they were not so permitted. As President Jackson mockingly remarked: "John Marshall has made his decision. Now let him enforce it." The Indians, however, were even more decisively prevented from holding back the power of Georgia by the central fact that two largely different ways of life were in conflict. And, as in Colombia and Brazil, in Switzerland and Russia—indeed,

38. William Gouge, *The Financial History of Texas* (1852), p. 22.

39. Volney, *A View of the Soil and Climate* (1804), p. 384.

40. The aboriginal population about 1500 is presumed to have been "nearly 850,000." Wendell Oswalt, *This Land Was Theirs* (1966), p. 510. The effects of exposure to disease brought by the Spaniards and French is suggested by the population decline in Central Mexico (for which there exist tolerably good measures). The numbers fell from 25 to 3 million between 1518 and 1568, and then to 0.7 by 1620. Cf. Sherburne Cook and Woodrow Borah, *Essays in Population History: Mexico and California* (1979), pp. 1, 100. For the area of what is now the United States, the Indian total in 1820 can be more reliably estimated at about 470,000; by 1960 the U.S. total (excluding Alaska) was about 530,000. Ibid, p. 510, and American Bureau of Ethnology, *Eighteenth Annual Report*, p. 537, and Oswalt, op. cit., p. 510.

41. *Cherokee Nation* v. *State of Georgia*, quoted in James B. Scott, *Judicial Settlement of Controversies between States of the American Union* (1919), pp. 101–02.

in nearly every nation of Europe and the Americas—the hunting and gathering way of life gave way to the European. The hunting and fishing peoples of Asia, Latin America, Africa, and Europe had been largely destroyed centuries before.[42] In the nineteenth century that history was repeated in the new colonies of Australia, Canada, and the United States.

By 1700 two European nations had carved out substantial pieces of North America. France and England confronted each other throughout the eighteenth century in America, as they did in India. At first, the French were sure they would be the final conquerors. (After all, Frenchmen had conquered the Saxons of the British Isles seven centuries earlier.) La Salle took possession of Louisiana "in the name of the most high, mighty, invincible and victorious Prince, Louis the Great."[43] But the French proved vincible, losing the war to the British in 1763. (They did get some of their own back by financing and providing military advisers to the American revolutionaries against the British twenty years later.) The result of "the United war with France and America," as a British journal called the Revolution, "gratified the American colonies with independence."[44] Because neither Britain, France, nor Spain still sought alliance with the Indians against the Americans, the Indians' primary power on this continent inevitably ended. As many developing nations would discover in the twentieth century, the expulsion of ethnic minorities left the new nation with one less scapegoat (real or imaginary) to account for its economic problems.

Appendix

Appendix A

R. J. Braidwood and C. A. Reed suggest 1.25 people per 10 square miles during the Mesolithic adaptation to post-glacial environments, and before mixed food getting plus specialized food collection (which, in turn, preceded village farming): "The Achievement and Early Consequences of Food Production," Cold Spring Harbor Symposia on Quantitative Biology, *Population Studies* (1957), 23:21–22, 24. Referring to A. L. Kroeber ("Native American Population," *American Anthropologist*, January-

42. G. P. Murdock, in "The Current Status" in Lee and DeVore, *Man the Hunter*, Ch. 2, states: "Ten thousand years ago the entire population of the earth subsisted by hunting and gathering." All were subsequently destroyed and/or superseded. He lists the few remaining such peoples, none in Europe.
    Cultural and religious factors that may have been associated with the supersession of the Indians are beyond the scope of an economic history. But one should reference a study given the American Historical Association's Bancroft prize. It contends the Indians had "an alien ideology of land use which is antithetical to the central dogmas of Christianity." Calvin Martin, *Keepers of the Game* (1978), p. 188. Martin's views are reviewed in Shepard Kreech, ed., *Indians, Animals and the Fur Trade* (1981).
43. Isaac J. Cox, ed., *The Journeys of Réné Robert Cavelier Sieur de La Salle* (1905), 1:16.
44. *Gentleman's Magazine* 70 (1800), pt. 1:iv.

March 1934) on the United States and Canada, they suggest that 2.16 persons per 10 square miles is "an overestimate . . . [for] a primitive hunting-collecting people who must depend on a forest environment for survival throughout the winter."

Sir Arthur Keith, *A New Theory of Human Evolution* (1948), p. 270, surmises that 10 square miles per head—i.e., 6,400 acres—were required by Europe's mid-Pleistocene population. Cf. also W. B. Hinsdale, *Primitive Man in Michigan* (1925), p. 16.

Appendix B

Cessions by individual treaty and tribe to 1820 are given in 16th Cong. 2d sess., *Quantity of Land Purchased from Indians . . .* , and in *American State Papers; Public Lands*, 3:461–62. Estimates of the number in each tribe, and the acreage claimed as of 1825, appear in *Plan for Removing the Several Indian Tribes, American State Papers: Indian Affairs*, 2:545–47. Because cessions 1820–25 are not included, we slightly understate Indian land requirements. The 1825 tribal counts are consistent with the variety of figures in John R. Swanton, *The Indian Tribes of North America* (1952).

The data for acreage of Creeks, Cherokees, Choctaw, and Chickasaw are from *American State Papers; Indian Affairs*, 2:499, and *American State Papers: Public Lands*, 3: 623. These provide contemporary and consistent data in a notably confused pattern of overlapping cessions.

Appendix C

"The average produce of an acre of ground, planted with potatoes, may be taken at about 300 bushels. Half an acre of allotment, therefore, will yield enough to give a family 160 pounds of potatoes a week during the whole year, or about 3 pounds a day each to a family of eight persons. . . . In the majority of cases there may be about half an acre to six or seven persons. . . . A portion [is] very commonly used for the growth of other vegetables, and frequently of a little corn." Report of A. Austin on Wilts, Dorset, Devon, and Somerset, in *Reports of Special Assistant Poor Law Commissioners on the Employment of Women and Children in Agriculture* (1843), p. 15.

Appendix D

Corn: J. D. B. De Bow, *Statistical View of the United States* (1854), p. 178, gives census data for Tennessee in 1850 when, if anything, returns were lower than, e.g., 1750. An 1839 U.S. average of 33.5 bushels is estimated by William Parker, "Productivity Growth in Grain Production," in Conference on Research in Income and Wealth, *Output, Employment, and Productivity in the U.S. after 1800* (1966), p. 542.

Tennessee: Andrew R. Aandahl, "Productivity Potential of Selected Soil Types" in Harold Halcrow, ed., *Modern Land Policy, Papers of the Land Economics Institute*, (1960), p. 93. Some farmers produced 52 bushels per acre.

Human consumption: *Niles Weekly Register*, June 28, 1817, and December 2, 1815.

Corn-pork conversion: Illinois Department of Agriculture, *Annual Report, 1871*, p. 361. A bushel of New England Indian corn weighed 61 pounds, yielded 50 pounds of meal. Benjamin Count of Rumford, *Essays, Political, Economical and Philosophical* (1798), 1:175.

Acreage: Hay: Report of the Secretary of the Treasury (1845), p. 194. Oats, De Bow, *Statistical View*, p. 178.

Horses: 50 bushels of grain and 2 tons of hay yearly. Cf. Elkanah Watson, *History of the Rise, Progress and Existing Condition of the Western Canals* (1820), p. 94. One horse could cultivate 12 acres, or six times the area needed to grow food for one person. We therefore estimate one-sixth of the acreage required for hay (at 1 ton per acre) plus one-sixth of that for the horse's grain (at 20 bushels of oats per acre), or, say, half an acre.

Appendix E

We assume that one horse could cultivate 12 acres, assuring food for six persons. The 1.94 acres required per capita is rounded to 2, thereby allowing for corn for whis-key. An average of 4 acres per person, based on lower grain yields, etc., is estimated for Concord, Mass., about 1750 by Robert Cross, *The Minutemen and Their World* (1976), p. 214.

Per capita requirements in China were 3.5 in 1770 (and 3.16 in 1913). D. W. Per-kins, *Agricultural Development in China, 1368–1960* (1969), p. 16. The average in an-cient Rome was 5 acres per family or 14 acres if they kept animals. K. D. White, *Roman Farming* (1970), p. 336.

Appendix F

Based on Tables 2.1, 2.2, and Appendix A. William Denevan has stipulated 1.5 persons per square mile for the tropical interior of South America as the aboriginal population density before European contact. His figure applies to areas of shifting ag-ricultural population under tropical conditions, representing far lower land require-ments than among people largely adapted to a hunting and fishing culture. William Denevan, "The Aboriginal Population of Tropical America: Problems and Methods of Estimation," in Paul Deprez, ed., *Population and Economics* (1970), p. 260.

Appendix G

Quebec: Edward Rogers, *The Quest for Food and Furs* (1973), p. 7. Boyce Richardson, *Strangers Devour the Land* (1976), pp. 322, 366. Glynn Isaac refers to the "relatively low" density of "most nonagricultural human societies—for example, 1 per square mile maximum for Australia," Glynn Isaac, "Traces of Pleistocene Hunters" in Lee and DeVore, *Man the Hunter*, p. 260.

Appendix H

Cities: National Commission on Urban Problems, *Three Land Research Studies*, Re-search Report 12 (1968), p. 12. Cities with 10,000 population in 1960 included more than one-third of the U.S. population. The median city in that group had 1,301 acres per 10,000 population, of which 443 were residential. We assume urban requirements did not reduce rural ones.

Appendix J

Massachusetts: Cf. Massachusetts Society for Promoting Agriculture, *Answers to Agricultural Inquiries* (1807), p. 10, A copy of this study is in the Sturbridge Village

Collection. The range of acreage reported was from 50 to 150. Cf. also Max Shumacher, *The Northern Farmer and His Markets During the Late Colonial Period* (1975), pp. 13, 37. William Cooper, *A Guide to the Wilderness* (1810, reprint ed., 1970), p. 7, refers to typical New York State farms as 100 acres.

Pennsylvania: James T. Lemon, *The Best Poor Man's Country* (1972), p. 89, finds averages in Chester and Lancaster counties (Pa.) of about 125 in 1760 and 1782, with a still higher average around 1710. Cf. also Duane E. Ball, "Dynamics of Population and Wealth in Eighteenth-Century Chester County, Pennsylvania," *Journal of Interdisciplinary History* (Spring 1976), p. 629.

There is America—which . . . serves for little more than
to amuse you with stories of savage men and uncouth
manners; yet shall, before you taste of death, show itself
equal to the whole of that commerce which now attracts
the envy of the world. Whatever England has been growing to . . . in a series of Seventeen Hundred years, you
shall see as much added to her by America in the course
of a single life.

—EDMUND BURKE, *Speech on Conciliation with America*

3

A New Nation

OVER many decades the British colonies in North America recruited
peasants from Europe as settlers, plus a sprinkling of convicts, religious
sectaries, and African slaves. That improbable collection, working in a new
range of freedoms, created an economy whose workers and farmers eventually earned real incomes greater than those of any other nation in the world.
In 1789 that prospect was still hidden by their raw, coarse, and penurious
existence. The character of that life is best seen by contrast with contemporary eighteenth-century reality.

The peasant origins of most Europeans who stocked the United States
lay far from the eighteenth-century of Enlightenment and high culture of
Haydn and Mozart, Hume and Smith, Helvetius and Voltaire. The harsh-
ness of that Europe has been all but forgotten. Portugal in 1766 still burned
men and women at the stake in city squares because they worshipped God
with a difference. Thirty years after the last witches were executed in Salem
they were still being killed in Scotland.[1] A century later men and women

---

1. Thomas Pennant, in John Pinkerton, ed., *General Collection . . . Voyages and Travels*
(1809), p. 83. In 1840 Ireland still had a law against witchcraft. Archer Poulson, *Law and Lawyers*
(1841) 1:289.

were still burned at the stake in England.[2] Frenchmen were accustomed to public executions, the bodies dangling at the gates of the major cities.[3]

The daily tasks for virtually all eighteenth-century Europeans make today's concerns about alienation, unemployment, relative deprivation seem like a happy dream. In Scotland men sold themselves into slavery because of poverty, and worked in the salt and coal mines.[4] In France travelers could describe the ragged peasant who yoked his plow with a donkey in one trace and his wife in the other.[5] In Switzerland women filled buckets with urine and manure, yoked them across their shoulders, and carried them uphill to fertilize the fields.[6] Highland women did the same in Scotland.[7] In 1816 a traveler in France saw "washerwomen in the river, standing up to their waists in casks fixed in the water"; in what is now Czechoslovakia, women "walking about without shoes or stockings on weekdays"; in Switzerland meat, even bread "considered luxuries by the simple people, who had them only on holidays.[8] In the most prosperous nation in Europe, thousands of young children made their living by sweeping the mud and horse droppings away from London street crossings in return for halfpennies from occasional passersby. Children also worked regularly in the mines. (Many years later a Royal Commission was still told of 12-year-old boys hacking away at the coal face, and 6-year-old girls picking up the loose coal and "hurrying" it away in baskets on their backs.[9]) And the rest of Europe? A widely traveled farm expert described the "absolute slavery of the peasants in some parts of Germany, in Denmark and in Poland and in Russia.[10]

In ordinary European houses rushes still covered the floor. They remained there indefinitely, accumulating the excrement of cats and dogs, the vomit of drunkards. Rats scurried through at intervals, and vermin were omnipresent. The Duke of Wellington, millionaire and first citizen of Europe, described his ingenuity in fitting out his traveling carriage with a light colored

2. M. Dorothy George, *Life and Labour in Eighteenth Century London* (1925), p. 370. The public hangings, said a contemporary, "were considered a public holiday;" ibid., pp. 208, 376.

3. Tobias Smollet, *Travels through France and Italy* (1776), letter 9: "We saw one body hanging quite naked and another lying broken on the wheel."

4. Pennant, *General Collection*, p. 453; *Edinburgh Review* (January-March 1899), p. 119.

5. Louis Simond, *Journal of a tour and residence in Great Britain . . . [with] an Appendix on France* (1817) 1:362.

6. Louis Simond, *A Tour in Italy and Sicily* (1828).

7. Pennant, *General Collection*, p. 89. "The tender sex . . . are the only animals of burden: they turn their patient backs to the dunghills, and receive in their . . . baskets as much as their lords and masters think fit to fling in with their pitchforks, and then trudge to the fields in droves of sixty or seventy."

8. Richard Edgcumbe, *The Diary of Frances Lady Shelley* (1912), pp. 161, 267, 287.

9. British Parliamentary Papers, *Industrial Revolution, Children's Employment*, vol. 7, Session 1842, pp. 288, 291 (Irish Universities Press, Parliamentary Papers).

10. Arthur Young, *Political Arithmetic* (1774), p. 202.

silk mattress cover. In that way he was able to spot, and capture, the lice more readily.[11]

What did the United States promise as compared with Europe? The threat of death by Indians or bears was certainly greater. But it hardly exceeded the odds of dying from the warfare that ranged persistently over the European plains. Or from the typhus, typhoid, and consumption that flourished amid concentrated populations who lacked clean water, sanitation, sewage systems.

European families could expect a daily diet of porridge, of potatoes and milk, or dried vegetables (except on Christmas). Americans were accustomed to meat every day. Most Europeans were peasants, subject to taxes by central and local governments. They were also subject to even more rigorous charges imposed by landowners who took a substantial portion of their grain as payment for milling the rest into flour, forbidding them to do their own milling. Americans averaged less than a dollar a year in taxes.[12] And anyone was free to set up a mill.

Most potent, however, was the life prospect faced by most Europeans. They could not own their own land. Nor could they even hope that their children might. In the New World, however, it was possible to buy a small farm after working and saving for a year or two. With the coming of independence, the British limitation on western settlement (beyond the Quebec line of 1763) was removed. More important, the Congress began selling the public domain for $2 an acre (and eventually less). A day laborer earned from $6 to $8 a month, plus room and board. He, and certainly his children, might expect to own a farm of their own. They could live independently of lords or feudal landowners. They were free from the close control that characterized older social and economic systems.

The development task confronting the new nation in 1783 was highlighted by a single fact: it had only one family per square mile.[13] The new nation consisted of isolated settlements, plus a few coastal centers scattered from Boston to Charleston. Roads between the settlements had been laid out by

11. Elizabeth Longford, *Wellington* (1975), p. 125.

12. An estimate for per capita meat consumption in Flanders in 1800 is 22 pounds a year compared to 360 in the United States. A speculative estimate for Europe in 1850 is 44 pounds. Cf. Henri Baudet and Henk van der Meulen, *Consumer Behavior and Economic Growth in the Modern Economy* (1982), pp. 31, 254.

"The people of this extensive country have . . . enjoyed all the essential benefits of society, on very easy terms. A man with five or six hundred acres of land is scarcely called upon for a dollar of taxes in a year." James T. Callendar, *The History of the United States for 1796* (1797), p. 58. "The fair average tax for a well seated farmer on an hundred acres is about the produce of one-sixth of an acre per annum." William Cooper, *A Guide in the Wilderness* (1810, reprint ed., 1970), p. 36. At perhaps 15 bushels of wheat per acre and 50 cents per bushel as the farm value, the tax per farm would have been $1.25.

13. The first census showed 4.5 persons per square mile in 1790.

deer and buffalo as they went from one stream or salt lick to another. Some eventually became Indian trails. Some were eventually worn into primitive roads by European settlers, through mud and fallen timbers. The cost of bringing goods along such routes into the pioneer settlements, or selling their output, condemned the settlers to continued isolation. For travel time was endless. Nearly a third of a century after independence, Mr. Drenning set out from Chillicothe, Ohio for New York City, driving 200 head of cattle. After walking 1,000 miles, he arrived a year later. (There he sold off the surviving cattle, profitably.[14]) It took two days to go a mere 35 miles in rural Ohio "in good weather, and a great deal longer if the roads were bad."[15]

The alternative was travel by water—ocean, river, lake. Improvements here were more feasible. The task was to shorten the time—and hence the cost—of shipping goods. That advance was achieved by technological change, and by the general growth in the economy. Both factors were evident in shipment of the major colonial product: tobacco. To ship tobacco to the United Kingdom[16] required about 6 months:

> 2 months sailing,
> 1 month loading and discharging cargo,
> 3 months waiting to assemble the cargo in Virginia.

The obvious target for cost cutting was assembly time, during which the ship's investment earned nothing. Buyers began to hold inventories at central points to be immediately available when ships arrived.[17] Improvements in ship and sail design, in charting sailing routes, became a further point at which entrepreneurs hammered away. The maturing commercial networks and technological innovation then combined to drive down costs and push up incomes.

One measure of the outcome of those many decades appears in Table 3.1. Even in 1783 real per capita income in the United States was high: It probably exceeded that in every other nation but Britain.[18] The nation retained that lead, and then increased it for nearly two centuries.

14. Thomas DeVoe, *The Market Book* (1862), p. 411, quoting the *New York Press*, June 1817.

15. William Cooper Howells, *Life in Ohio from 1813 to 1840* (reprint ed., 1963), p. 138.

16. Data from Ralph Davis, *The Rise of the English Shipping Industry* (1962), pp. 286–87. Davis reports that "the homeward freight of tobacco . . . represented nearly the whole of the ship's earnings for the year."

17. Cf. note 27, Chapter 4, this volume.

18. Cf. Robert Gallman's judgment in Lance Davis, Richard Easterlin, and William Parker, *American Economic Growth* (1972), pp. 21, 40.

TABLE 3.1
PER CAPITA PRODUCT, 1975[a]

Country	Per capita product
United States	$7,176
Africa	
Malawi	352
Kenya	470
Zambia	738
Asia	
India	470
Iran	2,705
Japan	4,907
Western Europe	
Ireland	3,049
United Kingdom	4,588
France	5,877
Denmark	5,911
West Germany	5,953
Eastern Europe	
Rumania	2,387
Poland	3,598
Soviet Union	4,700

[a]Gross domestic product in U.S. dollars converted at international prices.

Source: Gross domestic product figures in international dollars, with one exception, are from Irving Kravis, Alan Heston, and Robert Summers, "New Insights into the Structure of the World Economy," *Review of Income and Wealth* (December 1981), Table 1. The estimate for the Soviet Union is computed at 148 percent of the average for Poland and Rumania using data from Thad Alton reported in Paul Gregory and Robert Stuart, *Comparative Economic Systems* (1980), Table 10-1.

4

Colonialism

IT is four centuries since Britain founded its first colony in North America. And two centuries since the American Revolution began to destroy Britain's empire. The first two centuries (before the Revolution) were not ones of dutiful submission. Indeed, as John Adams observed, the eventual independence of the thirteen states began "with the first plantation in America."[1] Moral and political factors contributed to that outcome. So did two powerful economic forces.

One force involved the way the colonists earned their living. Most were independent farmers, artisans, merchants. Their livelihood did not depend on landowners whose social bases lay in the church, the nobility, or the state. Moreover, many American farms were physically removed from the immediate purview of British officials. True, planners sought to keep the colonists together. Virginia even passed a Cohabitation Act in 1680; by cutting taxes for town dwellers it tried to induce Virginians to live in selected towns. But the act failed to prevent migration. Southern planters, as Northern yeomen, continued to scatter. Americans settled wherever they found the most productive land within tolerably close reach of military protection. Physical independence came from economic choice. Political independence tended to follow.

A second and related economic force was at work. After the failure of communal land cultivation in Massachusetts Bay, virtually every white family owned its own farm. By 1774, of every four free families, three owned their own farm.[2] This was not merely an interesting statistical fact. For it led directly to a vital political consequence: Property ownership gave "political independence to the average American. In every colony that was to join the Revolution there was a representative assembly, elected by the property own-

---

1. "The principles and feelings which contributed to produce the revolution ought to be traced back for two hundred years, and sought in the history of the country from the first plantations in America." Quoted in Mellen Chamberlain, *John Adams* (1898), p. 15.

2. Computed from Alice Jones, *Wealth of a Nation to Be* (1980), pp. 39, 194. Examination of her southern data suggests that the true ratio might even be closer to 80 percent.

ers, which made the laws and levied the taxes."[3] That continuing experience in self-government made it less and less likely that the colonists would ever accept the increased taxes and obligations that Britain sought to impose after the war with France ended in 1763. Independent and isolated farming led to independent decision making.[4] Unlike the political ruptures on other continents down to the twentieth century, the Revolution of the colonists did not begin by creating such independence. It simply extended such freedoms further.

As so many before them, the British colonies in North America had been founded chiefly on dreams. Their predecessors and competitors, established to collect gold, or to trade in furs and exotics, yielded little. And then disappeared into nothingness. (From 1620 to 1770 more than a century of heroically greedy endeavor took place. By its end the colonists were gathering so few furs that the export value of furs did not even equal that of candles.[5])

Two other types of colony, however, did survive. One was the planned society, driven by a dream of righteousness and organized by regulations attributed to the Deity. The Massachusetts Bay colony rested on the shared and powerful faith of the Pilgrims; Pennsylvania, on that of the Quakers and Mennonites. General Oglethorpe and his Georgia colleagues likewise ran a planned society. But theirs rested on humanitarian and technocratic principles, anticipating that of many later visionaries. Its goal? To elevate Britain's "honest poor" by creating homes for them in the new land. Believing that "Georgia never can . . . be a flourishing province without negroes are allowed" the Reverend George Whitefield, Britain's great evangelist in the 1740s, persuaded the proprietors to introduce slavery into the province. Despite its "temporal inconveniencies."[6] In both types of planned colonies, religious and secular, rules and regulations flowed in a steady stream from London.

Most colonies, however, followed a different course: helter-skelter development. True, North Carolina had been elegantly planned by no less a mind than John Locke. And Maryland's Proprietor viewed that colony as a

---

3. Edmund S. Morgan, *The Birth of the Republic, 1763–89* (1957), p. 7.

4. Size contributed to such distance in the United States, as altitude did in the highlands of Scotland, Switzerland, and Montenegro.

5. Lawrence Harper, "Mercantilism and the American Revolution," *Canadian Historical Review* (1942), n. 16, provides data for 1770. Prior to 1804 the few furs that came from British settlements west of the Appalachians were disproportionately exported through the non-British port of New Orleans.

6. The trustees originally forbid slavery and hard liquor. Justin Winsor, ed., *Narrative and Critical History of America* (1887), 5:387. Whitefield wrote "that hot countries cannot be cultivated without negroes. What a flourishing country might Georgia have been, had the use of them been permitted years ago? How many white people have been destroyed for want of them, and how many thousands of pounds spent to no purpose at all? . . . I trust many of them will be brought to Jesus, and this consideration, as to us, swallows up all temporal inconveniencies whatsoever." Cf. *Works of the Reverend George Whitfield* (1771–72), 2:404–05.

refuge for Roman Catholics. But even these colonies began to fill with a curious mixture of migrants. Their growth reflected extremes of individualism in both society and polity.

So far as economic development was concerned, however, these varied colonies were identical, for they were overwhelmingly devoted to direct subsistence. For two centuries after 1585, when the first colony on Roanoke Island began its brief life, the colonists directed less than 5 percent of their labor to exports.[7] Nonetheless, the British Board of Trade and Plantations continued to believe that the colonies' raison d'etre was to generate exports.[8] As colonial exports of tobacco, rice, and indigo grew, Britain discovered an American import market for slaves to grow those crops. (It is at least possible that slaves would never have been substituted for free, or indentured, labor in the South but for the profitability of tobacco, indigo, and rice exports.) Despite violent American protests, Britain then insisted on the right of its merchants to sell slaves to the colonies. Such forces helped develop an export-oriented, slave-based plantation economy in the South.

These imperatives cast a long shadow before them. Eventually they generated a civil war. But their more immediate impact became evident in the Revolutionary War. By one of history's finer ironies, Britain helped guarantee widespread and powerful support for the American Revolution. Not even the powerful leadership of Virginia planters, from Washington to Jefferson and Mason, could have guaranteed uniform, or intense, southern support. But Lord Dunmore, royal governor of Virginia, set a match to the tinder as soon as the Revolution commenced. "No single event did more to propel the uncommitted Southern planters into the camp of rebellion than Lord Dunmore's call summoning Negro slaves to the British cause with a promise of freedom."[9] Yet the very existence of Negro slavery, as Jefferson noted in his draft of the Declaration of Independence, had been imposed on the colonies by Britain.[10] And, when the Virginia House of Burgesses tried to end slave trading, Britain overrode that legislation. Similarly, Britain raised up enemies

7. Even by 1772 the ratio of merchandise exports and invisibles to national income ran under 2 percent. Income and export figures from Jones, *Wealth*, pp. 51, 63; J. F. Shepherd and G. M. Walton, *Shipping, Maritime Trade and the Economic Development of Colonial North America* (1972), pp. 115, 128, 134.

8. "Administration of the colonies was left to the King, who turned it over to his Secretary of State for the Southern Department . . . [who] left it pretty much to the Board of Trade and Plantations, a sort of Chamber of Commerce with purely advisory powers. The Board of Trade told the Secretary what to do; he told the royal governors; the governors told the colonists; and the colonists did what they pleased." Edmund Morgan, *The Birth of the Republic, 1763–89* (1956), pp. 10–11.

9. Richard Morris, *The American Revolution Reconsidered* (1967), p. 74.

10. For Jefferson's draft, cf. Dumas Malone, *Jefferson the Virginian* (1948), p. 141. The ambivalence of Jefferson, Henry, and others on the subject is well known.

in the North. There, Hancock, Low, Beekman, and other merchants provided the leadership, status, and financial support essential to win the Revolution. But their power would have been trivial had Britain's pressure for colonial exports not raised them to affluence.

From their earliest days, the British colonies typically sent their exports to England (whether gold captured from Spain, or furs, fish, and flour). Whatever imports they could afford were likewise bought from England. Habit ruled their foreign mercantile policy. But during Britain's Civil War (1642–49), the colonies began trading directly with The Netherlands, France, and Russia. As soon as the Puritans won their Civil War, however, they passed a succession of Navigation Acts requiring that European goods destined for American markets had first to be sent to Britain. Although Charles II overthrew the Puritans in 1660, he did not end their policy of benefiting London merchants at the expense of the colonies. He extended it further.

The central British theme never changed. Americans were to sell their tobacco, rice, etc., to Europeans—in Britain—and to buy their European products—in Britain.[11] In that way British merchants collected extra commissions on tobacco inward and on French textiles outward. Longshoremen found jobs transshipping all these goods. And the king's exchequer picked up import duties as well.

How severe, in fact, was the burden of the Navigation acts? Typically historians have concluded that "British policies placed a heavy burden upon the colonies";[12] indeed, after 1763 they were "restrictive, injurious, negative; etc."[13] Robert Thomas, however, systematically estimated the total burden of these acts (Table 4.1).

But along with burdens, Britain also provided subsidies (Table 4.2). It offered bounties to those who grew indigo, provided tar and other naval stores.[14] While the British soldier protected the colonies against Indians, the

---

11. The minutiae were endless. European vessels could not ship goods directly to the colonies, although doing so would have reduced the cost to the colonists. The Navigation Acts of 1660–62 required American tobacco, indigo, and other items to be exported only to England, Ireland, or Wales. Later, the export of wool and hats were limited. Then the construction of iron slitting mills, which made nails, was restricted. In 1733 the Molasses Act put so high a duty on imported molasses from the French and Dutch West Indies that most of the Massachusetts distilleries, which converted molasses into rum for export, would have been closed down. The protest was so great that John Adams later did not "blush to confess that molasses was an essential ingredient in American independence."

12. Harper, "Mercantilism," p. 3.

13. Curtis Nettels, "British Mercantilism and the Economic Development of Colonialism," *Journal of Economic History* (Spring 1952), p. 114.

14. That the bounties for indigo were all net contributions is indicated by the abrupt end of colonial production after independence.

TABLE 4.1

BRITISH "BURDEN" ON THE COLONIES, 1763–72
(ANNUAL AVERAGE OF EXTRA COMMISSIONS,
TRANSSHIPMENT COSTS, ETC.)

Commodity	Cost (£ 000)
Tobacco	207
Rice	139
Other exports	35
Imports	144
Total	525

Source: Robert Thomas, "A Quantitative Approach to the Study of the Effects of the British Import Policy Upon Colonial Welfare: Some Preliminary Findings," *Journal of Economic History* (December 1965), p. 626. According to Thomas, if shipped directly to the Continent, tobacco would have sold for 34 percent more and rice 105 percent more. Tea and pepper, the major imports, would have cost the colonists 16 percent less had they been able to buy directly in Europe or Asia.

TABLE 4.2

BRITISH "CONTRIBUTIONS AND SUBSIDIES"
TO THE COLONIES, 1763–72

Contribution	Cost (£ 000)
Bounties (indigo, tar, etc.)	35
Preference on imports	39
Protection: British army	145
Protection: British navy	206
Total	425

Source: Robert Thomas, "A Quantitative Approach to the Study of the Effects of the British Import Policy Upon Colonial Welfare: Some Preliminary Findings," *Journal of Economic History* (December 1965), pp. 626, 634, 635.

British sailor protected them against pirates at sea. (True, the military protected British possessions at the same time. But the colonists did not pay for the soldiers, as they later would. Moreover, once the colonists were independent the higher insurance rates they had to pay for American shipping reflected their loss of protection by the British navy.) Thomas reached a striking conclusion: when the burden of British regulations is totalled, and all contributions deducted, the net loss to the colonists was some "36¢ a person . . . say 1 percent of national income."[15]

But does that trivial figure tell us whether the net burden was significant politically, or even economically?[16] Not at all. It could have been significant politically merely because of the way in which it was imposed or its rate of change: imagine the Treasury increasing colonial receipts fifteenfold within a few years.[17] As a brilliant "traditional" historian wrote:

> Britain placed a duty of 3d per gallon on molasses, and when it encountered opposition, reduced it to 1d. It provided for a Stamp Act and withdrew it in the face of temper tantrums. It provided for external taxes to meet the colonial objections and then yielded again by removing all except one. When it finally attempted to enforce discipline it was too late. Under the circumstances, no self-respecting child—or colonist—would be willing to yield.[18]

The economic elements, narrowly considered, are another matter. Matching a "burden" figure against the total colonial income is hardly more relevant than relating it to the total number of colonial mules. Consider, for example, the "burden" of extra commissions paid on tobacco and rice. What Britain had done was to reduce the net profit that planters could get from their lands and slaves. That reduction, in turn, reduced the value of those lands, which now capitalized the lower expected future prices for tobacco and rice. But Britain had "enumerated" tobacco and indigo for ninety years, and rice and naval stores for almost as long. After so many decades, the value of tobacco and rice lands had long since reflected the impact of such British legislation.[19] Thus, by the eve of the Revolution, colonial planters were no longer "burdened" by the Enumeration acts. They earned a "normal profit" on those lands despite the acts. Yet if they were not burdened by the acts the rest of the population, which accounted for most of "the national income" surely was not. "Burden" as a ratio to national income meant little.

15. Robert Thomas, "A Quantitative Approach," pp. 637–38. The procedures have been refined in Roger Ransom, "British Policy and Colonial Growth," *Journal of Economic History* (September 1968); Gary Walton, "The New Economic History and the Burden of the Navigation Acts," *Economic History Review* (1971). The approach was pioneered, less rigorously, by Lawrence Harper in Richard Morris, eds., *The Era of the American Revolution* (1939).

16. Gary Walton and James Shepherd, *The Economic Rise of Early America* (1979), p. 174, describe its "insignificant proportions."

17. From about £2,000 a year before the close of the French and Indian War in 1763 to about £30,000 a year after 1769. Edwin Channing, *History of the United States* (1912), 3:36, 90.

18. Harper, "Mercantilism," p. 14.

19. Year to year changes in legislation would, of course, have changed the expected sequence of future impacts. But such consequences would account for a trivial share of the aggregates shown in the Thomas estimates.

The economic interest of the tobacco and rice landowners, however, included the future quite as much as the past. If such acts were canceled by revolutionary protest, the value of their lands would rise.[20] Moreover, southern
landowners could then shrug off their huge debts to Scots factors and English
merchants. As of 1776, the South owed them 2 million, used to buy land,
slaves.[21] In 1783, "when news reached America that the Treaty of Peace provided that creditors . . . should meet with no lawful impediment to the recovery . . . of their debts, there was a furor in Virginia." As George Mason
wrote, Virginians were asking: "If we are now to pay the debts due to the
British merchants what have we been fighting for all this while?"[22] Patrick
Henry himself "sweat at every pore" when opposing the Virginia legislature's
decision to comply with this article in the treaty.[23]

During the colonial centuries the Americans steadily expanded their export markets. The overall American advance in distributive efficiency is defined in a deft analysis by James Shepherd and Gary Walton.[24] They showed
the difference between tobacco prices in Amsterdam, the major export destination, and in Philadelphia, thus measuring the total cost of transatlantic
shipping. That cost as a percent of the Amsterdam price ran as shown in
Table 4.3. What forces cut shipping costs so dramatically? Two political elements and two economic ones were at work.[25]

---

20. A century and a half later the mirror image of such legislation's impact appeared under
the New Deal. At that time owners of tobacco land saw its value jump as the government limited
the amount of land on which tobacco could be grown and qualify for Agricultural Adjustment
Act payments. In less than a decade thereafter, however, land values had capitalized the presence
of such legislation, i.e., the "right" to AAA payments. Thenceforth, buyers of such land could
expect to earn only "normal" profit rates from it.

21. Northern colonies owed £0.6 million. Cf. Shepherd and Walton, *Shipping*, p. 132, and
Jacob Price, *Capital and Credit in British Overseas Trade* (1980), p. 10. Thomas P. Abernethy, *Western Lands and the American Revolution* (1937), p. 161, argues that the "conservative tidewater gen-
try," who owed most of the debts, "went over to the cause of independence as a last resort."

22. Morris, *The American Revolution Reconsidered*, p. 82. A systematic argument on this point
appears in Lawrence Gipson, *The British Empire Before the Revolution* (1965), 12:199–207, and
idem, *Coming of the Revolution, 1763–1775* (1954), ch. 4.

23. In December 1787 Virginia finally repealed the laws standing in the way of the collection of debts of British and Scots merchants—the last state to do so. In the final debate one observer "reported that his anxiety could not be concealed—[and] made him sweat at every pore."
Merrill Jensen, *The New Nation* (1950), p. 281. It was Patrick Henry and his "yeomen" who fought
the proposal and specified that it would not apply until Britain paid for confiscated slaves and
evacuated their western outposts. Abernethy, *Western Lands*, p. 364.

24. Cf. *Economic Rise*, p. 117.

25. The data and quotations in the next two paragraphs are from Walton and Shepherd,
Rise, ch. 6. A measured and broad perspective was first offered by Douglass North, "Sources of
Productivity Change in Ocean Shipping, 1600–1850," *Journal of Political Economy* (September-
October 1968).

TABLE 4.3
TOBACCO DISTRIBUTION COSTS AS PERCENT OF AMSTERDAM PRICES, 1720–72

	1720–24	*1740–44*	*1760–64*	*1770–72*
Cost (freight, duties, etc.)	82.0	77.0	70.0	51.0

Source: Gary Walton and James Shepherd, *The Economic Rise of Early America* (1979), p. 117. Costs include freight, duties, warehousing, factors margins.

In 1720 piracy was still rampant on the seas: "The swarming of pirates not only on these coasts, but all the West Indies over . . . doth ruin trade ten times worse than a war." As late as 1718 pirates still operated from North Carolina inlets, looting vessels that traded out of Charleston. "Every month brought intelligence of renewed outrages, of vessels sacked on the high seas, burned with their cargo, or . . . converted to the nefarious uses of the outlaws." Colonial demands for help finally stirred the Royal Navy into action. By 1742 a report declared that "the pirates on the coast have been completely exterminated, and vessels came and went, unarmed and unguarded." Insurance rates between Jamaica and New York fell 20 percent between 1720 and 1773. In the earlier decades even small vessels had to carry guns, raising their capital cost and cutting down on space for paying cargo. By the 1740s, however, greater safety at sea had ended that need. These combined results cut the tobacco freight margin from 82 percent to 77 percent—a distinct, if modest, decline from the 1720s.

The most significant decline, however, occurred in a single decade. Between 1760 and 1770 the margin fell by nearly 20 percent. The obvious cause was the defeat of France in 1763. France withdrew from the war, and denied even covert support to the pirates who once operated from her West Indian ports.

These political forces contributed significantly to the productivity rise of some 7 percent a year in ocean transport (Shepherd-Walton estimate for vessels trading between Maryland and Virginia).[26] But two economic forces contributed to the same end. Neither involved great technological advance. (Ingenious changes in ship's hulls and rigging were indeed made, but they contributed little.) Neither force involved heavy capital investment. (In fact investment per unit of output fell.) One economic force for productivity gain was that the planters learned how to pack 5 times as much tobacco into a

26. The most obvious impact of new hull shapes, etc., would have been on average speed. Yet average speed changed hardly at all in the century ending in 1765. It is, however, possible that they improved handling in emergencies. If so, part of the reduction in insurance rates is to be attributed to such technological change.

hogshead in 1776 as in 1620.[27] The second economic force was the reduction in the time vessels spent idling in port in Maryland or Virginia. It fell from approximately 100 days in 1700 to 50 days by the time of the Revolution. Payments to captain, first officer, bosun, and carpenter for hanging about in port were cut in half. And the vessel's capital investment, which earned nothing during 100 idle days in the early period, did so for only 50 in the later.[28] That reduction in port times did not just happen. It was linked to the entrance of Scot factors into the trade after 1707.[29] They apparently settled old debts and thereby collected new crops from the planters more expeditiously. By gathering the crops in a few barns and warehouses, instead of continuing the older practice of sailing from one plantation to another to pick up each load separately, the Scots shippers loaded the vessels more quickly.

27. Russell Menard, "The Tobacco Industry in the Chesapeake Colonies," *Research in Economic History* (1980), 5:146. In the single decade 1625–35 rates were cut in half when hogsheads replaced tobacco packed loosely or in random containers.

28. Shepherd and Walton, *Shipping*, p. 198.

29. The French contracted with London to ship tobacco to them, war or no war. With this guaranteed market, Glasgow merchants began to buy "in advance of their shipping," turned around "their vessels . . . in weeks instead of months, and saved considerably on freight." Jacob M. Price, "The Economic Growth of the Chesapeake and the European Market, 1697–1775," *Journal of Economic History* (December 1964), p. 509. Cf. also James Soltow, "Scottish Traders in Virginia, 1750–1775, *Economic History Review* (August 1959), p. 89.

5

The American Revolution

W HY did the American Revolution break out? One of the Minutemen of
April 19, 1775, was later asked whether he had fought because of oppression? The Stamp Act? Tea?. No, he replied stubbornly. It was because
"we always had governed ourselves and we always meant to. They didn't
mean we should."[1] It would be hard to find a better, or more succinct, de-
cription.

The Americans were aggrieved, as colonists before and since, by their
subordination to a governing power. Their grievances were real enough. Yet
as each grievance was removed another took its place. The exact contribution
of purely economic factors cannot be determined. But a few may be noted.

British taxation stung the Americans as forcibly as the tiny ship money
tax of King Charles, which had begun a revolution in 1688. As late as 1774 the
Continental Congress declared that it would even admit Parliament's right to
regulate "our external commerce for . . . commercial advantages . . . to the
mother country," provided Parliament ended "taxation . . . on its subjects in
America without their consent."[2]

The Stamp Act alone infuriated two of the most voluble groups on the
continent—lawyers and publishers—even though its rates were low. Its passage created "a domination of lawyers . . . carried on by the same wicked ar-
tifices" that previously had allowed the "Domination of Priests"; they, in
turn, stimulated "the brutal rage of the Mob."[3] It was emotionally and politically irrelevant to the colonists that taxes per capita under British rule were

1. Mellen Chamberlain, *John Adams* (1898), p. 249. While attending Dartmouth in 1842
Chamberlain talked to Captain Preston, a survivor of "the Lexington fight."

2. Declaration and Resolves of the First Continental Congress, October 1774. Reprinted in
Samuel Eliot Morison, *Sources and Documents Illustrating the American Revolution* (1961), p. 118.
The full text, of course, had qualifications. Moreover, it is hardly likely that the colonists would
have acceded to close enforcement of any tax system.

3. Lieutenant Governor Cadwallader Colden of New York, quoted in the Introduction to
Esmond Wright, ed., *Causes and Consequences of the American Revolution* (1966), p. 45.

only one-seventh as great as those eventually imposed by an independent United States.[4]

In 1763, the victorious British had their choice between pieces of real estate they might take from the defeated French: Canada or the sugar islands. Because Britain's West Indian sugar planters feared competition, Canada was chosen. Having done so Britain then established a government for Quebec. The Quebec Act of 1774 outraged the colonists. By providing religious freedom for Catholics, it particularly infuriated the indignant Protestants of New England. The famous Suffolk Resolves had been quite explicit: "The late act of Parliament for establishing the Roman Catholic religion and the French laws in . . . Canada is dangerous in an extreme degree to the Protestant religion, and to the civil rights and liberties of all America."[5]

No less intense was the antagonism created by the 1764 Proclamation Line. To persuade the Indians to desert their French allies, the British had guaranteed their security in the Trans-Appalachian lands. After the war the British tried to halt American settlement beyond a line marking out those lands, whether or not any Americans had made treaties with local Indian tribes. This outraged Patrick Henry, Richard Henderson (for whom Daniel Boone explored and surveyed new lands), and thousands of others determined to settle on Indian lands or to profit from their sale.[6]

Finally, the cost of such expanded glories of empire led Britain to extend its surveillance over the Americans in numerous irritating ways, which culminated in what were simply termed the "Intolerable Acts": closing the port of Boston until the town paid for the tea dumped by the Boston Tea Party, annulling the Massachusetts Charter, prohibiting the cutting of white pine, stationing a "large, unrequested and ineffective body of British troops" in America, etc. Such acts, in the 1772 religious perspective of Samuel Adams, infringed on "the Rights of the Colonists . . . as men, as Christians, and as subjects."[7]

This accumulated history of dissent and expectation ended in April 1775 when the shooting war began on the Lexington green. The economic burden

4. Lawrence Harper in Wright, ed., *Causes and Consequences*, p. 163. John Adams could note later that Americans were simply "not used to great taxes, and the people are not yet disciplined to such enormous taxation as in England." John Adams, *Works* (1852), 7:294.

5. Peter Force, "Suffolk Resolves," *American Archives*, 4th ser., 1 (1837):778. It was not many years later that the Gordon riots in London took place because the Parliament made the most modest gesture toward granting Catholics more equal civil rights. The "Resolves" were first put forward in Massachusetts, then adopted by the Continental Congress.

6. True, as Gipson noted, frontiersmen did settle on Indian reserves, for Britain, in time, permitted such treaties. But the general limitation was a standing, a vast, and a public affront. Cf. Lawrence Gipson, *The British Empire Before the Revolution* (1954), 9:41–54.

7. Quoted in Morison, *Sources*, p. 88. Bernard Knollenberg, *Origins of the American Revolution, 1759–1776* (1960), details the extensive list.

on the Americans was sustained chiefly by the civilian population. But, given the "widespread apathy" of most Americans,[8] the real burden of the war, the fighting and dying, was assumed by a small group of soldiers. The perilous inevitabilities of war killed or wounded 10 percent of the American soldiers.[9] (American battle deaths per year of service in the Revolution were about twenty times greater than in Vietnam or World War II.[10])

The economic burden of the war appeared in the reduced consumption of food, clothing, etc. by Americans, then and later. Of that burden the greatest sacrifice was clearly sustained by those living at the Revolution.[11] Supplies of food were cut as soldiers fought over fields where wheat used to grow. Demand shifted. Congress attempted to feed its soldiers better than civilians had typically been fed and the French and British offered good hard currency to feed their soldiers and sailors so far from home. Prices, therefore, could be expected to rise somewhat. But they actually soared (see Figure 5.1). The Continental Congress had neither taxing power, gold, nor silver to back the money it printed almost endlessly. "Not worth a Continental" became a phrase embedded in history. Soldiers could do little about the disappearing value of their pay. But civilians increasingly refused to accept such currency. (Rhode Island actually sued a butcher because he would not exchange his meat for the worthless money that state had been printing.) There was one virtue in all this, however, at least for the Congress and the States: Inflation simply wiped out much of the monetary cost of the war. (It was the politically feasible way of trying to bid for the same resources.) As George Mason fretfully observed, "the late war could not have been carried on otherwise."[12]

Inevitably, popular demands led to state price controls. (Two centuries later a commentator noted that one American in two still believed in angels, in extrasensory perception, in unidentified flying objects—and in wage and price controls.[13]) With the long colonial heritage of price fixing, and two cen-

8. J. Franklin Jameson, *The American Revolution as a Social Movement* (reprint ed., 1961), p. 48. This view may, on closer study, prove to be an exaggeration. It is, however, the present judgment of specialists on the war. Cf. Don Higginbotham, *The War of American Independence* (1971), chap. 15.

9. This is the ratio for the Hessians, from Appendices A, B in Robert Atwood, *The Hessians* (1980). An estimate of 12.5 percent for military and naval deaths is offered by Howard Peckham, *The Toll of Independence* (1974), p. 133.

10. The average duration of service in Vietnam was twenty-three months. *1981 Statistical Abstract of the United States*, p. 364. One can estimate about the same duration for the Revolution, using data from *American State Papers: Military Affairs*, vol. 1, no. 3, and Peckham, *The Toll*, p. 130. Personnel and deaths are from the same sources.

11. Even ignoring the dynamic consequences for the economy, the real incomes of those living at the time sustained a greater proportionate reduction than those living in later decades.

12. Jonathan Hughes, *Social Control in the Colonial Economy* (1976), p. 153.

13. *Fortune* (December 1978), quoted in Alan Blinder, *Economic Policy and the Great Stagflation* (1979), p. 107.

FIGURE 5.1
PRICE INFLATION, 1776–80

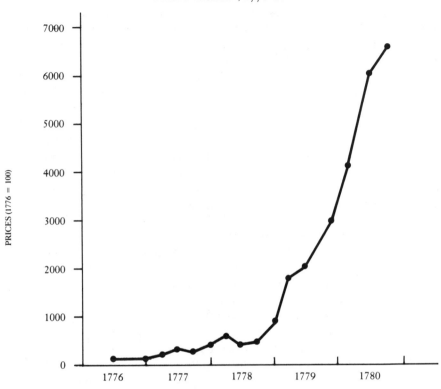

Source: Scale of depreciation set by the General Assembly of Pennsylvania, December 1780, for payments to the Pennsylvania Line, *Pennsylvania Archives*, 3rd ser., 3:763

turies less experience in the futility of such controls, the attempt was not surprising.[14]

The "avaricious conduct of many persons," the "exorbitant prices" of necessities, were challenged. But the wartime shortages were inevitable. Laws were then passed, meeting some emotional needs. But, as James Wilson wrote, "there are certain things which Absolute Power cannot do."[15] The saga of price controls brought its traditional effects. Farmers reduced the sale of their food in cities, where price controls were most effective. In some instances they left farming for better paying activities, thus reducing the supply

14. The colonial heritage is expounded with precision and saturine wit in Hughes, *Social Control.* See also Richard Morris's monumental *Government and Labor in Early America* (1946).

15. James Wilson quoted in Evarts Greene, *The Revolutionary Generation* (1946), p. 263.

still further. Merchants had to buy unnecessary items to increase the real price of necessary items: "I cannot purchase any coffee without [also buying] claret . . . and . . . sour . . . sugar." Moreover, the army, shocked by the starvation at Valley Forge in the winter of 1778, bought so much in 1779, said a contemporary, that it inventoried more food than " the armies can consume before it will be perishable."[16]

War shortages and inflation had their most apparent and long-lasting impact on the soldiers. The states and the Continental Congress had made them a set of financial promises. Soldiers' pay consisted of five items: an annual suit of clothes, promised title to 100 acres of land in the West, money pay, an $80 bonus if they fought till the war's end, and maintenance during the war.[17]

The suit was real and immediate. The acreage was far away and hypothetical. The actual maintenance for American soldiers while in service can be extrapolated from that of the far better provisioned British officers: "Broiled salt porc for breakfast, boiled salt porc for dinner, cold salt porc for supper. . . . The only thing which I found a little disagreable was lying five nights in the midst of a putrid marsh up to the ankles in filth and water. The heat . . . begins to be extream . . . and the rains . . . are now becoming very frequent."[18] Soldiers' pay and bonuses eroded to nothing in the ongoing inflation. In 1781 one desolate soldier wrote to Madison: "Dead is a Nothing to Compare against that Miserable life I must leve in, all for my True and Faithfull Service [the] pass Five years."[19]

The war eventually destroyed thousands, wounded other thousands. It nullified old titles to wealth and created new ones. During the course of the war the Continental Congress created a variety of new claims by borrowing and a new pattern of expectations by the inflation over which it presided. The outcome of such a Revolution was revolutionary economic change.

16. Anne Bezanson, "Inflation and Controls in Pennsylvania, 1774–1779," *Journal of Economic History, Supplement* (1948), p. 16.

17. *Laws of the United States Respecting Public Lands* (1828), p. 337. The bounty proposed by Washington in 1776 was only $20, but he had also specified "all plunder they shall take from the enemy to be equally divided . . . according to their pay." Quoted in *Record of Connecticut Men in the Military and Naval Service*, Henry B. Johnston, ed., (1889), p. 126.

18. Eric Robson, *Letters from America, 1773 to 1780* (1951), pp. 29–30.

19. The bonus was voted on May 15, 1778. *Journals of [Continental] Congress* (Philadelphia, 1778), IV:288. In 1780 Virginia raised a militia of 2,500 infantrymen, paying them in tobacco. (Hening, *Statutes*, X:221–26, quoted in W. T. Hutchinson and W. M. E. Rachal, *The Papers of James Madison* (1962), II:101. These and any others paid "in kind" would have been protected against the full blast of inflation. They could not have been many. A Virginia major wrote to Madison in January 1781 saying: "Dead is a Nothing to Compare against that Miserable life I must leve in, all for my True and Faithfull Service pass Five years . . . [over] Sixty Thousand dollars is due me [but] if . . . 100 Pound may be granted as advance . . . I shall be Extremely Glad.") Hutchinson and Rachal, *The Papers of James Madison*, p. 275.

Economic Consequences of the Revolution

The multiple and far-off consequences of the Revolution on the American economy would justify many volumes, of which most have yet to be researched. Several elements would loom large in such studies.

The transformation of the thirteen colonies into a continental nation had begun previously. But war and revolution speeded it up, as shown in Table 5.1. The Frontier portion of the United States had grown swiftly after the French defeat in 1763, as the pioneers moved north to Vermont and Maine and south to Kentucky and Tennessee. Now the Revolution nullified British laws and cancelled later attempts by Pennsylvania and Virginia to slow westward migration.

Production and Markets

The production of wheat, pork, and whiskey likewise moved westward with the population. The ending of British subsidies ended indigo production in South Carolina and Georgia, and North Carolina's export of timber to make masts for the king's ships. Subsistence farmers in Kentucky, Tennessee, western New York, and Pennsylvania began to "export." They did more than simply feed their families. Together they supplied potash, flour, and lumber for urban markets, indeed more than all the large-scale export-oriented farms of the East Coast supplied. Their increasing number expanded the market for horses, iron (for plows, axes, etc.), salt, and wagons more than

TABLE 5.1

POPULATION GAINS BY COLONIAL REGION (IN PERCENT)

	1750–60	1760–70	1770–80
Frontier territories	79	99	72
Coastal colonies	19	23	15
Border colonies	49	34	30
Cities	33	51	− 10

Frontier: Maine, Vermont, Kentucky, Tennessee, North Carolina, Georgia.

Coastal: Massachusetts, Rhode Island, Connecticut, New Jersey, Delaware, Maryland.

Border: All others.

Cities: Places of 5,000 and over.

Source: Computed from state estimates by Stella Sutherland, in U.S. Census, *Historical Statistics . . . to 1970,* p. 1156; and U.S. Census, *A Century of Population Growth* (1909), p. 15.

the equivalent increase of families on existing eastern farms. Moreover, war opened a path to new entrepreneurs. Goods once supplied by Britain now began to be manufactured in the United States. By 1788, Washington could write: "Not only agriculture but even manufactures, are much more attended to than formerly."[20]

The outward orientation of the economy shifted away from British ports whether in England or in the West Indies. These had taken 85 percent of colonial exports in 1768–72 but only 47.5 percent by 1790–92.[21] Exports to France, The Netherlands, and their West Indies, which amounted to almost nothing in the earlier period, rose to almost 40 percent in the later period. The monopoly nexus to Britain was broken. Moreover, Parliament put in new obstacles to break that trade. Yet a substantial trade continued despite a heritage of hatred and war. For language, traditional connections, knowledge on both sides of the transaction, still made that trade highly profitable.

The South's export total hardly changed over these decades. Export sales of indigo fell off and tobacco rose somewhat. While New England and the Mid-Atlantic nearly doubled their exports, chiefly in wheat and corn,[22] the South lost its dominance in export markets.

Wealth Distribution

Before his fellow French revolutionaries carted him off to be guillotined in 1794, Georges Danton had described his purpose: "to put on top what was below." "The Revolution," he declared forthrightly, "is like a battle. Shall it not be followed like all battles by a division of the spoils among the conquerors?"[23] To achieve that goal, he and his colleagues in France found it necessary to kill a multitude of peasants and workers, plus a handful of nobles, nuns, and teen-agers. American revolutionary leaders expressed no similar zeal, even though perhaps a quarter of the population were counterrevolutionaries.[24] Indeed, three-quarters of the Loyalists remained in the United States after the war.[25] The United States lacked a national church with lands and rich altars that could be confiscated. It also lacked an anciently estab-

20. To Thomas Jefferson, August 31, 1788, *Writings*, J. C. Fitzpatrick, ed., 30:83–84.

21. From the elegant, compact study of these early years by Gary Walton and James Shepherd, *The Economic Rise of Early America* (1979), p. 190. Data in constant dollars.

22. Walton and Shepherd, *The Economic Rise*, pp. 194–96.

23. Quoted in Stanley Loomis, *Paris in the Terror* (1964), p. 157.

24. John Adams wrote that by 1775 Britain had "formed . . . a party" in its favor, having "deluded nearly one third of the people of the colonies." To Morse, December 22, 1815. C. F. Adams, ed. *The Works of John Adams* (1856), 10:193. Paul H. Smith, *William and Mary Quarterly* (1968), pp. 259–77, surmises that the Loyalists composed 20 percent of the population.

25. Given a population of 2 million, a 25% figure implies 500,000 Loyalists. W. H. Seibert's data suggest about 100,000 migrants, including British soldiers and Loyalists per se. Cf. his "The Dispersion of the American Tories," *Mississippi Valley Historical Review* (1914) pp. 186–194. Loyalist enlistment in the Provincial line (men from the provinces) ran from nearly 1,000 at the end of 1775 to 10,000 by the end of 1780. Paul H. Smith, *Loyalists and Redcoats* (1964), pp. 76–77.

lished ruling class of robe and sword whose possessions could be redistributed to a new class. (Hardly any were executed or tortured.)

These signal differences meant that the economic consequences of revolution in the United States differed greatly from those in France. Few Americans could delude themselves with visions of riches from redistribution. True, the individual states confiscated the land holdings of the royal governors (e.g., Wentworth of New Hampshire, Hutchinson of Massachusetts, Johnson of New York). They could, and did, take over the massive holdings of King George III. And they confiscated the estates of wealthy Loyalists, chiefly those who fled. But these opportunities were limited. In the end, according to Jackson Main, "less than 4 percent of the nation's real and personal estates changed hands."[26]

The states might have accelerated wealth redistribution by distributing their confiscations to the poor, either then or after the war. They did neither. The financial crisis of 1779–80, and later emergencies, forced them to sell these estates. Farmers and other suppliers were no longer willing to provide the state militia with food and equipment for tax anticipation notes. They wanted specie or something more reliable. To finance a continuation of the war, the states had to tax everyone or to monetize the estates. The more ardent revolutionaries pressed the states to sell the estates. So did those "most anxious to lighten the tax burden and reduce the debt painlessly, such as the New York Clintonians and the settlers in the Carolina uplands."[27] To sell for securities that would be of real value, however, the states necessarily "restricted credit to purchasers with good security. Most of the property was therefore sold to men of cash, credit or influence."[28] To the extent that such purchasers paid market prices, of course, they exchanged one form of wealth for another. Once confiscation occurred, the wealth distribution was not changed by such sales.[29]

Main's extensive study of nearly 6,000 estates showed that the share "of the nation's wealth owned by the richest tenth of the population probably de-

26. Jackson T. Main, *The Sovereign States, 1775–1783* (1973), p. 330. Main's is the primary study on the subject. Pennsylvania confiscated some Loyalist estates but paid the Penns £130,000 for their holdings. Virginia allowed Lord Fairfax to retain his immense holding, of more than 5 million acres, and rent it until his death. The state finally confiscated the bulk of it when he died though he willed it to his brother in England.

27. Ibid., pp. 314–15.

28. Ibid., p. 319. Main observes that "in the end the states took over property worth around £5 million sterling but the treasuries of the taxpayers realized little benefit . . . possibly only a tenth of that amount" (p. 315). If the true value at sales time were indeed ten times as great, an immense squabble must have taken place among the happy beneficiaries during the auctions.

29. One Loyalist declared that the new bureaucracy skimmed off the difference between true and market prices: "Not twopence in the pound have arrived to the public treasury of all the confiscations." G. Ward, *Journal and Letters of Curwen* (1842), p. 417. Cf. similar doubts in Allan Nevins, *The American States* (1924), p. 509.

clined slightly (about 2 percent) between 1770 and 1788."[30] But if we include the confiscation of property once held by the British governors, the share of the upper tenth undoubtedly fell still more. Moreover, the most significant change in wealth distribution is ignored in most estimates, which refer only to the free population. What about all families, not just those that were free before the war? Ex-slaves had joined the ranks of free men and women.[31] Some 20,000 northern slaves were freed by 1790, and 10,000 "soon thereafter." (The remaining 30,000 northern slaves had to wait for the gradual breakdown of slave support over the next quarter century.[32]) If we reckon in the freedom that most northern slaves achieved by the revolution, the confiscation of the great estates, as well as the shifts among smaller owners, it becomes clear that the Revolution did generate socially significant changes in the distribution of wealth.

30. Main, p. 347.

31. Vermont abolished slavery in its constitution of 1777, Massachusetts in 1780, declaring all men born equal and endowed with freedom, and New Hampshire in 1784. Connecticut, Pennsylvania, and New York provided for gradual abolition by specifying that males born after a given date would be freed when they reached the age of 25 (Conn. in 1784) or 28 (Pa. in 1780; N.Y., in 1799). Cf. Arthur Zilversmit, *The First Emancipation, the Abolition of Slavery in the North* (1967), pp. 123, 128, 131, 182. In New Jersey in 1809 a 13-year-old boy was valued at $225 for his remaining fifteen years of service. Ibid., p. 200.

32. Main, *The Sovereign States*, pp. 338–40.

6

Confederation and Constitution

BY 1781 the war slowly began to end. (About 1,000 colonial soldiers were killed in both 1780 and 1781, 300 in 1782, and only 1 in 1783.)[1] Not coincidentally it was also 1781 when the new Confederation of states replaced the Continental Congress that had fought the war. Thirteen states had waged a common war against a common enemy. But that cement to their unity dissolved when the war ended. Without that unity an uncertain prospect awaited them, even if they had been freed from the burdens that Britain imposed. Answers to four questions about government policy decisively shaped private expectations about investment, the migration of men and money, and hence the prospects for national growth. Could the new government safely be granted the power to tax, and to regulate trade? Would it pay its debts? Would it provide physical security for its citizens? And, could it reduce the burden of private debts?

Could the new government safely be granted the power to tax, and to regulate trade? Such powers had been anathematized in a hundred protests against British control. The answer in the new nation was an obvious "no." The Confederation, therefore, had to depend on revenue sharing with the states. Nearly two centuries later sharing provided a bountiful flow from the federal income tax to state governments. In 1781–89, however, the (Federal) Confederation sought contributions from the states. In the immediate aftermath of the Revolution the results were, perhaps, wholly predictable. In 1785 the Confederation billed the states for $3 million, to pay its few employees and to begin reducing the war debt.[2] Two years later it had received less than 4

1. Howard Peckham, *The Toll of Independence* (1974), p. 130.
2. Curtis Nettels, *The Emergence of a National Economy, 1775–1815* (1962), p. 98. From 1781 to 1786 New Hampshire, North Carolina, South Carolina, and Georgia had all refused to pay any of the requisitions by Congress. Cf. Joseph Story, *Commentaries on the Constitution* (1851), 1:177. Almost 60 percent of the payments of the states to the Confederation from 1784 to 1789 consisted not of cash but of "indents"—money which the states simply printed themselves. These had value to the extent that the states would eventually accept them in payment for their own state taxes.

percent of that amount. Desperate for revenue to pay its ministers abroad in 1781, and the interest due on Revolutionary debts, the Congress tried to impose a 5 percent tariff on exports. Most states agreed. But Rhode Island quashed the attempt. In 1783 and again in 1786 a similar proposal was approved by the other states, but then stopped by New York's objection.[3] Presumably, the fact that both states were major importing centers and relied on income from their own tariffs led them to object. New York collected half its state income from tariffs. If it lost such revenue it would have had to increase taxes on its farmers.[4]

The Congress, in Adams' words, proved to be a mere "collection of ambassadors from thirteen sovereign states."[5] As Oliver Ellsworth of Connecticut fumed: "A single state can . . . veto the most important public measures." Hence, "a minority, a very small minority, has governed us."[6] So futile did the Confederation become in its final years that its Congress rarely could even muster a quorum.[7] Apparently it could be counted on to decide nothing; the states had little to fear if their representatives were absent. There was as little to hope for as to fear from taxation, regulation, or subsidy by that government.[8]

Would the Confederation pay its debts to its soldiers? Privates and non-commissioned officers were promised bonuses to enlist. Their monthly pay was printed up by the Continental Congress and by the states. In fairly short order the flood of money thus created became worthless. Soldiers discovered that they were serving for little more than intermittent meals of bread, cold pork, and vinegar.[9] A good many farmers, millers, and merchants who had sold their food and material to the Army were diddled in the same way.

Officers represented a greater political problem. Congress in 1778 had promised them half pay "for seven years, if they live so long."[10] During the hard winter of 1780 at Valley Forge numbers resigned. Washington noted

---

3. *Journal of Congress*, February 3, 1781 and August 23, 1786.

4. Nettels, *Emergence*, p. 95.

5. Cf. C. F. Adams, ed., *The Works of John Adams* (1856), 10:413.

6. Jonathan Elliot, *The Debates in the General State Conventions* (1836–45), 2:197.

7. Charles King, *The Life and Correspondence of Rufus King* (1894), 1:133–34, 154.

8. Cf. Merrill Jensen, *The New Nation* (1850), Part V. Jensen emphasizes "The Achievements of the Confederation." His finding, however, seems to be that a, if not the, "major achievement of the Confederation was the creation of a bureaucracy." Another achievement was that its employees put in order the scattered debt papers of the Continental Congress, and established just which of the many claimed debts against the Confederation were warranted. (In later wars debts were either paid fairly promptly or wended their way through the courts.) Once established, however, the Confederation did not pay them, because it could not.

9. In 1780 the Congress indirectly admitted this fact when it bought in the old continental currency at about 2¢ on the dollar (40 to 1), although the true market value then was less than 1¢ on the dollar. By the end of 1781 continental scrip brought 1/10 of one cent per dollar. Jefferson, *Writings*, Paul Leicester Ford, ed., 4:154.

10. *Journals of Congress* (Philadelphia), 4:288.

that few Pennsylvanians resigned, officers from that state having been promised half pay for life after the end of their service.[11] He, therefore, recommended, and Congress eventually promised, half pay for life to all officers
serving until the war's end.[12] In March of 1783, with that end clearly in sight,
the chickens came home to roost. The officers noted that in three years no action whatever had been taken to make good on that promise. (Indeed, Rhode
Island instructed its delegates "to exert themselves against half pay to retir-
ing officers."[13]) The threat of an 'officers' revolt" led Congress to print up
new certificates to provide the promised half pay. (The value of these certificates, however, was to be distinctly less than the original promise of half pay
for life.[14])

Taxpayer opposition at once flared in New England. It produced "almost a general anarchy," Madison said.[15] Sam Adams spoke for the Massachusetts legislature: such payment—about $1 a day for five years[16]—was
"inconsistent with that equality that ought to subsist among citizens of free
and republican states.". . . [It was] calculated to raise and exalt some citizens
in wealth and grandeur, to the injury and oppression of others." And it was
"more than an adequate reward for their services."[17] Indignant democrats
concluded that the officers would collect the money due them only "at the expense of the sufferings of their fellow citizens."[18]

A tax of $2 a year per family would have provided for the entire cost.[19]
By modern standards that does not seem excessive. After all, as Washington
remarked of the original half-pay promise in 1780: "it was part of your hire; I
may be allowed to say, it was the price of their blood and of your indepen-
dency."[20] However, a semi-grateful people did not even pay in 1783. Congress then only issued commutation certificates, which promised payment.

11. W. C. Ford, ed., *The Writings of George Washington* (1890), 8:484.
12. Washington also urged dispelling their "apprehension of personal distress [at] the termi-
nation of the war, from having thrown themselves [out] of professions and employments they
might not have it in their power to resume," as well as the fate of their widows should they die.
Writings, 6:304.
13. Rhode Island (Colony), *Records of the State of Rhode Island* (1864), 9:612.
14. The promise of half pay for life became one of five years pay or securities earning 6 percent "as congress shall find convenient," *Journals of Congress*, 8:162.
15. H. Gilpin, ed., *Madison Papers*, 1:572.
16. The Paymaster General reported that 2,480 officers were entitled to half pay or commutation. (19th Cong., 2d sess., H.R. 6, *Revolutionary Officers* (1826), p. 12.) Congress estimated the
commutation would cost $5 million. (Glasson, *History*, p. 19; *Journals of Congress*, IV:178–79.)
This works out to $1.10 per day for five years.
17. Glasson, *History*, p. 20.
18. John S. Barry, *The History of Massachusetts, The Commonwealth Period* (1857), p. 223. Barry
reviews other objections raised during the period of Shays Rebellion.
19. Congress estimated the cost over the five-year period at $5 million (*Journals of Congress*,
IV:197). There were then about 500,000 families in the United States. $2 equalled the cost of 2
gallons of whiskey at that time. (Cf. American State Papers, *Military*, I:38, 43.)
20. John Fitzpatrick, ed., *Writings* (1938), 26:492.

The states subsequently provided no money to back up these certificates. Nine years after Congress made these fresh promises not one dollar had been appropriated or paid.

Thus, most soldiers were discharged after their service with neither back pay, income, nor work. They, therefore, threw the certificates on the market for whatever they could bring. That averaged 12½ cents on the dollar.[21] The market thereby revealed that thousands of buyers and sellers agreed on one forecast: there was only one chance in eight that the Congress would ever pay off the certificates.

Would the Confederation, could it, provide physical security to its citizens? The answer was hardly a resounding "yes." After 1783 the outlying frontier settlements (south and west) continued to be attacked by Indians, the latter still protected by the British. Virginia refused to allow its courts to enforce the collection of debts due to the British, as required by the peace treaty. Great Britain therefore continued to hold military forts near the Canada–U.S. line—equally illegal under the treaty. Dangers seemed to appear everywhere. Virginia frontiersmen in the early 1780s even petitioned the state not to have their lands surveyed, though inaction would delay their getting secure legal title to the lands. Doing so, they warned, would involve them "in all the horrors and calamities of an Indian War."[22] A national army, however, could do what the state militias could not: provide "peaceable Possession, especially of back waste vacant Lands [as] a Kind of Right."[23] Moreover, Spain insisted on controlling the lifeline of Trans-Appalachia, the Mississippi, by limiting the exports that floated down to New Orleans. (Eventually it forbid them altogether.) Together, Britain and Spain menaced the lives and the livelihood of the frontier settlers.

New Englanders were accustomed to shipping wheat and lumber to the Mediterranean under British flags. They now found their ships captured by pirates from Algiers and Morocco, their sailors sold into slavery. (True, the enterprising North African states offered to stop their piracy. But their price

21. A Congressional report declared that the certificates, "from inability to pay in the maker [i.e., the Congress], and to wait in the holder, were thrown in the market for cash, and soon fell to 12 ½ cents on the dollar." 19th Cong., 2d sess., H.R. 6, *Revolutionary Officers* (1826), p. 12.

22. 24th Cong., 1st sess., H.D. 189, *Land Warrants and Scrip for Revolutionary Services* (March 1838), p. 4. The "horrors" were endlessly publicized: "they took one of the Prisoners and with a Knife ript open his Belly, took one end of his Guts and tied to a Tree, and then whipt the miserable man round and round till he expired; obliging me to dance" meanwhile. Thomas Brown, *A Plain Narrative of the Uncommon Sufferings* (1760), p. 13, reprinted in *The Magazine of History with Notes and Queries* (1908), Extra Number 1–4, V. 1.

23. Quoted from a document by the North Carolina Regulators. A brief review of the nine back country rebel movements in this period, from the Regulators to Shay's Rebellion, appears in Richard Brown and Don Fehrenbacher, "Back Country Rebellions and the Homestead Ethic," in their *Tradition, Conflict and Modernization* (1977).

was too high. The Confederation lacked money to pay the substantial blackmail they demanded.[24] Nor did it have enough to outfit a navy that could command their neutrality.)

Equally disturbed by the lack of security were the thousands of Americans, in all parts of the country, and from many social classes, who speculated in western land. Their land was worthless until potential buyers felt safe settling on it.

Would the government drastically reduce the burden of private debts? This was the most urgent question for all speculators and/or aspiring businessmen. Would it issue large amounts of paper money (thus rendering the debts smaller or trivial in real terms) and/or block legal suits for debt recovery? (The very poor, of course, were not really involved. For they contracted few debts. What tough-minded, shrewd lender ever lent to such persons?) The really substantial debts were incurred by businessmen and land buyers, particularly those trying to expand their operations.[25] As in later American wars, a host of Americans saw the price of wheat, pork, and other farm products rising during the war. They, therefore, borrowed money to buy farm land. (The celebrated Captain Shays, who led Shays Rebellion, apparently had borrowed for not one but two farms. His expressed goal was to close the courts, thus blocking suits for debt.)

Such speculators had saddled themselves with interest rates geared to the inflationary prices in the war and the immediate postwar boom. But after the war farm prices and therefore land prices collapsed. These sanguine borrowers then saw the real burden of their debt rise. Major speculators—Morris, Duer, Phelps, Gorham, and others—ended up penniless, some in debtor's prison. Lesser investors found the value of their land holdings collapsing while their interest payments continued, being geared to the older price level. (City workers were not equally afflicted; the cost of living fell dramatically, so their real incomes had actually not fallen much.[26])

The outcome was inevitable, if more extreme in certain frontier areas: mortgage "foreclosures and judgments for debt in central and western Mass-

24. Speaking for the pirate states the Moroccan ambassador proposed payment of a bit over a half-million dollars, plus a 10 percent bribe for himself. Cf. Henry P. Johnson, ed., *The Correspondence and Public Papers of John Jay* (1892), 3:197. Congress did not object to the ethics of such "bribery," but to its cost.

25. Larger investors and farmers were more likely to be both debtors to some lenders and also creditors of other borrowers. Recent writers of populist sympathies have arbitrarily assumed that those who wished to prevent debt recoveries were impoverished proletarians and subsistence farmers.

26. Flour and pork—the main ingredients in their diet—fell by about 10 percent from 1784 to 1787. A. Bezanson, et al, *Wholesale Prices in Philadelphia* (1936). Had money wages fallen 10 percent, they would have held their own.

achusetts . . . reached an all time high."[27] Suits for debt recovery were not always successful.[28] But enough were that Captain Daniel Shays led a brief uprising in western Massachusetts in revolt against the suits, put down by the state militia. The role of state taxation in producing this outcome has been somewhat exaggerated.[29] But the intensity of discontent was undoubted.

Year after year the Confederation failed to meet the demands for protection or payment. It did not lack good intentions; it lacked money. Justice Story observed that the Congress did not then have

> the power to raise any revenue, to levy any tax, enforce any law . . . [They] could contract debts; but they were without means to discharge them. They could pledge the public faith; but they were incapable of redeeming it. They could enter into treaties; but every state in the union might disobey them with impunity . . . All powers which did not execute themselves were at the mercy of the states.[30]

Finally, in 1789, the Confederation was replaced by a more centralized government that could both spend and tax. That shift to a more powerful government has often been seen as the product of plotting by Hamilton, Robert Morris, and others. But these men had offered their oratory, and logic, to the nation for years and years without result. In their "bitter contests [with] the party of inflation"[31] they persuaded few agrarians, democrats, or state legislators.

What eventually did change was the Confederation's status. Its financial string simply ran out. It could not pay its few ambassadors or any state militia it might have to call out. Having borrowed money throughout its life merely

27. Richard B. Morris, *The American Revolution Reconsidered* (1967), p. 139. He adds that "in the Valley of Virginia . . . executions (for bankruptcy) more than doubled between 1784 and 1788." However, reference to his source shows suits of execution being cut in half, not doubling.

28. Jensen, *The New Nation*, pp. 309–10, notes that 2,000 suits were instituted in Worcester County, Massachusetts, 100 people "jailed" for debt, a ratio of 5 percent. (If, as is likely, each debtor had multiple suits, the reference to 2,000 is no guide to the number involved. "Jailing for debt" in the early nineteenth century, tended to mean confinement to the debtor's house, or the town limits, for two weeks.

29. Jensen, *The New Nation*, p. 308, concludes that Massachusetts "levied enormous taxes," shifting the "burden onto the farmers who were least able to pay it. It is estimated that at least a third of an average farmer's income went in taxes after 1780." This improbable statement apparently ignores the consumption of food and the rental value of the farm home, both of which accounted for the bulk of farm income. He asserts that "taxes averaged more than three pounds a year for each of the 90,000 adult males in the state;" that "even propertyless males were expected to pay more than one pound a year through the poll tax;" that from 33 to 40 percent of the taxes levied were poll taxes." But 35 percent of (90,000 times £3) implies that well over 100,000 "propertyless" males paid poll taxes of £1 a year—although the total count for all adult males was only 90,000.

30. Joseph Story, *Commentaries on the Constitution of the United States* (1851), 1:168.

31. Quoted in Davis R. Dewey, *Financial History of the United States* (1920), p. 58.

to pay the interest on its debts, the day finally came when it had either to begin paying off some of those debts or repudiate outright. If it simply repudiated, of course, neither the United States nor the individual states might ever be able to borrow a cent in the future.[32]

Given that bleak prospect the states split ranks. Some ceased to oppose a central government, realizing they might make a financial killing. Their logic was simple. A stronger central government would almost certainly begin to pay off some of the debt created by the Continental Congress. Whoever then controlled that debt would see their certificates boom in value. The states, therefore, began to follow the farsighted Dutch bankers, buying debt certificates in the expectation of a rise.

Maryland's delegates to the Congress, noting the trend, "urged Maryland to buy as many final certificates as it could . . . By the spring of 1787 Arthur Lee of the [National] Board of Treasury was urging the governor of Virginia to . . . buy secretly and rapidly." Pennsylvania, New Jersey and Massachusetts likewise bought U.S. debt certificates.[33] Lee's conclusions were similar to those of private speculators, if not their source. They too began buying up certificates in the hope of public repayment.[34] And in 1787 the Constitutional Convention began.

The Constitution

"The Federal Constitution," John Adams wrote, "was the work of the commercial people in the seaport towns, of the slaveholding states, of the officers of the Revolutionary Army, and the property holders everywhere."[35] Adams specified "property holders everywhere." For he, as his contemporaries, recognized that by funding its debts and paying to defend its frontiers government would enhance the value of farms and land,[36] as well as other property throughout the nation. Many years later Charles Beard and a succession of historians wrote as though that support had been restricted to holders of debt certificates, one of many species of property.[37] That some-

---

32. The ingenuity and affluence of the west had not yet developed international agencies and huge banks that could attempt to "roll over" national debts, a process that worked, for a time, two centuries later.

33. Jensen, *The New Nation*, pp. 386–97; Ferguson, *Power*, p. 274. One Virginia legislator wrote: "We wish to possess ourselves of a large proportion of public securities before an appreciation takes place under the new government." Jensen, p. 397.

34. Later historians have indignantly attacked Morris and Hamilton for their public support of redemption, for redemption would benefit private legislators. These historians have seemed untroubled, however, by the actions of Lee and the Maryland delegates behind the scenes.

35. Quoted in the E. L. Bogart, *Economic History of the American People* (1933), p. 244.

36. H. C. Lodge, ed., *Hamilton's Works*, II:54.

37. Charles Beard, *An Economic Interpretation of the Constitution of the United States* (1913). Beard's interpretation put substantial emphasis on the advantages of adoption to those who

what myopic view has obscured the fact that over three-fourths of all American families owned property (land, farms, debts, certificates, etc.) and that nearly every species of property was likely to rise in value.[38] The reality may be still more complex. Holmes believed that "they wanted to make a nation and invested (bet) on the belief that they could make one, not that they wanted a powerful government because they had invested.[39]

On what terms were the certificates issued by the old Congress to be paid off? That issue was openly debated from the start of the Convention (1787) until 1791. Hamilton proposed, and the Congress eventually agreed, to pay off at the rate of 100 cents on the dollar. The first reason for doing so was crude, but persuasive. If Congress did not do so, it would darken its prospects of borrowing any money in the future. Who would then loan money to a nation that had just refused to pay its financial promises dollar for dollar?[40] The second reason was an argument from equity. In the long years when the Congress was refusing to pay them, many original holders had to sell their certificates in order to live. Congress's refusal had made the certificates of dubious value. Their holders were typically offered a mere 25 cents on the dollar, or even 10 cents. Madison argued that those who held certificates in 1790 should only be paid off at such market prices, with the balance of the face value then going to the original holder. Two centuries later his view was still being pro posed with fervor.[41] But in the 1790s Justice Iredell of the Supreme Court noted that, had Congress continued to refuse payment of the certificates,

owned "personality"—securities, debts, factories—by contrast to those who owned land. Since both groups would, and did, benefit from adoption, his prolonged argument achieves little. The validity of his factual presentation and consistency of argument have been devastatingly reviewed by Robert Brown, *Charles Beard and the Constitution* (1956), and Forrest McDonald, *We the People* (1958).

38. The greatest speculators, however, lost money. They had planned to buy millions of acres from the United States using U.S. certificates at bargain prices. The decision to fund drove up the certificate prices against them. Cf. Joseph S. Davis, *Essays in the Earlier History of American Corporations* (1918), I:142, 250.

39. Max Lerner, ed., *The Mind and Faith of Justice Holmes* (1951), p. 448.

40. Hamilton saw the government having to pay a higher margin on future loans: "For this dimunition of the value of stock every person . . . about to lend to the Government would demand compensation, and would add to the actual difference between the nominal and market value an equivalent for the chance of greater decrease." Samuel McKee, *Alexander Hamilton's Papers on Public Credit, Commerce and Finance* (1957).

A "great difference in the moral qualities between the Americans of the Northern and . . . Southern States" had been remarked upon by the Scotch creditors. By 1801 they were noting that of the prewar debts: "little has been obtained from the Southern but a considerable sum from the Northern States." Joseph Farington, *The Farington Diary* (1923), I:333. The availability and terms of further loans were affected.

41. Cf. Jensen, *The New Nation*, pp. 393 ff. Since close analysts such as Jensen still emphasize the gap between the original holder and the holders as of 1787, it should be noted that there were intermediate holders. Since no record for them existed, the gains by all 1787 holders could not, in fact, be ascertained.

those who had bought them on speculation "could not have applied for reimbursement from the original holder." Hence, "when the securities rose in value in consequence of an extraordinary resolution (which no man living at the time of the contract had any reason to expect)" it was unjust to demand that "the purchaser should refund the profit he had thus fairly acquired."[42] The original recipients of hollow Congressional promises had to live from 1780 to 1791, when redemption finally took place, using whatever trivial sums they had gotten from the speculators.

Suppose Congress had adopted Madison's position in 1780. Who on earth would then have offered the soldiers anything at all for the elegant certificates that Congress had foisted on them?[43] From 1780 the certificates plummeted, being worth 12 cents on the dollar by 1786. Then the triumph of property, and perhaps of "personalty," in the Constitutional Convention pushed them up—to 19 cents. After enough states ratified the Constitution to assure its passage, they reached 25 cents, briefly. "Those who had bought two years earlier had gained 40 percent," a tidy profit.[44] Perhaps half of the certificate owners held less than $500, therefore made not over two hundred dollars.[45] But they were surely as delighted as the large holders. (It should be noted that the market was still asserting that the U.S. Congress would probably *not* pay its debts: 22 cents on the dollar meant that the odds of payment still ran less than one in four. Better odds were actually offered for Confederate bonds a week before Lee surrendered.[46])

The nation's ability to borrow, thus created during Washington's first term, created a cornucopia in later years. It was almost immediately utilized by Hamilton's great opponent, Jefferson, to buy all the land west of the Mississippi. Had it been otherwise, Britain might well have extended Canada, Spain expanded Mexico, and France continued its huge Louisiana colony. Moreover, the ability of the nation to create a substantial national debt in the twentieth century might also have been lacking.

42. Griffith J. McRee, *Life and Correspondence of James Iredell* (1857, reprint ed. 1949), p. 314 (slightly adapted).

43. An additional technical difficulty was obvious. It was impossible, in 1791, to decide from whom the 1791 holders had bought the certificates they held, or at what price. Some bought from the original holder, some from second parties, some from third parties, and so on. Congress, it should be noted, had many years to compensate the original note holders for their losses, assuming say a typical loss of 80 percent because of its failure to pay. It never did.

44. Market values for 1786 and 1787 appear in Joseph S. Davis, *Essays in the Earlier History of American Corporations* (1918), 1:197, 250. Later data, and the quotation, are from E. James Ferguson, *The Power of the Purse* (1961), p. 256. Those who bought prior to that two-year interval, having earned nothing on their investment in all those years, achieved smaller profit rates.

45. Ferguson, *Power*, pp. 273–82 gives data for individual states from which one can surmise that about 45 percent of the holders owned less than $500 apiece in the issues he analyzed.

46. Cf. Richard I. Lester, *Confederate Finance and Purchasing in Great Britain* (1957), p. 207.

Part Two
1783–1860

What a pity we are not at Boston! You would be at peace,
I useful and esteemed, our daughter an American—born
. . . into the most worthy nation in the world!
—MIRABEAU, 1778

7

The Economic Problem, 1783–1860

ONCE independence removed colonial rule, the new nation faced its
economic problems directly and starkly. It could not convincingly
blame colonial rule for the most ancient of them all—how to acquire more
goods with less labor. Perhaps no philosopher, and certainly no economist,
has believed that the high and noble goal of human life was to produce ever
more gross national product. Just as certainly, however, the chief task of
human economies has been to produce whatever goods and services human
beings seek. The persistent and primary elements in the history of any
economy must then be its degree of success in creating more product, distributing it among the participants in the economy, and keeping down the required cost in human effort and suffering. The simplest basic facts about the
growth of U.S. product are presented in Table 7.1.

Indian societies did not focus on changing the standard of living. In
steady-state existence, their per capita incomes did not rise over the long
term.[1] Hence, the rate of growth in America from 1600 to 1700 must have
been as near zero as possible. Settlement by a population with different values, and a different way of life, then sharply increased the rate of growth in
U.S. per capita product. That rate in the long era of independence from 1800

1. Deaths by disease reduced the Indian population in New England just before the arrival
of the Pilgrims. The arrival of the Pilgrims affected total output but did little to the per capita
output of the surviving U.S. population. The new arrivals were few. Their problems in learning
how to survive in the new land were great. They could not have notably increased U.S. product
per capita during the period 1700–1800.

TABLE 7.1
ANNUAL RATE OF GROWTH OF U.S. NATIONAL
PRODUCT PER PERSON,
1700–1967 (IN PERCENT)

Year	Percentage
1700–1800	+ 0.4
1800–1860	+ 1.1
1860–1967	+ 1.7

Source: The basic estimates for years prior to 1860 are from Robert Gallman who created the first, and still standard, estimates of U.S. national income in the nineteenth century. These are cited, as well as his estimate for 1700–1800. in his basic and wide-ranging review, "The Pace and Pattern of American Growth," in Lance Davis, et al., eds., American Economic Growth (1972). Figures for 1860–1967 are adapted from Moses Abramowitz and Paul David, "Economic Growth in America," De Economist (1973). Terry Anderson estimates a slower rate of growth in 1660–1800 largely because he finds acreage in Hampshire County, Massachusetts, changing little from 1700 to 1739, quadrupling in the next decade, and then declining in 1770–79. That improbable sequence helps account for his estimate of slower growth. His analysis, however, and his discussion of basic work by Egnal, Main, McCusker, Ball, and Walton, plus comments by Paul David and Robert Gallman, provide a keen introduction to the estimation issues. Terry Anderson, "Economic Growth in Colonial New England," Journal of Economic History (March 1979).

to 1860 practically tripled that of the colonial century. The actual number in Table 7.1 may seem trivial, even piffling. Perhaps its importance can be seen by noting that real incomes for Lincoln's generation (born 1809) gained at three times the rate they did in Benjamin Franklin's (born 1706).

The elements of growth are examined in Table 7.2. Much attention has recently been lavished on the role of productivity, human capital, and research and development in economic growth. This irresistibly led to a belief that it was primarily such forces that drove real output up during the first century of independence.[2] Analysis of the still crude estimates of nineteenth-century output, however, warrants the judgment by Abramowitz and David: "Over the course of the nineteenth century the pace of increase of the real gross domestic product was accounted for largely by the traditional, conventionally defined factors of production: labor, land, the tangible reproducible capital."[3] As Table 7.2 shows, the advance in productivity did not actually contribute much more than one-tenth to the nineteenth century's gains.

2. Cf. the incisive presentation of this view in Douglass North, Growth and Welfare in the American Past (1966), pp. 9–11, 86–88.
3. Moses Abramowitz and Paul David, "Economic Growth in America," De Economist (1973), NR 3.

TABLE 7.2

GROWTH RATES OF U.S. GROSS NATIONAL PRODUCT, 1800–1967

(IN PERCENT)[a]

Year	Real product	Productivity	Per capita real product
1800–1855	4.2	0.4	1.1
1855–1905	3.9	0.5	1.6
1905–1927	3.3	1.5	1.7
1927–1967	3.2	1.9	1.8

[a]Average annual percentage rates for the private domestic economy: (1) real gross product and (2) productivity of manhours and net capital stock.

Source: These data are from the fundamental and deeply perceptive analysis of Moses Abramowitz and Paul David, "Economic Growth in America," *De Economist* (1973), NR 3, with some revision from Paul David's essay in Karl Brunner and Allan Meltzer, eds., *International Organization, National Policies and Economic Development* (1977).

The spare simplicity of a "labor input" series summarizes the market's valuation of the sacrifices in energy and effort made by the pioneer farmers, indentured servants, and slaves. A "capital input" series similarly measures (in financial terms) the extent to which they denied their families such tiny luxuries as sugar and coffee, such conveniences as cabins chinked well enough so that snow did not blow in through the logs. Such sacrifices were made because farmers used their time and energy to clear the land of trees and stumps, to repair farm tools, and used their savings to buy still other capital inputs. Indeed, families saved perhaps 12 percent of their incomes in order to make such investments, thus reducing their consumption at more than twice the rate their wealthier descendants did in the twentieth century.[4] These were the basic elements in economic growth. They continued to be basic as the twentieth century began.

But once such central "economic" contributions to growth are recognized we must turn to the contribution made by the values of the people themselves. These values drove the "productivity" gains, for they prompted the American willingness to accept persistent novelty in production. Without such willingness Americans would never have put up with the costs of growth—job turnover, migration, high depreciation of machinery, destruction of business investments, and the harsh obsolescence of human skills and training.

Visitors to the United States have long remarked how unusually willing Americans were to accept novelty in the economic process. (Only in recent

4. Cf. Appendix A, this chapter.

years have nations such as Japan, Taiwan, and Singapore come to rival, and even exceed, the United States in that respect.) Such open mindedness brought a near endless series of innovations which persistently drove up the nation's productivity.

As Schumpeter emphasized,[5] it is not a single class of innovations that generates productivity gains—not even the adoption of new techniques for production. Innovations must also include the searching out of new locations; putting into place new methods of organization (the corporation, the cooperative, the Post Office); creating new products (good and bad) to replace older ones (cotton gins for hand picking, cradles for scythes, and harvesters for cradles); creating brand new consumer products (canned milk, packaged sugar, sulkies, and high button shoes). Almost every change created private losses. It often created social costs as well. The corporation bankrupted private entrepreneurs. The automobile made carriage factories obsolete. The numerically controlled machine made machinists' skills all but useless. (Those able to view the process from on high also might judge some new products inferior to the old—the Hudson River school to Renaissance art, parlor music to baroque, wonder drugs to folk remedies.)

Some innovations "embodied" productivity advance in capital inputs. Thus when one grain cradle replaced four worn-out sickles, productivity gained without any net increase in capital.[6] Gross investment had "embodied" a new technology, advancing productivity. But when one harvester then replaced five worn-out cradles, both net and gross investment increased.

Some innovations required no additional inputs at all. Their impact was spectacular even in the first stages of an industry. When the new Liberty ships were created in World War II, the persistent increase in ship building productivity, with no increase in labor or capital inputs, signaled the importance of simply "learning by doing."[7] As Koopmans has written, "any application of technological knowledge contains a necessary and productive element of learning from experience."[8] Tracking back, historians have rediscovered the fact that nineteenth-century Americans learned how to produce more steel without more machinery or labor, more textiles by having workers tend two spinning machines instead of one, and so on.[9]

This process of innovation, however marvelous, however beneficial to society, did not benefit everyone. As always, there was a price. Business failures never ended. Thousands of items laboriously invented and patented

---

5. Cf. Joseph Schumpeter, *The Theory of Economic Development* (1934), ch. 2.
6. Ratios computed from data in Leo Rogin, *The Introduction of Farm Machinery* (1931), pp. 124–26.
7. Cf. BLS Bulletin 824, *Wartime Employment . . . in Shipyards* (1947).
8. Tjalling Koopmans, *Three Essays on the State of Economic Science* (1957), p. 125.
9. Paul David, "The 'Horndal' Effect in Lowell, 1834–36," and "Learning by Doing," in his *Technical Choice, Innovation and Economic Growth* (1975).

were never produced. Yet the willingness to hazard changes continued. The successful ones proved so numerous and so vital that their introduction drove and dominated the U.S. growth process. The elements that were vital to U.S. innovation, however, were not inevitable preconditions for economic growth elsewhere. (Japan and Taiwan achieved a forceful rate of productivity advance in a vastly different social context.) These American elements included the freedom for entrepreneurs to innovate in production, distribution, and consumption; the willingness of investors to opt for increasingly long-lived capital goods, deferring their financial return further and further into the future. They included entrepreneurs, great and small, who persistently ventured their time, their savings, their health in the hope of gain and distinction, however many the previous failures in the same industry, the same area.[10] They included workers who accepted innovation, and effectively worked with ever-changing techniques and equipment. The end result was more production, requiring less and less effort and energy per unit produced.

In the above perspective forces work in a social matrix: increased inputs are combined with productivity advance by a nation receptive to innovation. Scholars have, however, proposed more purely economic explanations of American growth. These do not exclude the social matrix, but they do not emphasize it. Chief among these is the "staple theory." As most elegantly presented, by Douglass North, it emphasizes one central factor from which the growth process took its primary stimulus: expanding foreign markets for American raw cotton. "There are few exceptions to the essential initiating role of a successful export sector in the early stages of accelerated growth of market economies."[11] At the beginning of the twentieth century, Britain swiftly expanded its cotton textile industry, and with it, purchases of American cotton. As North outlines it, southerners invested their returns in slaves and new lands, thus developing Mississippi, Alabama, and a new tier of states. Northerners participated, too, by shipping cotton overseas. They invested in ships, wharves, chandleries in New York City (and other locations). In turn, this stimulated investments in the Erie Canal and in building cities farther west. By the familiar multiplier process, such investments made jobs in construction, thence ironworking, thence on farms to feed and clothe the ironworkers, and so on. Pushing up the price of cotton and wheat, these then led to further farm investment.

The development of an export staple market was unquestionably a significant innovation. But it was only one among many. Bale for bale the ex-

10. Two fundamental, and lively, studies are those by Jonathan Hughes, *Industrialization and Economic History* (1970), and *The Vital Few* (1973).

11. Douglass North, *The Economic Growth of the United States, 1790–1860* (1966), p. 10, ch. 1. This modern classic had its predecessors on the staple theory: Harold Innis, *The Fur Trade in Canada* (1956), and Robert Baldwin, "Patterns of Development," in *Manchester School of Economic and Social Studies* (May 1956).

panding U.S. market for raw cotton (e.g., in Lowell textile mills, in Philadelphia and New York City mills) generated the same kind of multiplier–accelerator consequences as the expanding foreign market. Moreover, the markets for Ohio wool, Kentucky horses, Indiana wheat, that appeared among the growing populations in Boston, Philadelphia,[12] Baltimore, and New York City required similar investments in transport, retail stores, warehouses, eventually in farms.

More generally the U.S. market expanded rapidly as millions immigrated from Europe. The per capita income of Americans exceeded that of many Europeans and Asians who bought British textiles. Reckoning with these facts could imply that domestic demand was a far more powerful force in growth than foreign demand. But we are not required to choose. Both foreign and domestic demand shifts were at work. Both contributed to making markets for America's newest innovations, and its oldest products.

Another comprehensive view argues that output growth escalated so much after a given date that a U.S. "take-off" into sustained growth took place.[13] That view developed such intense interest among scholars that it led to a "take-off in sustained controversy."[14] Though it has had few recent advocates its muted form does well in emphasizing the role of persistent investment growth during the 1840s, particularly in railroads and the factories supplying material to them.[15] Such overstatement in turn led to contrary overstatements. Yet, as with exports, an important, if partial, truth is being noted: expanding investment surely expanded national income through the multiplier-accelerator process and thereby stimulated economic growth. Railroad investment surely made large and volatile contributions to that growth.[16] But other industries—from simple flour mills and shovel factories to canals—expanded investment even more. There is little basis for concluding that a dollar of railroad investment was peculiarly powerful. It did create significant backward linkage, for example, generating demands for iron, hence for iron ore, hence for shovels, etc. But it was not obviously greater than the linkages from farming investment or even primitive home building. The tables of inter-industry relationships for more recent decades point to no such priority.

12. Cf. Diane Lindstrom's acute discussion of growth in the Philadelphia area in "American Economic Growth Before 1840," *Journal of Economic History* (March 1979). Lloyd Mercer carefully concludes that "at the margin Southern demand for Western products contributed significantly to Western growth." Cf. Roger Ransom et al., *Explorations in the New Economic History, Essays in Honor of Douglass C. North* (1982), p. 95.

13. Walt Rostow, *The Stages of Economic Growth* (1961).

14. The phrase is from an admirable review by Henry Rosovsky in the *Journal of Economic History* (June 1965). Cf. also Felix and Rostow in *Journal of Economic History* (March 1970).

15. Rostow, *The Stages*, pp. 38, 55.

16. The contribution of the railroads, and indeed the structure of antebellum growth, are outlined in a beautifully judicious study by Albert Fishlow, *American Railroads and the Transformation of the Ante-bellum Economy* (1965). The still noteworthy analysis in Robert Fogel's pioneering *Railroads and Economic Growth* (1964) deflates exaggerated notions of their role.

Where, then, was all the investment expansion and increasing income taking place? Was it chiefly the accomplishment of industrialization? Table 7.3 indicates it was not. From its very beginning the U.S. economy had been agricultural. By the outbreak of the Civil War agriculture still employed more than half the entire labor force. The income rise of 1783–1860 that drew an ever increasing flow of European immigrants did, of course, reflect in part the sharp rate of increase in manufacturing and mining. But it was primarily the performance of the farm economy that drove U.S. incomes upward. Farming was, and is, more capital and land intensive than most other sectors. Hence, it not only used the large share of the labor force shown by Table 7.3, but an even larger proportion of total inputs. Moreover, little of that labor involved a wage earning class. (Northern farming relied primarily on members of farm families. Southern farming relied chiefly on slave labor.) And it was nearly all on a noncorporate basis.

Adelman and Morris recently asked why nations across the world developed economically at such different rates. One prime reason, they discovered, was the pattern of land settlement and holding. The slower developers had concentrated, or parcellized, land holdings. Or their "choice of crops and methods" was communally decided upon.[17] Neither obstacle was present in the United States. Millions of untilled acres were available for sale from the earliest days of the nation. Three-fourths of American families owned their own farms even in late colonial days. Farms ranged from 100 to 150 acres, and almost none held the tiny 5 acre parcels of many nations. Farmers could see what crops had done well, could make their own judgment of market prospects. They could vary their crop combinations and production techniques from year to year as they chose. Neither chiefs, landowners, village elders, nor the commune had to agree before a change could be made.

Level of Living, 1783

What were living conditions like in the world of 1783? American homes, of course, had no central heat. They relied primarily on one open fireplace, which was fed about 6 cords of wood a year.[18] (Students at a leading north-

17. Great Britain, Germany, France, United States, Sweden, Japan, and Canada all showed "a substantial rise in agricultural output per head . . . during at least several decades . . . prior to the first major spread of mechanized industry; subsequently there was a significant interaction between the spread of industry and the growth of the agricultural sector." Irma Adelman and Cynthia Morris, *The Role of Institutional Influence in Patterns of Agricultural Development: A Cross Section Quantitative Study* (September 1978).

18. *Niles Weekly Register*, June 28, 1817, p. 278, estimates 1 cord consumed per person. In 1831 records for Rhode Island cotton factories show about 8 cords per family. *Niles Addendum* to vol. 41 (1831), p. 62, and *Documents Relative to Manufactures*, pp. 94, 386, report 4 and 9, respectively. The *Patent Office Report for 1847* estimates 6 cords per family, H.D. 54, p. 559.

TABLE 7.3
THE LABOR FORCE, 1800–1960[a] (IN THOUSANDS)

| | Labor force (10 years and older) | | | | | | | Employment[a] | | | | | | | |
| | | | | | | | | | Manufacturing | | | Transport | | Service | |
Year	Total	Free	Slave	Agriculture (10 years and older)	Fishing	Mining	Construction	Total persons engaged	Cotton textile wage earners	Primary iron and steel wage earners	Trade	Ocean vessels	Railway	Teachers	Domestics
1800	1,680	1,150	530	1,400	5	10			1	1		40		5	40
1810	2,330	1,590	740	1,950	6	11		75	10	5		60		12	70
1820	3,135	2,185	950	2,470	14	13			12	5		50		20	110
1830	4,200	3,020	1,180	2,965	15	22			55	20		70		30	160
1840	5,660	4,180	1,480	3,570	24	32	290	500	72	24	350	95	7	45	240
1850	8,250	6,280	1,970	4,520	30	102	410	1,200	92	35	530	135	20	80	350
1860	11,110	8,770	2,340	5,880	31	176	520	1,530	122	43	890	145	80	115	600
1870	12,930			6,790	28	180	780	2,470	135	78	1,310	135	230	170	1,000
1880	17,390			8,920	41	280	900	3,290	175	130	1,930	125	416	230	1,130
1890	23,320			9,960	60	440	1,510	4,390	222	149	2,960	120	750	350	1,580
1900	29,070			11,680	69	637	1,665	5,895	303	222	3,970	105	1,040	436	1,800
1910	37,480			11,770	68	1,068	1,949	8,332	370	306	5,320	150	1,855	595	2,090
1920	41,610			10,790	53	1,180	1,233	11,190	450	460	5,845	205	2,236	752	1,660
1930	48,830			10,560	73	1,009	1,988	9,884	372	375	8,122	160	1,659	1,044	2,270
1940	56,290			9,575	60	925	1,876	11,309	400	485	9,328	150	1,160	1,086	2,300
1950	65,470			7,870	77	901	3,029	15,648	(350)	(550)	12,152	130	1,373	1,270	1,995
1960	74,060			5,970	45	709	3,640	17,145	(300)	(530)	14,051	135	883	1,850	2,489

[a]Persons engaged (employees, self-employed, and unpaid family workers), except as specified. Age 10 years and older.

Source: Taken from Stanley Lebergott, *Manpower in Economic Growth* (1964), p. 510. We have corrected the 1800 total and free labor force figures shown there for an arithmetic error noted by Paul David, and adopted a superior estimate of Albert Fishlow for railway employment in 1870.

eastern college consumed about 2 cords of wood each winter.)[19] By contrast, families that relied on wood heat in 1980 also consumed perhaps 6 cords, but in houses that had far better insulation and far more efficient stoves.[20]

Houses, of course, lacked plumbing. They had no hot water. Nor did they have running cold water, except in Boston and Philadelphia.[21] Toilets were outside shacks, enclosing a privy. A pitcher of water and a basin served for washing. On frosty mornings the frozen water discouraged excessive washing and shaving.[22] It is no wonder that even as late as 1850 a farmer's journal could stipulate that a healthy adult farmer might safely take a bath—once a week.[23]

Lacking plumbing, the house also lacked electricity or gas. Lighting came from candles, which were used so sparingly that one provided an evening's illumination.[24] The bedroom had a bed (without springs) but no chairs, lamps, end tables, dressers, counterpanes, mirrors. In homes, as in taverns and hotels, two persons customarily slept in a bed.[25] (European hospitals put three to a bed.)

The kitchen, lacking electricity, had no electric lights, no refrigerator—nor toaster, blender, coffeemaker, dishwasher, grill, and so on. It had no can opener: more than a century was to pass before even a handful of families used canned food. And half a century more before frozen food was stocked in groceries.

The housewife was expected to bake over half a ton of bread a year. (As late as 1900, after bakeries had multiplied, the figure was still half a ton.) She also had to kill the chickens; help butcher pigs; put up pork and beef in brine; clean, peel, and prepare all vegetables, serving some fresh and preserving the rest in jars. She likewise made whatever pickles, sauces, preserves, jams,

19. Williams College. Cf. *The Quarterly Register of the American Educational Society* (May 1831), p. 298.

20. State of Vermont, Energy Office. *Final Report on the Use of Wood as a Heat Source* (June 1978), p. 15, and U.S. Department of Agriculture, Forest Service, *Prospectus: Firewood Manufacturing and Marketing* (1980), p. 17.

21. U.S. Commissioner of Labor, Fourteenth Annual Report, *Water, Gas and Electric Plants* (1900), Table 1, p. 45.

22. A contemporary describes "having broken the ice in your basin to wash your hands" and "going up to the washing stand [to find] the water frozen to the centre of every bottle." James Beresford, *The Miseries of Human Life* (1807), pp. 156, 160.

23. Quoted in *Agricultural History.*

24. Records for 1831 show that two workmen in a craftsman's shop burned half a candle a day between them. Cf. (McLane Report) *Documents Relative to Manufactures* (1833).

25. A leading New York editor reported that hotels, about 1824, lacked "single lodging rooms or even single beds." "In country inns, a traveler who objected to a stranger as a bedfellow was regarded as unreasonably fastidious. Nothing was more common . . . than to be awakened by the landlord . . . showing a stranger into your bed." Harriet Weed, *Autobiography of Thurlow Weed* (1883), p. 143. On the frontier two to four persons shared a bed. Ray Billington, *America's Frontier Culture* (1977), p. 93.

ketchup, cakes, and donuts the family consumed. During most of the year apples were the only fresh fruit. Nearly all families subsisted on a diet that included salt pork, salt beef, lard (instead of butter or margarine), corn meal, and molasses (instead of sugar or other syrups). This was true as late as 1900. It was truer a century earlier. Of the 8,000 items available in today's supermarket,[26] hardly any were available to even the 5 percent of all Americans who lived in villages and cities in 1800. Of the 9,000 items in today's drugstore, only a similarly tiny proportion was available. If a patient needed to consume one of the dubious items in the formulary at the time—only the well-to-do did so—he had to mix the ingredients himself. Pharmaceutical companies were not yet sending detail men around, and pharmacists did not always provide such combinations.[27]

Changes, 1783–1860

How had this primitive level of living changed by 1860? Farm workers, both free farmers and slaves, retained their traditional workday. They continued to labor in the tradition of "first light to dark" and even beyond, amid the urgencies of the wheat harvest or sugar boiling. But by 1860 half the free labor force was engaged in nonfarm pursuits. The workday in many factories, shipyards, and shops had been cut from the average of thirteen hours in the early factories. A competent observer declared that "ten hours is the common usage."[28]

A three-hour decline sounds trivial in an era when most employees work eight, minus coffee-break time, and minus long lunch hours. Its importance can, however, be measured by the foregone consumption it represented. If hours had not fallen, nonfarm workers would have had something close to 25 percent more goods and services each year than they actually did.[29] Workers gave up that possible increase in their standard of living in return for a significant reduction in the effort, attention, and boredom of their workweek. No similar exchange was made in the twentieth century, which suggests how strongly the nineteenth-century worker valued a shorter workday, even

26. *Progressive Grocer* (April 1981), p. 101, reports 8,085 "warehoused items in the typical depot."

27. "Labouring in vain to disentangle your medicine scales; till after fretting, twisting, and twirling, for half the morning, to no purpose, you are at last obliged to weigh your dose (Tartar emetic or James' powders) as you can, with all the strings in a Gordian knot—one scale topsy-turvy and the other turvy-topsy." Beresford, *The Miseries of Human Life* (1807), p. 175.

28. Alexander Delmar, *Statistics of the United States, Compiled under the Authority of the Secretary of the Treasury . . . For the Paris Exposition of 1867* (1867), p. 18.

29. Three hours represents 33% of the 10-hour average in 1860. But there were surely some offsetting gains in work efficiency per hour. We consider 25%, therefore, a more realistic estimate of forgone output.

though he enjoyed far fewer goods and services than his twentieth-century counterpart.

What of the trend in measured incomes? Table 7.4 reports the income trend for farm laborers. That group is chosen as significant because most Americans were either farmers or farm laborers. Small farmers and urban laborers were continuously recruited from the farm laborer group, while many farmers did intermittent day work for their neighbors. Hence, the trend in earnings of the large farm laborer group should mark the income trend of a considerable group of workers. (And we have tolerably reliable data for it.)

For items other than food and lodging, bought by the cash wages in column 1 of Table 7.4, a significant real income gain came from rapid productivity advances. These advances brought a precipitous decline in the cost of textiles, a milder decline in the price of shoes, hats, and woolen cloth. Dorothy Brady's estimates show that, between 1809 and 1860, prices for a wide range of consumer items—from bedspreads to carriages, from books to tables—were cut in half.[30] (In the two centuries after the landing at Jamestown the world's clockmakers had cut the daily error in clocks from perhaps 500 seconds a day to one-tenth of a second.[31] But that technical advance was totally irrelevant to Americans until Chauncey Jerome's innovations, which cut the price of clocks by two thirds and made cheap clocks available to American households.)

The cost of food also fell, as indicated by the cost of board. (Since labor rates were rising, the cost of raw food per se must have declined dramatically. Presumably the swift improvement in farm productivity was responsible.[32]) As the cost of food fell, the quality of the diet rose. Most revealing was the increase in the primary luxuries of the masses: sugar and coffee. As Senator James Buchanan (later president) remarked in 1842: "Though not an old man I can remember the time when coffee and tea were considered articles of luxury: But now their use is universal."[33] Obviously these generalizations apply only to the free labor force. The daily ration of corn and pork did not change for slaves. Nor were their shambling one-room cabins improved.[34]

30. Cf. the price detail in Dorothy Brady's "Price Deflators" in Conference on Research in Income and Wealth, *Output, Employment and Productivity in the United States After 1800* (1966), pp. 106–09.

31. Carlo Cipolla, *Clocks and Culture* (1967), p. 59.

32. According to William Parker, labor required per bushel of wheat in the Northeast in 1839 was 8% lower in the West and 20% lower in the South. Cf. his "Productivity Growth in Grain Production," in Conference on Research in Income and Wealth, *Output . . . After 1800* (1966), p. 545.

33. 62d Cong., 1st sess., S.D. 21, *Customs Tariff of 1842*, p. 142.

34. This somewhat speculative judgment rests on the apparent lack of change over time in conditions as described in manuals for planters, contemporary articles, and assorted plantation records. However, when Louisiana was held by the French (prior to 1808), its slaves often had no meat in their diet. Some slight upward trend therefore probably did occur.

TABLE 7.4

TRENDS IN THE LEVEL OF LIVING, 1800–79

| | Monthly earnings farm labor (excluding food, lodging) | | Price of board (index) | Food consumption (pounds per capita) | | | | Percent of families with stoves |
	Current prices	1860 prices	(1860 = 100)	Meat	Flour, potatoes	Sugar, molasses	Coffee	
1800	$10.00	$ 6.62	110	175	365	15	2	1
1818	9.45	6.18						
1830	8.85	7.97	68					
1850	10.85	11.54	77					
1860	13.66	13.66	100					
1879	11.70	9.51		173	584	40	8	67

Source: Earnings, price of board: Lebergott, *Manpower*, pp. 257, 539–40, 548. Consumer Price Index: Paul David and Peter Solar, *Research in Economic History* (1977), 2:16. Food: *Niles Weekly Register*, December 2, 1815, p. 230. (Molasses converted at 1 gallon = 8 lbs of sugar.) Food Research Institute, *Studies* (May 1961). Coffee imports and population figures for per capita estimates from *Historical Statistics . . . to 1970*, pp. 14, 902. Stoves: Chauncey DePew, *One Hundred Years of American Commerce* (1897), 2:361.

Housing changed little in terms of simple comfort.[35] Most families lived in wooden houses in 1783. Most still did so in 1860. (Even in one of the more urbanized states, New York, 91 percent of all dwellings were still wooden.[36]) Of course no homes had electricity. Few had gas. Fewer still had hot running water. Indeed, not even 2 percent had indoor toilets and cold running water.[37] The one significant advance in housing was that stoves replaced open fireplaces. As cities grew and the trees around them were cut down for firewood, the price of wood rose steadily. When careful inquiry demonstrated that a sheet-iron cylinder stove required only one-tenth as much wood and gave as much heat as an open fireplace,[38] the cost incentive proved irresistible. While almost no American families had stoves in 1789, about two-thirds did by 1860.[39]

Such gains were more potent in reality than impressive in any summary measures—a marked shortening of the workday, a warmer house in the winter, more clothing (with less labor for the housewife), more minor luxuries such as sugar and coffee.

What can be said of the distribution of wealth, and income, in the United States before the Civil War?

Since such distributions have been unequal in every nation for which data are available, the United States was not likely to have been an exception. The basic study by Alice Jones for 1774 shows it was not. The richest 10 percent of households held half the wealth.[40]

Was the 1774 distribution "greatly" unequal? Oddly, some historians have found it "comforting . . . to [think that the U.S.] distribution of income and wealth was greatly unequal well before era of industrialization." But was it "greatly" unequal as compared to any other nation at the time? There is little evidence that it was or was not; other distributions are lacking. (A few city distributions have been derived with great effort and zest.[41] But these data tell us less about the United States as a whole than about the nesting habits of the

35. Heavy timber framing, post-and-beam construction, was replaced by balloon construction (using 2 × 4's and 2 × 6's) in the 1820s, but not substantially until after 1860.

36. *Census of the State of New York for 1865* (1867), p. 271.

37. Stanley Lebergott, *The American Economy: Income, Wealth and Want* (1976), p. 226. Data collected by Edgar Martin for the proportion of houses with water closets show 10 percent for New York city, about 2 percent for Albany, and Charleston, and 30 percent for Boston.

38. *Transactions of the American Philosophical Society*, n. s. 3 p. 63.

39. Even as late as 1830 less than 1% had stoves. Ownership is estimated here by applying a 10% annual depreciation rate to production data from Chauncey DePew, *One Hundred Years of American Commerce* (1897), 2:361.

40. Alice Jones, *Wealth of a Nation To Be* (1980) 164. Earlier studies by Jackson Main, "Trends in Wealth Concentration Before 1860," *Journal of Economic History* (June 1971), p. 445, give a similar result.

41. Cf. the comprehensive reviews by Jeffrey Williamson and Peter Lindert, *American Inequality* (1980), ch. 2, Edward Pessen, *Riches, Class and Power Before the Civil War* (1973).

rich as they moved into Boston or New York City in one period, out of it in another.)

How had the wealth distribution changed by 1860? Unfortunately the existing studies are not comparable enough to tell us much about that comparison.[42]

Many historians have been fascinated by de Tocqueville's assertion (in the 1830s) that men could rise in the economic scale more readily in the United States than in Europe. Implicitly accepting his point they have gone on to ask about the odds of becoming very wealthy in America. Data for New York City and Boston tell us something about that prospect during the very years de Toqueville was writing. They show that in 1828 New York City had 520 residents with $50,000 or more in wealth, while Boston in 1833 had 303 with $40,000 or more. If analyzed with care, their data show that in the course of the next 15 years, about 40 percent of those people dropped to lower wealth levels.[43] Hence the top slots became open. But meanwhile incomes and wealth had risen. Therefore, new men and women had replaced those in the top wealth ranks, but, in addition, still others had joined them.

However, one simple fact proved far more important to the 99 percent of Americans who were never in or near those lofty wealth categories: average real income in the United States exceeded that for the rest of the world. That accomplishment, hard won, was achieved by developing the land to the needs of a largely agricultural economy.

Appendix

Appendix A

The average household in 1805 had about $360 in homes, barns, tools, and apparel (Samuel Blodget, *Economica* (1806), p. 196). At that time the typical American in the labor force was a farmer, and earnings of farmers would have been something close to the $120 a year plus board (Lebergott, *Manpower*, p. 257) earned by farm laborers. Or even less, since the expectation of capital gains was a significant make weight for farmers.

The average family head in 1800, as a male 16 years and older, was about 35 years of age. If he saved $14.59 a year, earned 6 percent on his savings, the compounded amount in 15 years would been about $360. The implicit saving rate of 12 percent is almost double the 5 to 8 percent savings rates from personal income 1929–1980.

42. Cf. Appendix B, this chapter. They imply an unreasonably great increase in concentration by 1870, and, therefore, a great decrease thereafter.

43. Tabulated, from the extended studies of Edward Pessen, in Lebergott, *Wealth and Want* (1976), p. 204. We say "about 40 percent" because Pessen's data do not permit exact comparison. They show 219 of the 520 New Yorkers with under $45,000 by 1845, and 129 of the Bostonians under $50,000 by 1848.

Temperate and industrious workmen in Massachusetts might well "lay up $50 a year of $250 earnings, for sickness, old age, or future comforts." Luther Hamilton, ed., *Memoirs, Speeches and Writings of Robert Rantoul, Jr.* (1854), pp. 571, 573.

Donald Adams estimates savings rates of about 15 percent for about 40 workers in a Delaware woolen mill 1813–60, the company paying 6 percent. Cf. Tables 2 and 3 in his "The Standard of Living During American Industrialization," *Journal of Economic History* (December 1982).

Appendix B

Some historians have compared the fundamental study by Alice Jones for 1774 with that for Lee Soltow for 1850–70 to conclude that "there was a sharp advance in the concentration of wealth between 1774 and 1860." Jones' probate data indicate that less than 2 percent of wealth owners had zero assets or negative net worth. (Cf. Alice Jones, *Wealth of a Nation To Be* (1980), p. 162, and her *American Colonial Wealth* (1977), 3:2105. Unpublished tabulations kindly provided by Professor Jones facilitated this comparison.)

Lee Soltow, *Men and Wealth in the United States, 1850–1870* (1975), p. 188, however, estimates that 34 percent of free persons reporting in 1860, and 39 percent in 1870, had less than $1 in wealth. Now, given the upward trend in incomes and farm values over the decades, it is quite unlikely that these figures are comparable with the Jones data. Probate records were based on a careful evaluation of individual asset items by third parties while settling estates. (Moreover, the 1774 figures relate to an era before inheritance taxes would bias such findings.) By contrast, the Population Census reports for 1850–70 represent off-the-cuff responses made to government enumerators, with corroborative detail neither requested nor expected. To take one example from the 1850 Population Census records, in Pulaski County, Kentucky, 4 successive farmers reported as follows: Rufus Meece, age 32, no property; Aaron Meece, age 25, $300; William Nunley, age 38, $800; Richard Goff, age 40, no property. Entries for the Scollay Square area in Boston in the same Census cite grocers whose wealth was zero and also one whose wealth ran to thousands of dollars. There is little basis for assuming that "no entry" in these Census reports means zero dollars, rather than failure to ask a difficult question or failure to offer an answer to it.

The Population Census data are undoubtedly of value for suggesting differences between various population groups, at a given time, as Soltow's analysis suggests. But they are not sufficiently comparable with the probate sample for 1774 to provide reliable measures of change. (Cf. the more affirmative view in Jeffrey Williamson and Peter Lindert, *American Inequality* (1980), pp. 38–39.)

8

Land Policy and The Public Domain

AMERICA, Emerson wrote, begins with the Alleghenies. He was referring to "The Great Western Territory," which then constituted the public domain of the new national government.[1] That domain was created by two
major wars, followed by an unconstitutional land deal with a dictator. "No
problem so continuously absorbed the attention of Congress for the next century as the management, sales, and donation of this great empire."[2]

In 1763 Britain finally defeated the French in North America, and then
established the "Proclamation Line" to prevent the westward flow of migration. But that legislation proved nowhere near as effective a barrier to settlement as the French and their Indian allies had previously been. Britain's
victory proved a disaster for her traditional colonial policy. For that policy
had sought to draw raw materials from the United States and in return use it
as a dumping ground for convicts and religious fanatics. "The Great object of
colonizing upon the Continent of North America has been to improve and extend the Commerce, Navigation and Manufactures of this Kingdom, upon
which its strength and security depend." The promotion of fisheries, "the
growth and culture of Naval Stores," and "securing a supply of lumber, provisions and other necessaries" were all designed to that end. And "to answer
these Salutary purposes it has been the policy of the Kingdom to confine her
settlements as much as possible to the Sea Coast." All of which offered

> a very strong argument against forming Settlements in the interior country
> more especially where every advantage derived from an Established Gov-
> ernment would naturally tend to draw the stream of population; fertility of
> Soil and temperature of Climate offering superior enticements to settlers
> who, exposed to the few hardships and struggling with few difficulties,
> could with little labour earn an abundance of their own wants but without a
> possibility of supplying ours with any considerable Quantities.[3]

1. 20th Cong., 2d sess., H.R. 95, *Distribution of the Proceeds* . . . , Table 1 (SS190).
2. Paul Gates, *The Farmer's Age: 1815–1860* (1960), p. 51.
3. Lords of Trade to the Kingdom, "The General State of Indian Affairs and the Establish-

That forecast was verified in a few short years. For the settlers became increasingly restive as they spread beyond colonial restraints. And then the Revolution came. In its aftermath the soldiers picked up booty from the fields of battle. And the states picked up the fields themselves. States along the seaboard took nearly 380 million acres,[4] acres that were once the private property of "the most serene and most potent prince, George the Third, by the Grace of God King of Great Britain, France, and Ireland, Defender of the Faith, Duke of Brunswick and Luneburg, Arch Treasurer and Prince Elector of the Holy Roman Empire, etc."[5] Pennsylvania quietly absorbed 18 million acres that had belonged to the Penns; North Carolina took 22 million acres once the property of Lord Granville; and so on.

States that acquired no such lands within their own borders objected. They refused to ratify the Articles of Confederation in 1778 because those articles did not make such lands the common property of those who fought the war. New Jersey sought to turn over to the Congress those "vacant and impatented lands, commonly called the crown lands," to be then sold to pay off war debts or "for other public and general purposes."[6] Eventually New Jersey gave in, agreed to waive its demand in order to get the Confederation going.

Maryland continued to refuse. It felt that Virginia was "ambitiously grasping at territories to which . . . it had not the least shadow of exclusive right." By selling off a piece of "that extensive and fertile country to which she has set up a claim," Virginia could collect "vast sums of money." She could then cut her taxes. But when her taxes fell below those in Maryland, she "would quickly drain [Maryland] of its most useful inhabitants, its wealth." Maryland's "consequence in the scale of the confederated states would sink of course." Moreover, the Virginia land, they argued, was "a country unsettled at the commencement of this war, claimed by the British Crown." It was then "wrested from the common enemy by the blood and treasure of the thirteen states [and] should be considered as a common property, subject to be parcelled out by Congress into free, convenient, and independent governments."[7]

At first Virginia was unmoved by this logic. But five years later it conceded these lands to the United States. The reason was a persuasive one: the attitude of the Indians. For when the state tried to survey the lands preparatory to selling them off, "the settlers . . . earnestly represented to the Legisla-

ment of Posts" (March 1768), in E. B. O'Callaghan, *Documents Relating to the Colonial History of the State of New York*, 8:27–30.

4. Curtis Nettels, *The Emergence of a National Economy, 1775–1815* (1962), p. 138.

5. U.S. Laws—Public Lands (1828), *Treaties . . . Relative to the Public Lands*, p. 2.

6. 23d Cong., 3d sess., H.D. 213, *Resolutions of the Legislature of New Jersey* (February 1839), p. 2.

7. Instructions of the General Assembly of Maryland, 1779, quoted in 27th Cong., 3d sess., H.R. 296, *Relief of States—Public Lands, Report of Wm. C. Johnson*.

ture of Virginia that if the surveys were persisted in, the infant and defence-
less settlements . . . would be involved in all the horrors and calamities of an
Indian War."[8] Virginia turned its claims over to the United States in 1784.
Eight years later, Georgia also turned its lands over, declaring that they "shall
be considered as a common fund for the use and benefit of the United States,
Georgia included, and shall be faithfully disposed of for that purpose."[9]
However, unlike the other states, Georgia attached a rider: The United States
had to pay off both the Indian claims against Georgia and the claims resulting
from the fantastic Yazoo speculation by the Georgia legislature. (Eventually,
the United States paid $4,750,000 under that proviso.)[10]

The third massive action that led to westward expansion was, of course,
Jefferson's decision to buy the Louisiana Territory from France. Though he
thereby helped finance Napoleon's further wars across Europe, Jefferson
added 827,000 square miles to the 889,000 in the United States of 1783.[11]
That a president who believed his action was unconstitutional[12] would secretly make so vast a commitment pointed to the powerful new forces in
American life: "Hamilton and Jefferson, who agreed in nothing else, were an-
nexationists."[13] Americans had decided, very early, that "This Land Is Our
Land."[14]

Disposing of the Public Domain

Few useful precedents could guide the new democracy in disposing of so
vast a domain. Conflicting interests, differing goals, all surfaced as Congress
attempted to develop a public land policy.

The first issue was: should the public domain be sold at wholesale or retail? As Hamilton told Congress:

> Purchasers may be contemplated in three classes: moneyed individuals and
> companies, who will buy to sell again: associations of persons, who in-
> tended to make settlements themselves; single persons, or families now resi-
> dent in the Western country, or who may emigrate hereafter. [It is] desira-
> ble, and does not appear impractical to meet the needs of all three.[15]

8. 24th Cong., 1st sess., H.D. 189, *Land Warrants and Scrip for Revolutionary Services* (March
1838), p. 4.

9. 23d Cong., 3d sess., H.D. 213, *New Jersey—The Public Lands* (1839), p. 3.

10. Nettels, *The Emergence*, p. 154. The state sold millions of acres to private land companies,
companies in which Georgia legislators were major stockholders.

11. Land area from U.S. Census, *Historical Statistics of the U.S. . . . to 1970*, 2:236.

12. Joseph Story, *Commentaries on the Constitution of the United States* (1851), 1:384.

13. Lyon G. Tyler, *The Letters and Times of the Tylers* (1896), 3:115.

14. The title of a song that became popular after Paul Robeson sang it at the National Convention of the Republican party.

15. *American State Papers: Public Lands* (1790), 1:9.

The Continental Congress had tried to turn the entire sale over to wholesalers—the "moneyed individuals and companies." These would then deal with millions of individual purchasers. By so doing, no large bureaucracy need be created, offering a high prospect of corruption or special favors to those placed in either the executive branch or Congress.

That dream failed. In 1787 Judge John Symmes had contracted for 1 million acres. He succeeded in buying only a quarter of that amount and settled few people.[16] Robert Morris of Philadelphia and General Robert Harper of South Carolina were among the leaders in the North American Land Company. They bought 6 million acres outside the public domain up and down the East Coast (from both private sellers and the states). They too failed. As Curtis Nettels sharply put it: "The most regal operators—William Duer, Alexander Macomb, Robert Morris, John Nicholson and Henry Knox—ended their careers in bankruptcy."[17] Developing a continent proved too great a task for private investment companies. For, once their capital was locked up in land they earned nothing until the land was sold. Their profit turned on capital gains—usually pocketed only after a long period of time. Had that period been short, the investment could have been very remunerative. But settlers were free to "squat" on any of 100 million other acres still held by Congress. How many squatters would then pay a price that included substantial capital gains to large land speculators? Too few to compensate most such speculators for years with no return on their huge investments.[18] Hence, sometime in the 1790s Congress itself turned to selling the land. Beginning in Chillicothe, Ohio, and Marietta, Georgia, it established western land offices where buyers could choose their plats and make their payments.

A second question confronted the Congress: at what price should the land be sold? Present day values, of course, are not decisively relevant. It is common to describe how spectacular a bargain the Dutch got when they bought Manhattan from the Indians for $24 in trade goods and beads. Indeed, the prices originally paid to the Indians might reflect only the superior firepower of the Europeans. But a subsequent series of land transactions reveals the value of such land in a reasonably free market between European adventurers. And it proved not at all high by present standards.

Thus, in 1644 "the Connecticut adventurers purchased of Mr. Fenwick, agent for Lord Say and Seal, and Lord Brook, their right to the colony of

16. Ibid., p. 105.

17. Nettels, *The Emergence*, p. 154. The failure was not for want of good connections. Knox had been secretary of war; Duer was a close friend of Hamilton, secretary of the treasury; Morris, superintendent of finance during the war; Nicholson, controller general of Pennsylvania.

18. A speculator with 1 million acres, bought, say, for 30 cents an acre, had to earn $18,000 profit each year merely to equal the return from investing the same sum in U.S. 6% securities. This meant that even if he sold his land at 20% profit—a fairly high rate—he had to sell off nearly one-third of his holding every year. Few major speculators ever sold off anything like that proportion of their huge holdings.

Connecticut, for £1,600."[19] That worked out to about 8 acres for a penny.[20] Nearly two centuries later (in the 1790s) New York State sold off land to firstcomers: 4 million acres at 8 cents an acre and 6 million acres at 1.5 cents an acre.[21] Also in the 1790s, Patrick Henry and some associates bought nearly 16 million acres of the Dismal Swamp from North Carolina for a bit over 1 cent an acre.[22] And when Maine split off from Massachusetts in 1820, the latter offered the new state the unsold land in Maine for 2.3 cents an acre.[23] In 1812 the Holland Land Company valued its 116,000 acres of western New York (near the Pennsylvania line) at 25 cents an acre.[24] And between 1785 and 1821 the state of Massachusetts sold about 5 million acres at an average of 20.5 cents an acre.[25]

When the United States began selling off the public domain, the competition of these many other sellers had to be considered. As of 1812, individuals held some 30 million acres beyond the Alleghenies.[26] In addition, Massachusetts, Pennsylvania, and Georgia were each offering millions of acres for sale. Congress chose to price its land at $2 an acre beginning in 1796, although states and individuals were asking far less for land that was much closer to markets and transport. The difference suggests something more about cross purposes in Congress than the true value of the land.[27] One theory argues that "Congress . . . was determined to set a figure that would at one stroke shut out speculators and increase the revenue."[28]

In any event, little land was sold at that set price, even though Congress provided credit. But as the tide of settlement flowed westward, more and more voters appeared who favored cheaper land—and voted their opinions. Representative was the True American Society, which "complained that they were poor and suffering . . . that thousands of acres of land . . . were lying unoccupied . . . and that every man was entitled 'by nature to a portion of the

---

19. Jedediah Morse, *The American Geography* (1789), p. 237.

20. In addition to Connecticut's own 3 million acres of land, the deal included another 3.8 million in the Western Reserve (in Ohio). Cf. Paul Gates, *History of Public Land Law Development* (1968), p. 52.

21. John Krout and Dixon Fox, *The Completion of Independence, 1790–1830* (1944), p. 54.

22. C. P. Mcgrath, *Yazoo* (1966), p. 4.

23. David Smith, "Maine and Its Public Domain," in David M. Ellis, ed., *The Frontier in American Development* (1969), p. 115.

24. Buffalo Historical Society, *The Holland Land Company and the Erie Canal* (1910), p. 28.

25. *North American Review* (April 1844), p. 312. A lower figure, 17 cents, is quoted by B. Hibbard, *A History of the Public Land Policies* (1924), p. 78.

26. *American State Papers: Public Lands*, 2:440.

27. It has been argued that congressional policy reflected the conflict between different groups of large land holders. One group wanted a low price and another, a high price.

28. Hibbard, *A History*, p. 76. Given a high price, speculators would have to tie up so much money that they would turn to other investments; sales to many small farmers, at $2, would produce a large amount of revenue for the new government.

soil of the country.'"[29] By 1820 they had their way; Congress cut land prices to $1.25 an acre, at which official level (for the standard cash sale) they remained until 1862. One way to dimension that figure is to compare it with what common farm labor earned at the time for a day's work—about 80 cents in New England and 50 cents in New York.[30]

Hence a week's work would buy enough land for subsistence. However, in 1785, when Congress began to sell off the public domain, it required the buyer to contract for a minimum of 640 acres. The Congressional vision of a relatively prompt wholesale disposition of the public domain had not yet totally disappeared. The law of 1800 reduced the minimum size tract to 320 acres, while the act of 1820 further reduced the minimum to 80 acres—a far more feasible amount for the small farmer. That 80-acre minimum remained in force until the Homestead Act was passed in 1862.

Federal policy offered "a bounty, indelibly written in the text of the laws themselves, in favor of agricultural pursuits. Perhaps no enactment of legislative bounties has ever before operated upon a scale so vast, throughout a series of years, and over the face of an entire nation, to turn population and labor into one particular channel."[31]

While land policy fixed a single selling price, the lands differed in quality. As one of the first great American speculators wrote, "The value of unsettled land . . . will be regulated by . . . the facility with which inhabitants may be introduced, the healthiness of the climate, the aptness of the soil for useful productions, and the facility of exportation."[32] Such factors made the value of land vary from one county to another. Thus, for example, the Registers of Land judged in 1828 that U.S. land in Indiana offered for sale in the Jeffersonville Land Office averaged 44 cents in value, while that in the Crawfordsville office was worth $1.25.[33] But Federal policy offered both at the same price. Inevitably farmers settled on the best land first. Why choose sandy and barren soil for $1.25 an acre when land with trees (for firewood, fencing), and springs to water animals and humans, could be had for the same price? Hence: higgledly-piggledly settlement instead of the tight compact settlements commended by so many writers on agricultural policy.

Was Congress full of city slickers, innocent of the geological facts of farm life? Or were they indifferent? Probably neither. Most Congressmen before

29. Hibbard, *A History*, p. 78.

30. Lebergott, *Manpower*, p. 260.

31. Richard Rush in Guy Callender, ed., *Selections from the Economic History of the United States, 1765–1860* (1965), p. 559.

32. (North America Land Company) *Observations on the North-American Land Company* (1796), p. 106.

33. 20th Cong., 2d sess., H.D. 19, *Statement, Showing the Quantity, Quality and Average Value of the Unsold and Unsaleable Public Lands* (December 30, 1828), p. 2. They declared the Illinois land sold out of Springfield was worth 12 cents on average, that of Edwarsville, 48 cents, and Shawneetown, $1.

the Civil War actually owned farms. The uniform price policy they chose was, however, immensely simple administratively. If Congress had directed that every one of the millions and millions of public acres be valued, that valuation would have taken decades. Moreover, the values set in one year would have changed the next, as the "facility for exportation" changed or European demand did. The uniform price policy settled Americans across the landscape far faster than any carefully tuned price policy could have done. It thereby achieved a major political–military purpose: it swiftly provided a chain of American outposts far across the new nation. That scattering of settlers precluded the confident occupation of portions of the west by either Britain, Spain, or France, although all three countries had a foothold on the continent. The result helped satisfy the territorial imperative emphasized by Washington, Jefferson, Calhoun, and Adams.

A third policy issue confronting the Congress was: cash or credit. Land was sold by the Continental Congress on so lordly a scale—1 million acres, a half million acres—that credit was taken for granted and terms proposed. By 1800 the credit terms the United States offered (for the minimum tract size of 320 acres or more) were: one-quarter to be paid within forty days, another quarter within two years, and the rest within four years.[34] But, in 1820, under that generous loan policy, the U.S. government found that its citizens owed it $20 million dollars. Buyers had planned to settle, to speculate, or both, but were caught by the depression of 1818–19 and the collapse of the land boom.[35]

Federal financing of land purchases ended with the crash of 1819. "Its abandonment rather than . . . reform" has been sharply criticized: "The usual frontiersman who was trying to create a farm for himself in the wilderness had little or no capital with which to operate. Farm making called for considerable capital," however, and "a frontiersman . . . was [thereby] deprived of much needed working capital."[36]

Two dilemmas were present in the credit system from the beginning: The private market could provide plenty of loans for land investment at market rates. Hence, the taxpayer's contribution was evidently to make capital available at below market rates. But if he did so he would be subsidizing large land buyers. Large-scale speculators then could—and did—buy land on credit from the government, then being able to use their own funds to invest in still more remunerative ventures. Thus, the government both provided them

---

34. Hibbard, A History, p. 83, quoting U.S. Statutes at Large, 2:74.
35. American State Papers: Public Lands, 3:561.
36. Gates, The Farmer's Age, p. 64.

with capital at below market cost and subsidized their other ventures.[37] Was this sound policy?

But suppose credit were somehow restricted to small investors. Should the government subsidize citizens who bought farms in the west, but not those who bought farms in the hills of Appalachia, western New York, or up-country Georgia? And should the government assist those who wanted to enter one kind of business (farming) but refuse credit to other essential business—millers, cobblers, blacksmiths, wheelwrights, bakers? And what of workers who could never hope to buy farms or businesses but desperately needed credit to buy food and pay their rent while they were unemployed or sick?

Many later writers have argued that the land should have been sold only to actual settlers, to small holders, thus keeping out the "speculators." The administrative problems of implementing that restriction prevented direct legislation, albeit not decades of editorial perturbation. How could federal officials exclude only those who were buying land for speculation. By psychoanalyzing every buyer? But even suppose it were somehow decided that the buyer, in his heart of hearts, intended to farm and settle. What was to be done if subsequent illness, crop failure, or the request of parents back east for his return made him sell his land? Were all buyers to be forbidden to sell and make any speculative profits—by making their land "inalienable" (not salable), as so many later writers proposed? If so, an endless tide of special legislation would appear. That result could be anticipated, given the succession of special acts that Congress had passed over the decades to legalize illegal "squatting" on the public domain (i.e., the Preemption acts).

Moreover, western settlers typically took up more land than they could actually farm, hoping for a rise in land values, hoping to provide land for their children when they came of age. Such land was a speculative investment quite as much as any other holding that the law could define as speculative. Yet most farmers toughly defended their right to sell off any and all holdings as it might please them.

The most that the federal government could do was somehow to attempt to block purchases larger than a given amount—above, say, 3,000 acres.[38] As it turned out, however, at any time the giant landholders—say, those with over 5,000 acres—had only a trivial proportion of the total public domain.[39]

37. Cf. the discussion on tax liens in Robert Swierenga, *Acres for Cents* (1976). Cf. also the discussion in Gates, *The Farmer's Age*, p. 62, of large investors "anxious to lend funds at the high rates of interest obtained on the frontier" who "purchased heavily on the generous terms of credit that the government . . . granted."

38. A figure of 3,000 is chosen, with some arbitrariness, on the assumption that no congressman or land activist apparently objected to 640 acres per person. Given five persons in the average U.S. family, the family could assign 640 to each and thus hold 3,200 acres.

39. The big holdings identified on various pages in Gates, *The Farmer's Age*, total less than 5 percent of the public domain.

TABLE 8.1

REGIONAL MIGRATION RATES, 1800–1960 *(percent of mid-decade population)*

	1800–1810	1810–1820	1820–1830	1830–1840	1840–1850	1850–*1860
Northeast	− 1.0	− 2.0	0.7	1.0	4.0	3.7
Middle Atlantic	3.1	0.5	1.6	1.1	3.3	− 0.8
East–North Central	50.0+	50.0+	50.0+	50.0+	50.0+	50.0+
West–North Central	50.0+	50.0+	50.0+	50.0+	50.0+	50.0+
South Atlantic	− 4.7	− 5.1	− 3.6	− 5.3	− 2.6	− 1.7
East–South Central	12.7	0.6	2.3	1.5	− 1.9	− 8.1
West–South Central		50.0+	50.0+	50.0+	7.1	50.0+
Mountain					50.0+	50.0+
Pacific					50.0+	50.0+

*Native white.

Source: Stanley Lebergott, "Migration within the U.S., 1800–1960," *Journal of Economic History* (December 1970), p. 845.

The fifth problem was never resolved: how could a handful of soldiers keep millions of footloose men from moving onto unsettled land? True, the consequences ranged from bad to disastrous when settlers were not kept within the domain purchased from the Indians by treaty, surveyed and offered for sale. Such settlement inevitably led to sniping, massacres, and eventually to fairly large-scale Indian wars. Moreover, settlement on lands that had not been properly surveyed, or even bought, meant that many land titles were insecure. Anyone buying land from the federal government might discover squatters already on their land ready to fight for it. Similar problems had, of course, arisen when the Romans moved into Switzerland and Syria, the Bantu into southern Africa, the Dutch into Bushman country, the English colonists into Canada, the Norwegians into Lapland. Those conflicts had an outcome, usually forceful and disastrous. But no solution.

In 1768 Governor William Penn of Pennsylvania proposed the ultimate law. A flood of migrants had poured onto Indian lands in Redstone Creek and the Cheat River area. They had been forcibly removed by the soldiers, but soon there was "double the number of inhabitants in those two Settlements than ever was before." The governor, therefore, under his royal powers, proclaimed the death penalty for anyone settling on those Indian lands.[40] Failure to enforce that law might have been anticipated. A few decades later settlers in the same regions once again disturbed the Indians on their own territory. General George Washington ordered them removed. Soldiers then

40. Solon Buck and Elizabeth Buck, *The Planting of Civilization in Western Pennsylvania* (1939), p. 142.

TABLE 8.1 (CONTINUED)

REGIONAL MIGRATION RATES, 1800–1960 (*percent of mid-decade population*)

1860–* 1870	1870– 1880	1880– 1890	1890– 1900	1900– 1910	1910– 1920	1920– 1930	1930– 1940	1940– 1950	1950– 1960
7.1	4.1	10.1	10.9	9.1	4.9	0.6	−0.5	0.0	0.2
2.9	1.9	8.3	8.9	12.3	4.6	6.0	0.5	−0.4	1.0
1.4	0.1	3.5	4.6	3.2	7.2	5.8	0.3	1.6	2.1
19.2	20.0	16.3	−1.6	−1.3	−2.9	−6.0	−4.8	−7.6	−5.5
3.7	−1.2	−2.6	−2.9	−1.7	−1.5	−5.6	−0.2	0.3	2.7
−3.6	−5.5	−5.7	−4.1	−6.8	−8.8	−7.4	−4.1	−11.1	−12.4
−3.0	10.7	8.0	8.6	9.1	0.2	−0.5	−4.2	−7.8	−3.7
50.0+	45.4	38.8	17.4	30.0	9.8	5.8	0.1	3.1	9.3
50.0+	28.1	40.4	16.9	46.0	22.4	30.9	15.0	28.7	18.1

destroyed their cabins. But within a few months the settlers were once again back on "their" lands.[41]

The tide of pioneers migrating westward in the United States (Table 8.1) became, by the creed of democracy, voters equal in every respect to voters from the older states. They acquired their own senators and congressmen. And they knew their interests. Their legislators fought legislation that favored Indian rights when "Christian men" had no lands of their own. They fought, persistently and effectively, for preemption laws that legalized prior squatting on Indian and federal lands. (Thirty-three special Preemption acts passed between 1799 and 1830 were followed by the Acts of 1832, 1834, 1838, and 1840. By these Congress "forgave illegal trespass on public lands by granting preemption rights to settlers."[42] The frontiersmen elected Andrew Jackson as president. He had supported the Georgia settlers in their guerrilla wars against the Indians. As president, he then used federal moneys to "remove" the tribes from their ancient lands to new ones across the Mississippi River. Jackson, symbol for decades to come of vigorous populist democracy, was the most flamboyant major leader of the New West. But he had many followers. They traded support on other measures with other political leaders to get approval for a wide open land policy.

The sixth problem was how to reconcile the conflicting interests of the old and new states. Land in the new states promised farmers higher yields per acre. That factor alone threatened the prosperity of the old states as an exodus to the new began. It was cheaper to quit the old farm than to restore its fertility. It was estimated, for example, that one could buy three acres of land in

41. *Annals of Congress, The Debates and Proceedings* (1834), 1:412, May 1789.
42. Gates, *The Farmer's Age*, p. 67.

the New West for no more than the cost of sufficient lime to restore an acre in the Old South.[43] And every cut in the price of federal land made the West still more attractive.

Yet every move to the West inflicted capital losses on eastern farmers: The value of their land, and hence of their farms, fell. Every move to the West tended to drive up the wages that eastern manufacturers had to pay. And every such move tended to drive down the interest rates received by investors in the East. (Also, the demand for funds to operate eastern farms and related blacksmithies, wagoning companies, etc., tended to weaken and fall.) Finally, westward migration tended to reduce the importance of East and South in the houses of Congress.

These conflicts continued over the decades. The Northeastern and Middle Atlantic states successfully shifted out of farming into manufacturing, trade, and finance. That shift compensated—indeed, more than compensated—for the economic losses noted above. But in the South Atlantic states the steady decline in land values, in political influence, became a running sore. It contributed to the secession of South Carolina in 1833 and, eventually, to the secession of South Carolina and the Lower South in 1860–61.

43. Alfred G. Smith, *Economic Readjustment of an Old Cotton State* (1958), p. 97. The fierce effectiveness of early squatters against later purchasers is well described in Allan Bogue, "The Iowa Claim Clubs," *Mississippi Valley Historical Review* (June 1958).

9

Westward Ho

ACCEPTING Shelley's declaration that "poets are the great unacknowl-edged legislators of mankind," T. S. Eliot advised that "on the whole it would appear to be for the best that the great majority of human beings should go on living in the place in which they were born."[1] D. H. Lawrence likewise enjoined against migration, with even greater sonorousness: "Men are free when they are in a living homeland not when they are straying and breaking away. . . when they belong to a living, organic *believing* community . . . not when they are escaping to some wild west."[2] But most Americans did not heed the lesson of humane letters.

They harkened instead to the terse judgment by one of America's earliest civil engineers, Loammi Baldwin: "Every man will endeavor to improve his circumstances by a change of occupation or by a change of place. He fixes a standard mark of enjoyments by comparison of his present situation with what the new and unpeopled district holds out to him."[3] And for Americans, decade in and decade out, the change meant moving to the West.

As early as 1796, Albert Gallatin (secretary of the treasury under Jefferson and an emigrant from Switzerland) judged that "about ten thousand families migrate every year to the westward of the Alleghany Mountains"—three-fourths to Tennessee, Kentucky, Virginia and Pennsylvania, and about one-fourth to "the lands of the United States" (i.e., what was to become Ohio).[4] But later that year when the Treaty of Greenville was signed, the Indians relinquished their claims to the upper midwest. As Congressman John J. Hardin observed: "Now the Indian War is over a vast population is . . . and will be for years, rolling from the East to the West."[5] Indeed, more than

---

1. Quoted in Frank Musgrave, *The Migratory Elite* (1963), p. 104. As an immigrant to the United Kingdom himself, Eliot carefully refers to "the great majority."

2. D. H. Lawrence, *Studies in Classic American Literature*, p. 9. Lawrence, who left his native valley for wanderings to London, Santa Fe, etc., was, of course, likewise a migrant.

3. Loammi Baldwin, *Thoughts on a Study of Political Economy* (1809), p. 15. Baldwin, an early economist and civil engineer, discovered the Baldwin apple.

4. Henry Adams, ed., *The Writings of Albert Gallatin* (1879), 3:155.

5. 14th Cong., 1st sess., *Congressional Debates* (January 1816), p. 751.

60,000 people a year migrated westward during the next few decades.[6] By 1850, 51 percent of the residents of Michigan had been born outside the state; and, for Illinois, 47 percent; Wisconsin, 46 percent; Missouri, 42 percent; and Indiana, 41 percent.[7]

The magnet, as Baldwin indicated, was "a standard mark of enjoyments"—that is, all the advantages offered by the new regions. To many men the key advantage was that of becoming an independent farmer. True, as Clarence Danhof has demonstrated, few migrants arrived with enough capital to buy farms and implements and begin at once as full-fledged farmers.[8] Instead, they worked their way west, collecting a grubstake. The "active, aspiring mechanic, born in Maine or New Hampshire, migrates to New York or some other Middle State soon after reaching his majority; reaches Illinois or Missouri two or three years later; and will often be found traversing Montana or Illinois before he is thirty."[9] At each stop he worked, usually as a laborer, planting corn, digging cellars, harvesting wheat, taking whatever job was available. English visitors described the wandering. Morris Birkbeck met some who walked all the way west, stopping to work when necessary. Harriet Martineau met others "working their way into the back country and glad to be employed for a while at Detroit to earn money to carry them farther."[10] Some worked in cities. Some were farm laborers. Some did both. From 1804, when the price of government land was pegged at $1.25 an acre, such workers could acquire a farm, cabin, horses, and implements for perhaps $600.[11] In fact, not all paid such sums. Some were squatters, who farmed open land for years, neither buying nor renting it. After 1850 many bought land using military bounty warrants at prices of 50 cents to 80 cents an acre. If they borrowed the entire sum at 10 percent, they could get through their first year with no more than $100 in cash ($60 for interest, plus $40 for payment on principal). By the next year their crops would be in. The typical farm worker (who was paid $8.85 a month in 1830, plus room and board[12]) could accumulate the first year's grubstake in two years of hard work.

6. In 1850 some 1.5 million persons reported that they were living outside the state in which they were born. 1900 Census, *Supplementary Analysis*, Table 28. Assuming a median age of 40 years for that group gives about 60,000 a year. In addition, of course, among those, some did not survive to the census year.

7. Census of 1850, p. xxxviii. The data are for the male white population, but rates for the entire population of those states would be much the same.

8. Cf. Clarence Danhof's classic discussion, "Farm-Making Costs and the 'Safety-Valve': 1850–1860," *Journal of Political Economy* (1941), pp. 317–59.

9. Horace Greeley, *Essays on Political Economy* (1874), p. 286.

10. Quoted by Joseph Schafer, "Was the West a Safety Valve for Labor?" *Mississippi Valley Historical Review* (December 1937), pp. 305–06.

11. 80 acres at $1.25 an acre; 40 acres of timber; cabin; plow; horses, etc.

12. Lebergott, *Manpower*, p. 539.

But in the West, a farmer's tasks proved even harsher. As Solon Robinson warned in 1845:

> I can never advise an eastern farmer who is able to make both ends meet to become an emigrant, for if he will exercise the same frugality and cheap mode of living that he will be compelled to when he gets into his new log cabin, he can remain comfortable where he is. . . . All those rich acres are only the raw material out of which farms are to be created.[13]

Or, as the Duke of Wellington shrewdly noted, "the fact is men cannot bear those sacrifices in the presence of their neighbors and friends which they do not scruple to make before strangers, or in a forest . . . in America."[14] Even those who paid nothing at all for their land during the first year or two—buying on "long credit" from the railroads—had to make similar sacrifices by living in the wilderness.

Why then did they go? First, the long-range inducement, of course, was the farmer's chance to assure his livelihood for the remainder of his life and to provide a goodly inheritance for his children in the form of a productive farm. Second, the ever-present prospect of a rise in land value offered a powerful inducement. One writer described a 70-acre lot bought for a jackknife, a paper of pins, 2 quarts of molasses, and a dozen needles as worth $3,000 a century later, in 1812. Land in general, he added, had "risen by 100 percent within the memory of the present generation."[15] Third, farmers could monetize their time more effectively than urban workers. When western New York was being settled in the 1830s, the state had 449,000 acres up for sale. Such raw lands were valued at 29 cents to 49 cents an acre. After the settlers had cleared the land of trees and bush, however, it became worth $10 an acre.[16] Such land clearing, once the first few critical acres had been planted, could be done whenever the farmer had a break in his other work, thus effectively turning his free time into money.

Still other attractions drew many to western mines, canal work, etc. The migrants did not intend to become farmers, or not immediately. Their prospect was signaled by the difference in wage rates between East and West. De-

---

13. Herbert Kellar, ed., *Solon Robinson* (1936), 1:518.

14. "There is a great advantage certainly in obtaining land at a low price. But . . . what is the sacrifice of property, of time and of comfort . . . and the . . . time which must elapse before his new property can become productive? Compare that sacrifice with the produce of a similar sacrifice of luxury and appearance at home . . . if those who go into the colonies to economise would submit to make the same sacrifice at home . . . they would find that they can subsist as cheaply." Philip Stanhope, *Notes of Conversations with Wellington* (1888), pp. 34–35.

15. Azel Backus, *Connecticut Towns: Bethlehem, 1812 and Watertown 1801* (reprint ed., 1961), pp. 3, 8.

16. New York State Senate, S.D. 61, *Report of the Canal Board Relating to the Survey of the Hudson River* (March 10, 1840), pp. 6, 10.

cade after decade migrants moved from states with lower wage levels to those with higher levels.[17]

The "Safety Valve" and Wage Equalization

During the nineteenth century the Western European nations that supplied the United States with its migrants were marked by unrest, riot, and revolution. Indeed, a classic description of Europe in 1848, *The Communist Manifesto*, begins: "A spectre is haunting Europe": the spectre of revolution. In 1848 revolution erupted again in France, and in Germany, Austria, Hungary, and Italy (revolutions had occurred in 1830 in France, Poland, and Belgium). Marx and Engels foresaw an immense and almost immediate convulsion of the European world. By comparison, the United States proved to be remarkably free from such intense strife. One explanation of that difference was offered in an 1875 study of American communism: "Our cheap and fertile lands have acted as an important safety valve for the enterprise and discontent of our non-capitalist population."[18] The phrase "the safety valve" has been used ever since to indicate that both "enterprise and discontent" would find their way west, thus enabling the nation to skirt revolt and revolution.

In fact, even that more modest expression of working-class discontent, union organization, was virtually nonexistent until the twentieth century. As late as 1910, half a century after the first national trade union was organized, less than 6 percent of the U.S. labor force were union members.[19] Even at its peak between 1910 and 1920 the syndicalist International Workers of the World enrolled fewer than 5,000 members. The common explanation is that potential leaders and activists had headed in a new direction—they had become farmers, industrialists, and political leaders in the new regions.[20]

The safety-valve theory, as developed by Frederick Jackson Turner, implied a further consequence. The opportunity that workers had to move west tended to keep up wages in the East. And it seems reasonable that it did. It was unnecessary for any great number of workers to move, just enough to remind employers that workers could and did move.[21] Such recognition led to

17. Estimates available, in current dollars, show this result for the decades beginning with 1850. Allowing for differences in cost of living would give similar results, for the wage data used are for monthly farm wages, plus food and lodging, costs of the latter not differing largely between East and West.

18. Charles Nordhoff, *The Communist Societies of the United States* (1875), p. 12.

19. Cf. Stanley Lebergott's estimate in Lance Davis et al., *American Economic Growth* (1972), p. 220.

20. Cf. Selig Perlman, *A Theory of the Labor Movement* (1949).

21. Fred Shannon's lively attack on the safety-valve theory appears in his *The Farmer's Last Frontier* (1961), pp. 356–59.

higher wages than would have existed if the nation had been hemmed in by the Alleghenies. Did more workers move in depression than in prosperity? It is hard to know. But two indicators suggest they did not. First, the number of westward travelers seems to have declined in the recessions of 1857 and 1873.[22] Moreover, recent experience shows that migration slows down during recessions and depressions.[23] The reasoning is simple: Why break up one's home and way of life to be unemployed in a strange city or place? One might as well be unemployed in familiar surroundings among friends and relatives.

One final note: The opportunity of the West itself drew some immigrants to the United States who would not otherwise have come, as Fred Shannon has argued.[24] And that flow canceled some of the gains in eastern wages achieved by the actual westward movement of natives. (Most immigrants, however, would probably have been drawn to the freer, better paid life of the United States even had the West not existed. The incremental attractions of the West may not have drawn many except perhaps for the Scandinavian immigrants.)

A second range of consequences brought about by migration was the gradual equalization of wages throughout the nation. California rates had long exceeded those in Kentucky, for example. But the migration process narrowed the range of the difference decade after decade. In 1840 common labor earned $16 a day in California and 50¢ in Kentucky. By 1860 California workers earned only 2.5 times as much; by 1890, only 1.5 times as much.[25] Decade after decade the variation for farm labor wage rates among the states declined—except for the decade of the Civil War.[26]

When the Civil War broke out, when new mineral deposits were discovered, and when other major economic innovations were made, wage differences, of course, increased. But then the migration process would resume its whittling away at the new set of differences. These differences narrowed substantially over the entire period from 1850 to 1960.[27] They were narrowed by workers moving to locations where they could be more productive and hence could earn higher real wages. Such moves advanced productivity. In time, they lowered prices for final consumers.

22. Cf. Lebergott, *Manpower*, pp. 41–44.

23. Cf. Jacob Marshak's classic work on migration to and from Oxford in Helen Makower, ed., *Studies in the Mobility of Labour* (1938).

24. Frederick Shannon, "A Post-Mortem."

25. Lebergott, *Manpower*, p. 541; E. Gould Buffum, *Six Months in the Gold Mines* (1850), p. 85; John Hale, *California As It Is* (1954), p. 52.

26. Lebergott, *Manpower*, p. 135. The coefficient of variation clearly fell.

27. The differences in wage rates adjusted for cost-of-living differences were, of course, less extreme at the beginning. Nonetheless, real wage differentials have likewise narrowed.

Migration provided the pioneers who broke the plains. It peopled the new territories, creating new states. It provided labor for new farms and industries. But its immensity depended on the extent to which transport costs were cut. And its timing depended on the rate at which they were cut, for such costs metered the flow of people to the new frontiers and of their products to the older states and Europe.

10

Transport

IN August 1799 a courier set out from Detroit to deliver U.S. Army muster rolls to headquarters in Pittsburgh. His trip took fifty-three days of hard riding.[1]

In the 1830s Captain Henry Shreve began his life's work: trying to clear the Mississippi river system of fallen trees. From primeval times, enormous "rafts" of trees, branches, and dead animals had bunched together in those rivers. The one obstructing the Red River in 1828 actually stretched upstream for more than 200 miles.[2]

In 1844 Cyrus McCormick shipped his first harvesters to the great grain fields of the Midwest. They went on wagons "from Walnut Grove to Scottsville, Virginia; then down the canal to Richmond; then by water down the James River, into the Atlantic and around Florida . . . to New Orleans; up the Mississippi and Ohio rivers to Cincinnati."[3]

Three powerful interests eventually "made the ways smooth and straight." One group seeking to reduce these incredibly long and arduous trips included the army and its supporters. To move troops promptly to block foreign invaders, what more appropriate advance preparation than for the Army Engineers, then called the Topographical Corps, to clear rivers, lay out railroad routes, and design roads. Could private enterprise alone guarantee that the troops would arrive in time, rather than after the campaign was actually over?

> Defensive measures of the United States . . . [require] the construction of good roads. [We know] the importance . . . of procuring the earliest intelligence of the force and movements of an enemy. [Consider] the enormous pense incurred [in 1814] for the security of the much exposed frontier of Ohio, from the allied British and Indian forces which so long threatened its

1. *Message from the President of the United States Accompanying a Statement of Expenditures from the 1st of January 1797, by the Quartermaster General and the Navy Agents . . . 23 Dec. 1802* (1803), p. 110.

2. Report of Lieutenant Bowman, Army Engineers, 25th Cong., 2d sess., S.D. 1, *Message of the President* (1837), p. 353.

3. U.S., Department of Agriculture, *Yearbook, 1899*, p. 376.

safety; and from the unfortunate, not to say disgraceful, surrender of Detroit. . . . A single good road from the river Ohio to Detroit . . . would have
afforded complete security to that frontier, at a fourth part of the cost actually incurred in its defense, and have effectually preserved the honor of the
American arms.[4]

Similarly,

for seven months in the year [the proposed road from Chicago to Green Bay
would be] the only practicable route by which the troops stationed at Fort
Howard could be taken to the south or east . . . and without . . . the road . . .
it would be the labor of many days to get the troops only to Chicago, while
no munitions of war could be taken whatever.[5]

Indeed, for every $400 spent buying a cannon in Washington in 1814,
$1,500 or $2,000 had to be added to transport it to the northwest frontier of
Ohio. The western garrisons were then fed with flour costing $100 a barrel
and pork at $127 a barrel, although these same foods had sold for a mere $10
to $20 a barrel on the East Coast.[6] Primitive transport had added strikingly to
costs. Thus, the search for military advantage produced spin-offs that benefited civilian economic growth. These probably exceeded in importance the
better known side effects of military research many decades later in the 1940s
and 1970s. The program of land exploration by the Army Engineers provided
the basis for an enduring commitment to road, river, and harbor development.[7]

The second powerful force was commercial. It included every producer
who sought a wider market, and thereby a better price. Drover Drenning
walked a thousand miles with his herd of cattle for a single reason: He could
expect 12.5 cents a pound in New York, whereas the price back in Ohio came
to only a third of that figure.[8] Anthracite coal was worth $1.35 a ton at the
minehead in western Pennsylvania but almost four times as much ($4.50) in
Philadelphia.[9] Reduced transport costs expanded McCormick's harvester

4. 20th Cong., 1st sess., H.R. 91, Road—Washington to . . . Northwestern Parts of New York and
Pennsylvania (1828), p. 1.

5. 24th Cong., 1st sess., H.D. 141, Memorial of the Legislative Council of Michigan Territory
(1836), p. 3.

6. Elkanah Watson, History of the Rise, Progress and Existing Condition of the Western Canals
(1820), p. 22.

7. The work is richly presented by Forrest G. Hill, Roads, Rails and Waterways: The Army
Engineers and Early Transportation (1957).

8. Market beef (not beef on the hoof) cost 5 cents to 6 cents a pound in Chillicothe in April
1817. David Warden, A Statistical and Political Account of the United States of North America (1819),
2:262. James Flint, Letters from America (1822), reprinted in R. G. Thwaites, Travels (1904), 9:126,
gives 4 cents a pound for beef and pork in Middletown, Ohio, in 1818.

9. "Resources of Pennsylvania," The Merchants' Magazine and Commercial Review 12 (1845),
p. 253.

market in the Middle West, the Ohio cattle raiser's market in New York, the Pennsylvania coal miner's market in Philadelphia and Baltimore. Then there were the farmers. Those who owned land near a new canal or railroad route had a guaranteed way to wealth. Their land inevitably jumped in value. The reason was obvious. When such a route was decided upon it cheapened the cost of transporting to eastern or other markets the wheat or corn grown on that land. It did so not merely for one year but far out into the future. The landowner could capitalize that endless stream of savings into an increased value for his land and promptly did so.

The gains were hardly minor. In 1774 land in Virginia along the James River averaged £15 an acre, while away from the river it averaged only £10.[10] Coastal land in South Carolina averaged £17 if on a river, £11 if not. Land-owners simply capitalized in the value of their land the potential stream of saving in future shipment of the products of that land—rice, tobacco, cotton—to market year after year. It becomes understandable why Lincoln and Douglas lobbied to have the Illinois Central run through one Illinois town rather than another. And why the general commissioners of Rowan, Iredell, and Catawba counties in North Carolina agreed to subscribe $100,000 toward building the West North Carolina—"provided." Their proviso was that "the terminus not be located in the woods . . . thereby subjecting the community to much inconvenience," but rather in "the town of Morganton"—incidentally pushing up land values there.[11] For many farmers there was even lagniappe: They could earn still more money by contracting to clear the trees along the route, or grade the road, or dig the canal. Even the poorest farmers could do some of the actual work, at unusually high cash wages, between farm chores or in their off season.[12]

A third interest pressed for improved transport. Beyond the military and commercial motives, there was a political, a nationalistic one. From Washington on down political leaders believed that improving physical union of the states would help guarantee political union. The western settlers, Washington wrote in 1784, stood "upon a pivot. The touch of a feather would turn them any way. They look'd down the Mississippi until the Spaniards . . . threw difficulties in their way."[13] As matters then stood, westerners could ship their products eastward only at prohibitive cost, wagoning over primitive trails. Their primary highway, instead, was the Mississippi, even though they could not afford to ship their corn as grain but had to convert it into more portable pork or whiskey. The river flowed far down to the great export cen-

10. Alice Hanson Jones, *American Colonial Wealth: Documents and Methods* (1978), Table 3.10, p. 1750.

11. *Proceedings of the General Meeting of Stockholders of the Western North Carolina Railroad Company at Salisbury, August 30, 1855*, pp. 3–4.

12. "The contracts being generally awarded to gentlemen engaged in agricultural pursuits." Western North Carolina Railroad Company, *Third Annual Report* (1857), p. 10.

13. George Washington, *Writings of Washington*, ed., John Fitzpatrick (1938), 27:475.

ter, New Orleans. John Jay had all but worked out a widely advantageous treaty with Spain in the 1780s, only to find everyone from Adams to Jefferson pointing out that any possible blockage of the exports from Kentucky, Tennessee, and Ohio to New Orleans would stimulate the New West to create a nation of its own.

To forge a single nation that retained both eastern and western states was the goal. It appeared to require transport advance stimulated by the federal government. True, President Monroe and many others doubted that the executive branch had the constitutional power to sponsor any such program of "internal improvements." But that did not mean opposition to the program, as many historians have inferred. Merely passing an amendment would create the requisite federal power. As of 1814 the states had just finished approving a dozen such amendments to the new Constitution. Monroe therefore proposed a further amendment in his address to Congress. Meanwhile, he approved the use of the Army engineers (the "Topographical Corps") to survey canal routes, railroad routes, harbor improvements, all over the United States and the territories. (That was almost all the federal government could finance in those years.)

John Quincy Adams, the next president, proved to be an even more determined supporter of "internal improvements." Indeed, John C. Calhoun, eventually the South's great theoretician of secession, warned in 1817: "We are under the most imperious obligation to counteract every tendency to disunion. . . . Let us then bind the republic together with a perfect system of roads and canals."[14] Even Andrew Jackson's celebrated veto of a road to Maysville, Kentucky, did not end the period of federal spending on transport, as has often been asserted. (He may really have objected to the road because it lay wholly within the home state of Henry Clay, his major political opponent.) The level of federal spending on rivers and harbors did not end during Jackson's tenure in the White House, though legend has it so. Actually, it continued to rise, particularly in the South's great river system (see Table 10.1).

To reduce the cost of transport, nothing more was needed than millions of dollars plus a sensible plan. After a few decades, the country could then rely on a linked road and canal, or road-canal-railroad, system. True, no country before or since has done all this. But that should have constituted no particular deterrent.

The grand concept was not lacking. Albert Gallatin, second U.S. secretary of the treasury, had outlined a national plan for river and harbor im-

14. "Whatever impedes the intercourse of the extremes with the centre of the republic weakens the nation. The more enlarged the sphere of commercial circulation . . . the more inseparable are our destinies." John C. Calhoun, *The Works of John C. Calhoun*, ed., Richard Cralle (1853), 2:190.

TABLE 10.1
FEDERAL AID TO INTERNAL IMPROVEMENTS, 1802-60

	Expenditures ($000)			Acres granted to railroads (000)
		Rivers and Harbors		
Year	Roads and canals	Total U.S.	Mississippi and related rivers	
1802	–			
1803	2			
1804	3			
1805	–			
1806	2			
1807	12			
1808	11			
1809	3			
1810	56			
1811	31			
1812	68			
1813	78			
1814	73			
1815	114			
1816	109			
1817	361			
1818	349			
1819	510			
1820	147			
1821	84			
1822	41			
1823	38			
1824	110	26	3	
1825	363	40	11	
1826	563	87	16	
1827	352	136	36	
1828	401	188	53	
1829	782	530	57	
1830	639	576	59	
1831	363	653	157	
1832	695	540	86	
1833	1,053	710	87	
1834	867	606	56	
1835	1,233	595	71	
1836	1,218	873	114	

TABLE 10.1 (CONTINUED)
FEDERAL AID TO INTERNAL IMPROVEMENTS, 1802-60

	Expenditures ($000)			Acres granted to railroads (000)
	Roads and canals	Rivers and Harbors		
Year		Total U.S.	Mississippi and related rivers	
1837	944	1,389	367	
1838	457	1,066	360	
1839	397	788	119	
1840	357	151	22	
1841	48	79	0	
1842	260	82	16	
1843	137	112	66	
1844	123	322	177	
1845	37	548	252	
1846	44	230	51	
1847	254	45	22	
1848	90	24	4	
1849	94	26	–	
1850	235	43	1	3,752
1851	74	70	35	–
1852	113	43	16	1,765
1853	185	498	81	2,682
1854	199	960	306	–
1855	371	837	174	–
1856	391	169	–	14,560
1857	539	274	4	5,118
1858	670	465	204	–
1859	357	295	61	–
1860	555	232	121	–

Source: Tabulation of individual expenditure items listed in U.S. 47th Cong., 1st sess., S.D. 196, *Statement of Appropriations and Expenditures 1789 to 1882* (1882), and, for railroads, Thomas Donaldson, *The Public Domain* (1884) 1:273. Net expenditures except for Mississippi, which are expenditures by warrants.

provements as early as 1808.[15] Was it necessary to wait half a century for the world's knowledge of engineering, strength of materials and new technologies to develop? Hardly. After all, as far back as the Emperor Domitian's day engineers built a new road from Rome to Baia so solid and so smooth that "what was a whole day's journey has become scarce two hours travel."[16] And the first railroads had been laid down for British coal mines when Shakespeare was still alive.[17] Canals? Twelve centuries earlier the Chinese had built the Grand Canal.[18] And, as envoy to France, Thomas Jefferson had enthusiastically described gliding down the great Languedoc canal, built by Louis XIV in the seventeenth century.

What the United States lacked was not knowledge, nor a plan, nor technology. It lacked the resources to invest in roads, canals, railroads, steamboats, piers. More accurately, it lacked the will to divert so enormous a portion of consumption to investment. For such investment in "social overhead capital" required an almost interminable period of expenditure before any returns could be expected.

Three alternatives faced the developing nation then as they face others today. First, the nation could do without transport advance. Unthinkable. Second, the investment could be made by the government, which would tax its own people or borrow from Europeans. Third, the investment could be made by private individuals.

Each investment route was tried, depending on the period and the transport method, but unquestionably the primary source was private investment. This meant that improvements first appeared where profits could be expected, not where military needs or a general plan for national unification dictated. Expected profits, in turn, seemed most glowing in areas where concentrations of people to ship goods or buy them already existed. But to some entrepreneurs, the fitful glow of profits also appeared in those areas where new transport itself, like Cadmus, would magically sow the earth with people.

The history of mixed private and public enterprise in the new nation may well claim to begin with the turnpikes. Built from Philadelphia to Lancaster (1792), from Baltimore to Boonsborough (1804), and from Albany to Schenectady (1802), these were private ventures.[19] Enough footloose Ameri-

15. Cf. Carter Goodrich et al., *Government Promotion of American Canals and Railroads, 1800–1890* (1960), p. 27.

16. Publius Statius, *The Silvae of Statius*, ed., D. A. Slater (1908), Book IV, 3, l. 36, 37.

17. Bertram Baxter, *Stone Blocks and Iron Rails* (1966), p. 20. A wooden "rayleway" was built near Nottingham in 1604 for a colliery. By 1750 there was scarcely an important mine without its accompanying railroad. Ibid., p. 22.

18. "Water Transport," *Encyclopedia Brittanica*.

19. Cf. Curtis Nettels, *The Emergence of a National Economy, 1775–1815* (1962), p. 251. Joseph Durrenberger, *Turnpikes* (1931), pp. 52, 59.

cans, or fascinated foreign visitors, strolled and rode horseback along them to pay the toll keeper's salary, plus a bit more. What made the growth of turnpikes feasible was not the trivial 2 percent or 3 percent rate of return they paid their investors. As Henry Clay declared in 1818:

> The capitalist who should invest his money in [turnpikes] might not be reimbursed three percent annually upon it: and yet society, in various forms, might actually reap fifteen or twenty percent. The benefit resulting from a turnpike road made by private associations is divided between the capitalist, who receives his toll, the land through which it passes, and which is augmented in value, and the commodities whose value is enhanced by the diminished expense of transportation.[20]

Pecuniary economies (in the form of reduced transport costs) fail to measure the total social advantage of better transport. Nor were the real external economies achieved by the transport industry itself. Only the sum of Clay's three classes of benefits make up what Jacob Viner termed the net technical external economies accruing to the national economy.[21]

The Returns from Transport Advance

In 1851 the Reverend Thomas King preached that "Man was put here to subdue nature. It is just as truly a part of God's call to man to lay rail tracks as to build churches."[22] And the country seemed to agree. Each major transport advance offered more speed and/or more reliability. Turnpikes offered more speed than common roads. Canals offered more regularity and more certainty of delivering freight and passengers on schedule. Railroads offered still greater speed and still greater security against damage and late arrival.

What was the economic value of all this speed and security? A compact answer was given in 1854 by Congressman James McDougall.[23] A railway from the East to the Pacific, he declared, should be built. It would cut transit time from five months (around Cape Horn) to ten days (across the United States). It would thereby save

> $4.6 million in interest—for during transport "the merchandise is dead capital and properly chargeable with interest" (at 1 percent a month);

> $4.0 million in time saved by passengers (valued at $2 a day).

20. *Annals of Congress*, March 1818, col. 1377.

21. Jacob Viner, "Stability and Progress: The Poorer Countries' Problem," in D. C. Hague, ed., *Stability and Progress in the World Economy* (1958), p. 57.

22. *The Railroad Jubilees: Two Discourses Delivered in Hollis Street Meeting House* (1851).

23. *The Merchants Magazine and Commercial Review* (1854) 31:633–35.

These same factors are still used—perhaps more precisely—to decide on the advantage of building new roads along the Andes, new railroads in Tanzania, etc. Goods in transit to the consumer have a capital value locked up in them, which is earning no return. Goods held in regular inventories must be charged for interest foregone; so must goods in transit.[24] And, similarly, passengers are clearly willing to pay a premium to get there faster (by plane instead of train, by turnpike instead of routes through towns). And they will value their time perhaps at what they could earn in the time saved. (In 1849 the steamer from New York to New Orleans took 13 days less than the sailing ship, at $10 extra.[25])

The economic value of security in transport was also estimated by Congressman McDougall:

$4 million in insurance—because of the lesser risks by land;

$7 million reduction in losses not covered by insurance;

and "almost every article of merchandise that in the course of a long (sea) voyage has to pass twice through the tropics" arrives "less in quantity or injured in quality."[26]

The dangers of cargo destruction at sea are ancient and immemorial. Ships buffeted by storms were driven onto hidden rocks or shoals. They sank when badly caulked wooden hulls did not prevent marine worms from eating into them, when copper flashing ripped off, etc. The danger that road cargoes would be destroyed when wagon axles broke, when wagons foundered in the spring mud of a primitive land, were equally obvious. The insurance charges measure fairly well the loss to be expected for insured goods—to which one had then to add losses not covered by insurance.

Adding together these economic valuations of greater speed and enhanced security creates a measure of the reduction in real costs that society gains from improved transport. In a centrally planned economy such an estimate may suffice for most decisions to invest in transport advance versus some alternative. In a private market economy, however, the problem is more complex. As Henry Clay noted, we must consider the summed advantages to capitalists, landowners, and consumers.

24. The modern discussion of these elements in American history began with Robert Fogel, "Railroads in Economic Growth," *Journal of Economic History* (June 1962), pp. 163–97; and Albert Fishlow, *American Railroads and The Transformation of the Ante-Bellum Economy* (1965).

25. Sailing ships charged $50 for the trip from New York City to Galveston. Steamers charged $60 for virtually the same distance, from New York to New Orleans in first class, and $50 in second. Cf. Edward Smith, *Travels in Texas*, (1849), p. 6.

26. *The Merchant's Magazine and Commercial Review* (1854), pp. 633–34.

The consumer was the ultimate beneficiary of these new transport modes. Transport improvement almost always brought more competition into the markets he used: New sellers offered goods for sale, often driving down the price the consumers had to pay. In addition, more sellers usually meant a wider variety of goods from which to choose.

Not all economic groups benefited from the production of new modes of transport. Opposition there always was—although it never reached the state that it did in China where the indignant opposition actually tore up the first regular railroad and shipped its rails out as scrap. In the United States, opposition came from those with vested interests in the older mode. Thus, when the railroad replaced the road, thousands who had made a living driving cattle overland from the Midwest to the great cities of the East or up from Texas to the single cross-country railroad lost their economic reason for existence. So did the inns where they stopped each night to feed and water their cattle. Stagecoach companies were similarly menaced. So were the thousands of workmen who built stagecoaches, the blacksmiths who repaired them, and conservative souls in general.[27]

Each new technology competed with an older one—turnpikes with roads, canals with turnpikes, railroads with canals. Those who supported each change discovered that those with investment (money or skill) in the older modes tried to use the government to delay such advances. Typically, private entrepreneurs who owned the early short-line canals or turnpikes failed in that endeavor. But when the state itself was involved the odds improved. Thus when the Erie railroad began building across New York in the 1830s, the first railroad to serve so great a part of the state, it found a powerful vested interest: the state itself. The legislature actually passed a law requiring that any railroad within 30 miles of the Erie Canal had to hand the state Canal Board the equivalent of canal tolls from its fares. (That law was not repealed until 1851, almost a quarter of a century after railroads had begun spreading across the United States.)[28] These offsetting forces sometimes halted the building of canals and railroads. Sometimes they merely diverted their route.

The process by which the transport network of the nation was built, in response to these incentives, falls under two headings: private and public. The development path pursued by private enterprise was very clear, very petty. No roads to connect strategic parts of the union. Not even a set of railroads to bind one end of a state to the other. No canal or railroad system of majestic dimensions. And surely none from coast to coast or from North to

27. Josiah Quincy offered a resolution at a town meeting in Dorchester, Massachusetts, in 1842: "Resolved that our representatives be instructed to use their utmost endeavors to prevent if possible so great a calamity to us as must be the location of any railroad through it." Quoted in Charles B. George, *Forty Years on the Railroad* (1886), p. 45.

28. David M. Ellis, *Landlords and Farmers in the Hudson Mohawk Region* (1946), p. 175.

South. Instead, private enterprise built hundreds of very short lines, intended to move particular areas of land closer to existing markets.

The first turnpikes were built over short stretches—five, ten, twenty miles. The early canals were likewise short: The Merrimac, built in 1803, along the river from Boston to Lowell, ran only 27 miles. Nor did railroads extend hundreds of miles. The first U.S. railroad in 1827 was a mere 3 miles long: it carried granite blocks from the Charlestown Harbor to build the Bunker Hill monument. Next was the 9-mile Mauch Chunk and Summit Hill. That carried anthracite coal from the mine mouth to the nearest river. Of the key railroads built before 1831, all were less than 17 miles in length. And they typically carried coal from mine to river port.[29] Indeed, the average railroad begun in the 1840s, the first great decade of railroad construction, was a mere 43 miles in length.[30]

Why were railroads of such limited trackage built? The answer is much the same as that to another question: why were they built where they were? Private enterprise aimed to improve transport where the greatest volume of traffic, hence the largest profits, could be expected in the near future. Most early railroads were built where they were almost guaranteed a heavy traffic flow. For example, the Albany and Schenectady, built in 1831, and the Boston and Lowell, 1835, connected nearby cities, each line generating much traffic. Bales of raw cotton were continually shipped from Boston to the great new Lowell mills, and virtually the same tonnage of finished textiles was shipped back to Boston for sale.[31] Still other roads carried only coal from the mine to market but did so in immense volume.

The most reliable general index of potential traffic for a road or canal was population density. Farm products were shipped out and/or in to areas and manufactured goods were produced or consumed in some proportion to population. It might be more accurate to say in proportion "to the free population." One reason that canals and railroads developed little and late in the South was, of course, the lack of manufacturing and mining development. But it was also significant that shipments from plantations to Charleston or Richmond or New Orleans were not matched by any substantial volume returning. For the large slave populations offered only a trivial market, as compared with an equivalent free population. Slaves consumed little more than three "suits" of cotton and wool clothing each year, plus a pair of shoes. Investments in early southern railroads came perilously close to returning a profit only half the time, that is, on shipments one way. And fixed costs on

29. *Poor's Manual* (1900), p. xxxii. Their names reflected their focus: Carbondale, Port Carbon–Tuscarora, Mill Creek, etc.

30. Computed from the 1880 Census, *Report on the Agencies of Transportation*, Table 8. The average line in the United Kingdom by 1847 was no longer than a mere 15 miles. Cf. John Lansing, *Transportation and Economic Policy* (1966).

31. Cotton loses 10 percent or less of its weight in spinning.

such deadhead trips were far greater for canals or railroads than for steamboats. Hence, the prewar South relied on the latter. After all, the right of way for steamboats had been created by the Lord, and was maintained by the Army Engineers.

To build "developmental roads" to energize the economy of an entire state or region was quite another matter. Traffic on such lines would not build up for years, perhaps for decades. Investment in them meant a quick bankruptcy. Their builders would have to pay off interest charges on such investment year after year while the road's revenue was hardly sufficient to pay operating costs. Canals and railroads cost about $25,000 a mile in 1830–50. They had to earn perhaps $2,000 a mile to cover interest costs alone. To do so required far more traffic than could be achieved outside New England and the Mid-Atlantic states (and not even in all those states).

The Capitalists Guide for 1859 declared that if the Illinois Central Railroad could "be made self-sustaining, it would be one of the most magnificent enterprises of modern times; but such is not the case; and the query with capitalists is, how long can the road continue its traffic at a loss of a million to a million and a quarter dollars annually. . . ." The *Guide* bluntly compared its net earnings from operations with its costs (Table 10.2). "Loss in operating the road in four years . . . $4,251,912."[32] Thus stated a contemporary evaluation of a railroad that did eventually become enormously important to Illinois, and profitable for decades.

To the extent that it was built ahead of demand, even so well located a road as the Illinois Central became subject to a knife-edge dilemma. Without borrowing, the road could not be built. But with borrowing, huge expenditures for construction costs and interest were required years before traffic built up enough to create revenues. During those years developmental roads, canals, and railroads required public support. The boundaries of what private enterprise would provide were clear. What could public enterprise offer?

Public Aids to Transport

The first and most important public aid to transport was the creation of political order, so that travelers and goods could travel with moderate safety. When travel was dangerous, passengers were few and shipments of goods were still fewer. As a historian of another nation developing in the Americas noted: "To the poor material condition of the roads as a hindrance to cargo and passenger movement must be added widespread and endemic brigandage." From 1782 to 1808 a special Mexican court "meted out summary justice, frequently crucifixion, to unrecorded thousands" of highwaymen, while

---

32. *The Capitalists Guide and Railway Annual for 1859* (1859), p. 386.

TABLE 10.2
NET EARNINGS AND COSTS OF THE
ILLINOIS CENTRAL RAILROAD, 1855–58 ($ 000)

Year	Net Earnings	Costs
1855	$562	$1,270
1856	994	1,784
1857	503	2,043
1858	557	1,771

Source: *The Capitalists Guide and Railway Annual for 1859* (1859), p. 38.

"almost 14,000 dangled from the public gallows"—all to make travel safer.[33] Early travel in the United States involved dangers only somewhat less common. When packet service on the Ohio River from Cincinnati to Pittsburgh was announced in 1793, its safety was emphasized: "No danger need be apprehended from the enemy [i.e., Indians] as every person on board will be under cover, made proof against rifle or musquet balls." What was more, "convenient port holes for firing out of" were available.[34]

Public order was created by various levels of government. It could not be achieved economically by the private market.[35] But once public order had been achieved, a second range of public aids to transportation, and thereby to the development of markets and greater efficiency, opened up. The government could create, or invest in the creation of, the actual instrumentalities of transport. Adoption of a comprehensive approach (taken by most developing nations since World War II) would initiate a grand national plan for transportation.

The earliest substantial U.S. proposal of this sort was made in Gallatin's *Report on Roads and Canals*. Called "the earliest and most distinguished attempt to formulate a comprehensive national plan of internal improvements,"[36] it was early. It was distinguished. And it was disregarded. What John Quincy Adams commended as "the system of internal improvement by means of national energies," and fought for during his presidency, was rejected as both costly and "a dangerous advance 'toward monarchy.'"[37] For no national plan

33. Charles C. Cumberland, *Mexico, The Struggle for Modernity* (1968), pp. 160–61. Robberies on the main road from Vera Cruz to Mexico City became so common that an emergency supply of blankets and clothing was kept at each stage stop for passengers robbed of their clothes. Ibid., p. 162.

34. *Centinel of the Northwest Territory*, quoted in E. L. Bogart, *Internal Improvements and State Debt in Ohio* (1924), p. 5.

35. To provide guards for every stage and for every shipment was surely possible. But it was an expensive use of resources and could hardly induce the freedom of exchange that ordinarily precedes and stimulates economic development.

36. Goodrich, *Government Promotion*, p. 19.

37. Ibid., p. 19.

could be put across by one or two politicians in a country with so intense a variety of vested interests. To do so required a long process of political brokering through the Congress. Later years saw such a development: "pork-barrel legislation" was bargained out in the Congress, then carried through by the Army Corps of Engineers, giving each state its pet river, harbor, or road improvement over a stretch of time. But no one man could work out a politically balanced slate of projects. This was particularly true at so early a stage in the nation's development. For who could foresee the future with much assurance? Who yet had any idea which state, which region, which seaports were destined to become serviceable, to lead the rest? Furthermore, why should New York, better located than other states to tap the western trade, support a plan to help them? Why should South Carolina help new areas to become competitors in growing cotton? "The greatest improvements in Gallatin's report . . . were designed to overcome the Appalachian barrier. . . . They brought little benefit to the southern states and to the Lower South, none at all."[38] Programs to advance "the general welfare" could not be distinguished from those that aided some areas more than others. Another difficulty lay in financing. Gallatin proposed to rely on revenues from the tariff, that source for 90 percent of federal revenues during the entire pre–Civil War period. But the South was powerfully opposed to the tariff and reliance on its revenues.

Public aids to transportation did eventually proliferate. But not quite as Gallatin had planned or as Henry Clay had hoped. They turned out to reflect a battery of local interests. States, counties, and even cities gave subsidies and bought stock in the new transport modes. The state of New York levied taxes, borrowed money, and made the first grand commitment by building the Erie Canal (completed in 1825) from the Hudson River to Lake Erie. Philadelphia bought stock in the Pennsylvania Railroad; Baltimore, in the Baltimore and Ohio. (Nashville, lost in the race, even built its own railroad to Louisville. Cincinnati, bypassed by private entrepeneurs, also financed its own railroad.) Federal assistance eventually accumulated to a substantial amount. But the government's construction of a turnpike from Baltimore westward ('The National Road') was incredibly slow. Authorized in 1806, that road finally reached the middle of Indiana by the middle of the century (1852). There it expired in the mud. Subsequent federal aid for land transport largely went to the major transcontinental railroads, though considerable sums went for rivers and harbors decade after decade.

The public aids that actually financed transport in the years up to the Civil War turned out to reflect the vested interests of competing cities and states. A harbinger of that development was a conversation between George Washington and Elkanah Watson in 1785. Washington, the latter wrote, was intent upon linking "the western waters [e.g., the Ohio] by canals with his favorite Potomac . . . principally with a view to diverting the fur trade from

38. Ibid., p. 46.

Detroit to Alexandria instead of going to Montreal as heretofore."[39] For this purpose he supported removing obstructions in the distant Ohio River as well as those in the Potomac, the river flowing past Mount Vernon.

But, in fact, the first great attempt to attract the trade away from Montreal was made much farther north—the Erie Canal. Its success was overwhelming. No longer did shippers have to export from Montreal, whose port was closed by ice for 128 days a year.[40] They had an all-year open water port in New York City. Consequently, they were no longer uncertain as to whether their goods would clear the port before it was frozen in. Nor would their capital (in flour, furs, or other goods) remain locked up in a warehouse over the winter, earning nothing. Moreover, charges in New York for use of its wharves and other port facilities were less than those in Montreal, for those facilities were used a full year rather than two-thirds of a year.

But the opening of the Erie did not simply award the transport prize to New York. It initiated a chain of competitive responses by other state governments.

> It was on the success of this great public work that the western and eastern states immediately undertook the construction of similar works. Bostonians wanted to maintain their city as a commercial centre [but could not withstand the] power of the Erie Canal to draw the trade to New York. The question confronting the Boston merchants was then how to overcome or at least to counteract the natural disadvantages of their state.[11]

In the very year the Erie was to be finished, Massachusetts established a commission to plan a canal that would run from Boston to meet the Erie at Albany. The goal? To get the eastward trade to continue on from Albany to Boston rather than go south to New York. What eventually happened was quite unexpected: the gradual extension of railways, with a proposal in Boston in 1840 to extend the Massachusetts Railway from Boston to the Hudson. The inevitable parry by the New York City Council warned against such

> efforts to divert to seaports in other states a portion of the trade and travel which concentrates at Albany. . . . The immense trade and travel between manufacturing districts of New England and the grain producing regions of the West [will] be conducted, not through the city of New York, as in years past, but by 15 hours railway from Boston to Albany.

The City Council therefore urged vigorous efforts "in the construction of the

---

39. Watson, *History of the Rise*, pp. 8, 87.

40. 54th Cong., 2d sess., H.R. 192, *Report of the U.S. Deep Waterways Commission* (1897), p. 226.

41. Anon., *History of the Old Colony Railroad* (1893), p. 13.

New York and Albany railroad, which may be done to retain the trade between the east and west to its accustomed channel." [42]

An equally blunt response by another threatened city was reported in
1858.

> The immediate inducement to this, as well as to many other like under-
> takings, was a local interest, in this case a city of Hartford interest. The
> principal object was to attract new business, and to retain as far as might be
> the ancient connection of Hartford, in its trade, its manufactures, its banks,
> its insurance . . . with the eastern and western parts of the state. [For all
> other projected railroads were running] North and South, so as to divert
> trade and travel away from Hartford. [43]

To invest for such "prospects of remote and moderate profit," to quote
Gallatin, hybrid private–public schemes were often worked out. The merchants and landowners in seacoast cities created private companies in which
they invested and also lobbied their city and/or state into investing. Thus
Richmond subscribed $650,000 and Lynchburg $100,000 to the James River
and Kanawha Canal Company. Baltimore subscribed $500,000 to begin con-
structing the Baltimore and Ohio Railroad. By 1886 it had subscribed $5.5
million. The state of Pennsylvania borrowed $11 million to build the main
line system of canals and railroads between Philadelphia and Pittsburgh. [44]
The reasoning was simple. Businessmen could pick up and move to locations
with better transport. So could consumers. But landowners and businessmen
with investments in good-will at particular locations could not move without
considerable losses. They therefore had strong incentives to improve the
transport facilities right where their land was located. If public subscriptions
could be gotten, so much the better, and the project completed so much the
sooner.

Time after time those who sought public subsidy contended that such
support would actually be costless. Why? Because transport advance really
gave something for nothing. Thus, in 1825 a Select Committee of the House
of Representatives approved a

> memorial of the General Assembly of the State of Illinois, praying for aid
> from the United States in opening a canal to connect the waters of the
> Illinois River and Lake Michigan. . . . If, as the committee beg to recom-
> mend, a strip of land, of the width of two miles on each side of the canal

42. *Report of the Joint Special Committee on the Communication of His Honor, the Mayor, Relative to the New York and Albany Railroad, New York City Common Council* (July 24, 1840), p. 124.

43. *Report of Sundry Directors of the Hartford, Providence and Fish Kill Railroad Company* (1858), p. 4. Frederick Cleveland and Fred Powell, *Railroad Promotion and Capitalization in the United States* (1909), chap. VII, describes a host of these competitive endeavors.

44. *The American Almanac, 1840* (1840), p. 104.

shall be granted to the legislature of Illinois . . . the State would be able to raise [the sum required]. . . . The increased value not only of the immediately adjacent public lands, but of those throughout . . . Illinois and Missouri would not only reimburse the Treasury, but would much more than do it.[45]

The same argument had been proposed earlier for the Erie Canal.[46] And it continued to live in the halls of Congress. Legislation to subsidize the Union Pacific and Central Pacific railroads in the 1860s provided that the government would retain ownership of alternating land sections along those lines as compensation for its assistance.

Canals versus Railroads

It has been demonstrated that a system of canals could, in fact, have replaced most of the railroad lines east of the Rockies.[47] This raises the question of why the 1825–45 canal boom did not continue on to a time—in Robert Fulton's poetic language—when "canals should pass through every vale, winding round each hill, and bind the whole country together in the bonds of social intercourse."[48]

The technical feasibility of both systems had been apparent since 1825. For in that year the Erie, the first major U.S. canal, was completed, and England's first real railroad, the Stockton and Darlington, opened for business. In the early 1830s, when Philadelphia investors had to choose between the two modes for its main line, they sent an engineer, William Strickland, abroad to compare British canals and railroads. On his return he recommended railroads. (Pennsylvania chose canals nonetheless: the choice was to be made in an election year and canals provided more jobs).[49]

It was obvious that railways, in Wordsworth's phrase, were "injurious to morals" and destroyed the peace of rural districts.[50] But commercial considerations were no less obvious. In 1871 an Illinois writer testified to the value of rail transport:

45. 18th Cong., 2d sess., H.D. 53, *Report . . . Illinois River* (February 1825), pp. 1, 5.

46. The alternating arrangement had earlier been proposed by the Holland Land Company: By giving alternate sections along the way to the state, it would help get the Erie Canal built, yet make up the gift by the increase in value of its remaining land. Cf. Buffalo Historical Society Publications, *The Holland Land Company and Canal Construction in Western New York* (1910), 14:127.

47. Robert Fogel, *Railroads in American Economic Growth* (1964).

48. Cadwallader Colden, *The Life of Robert Fulton* (1817), p. 201.

49. According to the *Recollections of John Jay Smith, Written by Himself* (1892), p. 72: "We never could carry the elections and the railroad system, and Strickland agreed to report in favor of canals."

50. Philip Magnus, *Gladstone* (1954), p. 67. Wordsworth had written to Gladstone in 1844, hoping to check their spread.

One night's frost locked the [Erie] canal so as to embargo five hundred canal boats, all loaded with Western products bound for New York, the value of which is five million dollars, and which has to remain unmoved for four months. [But] not one solitary boat . . . moving West can be found caught in this commercial trap—it paying even the makers of stoves and heavy goods to move them west on railroads.[51]

The disastrous consequences for those shipping goods to the Midwest, or wheat and corn from it, were clear.

Two developments eventually ended the canal era, and frustrated Gallatin's plan. One was political, and all but inevitable. The other was economic. It was not at all inevitable.

The political factor was simple. The Erie cut the cost of transport from New York to Buffalo from $100 a ton by wagon to $8 a ton by canal. It had been financed by the entire state population, by taxes on salt and on goods sold at auction. As the counties on the canal line began to boom, their land values soaring, their cities expanding, the inevitable political question was asked. If it's good for New York City, Syracuse, and Buffalo, and for the farms in between, why isn't it good for the rest of the state? The legislature was duly moved to build other canals: the Oswego, linking to the Erie at the eastern border, the Genesee at the western border, and so on. Most of the subsequent canals did not share in the powerful growth of trade from the New West on to New York and the coast. Some participated in almost no trade at all. With losses on almost every other canal the state soon discovered its "canal system" to be a losing business.

Pennsylvania came along later. It moved swiftly to compete, once the Erie had been completed. But by then the race was over. The channels of trade to the West had been deepened and fixed along the Erie. Even if that had not been so, the Pennsylvania "main line" proved to be an expensive, a slow, and an odd arrangement. It provided worse service than the Erie, at higher cost. This was because it had to rise 2,200 feet over the Alleghenies (the Erie rose only 650 feet) to get to Ohio and the West. To do so it relied on a Rube Goldberg arrangement: Goods were taken by train 81 miles westward from Philadelphia at a not very swift average (3 miles per hour). At that point they incurred the cost (and breakage) involved in transshipment into a canal boat. The boat then went by stages until it was actually lifted up over the Appalachians by a series of long steel cables, with the canal boats hinged to split in half to take the bends. After further costly transfers, the goods eventually arrived in western Pennsylvania. That engineering feat became a triumphant commercial failure. Its costs were too high and time consumption too great. Moreover, Pennsylvania then had to build supplementary canals, even lower-

51. *Transactions of the Department of Agriculture of Illinois . . . 1871* (1872), p. 101.

use canals, to quiet the voters in the rest of the state. Even the main line became a losing proposition. Adding in the cost of the others promptly and
naturally led the state into bankruptcy in the late 1830s; it became unable to
pay interest on its bonds, much less make payments of principal due. Lacking
the help provided in later years (e.g., to New York City in the 1970s when it
overspent), the state went bankrupt. So did other states, from Michigan to
Mississippi, that had likewise engaged in big public investment programs to
induce swift economic development.[52] A private entrepreneur could build a
canal from one county to another, then call it quits. A state in a democracy
had no such option. Other counties demanded equal treatment.

The key economic reason for the end of the canal era was simply the development of the railroad. The superiority of the railroad rested on a simple
set of numbers, presented in Table 10.3. In round numbers the Army's
Topographical Bureau stated that the "appropriate load" for one horse was 10
tons on a railroad but only 1 ton on "an ordinary level turnpike."[53] Thus the
same investment in horse and wagon, the same cost of labor, carried a far
greater load on a turnpike than on a common road; on a railway than on a
canal; on a canal at 3 miles per hour than at 2.5 miles per hour. (Therein lay

TABLE 10.3

POUNDS OF FORCE REQUIRED TO MOVE ONE TON, 1800–60

Transport	Pounds of force
Common road	145.0
Level turnpike	111.0
Railway at 2.5 mph	8.5
Railway at 10 mph	8.5
Canal at 2.5 mph	3.0
Canal at 3 mph	6.0
Canal at 10 mph	*

*Not feasible because canal walls would wash away.

Source: Report on Steam Carriages, 22d Cong., 1st sess., H.D. 101 (1832): 14,
150, 152, 244. Wind resistance on canals was four times that on railroads
using the newer railway carriages at 3.5 mph and one hundred times greater
at 16 mph. Cf. James Espy, "On the Power Required to Propel Carriages,"
Journal of the Franklin Institute, n.s. 5 (1830):141.

52. A closely reasoned analysis of canal development and failure appears in Roger Ransom,
"Social Returns from Public Transport Investment: A Case Study of the Ohio Canal," Journal of
Political Economy (September–October 1970), and Albert Fishlow, in Lance Davis et al., eds.,
American Economic Growth (1972), pp. 475–85.

53. 24th Cong., 1st sess., H.D. 169, Road—Portsmouth and Linville (1836), p. 27.

the incentive to improve transport.) And no larger railroad investment was needed to carry a load at 10 miles per hour than at 3 miles per hour; whereas increasing canal speed by a mere half a mile per hour cut the load in half. (Therein lay the reason for the eventual switch from canals to railroads.)

As early as 1840 U.S. railroads could carry four tons of freight for the same real cost (in labor and capital use) that the canals required to carry only one ton.[54] In time that margin increased. For canal speeds were limited to six miles an hour. If the boats went any faster their waves broke the mud wall of the canal. But locomotive speeds increased year after year. Their round trips soon took no more time than canal boats needed to go only one way. (The actual speeds achieved in these various transport modes are reported in the historical literature and appear in this chapter's Appendix, Tables 10.4–10.6.)

The railroad offered two additional advantages. It delivered passengers and freight far more reliably than the canals could, given unpredictable freeze-ups in the winter, breaks of canal walls in the spring and fall.[55] Moreover, the railroad speeded development of the mountain and plains states, integrating into them a single economy with East and West. (Their natural stream and spring flows were insufficient to compensate for the tons of water that evaporated from canals every day.)

Private investors in the 1840s, as socialist planners in the 1980s, compared the effectiveness of investments in railroads with that in other modes of transport. What counted for them was the margin of advantage of one over

54. Stanley Lebergott, "United States Transport Advance and Externalities," *Journal of Economic History* (December 1966), p. 455. A too hasty reading has led one writer to see that as a comparison of "technologically possible" railroad freight rates rather than "economically attainable" ones. (Robert Fogel, "Notes on the Social Saving Controversy," *Journal of Economic History* (March 1979), pp. 8-10.) That comment is both incorrect and irrelevant. It is incorrect because the original calculation was for railroads operating at their economic "potential," defined as only 50 percent of their actual technical capacity. (Lebergott, "United States," p. 443.) Some highly profitable 1840 railroads actually operated at a far greater percentage.

The question addressed by that study was: "by how much the railroad reduced real costs of transport from those that would have prevailed under a regime of wagoners and boatmen." If one wishes to assume a still lower "intensity of track utilization" at potential than 50 percent, it is necessary to do the same for canals as well. The margin of advantage remains vastly in favor of the railroads. For the 4-to-1 ratio explicitly had assumed no economies of scale in operating railroads (though there clearly were) in order to understate railroad advantage. This secondary issue does not arise unless one were not interested in comparing railroads with the canal-road alternative, but only in deriving measures of "social saving."

55. Producers valued regularity of transport. Early textile manufacturers in Britain carted their cotton by road, rather than canal, even at much higher rates: "because speed and certainty are of the first importance." Henry Booth, *An Account of the Liverpool and Manchester Railway* (Philadelphia, 1831), p. 128. The "fear of not being able to sell inventory by the end of the finite planning horizon" was noted by Arthur Nevins: "Some Effects of Uncertainty," *Quarterly Journal of Economics* (February 1966), p. 82.

the other. Recent scholars have compared the railroad advantage, instead, with the entire national income. They have thus discovered, for example, that "the social saving attributable to the railroad in the interregional transportation of agricultural products was about six-tenths of one percent of national income."[56] That conclusion is startling—but uninteresting. A tiny percentage may be economically very significant. If, for example, such products were transported by magic carpet, at absolutely zero cost, the "social saving" would still compute to less than three percent of national income. Similarly, tiny numbers would describe the "social saving" from the coming of electricity, the automobile, hybrid corn, or anything else. Which only means that we cannot get much useful insight into the economic significance of any innovation by whether it produces an apparently tiny "social saving" number. Using our overall knowledge of economic savings, and social change, we can instead judge whether an apparently tiny "social saving" number does in fact reflect highly significant change. It did for the railroads.

Railroads enjoyed a substantial margin of commercial advantage over the alternative—wagon roads plus canals and rivers. That margin may have guaranteed their eventual expansion, but not the timing. Railroad mileage changed little from 1837 to 1847. It suddenly doubled in 1848, and then continued to rise. The motive force was a shock exogenous to the U.S. economy: the Irish famine of 1845–47 and the end in 1846 of the Britain's tariff keeping out U.S. wheat. When wheat shipments to Ireland and England soared in 1847 the Erie canal raised its "freight charge on a barrel of flour from Buffalo to Albany" from 45 cents to $1.12. The signal was clear, and "the railroads leapt into the breach."[57] The consequences for later regional growth (moving the center of wheat production westward from the East to the North Central regions) and for later industrial growth (milling the wheat in the United States to reduce transport costs) were many and momentous.

The coming of the railroads inevitably brought a variety of changes in modes of operation and sources of supply. Their physical scope required the development of new systems of supervising employees at a distance, more detailed than the rather simple combination of supercargo and captain that controlled a distant ship.[58] They also transformed the iron-rolling industry.[59] But their contribution to a new era in finance was almost as striking. The average farm or mill had required well under $10,000 in capital. The average

56. Robert Fogel, *Railroads and American Economic Growth* (1964), pp. 47, 223.

57. Paul Cootner, "The Role of the Railroads in United States Economic Growth," *Journal of Economic History* (December 1963), p. 497.

58. Cf. Thomas Cochran, *200 Years of American Business* (1977), chap. 4.

59. Railroads took 42 percent of the output of iron and steel-rolling mills. Cf. Robert Fogel, *Railroads and American Economic Growth* (1964), p. 142.

turnpike, perhaps 20 miles in length, had not cost over $20,000; the average whaling ship, fully equipped for sea, cost under $25,000. Even the giant Lowell textile mills required only $500,000 to $750,000.[60] But, the early railroad (typically a mere 30 to 40 miles long) required about $1,000,000 in capital.[61] It therefore opened a new era in finance for bankers, investors, and for other industries that could use this new financial structure.

60. For the whaling ship and the Lowell mills as of 1832, see (Louis McLane Report), *Documents Relative to the Manufactures in the United States* (1833), pp. 182, 340. For the turnpike, see Fishlow's estimate in Davis, *American Economic Growth*, pp. 473, 474.

61. Cf. Lebergott, "United States Transport Advance," p. 456. The railroad data are from the 1880 Census, *Railroads*.

Appendix

TABLE 10.4
FREIGHT SPEEDS AND LOADS, 1800S

Transport	Tons per horse	Miles per hour
1. Common road, Ohio, 1820s	0.60	1.0
2. Best road, Virginia, 1832	0.75	
Turnpike, Virginia, 1832	1.00	
3. U.S. turnpikes, 1820s	0.70	
4. Middlesex Canal, 1807	10.00–24.00	3.9
5. Baltimore and Ohio Railroad, 1832	20.00	6.0

Source: 1. William Cooper Howells, *Life in Ohio from 1815 to 1840* (reprint ed., 1963), p. 138. 2., 4. *American State Papers: Miscellaneous,* 1:828, 910, 918. 3. Joseph Durrenberger, *Turnpikes* (1931), p. 118. 5. *New England Magazine* 1 (1832).80.

TABLE 10.5
PASSENGER SPEED, 1840

Transport	Miles per hour
Sailing vessels	2.5
Canal boats	3.9
Stages and sleighs	4.9
Railroads, horse	6.0
Steamboats, rivers	9.0
Steamboats, lakes	10.0
Railroads, steam	15.0

Source: The American Almanac, 1841, p. 87. Based on a report of a "foreign gentleman" who traveled 10,330 miles throughout the United States.

TABLE 10.6
TRAVEL HOURS REQUIRED, NEW YORK TO ALBANY, 1817–41

Year	Transport	Hours required
1817	Sloop	36
1807	Steamboat	33
1841	Steamboat	10

Source: Autobiography of Thurlow Weed (1883), 1:62, 487; *Niles Weekly Register,* June 27, 1835, p. 299.

Now sits expectation in the air.

—HENRY V

I want what I want when I want it.
—VICTOR HERBERT, *Mlle. Modiste*

11

Finance and Investment

"WHY," asked Thackeray, "have the United States been paying seven, eight, ten percent for money for years past, when the same commodity can be got elsewhere at half that rate of interest?"[1] And why, asked Wordsworth, in an ode hurled "To the Pennsylvanians," was Penn's name

> abandoned by degenerate Men
> For state-dishonour black as ever came
> To upper air from Mammon's loathsome den[2]

Both writers had obviously loaned money in the United States. And been burned.

No economy can develop, can become ever more productive, without investing—in roads, in machinery, in inventories. But to do so requires the nation to throttle its consumption down in favor of its investment. Thus, some five thousand men who were busy digging the Erie Canal in 1817 could instead have transported goods along that route by wagon, and thereby made more transportation service available in that year. Instead they dug a canal that carried no goods at all in 1817. Nor in 1818. Nor in 1819. But when the great work was completed, in 1825, the nation had a new transport facility that could carry far more goods in any year, with far less human effort, than wagon transport. And it did so for decades after 1825. The social cost of U.S.

---

1. "Half a Loaf," *Roundabout Papers* (1884), p. 176.
2. *Poems* (Oxford edition), p. 515.

canal transport came to perhaps 5 percent of road transport for many decades after 1825. Huge investments were required to build the nation's canals, railroads, and machinery. But once in place, these improvements provided more service, at lower cost, than if the labor used to build them had been directly devoted to transporting goods.

Other types of investment were no less productive. Every year the amount of clothing worn out from January to March was much the same as from March to May. And the amount of textiles needed to replace it was much the same in each period. But fully two-thirds of the U.S. cotton grown each year was picked between January and March.[3] Hence, thousands of cotton bales had to be stored for months until the factories worked them into textiles. Wheat was also harvested in just a few months, but consumed over the entire year or less. Iron was produced in only part of the year[4] yet it was used steadily throughout the year by blacksmiths to produce stoves, wheel rims, and plow points. Investment in inventories of iron was therefore necessary.

To make such investments in cotton, wheat, and iron, some system of finance was required. Incentives were therefore needed to induce Americans to consume less than they would otherwise and divert that saving into longer term investments. The prudent nation, the reasonable tribe, could, of course, calmly reduce its standard of living long enough to accumulate real resources. These it would then convert into capital investments—fishing spears, windmills, railroads. Such investments would permit it to enjoy a distinctly higher standard of living thereafter: The roundabout method of production typically offers so much more efficiency than the direct. History, however, fails to record the names of many such prudent nations. More commonly it describes command policies that coerce the people into keeping their standard of living low. Still more often it describes a long process in which savings are laboriously accumulated, and slowly translated into investments, which then transform the economy. So it was for the United States.

Few U.S. capitalists were willing to loan money to would-be investors without exacting a price. That price covered the risk of borrower defaulting. But it covered more. The lender did not have the use of his capital for the period of the loan. He was prevented from spending it on enjoyable wild excess or lending it to some other borrower.

The risk of default is higher in societies where assault, theft, and murder are not effectively kept down by the government. Long-range investment is peculiarly sensitive to the growth of such security. As government expands its policing ability, investment too expands, for interest rates then tend to fall. In 1817 interest rates of 33 ⅓ percent were paid to Ashantee investors—every

3. Lewis C. Gray, *History of Agriculture in the Southern United States to 1860* (1933), 2:715.

4. McLane Report, *Documents Relative to the Manufactures in the United States* (1833), vol. 2. Some furnaces worked six months a year (p. 312), nine months (p. 363), or ten months (p. 334); others ran except "when stopped by cold" (p. 313).

forty days. And "when the patience of the creditor is exhausted, he seizes the debtor, or even any of his family, as slaves, and they can only be redeemed by the payment."[5] Given such harsh mores few persons came forward to borrow for long-term investment even though it could have improved the nation's transport or manufacturing. The interest rate was too great. And the dangers of failure, even greater. But social order developed in the United States; the risk component of interest rates fell; and with it, the supply price of capital.

The contribution of government to investors could have been much more direct. It could have "loaned its credit." It occurred to many that the federal government was borrowing at only 5 and 6 percent, while individual Americans had to pay 10 and 12 percent. What is more reasonable, said Gallatin in 1810, than for the government to loan its good name?

> Since . . . the want of capital is the principal obstacle to the introduction and advancement of manufactures in America . . . the most obvious remedy would consist in supplying that capital. . . . The United States might create a circulating stock, bearing a low rate of interest, and lend it at par to manufacturers. [Five to twenty million a year could be lent] without any material risk . . . and without taxing or injuring any other part of the community.[6]

That sanguine forecast, however, was sharply contradicted within a decade. Federal credit was extended to land buyers in 1800–17 with disastrous results. In 1819–20 millions of acres were returned to the federal government without payment. Buyers pressured for the return of even their down payments in every session of Congress. An enormous total of unpaid bills due the federal government had to be canceled. That ended the land credit policy in 1820. The United States likewise extended credit to importers until 1842 by not requiring prompt payment of tariff charges. Such loans to only one part of the business community, at the expense of the others, proved only slightly more acceptable.

The Bank of the United States constituted an early alternative to direct Treasury lending. It helped finance the War of 1812. The second Bank of the United States also helped Treasury financing. However, the bank's huge size and widely dispersed branches enabled it to restrict the growth of local banks by sending their bank notes promptly back to them and demanding specie. The local banks typically made their profits by making loans, which they did mostly by printing up their own bank notes, sometimes by merely establishing demand deposits for borrowers. The new banks that sprouted around the

5. T. Edward Bowditch, *Mission from Cape Coast Castle to Ashantee* (1819), p. 257. In ancient Athens annual interest rates of 36 percent (and even 18 percent for long-term investment in manufacturing) were quoted. Cf. Athenaeus, *Deipnosophistae* (Loeb Library, 1937), Book XIII, p. 297.
6. Albert Gallatin, *American State Papers: Finance*, 6:430–31.

nation in the 1820s found the Bank of the United States persistently redeeming their notes, thereby restricting their earnings. Nor did most of them schedule their loans as the banks of Boston and New Orleans tended to do, so they would be repaid at a steady rate through time. As a result, when under pressure from financial panics, or the Bank of the United States, they were at times unable to pay out specie to those presenting the banks notes for repayment, and were forced into bankruptcy. And when they failed, they inflicted losses on citizens caught holding the "wildcat" bank notes they had printed. Such restriction may have been a very worthy goal, particularly when no Federal Reserve System existed to do that job. But it hardly endeared the bank to the many small banks, or to the host of entrepreneurs who hoped to borrow money from those banks.

The Achilles' heel of the Bank of the United States was a political fact. As of 1809, about 75 percent of its stock was owned by foreigners.[7] And by 1832, when President Andrew Jackson proposed to end its charter, foreigners still owned 20 percent of its stock.[8] Journalist Thurlow Weed, partisan of the bank though he was, noted two decisive sentences in Jackson's veto message. One declared that the government "was endangered by the large amount of the stock of the Bank of the United States owned in Europe." The other asserted that the bank was a contrivance "to make the rich richer and the poor poorer." These sentences, he said, would carry 10 electors against the bank for every one whom Senator Daniel Webster could persuade to support it.[9] And, of course, Weed was right. Jackson vetoed the bank's charter. It then limped along to bankruptcy after a few more years, with a Pennsylvania charter.

Next best to federal credit was state credit—because the next lowest interest rates. Originally, the states had accumulated debts to pay soldiers for fighting in the Revolution. Those debts had almost completely been taken over ("assumed") by the national government in 1790, as Alexander Hamilton proposed.[10] For the next forty years, the states added very little debt. The real rise came in the 1830s (Table 11.1).

In what did the states invest huge sums? Illinois, Michigan, and the Midwest generally chose canals and railroads, as did New York and Pennsylvania. The border states, from Maryland to Kentucky to Missouri, also spent chiefly on transport—roads, canals, and railroads. But not the Cotton South—which issued 91 percent of its state bonds to create or benefit banks.[11]

The North needed transport to open up new land for farming, to make it possible to ship farm products to major markets. In the Cotton South (i.e.,

7. *American State Papers: Finance*, 2:351.

8. 22d Cong., 1st sess., H.D. 95, *Memorial of Citizens of Massachusetts* . . . (1832), p. 1.

9. *Autobiography of Thurlow Weed* (1883), p. 373.

10. Some $18 million of $22 million in state debt was assumed. Cf. 1880 Census, *Valuation, Taxation, and Public Indebtedness*, p. 523.

11. Ibid., p. 526.

TABLE 11.1
Stocks Issued by the States
(millions of dollars)

Year	Total[a]	Banking	Transport
1820–25	$ 13		
1826–30	14		
1831–35	40		
1836–38	107		
1820–38	174	$53	$119

[a]Miscellaneous debts included; redemptions excluded from the total.

Source: Period data: 1880 Census, *Valuation, Taxation, and Public Indebtedness,* p. 523. Data by type: *The American Almanac, 1840.*

the "Lower South") men wanted loans to buy land, to open new plantations, to buy slaves from the Upper South. By setting up state (or state-sponsored) banks, they financed such purchases through their states. Of the vast battery of state bonds issued in these years, Europeans bought three-fourths.[12] The Europeans, therefore, provided the essential financing for the great American canal boom of the 1830s and for the purchase of slaves and raw southern land by the planters of the New South.

The distinctive American contribution, other than using the mantle of state credit to secure foreign funds, was the growth of state banking. That helped flood the country with an increased money supply. By May 1838 the states had actually issued $51 million in stocks and bonds for bank capital.[13] Even had that all been supplied by foreigners, it would account for but a small share of the $320 million in bank capital as of that date.[14] Of that total, an enormous portion had been created since the end of the Bank of the United States, thereby throwing open the door for multitudes to charter banks and print bank notes without the discipline of a central bank.[15]

12. 25th Cong., 3d sess., H.D. 227, *Condition of State Banks* (February 1839), p. 201, reports that the states actually issued $124 million. (A further $50 million had been authorized but not issued.) A report of the Missouri General Assembly found that $95 million in state and other bonds had been sold to Europeans by mid-1837; ibid., p. 604. But private securities had not yet developed a ready market in Europe. G. Callender, "Early Transportation and Banking Enterprises . . .," *Quarterly Journal of Economics* (November 1902), p. 153. Therefore, virtually all of the 77 percent was on state account.

13. 25th Cong., *Condition of State Banks,* p. 210.

14. *Journal of Banking* (June 22, 1842), p. 386, reports $318 million paid in bank capital as of January 1838 and $327 million as of January 1839.

15. Bray Hammond, *Banks and Politics in America from the Revolution to the Civil War* (1957). Hugh Rockoff, "The Free Banking Era," *Journal of Money, Credit, and Banking* (May 1974), pp. 141–68.

Could anyone have predicted the results of placing a money printing press within reach of a handful of men subject to no discipline in the way of strong banking traditions or legislative limits? The state Bank of Alabama collapsed, having loaned money to eighty-eight members of the legislature. (When denied a loan, Representative Samuel Rice denounced "the conduct of a bank that would not lend money to the people, and avowed his purpose to bring the subject up in the legislature." He promptly got the loan.)[16] Some legislators had borrowed quite modest amounts. Others had accumulated far larger obligations.[17] They had invested in more land and slaves than the market warranted. After the crash in 1839 the state bank ended up with a useless collection of notes due. And it did not prove easy for the legislators to investigate themselves.

State investments in transport proved sounder. Private funds had been borrowed to build dozens of small New England canals and turnpikes between the 1780s and 1817. But private funds and management had improved only bits and pieces of streams. Two private companies had tried to build a canal westward across New York—and failed. The state itself then issued bonds, hired contractors, and trained engineers. From 1817 to 1825 it "built the longest canal, for the least money and in the shortest time" that the United States—and perhaps the world—had ever seen. As sections of the canal were finished, mule-drawn boats began a profitable business of transporting goods between Syracuse and Rome, between Rome and Schenectady, and so on. When the canal was completed, shipments, and thereby tolls, began to soar. New York State found the tolls flowing in so generously that by 1838 it had paid off $4.5 million of the $7 million it had borrowed between 1820 and 1825.[18] The magic financial formula had apparently been found.

Those who supplied these funds, by buying state bonds, included many foreigners. A nation in a world of other nations always has the enticing prospect of drawing upon the savings of other nations to finance its own development. The most obvious tactic is to monetize the faith and credit of the nation, thus creating a national debt backed by the national government. After all, both the Dutch and the British had done so most successfully. By a turn of the wheel, they themselves had become a source of investment funds. The previous sale of U.S. federal bonds in Europe had shown that some Europeans, at least, were prepared to bet on the United States.[19] By the end of the ebullient 1830s, 70 percent of Pennsylvania's debt was held by Britons

16. John du Bose, *The Life and Times of William Lowndes Yancey* (reprint ed., 1942), 1:117, 119.

17. Ibid. Cf. also 26th Cong., 2d sess., H.D. 111, *Condition of State Banks* (1841), pp. 538, 555.

18. 1880 Census, *Valuation*, p. 523.

19. In 1800 some 14 percent of U.S. public debt was held by foreigners. *American State Papers: Finance*, 2:289.

and Europeans.[20] Some 80 percent of the money that built the Erie and Champlain canals was loaned by foreigners at from 5 percent to 6 percent.[21] One contemporary went so far as to guess that all the state bonds were sold abroad.[22] However, a reliable estimate, as of 1856, shows about 40 percent of state bonds (and 20 percent of municipal bonds) were indeed held by foreigners.[23]

One reason why foreigners fell so completely for the state bonds, and exercised little more caution than the borrowers, was their failure to understand the federal system.[24] When Europeans learned that the United States had paid off its national debt, they inferred that here at last was a nation that was truly prudent financially. The United States lacked a large army or navy, spent less than it collected in revenue from tariffs and other taxes. U.S. bonds appeared, then, to be an unusually safe investment. But Europeans seemed to be pleasantly confused about the relation between the federal government and the states. Perhaps they assumed that Congress would take over the debts of the states if need be (as it had in 1790). Or at least that it would somehow guarantee them.

But the debts were owed to foreigners. And Congress took no action. The states simply refused to pay interest for some years: Raising taxes would be too uncomfortable. Mississippi asserted various technicalities, repudiating its debt altogether.[25] The natural result was that for many years thereafter the states had to pay exorbitant rates to raise money. Pennsylvania state bonds once commanded a premium of 20 percent more than their face value, but sold at 34 percent below face value by 1840.[26] South Carolina, Mississippi, and Alabama bonds were all sharply discounted, and Indiana's were even more sharply discounted. Meanwhile, Massachusetts, prudently borrowing little and spending carefully, found its bonds worth 100 cents on the dollar.[27]

Ministers of finance might shrewdly emphasize how the influx of foreign capital "knocks down the immoderately high level of profits to which our

20. *The Merchants' Magazine and Commercial Review*, (1849) 20:268. In July 1842 some $24 million of $35 million of Pennsylvania stock was held by foreigners. Since almost no state securities were sold abroad after mid-1839 (1880 Census, *Valuation*, p. 526), the 1842 proportion reasonably reflects the 1838 ratio.

21. New York State Assembly, *Annual Report of the Commissioners of the Canal Fund of the State of New York . . . January 1837* (1837), p. 11.

22. *Missouri General Assembly Report*, reprinted in 25th Cong., 3d sess., H.D. 227, *Condition of State Banks* (1839), p. 604.

23. 34th Cong., 3d sess., S.D. 3, *Report on the Finances* (1856), p. 426.

24. Although they had loaned millions to the states by 1840, Europeans made loans to not over a dozen private corporations. Cf. Callender, "Early Transportation and Banking Enterprises of the States . . .," *Quarterly Journal of Economics* (November 1902), p. 153.

25. William A. Scott, *Repudiation of State Debts* (1893), p. 33.

26. 26th Cong., 2d sess., H.D. 111, *Condition of State Banks* (1841), p. 1377. The impossibility of marketing any of Missouri's bonds abroad in 1840 is indicated by a letter in ibid., p. 1378.

27. 26th Cong., 3d sess., H.R. 296, *Relief of the States* (1843), p. 457. Virginia and Florida had only 10 percent discounts.

monopolistic entrepreneurs are accustomed, and forces them to seek compensation in technical improvements, which, in turn, will lead to price reductions."[28] But foreign investors had no great interest in making such a contribution. They were, as we have seen, avidly interested in certain state, canal, and railroad issues. But in the aggregate, foreign investors contributed only trivially to domestic U.S. capital formation. As of 1805 (and indeed as late as 1853), they accounted for only about 3 percent of the total.[29]

The primary source of U.S. finance over the decades proved to be neither foreign nor federal nor state. It was private. And, inevitably, the ancient conflict between borrowers and debtors appeared and reappeared. Would-be borrowers always hoped that credit could somehow be extended with neither charge nor limit. And in the decades before the Civil War many believed that commercial heaven could be achieved if only banks were forbidden to exist. Thus, the criminal code of Nebraska, adopted in 1855, actually declared that anyone helping to form a bank would be imprisoned and fined "not less than one thousand dollars." A charter granted at the very same session, however, permitted the Western Exchange Fire and Marine Insurance Company to "receive deposits and issue certificates therefore."[30] These certificates of deposit inevitably began to function as bank notes. (Bankers from other states profited, supplying bank notes that Nebraskans needed for their transactions.) It took decades before Western Exchange became a major bank. But it, and other unincorporated banks, performed the usual banking functions for decades before that.[31] For where there were those who wished to borrow in order to invest—in land, in factories, in stocks of goods—lenders appeared.

Major purveyors of credit in the United States before the Civil War operated outside the formal commercial banking system.[32] They included a

28. Sergei Witte, quoted in T. von Laue, "Document," *Journal of Modern History* 26 (1954): 69.

29. An 1805 valuation of $2.5 billion is given by Samuel Blodget, *Economica* (1805, reprint ed., 1963), p. 196. He stipulates a value of $2 for acreage away from populated areas, which we reduce to 40 cents, the latter figure being closer to actual sales of millions of acres in Maine and Ohio about this date. A foreign debt of $73 million in 1805 is estimated by Douglass North in Conference on Research in Income and Wealth, *Trends in the American Economy* (1960), p. 600. For 1853, a $10 billion national assets total is given by Raymond Goldsmith, *Institutional Investor Study Report of the Securities and Exchange Commission* (1971), supplementary vol. 1:30, and a foreign balance of $301 million in that year is estimated in North, *Trends*, p. 620.

30. *Nebraska History* 6 (October-December 1923):112.

31. Cf. the expert study by Richard Sylla, "Forgotten Men of Money: Private Bankers in Early U.S. History," *Journal of Economic History* (March 1976), pp. 173–88.

32. Note 29, this chapter, suggests that national wealth rose by $7.5 billion in 1805–53. But from the 1830s to 1853, the level of bank loans changed little. U.S. Census, *Historical Statistics . . . to 1970*, p. 1020. It is unlikely that the real estate loans were paid off in less than three years and the other loans in, say, two. If so, the banks financed not more than half of such investments. Since they undoubtedly financed some inventories, their share in financing the increase in total wealth ownership would have had to be less than half.

motley variety of individuals and businesses: storekeepers—who let their customers run up bills, paid off in kind (furs, skins, butter, eggs, potash);
wholesalers—who supplied grocers and other retailers with long-term credit;
manufacturers—who provided pig iron, textile yardage, or railroad cars to
other producers, also on time. But the largest amount of credit was undoubtedly extended to farmers and planters, who constituted the bulk of the
population. Innumerable sellers of land, plows, horses and slaves, farm implements and wagons sold them on time. But land financing likewise drew
funds from thousands upon thousands of clergymen, doctors, and lawyers, as
well as canny farmers and workers who placed their $50 or $100 with local
moneylenders and "mortgage sharks."[33] The very multiplicity of such
sources suggests a competitive market in funds, more so than in many
localities during later periods when suppliers were fewer. But the borrowers
in the 1830s and 1850s expressed the same desires as borrowers in the New
England of the 1780s, the Midwest of the 1890s, and the South of the 1930s.
They sought lower interest rates, debt relief, interest deferral, plus a flood of
paper money to reduce the real burden of debt. Public intervention to satisfy
such desires during 1789–1860 seems, however, to have been far less frequent
than in other such periods. Usury laws were indeed passed, particularly in
the Midwest. These kept down nominal interest rates. But there seems to
have been little enforcement. More important, as in other similar attempts in
world history, the development of premiums, points, and other side arrangements seems to have nullified the formal constraints. However, it is likely
that not all would-be borrowers were accommodated even with such conditions. The less established and younger persons, who hungered for land and
entrepreneurial opportunity, were afforded the empty satisfaction of not
being charged "excessive and unreasonable" rates—because they were not
granted loans in the first place. Since such people were indeed dubious risks,
the law probably protected competing and greedy lenders in spite of themselves, preventing their recklessly making bad loans to such borrowers.

The formal history of U.S. commercial banking and monetary supply is
replete with dramatic and improbable episodes. But the drama of Jefferson
and Jackson making sure that Federal funds were deposited in politically
"right" banks and of Jackson and his hard money friends letting loose a host of
individual banks to replace the staid Bank of the United States appears to have
little affected the main trend in the finance of U.S. investment.[34] The major

---

33. Allan Bogue, *Money at Interest* (1955), describes, in brilliant detail, how such lenders
judged their risks, decided on rates, placed loans, and called them in.

34. The saga of the Jackson years and the hard money men is elegantly and succinctly
analyzed by Peter Temin, *The Jacksonian Economy* (1969), a study that supersedes most earlier
work on the topic.

inadequacies of the banking system thus developed will be further examined in connection with the role of the Federal Reserve System in the Great Depression.

Finance was but one element in the new era of industrialism and economic modernization. A primary element was surely manufacturing.

The cotton factory is an invention that could be made by
a greedy dog.
—GEORGE BERNARD SHAW, *Don Juan in Hell*

All manufactories were conducted with slaves, because
the occupation had a tendency to degrade and debase the
human mind . . . [factories] would prove destructive to
the liberties of this Republic.
—REPRESENTATIVE JOHN ROSS, 1816

[Only in British climate] could the human animal bear,
without extirpation, the corrupted air, the noisome exha-
lations, the incessant labor of those accursed manufactories. . . . We should have the yellow fever from June to
January, and January to June. . . . The climate of this
country alone . . . says "You shall not manufacture."
—JOHN TAYLOR OF CAROLINE

12

Manufacturing

IN 1796 Talleyrand, the world's leading diplomat, coldly described the
state of U.S. manufactures. America

> is but in her infancy with regard to manufactures: a few iron works, several
> glass houses, some tan yards, a considerable number of trifling and imper-
> fect manufactories of kerseymere [a coarse kind of knitting] and, in some
> places, of cotton . . . point out the feeble efforts that have hitherto been
> made [yet fail to] furnish the country with manufactured articles of daily
> consumption.[1]

Within half a century, however, American prowess in manufacturing was obvious to all the world.

1. *Memoir Concerning the Commerical Relations of the United States with England by Citizen Talleyrand* (1806). For once, the great foreign minister was between jobs. He took a trip to the United
States to canvass prospects there.

What brought the change? Only a few decades earlier Hamilton and Gallatin had described the lack of capital in the United States; Jefferson had italicized the high price of labor; and the *Federal Gazette* had declared that "the diffidence of our citizens" would long prevent their beginning any new industry.[2]

Before trying to answer the question, we must first recognize that manufacturing was not expanded by a universal effort but by a mere handful of entrepreneurs and investors. No more than a dozen investors provided virtually all the capital required to start the first giant textile mills in the United States, the Boston and Merrimac companies.[3] And the total number of investors in the major mills was remarkably small.[4] The advance of American manufacturing industry, then, turned on a few hundred investors and entrepreneurs who deployed their efforts and capital to manufacturing.

A powerful central force was the willingness of this handful of venturesome entrepreneurs to build and operate factories—new, different, and often larger than any in the colonial past. Such venturesomeness, however, did not rely on mere animal spirits. During something close to a quarter of a century, the importation of manufactured goods from England had been frequently interrupted, thereby opening the market to potential American suppliers. The Revolution had been the first interruption. The Napoleonic Wars, which raged, with some intermissions, from the late 1790s to 1815, provided a cumulative impact. The flow of raw materials to Europe was slowed by the dangers of the war and then banned altogether by Jefferson's embargo of all foreign trade in 1808. In addition, Britain had issued Orders in Council to seize any U.S. ship that carried goods (contraband or noncontraband) to France. One indignant but shrewd Briton foresaw what the Orders would lead to:

> The United States of America offer to Great Britain, a market which it would be her interest to secure at the price of all the other markets of the world. . . . Some branches of manufacture have already, since the American embargo was first resorted to, made a progress which proves that they are capable of rivalling the looms of Lancashire and Yorkshire." [Now] "the habits of Americans are as yet . . . agricultural. . . . As long as Europe shall consume their raw materials and not subject them to intolerable vexations . . . they will continue to cultivate them. . . . Nothing but a forcible obstruction in the highway by which their production seeks a market, will

2. The objections are rehearsed by Joseph S. Davis, *Essays in the Earlier History of American Corporations (1917)*, 2:279–81.

3. Cf. the stockholder lists in *The Merchants' Magazine and Commercial Review* (December 1858), p. 666; Caroline Ware, *The Early New England Cotton Manufacture* (1931), p. 146.

4. Lance Davis estimates there were about five hundred original stockholders in the eleven largest Massachusetts mills as of 1859. Cf. Robert Fogel and Stanley Engerman, eds., *The Reinterpretation of American Economic History* (1971), p. 294.

convert them from farmers to manufacturers. [But by] embroiling herself with the United States [England is] gradually losing posession of the first market in the world.[5]

His wisdom went unregarded. His prediction came true. Goods imported into the United States cost more as the war went on: Marine insurance rates rose to cover the danger of seizure or sinking by the warring powers. Delivery became uncertain. The American embargo, plus the British Orders in Council, drove shippers out of foreign trade. The consequence? Reduced foreign supply and higher prices for imported manufacturers. The opportunity for American manufactures became obvious. The results in Massachusetts, reported in Figure 12.1, are suggestive.

The first tentative beginnings of new textile factories resulting from the 1808 embargo were followed by a steady stream of entrants into the industry at the same time that the state's activity in foreign trade declined. The declaration of war on Great Britain in 1812 accentuated the growth. Similar trade declines occurred in other states. Rhode Island, in addition, enjoyed moral advance, and financial loss, from the end of the slave trade in January 1808. It thereby lost markets for its ships, and the rum that its distilleries used to make for the slave trade. It too shifted to the newer manufactures.[6] The creative impact of the interruptions of war stands clear in the record (Table 12.1).

The mechanism of possibility, however, is noted in Table 12.2, which contrasts the increasing margin between two prices—what producers paid for raw cotton and what they sold their textiles for. After that gross margin had remained at a new high for several years, new factories began to be established—over a hundred from the beginning of Jefferson's embargo until the end of the Napoleonic Wars. The closing off of European competition by the War in 1812 obviously, and immediately, induced entrepreneurs to rush into the industry. As soon as the Atlantic was opened for trade in 1815, however, Britain's textile industry dumped a total of 71 million yards on the American market.[7] (At this time the entire annual U.S. production came to about 90 million yards.[8]) One single ship, the *Princess Charlotte Turnbull*, arrived from Calcutta in June 1815 with 5 million yards of piece goods.[9] To American manufacturers it looked like more than happenstance. And, indeed, they could quote England's chancellor, Lord Brougham, who declared that "it was well worthwhile to incur a loss upon the first exportation [after the war] in

5. *Conciliation with America the True Policy of Great Britain, by a Friend to British Manufactures* (1811), pp. 9, 15, 16, 25.

6. Cf. George Howe, *Mount Hope: A New England Chronicle* (1959).

7. Lars Sandberg, "Movements in the Quality of British Cotton Textile Exports, 1815–1913," *Journal of Economic History* (March 1968), p. 16.

8. Gales and Seaton, (U.S. Congress) *Debates and Proceedings* (December 13, 1815, February 13, 1816), cols. 1647, 1673.

9. Ibid.

FIGURE 12.1
Tonnage in Foreign Trade and
Number of Factories Incorporated, Massachusetts, 1808–16

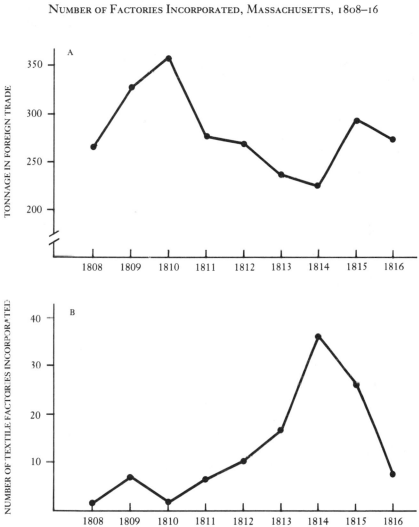

Source: Adam Seybert, Statistical Annals (1818), p. 322. Report of the Secretary of State, 18th Cong., 1st sess., S.D. 45, p. 15.

TABLE 12.1
NEW FACTORY ENTERPRISES, 1800–30

	Incorporations[a]				Factories established[b]	
	Total	Metal and machinery	Chemicals	Textiles	Cotton	Iron
1800	1	1				7
1801						
1802					5	
1803	2	1				1
1804						2
1805	3	2		1	2	1
1806					6	2
1807	4			4	4	3
1808	7	1		5	3	2
1809	26	1	5	18	6	2
1810	30	3	7	17	10	3
1811	41	5	5	30	9	3
1812	48	11	3	35	27	3
1813	66	5	1	57	23	3
1814	128	12	·5	105	43	2
1815	78	5	1	64	15	4
1816	26	6		18	6	5
1817	8	3		5	5	1
1818	12	2	1	10	5	4
1819	8	2	1	6	4	2
1820	8		1	5	7	14
1821					4	2
1822					11	2
1823					22	1
1824					17	8
1825					24	13
1826					24	12
1827					22	11
1828					48	12
1829					17	10
1830					24	11

[a]Data after 1820 not available. [b]Restricted to those still operating in 1832.

Sources: Incorporations: Computed from 18th Cong., 1st sess., S.D. 45, *Report of the Secretary of State* (January 27, 1824). A few mining and pottery firms were also included. The states included were: Connecticut, Massachusetts, New Hampshire, Vermont, New York, New Jersey, Pennsylvania, and Maryland. Cotton: Clive Day, "The Early Development of the American Cotton Manufacture," *Quarterly Journal of Economics* 39 (1925):452. Six New England states plus New York and New Jersey. Iron: Computed from 22d Cong., 1st sess., H.D. 308, *Documents Relative to the Manufactures in the U.S.* (1833), 2:115–22, 200–34, 239–301. Data are for Pennsylvania and New York.

TABLE 12.2
AMERICAN COTTON TEXTILES:
THE FORCING PERIOD, 1802–20

| Year | Price | | Factory gross margin | Number of factories established |
	Raw cotton (lb)	Cotton sheeting (yd)		
1802	19¢	16¢	11¢	5
1803	19	16	11	0
1804	20	19	14	0
1805	23	21	16	2
1806	22	22	16	6
1807	22	21	15	4
1808	19	22	18	3
1809	16	25	21	6
1810	16	22	18	10
1811	16	19	15	9
1812	11	19	16	27
1813	12	22	18	23
1814	15	23	19	43
1815	21	20	15	15
1816	30	19	12	6
1817	26	18	11	5
1818	24	17	11	5
1819	24	16	11	4
1820	17	16	12	7

Sources: Raw cotton and cotton sheeting: U.S. Census, *Historical Statistics of the U.S. . . . to 1970*, p. 209. Factory gross margin: Price of a yard of sheeting minus one-fourth the price of a pound of cotton. 22d Cong., 1st sess., H.D. 308, *Documents Relative to the Manufactures in the U.S.* (1833) U.S. serial set 222, pp. 175, 199, 298. One pound of raw cotton produced 4 yards of sheeting. Margin computed from unrounded price data. Number of factories established: Clive Day, "Early Development," *Quarterly Journal of Economics* 39 (1925):452.

order, by the glut, to stifle in the cradle those rising manufactures in the United States, which the war had forced into existence contrary to the natural course of things."[10] The "inundation of British goods, which have been sold under prime cost, I have heard,"[11] gave the Americans a very crude and very effective lesson in what was later called dumping. Their response to that lesson, an abrupt decline in new factory incorporations, is reported in Table 12.1.

10. *Edinburgh Review or Critical Journal* (February-June 1816), p. 264.
11. G. A. Lee, testimony in 1816 before a parliamentary committee, reprinted in great Britian, *Parliamentary Papers*, Command 397 (*Children's Employment*, vol. 1, 1968).

But the lull in textile factory start-ups lasted only half a dozen years. What induced the turnaround? Surely it was word of the profitability of such firms as Almy and Brown and the Boston Manufacturing Company. The latter was first of the large new companies. Instead of $14,000, the typical textile factory investment, it had invested almost thirty times that sum. Instead of 30 or 40 employees, it had 360.[12] And instead of modest profits, its dividends on capital ran from 17 percent to 30 percent (Table 12.3). Such rates of return were unparalleled. Ordinary loans for the decades 1820 to 1860 yielded only 7 percent; bank stock, 7 percent; canals, 3 percent; railroads, 8 percent.[13] The profit differential beckoned more and more adventurers into manufactures.

The Rise of Manufacturing

The initial growth of American manufacturing, between 1810 and 1840, was not significantly driven by the creation of new products. For that would have required reshaping the buying habits of consumers. Never simple, that task was almost insuperable in a nation whose markets were loosely connected (hence, low information flow), with little advertising, and with incomes too low to permit much venturesome buying of new and uncertain products.

Early manufacturers instead concentrated on the commercially sure thing: They produced goods already tested in American markets. (Of "the first cotton mill in America" George Cabot wrote Alexander Hamilton: "a number of gentlemen of this place associated . . . to manufact[ure] cotton goods of the kinds usually imported from Manchester." Nathan Appleton described the first, enormously profitable Boston Manufacturing Company: "the idea was to imitate the yard wide goods of India, with which the country was then largely supplied."[14] They were, in sum, pioneers—but by imitation.) The expansion of factory markets was compounded of three separate elements.

First was the mere growth of the domestic market to match the growth in population. As striking as any was the demand for iron and steel. When new

12. *American State Papers: Finance*, 4:397, gives data for 3,460 factories in 1820. These averaged $14,000 in capital. An average of 30 employees typifies most firms as late as 1832; McLane Report. Data for the Boston Manufacturing Company appear in Ware, *The Early New England Cotton Manufacture*, chap. 6.

13. A normal interest rate of 7 percent is quoted for 1820 in Neil McNall, *An Agricultural History of the Genesee Valley, 1790–1860* (1952), pp. 102, 35. Bank stock and canal rates for 1835 are from Anna Schwartz, Conference on Research in Income and Wealth, *Trends in the American Economy in the Nineteenth Century* (1960), pp. 436, 442. A Massachusetts investor with an $800,000 portfolio in 1827 averaged an 8.4 percent return for his railroad stock; 6 percent, loans; 7 percent, rents; 11.6 percent, insurance for the period 1833–58. His returns for the 1830s were much the same. *Bulletin of the Business Historical Society* (March 1933), p. 14.

14. Cabot: quoted in Robert Rantoul, "The First Cotton Mill in America," *Historical Collections of the Essex Institute* (January-June 1897), p. 39. Appleton: quoted in "Lowell and the Cotton Manufacture," *Hunt's Merchants Magazine and Commercial Review* (December 1858), p. 663.

TABLE 12.3
MANUFACTURING BEGINNINGS

	Dividend rate Boston Manufacturing Company	Number of major New England mills	Number of factories established	
			Cotton	Iron
1820	17	1	7	14
1821	20	1	4	2
1822	28	1	11	2
1823	25	1	22	1
1824	25	1	17	8
1825	30	2	24	13
1826	8	2	24	12
1827	9	3	22	11
1828	12	5	48	12
1829	7	6	17	10
1830	7	6	24	11

Source: Dividend rate and number of mills: Joseph Martin, *A Century of Finance* (1898), p. 128. Number of factories: see Table 12.1 *Sources*, this chapter.

farms were established—in Ohio, the Tennessee hills, or western New York—each farmer had to shoe his horses (or oxen), buy a plow, shovels, scythes, hoes, axes, and cartwheels for a wagon. Even one year's (1830) wear in horseshoes and other farm items required about 100,000 tons of pig iron. But total U.S. consumption of pig iron in that year was only about 200,000 tons.[15] As of 1840, the ratio was virtually the same.[16]

The growth of the great iron industry, the very center of early industrialization, turns out, then, to have been largely shaped by the gradual growth of farming—if not actually driven by it. The growth of other key factory industries was likewise linked to the growth of population and farming.

Second, manufacturing entrepreneurs increasingly entered into head-to-head competition with U.K. producers—the substitution of American for British goods. If Scotland could profitably produce cotton bagging and ship it all the way to the south, Kentucky entrepreneurs could surely do as well. If salt could be imported from Portugal, surely salt wells in the state of New York could be profitably developed.

15. Import data from 62d Cong., 1st sess., S.D. 72, *Tariff Proceedings* (1911), p. 2483. Bar iron is converted to pig iron at the ratio of 1.4 tons to 1. That ratio, and total U. S. production of pig iron in 1830, are derived from the *Report of the New York Convention*, in *Niles, Addendum* to vol. 41, p. 16. U.S. production of pig iron in 1840 from Robert Fogel and Stanley Engerman, eds., *The Reinterpretation of American Economic History* (1971), p. 154.

16. Import and production data from sources described *supra*. Lebergott, *Manpower*, p. 511, estimates 1,440,000 farmers. We here assume the same per farm consumption rate.

Kentucky planters started growing hemp, making bagging. Avid entre-preneurs on Cape Cod expanded the tanks in which they dried salt from sea water. The state of New York subsidized the use of its salt wells, while the state of Michigan required its salt producers to meet quality standards so that their product could more readily invade Eastern markets. Louisiana's planta-tion owners bought more slaves, used the invaluable rectifying process in-vented by Norbert Rillieux (trained in France and "free colored") to produce better sugar than the Caribbean islands. Lively New York publishers printed English best sellers without permission, making their import unnecessary. (In time Taiwan returned the compliment.) Rough estimates report how varied substitution proved for different products (Table 12.4).

Domestic products did not inevitably supersede foreign goods. For ex-ample, the proportion of hides that were imported (to make boots, shoes, and other leather products) changed not at all from 1809 to 1842.[17] For hides were simply the by-product of the primary use of animals—oxen to pull plows and cattle raised for milk and meat. Over those years farmers did not significantly improve the efficiency with which they produced cattle. Therefore, there was no reason for the price of domestic hides to fall relative to the price of im-ported hides and thus induce greater use of domestic hides for making shoes.

By far the most important market invaded, however, was a third. Fac-tory products substituted for those produced in the home, by manufacturing products for less than the unpaid housewife could afford to. Textiles offer the most notable example in the rise of factory production, as they did in Britain, India, and Japan.

From 1815 to 1833 the amount of cotton cloth produced in factories grew by 29 percent a year.[18] Some 3 percent of that gain represented sales to new consumers (population growth). Another 1 percent represented more cloth per consumer (income growth).[19] Hence, about 25 percent of the 29 percent annual growth in textile output was achieved by substituting U.S. manufac-tures for home manufactures and imports.

But how was it possible that women spinning and weaving in the factory could produce goods whose sale would pay for an immense stock of machin-ery, buildings, and waterpower facilities; pay their own wages; leave a profit for the owners; and still sell for less than the same goods produced by other women at home in their spare time?

The primary answer, of course, is the difference in efficiency between home and factory production. The typical housewife working at home took 10 hours to make a single yard of gingham, worth 11 cents in the market about

17. *American State Papers: Finance* 2:426,431. *The American Laborer* (June 1842), p. 83.

18. Robert Zevin, "The Growth of Cotton Textile Production After 1815," in Robert Fogel and Stanley Engerman, eds., *The Reinterpretation of American Economic History* (1971), p. 125.

19. Ibid., pp. 128–29.

TABLE 12.4

PERCENT OF U.S. CONSUMPTION IMPORTED, 1810–44

	Salt	Sugar	Bagging
1810	79		
1820		40	
1824			80
1831	53	33	
1844	52	44	13

Source: Salt: *American State Papers: Finance,* 2:430, 686. 22d Cong., 1st sess., H.D. 308, *Documents Relative to the Manufactures in the United States* (1833), 2:505. *Hunt's Merchants' Magazine* (April 1843), p. 358. Sugar: *American State Papers: Finance,* 3:535. *Niles Weekly Register* 61 (November 26, 1831):50. U.S. Treasury Department, *Quarterly Report . . . On Imports, Exports . . . March 1887* (1887), pp. 649, 664. Bagging: *Debates and Proceedings of Congress* (1824), cols. 1515, 1549. Charleston Chamber of Commerce (1845), in 62d Cong., 1st sess., S.D. 72, *Tariff Proceedings* (1911), pt. 3, p. 1864.

1832.[20] Which meant that in such work her labor was thus worth just a bit over 1 cent an hour. But in the giant Lowell mills women earned four times as much per hour.[21] That 4-to-1 ratio proved decisive, bringing about a steady decline in "home manufactures." Thus New York housewives wove 8 yards of cloth per person in 1820, but only half as much by 1835. By 1845 the figure was 2.7 yards, and by 1855, a mere 0.3 yards.[22] Moreover, as transport costs fell, textiles were shipped still farther west. Home manufactures declined on the frontier as well.[23] The overall productivity advance for cotton textiles is suggested by the increasing output per man year (Table 12.5). A major factor in the early decades was faster spindle speeds as belts replaced gears.

Factories did not automatically outcompete home manufactures. True, by 1840, most cotton textiles were made in factories. But few men's shirts were made in factories, and almost no men's suits, before the 1900s. True, flour production had been taken over by mills before the 1820s. But bread

20. Thirteenth Annual Report of the Commissioner of Labor, 1898, *Hand and Machine Labor* (1898), 1:40–41. The data used were for drills, gingham, and sheeting produced by hand. The labor requirements for gingham produced in 1835 did not differ noticeably from data for hand production in later years. For the 11-cent price, see *Documents Relative to Manufactures* (1833), 1:341.

21. *Documents Relative to Manufactures.* The mills averaged approximately 12.5 hours a day over the year, sold their cloth at an average of 11 cents a yard, paid an average of 50 cents a day.

22. Rolla Tyron, *Household Manufactures in the United States, 1640–1860* (1917), pp. 166, 289, 304.

23. Arthur Cole mapped the decline within the New York State. Those counties along the Erie Canal showed the greatest decline in home manufactures; those farther away, the least. Cf. his *The American Wool Manufacture* (1926), p. 280.

TABLE 12.5

ADVANCING EFFICIENCY IN COTTON TEXTILES, 1820–59

	Throstle revolutions (per minute)	Yards of output yearly	
		per spindle	per man year
1820	50	142	2,000
1831	8,000	185	3,707
1849		217	7,769
1859		219	9,410

Sources: Throstle: Leander Bishop, History of American Manufactures (1864), p. 399. Output: Lance Davis and H. L. Stettler, "The New England Textile Industry," in Conference on Research in Income and Wealth, Output, Employment and Productivity in the United States after 1800 (1966), p. 231.

production itself continued to be a monopoly of the home well into the twentieth century.

What principle explains this sequence of substitution? Chiefly that of comparative cost. We lack data on the saving in total costs (i.e., materials plus labor plus the rent of capital services). But the ratio of man-hours required by the competing methods is suggestive, since labor accounted for the bulk of factory costs: The ranking in Table 12.6 indicates the approximate order in which the production of various items moved out of the home and into the factory.

While labor production costs were thus being cut, other factors also lowered the cost of textiles. As production rose economies of scale developed. More product was produced annually with the same capital stock of buildings and equipment. Interest and depreciation costs were divided among an ever-larger number of units, making the cost per unit less. For firms began producing an average of six months rather than four, or ten months rather than six—as they did in iron manufacturing and distilling—which brought that result.

Transport costs were cut by the widening system of canals and railroads. By 1835 textiles could be shipped 100 miles westward from Albany for no more than it cost to ship them 8 miles in 1817–19; the Erie Canal had replaced the older wagon roads of mud and boulders.[24] They were further cut by improved transport technology. As steamboats replaced barges carrying goods

---

24. Rates of $108 a ton for 100 miles by wagon in 1817–19 and $8 a ton by canal in 1835 are taken from Hunt's Merchants' Magazine (July-December 1850), p. 387, (November 1858), p. 538; and State of New York, Assembly Document 296, Report of the Canal Commissioners (March 14, 1835), p. 44. The 1815– 24 rate is from Thomas Berry, Western Prices Before 1861 (1943), pp. 53, 55. Transport rates fell by 97 percent from 1815 to 1876. Anon., One Hundred Years of Progress of the United States (1876). Hence, the immense advance in transport efficiency was concentrated in the first decade.

TABLE 12.6
FACTORY MAN-HOURS AS PERCENT OF HOME MAN-HOURS
IN THE NINETEENTH CENTURY

Product	Percent
Cotton cloth	1
Hosiery	2
Soap	5
Overalls	10
Men's shirts	14
Underwear	19
Men's suits	36
Canned vegetables and fruit	42
Bread	72

Source: Computed from Commissioner of Labor, *Thirteenth Annual Report, Hand and Machine Labor* (1899) I, units 28–653. The ratios for individual vegetables and fruits were weighted by consumption in 1909, using U.S. Department of Agriculture, *Food Consumption in the U.S. . . . ,* Agricultural Economics Report no. 138, 1968, tables 16, 22.

upstream from New Orlean to St. Louis, between 1815 and 1824, transport costs fell by 80 percent.

Interest costs fell, first for the Boston Manufacturing Company and then for the other major Massachusetts mills. The success of these mills in pioneering mass production, and mass sales, yielded unusually rich profit rates. Such profits were then plowed back to expand facilities and sales effort further. In effect, profits served as low-interest loans.[25] Interest costs also tended to fall because improving capital markets in the East gradually increased supply.

Factory output did more than increase. It changed in range and quality. Beyond the substitution of U.S. factory products for those made in U.S. homes or imported from European factories was the creation of new products. European visitors were dazzled by the peculiarity of some. A visitor to Cincinnati could not get over his first view of a dumbwaiter, that substitute for waiters rushing up stairs and down. Others marveled at the Blanchard machine (1818) which enabled one semiskilled worker to carve sixteen identical gunstocks in the same time that a highly skilled European craftsman turned out one. (Britain and Russia bought the machine by the hundreds for use in the Crimean War.)[26] Charles Goodyear's marvelous new rubberized

25. The funds were not available at bargain rates. Rather, the entrepreneurs had a stronger basis, as insiders, for knowing how solid their prospects were. Outsiders would have had to add some further margin for the greater risk as they saw it.

26. 1880 Census, *Manufactures,* pp. 630–32.

fabric from which rainproof coats were made,[27] the bowie knife, machines that harvested wheat in a tenth of the time demanded by the sickle—these and a hundred other new products poured from the new factory system.

In time, factory products improved in quality. Improved versions expanded the market. For example, the steamboat *New Orleans* successfully descended the Mississippi in 1812, but could not return upstream. Neither its design nor its engine was effective against the powerful river current. By 1816, however, the *Enterprise*, fourth of the western steamboats, did just that. It ran upstream from New Orleans to Louisville—and in a mere twenty-five days![28]

The expansion of manufacturing began two dynamic processes. The first created a set of economic linkages. To open the new textile mills, a machinery industry had to be established—to make looms and spindles for those mills.[29] The machinery industry, in turn, set up a steady demand for steel. In time, importing steel from Sweden and Russia declined and an American steel industry developed alongside the older iron industry. Second, this current of novelty produced a furious rate of obsolescence. The "gale of creative destruction," announced by Joseph Schumpeter as characteristic of capitalism when working at full tilt, became apparent. David Anthony of Fall River wrote that one firm's machinery had declined one-third in value, from $60,000 to $40,000, "mainly owing to the depreciation in consequence of improvements made in machinery."[30] Bezaleel Taft of Uxbridge wrote that "expensive and well-constructed machinery had been entirely superseded by . . . new improvements, by which a saving of labor was to be obtained. . . . In this way garrets and out-houses of most of our manufactories have been crowded with discarded machinery."[31]

Manufacturing expanded on a broad front from the mid-1820s to 1860—textile firms, tanneries, iron forges, chemical and glass works. But it is well to keep in mind that the nation's comparative advantage still lay in agriculture (Table 12.7).

The ability of the United States to export wheat and soybeans to every corner of the world in the mid-twentieth century italicizes the enormous advantage the nation still had for farming. But once that fact has been recognized, the data in Table 12.7 point to the foundations of American industry, foundations laid more than a century ago, between 1810 and 1860.

27. The first pure gum rubber was imported in 1824 to cope with the slush of New England winters. Cf. J. Krout and D. Fox, *The Completion of Independence* (1944), p. 218.

28. E. L. Bogart, *Economic History of the American People* (1933), p. 329.

29. In some instances a single corporation combined both activities, as the Lowell Locks and Canal Company did. But combined or not, the textile industry set in motion a whole new machinery industry.

30. *Documents Relative to Manufactures*, p. 73.

31. Ibid., p. 80.

TABLE 12.7

PERCENT OF U.S. LABOR FORCE IN MANUFACTURING
AND AGRICULTURE, 1810–60

	Manufacturing	Agriculture
1810	3	81
1840	9	63
1850	14	55
1860	14	53

Source: Lebergott, *Manpower,* p. 510.

Appendix

How much iron and steel was actually used in farm production? One may begin with the lowliest, but commonest, item—horseshoes. The average farm had three work animals requiring shoes—horses, working oxen, or mules.[1] In reasonably heavy usage the shoes lasted only about five weeks.[2] But for average farm use we rely on a report that a canal "horse in service will require a new set of shoes every two months."[3] These shoes weighed 2-3/4 pounds when new, and 1-1/4 when removed.[4] Hence, 1-1/2 pounds per set were consumed every two months, or 27 pounds of iron per farm annually. To this figure one must add 2 pounds a year for horseshoe nails.[5] Including 10 percent for waste in the blacksmiths shop and for failure to retrieve shoes cast in fields would bring the average farm use of horseshoes to 32 pounds a year.

What of the other iron items on a farm? The main items averaged:[6]

Item	Pounds
Plough	75
Cartwheels	90
Shovel	5
Scythe	5
Axe	5
Hoe	2
Logchain, crowbar, harrow teeth, etc.	100

1. J. D. B. Debow, *Statistical View of the United States* (1854), p. 174.

2. 22d Cong., 1st sess., H.D. 101, *Report on Steam Carriages* (1838), p. 120.

3. 19th Cong., 1st sess., H.R. 228, *Chesapeake and Ohio Canal* (1826), p. 112.

4. Weight data from *Report on Steam Carriages*, p. 120: six sets at 1-1/2 pounds for three animals.

5. Eight nails per shoe, 128 per pound, based on data in U.S. Mounted Service School, *The Army Horseshoer, Manual for Farriers* (1912), pp. 67, 116.

6. The weight of the first six items is derived from reports on their production in 22d Cong., 1st sess., H.D. 308, *Documents Relative to Manufactures* (1833), 1:192, 476, 503, 510, 526, 1,030; 2:862.

If these items had a 1-1/2-year life, their depreciation would sum to 94 pounds a year. Adding 32 pounds for horseshoes results in an estimate of 126 pounds. As a check on that figure we may refer to an estimate in 1832 by Isaac Hill, of New Hampshire, that the typical farm consumed 200 pounds of iron a year.[7] (Since New Hampshire then averaged about 1 horse per farm, his estimate would imply 189 pounds of iron items other than horseshoes.) With 1,235,000 farmers in 1830, an average of the two estimates, 163 pounds, implies that 101,000 tons of iron were then annually needed to supply farmers needs. Total U.S. consumption of pig iron in 1830, however, was 201,000 tons.[8]

7. "On Clay's Resolution in Relation to the Tariff" (1832), in Yale's Sterling Library, *Pamphlets on Free Trade and Protection*, Vol. III.

8. Report of the General Convention of the Friends of Domestic Industry, in *Niles Register*, Addendum, XLI:3, 15. Bar iron imports are converted at the rate of 1 ton equalling 1.4 tons of pig iron.

Xerxes, ancient king of the Persians, "did not think that princes should use any foreign food or drink; whence a custom forbidding such use arose."
—ATHENAEUS. , *Deipnosophistae*

13

The Tariff

WHAT is the tariff in American history? Varied answers have been offered. John Randolph, the bitterest and most forceful spokesman for Jeffersonian Democracy and the Old South, stigmatized the tariff in 1816 as a

system of bounties to manufacturers . . . to encourage them to do that which, if it be advantageous at all, they will do . . . for their own sakes; a largess to men to exercise their own customary callings, for their own emolument. [Why should the] planters consent to be taxed, in order to hire another man to go to work in a shoemaker's shop, or even set up a spinning jenny? I will not agree to lay a duty on the cultivators of the soil to encourage exotic manufactures; because . . . we should only get much worse things at a much higher price . . . why pay a man much more than the value for it, to work up our own cotton into clothing, when by selling by raw material, I can get my clothing much better and cheaper from Dacca. . . . What [gives] those objects of the honorable gentleman's solicitude [any] claim to be supported by the earnings of others? The agriculturists bear the whole brunt of the war and taxation, and remain poor, while the others run in the ring of pleasure, and fatten upon them.[1]

Joseph Schumpeter, a great political economist, observed in 1940:

[Nothing] but confusion . . . can result from . . . [purely economic] analysis of the effects of protective tariffs without reference to the wider ambitions of the nation concerned. . . . First and last, what the American people wanted to accomplish when they decided to stake their all on inde-

1. John Randolph, *Congressional Debates and Proceedings* (January 1816), cols. 686–87.

pendence was to be a world unto themselves, to work out their own destiny, to be no longer pawns on the English chessboard; [and they] have consistently supported a policy of protection . . . refusing to listen to what mere economists might have to say about it.[2]

The primary economic characteristic of a tariff is clear. A tariff is an artificial ocean. It adds to the economic cost of the real ocean that goods must travel to the consumer from foreign countries. As Alexander Hamilton remarked in the earliest years of tariff protection: "The great distance of this country from Europe already imposes very heavy charges on all fabrics which are brought from thence, amounting to . . . fifteen to thirty percent of their value."[3] That, he inferred, was surely "a reason for moderating" the tariff rates being proposed.

Table 13.1 reveals how the artificial ocean compared to the real one: U.S. tariff duties on major products imported to the United States 1816–41 equaled between 100 percent and 369 percent of the cost of freight and insurance. Many duties were explicitly designed to prevent the shipment of large quantities of lower priced articles to the United States. They did so. The pro-tariff argument turned, rather, on long-run consequences.

Five powerful forces, economic and political, led the United States to levy tariffs.

1) First and most obvious: money needed to run the government. Some 93 percent of federal receipts came from the customs house. This was true in the first decade of the new government, 1790–1811. It was no less true in 1850–60, the last decade before the Civil War.[4] Congress had imposed other taxes. But they were few. And they yielded little. Money did come in from the sale of the billion-acre public domain. But, as we saw, Congress had fixed a low price to cheer voters; thus its sale generated little revenue. Congress relied almost solely on the tariff to finance the government: to pay Washington's salary, to refit navy frigates under Jefferson, and so on.

2) Federal aid to other industries. Believers in tariffs for manufacturing described how the federal government had helped other U.S. industries from its very beginning. Our largest industry was agriculture. In 1789, the very first year of the new government, Congress levied a tariff of 57 percent on cheese, 16 percent on indigo, and 12 percent on hemp and cotton. This, declared the bitter lobbyists for manufacturing, is the kind of "free trade" that

2. J. A. Schumpeter, "The Influence of Protective Tariffs on the Industrial Development of the United States," in *Proceedings of the Academy of Political Science* (May 1940), p. 2.

3. *American State Papers: Finance*, I:136.

4. Computed from Paul Trescott, "The United States Government and National Income, 1790–1860," Conference on Research in Income and Wealth, *Trends in the American Economy in the Nineteenth Century* (1960), p. 346.

TABLE 13.1

THE ARTIFICIAL OCEAN, 1815–41

	Freight and insurance to United States	U.S. duty
	(dollars)	
Northern products:		
Cottons (India): 1816		0.12
Nankeens per yard: 1819	0.014	0.025
Iron (Sweden, per ton): 1824	8.00	15.00
Iron (Pig, United Kingdom, per ton): 1828	3.60	13.30
Iron (Bar, United Kingdom, per ton): 1832	7.00	22.40
Rum (West Indies) per gallon: 1824		0.42
Calicoes: 1830	0.15	0.45
Salt (Turks Island): 1833	0.08	0.11
Southern products:		
Raw cotton (per pound): 1824	0.01	0.03
Hemp (St. Petersburg, per ton): 1824	30.00	30.00
Hemp (St. Petersburg, per ton): 1841	16.58	35.00
Bagging (Scotland, per yard): 1824	0.015	0.03

Source: 1816. Edwin Stanwood, *American Tariff Controversies* I:141 reports a 9-cent a yard price in India. The act stipulates a minimum value of 25 cents a yard for cotton goods whose original cost plus 10 percent (or 20 percent if imported from the Cape of Good Hope or beyond) comes to less than 25 cents per square yard. Cf. 29th Cong., 1st sess., S.D. 2, *Report on the Finances* (1845), p. 104.

1819: *American State Papers, Finance* III:418.

1824: Raw cotton: 18th Cong., 1st sess., *Debates and Proceedings* (April 1824), col. 2090 for freight (Webster, Wood). American State Papers, *Finance*, III:527 for duty. Thomas Ellison, *The Cotton Trade of Great Britain* (1886), Appendix for U.K. price. Iron: 22nd Cong., 1st sess., H.D. 264, *Tariff . . . Letter . . . Secretary of the Treasury* (June 1832). Hemp, bagging, rum: 18th Cong., 1st sess., *Debates and Proceedings* (1824), cols. 2065–2066 (hemp), cols. 1540 and 1557 (bagging), and col. 1491 (rum). Webster notes that hemp also paid $14 in port charges.

1828: 21st Cong., 2d sess., *Memorial of the Workers in Iron of Philadelphia* (1831), p. 124, and *Tariff Acts from 1789 to 1897* (1898), p. 73.

1830: Condy Raguet, *Principles of Free Trade* (1835), p. 332.

1832: *Documents on Manufactures*, H.D. 308 (1833), vol. 2, p. 224, and *Tariff Acts . . . from 1789 to 1897* (1898), p. 73.

1833: 29th Cong., 1st sess., S.D. 2, *Report on Finances* (1845), p. 548.

1841: 62d Cong., 1st sess., S.D. 72, Part 1, *Tariff Proceedings* (1911), p. 531.

agriculturists support. Over the years these rates had been pushed up still further. By 1820 they were 26 percent for hemp, 30 percent for cotton, and 37.5 percent for sugar. Such figures offer "full proof of the inequality of the system of legislation with which the government commenced, and of the care with which the agriculturists, who formed the great mass of the National Legislature, guarded their own interests."

The next largest 'interest' was 'the navigation interest.' The Philadelphia Chamber of Commerce opposed higher tariffs for manufactures, arguing, with free trade economists, that "the universal opinion of well informed men [is] . . . now that the greatest degree of national wealth is to be obtained by leaving every one to the unfettered use of his own labor, skill, and capital." But, the Pennsylvania Society for the Encouragement of American Manufactures countered: "This specious . . . theory accords but ill with the practice of our Government and the requisitions of our merchants."[5] Had the American shipping interests in fact been left to "the unfettered use of their own labor, skill, and capital, their tonnage would never have emerged from its insignificance. In the year 1789 it was only 201,562 tons." But it "rose in a few years to become second only to Britain." Why so? Because Congress laid

an enormous extra tonnage duty on foreign vessels engaged in the foreign trade, 700 per cent more than on American vessels; by subjecting foreign vessels engaged in the coasting trade to pay 50 cents per ton on every entry, whereas American vessels paid six cents once a year; by duties of teas imported in foreign vessels, which averaged 27 cents per pound, while those on teas imported in American vessels averaged by 12.[6]

Thus Congress awarded U.S. shippers an almost complete monopoly of the coasting trade (i.e., from one U.S. port to another). Foreign vessels paid about $600 a year. American-owned vessels were charged only about $6.[7] Moreover, it was pointed out, $3.3 million was being spent for the navy and $8.4 million for debt service. Most of the debt was incurred for the War of 1812 and for the annual blackmail payment by the Treasury to the pirate headquarters in Algiers and Morocco. Both were intended to "protect American Shipping."[8] Together these items made up the bulk of U.S. government expenditures.

3) Congress's inheritance of an obligation to the states that formed the new nation. Before the Constitution was adopted in 1789 those states had levied their own tariffs to raise money and to protect industries that legislators felt needed a little kindness in a cruel world. For example, Pennsylvania put a tariff of 56 cents a pound on cordage to protect its rope makers against Russian competition. Could the new nation suddenly cast them into the cold? As Senator William Maclay (of Pennsylvania) judiciously warned Congress: "To

5. Petition of the Pennsylvania Society for the Encouragement of American Manufactures, 1820, *American State Papers: Finance*, 4:527.

6. *American State Papers: Finance*, 4:487.

7. The rate per 100 tons of entry appears in *American State Papers: Finance*, 4:487, 489. The $50 charged foreign vessels per entry was multiplied by 12 (entries per year), the number estimated by Buchanan in 1824; 18th Cong., 1st sess., *Congressional Debates* (1824), cols. 2259, 2277. South Carolina vessels averaged 8 to 10 entries in 1789, according to Congressman Smith; *Annals of Congress* (May 1789) House Report, col. 260.

8. *American State Papers: Finance*, 4:14–15.

place the manufacturers of Pennsylvania, who had a claim to the faith of the state, on a worse ground than they stood before [the union of 1789] would be injurious to their property." Nay, it would "break the engagement the state had with them."[9] The new nation agreed on its first tariff in 1789. Thereafter importers paid the customs officer, on average, 21 percent of the value of the goods they brought in.[10]

Rhode Island did not, of course, join the United States in 1789. To raise revenue it too put on a tariff. If that had been set above the U.S. tariff, importers would never have landed at Newport or Bristol, but steered directly for the United States. On the other hand, a lower tariff would have drawn imports away from the United States and brought retaliatory action. The Rhode Island legislature therefore (in May 1789) "enacted . . . the same duties and imports . . . as may be ordered to be levied . . . [by] the said eleven states" that had "organized themselves into a new confederacy."[11] (When Rhode Island eventually ratified the Constitution in 1790, then, it did not need to change the protection rates its manufacturers had been receiving.)

4) National defense. During the War of 1812 with Britain the U.S. Navy could get cloth for uniforms only by buying from Britain. And to meet the nation's treaty obligations to Indian tribes, the War Department had to buy blankets from Britain. This humiliating experience was quoted by both Hamilton and Jefferson as reason for levying tariffs to protect infant U.S. manufacturing industries.

5) Nationalism. "Buy Persian" as a slogan was followed, after many centuries, by "Buy American."[12] Schumpeter's description of Americans desiring "to be a world unto themselves" simply describes the same feeling: Foreigners and foreign products are, in general, less to be desired than native products. A tariff helps achieve "independence" by keeping out foreign products. As in the developing nations of the twentieth century, the feeling existed that "dependence" on another nation was unmanly; it demonstrated that the nation was still a child, unable to stand on its own.[13] Moreover, even though the nation gained by importing foreign goods, some Americans lost their investments and jobs.[14] But even more powerful was the perception that profits could be made in non-existent industries—those developing because of

9. Edwin Stanwood, *American Tariff Controversies in the Nineteenth Century* (1904), 1:56.

10. Ibid., p. 101.

11. *The American Museum* 5 (June 1789): 380.

12. Athenaeus, *Deipnosophistae* (Loeb edition), 4:523. We have no source for the first use of "Buy American." But the practice began at least with the first "non-importation agreement," by which the Stamp Act Congress (1765) tried to prevent buying of British goods.

13. That no nation can be economically "independent" does not prove that such feelings are not politically vital—and effective.

14. When Prince Albert proposed a new design for the caps worn by the British army, the Duke of Wellington vetoed the proposal: It might throw the present cap makers out of work. Elizabeth Longford, *Wellington, Pillar of State* (1975), p. 432.

competition from foreign imports. The drive by such potential interests was vehemently emphasized by Representative John Holmes of Maine in 1824: "Kentucky wants to prohibit Hemp, scarcely a ton of which they do now produce."[15] The goal of future income, and the impulse to federal help, was as strong in these potentially vested interests as among vested interests.

Regional Interests

To get a tariff bill through the House of Representatives requires the votes of half the congressmen, plus one. To reach that number any agreeable set of constituent interests around the country will suffice. That set can shift from tariff bill to tariff bill, and did. Every Rhode Island congressman, for example, supported the Tariff of 1816; and every one opposed that of 1812. All Georgia congressmen supported the 1812 tariff; only half supported the 1816 tariff; and none, that of 1824. The tariffs of 1790 and 1833 were supported by more than half the congressmen in every southern state. But none of the southern states gave a majority to the tariffs of 1824 and 1828.

Yet the combination of constituent interests that passed tariffs before the Civil War has often been described in the simplest terms: a high-tariff North opposing a low-tariff South. The most casual examination of tariff votes suggests that such a description is grossly inaccurate. While the passage of the Tariff of 1832 did lead the South Carolina convention to secede from the Union, that tariff would never have been passed but for unanimous support by congressmen from three southern states (Mississippi, Tennessee, and Maryland), plus a majority of congressmen in each of four other southern states (Alabama, Kentucky, North Carolina, and Virginia).

It turns out that the steadiest members of the political coalitions that passed the many tariff laws from 1812 to 1832 came neither from New England nor the deep South. Indeed, the states that never gave a majority of their votes to those tariff laws were:

Massachusetts
Alabama
Louisiana

Persistent and effective support came instead from:

Ohio
Kentucky
New Jersey
Delaware
Pennsylvania

15. 18th Cong., 1st sess., *Congressional Debates and Proceedings* (1824), col 613.

(Ohio, indeed, was the only state to give 100 percent support to every tariff bill between 1812 and 1832.)

Was there a state whose producer interests did not seek tariff protection? Surely South Carolina, noted for her willingness to leave the union in 1833 over the tariff issue, qualified. Yet Robert Allston of South Carolina wrote scathingly of cotton factories in that state: They were "brought into existence by the patronizing countenance of the government, and stimulated by the temptation to share a portion of the immense profits derived from their peculiar tariff protection by the similar establishments at 'Lowell,' Fall River, Paterson and elsewhere."[16] Virginian fears for its coal industry, threatened by Nova Scotia imports, were forthrightly voiced by the "coal owners and ironmasters of Richmond." Even that redoubtable anti-tariff advocate John Randolph urged a higher coal tariff.[17]

Producer Interests: Agriculture

As the leadership of Ohio and the North Central states suggests, farmers proved to be persistent and powerful supporters of tariffs. The first U.S. tariff law, in 1789, had set high rates for cheese, hemp, and other farm products. Later tariffs protected wool generously, eliciting support from sheep farmers in Vermont and Ohio. But what of the southern farmers? We know that in the very first Congress Pierce Butler of South Carolina assailed tariff drawbacks for manufacturers, "threatening a dissolution of the Union . . . as sure as God was in his firmament."[18]

But beyond the rhetoric lies the legislation. That same Congress put a tariff on raw cotton. Its only beneficiary could be South Carolina and other cotton growing states. As Hamilton wrote two years later: "The present duty of three cents a pound, on the foreign raw material, is undoubtedly a very serious impediment to the progress of those manufactories."[19] The tariff that hurt the North Central states benefited South Carolina and the deep South. In 1824 John Randolph of Virginia attacked the pending tariff bill as marking

> us out as the victims of a worse than Egyptian bondage. It ought to be met, in the southern country, as was the Stamp Act, and by all those measures which produced the final breach with the mother country. . . . I bless God that Massachusetts and Old Virginia are once again rallying under the same banner against oppressive and unconstitutional taxation: for if all the blood

16. 29th Cong., 1st sess., S.D. 2, *Report . . . on the Finances* (1845), p. 582.
17. 29th Cong., 1st sess., S. D. 447, *Memorial of Coal Owners . . .* ; Stanwood, *American Tariff Controversies*, p. 154. U.S., Congress, *Debates and Proceedings*, 14th Cong., 1st sess. (January 22, 1816), col. 735.
18. Orrin L. Elliot, *The Tariff Controversy in the U.S., 1789–1833* (1892), p. 71.
19. Report on Manufactures, *American State Papers: Finance*, 1:141.

be drawn from out the body, I care not whether it be by the British Parliament or the American Congress.[20]

It is not as well known, perhaps, that the South had early sponsored high tariffs on textile manufactures. And that southern congressmen had introduced and vigorously fought through the system of "minimums" to increase textile tariffs.[21] And did so over the opposition of the giant textile manufacturers. For Francis Lowell, of Massachusetts, went to Washington in 1816 to declare that he did not support a higher tariff: His firm was "making a profit of 25 per cent, and stood in no need of further protection."[22]

Indeed, in 1832 a "large importer" remembered Lowell predicting

> that laying a heavy protective duty on cottons, would cause heavy investments to be made in manufactures, produce a ruinous competition, and ultimately reduce the value of the Waltham stock. Had he lived until 1829, he would have seen the stock fall from 60 per cent advance, to par, or under. . . . Our own manufacturers have much more reason to dread the effects of high protective duties than those of England, [for such duties] are sure to attract a heavy amount of capital from other branches of business less protected, which causes an excessive production of goods, creates a ruinous competition, and ends in bankruptcy and ruin.[23]

And an iron manufacturer matter-of-factly declared in 1832: "We would say let the duty remain where it is; if decreased, the competition would naturally increase; if reduced, we cannot make it a business worth pursuing.[24]

But John C. Calhoun spoke persuasively for southern interests. The War of 1812 had slashed southern exports of cotton to the United Kingdom, and Britain had blockaded its West Indian markets.[25] Calhoun supported the minimum:

> [Without it] our cotton establishments [would be] exposed to the competition of the cotton goods of the East Indies, which, it is acknowledged on all

20. U.S. Congress, *Debates and Proceedings*, 18th Cong., 1st sess., (April 1824), cols. 2360, 2379.

21. The minimum proviso stipulated that textiles coming into the U.S. market would be presumed to be worth at least so many more cents a pound and thus would be subject to the percentage ad valorem textile tariff. That William Lowndes of Virginia introduced the proposal for "minimums" is stated in "Memoir of Nathan Appleton," *Proceedings of the Massachusetts Historical Society* (October 1861), pp. 267–77.

22. Edwin Grosvenor, *Does Protection Protect?* (1871), p. 125. Cf. also the Remonstrance of the Philadelphia Chamber of Commerce, *American State Papers: Finance*, vol. 4.

23. 22d Cong., 1st sess., H.D. 264, *Tariff* (1832), pp. 4–5.

24. McLane Report, *Documents Relative to Manufactures* (1833), p. 189.

25. John L. Conger, "South Carolina and the Early Tariffs," *Mississippi Valley Historical Reviews* (1918–19):423. Conger notes that the planters "were eager to . . . be completely free from dependence upon English mills for a market for their cotton wool," particularly in view of the United Kingdom's blocking of their markets in the West Indies. Cf. also Samuel Slater, in *Documents Relative to Manufactures*, pp. 877–78.

sides, they are not capable of meeting with success. [Coming] from the South . . . [I have] no interest but in the cultivation of the soil, in selling its products high, and buying cheap the wants and conveniences of life. . . . [But] the recent war fell with peculiar pressure on the growers of cotton and tobacco . . . and the same state of things will recur in the event of another unless prevented by the foresight of [Congress]. . . . When our manufactures are grown to a certain perfection, as they soon will under the fostering care of the government . . . the farmer will find a ready market for his surplus produce; and . . . a certain and steady supply of all his wants . . . the people would be placed beyond the power of a foreign war materially to impair.[26]

After a few decades the South consolidated its dominance of the United Kingdom's cotton market. It continued to fight for a high tariff on its own raw cotton. But it now fought against the tariffs on cotton textiles. During the heated tariff bargaining of 1833 Henry Clay proposed to end the 3-cent tariff favoring raw cotton.[27] The reaction to his malicious proposal demonstrated that the South did favor high tariffs—for its own products. The proposal however, was struck down in committee. (The long established tariff on raw cotton reappeared in the compromise bill, testifying how hollow Jackson's victory over the South really was.)

Producer Interests: Manufacturing

Early manufacturing firms compared the rent they could earn on their investment if tariffs pushed their prices up with their loss in sales to producers attracted into the industry by such higher prices. If the technology of the new producers were better—and these industries were rapidly advancing—they could outcompete existing firms. Yet if their technology were inferior, the consequences would be even worse. For if they failed, their inventories and machinery would then be dumped on the market, where a still newer firm would buy them at bargain prices and be able to produce with unusually low capital costs. The total sequence forced prices down below those received by the earliest firms in the industry. Obviously, then, it was the new and the would-be producers and planters who sought high textile tariffs. At least in the first half century of American protectionism, from 1789 to 1849.

How much entry did the tariff induce into the most obviously profitable manufacturing industry, cotton textiles? How much impact, for example, did the 1828 "Tariff of Abominations" have? Its major impact would not have been on iron manufacturing. We may, therefore, take the number of new iron

26. Speech on the tariff bill, April 1816, in *The Papers of John C. Calhoun*, ed. Robert L. Meriwether (1959), 1:348–51.
27. Henry Clay, *Speeches* (Colton edition, 1857), 1:561.

factories established per year as a guide to how many new firms would have been founded as the result of the general expansion of industry, availability of finance, and entrepreneurial verve. We contrast that trend with the number of new factories in textiles in Table 13.2.

The ironworks incorporations suggest that the Tariff of 1828 drew perhaps seventeen additional textile factories into the field.[28] Among them were two giants: Appleton and Lowell. The total additional investment came to $1.2 million.[29] Hence, the $40 million total investment in the industry was increased only 3 percent in 1828 by the notorious Tariff of Abominations.[30] A host of entrepreneurs and capitalists put their money into other industries; the great boon provided by that tariff was evidently not as great as the years of rhetoric had suggested.

Consumer Interests

The benefits of tariffs to consumers can be assessed in precisely the same terms noted previously for producers. As John Randolph insisted, a tariff was likely to push up prices and reduce the real incomes of consumers. That conclusion was harsh, and inevitable. But it rested on a purely static analysis. Many tariff bills were offered under a dynamic theory: entry would actually drive down the real price of manufactures. First, the tariff would induce new producers to enter a monopolistic (or oligopolistic) industry. So, indeed, Henry Clay and others argued with respect to products turned out by certain U.S. industries. Second, if the new entrants adopted better technologies, then their competition would certainly drive down the price. All that was needed was time for competition to do its work.

Many politicians, such as Robert Toombs (in 1859), heatedly asserted, however, that we discriminated "for our infant manufactures . . . that we might prevent them from being crushed in their infancy. Well, sir, when is the iron manufacture going to get grown. . . . It has had . . . as much as one

28. Given a predicted annual average of twenty-four new cotton firms for 1828–30, on the basis of factors proxied by starts in iron, twenty-four "excess" firms appeared in 1828. Of these, seven were "borrowed from" 1829.

29. A search through the McLane Report data for Massachusetts, whose firms would be above average in size, yields figures of $518,000 for Appleton and Lowell and an average of $45,500 for eight other cotton firms. The latter average was assumed to apply to the seven other additional firms. It is virtually identical to the near $50,000 average for all mills indicated by the New York Convention data given in Timothy Pitkin, *A Statistical View . . . of the United States* (1835), p. 526.

30. 24th Cong., 1st sess., H.R. 146, *Cotton* (1836), p. 45. This report estimates $60 million for all capital. But the $40 million capital figure from the New York Convention (as of 1832) is more relevant here.

TABLE 13.2

NUMBER OF COTTON AND IRON FACTORIES

Year	Cotton factories[a]	Iron factories[b]
1822	11	2
1823	22	1
1824	17	8
1825	24	13
1826	24	12
1827	22	11
1828	48	12
1829	17	10
1830	24	11

[a]New York and Pennsylvania.

[b]The six New England states and New York and New Jersey.

Source: Documents Relative to the Manufactures in the United States, 22d Cong., 1st sess., H.D. 308 (1833), 2:115–301, and in addition, for cotton, the summary in Clive Day, "Early Development," Quarterly Journal of Economics (1925), p. 452.

hundred and fifty percent protection for forty three years. . . . Have they not had enough experience in making iron" by now?[31]

What, in fact, was the real world outcome? Relative product prices may be used as an indicator, given one key assumption. It is not unreasonable to assume that consumer demand was not shifting inward. If so, the decline in the real price of selected products (i.e., their price divided by an index of the general price level) would mark the efficiency change in a largely competitive set of markets. What was the price history of some of these protected items? The real prices of two major manufactured products and of the less (but nonetheless protected) farm sector ran as shown in Table 13.3.

Productivity advances and competition had indeed driven down the real prices of typical cotton textile and iron products.[32] They had done so while real farm prices rose, despite the pressures toward decline brought by the move into far richer western lands and to advancing technology. Factory prices might have declined still more if the tariff acts had not been passed. Perhaps advancing technology and domestic competition accounted for the entire deadline. But it is even possible that decreased ocean freight rates, plus

31. Ulrich Phillips, The Life of Robert Toombs (1913), p. 149.
32. Demand for both of these industries was most probably shifting outward, so that the results understate consumer gains from efficiency advances.

TABLE 13.3
REAL PRICE INDICES, 1820–60

Year	Cotton sheeting	Nails	Farm products
1820	100	100	100
1830	82	71	94
1840	71	68	119
1850	67	50	128
1860	65	38	121

Source: Price data for individual items are divided by Bezanson's wholesale price index. Cf. U.S. Census, *Historical Statistics . . . to 1970*, pp. 205, 209.

advancing technology in British textile and iron industries, together nullified the actual impact of American tariff protection. (See Figure 13.1.) A free-trade outcome under the umbrella of a tariff system may have been the ultimate irony of the long tariff debate.

Effective Protection

In January 1808 Paul Revere petitioned the Congress to increase the tariff, and also to decrease it. Take the duty off old (and scrap) copper, he urged, but impose one on new (sheet) copper. If Congress took his advice, he promised, domestic producers would soon be able to supply the entire country.[33]

Revere obviously sought to reduce the cost of the materials that he had to buy (scrap copper) and to increase the price of the finished product (sheet copper), which he had for sale. One was a cost; the other, a return. Ever since 1789 Congress has set tariff rates with a clear understanding of this difference between the published and the real rates. The real, the effective, tariff rates in any industry were those that protected the value added by the capital and labor in that industry. The effective rate differed from the nominal rate, often strikingly. How much did they differ for major commodities of interest to the North and the South? We hazard some estimates for a few of each in Table 13.4.

It will be noted how far rates on some manufactured products differ from those on their raw materials. Tariff protection on the process of textile production in New England was 40 percent. For southern raw cotton, which was bought by New England mills, it was 62 percent. The ostensible tariff on textiles—a combination of the two—was 47 percent. The apparent 92 percent

33. *American State Papers: Finance*, 3:268. Of the hollow-ware petitioners, Jacob Crowninshield of the Committee on Manufactures asked ironically: "Surely they do not wish to claim a monopoly?" *American State Papers: Finance*, 2:171.

FIGURE 13.1

TARIFFS VERSUS FREIGHT COSTS, 1821–60 (1821 = 100)

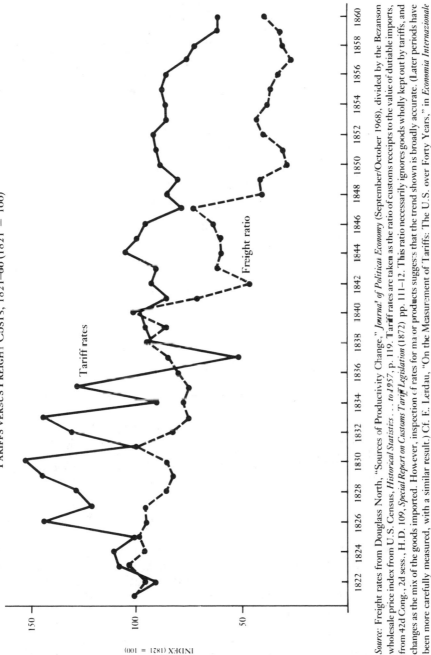

Source: Freight rates from Douglass North, "Sources of Productivity Change," *Journal of Political Economy* (September/October 1968), divided by the Bezanson wholesale price index from U.S. Census, *Historical Statistics . . . to 1957*, p. 119. Tariff rates are taken as the ratio of customs receipts to the value of dutiable imports, from 42d Cong., 2d sess., H.D. 109, *Special Report on Customs Tariff Legislation* (1872) pp. 111–12. This ratio necessarily ignores goods wholly kept out by tariffs, and changes as the mix of the goods imported. However, inspection of rates for major products suggests that the trend shown is broadly accurate. (Later periods have been more carefully measured, with a similar result.) Cf. E. Lerdau, "On the Measurement of Tariffs: The U.S. over Forty Years," in *Economia Internazionale* (March 1957).

151

TABLE 13.4

EFFECTIVE AND NOMINAL TARIFF RATES FOR
MAJOR COMMODITIES AND ACTIVITIES, 1845 (IN PERCENT)

Commodity or activity	Nominal tariff rate	Effective rate for labor and capital in activity
Cotton textiles[a]		40
Raw	66	
Manufactured	47	
Bar iron		30
Pig	49	
Bar	36	
Refined sugar		41
Clayed	105	
Refined	92	
Cordage		186
Hemp	39	
Untarred	84	
Shipbuilding		−11 to −12
Materials	18–23	
Ships	0	
Cotton growing		66
Purchased items	22	
Raw cotton	62	
Hemp growing	39	
Sugar cane growing	63	

[a]Not printed.

Source: Derived from data in *Tariff Proceedings and Documents, 1839–1857*, 62d Cong., 1st sess., S.D. 72, pt. 3:2121–22, 2130. The implicit rates are computed from data on expenditures for raw materials and value of product for individual firms. McLane Report, *Documents Relative to the Manufactures in the United States* (1833): cotton, 1:340; iron, 3:265–66; sugar, 1:469; hemp and cordage, 1:244, 418, 428. Cf. Appendix A, B.

protection received by refined sugar was derived from a rate of 105 percent on the sugar clayed in Louisiana (or Cuba) and a rate of 41 percent on the actual refining done in Boston. And though cordage manufacturing enjoyed a high rate, tar—a product of the South—benefited from an even higher rate. As the prolonged and complex process of tariff making indicates, the congressmen and their constituents were well aware of the impact of tariffs on raw materials in relation to those on the finished product.[34]

34. An inconsistency in the tariffs proposed for raw and refined sugar that threatened to lead to heavy importations of Cuban sugar in the form of molasses was noted, objected to, and prevented by Edmund Forstall of Louisiana in 1846 and is well described by him in 62d Cong., *Tariff Proceedings*, pp. 1963–67.

Geographic Differences

How heavily did tariffs actually burden the South? Two men who were obviously well informed on costs provide an initial perspective. One was a low-tariff South Carolinian; the other, a high-tariff man from Louisiana. Robert Allston, of South Carolina, declared that he had paid $296.20 in duties to operate his plantation in 1844, working about 100 hands.[35] A "native of Louisiana," probably Edmund Forstall, arguing for a high tariff, asked

> any honest cotton planter [to] take full account of foreign manufactures used by him for his negroes and plantation utensils, and my word for it, he will find the amount under $1,000, even with a gang of 100 hands; and supposing the value of these foreign goods to be enhanced 30 per cent by the tariff, he will see that his contribution toward the expenses of the Federal Government is a mere trifle.[36]

In other words, both men implicitly agreed that a plantation with 100 working slaves paid $300 in duties, or about $3 per hand. We derive a more specific estimate in Table 13.5.

The table indicates that in the antebellum period the planters would have increased their proceeds from the sale of raw cotton by 3 percent if they had not had to pay any tariff duties on their iron, bagging, slave clothing, and so on.[37] Put another way, an annual profit per hand, of say 10.0 percent, would have risen to 10.3 percent.[38] That a tiny increment in profit was, however, politically and arithmetically perceptible. It served as reason (excuse?) for the secession of South Carolina in 1832. But if the fervent tariff rhetoric of southern congressmen on the tariff were generated by so apparently tiny a reduction in their profit rate, surely a similar comparison would have to be made for northern investments. Were northern congressmen less vivid on the tariff because their constituents had all done so well by it?

No product, of course, typified the North, or the West, as cotton did the South. For none accounted for so large a share of the production in the other regions. But one industry was surely vital to northern "commercial interest" when tariffs first burgeoned. And that was ship construction. As Daniel Webster feelingly declared: "The shipping interest pays, annually, more than half a million of dollars in duties on articles used in the construction of ships." And the 1824 tariff before the Congress proposed "to add nearly . . . fifty

---

35. 29th Cong., 1st sess., *Report from the Secretary of the Treasury* (1845), p. 585.

36. Ibid., p. 755.

37. See Appendix A, this chapter.

38. Given an investment of $1,500 per hand—following Alfred Conrad and John Meyer, *The Economics of Slavery* (1964), p. 53—an annual return of $150 is estimated on the basis of the fairly typical 10 percent interest rate that traders charged for slaves sold on time. (See Table 18.1.) That figure would rise to $154.26 if the duties were added to the net.

TABLE 13.5
TARIFF IMPACT ON COTTON INCOME, 1824 (PER FIELD HAND)

Consumption	Input costs[a]	Input duties
	(dollars)	
Field hand		
Lowell, 15 yards	$1.50	$ .69
Linsey, 10 yards	4.00	.46
Blanket, 1	1.50	.30
Shoes, one pair	1.00	.30
Salt and medicines	1.00	.25
Total	9.00	2.00
Nonworking hand	6.00	1.35
Materials		
Hemp bagging		.16
Iron for hoes, plows, etc.		.15
Other		
Total		.91
Duties as ratio to cotton sales[b]	2.7%	

[a]Nondutiable costs: overseer and physician salaries, pork and corn, depreciation on buildings and animals, factor's commission, and transport to market.

[b]Sales: 4 bales produced per hand, 400 pounds per bale, 10 cents per pound, implies $160 in sales per working hand.

Source: Appendix A, this chapter.

percent to this amount."[39] New England's ship builders had no tariff protection, but had to pay higher prices for materials because of duties laid on them. (See Appendix B, this chapter.)

The duties on shipbuilding were substantial—12 to 22 percent. But they tell only half the story. Beginning with the very first tariff act, in 1789, the tariff paid on goods carried in ships built and owned by American citizens ran 10 percent less than on those in ships built and owned abroad.[40] There were such differential tariffs on teas, drawbacks on materials, and more. Moreover, the coasting trade—from one American port to another—was given over to American shipowners almost wholly beginning in 1789, and wholly so begin-

39. Annals of Congress, 18th Cong., 1st sess.; reprinted in George R. Taylor, ed., The Great Tariff Debate, 1820–1830 (1953), p. 20.

40. Winthrop Marvin, The American Merchant Marine (1902), pp. 38, 42. Between that year and 1828, the Congress "passed no fewer than fifty tariff or other laws intended directly or indirectly to protect American shipbuilding and shipowning."

ning in 1817.[41] The value of such a monopoly handsomely offset the negative protection on shipbuilding per se.

The South had done well in the tariff struggle. Old New England had done poorly, and was forced to shift out of what Santayana called its "blue water" stage of economic development. The new textile mills in Massachusetts, Pennsylvania, and New York did better. Doing best of all, perhaps, were the farmers of Ohio, Indiana, Vermont, and Kentucky. The persistent tariff protection they quietly achieved for their wool and hemp helped keep their investments profitable even in the face of vast efficiency advances by their chief competitor, cotton.[42]

Tariffs proved wonderfully attractive to those who benefited from them. Farmers who grew wool were protected against the harsh wind of foreign competition. So were planters who grew cotton. Both thereby increased their profits. Capitalists and workers in the iron industry, as in pottery, coal, vinegar, candy, and paper production, enjoyed tariff rates that ran to 50 and 60 percent. Protected from the cruel world, such "infant industries" were enabled to grow—or perhaps only to retain their infantile ways. For still other groups the tariff barriers offered a challenge, either to avoid or to evade. They included custom house personnel, auctioneers, American importers, and British manufacturers. The extent to which tariffs did provide net protection for the product of such infant U.S. industries therefore turned on the uncertain outcome of this protection, and this challenge.

In recent decades a charming and imaginary history of that outcome has been written. Its theme is that giving capitalist firms a monopoly somehow energized them. They thereby became ever more efficient, more devoted to production and to helping national economic growth. Lord Kaldor has described a kind of industrial biology: "industries are always inefficient at the beginning and they become efficient as a result of expansion and growth. . . . For a country like Mexico [in the 1970s] it was impossible under conditions of free trade. They cannot compete." Economists of this persuasion use the nineteenth century United States as exemplar of the "successful nurturing of heavy industry in a developing country"; tariff "protectionism used to allow infant industries . . . [such as] textiles to acquire the size and experience needed to compete in world markets."[43]

Yet conservative economists, as many a radical one, are dour and doubtful that giving capitalist adventurers a legal monopoly, via the tariff, benefited society. Suppose, improbably, that there was a natural history that each industry had to repeat, growing from inefficiency "at the beginning" to greater efficiency as a result of "expansion and growth." Yet it is still hardly clear that

41. Ibid., p. 359.
42. Labor required per cotton bale produced fell 40 percent 1800 to 1850, and slaves per unit of Southern crops produced fell 76 percent 1800 to 1860. Cf. Lebergott, *Manpower*, p. 156.
43. *New York Times* (October 24, 1982), p. 10–F.

the first nation in the market has an impressive continued advantage.[44] For the essential aspect of world economic history is not simple growth in a world of comparative statics. In the actual complex nineteenth century, British producers kept increasing their efficiency, driving down their costs and selling prices. U.S. tariffs did not rise correspondingly to protect each childish or infant industry. Even more significantly, productivity in ocean shipping advanced persistently, as it did in U.S. transport. Together these effectively kept reducing still further the price of British goods (and French, Saxon, Italian) landed on U.S. shores. Figure 13.1 marks the long downward trend in real ocean freight rates, and the actual decline in American tariff rates to 1860.

Nor was there a reversal in the next half-century. History instead reveals Andrew Carnegie shipping steel around the world, boasting that his industry needed no tariff protection; Standard Oil shipping the product of New Jersey refineries to Europe and Asia; Singer sewing machines sold in the depths of Central Europe.

The cost of traversing the ocean had long protected American industry from foreign competition. Tariffs added to that protection from 1789 onward. But British and continental ingenuity kept reducing the prices of their products at the same time. Their exports to the United States then increased decade after decade. Yet the United States did not fail to grow, nor its industry to develop. True, the typical industry that received solid protection might have led a life of sheltered ease. But the more typical U.S. response was different. Innovators, entrepreneurs, ingenious craftsmen, hard-working farmers and workers together revolutionized the technological parameters of the American economy. So doing they drove down prices, even those of the key protected products. (For example, the real price of cotton sheeting, archetypical product of the "infant" textile industry, was cut by 19 percent from 1820 to 1830, by 30 percent to 1860. The real price of nails, product of the great protected iron industry, fell by even more in the early decade, and by 62 percent by 1860.[45] In the process, industry happily widened its domestic markets, and began invading foreign ones.

---

44. Thus both British and American pioneers would have a period of learning, incurring costs but not realizing profits. The subsequent prices each charged would have to amortize such costs. That fact would no more deter intelligent entrepreneurs or financiers than the fact that funds have to be spent for machinery and factory buildings long before profits from production could repay them. The Japanese have well demonstrated that the advantage of being a follower (who avoids the mistakes, antiquated machinery, of the pioneer nation) can be potent. These considerations, however, are no more determinative than the infant industry argument. The dynamics and specifics of competition in particular fields must be established before the wisdom of any specific tariff policy can be judged, with due allowance for the politics of public gifts to private interests.

45. *Historical Statistics . . . to 1970*, pp. 205, 209.

Appendix

Appendix A

The estimates summarized in Table 13.5 and derived below indicate the effects of the tariff on income from the primary Southern product. We estimate the same $2.00 in consumption duties per non-working hand as per working hand, but allow for only 40 percent of all hands being non-working. The $4.26 in total duties per fieldhand comes to 2.1 percent of the $160 value of cotton produced per working hand.

1. The average working hand produced 2.5 bales of cotton in the Old South and 5 in the new, according to Treasury Secretary Levi Woodbury in 1836.[1] With cotton at 10 cents a pound, bales of 400 pounds, and, say, 4 bales per hand, each hand produced $160 worth of cotton (1,600 pounds) per year.[2] (An estimate of 2,000 pounds appears in *De Bow's Review*.[3])

2. For each bale, 5 yards of hemp bagging were required, each yard paying a 3-cent duty.[4]

3. Slave consumption per hand averaged 15 yards of Lowell a year, 10 yards of linsey, 1 blanket, 1 pair of shoes, and $1 worth of salt and medicines.[5]

4. For Lowell cottons averaging 10 cents a yard, duties are estimated at 4.6 cents per running yard. Those figures were derived as follows. In 1845 the Charleston Chamber of Commerce stated that low priced cambrics paid duties of 7 cents a square yard (i.e., 4.6 cents per running yard, as the statement elsewhere contrasts a 9-cent duty per square yard with a 6-cent duty per running yard). The chamber also reported that "Negro plains, Union cotton and wool"—which we take to indicate the linsey price—were imported at 31 cents to 40 cents a yard before duty and cost 40 cents to 55 cents after duty and markup.[6] Since they indicate a 10-cent margin for both cambrics and plains, the duty inferred for each is 4.6 cents. The result is $1.15 for the specified 25 yards of Lowell and linsey.

5. The duty on men's shoes was 30 cents estimated as 29 percent of the value of average shoes imported in 1844 (the latter's price being virtually identical with the $1 price estimated by Ware.)[7]

6. The duties on blankets valued at 75 cents or more was 25 percent.[8] Hence, a $1.50 blanket at retail,[9] minus a 20 percent distributor's margin, would have paid 30 cents in duty. As blankets were provided every other year, the annual duty was 15 cents.

1. 24th Cong., 1st sess., H.D. 146, *Cotton* (1836), p. 16.

2. Price and yield data from ibid., p. 18.

3. *De Bow's Review*, n.s. 19, no. 2 (1855):102.

4. James Hamilton of South Carolina and Thomas Cobb of Georgia provide these figures in U.S., Congress, *Debates and Proceedings*, 18th Cong., 1st sess., (April 1824,) 2:1540, 1544.

5. Nathan Ware (A Southern Planter), *Notes on Political Economy* (1844), p. 202.

6. 62d Cong., 1st sess., S.D. 72, *Tariff Proceedings and Documents* (1911), pt. 3:1862.

7. Ibid., p. 1626.

8. 29th Cong., 1st sess., H.D. 6, *Finance Report* (1846), p. 581.

9. Ibid., p. 702, reports a Louisiana planter paying $1.62. Ruffin's pro forma account indicated that a blanket worth $1.50 was provided each slave every two years; Edmund Ruffin, *An Essay on Calcareous Manures* (1844, reprint ed., 1961), p. 188. The Polk plantation paid $1.50 as well; John Basset, ed., *The Southern Plantation Overseer* (1925), p. 270.

7. With quinine valued at 40 cents an ounce (24 percent equivalent ad valorem) and opium, at $2.50, an arbitrary 25-cent duty is estimated for medicines.[10]

8. For iron consumption, we rely on three different estimates. James K. Polk's plantation expense record shows 550 pounds of iron and steel bought in 1852, 683 pounds in 1856 or, say, 600 pounds a year. Polk paid an average of 5.5 cents a pound.[11] The bar-iron tariff rate was 90 cents per 112 pounds.[12] Since the plantation bought 3 dozen pairs of shoes for slaves in both 1851 and 1852, we assume it averaged 30 slaves, with 60 percent of the slave population working hands. All of which leads to an average of 33 pounds of iron and a 27 cent duty per working hand.

James De Bow provides data that lead, in one case, to a figure of about 10 pounds, in another, to 30 pounds per hand. A plantation of 120 slaves consumed 500 pounds of iron worth $30 and spent a further $30 for hoes and spades; *Industrial Resources of the South and West*, 1:163). If half the cost of hoes and spades was for iron, we might infer, say, 10 pounds per slave. On the other hand, *De Bow's Review*, n.s. 19 no. 2 (1855):101) gives a pro forma account for a plantation with two-thirds working slaves, where $3.50 per working hand was spent for iron and blacksmith work plus $3 annual expense for tools, wagons, gears, etc., and averaging 2,000 pounds of cotton per hand.

An average of 20.8 pounds per slave can be inferred from data in Wendell Stephenson, *Isaac Franklin, Slave Trader and Planter of the Old South* (1938, reprint ed., 1968), pp. 280–96, using the approach noted above for DeBow's data.

Appendix B

Raw cotton had a 3 cents a pound duty, and sold for about 10 cents. Shipbuilding had no explicit protection. Cotton sheeting (Appendix A) averaged 46 percent for Lowells.

The sale price for a vessel built in the United States, equipped for sea, ran $60 a ton in 1820.[13] Daniel Webster provides most of the other data in Table B.1 on input requirements and duties.[14] We estimate that bolts of sailcloth, hemp or flax, average 40 pounds each; *Niles Weekly Register* 32 (August 11, 1827):391.

For estimating the effective protection rates shown in Tables B.2–B.4 two primary sources were used.

Detailed inputs, as well as output totals, are given for individual firms in a large-scale 1832 survey by the secretary of the Treasury.[15] These distributions, for 1832,

10. 62d Cong., *Tariff Proceedings*, p. 1623.

11. Bassett, *The Southern Plantation Overseer*, pp. 189, 196, 199, 270. The plantation also bought 100 pounds of nails in 1851, some portion of which should perhaps be allocated to subsequent years.

12. 62d Cong., 1st sess., S.D. 21, *Customs Tariff of 1842* (1911), p. 398.

13. According to the Mercantile Society of New York, quoted in *American State Papers: Finance*, 2:642.

14. George R. Taylor, ed., *The Great Tariff Debate, 1820–1830* (1953), pp. 21–23.

15. McLane Report, *Documents Relative to the Manufactures in the United States* (1833), vol. 1.

Data for cotton prints are from the Merrimac Manufacturing Company, the largest print works in the nation (pp. 340–41).

TABLE B.1
COST OF SHIP CONSTRUCTION AND TARIFF DUTIES, 1824
(COPPER-FASTENED SHIP OF 354 TONS)

Dutiable inputs	Duties
14 tons of iron @ $15	$ 217.50
10 tons of hemp @ $30	300.00
40 bolts Russian duck @ $2	80.00
20 bolts Ravens duck @ $1.25	25.00
Articles of ship chandlery	40.00
Total	$1,056.00

Source: Appendix B, first paragraph.

TABLE B.2
SHIPBUILDING DUTIES, 1845

Material inputs	Duty rates	New Bedford		Fairhaven	
		Cost	Input Duties	Cost	Input Duties
Oak[a]	30%	$ 6,479	$2,095	$ 2,160	$ 438
Plank[a]	30%	2,591	598	1,296	299
Spikes	3¢ per pound		195		99
Copper bolts	4¢ per pound		365		184
Swedish iron	$25 per ton		350		175
Total		$15,640	$3,603	$ 6,580	$1,195
Sales price: ships		$31,760		$16,240	

[a]The costs as of 1832 reduced 13.7 percent, using the 1832–45 decline in timber costs shown by A. Bezanson, in *Historical Statistics . . . to 1970*, p. 205.

Source: Appendix B.

are used to weight the tariff rates for individual input items. Insofar as the general trend in prices affected expenditures by such producers, the distribution of weights by 1845 would have been identical. Insofar as the price trends for one specific input—for example, belt leather versus harness twine or oak versus

Data for cotton sheeting, produced much more widely, are for a large manufacturing firm in Massachusetts but not one of the very large Lowell mills (pp. 198–99). The weights vary to such a limited extent that the use of data from a number of other firms gave virtually identical rates of effective protection.
Data for shipbuilding are from firms in New Bedford and Fairhaven (pp. 182–3, 188–9).

TABLE B.3
COTTON SHEETING DUTIES, 1845

| | Costs | Duties | |
		Rates	Aggregate
Material inputs			
Cotton (89,200 lbs)	$11,150	3¢ per lb	$2,676
Starch (5,330 lbs)	318	2¢ per lb	107
Oil	390	20%	65
Coal	160	69%	65
Belt leather	195	35%	51
Shuttles and peckers	245	30%	57
Harness twine	75	30%	17
Wood	25	20%	4
Iron	90	30%	21
Brushes, brooms	70	30%	16
Packing twine	18	30%	4
String leather	57	35%	13
Other	147	30%	34
Total materials	12,940		3,130
Cotton sheeting			
Sales:	$39,795		
Duties:	16,117		

Source: Appendix B.

plank—moved differently, the weights would be subject to some bias. Experimentation, allowing for differing price trends of major input items, showed the traditional result: Variations in index weights make remarkably little difference in the final index results. And, in this instance, the effective protection estimates changed not at all.

Duties on an ad valorem basis are available from estimates by the secretary of the Treasury for 1845.[16] However, for the major input items—raw cotton, copper bolts, iron—and for outputs of cotton sheeting and cotton prints, the actual charges per pound or per yard are used.[17]

16. 62d Cong., 1st sess., S.D. 72, *Tariff Proceedings and Documents, 1839–1857*, pt. 3:2120 ff.
17. For cotton sheeting the Act of 1842 rate was 30 percent of an arbitrary minimum of 20 cents a yard or 6 cents for goods selling for not more than 20 cents a yard. (Those of the Merrimac Manufacturing Company sold for 10.23 cents a yard in 1832 and about 15 cents in 1845.) For cotton sheeting, the similar minimum calculation gives a 6-cent tariff rate for goods selling at 8.5 cents a yard.

TABLE B.4
COTTON PRINT DUTIES, 1845

| | | Duties | |
	Costs/sales	Rates	Aggregate
Material inputs			
Cotton	$176,248	3¢ per lb.	$44,139
Starch	2,318	39%	650
Flour	2,200	33%	546
Wood	2,450	20%	408
Coal	2,900	69%	1,184
Oil	4,670	20%	778
Lime	1,820	26%	376
Copperas	5,700	100%	2,850
Potash	7,500	20%	1,250
Pearlash	960	(20%)	160
Pyroligneous acid	1,720	20%	287
Madder	31,130	free	0
Indigo	59,898	7%	3,919
Logwood	2,460	free	0
Berries	1,370	free	0
Blanketing	5,100	15%	665
Copper	3,200	free	0
Sulphur	5,800	free	0
Other	7,670	(20%)	1,320
Total			58,526
Sales: Cotton prints	660,600	9¢ per sq. yd.	

Source: Appendix B.

Locke sank into a swoon
The Garden died:
God took the spinning-jenny
Out of his side
—YEATS, *Fragments, the Collected Poems of W. B. Yeats*

14

Technology and Industrialization

I N the conflict between Civilization and Nature, technology has typically sided with civilization. Yeats' little effusion epitomized decades of objections—by Rousseau, Wordsworth, Madison Grant, by all who stood fast for Nature, Ecology, the Simple. And who, therefore, felt obligated to oppose mechanization, contrivance, industrialization. Since such values have been held so widely, why has technology nonetheless advanced so persistently? Original Sin? Possibly. But two other powerful reasons need to be considered.

Once expelled from the Garden of Eden man labored in the sweat of his brow—and hated nearly every minute of it. To make his daily bread, he had to grow the wheat. He had then to separate the wheat from the chaff. When prayers for wind failed to blow the chaff away, he resorted to artificial breezes: "Two persons took a sheet between them and by a particular flapping of the sheet produced a breeze that blew the chaff away." One nineteenth-century American declared that he had dug ditches, chopped trees, shoveled manure. But blowing chaff "was about the hardest work I ever performed." "Tradition states that the first persons who tried to produce an artificial wind were, by some, regarded as impiously invading the domain of Providence."[1] True, it was "unnatural." But so were a thousand technical changes, all introduced because human beings wished to do away with disagreeable chores—they hated to dig ditches with a shovel, empty privies, wash clothes by hand in freezing river water, pound corn in a wooden dish to

1. Leo Rogin, *The Introduction of Farm Machinery in Its Relationship to the Productivity of Labor in the Agriculture of the United States during the Nineteenth Century* (1931), pp. 154–55.

make meal. Technical change eventually substituted more agreeable techniques to achieve these tasks. It also reduced the sheer effort required for a thousand different tasks. Technology has proved to be the only way in which society can get something for nothing, that is, more goods and services without more human effort or real resources.

A second reason for the remorseless spread of technology was that it could perform magic. In the *Arabian Nights*, Sinbad's carpet took him wherever he wished, almost instantaneously. Canals and turnpikes, and later railroads, did just that. In 1797, kings could journey no faster than 14 miles an hour, even with fresh horses every 7 miles.[2] By 1847, railroads carried common laborers across the land three times as fast. The wealthiest queen in the nineteenth century had her first children in the traditional bed of pain. But the use of chloroform after 1848 permitted the safe, merciful absence of pain. Having witnessed perhaps the first operation using chloroform, a contemporary wrote: "I have no words to express my admiration for this invention. . . . All the [other] great discoveries of science sink into insignificance."[3]

The Sources of Technology

The first source of technological change was science—defined by a great novelist as "the absence of prejudice backed by the presence of money." It was science that led to the development of "machinery, which was the antidote of superstition, which was in turn—the exhalation of the archives."[4] Science, the great destroyer, continuously evolved new ideas that jostled away older ones. Money, as James noted, was essential. It paid scientists while they conducted research. And it implemented their discoveries. The evolving logic of science had its own dynamic. Perpetually suspicious of received wisdom, science raised fresh questions even after it reached new solutions. It opened new doubts after every, temporary, resolution of old conflicts.

Yet the United States provided little scientific leadership to the world during the century when it advanced from peasant colony to leading industrial power. As Carl Snyder noted, the entire history of science to the twentieth century could be written without referring to the work of more than one American, Yale's great physicist, Willard Gibbs.[5] What inference follows? That history demonstrated once more that knowledge was (almost) a free

2. Joseph Farington, *The Farington Diary* (1923), 1:211.

3. Philip Morrell, ed., *Leaves from the Greville Diary* (n.d.), p. 558. Greville, clerk to Britain's Privy Council, addicted to the turf, cynical about most things, is an ideal witness to the surcease from ancient suffering provided by that first safe, reliable, anaesthetic.

4. Henry James, *The Golden Bowl*, Bk. 1, chap. 1.

5. "Why is it that this people, now marching to the industrial conquest of the earth, has done so little, comparatively, in the realms of science? . . . It is perhaps just because of the rich prizes of business, that the Faradays and Claude Bernards are not to be found among us." Carl Snyder, quoted in *Literary Digest*, January 18, 1902, p. 81.

good. Once a scientist published his discoveries they became a gift to every nation in the world. Any economy could take the scientific work laboriously developed in a hundred other nations and turn it to its own purposes. It hardly needed to invest much in "research" as distinct from "development." U.S. history in the nineteenth century anticipates that of Japan and Hong Kong in the twentieth century: galloping productivity with very little investment in research.

But U.S. technological advance demanded more than "science." Trial and error was its second great component. The host of canny, crotchety inventors emphasized the role of alert empiricism. Cut and paste. Try and try again. Among the thousands of attempts and experiments, some proved successful. Centuries of empiric alchemism did lead to chemical discoveries; centuries of old wives' and old witches' experiments with herbs and potions did provide useful medicines.

Such empiricism was rampant in the United States. In 1802 a Louisiana planter imported a cargo of monkeys; cheap as slave labor was, perhaps monkeys could pick cotton even more cheaply.[6] In 1855, Secretary of War Jefferson Davis imported camels—for desert warfare in Utah, New Mexico, and California.[7] During its first year, the Baltimore and Ohio fixed up a railroad car with sails—and it coasted merrily along under the guidance of no less a personage than the Russian envoy to the United States.[8] Wade Hampton, general in the Revolutionary War, fed his slaves on cotton seeds to see whether a cheaper diet would serve—only to find his valuable slaves dying off "like rotten sheep."[9] Rice was Georgia's "staple commodity" in 1799. But tobacco was introduced as an experiment, and was expected "shortly [to] become the staple of this state. . . . [Tea was introduced and] now grows . . . in most of the fenced lots in Savannah."[10] In 1831 New Hampshire had thousands of mulberry trees. One grower, with 10,000 trees, raised 4,000 silk worms and manufactured 1¾ pounds of silk "of a superior quality."[11] But neither tea nor tobacco ever proved a feasible crop for Georgia. And New Hampshire never did prove able to compete with Japan.

A near infinite number of shrewdly designed, careful experiments, however, also took place. Each pitted one procedure against another. The results were examined and transformed into production techniques. In 1851 one

6. James H. Street, *The New Revolution in the Cotton Economy* (1957), p. 92.

7. His hopes for their "usefulness in the transportation of military supplies" appear in 34th Cong., 3d sess., *Annual Report of the Secretary of War* (1856), pp. 22–23.

8. William Prescott Smith, *A History and Description of the Baltimore and Ohio Railroad* (1853), pp. 25–26.

9. American Anti-Slavery Society, *American Slavery As It Is* (1839), p. 29; F. N. Boney, ed., *Slave Life in Georgia* (1972), p. 147.

10. John Payne, *New and Complete System of Universal Geography* (1799), p. 444.

11. McLane Report, *Documents Relative to the Manufactures in the United States* (1833), I:685, 826, 836.

shrewd farmer wondered whether the new-fangled seed drill was worth the price. How to decide? He sowed ten acres of wheat by drills. On another ten acres he broadcast the seed in traditional fashion. And he discovered that the difference in yield was significant. Another farmer selected two pairs of cattle: one to be fed on dry ground feed, the other on feed boiled in salt water. He found a 70 percent "weight gain in favor of cooked feed."[12] (After 1862, these primitive but sensible tests began to be done systematically by state Agricultural Experiment Stations.)

In 1832 a manufacturer sought to define "the comparative value of the Pictou (Nova Scotia) and Richmond (Virginia) coals, both deemed to be the best quality of their kind." He tried Pictou coal during the first and third weeks of the experiments, Richmond coal during the second and fourth; he discovered that the former produced more iron per unit of heat, yet required "0.97 bushels less coals per ton" of iron.[13] One railroad tried bituminous coals instead of wood in its locomotives, and discovered that a pound of coal yielded twice as much steam as a pound of wood.[14]

The Results of Technological Advance

Technological advance came in two forms: a new method of production and a new product. Each form wreaked havoc with older industry.

New methods of production in America's major industry, agriculture, involved continuous, unspectacular   but highly important—changes in the selection of species.[15] The selection for improved wheats had certainly begun back as far as the first settlers in Neolithic times who wandered about the ancient Middle East after The Flood, and picked out those emmer wheats that form the distant basis for today's wheats.

American farmers in the nineteenth century proved willing to pay for better, and then still better, varieties of seed. "'Hundred' seed, developed by Colonel Vicks of Vicksburg . . . sold, year after year, at two dollars a bushel . . . 'Mastodon' seed commanded five dollars a bushel . . . 'Banana' . . . seeds were sold at a dime each, or one hundred and fifty dollars a bushel . . . the famous 'Prolific' cotton originated from a single stalk, which was selected, and its seeds carefully preserved, by a Mississippi planter, who observed it in passing through his fields."[16]

12. *Letter from the Commissioner of Patents*, February 1853, pp. 115, 171.

13. 22nd Cong., 1st sess., H.D. 100, *Coal . . . Experiment on Foreign and Domestic Coals* (1832), p. 1.

14. Report of Mendes Cohen in *29th Annual Report of the Baltimore and Ohio Railroad* (1855), appendix. In a careful comparison he estimated that the pounds of water evaporated per pound of fuel were: wood, 2.9; piedmont coal, 4.9, 5.7; "American" coal, 6.0; swanton, 6.8.

15. "The Search for New Species" is reviewed in compact fashion by Paul Gates, *The Farmer's Age: 1815–1860* (1960), chap. 14.

16. *Report of the Comissioner of Agriculture for the Year 1866* (1867), p. 210.

As for the major crop of the North, corn: "The golden yellow maize of the cornbelt of the United States . . . which has become the very foundation of the Nation's agricultural economy . . . was not known to the Indians and came into being along with the cornbelt itself. . . . Maize as we know it in the United States is a gift of the pioneers. These cornbelt varieties were the creation of the nineteenth century. They came in large part from crosses between white Southern dents, mostly of Mexican origin; and the long, slender highland" of Guatemalan, Mayan, background.[17]

Improvement of the U.S. animal stock was no less steady and prolonged. The common sheep of the new nation yielded small amounts of coarse wool. But revolution and war broke up Spain's merino flocks, developed over centuries. When Charles IV abdicated the Spanish throne, Joseph Bonaparte seized it, while the local juntas declared for the heir apparent. Owners of valuable Spanish merinos promptly sold them before they could be lost by pillage. Americans imported some of the better rams. E. I. DuPont brought back the celebrated Dom Pedro in 1801, paying $60 for it. By the summer of 1810 sales were commonly made at from $300 to $500 per animal, some rams actually fetching a price of $1,000. William Jarvis of Vermont, then American consul in Lisbon, "purchased two thousand of the best blooded sheep in Spain." Some 18,000 were brought over by other buyers. This supply burst brought merino prices down to $100 by 1812. But by 1860 most of the nation's sheep descended from those imported 1810–20, and constituted a much improved stock.[18]

The incentive for the boom, of course, was the difference between the 1 to 2 pounds of wool one could get from "country sheep" and the 8½ pound clip from Dom Pedro.[19] (General Mason's merinos yielded 9 pounds apiece, while John Thelkeld, Esq. got 10 pounds from his flock.)[20]

The continuous "unnatural selection" doubled the fleece yielded by the average sheep from 1.3 pounds in 1810 to 2.0 pounds in 1840 and 2.7 pounds in 1860.[21] In half a century the persistent introduction of better varieties of sheep by American farmers had doubled the overall U.S. average.

17. Edgar Anderson and William Brown, "The History of the Common Maize Varieties of the United States Corn Belt," *Agricultural History* (January 1952), p. 2.

18. Details from Carrol W. Pursell, Jr., "E. I. DuPont and the Merino Mania in Delaware 1805–1815," *Agricultural History*, 36:91–100. We estimate $100 for 1812 on the assumption that a $6 rental of a sheep for a year implied a capital value, at 6 percent, of $100.

19. Ibid., p. 91.

20. *Niles*, VI (July 16, 1814):334.

21. The speculative 1810 figure, and the Census-based 1840 and 1860 averages, rest on data given in 50th Cong., 1st sess, H.D. 550, *Wool and Manufactures of Wool* (1888), pp. 13, 14. The Duke de Rochefoucault Liancourt in 1797 found even better sheep seldom yielding more than 3 pounds. Cf. Pursell, "E.I. DuPont," p. 91. A guessed average of 2.5 for 1832, obviously too high, is implicit in *Niles*, XLI (Addendum):33.

As for dairy cows, "up to the year 1800 the breed showed little improvement." Because of the high cost of labor, and the lack of scythes to cut hay, the breed deteriorated, and milk yield declined. Between 1800 and 1840, however, selection advanced the yield of an ordinary Massachusetts cow from about 2,500 pounds of milk to 3,225 pounds.[22]

Why were such improvements in plant and animal varieties important in economic history? Why did farmers pay such outlandish prices for choice varieties? The answer had little to do with the kind of interest that developed racing stallions or show dogs. It reflects rather the contribution of better varieties to farmers' profits. The orders of magnitude were impressive.

In cotton growing "the difference between the inferior grades and the first quality of seed is . . . in many cases . . . the difference between harvesting 400 and 200 pounds an acre."[23] If a cotton planter bought better seed, instead of simply using the seed he had left after ginning his cotton, what would it have been worth to him? As Table 14.1 indicates, yield doubled. Picking expenses rose only a small amount. Profits rose 25 percent. Any farmer would sensibly pay $15 to $20 a bushel for seed that yielded so much more saleable cotton. Tennessee green seed was gradually replaced after 1820 by Petit Gulf and other varieties.

These newer seed varieties were valued not merely because they were more fruitful. They were also distinctly easier to pick.[24] The upward trend in picking rates is evident in Table 14.2.[25] Some data relate to individual plantations that may not be widely representative (1825, 1841, 1895). But the 1810–60 trend for the remaining (contemporary) estimates, which seek to estimate a prevailing Southern average, is no less clearly upward.[26]

But the ease with which new varieties could be picked made it more certain that the crop could be gathered in before the first frost lowered its quality. And there was a still more powerful incentive. The maximum use of the slave labor force during the year occurred during the picking season. The fourfold increase in picking rates from 1800 to the 1850s meant that a planter could pick four times as much cotton with no increased investment in slaves.

22. T. R. Pirtle, *History of the Diary Industry* (1926), pp. 18, 26–27.

23. *Report of the Commissioner of Agriculture for the Year 1866* (1867), p. 210.

24. Mack Swearingen, "Charles Whitmore of Montpelier," *Journal of Southern History* (April 1935), p. 277.

25. Cf. Appendix B, this chapter.

26. Individual plantations did still better. Jefferson Davis had 11 pickers in 1853 who achieved 479 pounds apiece daily. And Bennet Barrow's slaves averaged nearly 250 pounds a day for many years in the 1840s. Cf. Dunbar Rowland, ed., *Jefferson Davis, Constitutionalist* (1923), 2:182, and Edwin A. Davis, *Plantation Life in . . . Louisiana* (1943), pp. 268–74, 337–68, 421–22.

TABLE 14.1
COST OF PRODUCING RAW COTTON, 1850 ($000)

| | Cost of seed (by type used) | |
	Average	Improved
Expenses: except seed	$ 3.40	$ 4.40
seed	3.60	19.20
Cotton sales		
at 122-lb per acre yield	$20.00	
at 244-lb per acre yield		$40.00
Profit	$13.00	$16.40

Source: Appendix A, this chapter.

TABLE 14.2
COTTON PICKING, 1800–1958

Year	Pounds per day
1800	50
1810	60
1825 (NC)	100–175
1841	107
1850–60	100 or more
1850s (Northup)	200
1850s (Louisiana)	200
1854 (Wailes)	200
1866	200
1868	100–200
1895	200
1896	240
1958	225

Source: Appendix B, this chapter.

No wonder the price of slaves rose. Planters could easily pay twice as much per slave in the 1850s as in 1800 and still make as great a profit.[27]

To mark the persistence of technological advance, and its results, few examples serve better than the cotton gin. Traditionally history describes Eli

27. Picking represented peak labor requirements. And slaves accounted for about $900 of the total value of investment per hand of $1,425 in the old South. (Data from A. Conrad and J. Meyer, *The Economics of Slavery* (1964), pp. 52–53.) The implicit share for labor, of 63%, may be contrasted with the 58% used by Robert Fogel and Stanley Engerman, *Time on the Cross* (1974) 2:132, 137.

Whitney's invention of the cotton gin in 1793 as causing the rise of "production of cotton . . . from 4,000 bales in 1790 to 333,728 in 1820."[28] On a visit to General Greene's plantation, Whitney, confronted by the problem, promptly figured out a vastly improved gin. It was variously claimed to clean 10 times as much cotton "as by any other mode," or even 1,000 times as much.[29] But we may take his own 1793 letter to indicate that by using it a hand could clean "60 to 80 weight per day"—or twice the prior average.[30] Whitney patented his "machine for ginning cotton" in March 1794. But that was hardly the end. Further improvements in the cotton gin came thick and fast. Cotton ginning patents[31] granted by the Secretary of State from 1794 to 1803 alone were as follows:

Machine for ginning cotton	Eli Whitney	March 1794
Improvement in cotton gin	Hodgen Holmes	May 1796
Metallic fluted rollers for cleaning cotton	Gurden Saltonstall	September 1801
Machine for ginning cotton	William Bell and Sam deMontmollin	April 1802
A saw mill for cleaning cotton	Gurdon Saltonstall	January 1803
Improvement to their roller cotton gin	Bell and Montmollin	February 1803
A rolling machine for cleaning cotton	Saltonstall	May 1803
Improvement in the cotton gin	William Bell	November 1803

In the 60-odd years after Whitney developed his gin, the amount of cotton that could be ginned in a day, because of his invention, rose to eight times the previous amount. By 1866 a "good gin" could easily separate three thousand pounds of lint from seed in twelve hours.[32] Gins, of course, had been used in India for centuries. But their output was low, as was their ability to grapple with the green seeds of upland cotton. In 1788 Richard Leake, of Savannah, became "an adventurer [and the first that has attempted it on any large scale] in introducing a new staple for the planting interest of this state; the article of

28. Marcus Jernegan, et al., *Growth of the American People* (1934), pp. 278–79. "Eli Whitney's cotton gin of 1793 solved the mechanical problem of separating the seeds from the cotton, and the way was open for large-scale production." Arthur Bining and Thomas Cochran, *The Rise of American Economic Life* (1964), p. 279.

29. The thousand to one ratio is implicit in Tench Coxe's *Digest* in American State Papers, *Finance*, II:669.

30. The tenfold advantage is described in a letter to his father in June 1793. It is quoted, together with the report of the early experience of one hand using it, in Allan Nevins and Jeanette Mirsky, *The World of Eli Whitney* (1952), pp. 66, 76.

31. American State Papers, *Miscellaneous*, I (1805):423.

32. *Report of the Commissioner of Agriculture for . . . 1866* (1867), p. 202.

cotton." He wrote to Philadelphia for one of those "gins or machines," supposed to yield 30 to 40 pounds of clean cotton a day. He intended to get one "whatever the cost may be" because he preferred to use his workers for "cutting lumber, ditching, and clearing land" in the winter.[33] A steady daily average of 25 pounds per man is reported in 1808 for the roller gin used on Carolina's silky, valuable, long staple cotton.[34]

This advance in output is summarized in Table 14.3. The economies in slave labor were internalized where the gins were used—on the plantations. The productivity advances in the grim planter–slave enterprise of cotton raising, therefore, were even worthy of comparison with the better heralded gains in cotton textile manufacture.

Since two-thirds of the U.S. cotton crop was sold overseas, advances in technology of distribution expanded the competitive potential of cotton just as advances in cotton growing did. Indeed, the early success of slave grown American cotton in replacing peasant grown Indian cotton in the British market came in part from lower transport costs. Not only was American cotton packed tighter (more pounds per bale) on the plantation.[35] But also, new,

TABLE 14.3

The Cotton Gin, 1788–1866

	Pounds of cotton cleaned per day
1788—by hand	2
1788 cotton gin—Philadelphia models	30–40
1793 cotton gin—Whitney model	80
1800 cotton gin—Whitney model	350
1866 cotton gin	3,000

Source: 1788 gin: Richard Leake, 1788, quoted in Niles, VI (July 16, 1813), p. 334.
    1788 hand, 1866: U.S. Commissioner of Agriculture, Report for 1866, p. 202.
    1793: J. Mirsky and A. Nevins, The World of Eli Whitney (1952), p. 76, quote Whitney writing to Jefferson, stating that a laborer cleaned 60 to 80 weight per day. On p. 66 Whitney is quoted to the effect that 1 man could clean 10 times as much as by any other method.
    1800: A writer in the Merchants Magazine (December 1861), pp. 562–63, who "entered an East India counting house in Philadelphia in 1804," states that as of 1800 Whitney's gin could clean 350 pounds, versus 1 pound by hand. A similar figure appears in Francois Michaux, Travels to the West . . . (1805), pp. 241–43, comparing 300–400 to 30 pounds "by the usual method"—presumably the more primitive gins.

33. Niles, VI (July 16, 1814):334.
34. David Ramsey, History of South Carolina (1858), 2:120–21.
35. Cotton "as packed by the Chinese occupies three times the bulk of an equal quantity shipped by Europeans for their own markets. Thus the freight of a given quantity of cotton costs the Chinese nearly twelve times the price to which . . . it might be reduced." Charles Babbage, The Economy of Manufactures (1832), p. 30.

powerful steam compresses reduced the bulk of the cotton bales further in the port cities. Both changes made it possible to pack more bales into each ship, thereby cutting transport costs. Table 14.4 marks the persistent trend of cost reduction in distribution. Between 1790 and the outbreak of the Civil War the weight per bale exported actually doubled; its bulk was cut in half.[36]

Accepting New Technologies

"Their keenly competitive spirit," observed a distinguished visitor from Britain, "and pride in their own ingenuity, have made them quicker than any other people to adopt and adapt new inventions: telephones were in use in every town in the West, while in the City of London men were just beginning to wonder whether they could be made to pay."[37] Since technological advance permits man to have more goods with no more work, the persistent U.S. judgment has been "let it rip." But that willingness has only been achieved in the face of powerful vested interests.

TABLE 14.4
COTTON BALES

Year	Bulk on shipboard (cubic feet)	Average weight (pounds)	
		in U.S.	in U.K. imports
1790	60–80	200	
1803		259	
1819		350	
1822			267
1832		345	311
1840			367
1850		450	388
1860		450	429
1866	32–33	450–500	369
1870			386
1880			444
1890			475

Source: Appendix D, this chapter.

36. It fell from 60–80 cubic feet in 1790 to 32–33 cubic feet in 1866. Because the United Kingdom obtained most of its cotton from the United States, the trend in weight of the bales it imported is suggestive of trends for the United States. That relationship, of course, was markedly interrupted during and immediately after the Civil War.

37. James Bryce, *The American Commonwealth* (1890), 2:284.

The first of these, and perhaps not least important, is a deep emotional vested interest in favor of stability. When the steamboat was first introduced near Seville, Spaniards ran along the banks crying "Sorcery, sorcery."[38] When the first automobile was introduced in Britain (in 1836) it was charged twelve times as much in turnpike tolls as horse-drawn carriages. And Parliament, right up until the twentieth century, required automobiles to throttle down to two miles an hour in any city, and to be preceded by a man on foot carrying a red flag.[39]

The first U.S. cast-iron plow was patented as early as 1797; but as late as 1837 New Hampshire farmers warned ominously that the iron would "poison" the soil.[40] When railroads came along in the 1840s, another fearful prospect was described: crops would wilt, horses would run away, and cows would calve prematurely.[41] In 1776 John Sears constructed a salt works on Cape Cod to evaporate salt from sea water—just as the Portuguese had done for decades. His neighbors contemptuously called it "John Sears' Folly."[42] And when Fulton came along with the first American steamboat in 1814, it was (with equal simplicity) baptized "Fulton's Folly."[43]

A second set of vested interests were intellectual and financial. Those trained in older ways were threatened with obsolescence. "Don't talk to me about iron ships," growled the chief architect of a British dockyard; "it's contrary to nature."[44] When the stagecoach companies and tavern proprietors found they would be obsoleted by new technology—the railroads—they got city councils to hamper railroad entrance into the cities. Trains entering New York, Philadelphia, and Baltimore had to stop at the edge of the city, have the locomotive "separated from the train, and horses . . . attached, of which 4 generally draw an 8-wheeled car."[45]

In 1867 Roebling proposed to build the Brooklyn Bridge, using steel wire. The opposition warned of collapse and catastrophe—arguments that actually led the English Board of Trade (in 1877) to "prohibit the use of steel in any structures."[46]

38. George Borrow, *The Bible in Spain*, chap. XLVI.
39. Charles R. Gibson, *The Motor Car and Its Story* (1927), pp. 84–5.
40. U.S. Department of Agriculture, *Yearbook, 1899*, p. 316.
41. John Stover, *The Life and Decline of the American Railroad* (1970), pp. 16–17.
42. McLane Report, H.D. 308, *Documents Relative to the Manufactures in the United States* I (1833):91.
43. W. S. Lindsay, *History of Merchant Shipping and Ancient Commerce* IV (1876):58.
44. Ibid., p. 84. When a Dantzig inventor developed a loom that could weave several breadths of ribbon at once, the city council concluded that many weavers would be thrown out of work. They therefore arranged to have the inventor secretely, but effectively, strangled. Abbot P. Usher, *History of Mechanical Inventions* (1929, reprint ed. 1959), p. 281.
45. Franz Gerstner, "Railroads in the United States," *Journal of the Franklin Institute*, n.s. XXVI (October 1840):300.
46. David B. Steinman, *The Builders of the Bridge* (1945), p. 309.

Some inventors themselves hampered the spread of the new technologies. For they sought to collect the full economic rent from their invention, rather than sharing it with the buyers. Eli Whitney refused to sell his gins. Anticipating the policy of the United Shoe Machinery company in the 1890s he did not sell his machinery but would only rent it. His price? The value of one in every three pounds of cotton it cleaned.[47] Which worked out to about $8 a day—eight times as much as the $1 cost of using the older methods.[48] Since his gin was mechanically very similar to other gins, the incentive to make a similar gin, and pay no royalty, was enormous. The South Carolina legislature did eventually appropriate $50,000 for Whitney to enable planters to use the gins freely. But the Georgians and Alabamans laughed at his claims. And though he spent years going from court to court, the gin was widely used throughout the South, with few payments made to him. Oliver Evans patented an improved flour mill, charged a moderate $33 for each license to use his machinery. The market took off. And after Congress renewed his patent (in 1808) he raised his price, reaching $3,600 by 1812.[49] Edison invented the first phonograph in 1877. But it spread slowly, its "use being . . . on a royalty basis."[50]

Where patents couldn't be gotten, other methods of enforcing monopoly were tried. Thus Fulton teamed up with Chancellor Robert Livingstone, a major power in New York politics, to monopolize the use of steamboats on the Mississippi. But they were confronted by the obstreperous Captain Shreve. Shreve simply went full steam ahead, in and out of New Orleans, time after time, refusing any compromise. Fulton and Livingstone carried the case to the Supreme Court. And there they lost, in the celebrated case of *Livingstone versus Ogden*. In both instances the claims were so broad that the development of a dozen states would have been at the mercy of a pair of individuals. The thousands of would-be entrepreneurs, and the workers and regions that would benefit from such development, could not be held back by transient legalities.

One entrepreneurial tactic to reduce the risk of innovation was to imitate another nation as closely as possible. When, in 1767, Dr. Turnbull sought to

47. James Sherer, *Cotton as a World Power* (1916), p. 164. The lint was then selling for 30 cents a pound.

48. His first gin cleaned about 80 pounds a day. One third of 80 pounds, with cotton at 30 cents a pound, meant an $8 rent. Slave labor could be hired at 50 cents a day, cleaning 80 pounds in 2 days.

49. American State Papers, *Miscellaneous*, II (1834), p. 225. The petitioners found that "he began to advance from exaction to exaction" and charging "twenty times . . . his former charge . . . threatens that he will rise still higher [and] from one of your memorialists . . . has demanded thirty-six hundred dollars."

50. 1900 Census of Manufactures, part IV, p. 181. Subsequent litigation over shoe machinery (United Shoe Machinery) and computers (IBM) involved more successful attempts to rent rather than sell.

plant mulberry trees and grape vines in Florida he did not hire native labor. Instead, he went to the expense of importing 200 Greek mountaineers, 100 Italians, and some residents of Minorca. These presumably had the required know-how.[51] In the 1780s the Philadelphia Society for Useful Manufactures advertised in Europe for skilled artisans to come over to America and reproduce the machines they were accustomed to making in Europe. Samuel Slater read their advertisement, did indeed come to the United States. He then developed the machinery for Almy and Brown of Providence, creating the first large-scale U.S. spinning mill. (Slater was offered in effect all the profits of innovation for the first seven years of his work.) In 1801 E. I. DuPont decided to establish his first power mill. To do so he returned to France, got both machinery and capital there to use back in Delaware.[52] Just after the Civil War, the Prudential Life Insurance Company sought to introduce insurance to the mass market—in the form of "industrial insurance" sold at 5 cents a week to wage earners. To do so they "adopted the essential principles" as well as life tables and data of the London company that had pioneered such insurance.[53]

The high salaries paid to foreign experts point out the importance attached to the transfer of technology. U.S. calico printing was first attempted in Dover, New Hampshire, and Taunton, Massachusetts, in 1826. It followed hard upon the first factory production of plain cotton sheeting.[54] John Prince, master printer of Manchester, England, was brought over to supervise the first print works of the Merrimac Company. He was paid $10,000 a year. That lordly figure exceeded the sum paid to Kirk Boot, general agent in charge of the entire mill operation, of which the print works was only part.[55] Transferring knowledge ("human capital") in this way enabled the United States to jump ahead quickly, as Japan, Korea, and Hong Kong were to do a century later.

The vigorous development of better species of food plants and animals affords an example of advances that could freely be introduced by any farmer who wished to do so. Moreover, to introduce them he had to do little more than plant one variety of seed rather than another, breed from one type of animal rather than another. But to introduce non-farm innovations often required changes in other productive inputs and techniques. And these were

51. L. C. Gray, *History of Agriculture in the Southern United States to 1860* (1933), I:111–12.

52. Francis DuPont in Chauncey de Pew, *One Hundred Years of American Commerce* (1895), p. 193.

53. John Dryden, *Addresses and Papers on Life Insurance and Other Subjects* (1909), pp. 40, 47. On the extensive consultations with English companies, see Frederick Hoffman, *History of the Prudential Insurance Company of America* (1900), pp. 60, 94.

54. E. J. Donnell, *Chronological and Statistical History of Cotton* (1872), p. 94.

55. William R. Bagnall, *Sketches of Manufacturing in Textile Establishments*, Victor Clark, ed. (1908), p. 2172. Typescript in the Baker Library, Harvard Business School.

bob-tailed, limited, or delayed in order to permit such integration. An obvious example is the use of locomotives to bring trains into the terminal sheds,
usually in the midst of a busy city. As already noted, railroad trains entering
New York, Philadelphia, and Baltimore had to stop at the edge of town, have
the locomotive "separated from the train, and horses . . . attached, of which
4 generally draw an 8-wheeled car."[56] Eventually, steam locomotives puffed
into new stations in new locations, saving time and cost. The locomotive
could be used most of the distance, yet the town was not completely disturbed by steam engines entering in the midst of horse carts, drays, and carriages. When the Philadelphia, Germantown, and Norristown railroad began
operation engines lacked an adequately enclosed cab. The railroad therefore
used "Old Ironsides" in fair weather, but used horses to draw the trains in
rainy weather.[57]

When Fulton took the first steamboat out of New York harbor in 1808,
the Clermont had "large square sails attached to masts"—insurance against
the failure of the primitive steam engine. And because the metal working abilities of the nation were still so infantile, no reliable steel boiler could be made.
Instead he used a wooden boiler, bound with heavy iron bands—which "contained the steam so inadequately that the boiler had to be covered with carpets
and blankets to keep some of the steam from escaping."[58] Whether Fulton's
was the first steamboat in the United States is arguable. Ramsey and Fitch apparently had invented boats that were propelled by steam for some distance in
the 1780s. Fulton propelled a scow by steam in 1807, but the Clermont was
apparently the first steam passenger boat.

When the first trains were introduced in the United States, the production of adequate steel rails was far off in the future. Ignorance of the chemis-
try involved and the lack of long years of experimentation did not actually
prevent the introduction of railroad transport. But the engines were designed
to work on iron straps nailed down onto wooden rails. On more than one occasion the engineering inadequacies of the enterprise brought shame to the
cheeks of the entrepreneurs. At the opening of the Boston and Worcester
Railroad the power of the locomotive, and the ability of its wheels to grip the
track, were such that it could not make the upgrade at nearby Westboro.
There the passengers got out and helped push it over the top.[59]

A bewildering set of inventions and innovations advanced U.S. productivity, and thereby investment, from such oddities as Ramsay's paddle steam
boat to Glidden's improved barbed wire. Science was at work, sometimes.
Coarse empiricism—try and try again—was at work, many times. (The dis-

56. Franz Gerstner, "Railroads in the United States," *Journal of the Franklin Institute*, n.s.
XXVI (October 1840):300.
57. John C. Trautwine, *The Philadelphia and Columbia Railroad of 1834* (1925), p. 160.
58. Hunt's Merchants Magazine (November 1858), p. 627.
59. Joseph G. Martin, *A Century of Finance* (1898), p. 232.

tinction between the laborious laboratory work of the one and the persistent, more random ventures of the other was not particularly obvious in the nineteenth century. Nor was it analytically clear at any time.) The willingness to adopt these novelties involved, in a critical way, the fact that Americans welcomed novelty—of innovations or of immigrants. Immigrants, however, brought in turn new ideas and challenged existing ways. Whether they did so on the basis of European wisdom, or mere ignorance, their arrival enhanced the competition of ideas, making the competition of markets persistently more effective.

Appendix

Appendix A: Sources

These estimates are a simplified version of those given in *De Bow's Review* (1850), pp. 435–37. They are sufficiently close in orders of magnitude to focus reasonably on the profit difference. We assume an increase in expenses because picking costs are doubled, given the opportunity cost of such time.

The seed price, and sowing rate of 2 bushels per acre, are from Commissioner of Patents, *Annual Report* (1848), p. 659. (A 75-pound average is reported for South Carolina. Lower figures also appear in the 1880 Census of Agriculture, *Report on Cotton Production* (1884), part 1, pp. 351, 813, and passim.)

Appendix B: Sources

1800 ("Early nineteenth century"), 1854: Wailes (1854) quoted in M. B. Hammond, *The Cotton Industry* (1897), p. 77.

1810, 1850–60: *Southern Cultivator* (1861) quoted in Paul Gates, *Agriculture and the Civil War* (1965), p. 14.

1825: *Niles*, XXIX (December 24, 1825):259; 100 for women, 175 for men.

1841, 1895: 13th Annual Report of the Commissioner of Labor, 1898, *Hand and Machine Labor* (1899), II:443.

1850s: Solomon Northup, *Twelve Years a Slave* (reprint ed. 1968), p. 125: "ordinary day's work is considered 200 pounds."

1850s: *Louisiana Historical Quarterly* (October 1950), 33:362.

1866 ("Fine weather"): J. Talboys Wheeler, *Madras Versus America: A Handbook to Cotton Cultivation* (1866), p. 96; Wheeler reports 7 to 10 pounds for the "usual days work" in India.

1868: Joseph B. Lyman, *Cotton Culture* (1868), p. 15; 100 for "slow" and 200 for "good" pickers.

1896: James L. Watkins, *The Cost of Cotton Production* (1899), U.S. Department of Agriculture, Misc. Bull. 16, p. 7, indicates for a large sample of Southern farms a cost of 44 cents for picking 100 pounds. A daily average Southern wage of $1.05 for common labor in turn implies a picking average of 240 pounds. (Wage data in Lebergott, *Manpower in Economic Growth*, Table A-23.)

1958: 85th Cong., 2d sess., House Committee on Agriculture, *Farm Labor*, p. 378. Mexican workers were paid $2.50 for 100 pounds, picking 225 pounds a day.

These data reflect standard tasks. Actual plantation records show time allocated to ginning, etc., during the picking season. Cf. Jacob Metzer, "Rational Management . . . ," *Explorations in Economic History* (1975), 12:136.

Appendix C: Sources

1788 gin: Richard Leake, 1788, quoted in *Niles*, VI (July 16, 1813):334.

1788 hand, 1866: U.S. Commissioner of Agriculture, *Report for 1866* (1866), p. 202.

1793: J. Mirsky and A. Nevins, *The World of Eli Whitney* (1952), p. 76, quote Whitney writing to Jefferson, stating that a laborer cleaned 60 to 80 weight per day. On p. 66 Whitney is quoted to the effect that one man could clean ten times as much as by any other method.

1800: A writer in the *Merchants Magazine* (December 1861), pp. 562–63, who "entered an East India counting house in Philadelphia in 1804" states that as of 1800 Whitney's gin could clean 350 pounds, versus one pound by hand. A similar figure appears in Francois Michaux, *Travels to the West* (1805), pp. 241–43, comparing 300–400 pounds to 30 "by the usual method"—presumably the more primitive gins.

Appendix D: Sources

U.S. weight—1790, 1832: 24th Cong., 1st sess., H.D. 146, *Cotton*, p. 5.

1803: Kinsey Burden in *DeBow's*, 19 (1803):125.

1819: American State Papers, *Commerce and Navigation* (1834), II.411 estimates typical shipping costs from New Orleans, using a 350-pound weight.

1850: *DeBow's*, VII (1850):559 quotes the *Charleston Mercury* as indicating cotton bales shipped at Charleston averaged 350 pounds—which we use as comparable with Burden's 1803 figure. Savannah cotton averaged 450 pounds.

1850, 1860: Exports to the United Kingdom averaged 423 pounds in 1850 and 447 pounds in 1850. *Merchants Magazine*, 45 (July 1861):9.

U.S. bulk: Commissioner of Agriculture, *Report for 1866*, p. 203.

U.K. weight: Average weight of bales consumed by mills: Liverpool Cotton Association, quoted in 53d Cong., 3d sess., S.R. 986, part 2, *Report . . . on Cotton*, pp. 157–58.

The whole of Elizabethan literature [is] strewn with gold
and silver; with talk of Guiana's rarities, and references to
that America—'Oh my America! my new-found land'—
which was not merely a land on the map, but symbolized
the unknown territories of the soul.
—VIRGINIA WOOLF, "The Elizabethan Lumber Room"

15

Immigration

WHY did five million people move from Europe, Asia, and Africa to the
United States between 1820 and the Civil War? The most ingenious
explanation was undoubtedly proposed by Dr. Raphael Dubois of the University of Lyons. The good doctor built a device to prove that man was irresistibly impelled westward, as a squirrel in a cage—because the earth ro-
tated eastward.[1]

A less ingenious, but testable, theory was put forward in 1809 by a great
American engineer (who incidentally, developed the Baldwin apple).
Loammi Baldwin wrote:

> Every man will endeavor to improve his circumstances by a change of occu-
> pation, or by a change of place. He fixes a standard mark of enjoyments, by
> a comparison of his present situation with what the new and unpeopled dis-
> trict holds out to him.[2]

For convenience one can imagine him comparing a Prospect in Europe with a
Prospect in the United States. A "Prospect" would include the total set of
economic and psychological returns that he could expect—from remaining in
Europe or from removing, say, to the United States. The prospect can be un-
realistically optimistic in one case, unduly pessimistic in another. But it will
nonetheless constitute the basis on which he decides whether to move. (As
with any consumer item it was not actual but anticipated joy that motivated

1. Robert Coates, *The Outlaw Years* (1930), pp. 11–12.
2. Loammi Baldwin, *Thoughts on the Study of Political Economy* (1809), p. 15.

the purchase of a ticket to America.) But, in fact, about 90 percent of those who migrated to the United States before the Civil War did remain. Only ten percent returned.[3] Moreover, not even all those who returned were discouraged or unhappy. Many had made their grub stake, then returned to Europe able to buy a farm, to pay a dowry, to get married.[4] For millions of Europeans, then, the prospect in the United States proved preferable to the prospect in Europe.[5]

What was the European prospect? Surely an enormously harsh one by present standards. But, more relevant, it was harsh by comparison with the United States of the same period. What about France in the 1840s—the France of fine wine, romantic poetry, of Lamartine, Chopin, Balzac, George Sand? Michael Chevalier compared life in France and the United States.

> In France nothing is more common in the countryside than to meet a poor woman crushed under the weight of a load of wheat or fuel. If you have been in the Pyrenees you would have seen them carrying the very harvest down from the mountain heights, returning with their shoulders laden not merely with fuel for cooking, but the earth that the rains have brought down . . . one even sees them hammering iron [as blacksmiths]. So sad a spectacle will never meet your eyes in England or the United States . . . women are completely freed from work requiring great physical effort."[6]

Russia? The Volga boatmen, of romantic legend, typically pulled huge barges along the river, towing them by ropes around their necks and shoulders.[7] (Men also pulled canal boats in Belgium and France as late as the twentieth century.) In Saxony, Hungary, and Poland as well, feudal remnants restrained life and choice as in Russia.

England? In 1842 Cobden declared that twenty-five thousand miners in Staffordshire were unemployed. "He knew of a place where a hundred wedding rings had been pawned in a single week to provide bread; and of another place where men and women subsisted on boiled nettles, and dug up the de-

---

3. Walter F. Willcox, *Studies in American Demography* (1940), p. 390.

4. In the depression year 1842 "out of 51,800 that arrived at New York, the Customs House reports show that the business depression caused the return of 9,521." In 1854, a prosperous year, the returnee total of 12,000 compares with immigration of 428,000. Thomas W. Page, "Economic aspects of immigration before 1870," *Journal of Political Economy* (January 1913), p. 54. The 3 percent returnee ratio for 1854 undoubtedly applied to most years in this period, the 20 percent ratio in 1842 to few. Therefore, these figures are consistent with Willcox's guess.

5. The 9 to 1 vote for the United States does not *per se* prove that the prospect in the United States worked out better: Some of the 9, faced with the costs of returning, would not or could not pay the emotional and financial costs. But the margin is so great that "by and large" seems a safe statement.

6. Michel Chevalier, *Cours d'Economie Politique* (1842), pp. 160–61. I translate "great physical effort" for Chevalier's "des travaux de force."

7. Cf. the photograph in *Soviet Russia Today* (November 1969), p. 23.

cayed carcass of a cow rather than perish of hunger." He went on to warn Parliament of the economic consequences.

> We are sowing the seeds broadcast for a plentiful harvest of workmen in the western world. . . . They are not going [i.e., emigrating] by dozens or scores to teach the people of other countries the work they have learnt—they are going in hundreds and thousands to those states to open works against our own machines, and to bring this country to a worse state than it is now in. There is nothing to atone for a system which leads to this; and if I were to seek for a parallel it would be only in the Revocation of the Edict of Nantes by Louis XIV . . . where the best men were banished from their country.[8]

England recovered from the depression of 1842. And it lost a smaller proportion of its population to the United States than a dozen other nations. Yet the prospect it offered thousands of its citizens seemed bleak indeed.

In European nations when small farmers died their land was typically divided among their children. As time passed, therefore, the typical size of farms became smaller and smaller, in many instances too small to permit even the eldest son to marry and support a family. This became increasingly obvious in southern Germany, Austria, Switzerland, and Norway in the first half of the nineteenth century.[9] "Many a farmer could not provide his sons with tools, much less a respectable tract of land."[10] Ireland, East Germany, western Russia, Sicily were dotted with great landed estates, and these were typically worked by landless peasants.[11] And these were ripe for emigration whenever the restraints of feudal life and ancient law were removed. When Italy and Russia ended their laws against emigration, their immigrants flooded into the United States.

A prospect in America, on the most elementary level, included a more reliable supply of food than in Europe. "Give us this day our daily bread" was an ancient and urgently meant prayer in Europe. Some 450 European famines were recorded between the year 1000 and 1855.[12] The ordinary U.S. diet was considerably more substantial than that in almost any European nation. For example, in France, that nation of haute cuisine, men in 1789 were accustomed to eating meat "only during the last days of carnival, on Easter and on birthdays."[13] But the average American ate meat daily.[14] When the president

---

8. Quoted in John Morley, *Life of Cobden* (1881), pp. 164–65.

9. United Nations, *The Determinants and Consequences of Population Trends* (1953), p. 112.

10. Marcus Hansen, *The Atlantic Migration* (1961), pp. 163, 221.

11. Ibid., p. 113.

12. "Famine" in *Encyclopedia of the Social Sciences* (1932).

13. According to the Cahiers of 1789. D. Avenel, *Paysans et Ouvriers*, quoted in P. Sorokin, *Hunger* (1975), p. 258.

14. *Niles Register* (Dec. 2, 1815), p. 230; (June 28, 1817), pp. 273–75.

of the Chesapeake and Ohio Canal Company sought workers to dig that canal he wrote to the U.S. Consul in Liverpool: "meat, three times a day, and plenty of bread and vegetables, with a reasonable allowance of liquor, and eight, ten or twelve dollars a month [should] prove a powerful attraction to those who . . . have a year of scarcity presented to them."[15] Many Europeans discovered that there was no place for them at Nature's feast: "The tables are all occupied—there is neither knife, fork nor wooden spoon to spare."[16] But in America "every necessary of life is sluttishly plentiful . . . it is not possible here to find a man hungry."[17] Millions reacted to that difference. They followed the advice given to the Irish peasant: "to work or beg his passage over . . . so that at all events he may quit his native island . . . that den of human wretchedness."[18]

Beyond the fundamental assurance of regular food, and better, America offered a chance to rise in the social and economic scale. That opportunity was not, of course, as Josiah Tucker airily described it: "estates for nothing and become gentlemen farmers."[19] Chevalier was closer to the truth: "Figure to yourself an Irish peasant, who at home could scarcely earn enough to live on potatoes . . . stepping ashore at New York finds himself able to earn a dollar a day by the mere strength of his arm. He feeds and lodges himself for two dollars a week, and at the end of a fortnight he may have saved enough to buy ten acres of the most fertile land in the world."[20] Europeans discovered the right to move freely across the nation without legal restraint, a right unprecedented in much of Europe, plus the no less unprecedented opportunity to buy land at low prices. These opportunities permitted men who were prepared to work and save to buy farms of their own. Equal application, hard work, saving, rarely afforded European workers any such opportunity.[21]

Those not dedicated to a life in farming discovered that the chance to rise from unskilled to skilled occupations in the United States, even to managerial and professional ones, was not as inevitably blocked off as it had been in Europe. (John Stuart Mill even described the European stratification system with "so strongly marked a line of demarcation, between the different grades

15. Mercer to Maury (November 28, 1828). Chesapeake and Ohio Letterbook, U.S. National Archives (1828), pp. 38–39.

16. John Regan, *The Emigrants Guide* (1846), p. 10.

17. James Caird, *Prairie Farming* (1859), p. 94.

18. Newnham Blane, *An Excursion through the United States and Canada during the Years 1822–23 by an English Gentleman* (1824), pp. 169–70.

19. Quoted in L. Hacker, *Shaping of the American Tradition* (1947), p. 193.

20. M. Chevalier, *Manners and Politics in the United States* (1836), pp. 143–44.

21. Ten acres would provide a functioning self-subsistence farm. Any time up to the Civil War they could be bought from the federal government for $1.25 an acre (or less)—the equivalent of the cash wages typically paid farm laborers for one month's work (above and beyond their food and lodging). Public credit was provided up until 1819. Private credit was available throughout the period. It was therefore possible for many a migrant to buy a cow, a few farm animals, and minimum equipment, as well as the land, over the course of a few years.

of labourers, as to be almost equivalent to a hereditary distribution of caste."[22])

Three other factors sped migration to the United States. First, a far brighter prospect awaited children. For they could begin life with all the expected advantages offered by the United States. That incentive particularly attracted young people just beginning to establish their families. (The typical U.S. immigrant before the Civil War was relatively young: immigrants aged 15–40 were six times as numerous as those over 40.[23]) Second, to Mormons, Quakers, Methodists, Jews, Communitarians, Dunkers, to every minor religious group, the United States offered a greater chance to practice its religion freely than European nations, most of which imposed state religions. Third, taxes in the United States were substantially lower. "One of the great advantages of the American government is its cheapness. The American King has about £5,000 . . . the Vice-King, £1,000. They hire their Lord Liverpool at about a thousand per annum and their Lord Sidmouth (a good bargain) at the same sum. . . . Life, however, seems to go on very well, in spite of these low salaries."[24]

In October 1641 the selectmen of Boston boarded the *Seaflower*, bound from Belfast for Philadelphia, but detoured by storms and lack of food. They found that the immigrants had been reduced "to such miserable circumstances that they were Obliged in Order to Sustain Life to feed upon the Bodys of Six Persons that Died in the Passage . . . as they were cutting up the Seventh, they Espied [a ship which] . . . supplied them with Men and Provisions sufficient to bring 'em into this port . . ."[25] Such ghastly voyages were few. Yet the fear of starvation, of death from disease, of shipwreck, deterred many immigrants, menaced the decision to migrate with fear and trembling. The dangers and terrors of the "mid passage" of slaves from Africa to the New World may have killed one slave in ten. But the death rates for free immigrants from Europe to the United States were probably greater: their deaths brought no financial loss to their owners.[26]

22. *Principles of Political Economy*, Book II, chap. 14.

23. *Historical Statistics of the U.S. . . . to 1970*, p. 112. The young, with many years ahead to compensate them for the break with family and homeland, were far more likely to migrate than the old.

24. Sydney Smith, "America," *The Edinburgh Review* (December 1818). "The Americans, we believe, are the first persons who have discarded the tailor in the administration of justice and his auxiliary the barber—two persons of endless importance in the codes and pandects of Europe. A judge administers justice without a calorific wig and particoloured gown."

25. Records of the Boston Selectmen, quoted by Marcus Jernegan, *Laboring and Dependent Classes in Colonial America* (1931), p. 206.

26. Mortality rates of about 9 percent for Portuguese slavers into Brazil 1795–1811, and 15 percent for French slavers out of Nantes appear in two fundamental studies: Herbert Klein, *The*

Probably the most notorious horrors marked the pell-mell migration from the Irish famine, in which more than a million people died. In May 1847 some 84 ships reached Montreal from Ireland. Not one was free of typhus. Of roughly 100,000 migrants who had left for Canada, an estimated 20,000 died, either at quarantine or shortly after their arrival in Canada.[27] Death rates in the migration to the United States proved to be nowhere near so spectacular. But some deaths on shipboard were almost inevitable. In 1867 the *Leibnitz* left Hamburg for New York. Cholera killed 20 percent of her passengers before they touched port.[28]

The arriving immigrants, of course, spread disease and death with their arrival—particularly before quarantine was tight. In the "cholera year" of 1832 "ships freighted with emigrants sick with cholera continued to arrive." As the immigrants

> speedily dispersed . . . throughout the states, the cholera followed as an epidemic. . . . Again in 1848–49, immediately after the arrival [at New Orleans] of cholera-infected emigrants from Havre . . . the epidemic took its course up the Mississippi . . . and in a single fortnight, at dates which in each river port correspond with the first week after the arrival of steamboats with the first cholera patients on board, the disease made its outbreak.[29]

The death rate in transit (for the decades prior to the Civil War) ran about 12 passengers per 1,000 during the two-month passage.[30] The death rate, therefore, at an annual rate, was about seven times as great as that for the United States in the 1970s. And by the mid nineteenth century it somewhat exceeded that for slaves imported from Africa.[31]

Middle Passage (1978), p. 55, and Philip Curtin, *The Atlantic Slave Trade: A Census* (1969), pp. 280–85. For the eighteenth century death rates for free immigrants on the shorter passage over ran to 15–20 percent (Klein, *Passage*, p. 70).

27. *Transactions of the American Medical Association* (1848), vol. 1. Some 14,000 died at Gross Isle, in quarantine; a further 5,000 in Montreal and Quebec. The estimate of one million deaths is from Joel Mokyr's "The Deadly Fungus," in Julian Simon, *Research in Population Economics* (1980), p. 248.

28. Report of the Commissioners of Immigration, printed in Edith Abbott, *Immigration, Select Documents and Case Records* (1924), p. 42.

29. "In river towns a thousand miles distant from each other, the epidemic made its appearance [when] the first cholera patients arrived by the steamboats." Dr. Elisha Harris, in *Reports . . . of the American Public Health Association*, reprinted in ibid., p. 47.

30. Based on a Treasury investigation of sailing ships in 1867, quoted in ibid., p. 48. Lower rates for passages from the United Kingdom, and for one season, appear in Klein, *Passage*, p. 91.

31. Warren S. Howard, *American Slaves and the Federal Law, 1837–62* (1963), p. 609, gives data for the number shipped and the number dying on the way. The data for numbers landed that are given in round numbers are likely to be vague guesses. We use instead the data for voyages where the number landed is reported in digits not ending in zero. The median rate for such voyages is 8 per 1,000. For a variety of reasons the Portuguese slavers had higher rates. These are cited in Klein, *Passage*, pp. 88–89.

No less important than the dangers of the transfer were the financial costs. These fell markedly. Steerage rates from Liverpool were cut by nearly two-thirds between 1816 and 1832.[32]

Packet boats introduced regular service in the 1820s. No longer did passengers have to wait until the vessel had collected a full complement of passengers. (Regular immigrant sailings, however, did not become common for decades.) Together with some changes in legislative provisions urged by Immigrants Associations, these worked to reduce the costs, uncertainties, and dangers of migration. Thus the decline in fares, plus such amelioration, steadily cut transfer costs in the nineteenth century.

The first wave of immigrants to the United States in the eighteenth century included many who could not scrape together enough money for the passage over. To make their passage possible they adopted an ancient labor market device—the indenture. Eighteenth-century parents, and early nineteenth-century ones, were accustomed to indenture their children for 6 or 7 years service to craftsmen or shopkeepers. In return, their employers would feed and clothe them and teach them the "mystery" of their crafts. Hence the precedent for "cash now, work later" was well known. Its application to emigrants made it possible for them to get out of Europe. (In a world where sailors did not charge for their services, pleasanter methods of finance would surely have developed. As nineteenth-century productivity advances in shipping cut fares, they did.)

Immigrants initially chose between ships sailing for the Caribbean or the mainland, since planters in the colonies competed for labor with planters in the Caribbean. As early as 1675 the Council and Assembly of Barbados regretted that "now we can gett few English, haveing no Lands to give them at the end of their tyme."[33] White servants preferred to pay for their passage by indenturing on the mainland. They were typically willing to indenture for 8 months longer in Maryland (where they could get land) than in Antigua (where they could not, and where death rates were higher).[34] When the vessels tied up in Baltimore, or another eastern harbor, the captain would put a notice in the papers stating that he had men and women with time for sale. Buyers who had read of the arrival in the *Post Boy*, or *Gazette*, would then come aboard and bargain over the indentures. Because some passengers "attempted running away privately with their Children and Effects," passengers

32. Marcus Hansen, *The Atlantic Migration* (1961), p. 198. Fares fell from £10 or £12 to £4 in ordinary trading vessels. Packets (which had begun regular, prompt service in the late 1820s) charged £6. The decline for the LeHavre to New York trip in the same fifteen-year stretch was similar.

33. Quoted in David Galenson, *White Servitude in Colonial America* (1981), p. 110.

34. As indicated by regression coefficients in Galenson, *Servitude*, pp. 110, 104.

were confined on shipboard until they struck a bargain with a purchaser, or until the captain had finally sold their services.[35]

By the time of the American Revolution over one-third of the white immigrants coming to the United States were indenturing themselves.[36] For an average term of 4 years, plus a customary suit of clothes as freedom dues, they were able to pay the usual passage cost of £5 or £6. (Some 16,000 Americans at that time were still indentured, while many others—e.g., Charles Thomson, Secretary of the Continental Congress—had only recently completed their indentures.)

The indenture route was used less and less as time went on. One central reason was that steerage fares declined substantially. As trade expanded, even more ships left for European ports loaded with lumber, cotton, tobacco, and wheat. But these ships returned from Europe with cargoes of textiles, tea, tin trays, drugs—high value with less bulk. The excess cargo space could be made to yield a profit—in "back freight." The motivation was not humanitarian. It was not cultural. "I have no motive in it beyond a back freight to ships I am interested in," a Liverpool forwarder told Parliament in 1826.[37] Furthermore, the back freight loaded itself aboard ship. Soon builders began to build ships specialized to immigrant transport, and these drove down fares even further. The fare from Le Havre to New Orleans was cut by two-thirds from 1818 to the early 1830s.[38]

Where did the immigrants go once they reached the United States? By and large they fled slavery as the plague. Hence, only 10 percent of the 1850 foreign-born population lived in the South, although that region contained 25 percent of the native-born population.[39] A survey of the immigrants crowding into New York in 1855–60 (where most immigrants to the United States arrived) asked their destination. A mere 3 percent declared it to be the Southern states (even fewer than the percent who planned to go on to Canada).[40]

One reason was their reluctance to go where labor was equated with slavery, and where the region's leaders had expressed their contempt for labor. Did not George McDuffie, John C. Calhoun's great lieutenant in Congress, refer to labor "bleached or unbleached [as] a dangerous element in the body politic"?[41] And did not a southern paper characteristically describe free soci-

35. *Pennsylvania Archives*, 8th Series, VII:5720.

36. See derivation of this figure in Appendix, this chapter.

37. Quoted in Marcus Hansen, *The Atlantic Migration* (1961), p. 179.

38. Maldwyn Jones, *American Immigration* (1960), p. 105.

39. Computed from J. D. B. DeBow, *Statistical View of the United States* (1854), p. 118.

40. Data from the Annual Reports of the Commissioners of Emigration given in Robert Ernst, *Immigrant Life in New York City, 1825–1863* (1949), Appendix Table 10.

41. *Congressional Globe, Appendix*, 52d Cong., 1st sess., vol. XXIII, part VIII.

ety as "a conglomeration of greasy mechanics, filthy operatives and small fisted farmers"?[42]

Immigrants likewise fled the plague and other diseases. The extremely high death rates in the South from yellow fever and malaria were universally feared.[43] "The dread of yellow fever and other maladies common among strangers in a southern climate" deterred immigrants from going south and even from going to the Midwest via the Mississippi.[44]

Most immigrants remained on the East Coast, where they had landed. Though in 1850 New York, Massachusetts, and Pennsylvania together contained 30 percent of the native-born population, they contained 50 percent of the foreign born.[45] Immigrants hesitated to pay the additional emotional and financial costs of moving inland. Most English and Irish immigrants stayed in the East. However, the other major wave of immigrants in the pre-civil war decades—the Germans—pushed on to the Midwest. (And virtually all Norwegian immigrants went on to the North Central region.)

Many immigrants, if not most, settled in cities. By 1850 about 40 percent of the foreign-born population lived in large cities.[46] But most Irish immigrants came from cottier farms. Many others had moved from rural areas. Why did they not seek the cheap farmland in the United States where they could utilize skills they already possessed? The attractions of living in East Coast cities was surely one factor. Many had their passage prepaid by those who went before them. (Perhaps half of all Irish migrants in 1834 did so; three-fourths by 1850.)[47] For them, living near or with the relatives who paid or loaned passage money was surely to be expected. There they could count on having neighbors who shared the same background, could speak the dialect (or language) of the old country. There too the other advantages of urban living spoke to them. The balance of urban attractiveness differed, however, between the different nationality groups. Thus, by 1860 Germans and Irish had come to the United States roughly in equal numbers. But from twice to ten times as many Irish as Germans lived in Boston, Albany, Troy, Providence, Philadelphia, and Brooklyn. Quite the reverse was true in St. Louis, Cincinnati, and Louisville.[48]

42. Quoted in *Congressional Globe, Appendix*, 35th Cong., 1st sess., March 20, 1858.

43. In November 1837 the ship Nestor sailed from New York to New Orleans with 212 passengers; 132 died of yellow fever. *Niles* (November 18, 1837), p. 192.

44. Thomas W. Page, "The Transportation of Immigrants," *Journal of Political Economy* (1911), pp. 736–37.

45. J. D. B. DeBow, *Statistical View* (1854), p. 61.

46. Ibid., p. 123, gives data for the English, Irish, Germans and Prussians—nationalities which then included many of the foreign-born population.

47. The percentages are from Oliver MacDonagh, "The Irish Famine Emigration to the United States," *Perspectives in American History* (1976) X:394–95.

48. 1860 Census, *Population* (1864), pp. xxxi,xxxii.

The migration flow to the United States until the Civil War rose massively decade after decade:[49]

1790–1800	50
1801–1810	70
1811–1820	114
1821–1830	143
1831–1840	599
1841–1850	1,713
1851–1860	2,598

Behind that flow basic factors were at work: the difference between an American and a European prospect, the costs of transfer both financial and emotional, and the amount of information a potential immigrant had about these matters. Added to these were the driving effect of shocks in Europe and Asia. These included revolutions in Poland in 1830, in France and Austria in 1848, the 1832 Reform Act in Britain and the ending of its Corn Laws in 1846—all of which sped migration.

Year-to-year timing of migration generated by these forces was a different matter. That variation proved to be largely set by three forces.[50] One was the year-to-year variation in aggregate incomes in the United States. (Immigration tended to slump a year after business downturns, such as in 1837, 1842, and 1857; it tended to rise a year after such high prosperity years as 1836 or 1853.) A second force proved to be changes in railroad construction. Thus the bunching of heavy immigration in a very few years, 1850–1854, reflected both the opportunities for employment building the new lines, producing the iron and lumber that the lines demanded, and producing for the future consumer markets expanded by such investment.[51] Finally, the changing financial cost of passage from Europe was a powerful force: the lower the price went, the more migration rose.

We know that some broad measures comparing conditions in the United States to those in both Europe and Asia should have been used; that jobs were

---

49. Estimates for 1790–1820 from U.S. Census, Eighth Census, *Population of the United States in 1860* (1864), p. 18; See also U.S. Census, *Historical Statistics to 1970* (1975), p. 106.

50. Annual migration = $90,050 + .754Im + 96.09RR - 1023ST$. Im is the quantum of imports into the United States; RR is the annual rate of change in the number of miles of railroads built; and ST is an index of freight rates, taken as a proxy for the trend in steerage rates. The coefficient of determination, $R^2 = .712$. The drama of the revolutions is captured in such studies as Peter Stearns, *1848: The Revolutionary Tide in Europe* (1974). But there is little basis for inferring any major contribution to U.S. immigration. Thus immigration from Germany in 1848–49, the aftermath of revolution and counterrevolution, differed little from levels in 1846 and 1847.

51. Westward expansion also resulted from the cut in price of federal lands (the Graduation Act of 1854 reduced land prices, which were further reduced as soldiers threw on the market their land warrants issued under the Acts of 1847–52 for service in wars going back to the Revolution); and from the discovery of gold in California.

available not merely in railroad construction but in other industries as well; that freight rates did not necessarily move in strict proportion to steerage rates, as we have assumed. The true correlation, therefore, is likely to be even greater than that reported here.

Mass migration to the United States shaped the U.S. economy in a variety of ways.[52] Most vital was the continuous instability it brought. Local monopolies of labor and enterprise were broken up by immigrants. Techniques of production were upset by the succession of new views and conflicting attitudes. Where business had a monopoly, where labor controlled entry to an occupation, where engineers promulgated a traditional method of production—there resources were unlikely to be used with high efficiency. But the free market in ideas, the persistent competition of novelty, kept surfacing ever more efficient production techniques, then got them adopted. It is no mere chance that the greater stability of production methods in the plantation South contrasted with continuous change, industrialization, and economic advance of the North. For the flow of immigrants to the North and West was never ending; that to the South was minuscule.

If the immigrants had all come from a single nation, social group, or tradition, no such conclusion would apply. For British production techniques, or Russian, or Cantonese, were unlikely to suit the development of, say, Omaha or Cleveland—given relative costs in the United States. But the mixture of immigrants from such differing backgrounds prevented any one group from imposing its procedures by mere reference to its tradition, its national authority. Men from Wales brought one technique for mining. They were confronted by men from Styria who brought another, and by still others from Italy, who brought a third. When the copper mines of northern Michigan were opened, or the coal mines of western Pennsylvania, these traditions came into conflict. All were tried, adapted, changed drastically. The combination suited to American resource patterns of the time had to be worked out.

All other things being equal—and they surely were not—the flow of immigrants would inevitably have hammered down U.S. wage rates. A greater supply of labor, as with any input, tended to push down its price. In addition, the immigrants from countries with far lower standards of living—China, Sicily, Ireland—accepted lower levels of incomes than that demanded by older Americans. They could survive on lower incomes and even save money; such incomes still exceeded those in their homeland.

52. The subject of the contribution immigrants made because their support during youth had taken place in foreign countries has been studied by Paul Uselding and Larry Neal, who conclude that in 1839–59 the value of such human capital came to at least one-half that of gross physical capital formation in the U.S. The subject is reviewed by Robert Gallman, "Human Capital in the First 80 years of the Republic," *American Economic Review* (February 1977).

This sequence helps explain why New England Yankees fought the Irish in the 1840s; why the Irish rioted against the New York blacks in the 1860s; why the blacks opposed Chinese immigration in the 1870s. And when the immigrant groups voted their way into stronger positions in the labor market, they generated further opposition.[53] (It will be remembered, however, that the actual U.S. wage trend was up despite the downward pressures of immigration. The countervailing forces were created by the steady drift to the frontier (helped by a cheap public land policy) and by the nearly incessant advance of productivity on farms and in factories.)

Immigrants disproportionately increased the supply of unskilled workers, and of the self-employed. The Society for the Encouragement of Faithful Domestic Servants in New York reported, in 1826, that 60 percent of those who applied to it for jobs were Irish immigrants—well before the great migrations of 1846–48.[54] Lowell factories in the 1830s filled most of their jobs with native-born women. But "much of the rest is furnished by immigrants. I saw English, Irish and Scotch operatives," wrote Harriet Martineau.[55] More generally, the foreign-born population concentrated disproportionately in common labor, mining, canal and railroad building.[56] They appeared less than proportionately in farming (whether as farmers or laborers) and in all the professional and managerial groups at the top of the social order.[57] Moreover, because their knowledge of English was limited many worked for themselves. They appeared much more often than native-born Americans as self-employed shoe makers, butchers, confectioners, grocers, and owners of restaurants, shoe-shine parlors, and every kind of retail store.

The variety of immigrant flows to the United States never ceased. Textile weavers, dancing masters, peasants, falconers, furriers, common laborers all left Europe. Arriving in the United States, many remained in their trades. Others became railroad track layers, miners, heads of giant steel companies,

53. In 1843 the Democrats gained control of the New York City Council. "Heretofore the markets had been under American control. Now the American meat-sellers found themselves with Irish competitors and subject to oversight by Irish clerks, weighers and watchmen. Nativism at once sprang into new life in the markets." Lewis Scisco, *Political Nativism in New York State* (1901), p. 39.

54. *First Annual Report of the Society for the Encouragement of Faithful Domestic Servants in New York* (1826), p. 21. Data for New York in 1830 appear in *Address to the Public of the Society for the Encouragement of Faithful Domestics, Philadelphia, July 20, 1830*, p. 10, and also indicate about 60 percent.

55. Harriet Martineau, *Society in America* (1834–36), II:53–55.

56. "Bog trotters from the West of Ireland . . . were set to work knee deep in the wet muck [of the Montezuma marshes through which the Erie Canal was dug]. 'They could wear no clothing but a flannel shirt and a slouch cap.' They were part of that great army of Irishmen which . . . dug America's canals." Quoted in A. F. Harlow, *Old Towpaths* (1926), p. 54.

57. E. P. Hutchinson, *Immigrants and Their Children* (1956), Table 21. Our first comprehensive data are for 1870. But the differences noted above appear to have prevailed in the previous century as well.

dentists, grocers, upholsterers, Nobel prize winners. Legal limitations on the flow began seriously in the 1880s (timed aptly for the 1886 dedication of the Statue of Liberty—with Emma Lazarus's inscription: "give me your tired, your poor, your huddled masses . . . "). The decisive reduction in the 1920s may, as Richard Easterlin has contended, have decisively altered trends in the American labor force, income distribution, and consumer markets.[58]

Despite their importance for economic advance and economic change, immigrants constituted only a small portion of each generation. (Persons born abroad never accounted for more than 15 percent of the national population—even as early as 1790.)[59] We turn now to the major changes in the prospects of life and death that marked the growth of the U.S. population as a whole.

Appendix

A highly speculative estimate of the number of indentured servants in 1774 was arrived at as follows: Alice Jones, *American Colonial Wealth* (1977), records the composition of 919 probate estates. For each sampling cluster—Litchfield, Conn., Suffolk, Mass., and others (listed on p. 1831)—one can locate those estates with a servant or slave (from the individual listings on pp. 2140–95). Reference to the specific probate records in the three volumes then makes it possible to locate those with servants having remaining time to serve. Weighting the percentages in each region by the number of probate wealthholders (pp. 1789–93) gives an estimate of 16,880 indentured servants.

The average term of service of indentured servants is estimated at 4.13 years by weighting the age distribution of servants by the regression coefficients for each age from David Galenson, *White Servitude in Colonial America* (1981), pp. 105, 199. The stock in any year consisted of four-quarters of those migrating in that year, three-quarters of those in the prior year, and so on. Dividing the above estimate of the 1774 stock by 2.5 gives an annual flow of 6,750 indentured servants in the years 1770–74.

James Shepherd and Gary Walton, *Shipping, Maritime Trade . . .* (1972), p. 147, estimate white immigration at about 11,000 a year during 1768, increasing to 19,000 by 1772. Our 6,750 figure for 1770–74 then compares with, say, 18,000 total immigration. The implicit ratio of 38 percent is well below the percent surmised by Abbot Smith (*Colonists in Bondage* (1947), pp. 3, 313) for indentured servants plus convicts.

The above estimate of indentured servants in 1774 is about 32 percent of the 53,016 estimated by Alice Jones (*Wealth*, pp. 1787) from a variety of secondary sources. In this case we prefer to rely on the unparalleled analysis she provides of the probate data rather than these secondary sources.

58. Richard Easterlin, "What will 1984 Be Like?," *Demography* (November 1978).
59. Richard Easterlin, "The American Population," in Lance Davis et al. *American Economic Growth* (1972), p. 124.

16

Population

IN 1939 the president of the American Economic Association, in a depressing address to its membership, reviewed the persisting decline in the U.S. birthrate. He concluded that the exhaustion of U.S. investment opportunities had arrived, and with it the end of long-term growth prospects. The eventual catastrophe was a mere matter of time.

On the other hand, from the eighteenth-century predictions of Thomas Malthus to the latest Zero Population Growth report, a contrary vision has been displayed: population expanding to the limit of resource support, bringing in its wake the end of basic resources, famine, death.

What does the American record tell us about these untidy and menacing alternatives? In 1789 the United States was surely a nation with vast resources of land, of forest and mineral wealth. In time its settlers discovered even more fertile land than that which they had already settled, even more dazzling mineral deposits. The population should then have grown at an extremely high rate. And it did. The rate of U.S. natural increase from 1790 to 1860 proved to be 50 percent greater than the rate at which world population grew in the 1970s, a decade when predictions of world population explosion and catastrophe were a dime a dozen.[1] U.S. population, below 3 million when George Washington was inaugurated, rose to 222 million by 1980.[2] That vast gain was primarily the result of births within the United States. What underlying trend in fertility had brought it about?

In 1800 the typical American mother had given birth to 7 children. That figure is "markedly higher than that ever recorded for any European country; it is equalled [in reliably recorded data] only by such unusually fertile populations as the Hutterites and the inhabitants of the Cocos-Keeling Islands."[3]

---

1. World population in the 1970s increased at 2 percent a year. The U.S. increase from 1790 to 1860 was 3 percent a year. Richard Easterlin in Lance Davis et al., *American Economic Growth* (1972), p. 123.

2. U.S. Bureau of the Census, *Historical Statistics of the U.S. . . . to 1970*, p. 756, and *Survey of Current Business* (November 1980).

3. Ansley Coale and Marvin Zelnik, *New Estimates of Fertility and Population in the United States* (1963), p. 36.

FIGURE 16.1
U.S. FERTILITY RATE
(AVERAGE NUMBER OF CHILDREN BORN PER MARRIED WOMAN)

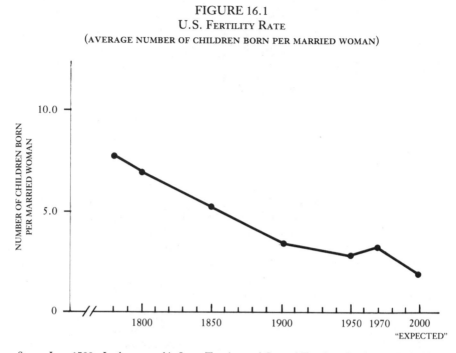

Source: Late 1700s: Lotka, quoted in Irene Taeuber and Conrad Taeuber, *People of the United States in the 20th Century* (1971), p. 356. 1800–1950: Coale and Zelnik, *New Estimates*, p. 36. 1970: Expected total births for wives aged 35–39 in that year is given in U.S. Census, *Fertility Histories and Birth Expectations of American Women* (June 1979), series P-20, no. 263, p. 8. 2000: The total births expected in 1982 by women then aged 18–24 was used, data from U.S. Census, *Fertility of American Woman* (May 1983), series P-20, no. 379, p. 4.

The religious beliefs of the Hutterites require adherence to the biblical exhortation "be fruitful and multiply." The fact that the entire United States had such a high rate in 1800 suggests national fertility near the natural reproductive limit. Yet since that time the decline has been continuing and massive, shown in Figure 16.1.

This decline did not reflect a rise in sterility or decisions to live without children, but rather a decline in the number of very large families as shown in Table 16.1. Half of all white women at the beginning of the nineteenth century had 7 or more children. But only about six percent of those born during the Great Depression did. For nonwhites the percent fell from about 52 percent to 13 percent, then rose slightly in the twentieth century.

What factors brought so persistent a decline in large families, and so vast an overall decline in fertility? An explanation is to be sought in James Fields' remark: "a man's standard of living is defined by the wants he insists upon

TABLE 16.1
WOMEN BY NUMBER OF BIRTHS

| | | Percentage of women | |
| | | giving birth to: | |
Year of mother's birth	Total	No children	7 or more children
White			
1800	100	N.A.	50
1840	100	8	35
1860	100	10	27
1900	100	20	7
1925	100	10	5
1934	100	7	6
Nonwhite			
1840	100	6	52
1860	100	9	44
1900	100	28	13
1925	100	18	16
1934	100	9	18

Source: 1800: Since the average American married woman in 1800 had given birth to somewhat more than 7 children, over 50 percent would have had 7 or more children. 1840–1900: Based on data in Taeuber and Taeuber, *People,* p. 378. 1925, 1934: U.S. Census, *Fertility of American Women, June 1979,* P-20, no. 358, p. 30. For nonwhites in this year, we use Census data for "Negro." All data refer to completed fertility of women aged 45–49.

satisfying before he is willing to enlarge his family."[4] It was, in other words, a choice between more children or more of all other goods (including leisure). What are some of the elements in the catalogue of alternatives?

Typical parents increasingly wished to spend more on their first child (or children) rather than having more children. Prior to the Civil War many children did not have shoes for regular wear until they reached their teens. (Hudson Maxim, the great inventor, who lived in rural Maine in the 1890s, did not get shoes until his teens.) Their clothing, housing, minor comforts, were equally scanty. Few went beyond the primary grades—even then averaging only a few months of schooling a year. (They could not be spared from farm work in other months.) As the decades passed parents began to spend for "higher quality" children rather than for a higher quantity of children.

Parents really wanted children, not births. But every increase in life expectancy meant that children would live longer. Parents of a baby born in 1800 could expect it to live 39 years; babies born in 1900 had a life expectancy

4. James A. Field, *Essays on Population and Other Papers* (1931), p. 231.

of 47 years; and those born in 1979, 74 years.[5] The advance of public water and sewage investment over the nineteenth century accounted for much of these marked increases. Hence, one birth in 1977 could provide parents with almost as many years of cheer (in their younger years) and consolation and help (in their old age) as two births in 1777.

The value of children as "producer's goods" steadily declined. "Happy is the man that hath his quiver full" (of children), declares Psalm 127. On family farms children were valued both for themselves and as a vital source of labor. They were, in effect, producer's durable goods. Their attractions as humans did not decline as economic development proceeded. But their productive contribution did. Table 16.2 indicates how the rate of population increase declined from 1810 to 1840—in close proportion to the increased density of population. Yasuba has emphasized the link:

> Where the supply of land is limited the value of children as earning assets is low, and hence the demand for children may not be so great as where there is plenty of open land nearby. The increased cost of setting up children as independent farmers and the fear of the fragmentation of family farms may further encourage the restriction of family size in densely populated areas.[6]

When density increased, in sum, birth rates fell.

TABLE 16.2
RURAL FERTILITY AND DENSITY

	1810		1840	
	Fertility Index[a]	*Population Density*[b]	*Fertility Index*[a]	*Population Density*[b]
East Coast				
Middle Atlantic	1,344	20.1	1,006	45.3
New England	1,079	23.7	800	36.1
North Central				
West	1,810	0.5	1,480	1.6
East	1,706	3.1	1,291	15.2
South Central				
West	1,557	2.2	1,495	4.6
East	1,701	3.9	1,424	14.3

[a]Children under 5 per 1,000 white females 20–44 years of age.
[b]Population per square mile.
Source: Fertility: Wilson Grabill et al., *Fertility of American Women* (1958), p. 17. Density: 1960 Census, *Population*, U.S. Summary PC-(1)-1A, pp. 1–20.

    5. 1800: Wilson Grabill et al., *Fertility of American Women* (1958), p. 10; *Historical Statistics of the U.S. . . . to 1970*, p. 55; *1981 Statistical Abstract*, p. 69.
    6. Yasukichi Yasuba, *Birth Rates of the White Population in the United States, 1800–1860* (1962), p. 159.

TABLE 16.3
WOMEN IN THE LABOR FORCE, 1830–1979
(PERCENTAGE OF POPULATION)

	White		Nonwhite	
	Total	Married	Total	Married
1830	8	0	90	90
1890	13	2	38	22
1950	28	21	37	32
1979	50	48	53	60

Source: 1830–1859: Stanley Lebergott in Universities-National Bureau of Economic Research, *Demographic and Economic Change in Developed Countries* (1960), pp. 389, 391. Data relate to persons 10 years of age and older. Data for 1979, relating to persons 16 years of age and older, are computed from BLS Summary of Special Labor Force Report, *Marital and Family Characteristics of the Labor Force, March 1979*, Table 3.

Womens' desire to enter the world of hired work rather than work within the family home or family farm was a further force. Such entry, of course, increased family money income. And provided its own satisfactions. But one typical association was clear; women in the labor force had fewer children than those who worked only at home.[7] In any event, the percent of women in the labor force rose substantially, as shown in Table 16.3.

And finally—though not necessarily least in importance—fertility rates fell because some women wanted to spend less of their lives bearing and raising children. After all, given an average of 7 children ever born, and adding at least a few miscarriages under those harsh, primitive conditions, the typical married woman in 1800 would have spent virtually all 23 years of her married life bearing and raising children.[8] The reduction (between 1800 and 1850) in the average number of children born from 7.04 to 5.42 would have cut close to 25 percent from those child-centered years.

Density

Increased population density, most obvious in cities, is a useful surrogate measure of advancing production efficiency. It is, therefore, worth noting the rate at which density increased in the United States, and when—shown in Table 16.4. Density just about doubled within 70 years after 1790; doubled

7. No assumption as to cause and effects are made here.
8. The life expectancy for females born in 1800 was 42 years. Cf. Coale and Zelnik, *New Estimates*, p. 9. The life expectancy at, say, age 19, when most married, would not have been much different, judging from Philadelphia data in Adam Seybert, *Statistical Annals* (1818), p. 51, and Massachusetts data in Irving Fisher, *National Vitality*, 61st Cong., 2d sess., S.D. 419, p. 648.

TABLE 16.4
U.S. POPULATION
(PERSONS PER SQUARE MILE)

1790	4.5
1860	10.6
1890	21.2
1930	41.2

Source: 1960 Census of Population, U.S.
Summary, PC(1) 1A, pp. 1–4.

again within 30 years after 1860; and again within 40 years after 1890. The shortest doubling period ran from the Civil War to 1890. That fact may be related to another—this was the classic period of American industrialization.

White–Nonwhite Shares

The nonwhite share in the total population totalled 19 percent at the first Census in 1790. It fell to 14 percent by 1800. The decline reflected, of course, the virtual end of slave importation while migration from European nations continued. What contribution did differentials in fertility make? Fertility indexes did not differ largely as between white and nonwhite, as shown in Table 16.5.

Indeed, Southerners made much of this differential as testifying to the mildness of American slavery. William Gilmore Simms discovered that "the slaves are very prolific, increasing in greater proportion than the whites; a sufficient proof of the mildness of their servitude and labor."[9] General Jubal Early found "the most conclusive answer to the slanders against Southern slave owners . . . in the rapid multiplication of the slaves by natural increase, which could not have taken place if such barbarities had been practiced or such immorality had existed as has been represented."[10] However, later experience revealed "a greatly increased birthrate . . . was one of the first results of emancipation," as it had been in Russia after the serfs were freed.[11] Which suggests that the increase among the slaves, while greater than in many British, Spanish, and French colonies, may also reflect the origins of American slaves; and was less than that group would have manifested if its children had been born into freedom.

Productivity Implications

We must note one immediate economic implication of increased longevity. That inference is surely less important than the human implications of

9. William Gilmore Simms, The Geography of South Carolina (1843), p. 21.
10. Jubal E. Early, The Heritage of the South (1915), pp. 113–114.
11. Walter Willcox, in 1900 Census, Supplementary Analysis, p. 417.

TABLE 16.5
CHILDREN UNDER 5 YEARS OF AGE
PER 1,000 FEMALES

	Native white	Nonwhite
1850	892	1,010
1860	905	965

Source: Estimates by Stanley Lebergott in Universities-National Bureau of Economic Research, *Demographic and Economic Change in Developed Countries* (1960), p. 394.

the fact that babies died less frequently. But it is important. In 1800 when the life expectancy was 39, the average American male remained dependent on mother and father until he entered the labor force at age 10 and worked until he died. For 35 percent of his life he was a dependent, and for three-quarters of it he produced goods and services.[12] By 1900 that proportion had hardly changed. (By the 1970s the dependency proportion reached 45 percent.[13] That more affluent society kept its children in school longer, supported its older people in retirement. But not before much higher incomes had changed national horizons.) Prior to the twentieth century persistent hard work was expected once the years of mere childhood had passed.

Social Structure

Spain's great twentieth century philosopher, social critic Ortega y Gasset's brilliantly describes the startling impacts of fast population growth on established societies in his *Revolt of the Masses*. More and more young people come of age, thrusting for more positions of status than society offers. The impact breaks apart the older social and economic order. That prospect was particularly ominous in the fast-growing United States. Prior to the Civil War, however, there was a live alternative to the young's breaking up the social order of the patroons along the Hudson river, or the old Quaker hierarchy of Philadelphia (though these gave way in time, too). Many of the vigorous young instead "hived off" to new territories. There they formed additional social structures, with prizes in jobs, status, and money. Most chose to farm. For on a farm young adults, as the new immigrants, could wrest income and wealth from the soil. And do so with much less restraint by others than was true for their fellows back in the East.

12. Women did not commonly enter "the labor force." They typically worked, in the home and for family enterprise, from an earlier age until they died.
13. *Monthly Labor Review* (March 1982), p. 17.

17

Regional Growth

T RAVELING near New Orleans in 1803, Dr. John Sibley came across a scene out of the Old Testament: "a pillar of smoke by day, a pillar of fire by night." For he passed "a high bluff or mountain of coal, which had been on fire for many years . . . [It] afforded always a light at night, and a strong thick smoke by day, by which vessels are sometimes deceived and left on the shoaly coast . . . ."[1] The production possibilities of coal had failed to interest the Caddos or other tribes in the area. Only after European settlers arrived were these production possibilities used to create new goods, to achieve different goals. This dramatic image emphasizes that mere natural resources do not generate economic development, however much they tilt regional growth.

When the *Mayflower* landed on the Massachusetts coast the Puritans came to a permanent halt there—a thousand miles from the most fertile lands in the nation. The food and foe of the day preoccupied them when visions of heaven and hell did not. New England became the place to live, to grow in grace, and (eventually) to be buried. Searching out the land's potential was a task for later generations.[2] The same experience marked the early settlers in North Carolina's "lost colony," in Georgia and in Virginia. Mere survival was a sufficient task for the first generation.

The European immigrants sorted themselves out along a narrow strip of the East Coast. They remained there, a European population, for generations. New recruits migrated from Europe. The (living) failures returned there. Europe supplied everything beyond simple subsistence. As late as 1768 George Mercer could write to his agent in England: do not "omit to send me a tutor for my children by the first opportunity . . . and a quantity of nails . . . 50 yards of haircloth . . . a drill plow with brass seed boxes for wheat . . . ."[3]

1. American State Papers, *Indian Affairs*, I (1806):722.
2. A lively and comprehensive review of U.S. exploration from Lewis and Clark onward appears in William Goetzman, *Exploration and Empire* (1967).
3. George Mercer, *George Mercer Papers*, Lois Mulkearn, ed. (1954), pp. 215, 219.

With the colonies still oriented toward Europe, population centered most advantageously in the ports of the East Coast. (It took two days to transport a load of farm products a mere 15 miles to a port city and to return home.)[4] The roads were still much as they had been when originally laid out by the deer and the buffalo. Of the various ports along the coast those near great stores of natural resources were, of course, preferred. Greatest of these was the Grand Banks, off Newfoundland. From time immemorial, Portuguese, Englishmen, Spaniards, Frenchmen had fished there to provide Europe with food. Among the most heated negotiations for America's peace treaty of 1783 with Britain was Adams' fight to establish more than the mere "liberties" of American fisherman on the Grand Banks. They sought "rights" to go there. Even then the bulk of the "law of the sea" involved nation tilting against nation.

The cities closest to the Grand Banks were all commercial: Montreal, Halifax, Portland, Boston, and New York. Increasingly, fishermen began to restock and refit in American ports, not European ones. Of these the Canadian ports were obviously the closest to their fishing grounds. Yet New York superseded them gradually and inevitably. The reason was the economic outcome of a geographic fact: Its superb natural harbor never froze over. Hence, "produce deposited there can be sent to market [for five winter months] during which, at Montreal, [it] lies a dead weight on the hands of the owner."[5] For investors to earn nothing on their inventories 5 months out of every 12 was indeed a chilling prospect. The heavy expenditures required to build wharves and port facilities would be deterred for the same reason. That simple but basic difference worked tirelessly and persistently against the growth of the Canadian ports and in favor of the growth of American ones.

As population in North America grew, and ocean-going vessels began transporting more and more goods to Europe, they began to concentrate their voyages on the ice-free ports south of Boston. What, then, explains the steady nineteenth-century decline in the relative standing of Charleston and Baltimore, and the rise of New York City? Vessel owners were increasingly drawn to ports where they could deliver full cargoes from Europe and return with full cargoes from the United States. To have "the homeward freight of tobacco [from Virginia] . . . represent nearly the whole of the ship's earnings for the year" meant earning only about half the sum possible if a lading from Europe could be delivered to the United States.[6] To come into Charleston with a cargo of bricks (as some French ships did), or partly in ballast, meant that one cargo, not two, had somehow to cover expenses and pay a profit.

---

4. Cf. Paul Gates, *The Farmer's Age: Agriculture, 1815–1860* (1960), p. 159.

5. New York State Canal Commissioners, *Public Documents Relating to the New York Canals* (1821), p. 27.

6. The quotation is from Ralph Davis, *The Rise of the English Shipping Industry* (1962), pp. 286–87.

British vessels began to concentrate their voyages to New York, Boston, and Philadelphia. For in these ports they could both deliver a full cargo of manufactured goods (to be consumed in the cities or sent along to the West) and also pick up return cargoes. The demand for manufactured goods and such luxuries as tea and coffee, however, grew far more slowly in such southern centers as Charleston, Savannah, and Wilmington. One reason was that much of the nearby population were slaves, consuming little in the way of manufactured goods. Another was that the new southern lands attracted far fewer immigrants and new settlers than the North did. As a result, southern cotton was increasingly shipped to New York, and only then transshipped for Europe. This shift further stimulated northern economic growth. (Northern income from the transport of southern farm products in 1859 was estimated, by one indignant southerner, at 14 percent of the value of those products.)[7] That expenditure would account for 6 percent of all the gainfully occupied persons in the North.[8] This growth increment was small—but helpful.

In the first century of the Republic a grand specialization developed.[9] The South grew cotton, tobacco, rice, and several other crops. The Northeast concentrated on manufacturing and shipping. The North Central region raised wheat, corn, and hogs. (Within each region there were, of course, other but lesser specializations.) How did this division develop?

The South

The plantation South of pre-Civil War days was created by other regions: by the northeastern United States, by the Caribbean, and by Europe. The contribution of the Northeast proved overwhelming. Opposed root and branch to slavery, the Northeast nonetheless guaranteed its survival in the South. It did so by the high moral accomplishment of forcing the South to accept the end of the external slave trade twenty years later (in 1808) as a condition of accepting the Constitution. Ending that trade immediately forced up the price of slaves, and kept them up. Slaves became an increasingly valuable

7. Thomas Kettell, quoted in Douglass North, *Economic Growth of the United States 1790 to 1860* (1961), p. 114. North displays the port charges for cotton on p. 115. With cotton at 9 cents a pound in 1840 (Alfred G. Smith, *Economic Readjustment of an Old Cotton State* (1958), p. 221) and assuming all shipping was in Northern vessels, one arrives at charges of $10 per bale worth $37.80. But since much shipping was in English vessels the 14 percent computed from Kettell's figures is more accurate for present purposes.

8. An annual average income in 1860 of $1 a day for 311 working days divided into Kettell's 63 million indicates 203,000 gainfully occupied in the transport of Southern goods. That number is 6 percent of the gainfully occupied in the Northern states in 1860. Cf. 1860 Census, *Population of the United States in 1860* (1864), p. 680.

9. The specialization has been outlined most persuasively by North, *Economic Growth*, chap. 9.

asset. So valuable that Southerners eventually broke up the Union fighting for it.

The second element shaping the South was the cumulated catastrophe of the Caribbean Treasure Islands. In 1791 their control by France's Old Regime collapsed. An invitation to revolt offered by the revolutionary French Convention persuaded the desperate slaves of Santo Domingo to slaughter most of the whites in the island. Once a major source of cotton, Santo Domingo ceased even to be an important source. The end of slavery in the other Caribbean islands in the 1830s proved more peaceable, largely because Britain bought the slaves their freedom. But once on their own, the economies of those islands declined similarly. They ceased being world centers of cotton, sugar, and tobacco production. The demand for these attractive products had not disappeared. Only their suppliers changed. These industries then moved to the American South. Emile Borel and other planters created a new sugar industry in Louisiana by 1795. And cotton, once grown in the gardens of Charleston as a pretty plant, became the base of one of the world's largest plantation enterprises.

The third force shaping the old South was Britain. Its industrial revolution made it into the world's great producer of cotton textiles. Millions began to buy its new machine textiles. They were cheap, durable, and could be washed far more readily than the old, often disease-ridden garments of wool, flax, or leather. British industry therefore created a massive market for cotton from the new South. Britain did, indeed, attempt to foster a competitive cotton-growing industry in one of its colonies, India. It even hired skilled American planters to do so. But it never ended its dependence on American cotton. Throughout the nineteenth century American slaves produced better, more marketable, and cheaper cotton than Indians or Egyptians.

The result of these forces appears in Table 17.1, showing export data for Southern crops. The most important increase reported by Table 17.1 is clearly that for cotton. Yet the rise in Louisiana sugar production was no less striking—from zero in 1790 to 10,000 hogsheads by 1810, 122,000 by 1840.[10]

Along with such rises, declines inevitably appeared. Cotton and rice production had replaced indigo, particularly when American independence cut off the British subsidy for producing this brilliant blue dye.

Among the first forays to new regions were those made by cotton and sugar planters. Refugees from Santo Domingo had fled to the French Territory of Louisiana, settling near New Orleans. They bought goods from the East and slaves from Virginia. These new planters discovered the Yazoo delta of the Mississippi. A hundred and fifty miles long, "every square foot of it riots in vegetable life . . . nature knows not how to compound a richer soil."

10. American State Papers, *Finance*, II:808; 1840 Census, Allen, ed., p. 359. Louisiana hogsheads contained a little more than 1,000 cwt. *Niles Register* (May 21, 1814).

TABLE 17.1

U.S. Exports (annual averages, 000 pounds)

Year	Cotton	Rice	Tobacco	Indigo
1790–1800	5	115	100	501
1801–1810	414	85	89	36
1811–1820	687	91	70	5
1821–1830	2,035	121	121	4

Source: Cotton 1791–95: Timothy Pitkin, *A Statistical View of the Commerce of the United States* (1835), p. 111. These figures include some re-exports. Other: 48th Cong., 1st sess., H.D. 49, part 2, *Exports . . .*, by Charles Evans (1884). Rice: 000 tierces.

For centuries the river's floods "came down loaded with skimmings from the great watershed above. Overtopping its banks, the enriched water spreads far and wide over the alluvial area . . . letting fall its sediment as it went. Thus the floods built up the valley year by year in layers of fatness."[11] Sugar and cotton grew at an astounding rate. Where a slave averaged 3 bales an acre in the older regions, he could produce 5, and even 8, in the new.

In less than twenty-five years the new region overtook the old, shown in Table 17.2. The East South Central region, its cotton production centered around the Mississippi, took over almost half of all U.S. production. The doomed older cotton region began to sell its slaves, thus stocking the new region. Its lands fell in value. And its leading state—South Carolina—vented its anger in 1832 by passing an ordinance to secede from the Union.

The Northeast

Nearly every American in 1789 lived on a farm. Even half a century later less than 20 percent of those employed in the North worked in manufacturing.[12] What still underpinned the economy of the Northeast was farming. Most Northeastern farmers found their markets in the growing cities of the east coast. They also discovered opportunities in expanding European and colonial markets. As early as 1789 Jedediah Morse could write: "the trade of Connecticut is principally with the West India Islands"; and "new markets for the produce of [Massachusetts] and other states, are continually increasing. The Cape of Good Hope, the Isle of France, Surat, Batavia, and Canton, have lately opened their ports to receive . . . beef, pork, bacon, butter,

11. Judge Robert S. Taylor, of Indiana, quoted in Frank Tompkins, *Riparian Lands of the Mississippi River* (1901), p. 234.

12. *The Compendium of the Census for 1840* gives data that indicate 28 percent for manufacturing and hand trades. We exclude hand trades by the ratio of a) 500,000 in U.S. manufacturing, from Lebergott, *Manpower*, p. 510, to b) 791,749 (1840 *Compendium*, p. 103).

TABLE 17.2
U.S. Cotton Produced by Region
(percent)

	South Atlantic	East South Central
1811	93	4
1821	66	28
1834	39	47

Source: Computed from the 1949 Census of Agriculture.

cheese, timber, ginseng."[13] Since the French had developed farming so little in Canada the New England colonies had supplied the French as well as the British West Indies. The trade continued under the new nation.

The North Central

Northward, the Erie Canal opened the way west in 1825. That opening shifted wheat production, the North Central States gradually replacing the traditional wheat farms of Maryland, Delaware, and Massachusetts. Perhaps as sharp a measure as any of this westward shift was the changing shipment of flour along the Erie Canal, as shown in Table 17.3. Exports peaked briefly in 1846, when England suddenly opened her ports to foreign wheat, but that did not stay the shift. The New York State consumer bought less and less of his wheat from New York State farmers. And the world bought ever more from the newer "Western" states: in other words, the East North Central region.

The West

The discovery of the main dimensions of the West was led, in large part, by the beaver. The mountain men pursued the beaver, up the major rivers, then back into the smallest tributaries, to supply furs to the great annual fairs at Leipzig. In so doing, they discovered the character of the new land: its soil, timber, and mineral resources. Some of its minerals, such as the lead mines on the upper Mississippi, not far from St. Louis, had been worked for years by the Indians. (These were taken over by the federal government after the Louisiana Purchase in 1803, and were rented out to miners for some years at so much per basket of ore.) Other minerals had remained unknown.

A second great discovery force, which eventually opened up the far West, was the lure of gold and silver. Gold had been discovered in Maine, Georgia, and North Carolina, drawing migrants to each state from older

13. Jedediah Morse, *American Geography* (1789), pp. 182, 215.

TABLE 17.3
BARRELS OF FLOUR PER YEAR FROM
TWO REGIONS (000 OF BARRELS)

Year	New York State	Western states
1836	776	317
1841	597	1,233
1846	929	2,723
1851	495	3,496

Source: Hunt's Merchants Magazine (April 1853), p. 481.

states. But this proved to be a brief mining boom. And a small one. An 1829 writer declared: "monied men from every quarter of the union are purchasing land" in the North Carolina gold regions. By 1830 "bodies of 100 hands" averaged 2 penniweights of gold a day—or $1.60.[14] These were high earnings at the time. But they hardly prepared the nation for 1848, when gold flakes were discovered near Sacramento, California, in the mill race of Captain Sutter's flour mill. A hundred thousand people rushed into California in the next year—sailing round the Horn from Boston, crossing the Isthmus of Panama, or even walking across the continent to San Francisco. That discovery did more to link the two coasts than all the transcontinental railroads and cartographers put together. Later key discoveries came after the Civil War—silver in Nevada, petroleum in Pennsylvania, sulfur in Louisiana. These too stimulated growth and drew new immigrants.

The most persistent attraction that drew men to strange and dangerous lands, however, was neither beaver nor gold. It was the incredibly fertile soil. Coming from a thousand years of agriculture, European settlers discovered new lands of unusual productivity. To sow an acre in wheat required an initial planting of about 2½ bushels in Britain and the Isle de France, somewhat less in Italy and Greece, and 2 bushels in Egypt and Palestine.[15] By contrast, 1⅓ bushels was about the right quantity on the prairies.[16] In other words, U.S. prairie farmers had to set aside far less of the previous year's seed for the new year's crop than did farmers in the ancient granaries of the Middle East, and only half as much per acre as did English farmers.[17]

14. Niles (May 16, 1829), p. 186; (July 27, 1829), p. 286; (June 19, 1830), p. 302.
15. A. J. P. Paucton, Metrologie (1780), pp. 513, 811.
16. Fred Gerhard, Illinois As It Is (1857), p. 325.
17. Thomas Tooke and William Newmarch, A History of Prices V (1857):106, find that the produce of the land averaged 9 times the amount of seed. But they estimate on p. 127 about 32 bushels yield per acre for 1815–25 and 1826–35, which would make seed requirements above 3 bushels per acre in that period.

The differentials within the United States were as great as those between the United States and other nations. In 1800 in Tidewater Virginia and Maryland wheat averaged 6 bushels per acre; in 1839 in the Midwest, 13 bushels, and in Ohio in 1853, 16 bushels.[18] Pounds of cotton per acre in 1850 averaged:[19]

Tennessee	300
South Carolina	320
Georgia	500
Alabama	525
Mississippi	650
Texas	750

Capital, labor, skill, all moved toward the areas of highest return. Drawn by high profits in new states and new cities, capital flowed from east to west. Drawn by high wages, labor did the same. But this very flow gradually drove down the high profits and high wage rates. Over the course of development, prices tended to equalize (as water in a pool tends to level off even though a stream may be rushing into one end). For example, wheat prices in New England exceeded those in the East North Central states[20] by 104 percent in 1840–46, but only 49 percent in 1871–75, and only 11 percent in 1911–15. (By 1959–63 the difference had fallen to a mere 2 cents a bushel.) As prices tended to equalize, so did wages. From 1830 to 1850 the coefficient of variation of farm wage rates decreased significantly; it decreased even further from 1850 to 1860.[21]

The resource shifts associated with the cost and profit differentials are dutifully reported in the data on farm production (Table 17.4). While the westward shift is obvious, it neither occurred at the same rate, nor with the same timing, for the different products. Each was responding to changes in the costs, and market opportunities, relevant to that product and that period.

Older regions gradually lost their dominance. So did cities. In 1819 a traveler discovered "two ruling passions in Cincinnati; enmity against

---

18. L. C. Gray, *A History of Agriculture in the Southern United States to 1860* (1933):819; see also William Parker in National Bureau of Economic Research, *Output, Employment and Productivity in the United States after 1800* (1966), p. 532; *Hunt's Merchants Magazine* 29 (December 1853):771.

19. J. D. B. deBow, *Statistical View of the United States* (1854), p. 178.

20. Computed from data in Conference on Research in Income and Wealth, *Trends in the American Economy in the Nineteenth Century* (1960), p. 113; United States Department of Agriculture Bulletin 594, *Geography of Wheat Prices* (1918), p. 22; United States Department of Agriculture, *Agricultural Statistics, 1966*, p. 3.

21. Lebergott, *Manpower in Economic Growth*, p. 135. For all 1830 states these coefficients fell from 23 percent to 18 percent between 1830 and 1850, then from 36 percent to 30 percent (for another set of states) from 1850 to 1860.

TABLE 17.4
MAJOR FARM PRODUCTS, 1840–1979 (PERCENT PRODUCED BY REGION)

	1840	1850	1860	1870	1880	1890	1900	1909	1919	1929	1939	1949	1959	1969	1979
Cotton:															
South Atlantic	37.0	37.4	23.7	29.3	31.3	31.3	28.3	37.7	35.7	20.8	19.5	10.8	9.2	6.5	2.2
East South Central	42.9	50.4	46.2	39.1	34.7	30.3	27.9	23.7	17.5	25.4	24.0	19.1	20.7	22.3	13.3
West South Central	20.0	12.2	29.3	31.5	33.7	38.2	43.5	38.1	45.3	48.9	46.3	53.9	46.6	48.3	50.5
Tobacco:															
South Atlantic	53.5	45.5	45.3	25.1	28.5	20.5	34.6	31.7	36.0	53.0	65.6	60.8	61.2	n.a.	65.3
East South Central	37.9	38.0	34.7	47.9	42.2	52.9	41.9	44.2	45.2	33.5	25.5	30.1	27.7	n.a.	29.4
Rice:															
South Atlantic	89.7	93.5	92.5	76.9	70.0	34.8	23.3	2.8	1.0	—	—	—	—	—	—
West South Central	3.5	2.6	3.0	23.1	20.0	58.7	72.2	96.8	79.6	85.1	82.0	75.4	73.1	79.8	66.8
Pacific	—	—	—	—	—	—	—	—	19.6	14.9	18.0	24.6	24.3	17.1	25.8
Wheat:															
Mid Atlantic	30.6	30.0	13.3	11.8	7.2	6.4	5.0	4.4	3.6	2.8	3.7	3.2	2.1	1.2	.7
East North Central	30.6	39.0	46.2	44.4	44.7	31.4	20.5	17.7	21.4	12.6	16.7	16.5	13.2	10.4	9.2
West North Central	1.2	5.0	8.7	23.3	27.2	37.4	46.6	56.0	44.8	46.9	41.2	38.3	41.4	47.8	45.6
Corn:															
East North Central	23.0	29.9	33.4	36.5	35.3	27.1	31.0	33.1	29.1	25.1	35.4	35.8	37.7	41.8	38.6
West North Central	5.0	7.6	15.0	21.3	37.9	48.3	41.8	39.0	38.2	47.4	39.3	43.7	46.7	45.7	47.1

Source: U.S. Censuses of Agriculture, 1950, 1959, 1969. U.S. Department of Agriculture, *Agricultural Statistics* (1982), pp. 6–99. Since production in regions of lesser importance is omitted, totals will not sum to 100 percent.

Pittsburgh, and jealousy of Louisville."[22] New Orleans competed directly, even if distantly, with New York as an outlet for the products of the Mississippi valley states. And it lost.

How was it possible for the less efficient farm regions to continue competing with the newer ones in growing, say, wheat? For the most part it wasn't. The older regions gave up the ghost. After specializing in wheat for more than a century both the Northeast and the Southeast abandoned it. Their capital and labor migrated to factories, or even went west. Some farms still remained in competition. But they could do so only on a different basis.

The Virginia farms that continued to produce wheat in the 1840s now became heavy users of fertilizers. (Cheap supplies of plaster, used as a fertilizer, became available once the James River Canal had been completed.)[23] These farms matched the yields reported from the newer regions: Virginia's average rose to 15 bushels an acre, as did that for Massachusetts.[24] At such figures they readily competed with Ohio and Illinois.

The older cotton plantations managed to remain in competition with the rich new lands of the Southwest on a similar basis. In the 1840s U.S. cotton plantations began to import the guano deposited by sea birds for thousands of years on islands off Peru. Heavy fertilizing with guano then made it possible for planters along the Eastern seaboard to remain in profitable production, even though the center of the industry had shifted irretrievably to the southwest.

In still other cases, farmers became most efficient in new and better-quality products. For example, producers in one New York county decided to take special care in making butter. They fed their cows on the best clover and bluegrass, emphasized cleanliness in processing, and controlled the temperature in churning and keeping. As a result "Orange county butter" acquired a reputation for quality, even in Europe. Its producers got 22 to 25 cents a pound, while common butter sold for 9 to 10 cents a pound.[25] Other areas switched products. Delaware had been a center of wheat production well into the 1810s. But as new areas developed it gave up wheat production. The Du Pont brothers even gave up their major wool manufactory. Much of the state shifted to explosives, to chemicals production. The growing efficiency of Iowa for growing wheat, of Vermont and Ohio for wool production, no longer mattered to Delaware.

22. Quoted by Richard Wade in *The Urbanization of America*, Allen Wakstein, ed. (1970), p. 2.

23. L. C. Gray in *ibid.*, p. 820.

24. Idem.; see also Henry Colman, *Third Report of the Agriculture of Massachusetts, on Wheat and Silk* (1840), p. 48.

25. Paul Gates, *The Farmers Age, Agriculture 1815–1860* (1960), p. 242.

Out of these ceaseless shifts—areas declining, farms and firms going out of business, men moving to the new high-return areas—what end result on that key measure of economic achievement, real income?

As the pioneers restlessly moved on to richer farm land, to brighter skies, the contribution of that advance to higher real incomes has long claimed attention. William Parker concluded early that "without technological change, westward expansion could have been accompanied by very little rise in productivity in agriculture."[26] Easterlin suggested more recently that the geographic shift increased farm output per worker about 6 percent from 1790 to 1840.[27]

One resistless tendency followed: an equalization of returns. Men moved from relatively low wage to relatively high wage states. They thereby raised wages in the former (fewer workers), and depressed them in the latter. Table 17.5 reports Easterlin's figures for income per agricultural worker, by region. The tendency to equalize incomes as time went on is apparent. For most regions the difference from the national average was gradually reduced, the most substantial differentials being reduced the most (as for West South Central).[28] The very moves which reduced the differentials necessarily shifted capital and labor to higher income states. It follows that incomes for U.S. workers as a whole tended to rise. In fact, real income per agricultural worker rose by 15 percent from 1840 to 1860.[29] And U.S. real income per worker rose by some 25 percent.[30]

Just as important as these actual changes is one that fails to appear in the data: Myrdal's "natural tendency to regional inequality." This tendency presumably produced "backwash effects" not counteracted by "the movements of labor, capital, goods and services."[31] Wherever any such mysterious "natural tendency" to regional inequality appeared it was surely not evident in these U.S. data. The antebellum period has been seen by some historians as one in which slavery was about to collapse because it "reached its natural limits." Others have described slavery collapsing as it was confronted by rising "bourgeois industrialism." Nonetheless, Southern per capita incomes rose from 1840–60 by 39 percent. (Northern incomes during the same period

26. William Parker and Judith Klein, in National Bureau of Economic Research, *Output, Employment and Productivity in the United States after 1800* (1966), p. 546.

27. Richard Easterlin in David Klingaman and Richard Vedder, *Essays in Nineteenth Century Economic History* (1975), p. 89.

28. Easterlin in ibid., Table B-2. An apparent exception appears in estimates for the West Central that include Texas. Cf. Robert Fogel and Stanley Engerman, *Time on the Cross* (1974), p. 248.

29. Easterlin in Klingaman and Vedder, *Essays*, Table B-1.

30. Net national product: Gallman estimates in Lance Davis, et al., *American Economic Growth* (1972), p. 34; labor force: Lebergott, *Manpower*, p. 510.

31. Gunnar Myrdal, *Rich Lands and the Poor* (1958), pp. 27, 30.

TABLE 17.5

INCOME PER FARM WORKER

Region as percent of U.S. (U.S. average = 100 percent)	Year	
	1840	1860
Northeast	86	76
Middle Atlantic	106	103
East North Central	107	110
West North Central	102	86
South Atlantic	82	77
East South Central	108	102
West South Central	158	139
U.S. average (in dollars)	$203	$234

Source: see Note 28, this chapter.

rose only by 29 percent.)[32] After the catastrophe of the Civil War the South's per capita incomes again gained more than the North's did both from 1880 to 1900 and from 1900 to 1930.[33]

Immigrants arriving, as men and women coming of age, pioneered in one state rather than another, took a job in one locality rather than another. Slave holders moved their chattels from the Atlantic Coast to one of the new teritories acquired under Jefferson, Tyler, or Pierce. In so doing, each brought supplies of labor plus alert, if not feral, ingenuity. Together, they drove down the cost of labor wherever they settled. These settlers brought less predictable changes as well. First, they discovered new mines, new modes of planting, and new products. Second, they voted for administrations favoring pre-emption or tariffs, building sidewalks or battleships. Yet, of all the regional changes they induced, those centering on slavery were surely among the greatest. Slaveholders insisted on their right to sell slaves in whatever region where doing so would yield the greatest capital gain. Free men, particularly in the Midwest, increasingly voted the contrary view.

32. Easterlin's data are weighted and combined with data for Texas in Robert Fogel and Stanley Engerman, *Time on the Cross* (1974), p. 248.

33. Richard Easterlin's figures in *American Economic History*, Seymour Harris, ed. (1961), p. 528.

But, as 't is,
We cannot miss him: he does make our fire,
Fetch in our wood, and serves in offices
That profit us—what ho! slave!

—The Tempest

18

Slavery

I N 1776 the British colonies of North America declared their independence. One of the articles in their Declaration charged the British King
with forbidding them to end slavery. Most of the world at the time still accepted slavery. In 1776 the religious Order of St. John of Jerusalem was still
selling captured slaves to their families back in North Africa, while the Moslem rulers of Algiers and Morocco were selling Christian slaves back to their
families.[1] Britain still had slaves in the salt and coal mines of Scotland. (The
last slave died in 1819.)[2] Nor did Britain abolish slavery in its Caribbean colonies until the 1830s. For many decades prior to 1776 the United Kingdom's
Royal Africa Company, chartered by the Crown, efficiently supplied slaves
to Spain, a country which then used them in its colonies.

When Napoleon became Emperor in 1802, France (which had abolished
slavery in 1797) reinstituted slavery in its colonies.[3] And long after abolition
in Europe, the slave trade continued in Arabia and Africa, Brazil and Cuba.
"Slaves were brought to Ashanti from the North, where they had been taken
captive in wars; were paid to the Ashanti as tribute; or bought from slave traders. . . . [indeed] this trade reached a new peak in the last quarter of the
nineteenth century."[4] Slavery actually remained legal in Arabia and Ethiopia
in the 1930s, and Saudi Arabia until November 1962. It would be far easier to
name those nations that did not have legal slavery in 1776 than the multitude
that did.

---

1. Jean Mathiex, "Trafic et prix de l'homme en Mediterranee aux XVIIe et XVIII ^e sie-
cles," *Annales* (1954), p. 162–63. The order of St. John charged $400 to $500 while Algiers and
Morocco charged three times as much—the ability of Christian and Moslem families to pay presumably differing in that proportion.

2. *The Edinburgh Review* (February 1899), pp. 119–48; John Pinkerton, *A General Collection of
Voyages and Travels* (1809), p. 453.

3. Las Cases, *Memorial de Sainte Helene* I (1961):248.

4. Nehemia Levtzion, *Muslims and Chiefs in West Africa* (1968), p. 41.

Slavery in the United States

The Indian tribes in what is now the United States likewise owned slaves, both before and after the white man appeared. Indians on the Pacific Coast bought and sold slaves at a standard price of one copper war shield for nine slaves.[5] At the other end of the nation, the Creeks warred with the Seminoles in Florida. Among the prizes of war the Creeks seized were black slaves owned by the Seminoles.[6] And in the middle of the continent the Miami Indians regularly owned slaves. They held that every man had the right "to kill his horse, his dog or his slave."[7] During the Civil War the Choctaw, the Cherokee, and the Chickasaw fought alongside the Confederacy, fearing that the North would abolish slavery.[8]

In the early days of the new government it looked as though slavery would eventually disappear, in part because of its own contradictions, sinfulness, and inefficiency, in part because independence now made it possible for the colonists to act against it. The first step was to end the external slave trade: The Constitution of 1787 implied that after January 1, 1808, no slaves would be brought into the United States.[9] That action grew out of a belief that slavery was sinful—a sentiment fostered by the evangelical sects in England and propagated by the Quakers in the United States.[10] It was also presumed that the presence of slaves menaced the free laborer or farmer.

But the existing stock of slaves owned in the South (only a handful were still owned in the North in 1789) proved to be the sticking point. To make all that "property" worthless, the South insisted was out of the question. Andrew Jackson declared, with some violence, that to free the slaves would cut the value of Southern lands by 75 percent. White people, he asserted, could not till the lowlands on which rice, sugar, and much cotton was grown.

---

5. James H. Gilbert, *Trade and Currency in Early Oregon* (1907), p. 33.

6. 25th Cong., 3d sess., H.D. 225, *Negroes, etc. Captured from Indians in Florida . . . Secretary of War Respecting* (1839).

7. John Tipton, *The John Tipton Papers*, Nellie A. Robertson and Dorothy Riker, eds., II (1942):300.

8. The 1860 Census (*Population*, p. 15) reports slave ownership by these tribes. Some owners had over 200 slaves apiece. The Church of the Latter Day Saints supported the Democrats as early as the election of 1856 because the free soilers and Republicans threatened to end two "institutions in the territories—polygamy and slavery." Cf. *The Suppressed Book About Slavery* (1864), pp. 112–13.

9. In fact, the Constitution forbid outlawing the trade before that date. But the legislative history of the Constitution had implied an agreement to do so then. This was, in fact, done.

10. Wilberforce argued in 1806 that ending the slave trade "would force the planter, from a sense of interest, to improve the situation of the negro." Quoted in Elsa Goveia, *Slave Society in the British Leeward Islands at the End of the 18th Century* (1965), p. 41. Many Southern planters were themselves infected by these sentiments. Cf. Henry W. Farnam, *Chapters in the History of Social Legislation in the United States to 1860* (1938), p. 169–71. Robert Toombs, great firebrand of the Civil War, declared in 1860 that Southern states had to pass laws forbidding the freeing of slaves by individual planters. Otherwise, he said, so many planters would have followed George Washington's example that there would have been no more slaves.

Moreover, to free the slaves "would produce scenes of Santo Domingo in our land."[11] (Freedom had come to that French colony in the French revolution. It was followed by civil war. The subsequent slaughter of most of the whites in the colony was described in Baltimore, Charleston, and New Orleans by a handful of survivors.[12])

The Constitutional Convention worked out a compromise that looked in opposite directions. Reacting to the rising tide of opposition to slavery, it considered forbidding the import of any more slaves.[13] Recognizing the extensive vested interests of planters in slaves, and in lands which they believed could be cultivated only by slaves, it did not abolish slavery within the United States. The Convention observed that planters in Georgia, Alabama, and Mississippi wanted slaves "to stock their lands." But they were not prepared to pay sizable capital gains to slave owners in the older states.[14] The Convention, therefore, deferred the end of importation until January 1, 1808. No other compromise seemed able to unite the new and old states under a constitution. The external slave trade was thus ended.

But slavery remained. Did it continue, as the planters contended, because of the "responsibilities of race discipline" (which they took upon themselves)? Did it remain because they expected that freeing millions of uneducated slaves would mean millions would go to plundering because they lacked proper skills and discipline? (That the American Colonization Society was organized by Henry Clay and supported over the years by Southerners suggests some element of fear: Southerners actually paid to ship freed slaves "back to," or to, Africa.)

History records that in 1791 the South agreed to forbid slavery in the Northwest Territory. It also records that the Kentucky Assembly, in 1830, failed by only a single vote "to fix a definite time, after which all [children]

11. Everett S. Brown, *William Plumer's Memorandum of Proceedings in the U.S. Senate, 1803–1807* (1923), pp. 250–51. This argument did not change its nature for the next half century: "The Southern states by their situation and climate required negro labour, and *must* have it, or cease to have any value. White free labor was necessarily exorbitantly dear, first, because the climate was unfortunate to the health of white labor; and secondly because the number of such labor was very small." Henry Middleton, *Economical Causes of Slavery in the U.S. and Obstruction to Abolition, by a South Carolinian* (1857), p. 31.

12. Cf. J. Thomas Scharf, *Chronicles of Baltimore* (1874), p. 266. About 1,000 whites and 500 "people of color flying from disaster" arrived in Baltimore in 1793. The French Convention "had freed all slaves who would take arms against the existing French Government of the island."

13. The treaty with Britain had only just been signed in 1783 when David Ramsey wrote Richard Rush his misgivings about the resumption of the slave trade: "The infamous traffic will be resumed without anything being said on the subject." Robert Brunhouse, "David Ramsey," *Transactions of the American Philosophical Society* N.S. 55, part 4 (1865).

14. Patrick Henry and others sought to halt the slave trade in 1788. Madison, however, recognized the position of South Carolina and Georgia. These states argued, he said, that they had bought much of their land "in contemplation of improving it by the assistance of imported slaves. What would be the consequence of hindering us from it? The slaves of Virginia would rise in value, and we should be obliged to go to your markets." Jonathan Elliot, *The Debates in the Several State Governments on the Adoption of the Federal Constitution* IV (1836):453–54.

born in the state should be free."[15] An equally close split appeared in the Virginia legislature in 1832 over a plan to end slavery in that state. And in 1832 Maryland forbid bringing any slaves into the state for sale.[16] These and related actions reflected the Southern fear lest a growing number of free blacks lead, as in Santa Domingo, to the massacre of all whites.

Did such fears account for the continuation of slavery, and not its financial profitability? The explanations are, of course, not alternative ones. They may each be correct, or incorrect. We consider only one here—was slave holding indeed a profitable investment? Economic analysis can cast some light on that question.

The Profitability of Slavery

Many owners defined slaves as so much property. As Robert Toombs told the Senate just before secession: the planters have the right to settle in any territory "with whatever property they possess, including slaves."[17] Typically they bought slaves as an investment. For example, the North Carolina Railroad matter of factly listed among its other assets: real estate, tools, "Negroes (two) . . . $1,550.00."[18]

American slavery demonstrated (had there been any doubt) that a system which Jefferson, Mason, Washington, and Taylor of Carolina felt to be degrading and inhumane, was nonetheless financially profitable. The market value of the typical slave suggests such profitability. For that value necessarily capitalized all the returns to be expected from owning slaves. (And it was net of all the shame, the dubious prospects, and the catastrophes from ownership.) In 1815 a typical U.S. slave was valued at $250;[19] by 1839 the price was $500;[20] and by 1860 it had climbed to $900.[21] Prices of slaves had almost quadrupled from the slave trade's end in 1808 to the outbreak of the Civil War in 1860. Underlying that increase was the quadrupling by 1860 in

15. *Quarterly Register of the American Educational Society* (November 1830), p. 125.

16. *New England Magazine* (1832), 2:433.

17. You seek, he warned them, "to outlaw $4,000,000 of property of our people." *Congressional Globe*, 36th Cong., 2d sess., pp. 270–71.

18. North Carolina Railroad, *Annual Report* (July 8, 1858). Similarly the Wilmington and Weldon Railroad: "Negroes—mechanics and laborers, $13,500," in its *Annual Report* (November 4, 1861), p. 18.

19. 1815: A figure based on the direct tax assessment of 1815 appears in Timothy Pitkin, *A Statistical View of the Commerce of the United States* (1817), p. 315.

20. 1839: In his speech of February 7, 1839, Henry Clay estimated slaves to be worth $1.2 billion. Dividing that figure by 1.5 million slaves enumerated in the 1840 Census gives $485. We assume that Clay, not knowing what the Census count would be, was using a round $500 figure.

21. 1860: Lee Soltow, *Men and Wealth in the United States, 1850–1870* (1975), p. 137. 1857: A $700 estimate by Major Beard, "the great slave auctioneer of New Orleans" is quoted in James Stirling, *Letters From the Slave States* (1857), p. 239.

The usual prices for prime males increased less; the premium for that group declined over time.

Southern crop production per slave.[22] Slaves had increased so much in value chiefly because they produced so much more in salable crops.

Investments are expected to pay a return, a return at least as great as alternative investments (of equal riskiness) will yield. Nothing in economic theory, however, requires that all of the investment return had to be in the form of money. Planters could have given up some monetary return for the seigneurial pleasures of ownership—anticipating humble bows, respectful treatment, instant admiration of their persons, their condescension, their jokes. Some may indeed have done so. But most planter investment was locked up in gangs of slaves who worked in distant fields. These were not very likely to provide such satisfactions. Moreover, such seigneurial returns should have been highest in the great centers of the old plantation aristocracy, clustered around Charleston, Augusta, Richmond, and in Southside Virginia. Yet these were precisely the areas that persistently sold slaves. They continued to do so from 1830 to 1860 as monetary returns fell below those to be earned in the Southwest.

Moralists have long argued that slavery had to be unprofitable, because under it labor was given so grudgingly, and in such slovenly fashion. But whether classical economists (McCullough), shrewd commentators (Helper), or alert "Marxists," their comments are not to the point. Who cared whether slavery was "optimally efficient"? Certainly not the slaves. And slaveholders asked only: did it pay; did it pay them at least as well as alternative modes of investment and living? It was the answer to such questions that helped explain the durability, as well as forecast the demise, of that ancient and ghastly system of production.

One can be even more specific about profitability. And three alternative paths lead to the same conclusions:

First, thousands of planters bought their slaves on credit, from traders. Few planters would have borrowed to buy those slaves, and pay interest on their borrowings, unless they could earn at least that much by putting them to work in the fields. (A butler here, a mistress there, a favorite child, would have been the exception. The profitability of "the institution" rested on the work of the great mass of slaves. And they worked in the fields.) Now, the interest rates charged by traders averaged 8 to 10 percent for most years between 1820 and 1860, as shown in Table 18.1. The figures are consistent with the assertion of the president of the South Carolina College in 1829: Given the cost of rearing slaves, "such property ought to bring at least 10 percent interest."[23] The 10 percent rate for the 1830s is consistent with Louisiana statements in 1829–30: "The conventional interest of this state [Louisiana] is ten percent . . . the rate of discount of the banks with endorsements or   ·

22. Lebergott, *Manpower*, p. 156.
23. Thomas Cooper, *Lectures on the Elements of Political Economy* (1829), p. 106. By "interest," Cooper meant rate of return on investment.

TABLE 18.1
INTEREST RATES CHARGED ON
SLAVE SALES IN NEW ORLEANS,
1825–60[a] (PERCENT)

1825	8	1846	—
		1847	8
1832	8	1848	8
1833	—	1849	—
1834	10		
1835	6	1850	8
1836	10	1851	8
1837	10	1852	7½
1838	9	1853	8
1839	10	1854	—
		1855	8
1840	10	1856	7
1841	10	1857	8
1842	10	1858	8
1843	10	1859	—
1844	9		
1845	8	1860	7½

[a]Median rate for the year.

Source: Tabulations of 181 sales recorded on the Fogel-Engerman tapes, which record sales in New Orleans over these decades, provide the basic data on interest charges. However, 10
percent rates are also reported for the major Alexandria partnership of Armfield and Franklin. Cf. Wendell Stephenson, *Isaac
Franklin, Slave Trader and Planter of the Old South* (1938), pp. 64,
65. An 8 percent rate is recorded in Joe Taylor, *Negro Slavery in
Louisiana* (1963), pp. 26–7.

mortgages [including charges] amounts to nine percent, and out of banks is
higher . . . generally planters have borrowed at 10 or 12 percent."[24] Few
planters would borrow money at 10 percent to invest in slaves unless they anticipated earning at least that much from their investment. The interest rate
charged by slave traders decade in and decade out suggests that planters did
indeed get at least a 10 percent return.

Second, many slaves were hired out by their owners: widows; estates
run by lawyers for the benefit of minors; and planters with a temporary
surplus of field hands. The rent charged by planters for these slaves measured

24. 21st Cong., 2d sess., H.D. 62, *Sugar Cane* (1831), pp. 25, 27, 36. A group of sugar planters calculated the rate of return for a typical sugar estate at 10-3/7 percent, and indicated that was
about a "normal" rate of return.

their investment return that year.[25] In 1850–60, for example, farm laborers in the South Atlantic were paid $9.64 a month, plus board and lodging; West South Central slaves rented for $13.90.[26] Such slaves sold for about $1,070 and $1,400, respectively.[27] Slaves in the Old South coastal states, then, earned about 11 percent of their value for their masters, while those in the New South yielded 12 percent.[28]

Third, a different approach to profitability was pioneered by Alfred Conrad and John Meyer.[29] It compares rates of return from slaveholding and other investments. They estimated the market value of prime field hands in 1850–60, plus the cost of the land and tools with which such hands worked to grow cotton. They then related that investment to the income from each slave—for example, to the bales of cotton grown per hand times the price per bale. And finally they discounted that income because they were relating the price of a 20-year-old prime hand to the income he would have produced over the years from birth to age 20.[30] The result of their calculations suggests a rate of return between 6 percent and 8 percent. They compared that rate to the alternative investment opportunities—Northern cotton textile firms, U.S. government bonds, and so on—which proved to yield somewhat similar rates of return. They concluded that slaveholding was economically profitable. More specifically, they countered the conclusions of some historians who held that the unprofitability of slaveholding was bringing "the institution" to its natural death, and that the Civil War was therefore "unnecessary." Insofar as "unprofitability" was invoked to assess the prospects for slavery's continuation as

25. Planters typically had to supply clothes for their slaves. (The cost averaged about $15 a year.) Cf. Nathaniel Ware, *Notes on Political Economy as Applied to the United States by a Southern Planter* (1844), p. 201. We deduct that sum from the gross hire to get the net rate of return *infra*.

26. We average 1850 and 1860 wages from Lebergott, *Manpower*, p. 539.

27. Data from Phillips as summarized by Robert Evans in his "The Economics of American Negro Slavery," in Universities-National Bureau, *Aspects of Labor Economics* (1962) p. 202. Evans' own price estimates, available for the upper South, 1856–60 only, are slightly higher.

28. Slaves did not normally work for 1 to 2 weeks at the end of the year. Evans (ibid.) pioneered the use of hire rates for estimating rates of return. We do not use his wage data because they were very largely based on data for railroad hires. Railroads, however, hired chiefly very vigorous and strong males, whose pay rates exceeded those for the average slave. Available purchase price figures apply, instead, to the more typical "prime hands."

29. Alfred Conrad and John Meyer, "The Economic Profitability of Slavery in the Ante-Bellum South," *Journal of Political Economy* (April 1958), pp. 95–130.

The tight coherent theory and empirical base of this classic study began "the new economic history." But the ground had been laid by at least one economist: L. C. Gray, *History of Agriculture in Southern United States to 1860* (1933); and by one historian: Robert Smith, "Was Slavery Unprofitable . . ." *Agricultural History* (January 1946).

30. With Y indicating the selling price of the slave, X indicating the net monetary return, and r the internal rate of return, they estimated:

$$Y_t = \frac{X}{(1 + r)}t$$

of 1860, they replied that no such conclusion would follow. (They did not, of course, purport to deal with the multiple other causes behind the outbreak of the war.)

One point in their estimates was noteworthy: Men and women fetched the same price in slave markets, yet women consistently earned less for their owners than men did when hired out in the fields. Since no one presumed that the labor market discriminated against female slaves, they sought to explain that difference in earning rates. And they concluded that it measured the owner's return from the babies that the women slaves would have. (Once raised, the babies could usually be profitably sold in Alexandria, New Orleans, and Richmond.) Thus their analysis demonstrated that the market for slaves was a technically "efficient" market.

But, as Yasuba noted, raising a slave from birth to maturity might nonetheless have been an unprofitable business.[30] Since an efficient market always adjusted prices to expected returns, the price of the slave would, in time, inevitably adjust up or down to yield the same rate of return as competing investments.[31] Yasuba, therefore, assessed "the viability" of slavery.[32] This he did by measuring the actual costs of raising a slave to the age of 20, the age when he could be sold for $800 to $1,200 (during most of the 1800–60 period). He thus concluded that raising slaves was a profitable business. Slavery per se was "viable"—that is, slave property could be profitably reproduced and sold. It followed that a supply of home-grown slaves to produce cotton, tobacco, and sugar would have been available indefinitely.

Despite these alternative modes of estimating, and wide testimony by many historians, the profitability of slavery has been challenged in recent years by one widely accepted "Marxist" view.[33] But the colorful premise on which that argument rests is most unlikely. For it stipulates that planters hazarded the lives of slaves (typically worth $1,000), reduced their net profits, and accepted less productivity from their slaves—all to save $3 a year on each slave's diet. It argues that planters fed slaves "abundant pork," but because that pork "was largely fat," their productivity was damaged. "The limited diet was by no means primarily a result of ignorance or viciousness . . . the problem was largely economics. Feeding costs formed a burdensome part of plantation expenses." But even if planters' records did not in fact show that planters typically bought leaner pork, they could at most have saved $3 a year per slave by using cheaper pork.[34] The argument that such "burdensome"

31. Yasukichi Yasuba, "The Profitability and Viability of Plantation Slavery in the United States," *The Economic Studies Quarterly* (September 1961), pp. 60–67.

32. His premise here is, of course, odd: an "efficient market" in which sellers unaccountably persist in producing products that yield losses. He does not explain the plausibility of that premise, granting he need not.

33. Eugene Genovese, *The Political Economy of Slavery* (1965), chap. 2 and *passim*.

34. The structure of the rather indirect argument is more fully reproduced in Appendix A, this chapter.

costs made slavery unprofitable is arguably "Marxist," and unarguably dubious.

The Efficiency of Slave Labor

The productivity of a slave's labor can be measured as the sum of two financial components: 1) profits taken by his owner and 2) the cost of his own subsistence.

We can measure the minimum yearly profits on the slave's work by multiplying the interest rate charged by sellers times the slave price. (Why, on average, borrow at X percent to buy field slaves, unless they earned at least that much?) For the period 1843–60 the median interest rate charged by slave sellers averaged 8 percent, while the median price in 1850–52 for males aged 18–27 averaged $950. Multiplying rate times price indicates that minimum money profits to the slave owner in 1850 averaged about $76 for prime-age males.[35]

But the risks facing traders and planters differed significantly. At worst the trader could repossess the slave he sold. But the planter could wring his profit from the slave only by persistent effort to make sure that he did not malinger, run away, or die; after persistent worry that cotton prices would fall, drought would hit his crop, and so on. A 2 percent further return for such risks would yield a very moderate figure, indeed, making a typical, but low, return to planters of 10 percent or $100.

An alternative estimate of slave owner profits is given by the records of what slaves who hired out their own time paid their owners. In 1820 Hodgson reports slaves paying their masters $3 a week,—$156 a year—"for permission to work for themselves and retain the surplus."[36] In another instance, a Florida blacksmith formed a partnership with a slave in 1863, the latter paying his master $600 a year out of his earnings.[37] (This extreme value undoubtedly reflects the superior skills of a blacksmith as well as wartime inflation.)

In New Orleans in the late 1840s slaves hired out at fixed prices and earned $20 to $25 a month for themselves.[38] Surely their master received at least as much for himself. In the mid-1850s Richmond tobacco factories hired

---

35. Tabulations of interest rates and prices are from the Robert/Stanley Fogel-Engerman tapes of New Orleans sales, prepared in connection with their basic study, *Time on the Cross.* I am indebted to Professor Engerman for kindly making these tapes available.

Given the proper age-price profile, the prices at other ages and for females should adjust so that a similar return would typically be earned from them. (However, for the very young and old the discounting may have been less precise, particularly as the war drew near.)

36. Adam Hodgson, *Letter to M. Jean Baptiste Say on the Comparative Expense of Free and Slave Labor* (1823), p. 17.

37. Helen Catterall, *Judicial Cases Concerning American Slavery and the Negro* 3 (1932):124.

38. Edward Smith, *Account of a Journey Through Northeast Texas* (1849), p. 83.

slaves, paying them piecework rates so that they averaged $3 a week income for themselves—about $150 a year.[39]

John McDonough, a New Orleans millionaire, paid his slaves for over-time work on Saturday afternoons and Sundays, putting that sum in an account enabling slaves to buy themselves out of slavery. He estimated that after 15 or 16 years the typical male, worth $600, could buy himself out—implying earnings of perhaps $39 a year by such extra effort.[40] (That figure does not measure the full margin a slave could earn, but only what he could earn by working the day and a half normally reserved for leisure.) At that rate a six-day week yielded at least 4 times 39, or $156.

Hodgson's $156 figure, Roberts' $150, and McDonough's $156 figure together suggest a far higher figure than the 10 percent minimum suggested above.[41] However, slaves who worked out on their own were surely more capable, responsible and probably more skilled than the average slave. We take owners' profits, then, to be on average 10 percent, recognizing that a plausible case could be made for a somewhat higher rate.

The yearly subsistence cost of slaves (derived in Appendix A) came to:

clothing	$15
cabin depreciation	6
medical care	1
food and preparation	36
pork $10	
corn $ 5	
taxes and waste	3
Total	$61

39. Joseph Roberts, *The Tobacco Kingdom* (1938), p. 204.

40. *A Letter of John McDonough on African Colonization* (1842), pp. 1, 5, 16. "The gain from their extra labor [that is, labor over and above that which slaves in general yield their owners] in the course of time—say fifteen years, will enable their masters to send them out and purchase in Virginia or Maryland, with the gain made from extra labor a gang of equal number to replace them. In addition to which, what amount of satisfaction . . . would he not enjoy in knowing that he was surrounded by friends, on whose faithfulness and fidelity he and his family could rely under every possible contingency." (p. 1). "It is your freedom in Liberia that I contract for, (for I would never consent to give freedom to a single individual among you to remain on the same soil with a white man) within the term . . . of 15 or 16 years or thereabouts." (p. 5). He estimated men were worth $600, paid them 62½ cents a day, 50 cents in winter (women $450 / 50 cents / 37½ cents). Thus 52 Sundays and 52 half-Saturdays times 55 cents gives $43 a year, or $600 in about 14 years—assuming no ill health or bad weather—as interest credited.

41. Hiring rates of about $150 are indicated in the pioneering and still basic study of Robert Evans, "The Economics of American Negro Slavery," in Universities-National Bureau of Economic Research, *Aspects of Labor Economics* (1962), p. 216. Some years ago Professor Evans was kind enough to give me his sources for these quotations. It was clear that the results were dominated by railroad hires. Such companies must have paid well above typical hiring rates: they demanded sturdier slaves, exposed them to far greater risk of injury and death.

Edward Everett, *Register of (Congressional) Debates* (June 25, 1832), and the *Farmer's Register* 4 (1837), pp. 577, 747 are among the many contemporary sources indicating rates of 10–12% for older farms, not well managed, and 15–20% for well-run plantations in the newer states.

Adding the $100 in profits, gotten by the owner, to the $60 in subsistence costs for the slave, indicates that slaves produced a total of about $160 a year. Thus field hands received about forty percent of the income they produced, not the improbable 90 percent suggested by recent writers.[42]

How did this figure compare with what free labor would have earned doing the same work? We have no direct answer to that question.[43] We do, however, have wage data for northern farm laborers, who did identical work in growing corn (the South's largest single crop), raising hogs, and growing wheat. And what we know of northern prices for corn, wheat, and pork suggests that northern prices were generally lower than those in the South.[44] The wages paid northern farm labor, therefore, suggest the value produced by northern labor when growing the same crops as many slaves did. Northern farm labor was paid approximately $10 a month, plus board and lodging valued at $6 a month.[45] Northern farm laborers therefore produced $182 a year, or about the same value produced by southern farm slave labor. There is little basis, then, for recent assertions that "Southern agriculture as a whole was about 35 percent more efficient than Northern agriculture in 1860."[46]

But if slave agriculture were not obviously much more "efficient" how could slave ownership nonetheless pay at least an 8 percent return? It did so by forcing the slave to subsist on about one-third of what the market yielded to a northern farm worker (i.e., $60 compared to $182).[47] Slave ownership almost by definition required that slave prices adjust at least to an 8 percent rate of return. For competing alternatives enticed southern investors: southern land, southern manufacturing; northern railroad bonds and factory stocks; English railroad securities. Given such alternatives, the sizable trade in slaves

42. Robert Fogel and Stanley Engerman, *Time on the Cross* I (1974):5–6, estimate that "the typical field hand received about 90 percent of the income he produced." Their method of estimate stipulates (I:153; II:124–25) that if slaves had never been paid any wages, or given any food or clothing in their entire adult life they still would owe their owners—for the food they consumed while being raised to become a saleable product. Plus the forgone interest their owners did not receive on that food (and which the slaves certainly did not receive).

43. The earnings of free labor in the old South do not provide a precise measure: Free labor may have worked more energetically.

44. *Conference on Research in Income and Wealth* 24:113, 118.

45. Monthly wage data from Lebergott, *Manpower*, p. 539. We estimate the value of board as the difference in daily wage paid to common labor with and without board in 1850, multiplied by 365 (see p. 541).

46. The quoted efficiency differential is from Fogel and Engerman, *Time* 1:192 and, in general, all of vol. 1, chap. 6.

47. For the wide difference between these estimates and those in *Time on the Cross*, see the review of that volume by Stanley Lebergott in the *American Political Science Review* (June 1975), pp. 697–700.

Of course total expected return to slaveholders included both current return and capital gains, the latter running about 2% a year 1840 to 1860.

would hardly have taken place unless investors in slaves could earn something close to the alternative 8 percent plus a premium to compensate for dealing with that "troublesome property."

Slavery as a way of organizing human labor and providing returns to those who were masters of power reaches far back in history, and lasted long after it ended in the United States. From the first day of separation from England, the profitability of slavery in America confronted a system of free labor. That conflict of political and moral interest appeared in other slaveholding nations. The United States did not continue slaveholding to the 1870s as did Brazil, or the 1960s as did Saudi Arabia. But it did not end slavery by choosing the commercial solution of Great Britain—buying out slaveholders. Nor did it adopt Russia's communal solution, in which the slaves slowly had to pay for their own freedom. Instead the United States split apart in armed conflict. And freedom sprang from civil war.

Appendix A: Maintenance Costs of Slaves

Food

We estimate an 1850 average of $3 a month: farm labor wages with board in 1850 ran 30 percent above the $10 a month rate without board. (Lebergott, *Manpower*, pp. 439, 541.) A $36 annual figure is close to the median board rate for various industrial enterprises in 1847–52 as noted by Robert Starobin, *Industrial Slavery in the Old South* (1970), pp. 296–97.

Slave holders would, of course, have reckoned in the cost of food preparation. Raw food costs of $21 are implicit in the calculation by Fogel and Engerman (*Time*, 2:117). That figure would be raised to $27 if one adopted instead the revised raw food figures of Richard Sutch (*Treatment*, cited *infra*)

Other food averages are as follows: $30, *Baton Rouge Gazette* (September 19, 1829); $24, James Sellers, *Slavery in Alabama* (1950), p. 98; $55 a year in slave boarding on railroad work (15 cents a day) and another estimate of 20 cents a day, or $73, in Charles Sydnor, *Slavery in Mississippi* (1933), p. 36; $73, or 20 cents a day boarding negro hands in a factory is recorded in *De Bow's Review* VII (1855):176, as contrasted with 30 cents a day for white hands. Robert Russell, *North America* (1857), p. 180, quotes Georgia planters to the effect that food and clothing cost from $30 to $40 a year. (If one takes a $15 figure for clothing, *infra*, food would come to $20.) The lowest estimate is probably that implicit for the sugar plantations under French ownership: the Louisiana ration in 1802 consisted of "1 barrel of maze, not pounded . . . some masters, more humane than others, add to the ration a little salt." John W. Davis, trans. *Travels in Louisiana and the Floridas in the Year 1802* (1806), p. 86.

Corn

William Parker and Judith Klein in Conference on Research in Income and Wealth, *Output, Employment and Productivity in the United States After 1800* (1966), pp. 549–51, offer data indicating that in the South 4 hours of work were required to produce a bushel of corn. The 30th Cong., 2d sess., H.D. 59, *Annual Report, Commissioner of Patents for the Year 1848*, p. 487, quotes a Virginia report that "ten bushels of corn, well ground, will make twelve bushels of meal, which gives per head the week little less than a peck." Ezra Seaman, *Progress of Nations* (1852), p. 274, states "the allowance to adult field slaves is usually one peck each per week, or thirteen bushels per year." Similar quantity allowances are reported by Gray et al. as noted in the comprehensive study: Richard Sutch, "The Treatment Received by American Slaves: A Critical Review of the Evidence Presented in *Time on the Cross*," *Explorations in Economic History* 12 (1975):360.

Robert Gallman and R. V. Anderson, *Slaves as Fixed Capital* (n.d.), p. 11, use data from nine plantations to estimate a work day averaging 10.53 hours. Taking the above data—4 hours per bushel, 10.53 hours per day, and, say, 11 bushels of corn (13 of meal) per year—gives 4.2 days required to produce a year's consumption of corn. The Southern farm laborer in 1850 earned about 70 cents a day (Lebergott *Manpower*, p. 539). Hence, the 4.2 days for corn were worth $2.95. If one adopts Parker's revised six-hour figure (Output, p. 532) one gets $4.45—virtually the same figure derived using Towne-Rasmussen's 40 cents a bushel value.

Pork

An estimate of 200 pounds per working hand appears in 30th Cong., 2d sess. (cited *supra*), H.D. 59, *Annual Report, Commissioner of Patents for the Year 1848*, p. 495. An average of 208 pounds is taken as an intentionally generous figure by Robert Gallman, "Self-sufficiency in the Cotton Economy of the Antebellum South," *Agricultural History* (January 1970), p. 18. A weekly average of 3–4 pounds—175 pounds a year—is reported by many nineteenth-century writers, and is used by Gray, Phillips and many others, as noted in Sutch, "Treatment," p. 360. On p. 380 Sutch himself estimates 150 pounds, following the exceedingly indirect method of using disappearance data, as pursued by Fogel and Engerman in *Time on the Cross*. It rests on a lengthy sequence of assumed values. (It adopts a sample average of 144 pounds for the dressed weight of the average hog, while a direct Virginia estimate of 170 pounds of pork per hog appears in the 1848 Patent Office *Annual Report*, p. 482.) More importantly, the extensive contemporary reports, indicating 3–4 pounds of pork per full-task hand, cannot readily be ignored in favor of a sequence of assumptions that yields a figure below the lower bound of this range.

We estimate pork as worth 5 cents a pound, the price for which it was purchasable on plantations. Wendell Stephenson, *Isaac Franklin* (1938), pp. 244–59 reports that Franklin bought bacon in 1846–49 (in hogsheads averaging 800 pounds) at a median price of 5¢ a pound. Nathaniel Ware, *Notes on Political Economy as Applied to the United States by a Southern Planter* (New York, 1844) p. 201 estimates 200 pounds of bacon or pork per slave costing $8. The cost of bacon for a slave owned by the Savannah and Charlestown Railroad was estimated at $15 (*De Bow's Review* 18 (1855):405). Edward Ruffin, *Essay on Calcareous Manures* (1842), p. 132, estimates $9 for plantation cost of "meat, fish etc." in 1828. A sale of some 300 pounds at 5 cents a pound is reported in *The American Farmer* 5 (1844): E. J. Forstall (quoted in J. C. Sitterson, *Sugar Country: The Cane Sugar Industry in the South, 1753–1950* (1953), p. 161) finds mess pork costing $12 a barrel in Louisiana, slaves consuming 9/10 of a barrel (a barrel presumably weighing about 200 pounds). James Hammond in 1841 estimated 160 pounds of bacon per slave, at a cost of $9. (John Van Deusen, *Economic Bases of Disunion in South Carolina* (1928), p. 269.)

A consumption rate of 3.5 pounds a week, at 5 cents a pound, leads to an annual cost of $9.10—as compared to the Hammond figure of $9, and Forstall's figure (for Louisiana) of $10.80. We thus take a round $10 figure for the entire South.

Clothing

We take a $15 expenditure figure for slave clothing using the median figure from 21 reports for enterprises that hired labor in the old South—iron works, plantations, railroads, etc.[1]

Rent

No rental figures are available for slave cabins. However, on more than one occasion slave owners sued for slave cabins destroyed by some type of government action. In 1820 suits were instituted for the loss of "a negro house" and cabins, whose values were specified at from $30 to $100. We take a mean value of $60 for "a negro house 12 by 12."[2] Cabin sizes recorded by Olmsted, Russel, and Weld vary around this dimension. At a 10 percent imputed rental rate (used in recent years for very different housing by the Department of Commerce, National Income Division, Thomas Juster, Leo Grebler, and others) the imputed rent was $6 a year. (At a then common interest rate of 7 percent,[3] plus repairs, the rent would have been similar.)

Medical

Estimates are $1: Nathaniel Ware, *Notes on Political Economy as Applied to the United States by a Southern Planter* (1844), p. 201; $1.35, for the Society Hill, South Carolina plantation, James L. Watkins, *The Cost of Cotton Production*, USDA Misc. Bulletin 16 (1899):44.

1. For 16 enterprises we use the summary in Robert Starobin, *Industrial Slavery in the Old South* (1970), p. 296–97. Other estimates were: $20, in "Superiority of Slave Labor," *De Bow's Review* 18(1855): 405; $8 in David Warden, *A Statistical, Political and Historical Account of the United States of America* (1819), p. 275; $17, in *Niles* (1822) 41 (Addendum), p. 49; $14, in Edward J. Forstall, *Agricultural Productions of Louisiana* (1845), p. 24. Thomas Cooper, *Lectures on the Elements of Political Economy* (1831), p. 106, estimates $40 a year for food, clothing, and medical care per hand. He records on p. 197 food as 9 quarts of corn and 3 pounds of pork a week, at $30. The clothing figure would then be about $9. Edmund Ruffin, *An Essay on Calcareous Manures* (1842), p. 132, estimates $7 for slave textiles, shoes, and blankets in Virginia in 1828–32. A $12 figure for Louisiana sugar plantations is given in the *Baton Rouge Gazette* (September 19, 1829).

2. 16th Cong., 1st sess., 1819–1820, S. D. 49, *Report, Committee on Claims . . . Joseph McNeil*, p. 6, and S. D. 51, *Report . . . Damages Occasioned by Troops of the United States . . .* , pp. 2–6.

3. Governor Miller of South Carolina declared in 1829 that "Upon the capital embarked in planting, few persons made more than four per cent; yet, upon all the contracts connected with the objects of agriculture, seven per cent is allowed . . . the planter who is now paying seven per cent interest is engaged in a losing business," quoted by Alfred G. Smith, *Economic Readjustment of an Old Cotton State* (1958), p. 107. Smith states on p. 107, "a common complaint between 1820 and 1860 was that the rate of return on agricultural investments was below the maximum legal rate of interest, which was seven per cent."

Appendix B

In a series of extended articles, collected into a major study, *The Political Economy of Slavery* (1965), Eugene Genovese developed the following analysis. "The economic backwardness that condemned the slaveholding South to defeat in 1861–1865 had its root in the low productivity of labor . . . Bondage forced the Negro to give his labor grudgingly and badly . . ." (p. 43).

Yet,

> However much the slaves may have worked below their capacity, the limitations placed on that capacity were even more important in undermining productivity. In particular, the diet to which the slaves were subjected must be judged immensely damaging. . . . The slave usually got enough to eat, but the starchy high energy diet of cornmeal, pork and molasses produced specific hungers, dangerous deficiencies and [an] . . . unidentified form of malnutrition. . . . Protein hunger alone . . . greatly reduces the ability of an organism to resist infectious diseases. . . . The abundant pork provided was largely fat. Since the slave economy did not and could not provide sufficient livestock, no solution presented itself. [p. 45]

(However, "not provide" and "no solution" are used in a very unusual sense, for p. 115 suggests that "the South [could and did] import substantial quantities of hogs and pork.") Nor, he adds, was "the limited diet . . . primarily a result of ignorance or viciousness on the part of masters."[4] What, then, *was* the reason behind the "limited diet" that led to the low productivity of slave labor? "The problem was largely economic. Feeding costs formed a burdensome part of plantation expenses. Credit and market systems precluded the assignment of much land to crops other than cotton and corn." (p. 46) "Southern attempts to increase nonstaple production and to improve livestock broke down in the face of enormous difficulties. . . . The planters had little surplus capital with which to buy improved breeds and could not guarantee the care necessary to make the investment worthwhile." (p. 117)

If neither ignorance nor viciousness nor inability to import pork explains planter behavior in feeding slaves, the implicit argument in all this is that planters tried to reduce "feeding costs . . . a burdensome part of plantation expenses" by buying cheaper, fatty pork. Even assuming that they did, how much could they save? Prime pork cost 4.5 cents a pound; the better "mess pork" cost 6 cents a pound.[5] What evidence is there

---

4. The views outlined in this study were not obviously superceded or touched on at all directly in Elizabeth Genovese and Eugene Genovese, *Fruits of Merchant Capital* (1983). At most it notes that slaves supplemented their diet by gardens, fishing, etc. (p. 56).

The failure of the slave diet to provide a proper balance of proteins was matched by the failure of the diet of most Southern whites to do so. Only after research by Atwater and others, and the life work and insights of Goldberger, was the basic ignorance on these matters swept away—long after the Civil War.

5. The price of pork is from Ezra Seaman, *Essays on the Progress of Nations* (1846), p. 304. The differential is inferred from wholesale prices in the *Annual Report of the Secretary of the Treasury* (1881), Table XXV.

that the bulk of slaveowners were so lunatic as to hazard the lives and lower the money productivity of their valuable slaves to save $3 a year?

Moreover, what evidence is there that planters chose cheaper meat so as to cut "burdensome expenses"? The obvious reason was ignorance of nutrition, dispelled only after the Civil War. But Genovese specifically excludes "ignorance" as the cause. Mess pork at $12 a barrel is referred to by Forstall as the standard slave food.[6] Fogel and Engerman estimate that the slave diet provided more than enough protein.[7] A recent extensive study agrees that "the standard ration" was "adequate to provide sufficient energy to work like a slave."[8]

6. Cf. J. Carlyle Sitterson, *Sugar Country* (1953), p. 161.

7. Fogel and Engerman, *Time on the Cross*, p. 114.

8. Richard Sutch, in Paul David et al., *Reckoning With Slavery* (1976), p. 268–81, suggests that the slave diet "may generally have been nutritionally balanced even when the slave ration provided by the master was not," thanks to slave gardens and pilferage. These garden sources were, in fact, widespread. Flanders declares "it was the universal custom in Georgia to allow slaves the privilege of raising small crops of their own." (David, p. 73)

What an incomprehensible machine is man! who can en-
dure toil, famine . . . death itself in vindication of his own
liberty, and the next moment . . . inflict on his fellow
men a bondage, one hour of which is fraught with more
misery than ages of that which he rose in rebellion to oppose. But we must wait with patience the workings of an
overruling providence, and hope that is preparing the deliverance of these, our suffering brethren.
—THOMAS JEFFERSON, 1786

19

The Hinge of Fate

O NE great and bloody event splits American history in two: the Civil
War. That war ended slavery. It began a massive sequence of moral and
social change. And it expanded the scope and potential of the economy. The
timing of the war, and in part its very occurrence, were fixed by a critical sequence of events from 1846 to 1848. Churchill once described the year 1942 as
"the hinge of fate," that turning point when the eventual outcome of World
War II became clear. In the same way the events of 1846–48 decided when the
Civil War would break out—and perhaps even whether it would.

The first of these critical events took place on the American continent.
The Mexican War occurred in 1846. As a result of that war, Texas was an-
nexed to the United States under Tyler, latest in the Virginia dynasty of presidents. That action, he declared, "gave to the U.S. a monopoly of the cotton
plant, and thus secured to us a power of boundless extent in the affairs of the
world. . . . The monopoly . . . was the great and important concern. . . . [It] places all other nations at our feet; an embargo of a single year
would produce in Europe a greater amount of suffering than a fifty year
war."[1]

Men were induced to enlist in the Mexican War by the promise of bounties. These were given in the form of land warrants, entitling the soldiers to

1. Lyon Tyler, *Letters and Times of the Tylers* (1855), 2:422, 483.

160 acres of land, which they could locate anywhere in the public domain (that had already been mapped). The political consequences of this offer were inevitable in a democracy and swift in arriving. Soldiers who had fought in prior wars, or their widows, pressed for similar bounties. If service in the Mexican War justified such a gift from the government, what about those who had fought in the Revolutionary War? Or the Black Hawk War? Eventually Congress had to give 37 million acres to the doddering relicts of the War of 1812, 4 millions to those of the Revolutionary War, and so on. Virtually all 53 million acres issued in land warrants were located in the newly developing North Central region. Over 400,000 families therefore may be estimated to have settled there.[2] And with settlement came the organization of new states, with votes in subsequent presidential elections.

The other major settlement that resulted from the Mexican War came when California was acquired by the Treaty of Guadeloupe Hidalgo. Almost immediately afterward, gold was discovered, in 1848, in the waters of Captain Sutter's sawmill, now officially U.S. territory. Hundreds of thousands of Americans, Europeans, and Asians began heading for California. Many gave up and settled part-way. But during the next year 40,000 succeeded in sailing into San Francisco Bay. Perhaps 100,000 walked overland all the way to California, some driving oxen on the way.

The second set of key events in 1846–48 took place in Europe. In 1846 Britain finally adopted free trade in grain. Henceforth American wheat entered English ports without paying duty. In short order American exports expanded enormously. Driving down the price of British wheat, helping to destroy much of the ancient landed aristocracy, they wiped out many of Britain's small farmers. As one result British migration to the United States began to rise, peaking in the 1850s.

In 1846–48 Ireland faced an unexampled series of potato crop failures. Since the population had grown steadily in the first half of the century to a point where there was no margin of safety, the crop failures meant widespread death—and migration to the United States.

In these same years revolution broke out in France, in Germany, in Italy, and in Hungary. (In 1848, the year of the Communist Manifesto, Marx and Engels saw revolt spreading so fast that the old European capitalist order was doomed. These revolutions turned out not to be the death knell of capitalism. But they did drive defeated revolutionaries to migrate to the U.S. And still other Europeans fled the disturbances the revolts brought.) These European catastrophes forcefully increased the flow of immigrants to the United States. Immigration had been 100,000 in 1845. It jumped to 200,000 in 1847, and continued to rise thereafter.

2. Bounty data are based on a sample tabulation of 4,190 warrant entries listed in the *Abstracts of Bounty Warrants*, now in the U.S. National Archives and Record Service. Since the typical warrant was for 120 or 100 acres, we assume one family settling per warrant.

As bounty warrants fluttered out of Washington in a nearly endless stream, and the pressures in Europe mounted, migration within the United States likewise rose. Men and women poured into the North Central states, and on to California, doubling and tripling the population of the thinly settled territories and states.[3]

Meanwhile, the old South lost population. Why was the migration rate into the South so different?[4] Two factors kept immigrants away. First, said Senator Stephen Adams (Mississippi) in 1856: "The whole education of foreigners, and their prejudices . . . are against the institution of slavery."[5] A second factor was the dramatic Southern death rate from malaria, typhoid, typhus, and yellow fever. (In New Orleans alone 7,849 people died of yellow fever in 1853, over 2,000 persons died of it in 1854 and again in 1855, and nearly 5,000 in 1858.[6]) Thousands of Irish laborers had died in digging the canals around New Orleans, and word had gotten back to Europe. (To dimension these numbers: annual deaths in the entire United States from all air and water pollution a century later about equaled New Orleans' yellow fever deaths in 1853–54.)

This sequence of events in 1846–48, and the migration it induced to and within the United States, created a population redistribution of major political importance. The U.S. population in 1830–60 was distributed as shown in Table 19.1. One aspect of these figures stands out: right up to the Civil War the North and South had an equal share in population—and in the U.S. Senate. As the North Central region grew, its vote in political battles came to be decisive.

The South read those political implications and decided that "it was time to calculate the value of the Union."[7] As Henry Wise (Virginia's Governor just before the war) put it:

> The [Mexican] war was prosecuted with enthusiasm and success and resulted in the acquisition of Texas, New Mexico and upper California. This vast domain, and the gold mines of Sacramento, changed the whole destiny of the United States . . . but the golden fruit was guarded by the dragon: the immense immigration to America, and the enormous addition of wealth . . . by the California mines, revived the Missouri compromise contention. . . . Two more free states were admitted, Iowa and Wisconsin, and the beam of the balance of the union was kicked against the South.[8]

3. Migration estimates from Stanley Lebergott, "Migration Within the U.S. 1800–1960: Some New Estimates," *Journal of Economic History* (December 1970), Table 1.

4. Most of the migration out of the old South probably went to the West South Central region, but some surely flowed North or West.

5. 34th Cong., 1st sess., *Congressional Globe* (June 26, 1856), p. 1413. Adams added: "by free immigration you are fostering a power destined to destroy the country."

6. Joseph Jones, *Medical and Surgical Memoirs* (1888) vol. 3, part 1, p. 296.

7. In the 1827 phrase of President Thomas Cooper of South Carolina College; David D. Wallace, *South Carolina* (1951), p. 388.

8. Henry A. Wise, *Seven Decades of the Union* (1872), p. 246.

TABLE 19.1
U.S. POPULATION DISTRIBUTION BY REGION
(PERCENT OF ENTIRE U.S. POPULATION)

	1830	1840	1850	1860
North	43	40	37	34
South	44	41	39	35
North Central	12	20	23	29

Source: 1970 Census, PC (1)-A1, *Number of Inhabitants, U.S. Summary* (1970), Table 10.

In 1861 Marx and Engels wrote: "The leaders of the South had never de-ceived themselves as to the necessity for keeping up their *political* sway over the United States. John Calhoun . . . stated distinctly . . . in 1847 'that the Senate was the only balance of power left to the South in the government,' and that the creation of new slave states had become necessary 'for the reten-tion of the equipoise of power in the Senate.' "[9] But few such states were created: immigrants did not go South and few Southerners moved out of the old South. In the end a political party less than ten years old, aided by a split between the inflamed states rights group and the Douglas Democrats, ended the South's long dominance in the federal government. And the war came.

9. Karl Marx and Frederick Engels, *The Civil War in the United States* (n.d.), p. 12.

Part Three

1860–1900

The period begins in barbarism, and ends in failure.
—ALFRED NORTH WHITEHEAD, *Adventures of Ideas*

20

The Civil War

THE war was the last, and most decisive, in a series of conflicts that reached far back in time. The Missouri Compromise of 1820; the South Carolina secession conventions of 1833 and 1851; the Mexican War; the Compromise of 1850; the pitched battles in Kansas; the Kansas-Nebraska Act. Each of these marked the conflict between North and South. Why did the entire South finally secede?

South Carolina seceded upon word of Lincoln's election in November of 1860. But other states lingered. Perhaps, as many times before, a compromise would give the South all it sought. Two days after Senator Brown's telegram reported the failure of the Crittenden compromise, Mississippi seceded.[1] Months later Virginia followed.

Southern constitutional theory argued that as each state had a right to unite, it had an equal right to secede. G. G. Memminger, Secretary of the Treasury in the Confederate States of America (CSA), had wisely noted: "While secession was a right . . . its exercise was not necessarily one that would not be resisted" by the other states.[2] These secessions, CSA General Jubal Early declared, ignored Lincoln's inaugural guarantee "that he would perform his duty" under the Constitution. And CSA General Braxton Bragg similarly saw the address as guaranteeing "peace and protection for our property, and [indicating] that the fugitive slave law would be faithfully executed." Virginia, therefore, was being placed "in this perilous condition solely from the action of those states that have seceded from the Union without having consulted our views."[3]

---

1. "On January 9, 1861, hardly six weeks after Governor John Jones Pettus had called upon the state to 'go down into Egypt while Herod rules in Judea' Mississippi fled the union." John K. Bettersworth, *Confederate Mississippi* (1943), p. 1. The first states formed the Confederate States of America in February 1861. Not until Virginia joined them later in 1861 was it clear that war was inevitable.

2. Henry Capers, *The Life and Times of G. G. Memminger* (1893), p. 227.

3. Beverly Munford, *Virginia's Attitude Toward Slavery and Secession* (1909), p. 266. Virginia's long delay has been ascribed to her waiting until the CSA finally adopted a constitution forbid-

233

The Decision

Two grand theories have been used to explain the South's secession. One describes a totally rational decision; the other, a vividly irrational one. It is fairly simple to imagine a "rational" calculation in which the prospective loss of income from slaves was found to exceed prospective money costs of the war.[4] But the South expected neither abolition nor the ending of slave income. As a Confederate delegation told Great Britain's Prime Minister in August 1861: "It was from no fear that the slaves would be liberated that secession took place. The very party in power has proposed to guarantee slavery forever in the States if the South would remain in the union."[5] And who would "rationally" calculate the cost of a war yet ignore its catalog of injuries and suffering?[6]

One of the nation's greatest novelists, and a Southerner, has compressed the irrational view into a single sentence: "Who else would have declared a war against a power with 10 times the area, and 100 times the men and 1,000 times the resources?"[7] His arithmetic was fantastically in error. But his imagery was crystalline: wounded pride; the "responsibility" for race guidance and discipline; and the mystic requirements that destiny laid upon a ruling class to combine liberty and responsibility. All these impelled the South. It knew not why; it had no choice.

Another view declares that the South was fighting to reopen the slave trade. But the facts controvert it. As early as January 1861, Mississippi's Secession Convention voted to secede. But it likewise voted that "it is not the purpose of the State of Mississippi to reopen the African Slave trade."[8] In March Virginia's Convention voted for a CSA Constitutional Amendment that would prohibit foreign slave trade.[9] And Article 1 of the Confederacy's Constitution forbade import of "African negroes from any foreign country."[10] (True, a handful of activists in some pre-war Commercial Conventions tried to reopen the trade. But the balance of Southern interests weighed heavily against a trade that would inevitably force down the market value of the slaves already owned in the South.)

ding (Sec. 9, Art. 1) the importation of slaves from Africa. Had those favoring importation won, the value of Virginia's slaves would have fallen.

4. Gerald Gunderson, "The Origins of the Civil War," *Journal of Economic History* (December 1974), pp. 915–50.

5. Yancey, Rost, and Mann to Lord Russell, in the *War of the Rebellion (Navies)* Series II, 3 (1922):244.

6. Gunderson measures the human costs by matching the forgone civilian incomes against the imputed incomes of soldiers. Deaths enter into this calculation only as an earnings diferential. Hence the deaths of white or free colored women, of men over 50, of children under 10 are all valued at zero.

7. William Faulkner, *Go Down Moses* (1942), pp. 288–89.

8. John K. Bettersworth, *Confederate Mississippi* (1943), p. 13.

9. Beverly Munford, *Virginia's Attitude Toward Slavery and Secession* (1909), pp. 271, 274.

10. 58th Cong., 2d sess., S. D. 234, *Journal of the Congress of the Confederate States of America, 1861–65* (1904), 1:95.

Did the war begin because the South feared the North would abolish slavery? Unlikely. On the Sunday before Lincoln was inaugurated, Congress actually passed a law forbidding the federal government from interfering with slavery in any slave state—and requiring three-fourths of the states to approve that law as a constitutional amendment. (The same session voted down then Secretary of War Edwin Stanton's "force bill" to give the President control over the state militias.)[11]

The attitude of the new administration was succinctly put by Lincoln's letter of December 22, 1860, to Alexander Stephens, soon to become vice president of the Confederacy: "Do the people of the South really entertain fears that a Republican administration would, directly or indirectly, interfere with the slaves, or with them about the slaves? If they do, I wish to assure you, as once a friend, and still, I hope, not an enemy, that there is no cause for such fears. The South would be in no more danger in this respect than it was in the days of Washington."[12]

Three primary and massive forces explain the South's decision to secede.

1) One powerful element was a frontier-feudal willingness to adopt a belligerent stance, personally and politically. That stance did not characterize regions where the family farmer or small craftsman was dominant. But from 1789 on, warfare with American Indians took place mostly in and for Southern territory: Florida (in 1819); the Creek wars in Georgia (in the 1820s); the war for the independence of Texas (in 1836); and the Mexican War (in 1848). The great arsenals and army bases were also mostly in the South. And U.S. army and navy officers were disproportionately recruited from the South.

Does this mean that the South's leaders were more belligerent than those of the North? At first glance, that conclusion seems unwarranted. The president of the CSA, Jefferson Davis, had "opposed headlong secession." He left his U.S. Senate seat "with gloomy forebodings of a 'long and bloody war.' "[13] Alexander Stephens (CSA vice-president), Herschel Johnson and Benjamin Hill—major leaders of the CSA—"gave up their fight for the union only after their state seceded."[14] Robert E. Lee, the great military leader of the South for nearly the entire war, had declared, years before, that "slavery is a moral and practical evil." And while the Virginia Convention was still pondering the desirability of seceding, Lee said: "I am one of those dull creatures that

11. Carl Sandburg, *Abraham Lincoln; The War Years* (1939) I:119.

12. John G. Nicolay and John Hay, "Abraham Lincoln: A History," *Century Magazine* (November 1887), p. 82.

13. Dunbar Rowland, *Encyclopedia of Mississippi History I* (1907):623–24; John K. Bettersworth, *Confederate Mississippi* (1943), p. 17. Rowland was the admiring and knowledgeable biographer of Jefferson Davis.

14. E. M. Coulter, *The Confederate States of America, 1861–65* (1950), p. 4.

cannot see the good of secession."[15] But other powerful leaders were in-flamed. Robert Toombs, Senator from Georgia who almost became president of the CSA, declared more than once: "He who dallies is a dastard; he who doubts is damned."[16] Toombs spoke for a large and vocal group described contemptuously by General Braxton Bragg of the CSA. Secession, Bragg de-clared, had been engineered by a set of "political hacks and barroom bullies . . . who could easily pull down a government, but inspired no confidence in setting up another."[17] Such heroes of the vigorous deed were hardly lacking in a region that tendered a formal dinner to applaud two Congressmen for beating Massachusetts Congressman Sumner with wooden canes while he was seated at his desk. Of course belligerent feelings were not restricted to the South. A well-known Northern minister declared that "the Sharpe rifle was a truly moral agency, and that there was more moral power in one of those in-struments, so far as the Slave-Holders of Kansas were concerned, than in a thousand Bibles. . . . They have supreme respect for the logic that is em-bodied in Sharpe's rifles."[18]

2) A second element was the fact that the entire nation had not yet been welded into a unit. The first loyalty of many Southerners was not to the United States, but to their own state. Emblematic was Major Richard Meade. A West Point graduate, he defended Fort Sumter when the South Carolinians began bombarding it. After its surrender he returned North. But when his home state seceded, Meade felt it his duty to resign from the U.S. Army. He then joined Virginia's military contingent to the CSA.[19]

Still other Southerners joined their local military companies for the most prudent reasons. By joining immediately, wrote one, he would be with men from his area, and of his quality: "It would be very disagreeable for me to go with those companies which would be formed afterwards as they would be composed of the dregs of the parish."[20]

3) But the entire South was rushed into a war by more than a combina-tion of military, feudal, and local loyalties and values. It was committed to a way of life that rested on the profitable ownership of slaves. This meant more than the simple fact that slaves yielded a steady income. Can one imagine a cool decision to break up the union, even to risk a "moderate" war, in order to continue earning 10 percent on slave investments? It is ridiculous not least be-cause the South could earn nearly as much in various other investments, and later proved it could do so.

15. Munford, *Virginia's Attitude*, p. 101, and *The Memoirs of Colonel John Mosby* (1917; reprint ed., 1959), p. 379.

16. Pleasant Stovall, *Robert Toombs* (1892), p. 205.

17. Quoted in Merton Coulter, *The Confederate States of America, 1861–1865* (1950), p. 328.

18. *Fanaticism and Its Results or Facts Versus Fancies* (by a Southerner) (1860), p. 14.

19. Francis Bradlee, *Blockade Running During the Civil War* (1925), p. 166.

20. " . . . and verily mortifying not only to me but to the whole family to have me drafted," quoted by J. Carlyle Sitterson in "The McCollams," *Journal of Southern History* VI (1940):295.

The explanation turns rather on the potential loss of individual investments in slaves. To earn 8 percent rather than 10 percent was no catastrophe. But to lose one's entire worldly assets was quite another matter. True, the slaves could have been bought out at market prices as Victorian Britain had showed.[21] But no Northern political party, church group, or Northern legislature had been prepared to make so great a financial sacrifice. (A leading Massachusetts Democrat inveighed against the proposal to "buy up the negroes of the South" in order to end slavery. Doing so would create "a great national debt, greater than Great Britain," thereby making "the republic [into an] empire," because of the "great patronage existing in the hands of one magistrate."[22]) And what about compensation for future capital gains? Every addition to the territory of the United States extended the area within which slaves could be used, and shifted the demand curve for slaves outward. No such capital gains could be expected by the South once the North Central and Northeastern states took over both Congress and presidency. Toombs warned the Senate on the day he left it for the CSA: "I will now read my own demands." Of these the first was "that the people of the United States shall have an equal right to emigrate and settle in the present or any future acquired territory with whatever property they possess, including slaves. . . . You seek to outlaw $4 billion dollars of property . . . in the territories of the U.S.; is not that a cause of war?"[23] So long as more and more slave territory could be added—California? Mexico? Cuba?—the market for the slaves of the old South would expand. And with expanding demand, slave owners would be able to sell off their slaves (and their slaves' children) at a rising price. To restrict slavery within its older limits was to permit other nations (e.g., Texas when it was still an independent republic, Cuba, Brazil, etc.) to use slave labor for growing cotton in even more effective competition with the South.

Suppose the North had proposed compensated emancipation at generous rates. Would the South have accepted compensation given its obsessive fear of a slave uprising? Of the emancipation proclamation, Mississippi's Senator Phelan remarked: "Our brutal foes . . . seek to light the baneful fires of servile war . . . a scheme so atrocious and infernal is unparalleled in the blackest and bloodiest page of savage strife; it surpasses in atrocious cruelty the most signal despotism that ever disgraced the earth."[24]

During the American Revolution the South had provided harsh rhetoric, but few troops, to fight the British. Few of its men traveled to the battlefields

21. Despised by generations of delicate and astute critics it was Britain's bourgeois Victorians who taxed themselves in the 1830s to buy out and thereby free the slaves in their West Indian colonies.

22. Luther Hamilton, ed, *Memoirs, Speeches and Writings of Robert Rantoul, Jr.* (1854), p. 809.

23. 36th Cong., 2d sess., *Congressional Globe*, pp. 270–71.

24. Quoted by E. Merton Coulter, *The Confederate States of America, 1861–1865* (1950), p. 265.

where the British were attacking Washington and his generals. They stayed in their homes, or nearby, because they feared "a servile rebellion." After all, the entire population of Haiti had been almost totally destroyed just a few years earlier in a slave revolt. A mere handful of survivors limped into Baltimore and New Orleans. That ghastly event had been followed by well-publicized "revolts" in the United States in 1816 and 1831. Southerners retained a looming image of catastrophe for over a century. (Actual destruction by slaves during the entire Civil War probably did not equal that of a single day in the 1967 riots. Yet such fears limited efficient use of slaves throughout the war.)

Horace Greeley and other Northerners proposed to tell the seceders: "Erring sisters, depart in peace." And Wendell Phillips, the great abolitionist leader, declared on April 9, 1861, that the principles of 1776 gave the South the "right" to a separate government.[25] But Abraham Lincoln felt, as did a majority of the North, that the constitution obliged him to keep the union together. He simply could not let the world's leading democracy break into bits.

Two sentences in a Lincoln letter of 1861 to Stephens went to the heart of the problem: "I suppose, however, this does not meet the case. You think slavery is right and ought to be extended, while we think it is wrong and ought to be restricted. That, I suppose, is the rub, it certainly is the only substantial difference between us."[26]

John Stuart Mill, a classical economist, offered a summary judgment: "The slavery quarrel in America . . . was in all its stages an aggressive enterprise of slave owners to extend the territory of slavery; under the combined influences of pecuniary interest, domineering temper, and the fanaticism of a class for its class privileges."[27]

Four years later the most penetrating inaugural in American history concluded: "Both parties deprecated war; but one of them would make war rather than let the nation survive; and the other would accept war rather than let it perish. And the war came."

The Conflict

How equally were the "belligerents" matched? William Faulkner contended that the North had ten times the area of the South. In fact, it had much the same area.[28] But mere land provides more than resources (a bene-

25. Quoted in Sandburg, *Abraham Lincoln; The War Years* I:182.
26. Nicolay and Hay, "Abraham Lincoln."
27. *Autobiography of John Stuart Mill* (1944), p. 187.
28. The territories required more military protection, and imports, than they contributed. But even including them would only make a 4 to 1 ratio. Cf. 1970 Census, PC(1) 1A, Number of Inhabitants, *United States Summary* (1970), pp. 1–52.

fit). It must also be defended (a cost). We must therefore look to more basic measures.

Of these, manpower was primary. The South's army averaged 414,000 men.[29] The North's averaged 680,000—many more but a far cry from Faulkner's "100 times."[30] Sickness and desertion also took their toll of both armies. About 80 percent of the boys in butternut gray were present in ranks at the end of 1861. The South still retained nearly 75 percent in ranks a year later (as did the North), despite bloody battles and sickness. But sickness and desertions steadily brought the rate down to 50 percent for the South (65 percent for the North) by the end of 1864 and, inevitably, still lower in 1865.[31] As early as October 1863 Secretary of War James Seddon declared that Lee's effective forces hardly ran more than 50 percent; even allowing for sickness, "one third of our Army on an average are [still] absent from their posts and may, with due efforts, be returned."[32]

The flow of men into the Confederate armies reflected the sharp variation of "patriotism" among the Southern states. A simple comparison between draft exemptions granted by the Carolinas (Table 20.1) is revealing. With about twice the white population of South Carolina,[33] North Carolina

TABLE 20.1
NUMBER OF MEN EXEMPTED FROM CONFEDERATE DRAFT
(UP TO NOVEMBER 1864) BY CAUSE OF EXEMPTION

	Physical reasons	Occupation	
		State officials	Medical doctors
South Carolina	1,571	105	324
North Carolina	28,055	13,101	956

Source: Exemption data quoted in *Richmond Examiner*, November 21, 1864.

29. U.S. War Department, *War of the Rebellion*, Series IV, I:822, 1176; II:278, 380, 530, 615, 1073; III:520, 989, 1182.

30. Frederick Phisterer, *The Army in the Civil War* (1883), vol. XIII; *Statistical Record of the Armies of the United States*, (1883), p. 62. Phisterer's data, from the *Report* of the Provost-Marshal-General, give the men in service at different dates, January 1, 1861–March 31, 1865. These were graphed and interpolated, to give an average for the 1861–64 period.

31. Rate computed from the abstracts of returns to the Confederate War Department cited in Note 29 above.

32. U.S. War Department, *War of the Rebellion*, Series IV, 2:995.

33. Population data from 1860 Census, in 1970 Census of Population, *Number of Inhabitants* United States Summary, Table 18.

granted 20 times as many physical exemptions. It exempted over 100 times as many state officials. Such differences testify to the well-known disaffection in North Carolina for the war. It was intense, though somewhat milder than the feelings that made the western counties of Virginia break away from the slave-holding, fighting South to become West Virginia.

The Southern advantage in experienced military men, however, was another matter. And a critical one in a war. More than a third of all U. S. Army officers deserted to the South—many before the war began.[34] And 90 percent of West Point graduates deserted.[35] The navy, however, was different. Its officers also deserted. But, as the Confederacy informed Britain's prime minister, they had so "high a sense of duty" that they first "honorably delivered [their ships] to the U. S. Government."[36]

Much has been made of the great difference between North and South in industrial power, in factory output, and in income. It is well, however, to recognize that the South fought on for four years despite these differences. (The shattering experience of American defeat in Vietnam emphasizes how morale, commitment, and willingness to die can win a war, can swamp differences in industrial might.)

How did differences in economic strength reveal themselves? In ability to produce munitions, food, clothing, railway material, particularly. Let us look at each. How did the South get its munitions? It began the war with 28,500 guns hurriedly bought from United States arsenals. These were bought in late 1860, after South Carolina seceded, but while James Floyd (soon to become a southern general) still headed the U.S. War Department.[37] 159,000 small arms were also seized from U.S. arsenals in the South.[38] Within six months the former U.S. arsenal at Harpers Ferry was producing 1,000 weapons a month. By February 1863 the CSA had received 131,000 stand of arms from London and Vienna. Another 53,000 stand were ready for shipment.[39] And from the battle of the first Manassas CSA soldiers picked up

34. Carl Sandburg, *Abraham Lincoln; the War Years* I (1939):7.

35. E. Merton Coulter, *The Confederate States of America, 1861–1865* (1950), p. 328.

36. Yancey, Rost, and Mann to Lord Russell, August 1861: The South "commenced its career entirely without a navy. Owing to the high sense of duty which distinguished the Southern officers who were lately in commission in the U. S. Navy the ships which otherwise might have been brought into Southern ports were honorably delivered to the U. S. government . . . and were now used to coerce one third of those who had paid for them." U. S. War Department, *War of the Rebellion (Navies)* Series II, 3 (1922):241. Whether the crews were equally sympathetic to the South, or the officers could single-handedly have sailed the vessels into Southern harbors, is not discussed.

37. 36th Cong., 2d sess., H.R. 85, *Forts, Arsenals, Arms* . . . (1861), p. 32.

38. Richard Goff, *Confederate Supply* (1969), p. 14.

39. U. S. War Department, *War of the Rebellion*, Series IV, II:383–84.

thousands of U.S. rifles from battlefields. The fact that only 300 vessels of the thousands entering Southern harbors through the North's blockade were loaded with arms or munitions indicates that the South's need for such supplies was not critical; many more cargoes could have been military.[40]

Was the Confederacy unable to feed its armies, or those at home? One CSA propagandist declared in 1863: "The grain crops of the South this year are very much greater than formerly, in consequence of the hands being employed in that description of agriculture, instead of cotton, tobacco, and sugar. Indeed, it is estimated that the Confederates have now two full years' supply."[41] Jefferson Davis observed in April 1863 that the CSA even had enough meat, though it was not well distributed.[42] When the union armies entered the South they discovered plenty of food in the aggregate, though localized shortages existed.[43] As Fulkerson reminisced:

> Flour, though scarce, could be had at some point in every state. Corn meal was to be had at home everywhere. . . . The Confederacy was pretty well supplied with sugar. . . . Sorghum was largely planted and furnished a good supply of molasses . . . the sweet potato was abundant, but the Irish potato was scarce. . . . Hogs were abundant, much attention was paid to raising them. Coffee and tea were luxuries which few persons were fortunate enough to enjoy.[44]

The South had its essential and customary foods (the shortage of tea and coffee hardly prevented military effectiveness.)[45]

Was there a general shortage of clothing? In 1864 a leading textile manufacturer stated that no new cotton mill had been established during the war—suggesting that the existing mills, plus homespun, met critical needs.[46] A Richmond paper referred to the "well known improvidence of our soldiers who throw away their overcoats and blankets in spring . . . expecting to take

40. Frank Owsley, *King Cotton Diplomacy* (1931), p. 290.

41. George M'Henry, *The Position and Duty of Pennsylvania* (1863), p. 29.

42. U. S. War Department, *War of the Rebellion (Navies)*, Series II, 3, p. 147.

43. Frank Klingberg, *The Southern Claims Commission* (1955), p. 137.

44. H. S. Fulkerson, "Confederate Cotton," *Mississippi Valley Historical Review*, (December 1937), 24:369–70.

45. Military hospitals occasionally were short of whiskey, as an analgesic. But there was no overall shortage of whiskey. The *Richmond Daily Enquirer* (October 17, 1864) reported: "The cavalry's loss of morale can't be blamed on John Barleycorn, and a valley which is running with apple brandy. I tell you, dear sir, there is nothing running in this valley like our cavalry . . . there was more brandy and more drinking and more good living in this valley in the glorious times of Jackson . . . and yet he took . . . a hundred of pieces of artillery from the Yankees." (That present campaign took only ten.)

46. E. Merton Coulter, *The Confederate States of America, 1861–1865* (1950), p. 212.

new ones from the Yankees before winter."[47] And the state of North Carolina had over 90,000 new uniforms in its stock when the war ended.[48]

Imports cost the South heavily in foreign exchange. And, with few exceptions, they supplied only those items the government allowed to be imported.[49] Hence, the thousands of cargoes imported through the blockade should therefore indicate what the major needs of the South were.

The most typical entering cargo was classified as "assorted."[50] The second most numerous cargo included arms and ammunition. The third consisted of those simply designated as "coffee." For the steamer *Stettin* we have a huge "assorted" cargo fully itemized (worth $177,000). The chief item it brought a beleaguered nation in arms was 9,219 gallons of brandy. It also brought 557 cases of gin; assorted champagne and schnapps; a shipment of colored lisle hosiery for the women; 57 cases of army brogans; 83 cases of "congress gaiters"; "enamelled sidelace gaiters"; drugs and toiletry articles. In addition, it brought hardware, the major item being 3,978 sad irons (used to iron starched shirts and ruffles). The largest item by weight consisted of 154,500 pounds of coffee.[51]

The inward flow of resources from foreign nations was sizable: over 1,000 vessels entered through the blockade in 1862–65.[52] Their cargo composition does not point back to major shortages of any one type, military or civilian, that would indicate critical overall differences in industrial might between South and North. (It should be remembered that the South, with smaller armies, and whatever drawbacks came from industrial differences, fought for four years—and with great effectiveness for most of those years.) Industrial might differed. So did manpower. Insofar as these slowly told over the years, they did so when Southern morale weakened, and when military defeats occurred. There is no evidence that the ability to produce iron rather than to import it (or yardgoods or ammunition or meat) was decisive in this interacting set of forces.

The South's basic industrial strength, its ability in terms of resources, was one thing. But its willingness to allocate those resources to the war—apart from young white males to the army—was another.[53] Warren Akin,

47. *Richmond Daily Examiner*, December 13, 1864.

48. Richard Yates, "Zebulon B. Vance as War Governor," *Journal of Southern History* (1937), pp. 43–75.

49. Most imports entered a few major ports under the protection of signals provided by the CSA military authorities, and their cargoes then paid duty after inspection by these authorities. Late in 1863 the CSA began requiring that half the cargoes contain more essential goods.

50. Of those itemized in the long list of U.S. Navy captures, 1861–65, and 38th Cong., 1st sess., H.D. 74, *Prize Cases in NY*.

51. *Prize Cases*, pp. 585–95.

52. Stanley Lebergott, "Through the Blockade," *Journal of Economic History* (December 1981) p. 879. Over 2,000 entered in 1861.

53. The following text draws upon a view more fully put forth in Stanley Lebergott, "Why

member of the Confederate Congress (in 1864), "noticed the strange conduct of our people during this war. They give up their sons, husbands, brothers and friends, and often without murmuring, to the army; but let one of their negroes be taken and what a howl you will hear. The love of money had been the greatest difficulty on our way to independence—it is now our chiefest obstacle." During the war the South created two great armies. One included almost the entire white male population from 17 to 50. The second army, mostly slave, and just as large, was devoted to growing nearly 7 million bales of cotton during the war. Members of that second army could have been used to grow corn, raise hogs. They could have released for battle soldiers assigned to repair railroad lines, team horses, or build redoubts. They could have performed a host of tasks that drained the Confederacy's manpower and, by forcing conscription, added to war weariness, loss of morale, desertion. But planters typically objected. They had their eye on postwar "monopoly" of cotton, as well as their individual wartime incomes. So they continued to divert critical manpower to growing cotton. Nor would they buy CSA bonds, or pay export taxes on whatever cotton they smuggled through the blockade—two bales going north for every one to the United Kingdom and Europe. Such unwillingness forced the central government into the command mode: it simply took away the corn, mules, food it needed. "Impressment," however, bore unequally on its citizens. It was easiest, if harsh, to take corn and mules from the small farms. These were often run by soldiers' wives, who then beseeched their husbands for help. The method of providing essential resources thus ended by increasing desertion and military weakness.

The Outcome

For some reason the experience of strategic bombing in World War II—such as the Plocsti oil fields—seems unknown to historians of the Civil War. Or even the record in Vietnam. Both show that human effort could substitute for economic potential. History has, however, followed the Southerners in using death and human desolation, the breakdown of their social system as proof that their economic potential was necessarily destroyed. Most recently, Goldin and Lewis have attempted to measure such destruction by the amount of reduced income flows.[54] Specifically, they find that the sheer destruction of physical capital accounted for about half the total reduction in income.[55]

---

the South Lost: Commercial Purpose in the Confederacy, 1861–1865," in *Journal of American History* (June 1983), and "Through the Blockade," *Journal of Economic History* (December 1981).

54. C. Goldin and F. Lewis, "The Economic Cost of the American Civil War," *Journal of Economic History* (June 1975), pp. 299–326.

55. Ibid., p. 308. This ratio is indicated by their "direct" measure of losses. The "indirect measure" is more comprehensive, but offers no way to get at this ratio.

(Accepting Temin's corrections of their estimates makes that percentage still greater.)[56]

But in what did this tremendous decline in Southern capital stock consist? The South's investment in fence rails, farm equipment, houses, and factories was rather small. Hence, the estimated decline must largely reflect a decline in the value of its real estate.[57] The underlying Census data Goldin and Lewis use report that the real value of Texas real estate fell by about 66 percent.[58] (Between 1860 and 1867 land prices fell 55 percent to 60 percent in five Southern states.)[59] The value of Southern real estate and farms therefore declined by some 60 percent. It is not surprising that Goldin and Lewis decided that (real) Southern capital stock fell by half from 1860 to 1865.[60] Yet the productive potential of the real estate stock simply could not have declined by that amount. How could the union armies destroy a third of the real estate in Texas? Scorched earth, perhaps. But volatilized earth? Which union armies operated in any strength at all in Texas?

Such numbers do not remotely report the destruction of the region's productive physical capital. They describe instead the revaluation of private claims by a revolution in social structure. Census data indicate that the number of improved acres in Texas farms actually rose by 10 percent from 1860 to 1870.[61] The rest of unimproved Texas acreage was still there. And the share of buildings and equipment in total farm value was trivial at both dates. Hence, figures that describe a vast decline in the capital stock must imply that the union armies (in attack) or the confederates (in retreat) destroyed the fertility of the soil. Put thus baldly, there seems little warrant for the proposition. The cultivated land did decline, by some 9 million acres, between 1860 and 1870. But since the South raised even more cotton in 1870 than 1860, what did that imply? Chiefly that the less fertile land had been set aside; the ex-slaves were producing even more per acre of land than they had as slaves.

---

56. Peter Temin, "The Post-Bellum Recovery of the South and the Cost of the Civil War," *Journal of Economic History* (December 1976), pp. 898–907.

57. Goldin and Lewis, "The Economic Cost," p. 308. Note "d" and their unpublished "notes" indicate a careful set of adjustments to Census wealth data—largely real estate—in 1860 and 1870.

58. The 1870 Census, *Wealth and Industry* III (1870):10, reports the current dollar values of real estate in both 1860 and 1870. If we apply the overall ratio of assessed to true value to the real estate totals we get 1870 as 50 percent of 1860. Goldin and Lewis adjust by the Warren and Pearson price index, which rises 1860–70 by 45 percent. Therefore, 50 percent divided by 1.45 = 34 percent. Texas real estate falls 66 percent by their procedure as compared with the Census' 50 percent decline. It fell by 65–70 percent in two other Southern states.

59. *Report of the U. S. Commissioner of Agriculture* (1867), p. 119.

60. Goldin and Lewis, "The Economic Costs." See "notes" p. xix. They estimate 53 percent.

61. 1900 Census, *Agriculture*, vol. V, part 1 (1900):692.

The destruction of Southern railroads has gotten great play in reminiscence and motion pictures. But the balance sheets of the major railroads showed remarkably small real losses. And the U.S. military, finding "their immediate operation being a military as well as a political necessity [promptly] sold them the necessary replacement material at appraised value."[62] The real capital stock of the South suffered far less than graphic reminiscence or heated statistics would assert.

The war sacrificed some economic groups, benefited others. Three groups most clearly benefited. Most important of them, surely, were nearly four million Americans transferred from slavery to freedom. Without the war their freedom would have been further delayed—for years, or even decades. (Even after two years of war, Lincoln felt that federal emancipation could only be justified as a military measure.) By that transfer the freedmen became able to earn a profit margin that had once gone to their owners.[63] The pioneering study by Ransom and Sutch demonstrates that it added significantly to their tiny real income.[64]

The second major group to benefit economically from the war were millions of Northern farmers. The military demands for food and wool drove up their current incomes, increasing the value of their farms as well. (Some Southern farmers fell into that category, particularly those who sold cotton during the war and salted away their profits in specie or greenbacks. Several thousand sold cotton at the war's end for incredibly high prices.)[65]

A third group, small but notorious, discovered sudden opportunities in the discontinuities that war markets and public policy created, acting to arbitrage them. It included those who exported or imported through the battle lines. It also included those who supplied material and products urgently demanded by the military, whiskey distillers benefiting from Congressional tax policies, and more.

62. The quotation is from 40th Cong., 2d sess., H.D. 73, *Southern Railroads* (1868), p. 4. For example, the Mississippi Central railroad company reported a loss of $113,000 in "track material" during the war—destroyed by marauding armies or merely worn from use. With pre-war construction costs of perhaps $7,000 a mile for such material (derived from data on Albert Fishlow, *American Railroads and the Transformation of the Ante-Bellum Economy* (1965), pp. 365–81), the per mile replacement by the U.S. army came to half that figure for many southern roads (*Southern Railroads*, pp. 4–29). Delayed maintenance alone would have accounted for much of that expenditure. That their slaves were freed, and CSA bonds became worthless, did not cut their real productive capacity.

63. The disorganization of the economy in the aftermath of war undoubtedly dissipated in dead weight loss some of the total margin created by the work of the slaves under slavery. But the freedmen received the balance.

64. Roger Ransom and Richard Sutch, *One Kind of Freedom* (1977), p. 219. They estimate an 1859–79 increase of 31 percent in real per capita incomes as slaves became tenants.

65. Cf. Stanley Lebergott, "Why the South Lost: Commercial Purpose in the Confederacy," *Journal of American History* (June 1983).

Other groups in the economy lost. Obviously and importantly, the men in the military lost. Even those who lived through the war without physical injury had their lives broken apart. Nearly all had their standard of living sharply lowered while fighting. Most Southerners likewise saw their consumption level cut during the war—by impressment, by a depreciating currency, by the higher cost of imports.

The outcome for Northern wage earners is uncertain. When the war broke out prices began to rise, producing the usual effects of unanticipated inflation. "Almost every owner of property found that the price of his possessions had increased and almost every wage earner found . . . his pay . . . advanced. Strive as people may to emancipate themselves from the feeling that a dollar represents a fixed quantity of desirable things . . . they are almost certain to feel cheerful over the large sums. . . . Habit is too strong for arithmetic."[66]

But two forces did cut real wage earner incomes. First was the government's diversion of production to munitions, uniforms, and more through increased excise, income, and tariff charges. Consumers were further burdened by the higher prices of imports—tea, coffee, clothing. Europeans hiked prices to compensate themselves for the fact that they were now being paid in greenbacks. Hence American dollars were worth less in international markets than U.S. currency had been when it was backed by gold.[67] War demands, however, reduced the amount of unemployment to which workers had been accustomed. The net impact of the war on the real incomes of Northern wage earners has yet to be assessed.

The Aftermath

Historians with a taste for paradox (or dubious economics) have discovered that the Civil War brought unprecedented economic growth to the United States. No longer hampered by the South's agrarians, Northern industrialism took over the nation after the war. Northern production surged forward.[68]

66. Wesley Mitchell, quoted in *The Economic Impact of the American Civil War*, Ralph Andreano, ed. (1967), p. 5.

67. Wesley Mitchell, among others, held that wage earner incomes were reduced in favor of profits during the war. The importance of taxes and import prices, however, makes it impossible to reach any conclusion on this point, as demonstrated by Reuben Kessel and Armen Alchian in their "Real Wages in the North During the Civil War," *Journal of Law and Economics* (October 1959).

68. That prevailing view was first brought to a systematic test by Thomas Cochran's primary study, "Did the civil war retard industrialization?", *Mississippi Valley Historical Review* (September 1961), pp. 197–210. The next major study, by Claudia Goldin and Frank Lewis, "The Economic Cost of the Civil War," *Journal of Economic History* (June 1975), pp. 299–326, expands the perspective with great skill. It measures the total decline in Northern production resulting from the war by assuming that total Northern per capita consumption without the war would have been the same after 1879, and prior to 1860.

This belief that the war did stimulate production rests on one observation: Northern production rose after the war. But output had been increasing for decades before the war. Did the rate of total U.S. output obviously speed up? The most dramatic cases of wartime expansion—in iron and steel, machinery, muskets and rifles—had only the slightest impact on the rate of total output.[69] But the question is not how the production changed when compared to prewar trends. Nor when compared to, say, trends after some arbitrarily chosen postwar year—say 1879 or 1889 or 1899. It is rather how it changed by comparison with the economy in which the war had not occurred 1860–65. That economy cannot be hypothesized by simply extrapolating prewar trends. Nor by simply assuming that the war's impact had been precisely neutralized by some given date, with the long trend then resuming. For the war had made major irretrievable changes.

The postwar decade had its own stimuli, new forces working to vary output as a result of changes both in Europe and the United States. Such changes may have speeded or slowed American industrialization. A look at the actual production record therefore fails to measure the war's impact. We can, however, infer that the war probably slowed American industrialization, had the alternative to war been yet another "peaceful" secession crisis. For death and suffering would not then have afflicted hundreds of thousands, North and South. Living on, and working, these workers would have lived to teach their skills to the next generation. And those who became entrepreneurs would have provided new productive ideas, otherwise lacking. (Their absence is most evident in the South, with its carry-over of elderly leadership in the white community.) The Northern armies had enrolled the equivalent of one person in every four from the labor force. Among them were those set to developing production facilities for ammunition, gunpowder, woolen uniforms, army wagons, rather than the investment that would have better met postwar needs. By diverting human and material resources away from civilian investment the war necessarily slowed such investment, and thereby postwar growth.[70] The human catastrophes of the war and the basic change in the

---

69. Richard Wacht has demonstrated that to produce all the muskets and rifles used by the North required no more than 1 percent of U.S. iron production. Cf. Richard Wacht, "A Note on the Cochran Thesis," *Explorations in Entrepreneurial History* (1966).

70. A focus on Northern industrialization per se would require some judgment on the relative slowdown of investment in farming versus nonfarm activity during the war. We surmise—though the point requires proof—that the immediate profit prospects from wartime food production diverted wartime investment both to farm development and to industries of military consequences, and away from civilian nonfarm industry.

The accumulation of debt and its repayment did generate some offsetting increase in capital formation. Engerman has worked through the magnitudes, and concludes that doing so increased the shares of net capital formation in GNP by less than 1 percent (and, of course, increased GNP by far less than that). Stanley Engerman, "The Economic Impact of the Civil War," a penetrating analysis that takes up the major elements that have been proposed, appears in Robert Fogel and Stanley Engerman, *The Reinterpretation of American Economic History* (1971), pp. 369–79.

condition of Southern slaves (and, in turn, whites) constituted more far-reaching effects of the war. But the probable slowing down of American economic growth, rather than speeding it, was one of its more narrowly economic outcomes.

Some men are born great, some achieve greatness and
others lived during the Reconstruction period.

—PAUL LAURENCE DUNBAR, 1903

21

Reconstruction

THE frustrated hopes of the Reconstruction period are encapsulated in
Dunbar's classic sentence. Yet a hundred histories of that period fail
when they ignore Reconstruction's central heartening and overwhelming experience: 3.5 million Americans began to live in freedom. However miserable
their lives, that move out of slavery marked a critical advance.[1] Histories that
emphasize the disorganization of economic life in the South typically offer no
realistic standard of comparison. What was to be expected after emancipation? In major British colonies production had declined spectacularly after
emancipation.[2] Production of sugar, British Guiana's chief crop, fell by over
40 percent. In Jamaica a major drop was also apparent.[3] But in the United
States, production of cotton did not fall similarly. Indeed, by 1869 the South
had actually regained its pre-war production average. And by the period
1870–79 Southern production was running 42 percent above its pre-war
level.[4] Such an advance for the South's major crop stood in striking contrast
to the experience in most other Caribbean colonies that had freed their
slaves.[5] The proportion of black females working fell from 90 percent to 40
percent; Southern capital and land inputs declined as well from the pre-war

1. In Dubois' words, "the enfranchisement of the freedmen after the war was one of the
greatest steps toward democracy taken in the nineteenth century." W. E. DuBois, *Black Reconstruction in America*, (1935), p. 43.
2. Alan Adamson, *Sugar Without Slaves* (1972), p. 40.
3. Michael Craton and James Walvin, *A Jamaican Plantation* (1970), p. 222.
4. *Historical Statistics . . . to 1970*, p. 518. For example, in 1850–59, 3,091,000 bales were
produced. In 1870–79, 4,397,000 bales were produced.
5. Cf. Noel Deer, *A History of Sugar* 2 (1950):377.

(1859) levels to those in 1876–80.[6] Since inputs fell output should likewise have plummeted. Yet production on Southern farms had returned almost precisely to its pre-war level.[7] Freedom and the qualities of those who survived the war, white and black, were surely basic to this unprecedented achievement.

"For several years after the close of the Civil War, the negroes of the South believed that the estates of the whites were to be confiscated . . . and that each head of a family would obtain from the property thus confiscated 'forty acres and a mule.' "[8] That expectation had multiple sources.

To "excite their own people to greater activity in the rebellion," Southern leaders spread the word that planters' lands would be divided among the slaves if the North won.[9] In 1864 Andrew Johnson, the poor white from Tennessee who became vice president, was declaring that "treason must be made odious" and the plantations divided up and sold.[10] (His pardon for most Southerners, which automatically restored their ownership of the land, was not to occur until a year later.[11])

In January 1865 General William Sherman issued Special Field Order No. 15. It ordered the "colonization on forty-acre tracts" of the refugees then

6. Labor force rates: Lebergott, *Manpower in Economic Growth*, pp. 59–62, 519. Virtually all black females were then in the rural South. Ransom and Sutch follow Lebergott's 90–95 percent rates for females under slavery, but estimate 50–67 percent rates for the 1880 "cotton South" using 1890 data in *One Kind*, pp. 227, 232–34.

7. Detailed output data from Eugene Lerner in *Agricultural History* (July 1959), pp. 117–25. These were weighted together using 1870 prices from Marvin Towne and Wayne Rasmussen in *Trends in the American Economy*, p. 295. A constant dollar index shows 1876–80 output at 99.6 percent of that of 1859.

An extensive study of "Growth and Welfare in the American South in the Nineteenth Century" nonetheless concludes: "even by 1879 . . . per capita output was only 81% of its 1857 level, and 71% of its 1859 level." (Robert Ransom and Richard Sutch, "Growth and Welfare," in *Market Institutions and Economic Progress in the New South 1865–1900*, Gary Walton and James Shepherd eds. (1981), p. 137.) Three reasons account for that more depressing view: (1) Its basic prewar benchmark (the Census cotton output figure for 1859) is unfortunately not comparable with its postwar figures from BAE-Latham, Alexander Co. (Roger Ransom and Richard Sutch, *One Kind of Freedom* (1977), pp. 257, 262.) But the underlying, comparable estimates (Latham Alexander and Co., *Cotton Movement and Fluctuations 1875 to 1882* (1882), p. 93) show cotton production in 1869 within 1% of its 1857 level, and within 10% of 1859 by 1870. (2) It emphasizes output for the 5 slowest growing of the 13 Southern states, the five whose income grew at half the South's rate in 1879-99. ("Growth and Welfare," p. 142.) (3) Emphasis on per capita money income necessarily puts a zero value on the marked decline in field work by women and children—a change that markedly increased the well being of the freedmen.

8. Walter Fleming, "Forty Acres and a Mule," *The North American Review* (1906), p. 721.

9. Testimony of General Saxton in 39th Cong., 1st sess., H.R. *Hearings of Select Joint Committee on Reconstruction* (1866), Part II, p. 221.

10. Fleming, "Forty Acres," p. 723.

11. Ibid., p. 726.

crowding into Union lines and needing support. The order located some 40,000 families on the Carolina sea islands. (That land had been abandoned and was part of half a million acres seized by the U.S. Army.)[12] Perhaps most persuasive was the fact that Congress confirmed Sherman's field order for those already located. It reserved three million acres "from unoccupied public lands" in the South. There the "loyal refugees and freedmen" could settle on land "not exceeding forty acres each . . . at such annual rent as may be agreed upon . . . based upon a valuation of the land."[13] (President Andrew Johnson promptly vetoed this law. That veto constituted one of the articles in his impeachment proceedings.)

These varied promises and expectations ended with only a handful of acres actually sold to the freedmen by the federal government. Nor were a greater number offered at "an easy rent" (to use General Saxton's words to the first freedmen on the Carolina sea islands).[14] Instead, as Ransom and Sutch put it: "The failure to carry forward plans for [land] redistribution appears as the great tragedy of this era."[15]

The explanation commonly given for this failure is that Andrew Johnson had vetoed the bill to give land to the freed slaves. But this is not much of an explanation. For Congress then failed to pass such a bill during the next eight years of the sympathetic Grant administration. One unvoiced congressional objection was surely that put by Charles and Mary Beard. They describe (incorrectly) "the complete destruction of about four billion dollars worth of 'goods' in the possession of slave owners [i.e., emancipation] as the most stupendous act of sequestration in the history of Anglo-Saxon jurisprudence."[16] That "expropriation and confiscation" had been at work was surely the view of both Communists and Southern leaders.[17] But there was a second factor. Nearly a quarter of a million Union soldiers had died in the war. No land had been given to their widows, nor to the thousands of wounded, nor to the hundreds of thousands who had served at the hazard of their lives. Instead, Congress had passed a general Homestead Act in 1862, making certain

---

12. Saxton in *Hearings*.

13. The Act is printed in Edward McPherson, *A Political Manual for 1866* (1866), pp. 72–74.

14. "Agents will locate your small farms of 40 acres, which you can hire at an easy rent," 39th Cong., 1st sess., *Report of the Select Joint Committee on Reconstruction* (1866), Part II, p. 230.

15. Ransom and Sutch, *One Kind*, p. 80.

16. Charles Beard and Mary Beard, *The Rise of American Civilization* (1930), p. 100. Such majestic, polysyllabic, words—"sequestration, jurisprudence"—may delude the unwary reader. It was not "sequestration," but defeat in war, and the war exigencies leading to emancipation, that freed the slaves beyond any possible recall by the planters.

17. The leader of the Communist International wrote: "When, after the great North American civil war, millions of slaves were emancipated, who had been the lawfully acquired property of their masters, without reimbursing the latter, this was done 'in behalf of the common welfare.' Our entire bourgeois development is an uninterrupted process of expropriation and confiscation." August Bebel, *Women and Socialism* (1910), p. 368.

U.S. land freely available to the soldiers and any other person—citizen or not—who was prepared to settle on it.[18]

Yet these considerations hardly constrained the independent state legislatures in the South during 1866–76, controlled as they were by ex-slaves, Northern carpetbaggers, and scalawags. Those legislatures did appropriate large sums of money—but for other objects. Thus, South Carolina increased its spending on free schools from $75,000 to $300,000, on "public printing" from $17,000 to $332,000, between 1859–60 and 1872–73.[19] Its legislature, however, made only one, limited, attempt to buy land for the freedmen. Their appropriation of $700,000 ended in futility. For it settled no more than a few hundred families; most of the money disappeared into thin air.[20] The other Reconstruction legislatures did even less.

Suppose Congress had indeed enabled the freedmen to "rent parcels . . . at such annual rent as may be agreed upon . . . based upon a valuation of the land." How much would that have helped sharecropper incomes? One may make an approximation from data in the 1880 Census and other sources.[21] In that year rents in South Carolina ran about 25 to 30 percent on the "valuation of the land."[22] Meanwhile, white farmers paid about 20 percent for short-term loans.[23] Since Southern investors surely shifted funds between investments based on their differing profitability, 5 to 10 percent approximately marks the difference between rates on comparable loans to whites and to blacks.[24] It likewise suggests that if black cash tenants had rented their land directly from the U.S. Congress at a "rent based . . . on valuation," they might have saved $12 to $25 (their annual net income being

18. It is surely likely that Congressmen shared the view expressed by Andrew Johnson: Congress "has never deemed itself authorized to expend the public money for the rent or purchase of homes for the . . . millions of the white race, who are honestly toiling from day to day for their subsistence." Quoted by John and LaWanda Cox in "Andrew Johnson and his Ghost Writers," *Mississippi Valley Historical Review* (December 1961), p. 469. Since nearly all voters were white, the political appeal of this claim must have been non-trivial.

19. 43d Cong., 1st sess., H.D. 34, *Counter-Statement to Tax-Payers Memorial*, p. 2, and 43d Cong., 1st sess., H.D. 233, *Petition of the Tax-Payers Convention of South Carolina*, p. 2.

20. Joint Select Committee, *Affairs in Late Insurrectionary States* 3 (1872):235. The testimony of Judge Carpenter, formerly candidate for governor, is not controverted by the testimony of Land Commissioner DeLarge, nor by any other statement in the *Report* of the Joint Committee.

21. 1900 Census, *Agriculture*, V (1900):695, reports $10 as the average value per acre.

22. 1880 Census, *Report on Cotton Production in the United States, part II*, (1880):516–22. $2, $3, $4, $5, $1.50 to $3; $1; $1 to $3; $2 to $4; $3 to $15; $1 to $5; $2 to $4. We use the rental figures applicable to cash rents.

23. Enoch Banks, *The Economics of Land Tenure in Georgia* (1905), p. 114. Banks' discussion relates to bank loans, which would have been primarily limited to white farmers. Most short-term loans were more likely made to small rather than large farmers.

24. Short-term loans would tend to yield more than longer term investment in land. On the other hand, loans to blacks, with lower assets, would be perceived as riskier than loans to whites.

$184).[25] Since landlords rented to both cash and cropper[26] tenants, the $12 to $25 marks the landlords' judgment of risks in renting to black rather than white cash renters. "Forty acres and a mule," then, could have helped the freedmen toward independence and a brighter future. But they would have alleviated their poverty only slightly.

Two distinguished historians concluded that "the overthrow of slavery, unattended by an heroic effort to settle the Negroes on the soil, let loose a flood of landless people destined to wage labor or tenancy."[27]

The freedmen, indeed, fiercely wanted land. As one declared: "We wants land—dis bery land dat is rich wide de sweat of we face and de blood ob we back."[28] The slaves were landless—as were most laborers in the North and West, as were the host of immigrants each year. Few workers who desired to own a business (farm or nonfarm) inherited money to achieve that happy status, whether they were black or white. Nor were they given funds to do so by a loving Congress. White or black, they had to choose between four routes to ownership.[29]

First, they could work as laborers. By consuming less than they earned they could laboriously save up enough money to buy a farm. Numbers of freedmen, of European immigrants, did just that. It was, of course, a hard and self-denying route.

Second, they could borrow—and pay interest—using the money to buy a farm. To do so they would first have to demonstrate credit worthiness to a lender. But white lenders had to be persuaded that black (or white) borrowers knew enough about farming to make a go of it and would actually pay off their debts on time. Surely very few freedmen, few European immigrants, and indeed, few Northern workers, could present a persuasive case on that point.

Some experts inferred that "black ownership [was] effectively prohibited."[30] But was it? By steadily saving and borrowing small amounts, an unbelievable number of freedmen actually did become owners. As of 1880,

25. Ransom and Sutch, *One Kind*, p. 216, give data from which one can infer that cash tenants averaged about the same 25 acres, and about the same $330 gross income as croppers.

26. Ransom and Sutch find that croppers paid $6 more for rent than did cash renters—presumably for greater risk. They stipulate a 50 percent share of crop product went to landlords. Since they estimate a $330 annual product per black sharecropper, and 24.8 acres per farm this works out to $5.87 per acre—i.e., some $75 more than at a $3.00 acre average.

27. Beard and Beard, *The Rise* 2:275.

28. Quoted in James M. McPherson, *The Negroes' Civil War* (1965), p. 297.

29. The four choices had more overlap than is here itemized. For a comprehensive discussion of these choices, see Robert Higgs, *Competition and Coercion, Blacks in the American Economy, 1865–1914* (1977).

30. "With the demise of the plantation system, and black ownership effectively prohibited, a new form of landlord-labor relationship had to be negotiated." Richard Sutch and Roger Ransom, "The Ex-Slave in the Post-Bellum South," *Journal of Economic History* (March 1973), p. 137. On p. 87 of *One Kind*, Ransom and Sutch say threats of violence "added costs and risk so great they virtually eliminated a market in land accessible to blacks."

20 percent of all black farmers in the cotton South had done so. (The most spectacular example, Benjamin Montgomery, farmed 4,000 acres from 1866 to 1880, once the property of Jefferson Davis's brother.[31]) They had worked as laborers. They had lived with prudence and frugality. And they had saved enough to make a down payment on a farm. Their names are now largely lost to history. But their steadiness and ability persuaded thousands of local lenders to lend them the balance, and enabled them to become farm owners. And by 1900 27 percent of black farmers in the entire South had become owners.[32] Surely that rise constituted a spectacular achievement on their part. The figures become still more striking for those who adopt the hypothesis that the heritage of slavery inevitably destroyed the freedmen's competence, or the hypothesis that the Ku Klux Klan represented a unified view of the white South.

Black ownership was the outcome of wide-ranging experience in private markets. Thousands of white land owners had decided (on the simplest economic basis) that one in every five freedman farming in the cotton South was indeed a skilled farmer; had demonstrated prudence, foresight, and reliability; and could be expected to pay off his loan.

Third, homesteading offered a route to ownership. The freedmen needed to borrow only enough money for some equipment, a horse or mule, and a few absolute necessities. (Such sums could be managed, with greater difficulty, by working and saving in advance or while homesteading.)

Yet under 40,000 freedmen chose to homestead.[33] And for very good reason. Before the war, the South's per capita income actually exceeded that of the North Central region, that rising center of Northern farming. And Southern incomes had increased faster from 1840 to 1860 than those in the entire North.[34] Such gains rested directly upon the effort, and farming skills, which the slaves lavished on Southern lands. Had the freedmen moved to homesteading states—the Midwest and far West—they would have had to junk many of their old skills. They would have had to learn the vagaries of new crops and new climates. And they would have had to do so in dangerous territory. (More farmers were killed by Indians in these years than were ever

31. Computed from Ransom and Sutch, *One Kind*, p. 84, based on their sampling of 1880 Census returns. The Southern black population was disproportionately concentrated in the cotton farming region they study (p. 281).

In one of history's high ironies Jefferson Davis's home address while in the U.S. Congress was "Hurricane, Mississippi." His brother's Hurricane and Briarfield plantations were farmed by Montgomery and his sons. Cf. Booker T. Washington, "A Town Owned by Negroes," *World's Work* (July 1907), p. 9131.

32. 1900 Census, *Agriculture* V (1900):4.

33. By 1880 only about 30,000 had moved to Kansas, about 5,000 to Iowa, and a handful to other homesteading states. 1880 Census, *Population*, Table XII. These data, for the entire "native colored population," would overstate the count of freedmen who migrated 1865–80.

34. Fogel and Engerman, *I:Time on the Cross*, p. 248.

lynched by mobs in the Reconstruction South.) Virtually all freedmen decided to remain in the South, utilizing their skills, experience, and familiarity with the ways of cotton, corn, tobacco, rice, and sugar. Their choice laid the basis for prompt recovery of cotton production after the war's end.

What of the other alternatives open to the freedmen? "Most negroes—next to owning—preferred to rent."[35] But renting was no simple matter. Gavin Wright emphasizes that landlords who wished to protect themselves against the risks of crop failure and price fall did see fixed-price tenancy as attractive. But, he adds, "in practice a tenant without assets cannot make such a guarantee credible"—either to his landlord or to another money lender.[36] It is nonetheless a fact that by 1880, 26 percent of all black farmers in the cotton South had somehow persuaded thousands of white land owners that they were indeed competent and reliable farmers.[37] (The 26 percent grew to 36 percent by 1900). Owners renting to any of those black tenants did so reasonably confident that they could collect the cash land rent due them at the end of the season. They therefore had to believe that the freedman did possess three critical qualities. First, he was competent in the hundred ways required of a farmer. Second, he had the energy and willingness to apply himself virtually every single day of the crop year. And third, he had the probity to remain on the farm until the end of the year and pay off his debt.

Finally, there was sharecropping. Though often taken to characterize the entire cotton South during Reconstruction, it nonetheless applied only to about half (54 percent) of black farmers. DuBois observed that cropping began its important role with a "widely adopted system . . . proposed as early as 1866 by a negro laborer" in South Carolina. The "laborer works 5 days in the week for the land owner, and has a house, rations, and three acres of land." He likewise has "a mule and plow every other Saturday to work [his 3 acres] when necessary and $16 in money at the end of the year."[38] Other proposals appeared directly after the war. The intense desire of freedmen for land ownership stimulated the growth of tenancy more than "planter conspiracy" did. The "*Southern Argus*, one of the most articulate and insightful voices of the planter class, admitted that sharecropping was 'an unwilling concession to the freedman's desire to become a proprietor . . . not a voluntary association from similarity of aims and interests.' "

Many writers have regretted that concession. "Whatever efficiency and planning, whatever virtues of proprietorship had resided in the old plantation

---

35. Vernon Wharton, *The Negro in Mississippi* (1947), pp. 63–64.

36. Gavin Wright, *The Political Economy of the Cotton South* (1978), pp. 176–77.

37. Ransom and Sutch, *One Kind*, p. 84. Some unknown number of these were "standing" renters, who paid a fixed amount of the crop standing in the fields—e.g., so many bales of cotton rather than cash.

38. W. E. B. DuBois in 1900 Census, *Supplementary Analysis* (1900), p. 522. The quotations are chiefly from 1880 Census, *Report on Cotton Production in the United States* II (1880):519.

system were largely missing from the sharecropper system . . . from a strictly economical point of view cropping was worse for the agriculture of the region then slavery had been."[39] Such judgments simply assume that the overseer's lash and gang labor must have elicited more labor effort than did the free family group plus the planter's usual 50 percent interest in the sharecropper's output. There is no evidence, however, that free labor was less "productive." There is instead considerable reason to believe that the "concession to the freeman's desire to become a proprietor" proved a central force in the resurgence of farm production even amid the turmoil of Reconstruction.

Sharecropping had, of course, its extended history. In ancient India the croppers gave up 20 to 25 percent of their crop in return for the use of the land and capital.[40] In eighteenth-century England close to a third went to the landlord.[41] This system developed in the South in the early nineteenth century, according to Joseph Reid's research, while it was already common in the North.[42] (The 1880 Census reported that half of U.S. croppers were outside the South.[43]

In sharecropping the landlord provided the land the cropper lacked. The landlord typically provided one or more of the following as well: the use of a mule, plough, and other equipment; food; housing; and more. In return, he received a share of the crop. In Mississippi in 1880, for example, that share was one-third of the cotton in alluvial counties, but only one-quarter in the uplands.[44] Why the difference? Presumably because an acre of rich alluvial land typically yielded much more cotton (347 pounds compared to 162).[45] With equal effort, then, the cropper would earn more. Hence, he was prepared to give a greater share to a landlord with alluvial land than one with poorer upland.

Why did sharecropping develop? Its variety of contract arrangements was surely bewildering when compared with the great simplicity of, say, hired labor. But it achieved two vital goals, in varying degree: It shared the risks of farming and it reduced the risks of farming. Amid the uncertainties of

39. Jonathan Wiener, "Class Structure and Economic Development in the American South," *American Historical Review* (October 1979), p. 976. "Whatever efficiency. . . .": John Blum *et al.*, *The National Experience* (1981), p. 24.

40. R. Shamasastry, *Kautilya's Arthasastra* (1915, reprint ed. 1960), p. 128. "Those who live by their own physical exertion may cultivate ["fields left unsown . . . owing to the inadequacy of hands"] for ¼ or ⅕ of the produce grown."

41. Richard Cantillon, *Essay on the Nature of Trade*, Henry Higgs, ed. (1892), p. 121. Cantillon notes that in the Milanese state the share was one-half and "doubts not" that in China the share was more than three-quarters.

42. Joseph Reid, "Ante-Bellum Southern Rental Leases," *Explorations in Entrepreneurial History* (April 1976).

43. 1880 Census, *Agriculture* V (1880):29.

44. 1880 Census, *Report of Cotton Production in the United States* II (1880):356.

45. 1880 Census, *The Productions of Agriculture* V (1880):274.

Reconstruction it proved attractive to many white farmers, as well as to black ones. (By 1900 the percent of white farmers in the South who were croppers was more than twice that in the rest of the nation.)

The decisive role of risk sharing in sharecropping was obvious.[46] Should the crop fail, the landowner would not sustain the entire loss, but only his share—typically one-half or two-thirds. Conversely, if the crop did very well, but the landowner had relied on hired labor, his workers might decide to strike at harvest time, or actually leave. (Both actually occurred to some owners in the transition years 1865–66). Sharecropping gave the workers a powerful incentive not to leave. For, if they did, they would forfeit the return from an entire year's work. An owner might well expect hired labor to soldier on the job when he was not around, and even fail to do tasks essential for getting out a large crop. But a sharecropper would not find it to his interest to omit such work (intentionally).

What about the sharecropper's view? Hired labor offered independence. In the early days this seemed preferable to many freedmen. But crop failure in 1866–67 led some owners to refuse to pay off hired labor; they had no net income from the crop. A further drawback existed even if owners paid regularly: hired labor could not expect to get work, and income, throughout the year. If the crop were damaged by weather in midseason, or the army worm attacked it, or the boll weevil destroyed it, the landowner needed no more labor. He would turn out his hired laborers. They then would have to look around for work and locate a planter not already provided for. Against such prospects of unsure payment, of intermittent unemployment, many laborers preferred sharecropping. It offered a reasonable guarantee of a steady supply of food and housing during the year, plus a share of the crop proceeds at the end.

These different factors were persuasive to some owners and freedmen, though not to all. (And they varied among the states. In 1880, for example, the percentage of farmers who cropped was almost twice as great in Alabama, Georgia, and Texas as in Florida, Kentucky, and Virginia. By 1900, the proportion of colored farmers who were croppers ranged from 10 percent in Florida to 25 percent in Alabama to 44 percent in Georgia.[47]) No general coordination or identity of class interest among white planters (or freedmen) made cropping uniformly preferred. Planter interests were multiple; freedmen's abilities were varied. Together these led to different tenure arrangements and to great variation even within sharecropping.

46. Emphasis on risk sharing appears in Stephen Cheung, *The Theory of Share Tenancy* (1969). Emphasis on risk reduction appears in Reid, "Ante-Bellum." Cf. also the best single study of the entire period, Wright, *Political Economy*, pp. 168–76.

47. 1880 Census, *Production of Agriculture* (1880), p. 63, and 1900 Census, *Agriculture* V (1900):6.

What fixed the actual returns to sharecroppers (and to tenants in general)? The simplest planter story was their antebellum one: generous, prudent, and thoughtful planters subsidizing barely competent, feckless, indolent workers. The simplest story told by some historians describes how the Knights of the Golden Circle and the Ku Klux Klan terrorized the freedmen into accepting just enough subsistence to keep them from actual starvation. (Recently, as Part IX will note, this view has been enriched by a modern version of the planters' complaint against the merchants throughout the Reconstruction period.)

Without denying some truth to either story what was the commonest market outcome? When landlord greed met cropper need the real restraints on both consisted of the many competing participants seeking to buy, and to sell, labor. Inevitably, landlords tried to stand together in a giant cartel. How well did they succeed?

Ex-slave holders began by trying to "limit the free market in labor and force freedmen to work on plantation gangs. Some turned to terror—to the Ku Klux Klan." They resolved that "all would offer the same terms to the freemen, and none would 'employ any laborer discharged for violation of contrasts.' " They passed "enticement" acts in every southern state. These made it a crime to "hire away . . . by offering higher wages to the blacks." Nonetheless, "the freedmen defeated the planters efforts. . . . In establishing decentralized family sharecropping as the prevailing organization of cotton production after the war, the planters made a major concession to the freedmen."[48]

But just how did freedmen "defeat the planters efforts"? By mere self-respect and determination? Hardly enough against the Ku Klux Klan and the Knights of the Golden Circle. The deeper answer is implicit in the Reconstruction legislation that defined the criminal. He was "not the black who left his plantations, but the planter who sought a free market in labor." The "criminals" were in fact those white planters who offered higher wages to attract labor. They included white landowners who offered croppers a better share, to get croppers, and thereby profit from their land ownership. They also included white lenders who loaned freedmen money to buy land. They even included corporations building railroads, who bid black labor away by offering higher wages.[49] Moreover, and importantly, they included planters in other states, who couldn't care less about the need for "docile" labor in a given state.

48. The quotations are from Wiener, *Class*, pp. 974–76.
49. "Disguised men" went to the railroad then being constructed to "take these negroes out and whip them, and force them from the road back to the farms to labor. They received higher wages for working on the railroad." Poiner quoted in *Report of the Joint Select Committee . . . Affairs in the Late Insurrectionary States* 3 (1872):27.

As early as 1864, planters from other states began seeking labor in Georgia. As General Tillson (then head of the Freedman's Bureau in that state) observed, Georgia planters were offering farmhands only $2 a month. But: "Men from Alabama, Mississippi, Arkansas say that [labor] is worth fifteen dollars, and stand ready to give it. . . . To permit [the freedman] to make contracts for very much less, is to permit him to be swindled. A little while ago, many of these [Georgia planters] were wishing the negroes all driven out of the State; and now they are in a great panic because I am allowing them to go."[50] Throughout Reconstruction the freedmen moved to those areas where planters sought labor to work their lands. The "feverish excitement" of the 1867 boom led Mississippi planters to pay wages 50 percent greater than in South Carolina and 27 percent greater than Alabama. By 1868 the boom had ended and these states were offering virtually the same wages.[51] But meanwhile they had bid labor away from nearby states. In a later year "some four or five thousand colored laborers" left South Carolina for "Arkansas, Alabama, Mississippi, where wages were much higher."[52] Between 1870 and 1880 alone about 20,000 freedmen moved into Mississippi. Equal numbers migrated to Texas and to Arkansas. Alabama lost over 35,000.[53]

Owners in the old South, therefore, had to increase their wages and their share offers if they were to keep their entire labor supply from drifting away. Conversely, of course, competition among freedmen tended to keep their wages and shares from going higher than they did. So did the exhortations of Frederick Douglass to stay in the old South and not move westward.[54] So did the postwar increase in the black birth rate.

The planter drive for more labor in the new states did not guarantee either a "reasonable return" to owners on their land investment, or "adequate wages" to sharecroppers. What it did do was keep the income of sharecroppers in line with the major alternatives open to croppers in the market. And it did so despite the desires that planters as "a class" might have had.

It has been contended that the "basic relations of the plantation economy which existed before the Civil War were permitted to continue to exist after

50. John T. Trowbridge, *The South*, pp. 495–98.

51. U.S. Commissioner of Agriculture, *Report* (1867), p. 416.

52. Joint Select Committee, *Report* (1872), p. 247.

53. Everett Lee, et al., *Population Redistribution and Economic Growth in the United States, 1870–1950* 1 (1957):Table P–1. We use nonwhite data in these instances as a measure of freedmen.

54. Douglass urged staying and fighting for "your rights" in his "The Negro Exodus from the Gulf States," *Journal of Social Science* (May 1880), pp. 2–21. Professor R. T. Greener urged moving west for higher incomes, safer lives, in his "The Emigration of Colored Citizens from the Southern States," *Journal of Social Science* (May 1880), pp. 22–35.

it."[55] Does a shift from slave to free labor really fail to qualify as a change in "basic relations of the plantation economy"? Surely the end of slavery did overwhelmingly change the economics of production as well as the lives of millions of freedmen.

New forces helped determine the incomes of freedmen—whether as owners, renters, or sharecroppers. They brought a rise in real incomes freedmen received over those for slaves—some 21 percent more, according to the Ransom and Sutch data.[56] That rise was pitiful in absolute terms ($43). But it was highly significant to freedmen as they rose above the slave standard of consumption.

As a cost it proved no less significant to the planters. To offset such cost increases landlords began to hire more and more whites for field labor. If the Knights of the Golden Circle and the Ku Klux Klan had been able to control black labor as effectively as many writers assert, landlords would have had little incentive to introduce white labor. But whites, who provided only 16 percent of cotton field labor before the war, constituted 40 percent by 1876, and 60 percent by 1900.[57]

Two shifts were obviously taking place. Those freedmen who proved most efficient as farmers and laborers remained in farming. And whites who were most efficient as farm laborers moved into such work. White planters who continued to farm and who held onto the best land from the old plantations achieved the highest incomes of all. But ex-slaves who remained in the fertile cotton belt during Reconstruction achieved the next highest incomes. In the areas outside that belt, incomes were lower. Moreover, on those poorer lands, blacks tended to surpass whites in productivity (and presumably in income from farming).[58]

---

55. Jay R. Mandle, *The Roots of Black Poverty* (1978), p. 17. The study does not indicate which person or agency had a choice of "permitting" "basic relations" to exist or end. One reviewer has taken this study as indicating "virtually nothing changed [from prewar to] the postwar South." Cf. Peter Kolchin, "Race, Class, and Poverty in the Post-Civil War South," *Reviews in American History* (December 1979), pp. 515–26.

56. Ransom and Sutch, *One Kind*, p. 219, provide a carefully detailed estimate of per capita real incomes of slaves—i.e., value of their food, clothing, and housing—and compare it with that of sharecroppers in 1879. They estimate a 28.9 percent rise for croppers. They reduce that figure to 13.8 percent if "all food was purchased at credit prices." Since they show that $29 worth of food per capita was in fact garden produce and pork production of the farm itself, it is impossible that all food was indeed "purchased at credit prices." Moreover the average size of the croppers' lien was $71 for the entire family, and was held for from 4 to 6 months. It is, therefore, unlikely that all purchased food was bought on credit. We average their 14 percent and 29 percent to provide a figure more consistent with their own data.

57. Labor data for 1860 and 1876 are from U.S. Department of Agriculture, *Report of the Commissioner of Agriculture . . . 1876*, p. 136. For 1900, data are computed from the 1900 Census, *Occupations*, Tables 32 and 41. For farmers, 1860 is assumed to be zero, and for 1900, see 1900 Census, *Idem*.

58. The conclusions on land-labor relations are developed by Stephen DeCanio, in his major study, *Agriculture in the Postbellum South* (1974), chap. 6.

The Soldier and the Storekeeper

The terms which planter and cropper could get in their share contracts were bounded by the alternatives each could find in the market. Those terms were shaped by two further, influential, forces during the Reconstruction period. One was a new presence—the U.S. Army. The other was the rural general store, described then (and now) as restricting the freedmen's choice.

The U.S. Army presumably offered powerful protection to the freedmen amid the terrors of the Reconstruction world. But how did it affect their economic welfare as the terms of sharecropper contracts were hammered out? The answer is less clear. More than once the army held the freedmen to terms and obedience well beyond what economic markets per se would have been able to. For example, Colonel Lambert, head of the Freedmens Bureau in Georgia, "fined a respectable planter $150" for tempting a freedman to break his contract by offering him 30 percent above the going wage rate. Such offers were, and are, a normal incident in private markets. Lambert, however, felt it to be "one of the worst offences we have to deal with."[59] In South Carolina Lieutenant Colonel Smith issued General Order No. 9 in 1866: Freedmen deserting legal employment would be arrested; plantation owners were urged to report freedmen not working according to their contracts, and so on.[60] A thousand miles away, General Kiddo, Assistant Commissioner of the Freedmen's Bureau in Texas, issued Circular Order No. 14. Its purpose? To "forbid enticing contract laborers from one employer to the other." The bureau's local agent in Marshall, Texas, similarly blacklisted freedmen who had left their employers, "notifying other employers not to hire them."[61] True, stationing military men in the South appealed to many Northerners. But belief in that policy surely required asking, "What kind of men?" W. E. DuBois considered the bureau "successful beyond the dreams of thoughtful men," defined "the two great obstacles which confronted the officers at every turn [as] the tyrant and the idler: the slaveholder who . . . was determined to perpetuate slavery under another name; and the freedman, who regarded freedom as perpetual rest."[62] Army personnel quite naturally put a high emphasis on regular work, order, stability, and contract adherence. Such values stand high in a military perspective. But they could only restrain freedmen attempting to benefit from the opportunities irregularly offered when planters competed with one another in the market for labor.

59. Trowbridge, *The South*, p. 465. The Army began by setting its own rates when Sherman hired freed men at Hilton Head. Cf. Laura Webster, The Operation of the Freedmen's Bureau in South Carolina (1916), p. 70.

60. As summarized in John H. Moore, *The Juhl Letters* (1974), p. 103. Children of such freedmen will be bound "to such persons as will take care of them and learn them habits of industry."

61. Charles W. Ramsdell, "Presidential Reconstruction in Texas," *Texas Historical Association Quarterly* (January 1909), p. 214.

62. W. E. Burghardt DuBois, "The Freedmen's Bureau," *Atlantic Monthly* (March 1901), p. 361.

The country merchants, who extended credit to the croppers, were central to the freedmen's advance. The credit they provided enabled croppers to escape from any oligopolistic control by the planters. Hence landlords claimed that it was really the merchants who ground down the cropper. The assertion was repeated with enormous vigor for more than a century, and was even taken up by radical critics of capitalism. Yet, even adding dialectic to feudal fervor does not make their case more cogent. Fortunately, extensive data recently developed by Ransom and Sutch permit us to analyze it more closely.[63] A study of the data indicates that, in a choice of Reconstruction villains, the merchant does not replace the planter or the structure of southern society.

What key conclusions can be drawn from a close reading of their data?[64]

"Our analysis of debt peonage and the power of the merchants to force farmers into overproduction of cotton has considerable appeal," Ransom and Sutch correctly note. But their scenario of massive and menacing effects rests on some strikingly improbable theses.

1. Ransom and Sutch describe an apparatus of merchant coercion that works by the most brilliantly improbable means—by forcing black sharecroppers to work 2.5 days less each year, and to commit 2.5 acres less to growing corn than "self-sufficiency" would require. (Croppers averaged 18 untilled acres apiece.)

2. The merchants utilized their "territorial monopoly" to squeeze a monopoly profit of at most $18 a year from each sharecropper. (The croppers' annual net incomes averaged $184 by their estimate.) Surely monopolists are made of sterner stuff.

3. The analysis of Ransom and Sutch implies that an "exploitative merchants monopoly" regularly and significantly forced down the rents of well over 100,000 white landlords who rented to sharecroppers. Yet we have no reports of landlord objection or public protests over a thirty-year period.

4. Ransom and Sutch likewise imply that over 50,000 "large farm" owners "were exploited through exorbitant credit prices and were susceptible to manipulations" by merchants. Yet these farm owners were far wealthier and had far higher status than the typical storekeeper.

5. The merchants charged "interest rates that must be judged enormous when compared with credit charges at other times and other places in American history"; interest that was "exorbitant," that "could not be justified by legitimate costs." Yet the attractions of such returns somehow failed to attract greedy outsiders into breaking the 7,889 merchant "territorial monopolies." For the South's ratio of rural merchants per farm did not increase during three decades after the Civil War.

63. Ransom and Sutch, *One Kind.*
64. These conclusions are developed in the Appendix, this chapter. They obviously differ from those of Ransom and Sutch, but rely directly on their data, and implications of those data.

6. As improbable as any is the underlying premise that the merchant cheated himself by this procedure. For if he forced the cropper to concentrate on the less profitable crop (i.e., cotton) the merchant slashed his own profits, since he took 50 percent of the crop. Suppose he were indeed the "monopolistic" supplier of furnishings to the cropper, at prices he alone "fixed," that Ransom and Sutch describe. By encouraging a more profitable crop mix he could get even more profits for his share, plus still more profits from greater sales of tobacco, textiles, whiskey, and notions to better off croppers.

The flow of blacks out of gang labor on plantations could not, in fact, have occurred without the rural and small town merchants. For these merchants provided a source of credit other than that provided by the landowners. Hence, they offered some competition in keeping down credit rates. It was that conflict between planter and merchant interests that explains the bitterness of planters about the Georgia crop lien law passed in 1867. That law permitted the cropper to mortgage a crop not yet even planted. As planter Hiram Hawkins said bitterly, it "opened up the flood gates . . . [and] turned over the fairest portion of the state to negro tenants. . . . Under this odious law the negro refused to be controlled or work under the direction of the owners. . . . The cotton raisers were forced to rent to the labor on their lands or to turn it out to the commons."[65] Charles Otken, the great critic of planter concentration on cotton and merchant credit, declared that "lien laws were enacted in all the Southern states enabled the negroes to be independent of the white man's supervision. . . . One of the first effects was to derange negro labor. He was desirous to be himself; to get away from his old master . . . the truth is, the old master was the negro's best friend and safest adviser."[66] The recent revival of attacks on the merchants repeats the planters' arguments of those decades. But, as DuBois more truly put the argument for the merchant and his crop lien: "The crop lien system was the only door of opportunity opened to the freedmen." And through it "thousands have advanced from penury to ownership."[67]

Appendix: Merchant's "Monopoly" in the Reconstruction South

Since colonial times merchants have been held responsible for many of the South's economic ills. Conventional historians, Marxists, and cliometricians have all pointed to the same target when explaining the tragedy of economic reconstruction

---

65. 53d Cong., 3d sess., *Cotton* (1895), p. 310.

66. Charles Otken, *The Ills of the South* (1894), p. 33.

67. 1900 Census, *Supplementary Analysis* (1900), p. 522. Indiana's lien law was successfully opposed from 1857 to 1881 by those who contended it was "in favor of capital, the rich, and against labor, the poor." Cf. Paul Gates in Walker Wyman and Clifton Kroeber, *The Frontier in Perspective* (1957), p. 149.

after the Civil War. The study by Ransom and Sutch offers a rare combination of urgent concern, close economic analysis, and extensive collection of basic data. Their work has therefore become central for any study of Reconstruction. We note below some of the implications that come out of a consideration of their findings.

1) Their description of how the merchants forced overproduction of cotton has a steady cumulation. The merchants "forced the farmer into excessive production of cotton by refusing credit to those who sought to diversify production." The merchants' "insistence . . . that the farmer forgo self-sufficiency obviously . . . served to inflate merchants' profits." Farmers were prevented "from practicing self-sufficiency as a means of escaping the merchants"; they were thereby "locked into cotton production." "Probably most of the farms that failed to produce 15 bushels of corn per family member were exploited through exorbitant credit prices."[1]

The analysis, therefore, turns on the catastrophic failure of farmers to achieve "self-sufficiency"—defined as growing 15 bushels of corn per family member for food. The actual average was only 9.7.[2] The gap was, therefore, 5.3 bushels of corn per family member. But what would it have taken croppers to grow that much? Four additional work days a year.[3] (Croppers usually worked 21 days a year less than did black wage hands.[4]) And it would also have taken three additional acres out of the 16 they actually cultivated or the 8 untilled acres they also had.[5] Even this small requirement dwindles if we do not rely on the 14 steps of the Ransom and Sutch estimating sequence to infer purchase rates. If instead we use the purchase rates reported in the same survey they used to compute costs we find only 29 percent (not 63 percent) buying corn in 1880.[6]

2) The total monopoly rent these calculations imply that the merchants extracted from the typical black sharecropper was between $8 and $18 a year. We can infer that range as follows. They estimate merchants charged an average of 60 percent interest whereas "the highest rate merchants could justifiably charge" would have been 22 percent.[7] They specify 15 percent as fully "justifiable" if one assumes no risk

1. Ransom and Sutch, *One Kind*, pp. 149, 161, 162, 164.

2. In ibid, p. 159, Ransom and Sutch contrast an actual figure of 9.7 with a "necessary" figure of 10, "a more plausible" one of 15. In further calculations they use, as we do, the figure of 15.

3. William Parker and Judith Klein, in Conference on Research in Income and Wealth, *Trends in the American Economy in the 19th Century* (1960), p. 532, estimate 26 hours were required in the South in 1907–11 to raise an acre of corn. On p. 184 in *One Kind*, Ransom and Sutch give data implying 2.035 workers per black family farm. Therefore, both workers could raise the required 30 bushels in two days.

4. Ransom and Sutch, *One Kind*, p. 235.

5. Given 5.17 family members (p. 219), and 15.0–9.7 bushels of corn required per person (pp. 15, 251), an additional 27.4 bushels were required. Ransom and Sutch state that "small scale family operated farms . . . in the Cotton South averaged . . . 11.3 bushels of corn per acre" (p. 167). That the croppers' farms averaged 24.78 acres is implicit in the figures on rent per acre (p. 100) and output (p. 216). Ransom and Sutch estimate 66 percent of the acreage was untilled (p. 183). The resultant figure of 8 untilled acres is the same as indicated by multiplying acres in crops per laborer (p. 100) and number of laborers (p. 184).

6. M. B. Hammond, *The Cotton Industry* (1897), p. 153.

7. Ransom and Sutch, *One Kind*, pp. 130, 131, 242, 243.

of default whatever (given the presence of supervision).[8] The liens averaged $78 and were for 6 months.[9] Thus, (60 percent − 15 percent) times $78 times ½ year sums to $17.55.

We have, however, a reasonable indication that the appropriate rate of interest in the market was greater than their "justifiable" 15 percent. For banks in the rural South charged white farmers 28 percent on small loans (less than a year in duration).[10] Even if banks considered the risk of a loan to black sharecroppers no greater than to white farmers the estimate of monopoly profits from black croppers would not be (60 percent − 15 percent) but (60 percent − 28 percent) or $8 a year. An $8 figure hardly indicates the merchant monopolist extracted a lordly amount from his dependent cropper's net income of $165.

3) The Ransom and Sutch analysis implies that the "exploitative merchants monopoly" regularly, and significantly, cut the rents received by about 150,000 landlords who rented to sharecroppers—but that the latter did not object or protest publicly in a thirty-year period.

The above implication begins to surface in their conclusion that the "farmer who paid credit prices for corn could have increased his income at the margin by approximately 29 percent simply by shifting from cotton to corn."[11] They were, however, apparently blocked by the merchant. He would refuse "to grant credit to a farmer who was not willing to [make] . . . cotton the principal crop."[12]

But they estimate elsewhere that only half the crop belonged to the sharecropper; the other half was taken by his landlord.[13] Hence, the landlord would lose, dollar for dollar, the same amount of money his tenant cropper lost whenever his income was cut by the merchants' policy of forcing him to grow cotton instead of more profitable grains.

8. Ibid., pp. 131, 243. Thus they find that 10 percent (for the opportunity cost of funds) plus 6.25 percent (for supervisory costs) plus 5 percent for risk of default "would justify no more than a 22.4 percent charge for interest." But, they add, "the sole purpose of the supervision was to lower the risk of default. . . . [Hence] it seems unlikely that the default rate would have been that high with a full time overseer" (p. 131).

9. The amount (derived from Hammond in the 1880 Census) is cited in Ransom and Sutch on p. 123. They use a hypothetical figure of $80 in their text, p. 131. On pp. 242–43 they carry through a calculation of "justifiable" versus actual interest costs, using a 6-month period. Had they, or we, used a 4-month term—also mentioned in their text—the dollar estimate of the "extortion" would, of course, have been still smaller. Hammond (p. 154) finds 6 months "a very liberal estimate."

10. Hammond, *Cotton*, p. 164, notes the newly established loan agencies charged interest plus points for small loans—$20 in fees plus $8 in interest, both off the top of a $100 loan. Hammond further notes that 18 percent was charged for short term loans with security other than crop liens. However, those liens were "about the only security which most of the farmers have to offer." Other sources describe rates of 20–24 percent charged white planters. Cf. *Harpers* (January 1874), p. 280, and *International Review* (January 1882), p. 77.

11. Ransom and Sutch, *One Kind*, p. 167.

12. Ibid., p. 163.

13. Ibid., pp. 89, 214, 216.

About 150,000 landlords[14] would have had to remain as silent in real life as they were stupid in this scenario for the "exploitative merchants monopoly" analysis to describe the real world. Neither seems terribly likely.

4) The analysis assumes that over 50,000 "large farms" were "exploited through exorbitant credit prices and were susceptible to manipulations by the merchant."[15] Their estimates on pages 159 and 283 indicate that 53,000 large farms fell into that total. "We can identify a large body of farms that must have been easy prey for the coercion of the credit monopolist. We know that at least three-fourths of all farms in Georgia purchased some fraction of their supplies on credit in the 1870s . . . [and] this figure was typical throughout the cotton South."

Even the large farmers bought "some fraction of their supplies" on credit. Did the "coercion of the credit monopolist" work on them as well? How "susceptible to manipulations of the merchant" were the large farmers? One indicator should be relative wealth. The large farmer had farms alone worth $12,000.[16] That figure compares with some $5,000 for the typical merchant, as estimated by Ransom and Sutch. The image of these large farmers cowering before the merchant is an improbable one.[17]

5) The analysis does not explain how the large farmers were persuaded, year after year, to accept a mere 6 percent and 10 percent on their farms without switching some funds into the nearby stores, where the merchants earned 25 percent to 60 percent.[18]

14. Some 166,998 farms in the cotton South were run by sharecroppers. Ibid., p. 283. Each had a landlord. From this total we must deduct those run by merchants, who need not have cared what they lost as landlords if they could recoup as merchants. The Mercantile agency listed about 8,000 general stores in "the rural cotton South" (p. 132), and Ransom and Sutch add that "a fraction (sic) of merchants owned more than one store" (p. 137). How large was "a fraction"?

The land worked by sharecroppers earned $5.87 an acre (p. 100). They estimate "a merchant with reasonable credit should have been able to borrow money at between 6 and 10 percent" (p. 240). (On pp. 131, 344 note 9 they use "a 10 percent opportunity cost of funds" for risk free investment.) Taking the mid-point, 8 percent, implies a land value of $73 per acre. (Farms run by croppers averaged 24.78 acres—implicit in the rent per acre, p. 100, and the contractual output total, p. 216. Hence, the farm land and capital used by the average cropper averaged $1,810.

Ransom and Sutch report that the stores of the 8,000 merchants in the rural South had a median net worth of about $5,000 (pp. 132, 138). We assume a further $5,000, a fairly generous amount in land investment. Dividing that figure by $1,810 per cropper implies 28 croppers per 100 merchants, or 22,000 in all, leaving 145,000 croppers not so tied.

15. Ransom and Sutch assert that "probably most of the farms that failed to produce 15 bushels of corn per family members (63.1 percent of all farms) were exploited . . . ." (p. 164).

16. That size distribution of farms (p. 69) and the U.S. aggregates (pp. 282–83) imply that the large farms averaged 201 acres. The rent paid the landlord per acre came to $5.87 (p. 100) and Ransom and Sutch estimate that "a merchant with reasonable credit should have been able to borrow money at between 6 and 10 percent" (p. 240), while they use "a 10 percent opportunity cost of funds" (p. 131) as the relevant risk free rate (p. 344, note 9). Capitalizing the rent makes the acreage and associated capital worth $59 an acre.

17. Ransom and Sutch report the stores of the 8,000 merchants in the rural South had a median net worth of about $5,000 (pp. 132, 138).

18. "A merchant with reasonable credit should have been able to borrow money at between 6 and 10 percent" (p. 240). They estimate a justifiable interest charge on the basis of a prevailing "short term interest rate of 10 percent" (p. 242). Long term returns in farming were surely smaller.

"Few opportunities in Southern farming were sufficiently profitable that the agricultural entrepreneur could afford to borrow at 25, 40 or 60 percent rates of interest to invest in his farm"

(It was, of course, quite unnecessary for the farmers themselves to run the stores, just as the farmers did not themselves do the cropping.) An even simpler tactic was available: "The writer buys their . . . provisions [etc.] for cash or short time—and his credit is nearly equal to cash—charges them to his hands, adding in moderate interest."[19]

6) The analysis implies that the merchants chose to exploit their "territorial monopoly" by driving their own net income below that which they could have achieved. This inference derives from several of their assumptions.

First, it premises a "merchants' requirement that he [the farmer] plant cotton" (p. 160); "cotton was required to secure a loan needed to finance the farm's operation" (p. 159); and "the merchants' insistence on cotton had the convenient effect of driving the farmer into increased dependence upon *purchased* supplies" (p. 161).

Second, the farmer could have made more money had he planted other crops, particularly corn. "It is a strange juncture of circumstances in which the great market staple of the State is selling at cost of production, while everything else raised on the farm sells at a handsome profit," mused Thomas Janes, Georgia's Commissioner of Agriculture" (p. 157). And, Ransom and Sutch estimate, "the farmer who paid credit prices for corn could have increased his income at the margin by approximately 29 percent simply by shifting resources from cotton to corn" (p. 167).

The merchants' insistence, therefore, led to reducing the real income produced by the farmer because he produced relatively less of the relatively more valuable crop (corn).

But, the analysis assumes that merchants also fixed the price of cotton sold by the farmers—and, hence, their incomes. They quote George Holmes: "The merchants . . . have replaced the former masters and have made peons of them and their former slaves" (p. 126). They later vary that point themselves: "The merchant could simply adjust the price of cotton and the farmers' income—to whatever level would keep the farmer at his job but never freed of the merchants' control" (p. 163).[20]

Now if the merchants could force the farmer to pay the prices they set for his purchases of corn, bacon, and more, and the prices he received for his cotton (and thereby "adjust . . . the farmers' income") why were they so altruistic? Specifically, why did they not let, or even urge the farmer to plant corn and other items that would yield a still more "handsome profit" and then skim off a still larger monopoly profit? By letting the cropper produce still more gross income the merchants would have garnered a still greater profit, and with their monopoly they could continue to fix corn, bacon, and cotton prices so that the cropper was still perpetually dependent on them. (Some of the 8,000 merchants could even have given part of the additional income to the cropper, thus enriching both themselves and the cropper.)

(p. 187). These figures relate back to their discussion on pp. 130–31, which estimates "justified" merchants' profits at 22 percent and actual rates ranging from a low of 40 percent to an average of 60 percent. The grandsons of Calhoun described merchants selling planters "places which have fallen into their hands, and which rent for 18 and 20 percent on their present value." Edward Atkinson, *Century Magazine* (February 1882), p. 563.

19. *Report of the Commissioner of Agriculture . . . 1876*, p. 132.

20. Ransom and Sutch continue: "This ultimate trade . . . was probably resorted to in only a fraction of the cases. But the lock-in mechanism . . . held income sufficiently low to prevent an escape into self-sufficiency. . . . [It] undoubtedly kept a majority of small farmers in a perpetual cycle of cotton overproduction and short term debt" (pp. 163–64).

The Octopus of mortgage indebtedness.

—Mary Lease

22

The Land

THE Civil War has been described as the triumph of northern industrialism, and the 1862 Homestead Act as one of the trophies of that
triumph. After the war, says Louis Hacker, "North and South were finally
united . . . nothing was to stand in the way of the quick industrialization of
the United States." The "grand design" at once took shape. "The Homestead
Act opened up the vast areas of the West . . . to free or easy settlement, and
permitted the quick exploitation of . . . natural resources."[1] Now the most
persuasive evidence of "quick industrialization" would have been a critical
shift of U.S. resources into industry. But the data actually point quite
another way: From 1840 to 1860 the labor force in farming declined from 63
to 53 percent of the total.[2] But the century-long shift toward manufacturing
and other nonfarm pursuits was abruptly halted in the next twenty years:
After 1860 farm labor dropped by only 2 points, to 51 percent. Instead, the
special advantage of the United States for producing immense exports of
wheat, corn, and cotton became evident: unusually rich land plus a railroad
boom that sharply cut transport rates.[3] (After 1880 the long decline in the
farm share resumed.)

Another analyst went further than Hacker: "In the North as in the
South, the Emancipation Proclamation had freed more white people than
black people. As a direct result of the war, the lands of the West had opened
to poor whites and rich white railroad operators."[4] The lands of the West,

---

1. Louis Hacker, *The Course of American Economic Growth and Development* (1970), pp. 172–73.
2. Lebergott, *Manpower in Economic Growth*, pp. 103, 510.
3. Stanley Lebergott, "Labor Force and Employment," in National Bureau of Economic Research, *Output, Employment and Productivity Growth in the United States After 1800* (1966), p. 130.
Cf. Jeffrey Williamson, *Late Nineteenth Century American Development* (1975), p. 196.
4. Lerone Bennet, *Prelude to Power* (1967), p. 48.

however, had been "opened" for nearly a century prior to the Homestead Act. How else had 10 million people come to live West of the Mississippi by 1860?

The great central concern of producers South and North was possession and use of the land. South and North. The South turned to reorganizing both legal claims and modes of production, forced by the freedom of four million ex-slaves. After decades of prewar expansion, the postwar South broke only a limited amount of new land to the plough (almost solely in Texas and Arkansas). In the North Central region, on the other hand, land grants and homesteading created a million new farms. This dramatic difference is shown in Table 22.1.

Most new farms in the old South were, of course, mere subdivisions of prewar plantations. But those in the North Central states represented new farm land—purchased from the federal government, railroads, states, private owners. In this acquisition process, the role of the Homestead Act was central. That Act gave title to 160 acres of federally surveyed land to anyone who would put up a house and live on the homestead for five years. The price? A minor fee while filing. After six months the farmer could take title by paying a $1.25 an acre "commutation fee." Just before the war began, millions of acres of federal land throughout the Midwest were selling for the cost of a bounty warrant—67 cents an acre.[5] (Common labor earned $1 a day.) The Homestead Act, then, cut the price of U.S. land from 67 cents an acre to 10 cents. But there was a proviso to that cut. The farmer had to stay on the homestead land for five years, come what may, before he got legal title to it.

To whom was such a cut in land prices important? Industrialists and business men? Surely that group was not defined as generously as William Jennings Bryan did in his Cross of Gold speech: "The man who works for wages is as much a business man as his employer . . . so are the miners who go down a thousand feet."[6]

The attractions of the Homestead Act even to prospective settlers are not to be overstated. For how was federal land actually disposed of during the first ten years under the act? From 1863 to 1872, ten times as many acres were sold for cash as were homesteaded. In the next decade three and a half times as many were sold.[7] Farmers continued to pay cash far oftener than they took

---

5. The bounty warrant price was given by President James Buchanan in his June 1860 message vetoing the first Homestead Act. Cf. John Basset Moore, ed., *The Works of James Buchanan* X (1910):447. Since an acre of land then cost less than the dollar a day that common laborers earned, the move from 67 cents to 10 cents an acre was hardly central to a "Second American Revolution."

6. Paolo Coletta, *William Jennings Bryan* (1964), p. 139.

7. During the next decade the ratio rose once again.

TABLE 22.1
IMPROVED LAND (MILLIONS OF ACRES)

Region	1860	1880	Percentage increase 1860–1880
North Central	52	137	163
South	60	86	43

Source: 1900 Census, Agriculture, V (1900):688, 692, 693.

up homestead land. And they bought land at $4.50 from railroads while good U.S. land could be had for $1.25.

The reasons they did so are suggested in Table 22.2. First, railroad land (closer to the railroad's right of way) was distinctly more valuable than U.S. land further away. For the less time a farmer needed to team his crop to (and from) the railhead, the more he had for work on the farm and the less he wore out his horses. That forgone income could be worth the difference.[8] Second, U.S. land that yielded even half a bushel of wheat more than free homestead land was worth more than its $1.25 cost.

As far as the railroad companies were concerned, they would have been incredibly shortsighted had they tried to hold their land off the market until they could charge more than it was worth.[9] First, because farmers could choose among millions of other acres—both land from the federal government (paying cash or homesteading) and land for sale by states and private sellers. Why should they pay the railroad a cent more than its land was worth? In fact, the reverse question arises. Why did new railroads in the North Central states offer 6 percent loans to would-be farmers when interest rates were generally far higher? (10 percent in Iowa was the legal limit, and 12 percent in Nebraska.)[10] Why did the Florida railroad, built after the Civil War, actually offer 40 acres free to any farmer who would settle and cultivate the land for two years?[11] The answer, of course, is net freight revenue. High land prices

8. The settler "should look to the quick and cheap access to the great centers of trade . . . corn which must be carted on common roads 170 miles, or wheat 300 miles, is worthless, as the cartage is more than it will bring in the market . . . one large western farmer demonstrates that the location of a Railroad Depot ten miles nearer to him than before saves him ten cents on each bushel of grain he has to sell. This would soon make up for a great difference in the price of land." United Emigration . . . Map of Colony Farm Lands at Banks, Delaware County Iowa (Broadsheet in Beinecke Library, Yale University).

9. "Speculators were generally able to secure the most desirable lands . . . the subsequent settler had the choice of buying at the speculator's prices, from the land grant railroads which held their alternative tracts at equally high prices." Paul Gates, "The Homestead Law in an Incongruous Land System," The American Historical Review (July 1936), p. 662.

10. Iowa and Nebraska Railroad Lands for Sale on Ten Year's Credit.

11. John H. Moore, The Juhl Letters to the Charleston Courier (1974), p. 200. Grants ranged from 20 to 80 acres.

TABLE 22.2
LAND INVESTMENT CHOICES, 1870S (NORTH CENTRAL REGION)

Cost and income	U.S. government land Homestead	Cash	Northern Pacific land
Yearly average (per acre)			
Gross income from wheat	$14.50	$15.00	$15.00
Interest on land purchase		$ .12	$ .27
Hauling crop to railroad	$ 2.40	$ 2.40	0
Gross income			
Less interest and transport	$12.10	$12.64	$14.63
Memorandum			
Land price (acre)	0	$ 1.25	$ 4.50
Wheat			
Yield (bushel)	14.5	15	15
Price (bushel)	$1	$1	$1
Interest rate		10%	6%

Source: Data from the Appendix, this chapter. The interest, hauling, and sales figures were discounted back to the date of purchase for comparability with the price data.

would delay settlement. But the faster freight revenues began to increase, the faster railroad profits would roll in.[12]

Thus the Iowa Railroad in 1871 offered "long credit" (i.e., for 10 years) "to actual settlers," for up to 160 acres. It offered 40 acres of land at $3 an acre, rather than the usual $5, to those who would settle and improve the land in three years.[13] The reason for its emphasis on settlement was obvious. An operating farm yielded a permanent source of revenue to the railroad. For, even if the first farmer went bankrupt, his successor would generate an equivalent rail revenue. Hence, despite widespread assertions, it rarely paid railroads to keep land off the market for a higher land price: too much would be lost in current revenue. (In counties or areas where sales prospects were rare, however, the railroads did so. They then benefited from holding land off the market because they did not become liable to state and county taxes on all land in that area. But refusing to sell to hordes of would-be purchasers was hardly to their financial advantage.)

12. As data in the Appendix indicate, each acre of land could grow 15 bushels, paying transport, say, at 15 cents apiece. Net revenue to the railroad was about one-third of gross, or 75 cents. Interest revenue at 6 cents on $4.50 per acre gave the road 27 cents. Even if $4.50 land doubled in price in 5 years the railroad would have lost money holding it for sale.

13. *Iowa Railroad Land Company, Farming Lands in Iowa and Nebraska: 1,880,000 Acres for Sale . . .* (1871).

The major complaints about the Homestead Act have been described many times, but rarely more pungently than by Fred Shannon and by Paul Gates. The Act failed to offer settlers free transportation from the East, or loans at low interest rates to "cover their needs." It did not provide for county agents to teach them how to farm. It did not provide them with "facilities for social and economic intercourse." "Lacking capital to purchase farms and . . . equipment [settlers] were frequently forced to become tenants on the lands of speculators. Thus farm tenancy developed in the frontier stage at least a generation before it would have appeared had the homestead system worked properly."[14]

What of these "defects"? A century later Congress did indeed provide low interest loans to farmers and other small businessmen, did provide extension agents to teach farming. But in 1862, and for many decades thereafter, the electorate was chiefly made up of small businessmen—farmers, artisans, miners, grocers. To provide capital, or even credit at below market interest rates, plus free transport and more to one group would only have brought demands from others. To provide for all was to subsidize most voters and would have required an immense increase in taxes. Only after small businessmen had become a minority was it possible to tax the majority of urban wage earners enough to achieve such purposes. Since the government would not set them up in business, many of those who wished to farm on the new frontier perforce rented farms, thereby becoming tenants rather than land owners. Penniless farm laborers who wished to own land in the East or South had long been accustomed to consider renting rather than owning. That option was now repeated in the Midwest.

A quite different objection found the homesteading policy too generous. Once a farmer had acquired a homestead title, perhaps only by a "commutation" payment after six months, he was free to mortgage the land, or even to sell it.[15] But families who had a run of bad luck (death, drought, grasshoppers) wanted to be free to mortgage or sell their farms. To limit such property rights was politically out of the question. It was equally out of the question for the government itself to buy farms or to loan money to buy farms. Confidence in merely the government's ability to make loans did not develop until the 1920s. And a willingness to subsidize farmers at the expense of the urban population did not develop until considerably later.[16]

14. These objections appear in Fred Shannon, *The Farmer's Last Frontier* (1961), p. 55; and Paul Gates, "The Homestead Law . . . ."

15. "Almost . . . as bad was the failure to provide for the cancellation of patents [i.e., land titles] if the homesteads were ever sold . . . or mortgaged to anyone but the government. Free farms were intended for the sole use of the patentees and their heirs forever." Shannon, *Frontier*, p. 55. Mortgages from the government, or federal willingness to buy any homestead offered for sale, would have required establishing interest rates, valuing each farm.

16. One of the obstacles, of course, was the fact that such loans did not benefit the millions of existing farmers, much less create even a trickle down to farm laborers. And the loans cost

As part of the generosity of urban residents toward their fellow farming citizens, the Congress passed the Timber and Stone Act of 1878. This act gave "the home maker a timber lot to be used in conjunction with his homestead." A buyer under that act declared "that he does not apply to purchase the same on speculation, but in good faith to appropriate it to his own exclusive use and benefit." For him to cut the timber as soon as he got title and sell it "for his own exclusive use and benefit" was acceptable. Not to cut it and sell was quite another matter. As the Conservation Commission complained, "far sighted lumber operators . . . began to take advantage of the Timber and Stone Act to acquire the best forests in the West." They "foresaw that the value of fine timber would increase for some time in geometrical progression." In some cases "they imported shiploads and carloads of their employees . . . furnishing them with the necessary funds to buy." In Modoc, California, more than 85 percent of the entries early in one year were transferred to others before May 1 of the same year. "Over 14,000 acres . . . went to one man" and about 10,000 to three others.[17] Companies, foreseeing that "the value of fine timber would increase," held it for future sale. They thereby conserved the forests, but drew down the wrath of the Conservation Commission. By passing the Timber and Stone Act, then, Congress inadvertently increased the amount of wood held to the twentieth century and reduced that burned in the nineteenth.

Land was not disposed of by resort to the ideal auction markets of classical economics. Had that been possible the people of the United States, as taxpayers, might have realized the full value of the hidden minerals, the great stands of timber, the rich bottom lands. But no such system was feasible in the actual historic context. Where it was attempted with ordinary lands (for which speculators might bid more than the settlers who had pre-empted the land, legally or illegally) it failed more than once. As William Parker wrote: "The settler-speculators, interested in opening lands or in holding them off the market, exercised strong pressures. And the squatters, with families, shotguns, and a strong sense of moral right, combined with local settlers to form a brooding, even a menacing presence as the bidding proceeded."[18] They would not let "their" land be bid up to the price that it could command in the market.

The Homestead Act, however, provided opportunities to claim rich lands, large stands of valuable timber, without even the formality of bidding. The typical objection recorded by historians does not challenge such give

urban workers. In later years even the definition of a farmer became a puzzle, when farm loan agencies loaned money to city policemen who ran small farms, to public employees who invested in ranches near the capital, and others.

17. All above quotes from 60th Cong., 2d sess., S.D. 676, *Report of the National Conservation Commission* (February 1909), p. 87.

18. Cf. his discussion in Lance Davis, et al., *American Economic Growth* (1972), p. 105.

aways to homesteaders. It objects instead to those homesteaders who did not, in fact, "intend" to stay on the farms for more than the 14 months legally required. However, few land office clerks were trained either as clairvoyants or as psychoanalysts. Inevitably they failed to discern the real "intent" of those who failed homestead patents. Nor did Congress offer any guide.[19]

Overall was the unwillingness of Congress to provide sufficient staff and sufficient tax money. Doing so would have promptly reduced the frauds perpetrated by all sorts of Americans—native and immigrant, individual and corporation.[20] Thus 11.6 million acres were disposed of by West North Central land offices in 1884 and 17.6 in 1885. The same office staff could not, however, sell almost 1 ½ times as many acres per year as they had been accustomed to, and also review each application so carefully as to prevent any fraud. Congress long had the option of adding enough staff and inspectors to reduce fraudulent transfers. The voters had the option of pressing for such action. Neither did so. Only decades later did a different set of values develop among some critics. There is, at least, no indication from experience in other vast nations—Canada, Australia, the Argentine, Brazil—that land has ever been sold to millions of landless people below its market value without a garish and rich variety of frauds taking place.

To sell a nation's land and prevent all fraud might, perhaps, have been feasible in Andorra or Luxemburg or some ancient city-state. But the United States found it impossible to prevent fraud while letting millions of people settle one billion and a half acres of widely varying quality.

19. That some 50 to 60 percent of initial homestead entries were patented 5 years later does not prove dubious intent. Farmers have failed before, and since, because of the weather, the grasshoppers, the boll weevil. Still others quit because of death, sickness, etc.

20. Cf. the lively discussion of such frauds in Raymond Robbins, *Our Landed Heritage* (1942), chap. 15, especially p. 245.

Appendix

Price

The Northern Pacific Railroad sold land at an average price of $4.50 an acre in 1877, and the Atchison, Topeka, and Santa Fe Railroads, at $6 in 1871–73, as compared with the U.S. cash price of $1.25.[1]

1. *Report of the Secretary of the Interior (1878) Annual Report of the Auditor of Railway Accounts*, table 13; Paul Gates, *Fifty Million Acres* (1954), p. 271.

Interest Rate

In 1871 the Burlington and Missouri Railroad offered land at 6 percent credit, noting that the legal rate in Iowa was 10 percent and, in Nebraska, 12 percent.[2] The B&M Railroad offered lands on short credit, or 2 years, at 10 percent interest, or long credit at 6 percent for 10 years—with the privilege of paying "any part of the principal you choose before it is due, and thus 'stop interest.' " They offered long credit lands at $12 an acre, with the same land at $8 if sold for cash.

Yield

An average wheat yield per acre as estimated by the Department of Agriculture was 15.6 bushels in 1877, 13 for the decade of the 1870s.[3]

Freight Revenue

The freight rate in 1859 per bushel of grain from a point 100 miles west of Hannibal to that city was 8 cents, 5 cents to St. Louis.[4] Hence, the local railroad could expect to gross 13 cents per bushel. In 1870 the through rate from Chicago to New York was 45 cents for 100 pounds, while the class rate in 1886 from Waterloo, Iowa, to Chicago (357 miles) was 28 cents for 100 pounds.[5] Since the average wheat bushel weighted about 60 pounds, the Waterloo-Chicago cost for a bushel of grain ran about 17 cents. We use a 15 cent gross revenue figure as a rough indicator.

Freight Profit

Profit is estimated as one-third of revenue. Fishlow's data for 1859 give a rate of about 45 percent, while the ICC data for 1890 give a ratio of 30 percent.[6]

Hauling Crop

A horse team could travel 25 miles a day on nineteenth century roads.[7] As of 1913, by which time roads had improved in many parts of the country, a USDA survey found that "a normal day's work in hauling to market with wagon for one man and two horses [loading, hauling, and unloading] covered about 12 miles with a ton and a

2. *Iowa and Nebraska Railroad Lands for Sale on Ten Years Credit* (1871). (Broadsheet in Beinecke Library, Yale University); C. J. Ernst in *Nebraska History* (January–March 1924), p. 21 for a $5.14 rate for Northern Pacific.

3. U.S. Department of Agriculture, Statistical Bulletin No. 158, *Wheat, Acreage, Yield, Production* (1955).

4. Broadsheet: *The Hannibal and St. Joseph Railroad Company . . . Over 600,000 Acres* (1859). The charge from St. Louis to New York was a further 25 cents.

5. Rate data from 52d Cong. 2d sess. S.R. 1394, the Aldrich *Report on Wholesale Prices . . .* , pp. 516, 645.

6. Albert Fishlow, *American Railroads and the Transformation of the AnteBellum Economy* (1965), p. 337; *Historical Statistics . . . to 1970*, p. 737. The Pennsylvania Railroad in the 1880s had a ratio of about 1/3. Cf. Paul MacAvoy, *Economic Effects of Regulation* (1965), p. 198.

7. The *Rural Carolinian* in 1870 estimated 25 miles a day. Ransom and Sutch, *One Kind*, p. 345. For Illinois in 1841, 28 miles a day is recorded for a two-wagon team from Peoria to Chicago loaded with wheat. David Schob, *Hired Hands and Plowboys* (1975), p. 52.

quarter of corn and small grain."[8] If half a day went for loading and unloading, the two figures are consistent.

The average daily wage of farm hands in 1877–79 in Iowa was 80 cents and in Nebraska, 89 cents.[9] The daily rate would then have been applicable to the value of a farmer's time during harvest, as he could have hired out on adjoining farms. Allowing for the hire of two horses and a wagon, the cost would have been about $3.

The load per wagon in 1831 on the main road from the Susquehanna to the Schuykill averaged one-half ton.[10] A two-horse wagon on Maine roads in 1840 would carry "from 10–12 cwt" (i.e., about one-half ton).[11] Assuming the wagon transported one-half ton, it would carry one year's product of one acre of wheat land (15 bushels, 56 pounds apiece) some 25 miles for $3. Hence, to carry an acre's product only 10 miles from farm to market and back would have cost $2.40.

8. U.S. Department of Agriculture, Bulletin No. 3, H.H. Mowbray, *A Normal Day's Work for Various Farm Operations* (1913), p. 41.

9. U.S. Department of Agriculture, *Farm Wage Rates, Farm Employment and Related Data* (January 1943), p. 26.

10. (Pennsylvania) *Report* of the Committee on Internal Improvements and Inland Navigation, January, 1831 (1831).

11. Maine, 20th Leg., H.D. 3, *Report* of the Land Agent (1840), p. 61.

"Falta caminos! falta gente!" (We need roads! we need people!) is the cry of the Yungeno and of the ambitious Bolivians.
—MARGARET A. WALSH, *The Bankers in Bolivia*

With all her 200,000 miles of railway America is not a country but a continent.
—ALFRED MARSHALL, *Minutes of Evidence . . . Indian Currency*

23

The Railroads: After the War

THE expansion of the U.S. railroad network after 1865 was driven by three powerful forces. Very similar to those that appear and reappear in the developing nations of the twentieth century, they were: mystic, military, and monetary. The mystic sense of national identity and purpose, vague though it may be, generates powerful political effects. In the United States, the catastrophe of the Civil War intensified the belief that "a house divided cannot stand," and strengthened the feeling that a truly national transport network was needed to bind the nation together. The military motive was long felt, and persistent. In the 1850s major exploring parties had been sent out by the then Secretary of War, Jefferson Davis, to lay out various transcontinental rail routes. The purpose? To enable the army to rush troops to the frontiers whenever war broke out—war with Britain (the Northern frontier), or with Spain (the Southern), or with the Indian tribes. Finally, the monetary motive was obviously decisive since private entrepreneurs developed nearly every rail route except the transcontinental ones.

The transcontinental roads constituted a separate problem. Political pressures for building such roads had been persistent, noisy, and sometimes important for decades before the Civil War. However, few capitalists were attracted to invest in a road to run thousands of miles through largely unsettled territory, dotted by menacing Indian tribes. True, the trains might pick up a small cargo in one county, deliver it five counties further on. They might pick up a passenger in one state and set him down in another. But that tiny revenue potential made few capitalists into zealots for transcontinental roads. The market price of the Union Pacific stock even after the road had been completed is suggestive.[1] True, the railroad had been given apparently huge government subsidies. It had a monopoly of rail traffic across the plains. It was the dominant corporation in seven states. And it was fettered by no ICC controls on what it could charge. Nevertheless, its stock sold for a mere 40 cents on the dollar from 1869 through 1876.[2] For the volume on Union Pacific traffic, from which profits had chiefly to come, was trivial. Only the prospect of profits could buoy up stock values. Every investor knew these simple facts. And stock prices reflected them.

The acceleration of railroad construction after the Civil War can be readily described (see Table 23.1). Over a billion dollars went to building railroads between 1870 and 1879, chiefly in the North Central United States—in a far smaller economy than today's.[3] That construction boom, particularly in the North Central and West, was not sparked merely by the enthusiasm of railroad stockholders for profit, or a national ardor for railroads. The underlying reason was that shippers, who provided every cent of railroad revenue, found them cheaper than the alternative. Wagoning wheat to markets on the crude roads of the frontier required more energy than did transport by railroad—the basic reason why railroad charges per ton-mile averaged under a fifth of rates by wagon.[4] Moreover, that differential offered millions of farmers, thousands of small manufacturers, and dozens of giant trusts the opportunity to expand their sales (and profits) by moving into new markets. Some of these new markets were a hundred miles from their base. Others were located thousands of miles away in Europe and Asia.

How was it all possible? To some extent the inflow of foreign capital was at work. U.S. indebtedness abroad rose by about $1 billion between 1861 and 1871. A goodly share of that increase went to snap up the bonds of the Erie Railroad (soon to be worthless), plus those of the Burlington and more reliable

1. The venturesome decision to build the road in the first place, and the contrast between its dubious prospects and the charges of excessive public subsidy and promoter profits, are reviewed in the classic study by Robert Fogel, *The Union Pacific Railroad* (1960). Later, and conflicting, views appear in Lloyd Mercer, "Rates of Return for Land Grant Railroads," *Journal of Economic History* (September 1970), and Heywood Fleisig, "The Union Pacific Railroad," *Explorations in Economic History* (Winter 1973).

2. Charles E. Ames, *Pioneering the Union Pacific* (1969), appendix Z, p. 555.

3. Albert Fishlow estimates that net capital stock (in 1909 dollars) rose by $1.5 billion from 1869 to 79; see Conference on Research in Income and Wealth, *Output, Employment and Productivity in the United States After 1800* (1966), p. 606.

4. George R. Taylor, *The Transportation Revolution 1815–1860* (1951), pp. 134–35, 442, compares a 15 cent wagon rate and a 2 cent railroad rate (in 1850 and 1860) as does Robert Fogel, in his *Railroads and American Growth* (1964), pp. 29, 56, 109; see also Peter McClelland, "Railroads, American Economic Growth," *Journal of Economic History* (March 1968), pp. 106–8.

TABLE 23.1

MILES OF RAILROAD BUILT BY REGION (000 MILES OF 000 PER DECADE)

Decade	U.S. total	North Central	New England	Mid Atlantic	South	West
1830–39	2	0	—	1	—	—
1840–49	5	1	2	1	1	—
1850–59	20	9	1	4	6	—
1860–69	16	6	—	4	3	3
1870–79	41	19	2	6	5	9

Source: Tabulated from 1880 Census, Report on Transportation (1880), table VIII. U.S. totals computed from unrounded data.

railroads. Foreigners increased their share of U.S. railroad ownership from about 10 percent in 1853 to 20 percent by 1873. And much of that increase took place in the early 1870s.[5]

Most U.S. railroad construction, however, was financed by U.S. sources. A small contribution was made in 1880–89 when the Treasury repaid nearly $1 billion of debt to investors in the Civil War. That debt had massively increased ($2.5 billion) between 1860 and 1869 while railroad construction was booming, and very little repayment had taken place during 1870–79.[6]

The major financing of new railroads, then, came directly from U.S. nationals invested rather than increasing their present consumption as they otherwise might. Who were they? Generally they were landowners who sold land to the companies; manufacturers who sold them rails and cars; plus sanguine widows and tough financiers who planned to make a quiet million.[7] When railroad stocks and bonds poured into the financial markets, these were the buyers. Railroads had earned roughly 8 percent from the end of the Civil War to 1872.[8] Increasing railroad shipments made their stocks appear absolute certainties. The result?

5. The 10 percent figure for 1853, and a 10 percent estimate by Wells for 1869, appear in Cleona Lewis, America's Stake in International Investments (1938), pp. 521, 523. The 1873 estimate is from Leland Jenks, "Railroads as an Economic Force in American Development," in Joseph T. Lambie and R. V. Clemence, Economic Change in America (1954), p. 59. Jenks reports Schumpeter claiming that foreigners financed the entire 1866–72 boom.

6. Data on Federal debt from Historical Statistics . . . to 1970, p. 1104.

7. Farmers along the line, who would benefit from better facilities for shipping their crops, also bought stock. One is quoted as saying: "See here; I can mortgage my farm . . . and go East, where I came from, to get money for it." Between 1850 and 1857 nearly 6,000 Wisconsin farmers bought $5 million in railroad stock. John Stover, The Life and Decline of the American Railroad (1970), pp. 32–33.

8. Historical Statistics . . . to 1970, p. 1003.

TABLE 23.2
FREIGHT COSTS, 1860–80

	Rail Chicago to New York City (cents per bushel wheat)	Ocean New York City to Liverpool (cents per barrel flour)
1860	35	62
1870	30	40
1880	20	40

Source: U.S. Department of Agriculture, "Changes in Railway Rates . . . ,"
Miscellaneous Bulletin 15 (1898), pp. 41, 51; also, unpublished estimates of
Douglass North.

In twenty years, from 1865 to 1885, the improvement of the U.S. transport system touched off a series of economic revolutions and social
cataclysms. These destroyed beyond recall portions of ancient economies
throughout Europe. Only slightly less portentous changes occurred in hundreds of established production centers within the United States.

The effect on European economies was foreshadowed by the precipitous
decline of U.S. freight rates to export markets, shown in Table 23.2. Ocean
freight rates declined from 1860 to 1870 as steam arrived, ending the sailing
ship era. Steam vessels were managed with fewer men than sailing vessels.
And ships with the new compound marine engines could move almost three
times as much freight as the old vessels, whose bulky engines and heavy coal
requirements used up much of their potential cargo space.[9]

The result of this transport advantage appeared in exports, shown in
Table 23.3. As a French commentator wrote: "Each mile of railroad constructed in a new country is a kind of centrifugal pump furnishing for exportation hundreds of tons of the products of such country."[10] To produce this
increase in exports of wheat and corn from 1850 to 1880 required something
close to 170,000 additional U.S. farms.[11] Now farms in Europe were less productive, acre for acre. They were smaller, and their production was less efficient than U.S. production. It is likely, therefore, that at least a third of a

9. David A. Wells, *Recent Economic Trends* (1890), pp. 35–37. Wells estimates that the
number of sailors for a 3,000 ton steamer fell from 141 to 84 between 1870 and 1885 in the British
merchant marine, while freight capacity rose from 800 to 2,200 tons.

10. Wells, *Recent Economic Trends*, p. 176.

11. The average North Central U.S. farm in 1870 had about 69 improved acres. 1900 Census, *Agriculture*, part V, p. 692. The average per acre yield in the West for 1866–75 was 14
bushels of wheat, and 31 of corn. (Cf. William Parker in Conference on Research in Income and
Wealth, *Output, Employment and Productivity in the United States After 1800* (1966), p. 537.) Hence,
the equivalent of 45,000 farms devoted to corn and 124,000 to wheat would have been required.

TABLE 23.3
Exports, 1850–80
(MILLIONS OF BUSHELS)

	Corn	Wheat
1850		11
1860		16
1870	1	45
1880	98	175

Source: Charles Evans, *Imports-Duties from 1867 to 1883, Inclusive* (1884), part 2, pp. 113, 115. The data shown are 3-year averages centered on the given year.

million European farms were closed down by American competition. (Wheat acreage in Britain alone was slashed 40 percent from 1869 to 1887.)[12] The destruction of European farms was not limited to a single European nation. Farms were scattered in a long arc from England and Denmark through Prussia on into Russia. (Only rarely did European farmers, as in Denmark, succeed in switching to other products.) The small capitalist farmers of North America hacked away at the economic base of the ruling landed classes in Europe more destructively than all the revolutionaries on the Continent.

Railroad extension brought no less spectacular impacts within the United States. Its primary result? Increased competitiveness of the U.S. economy, to a degree never seen outside the textbooks of classical economists. The United States had been pock-marked by local monopolies of blacksmiths, wheelwrights, millers, retail grocers, cigar workers, physicians, cobblers. Outsiders could not profitably ship their goods, or bring their services in, to compete with these monopolistic craftsmen and handicraft workers. Railroad expansion broke up their world, exposing them all to the harsh blasts of competition. Railroads introduced competing products from a dozen states into every county along or near their lines. (Between 1870 and 1880 the number of traveling salesmen quadrupled.[13] They carried the products of new competitors into every region in the nation.) The tonnage of raw material shipped into factories, and final products shipped out from 1859 to 1879, rose four times faster than the volume of GNP they produced.[14]

Producers who once led the nation in profit rates were submerged. Skilled workmen and professionals found their modest local monopolies

12. Wells, *Recent Economic Trends*, p. 88. Acreage fell from 4.0 to 2.3 million.
13. 1900 Census, *Occupations*, p. 1. The number increased from 7,000 to 28,000.
14. The constant dollar GNP figures of Robert Gallman are used together with tonnage data from Edwin Frickey, *Production in the United States, 1860–1914* (1947), p. 100.

broken up as new products were shipped in, as customers began travelling to county seats or urban centers for dressmaking, legal, repair services. (It all proved to be a harbinger of what the automobile would accomplish, even more spectacularly, when it arrived.) These displaced small entrepreneurs, and small craftsmen, became participants in the first great U.S. strikes (of the late 1870s); in the development of populist discontent; and in the leadership of a continuing, if small, labor movement.

Railroads first attracted this heavy volume of shipment because they were expanding into new areas. Their enormous superiority over wagon transport gave them the obvious edge. They reinforced that lead by persistent technical advance. In later decades, when the railroads became a classic example of sluggish technological change, it was hard to imagine that they once stood in the forefront of innovation. But they did. And their innovations enabled them to cut costs persistently. These costs, given the fierceness of competition prior to the Interstate Commerce Commission, were largely passed along to shippers as lower freight rates.

Two massive innovations accounted for most of the productivity advance. On road after road the old iron rails, though still serviceable, were torn up and replaced by steel rails. For steel rails could be expected to carry ten times as much tonnage during their useful life as iron ones.[15] Hence, the real costs of ripping up old rails and putting in new ones became relatively trivial. The second major factor that cut costs was the 100 percent increase in the tractive power of locomotives between 1870 and 1910, and 60 percent rise in the size of freight cars.[16]

The Erie railroad provided a graphic example. In this period the financial shenanigans of its chief officers, Daniel Drew and Jim Fisk, horrified a host of critics and journalists.[17] But meanwhile the railroad was installing new engines. Its "American" locomotives of 1874 pulled an average load of 106 tons, while the huge new "consolidation" type locomotives of 1883 averaged a 228-ton load.[18] The new compound engine did more than pull greater loads. Tests by leading railroads all over the East and Mid West showed that it cut coal consumption by about 25 percent.[19] Other technological advances, though multitudinous, made little difference in overall costs or prices. That

15. Albert Fishlow, in National Bureau of Economic Research, *Output, Employment and Productivity in the United States after 1800* (1966), p. 639. Engineering data he cites suggest a 25-fold advantage.

16. Ibid., pp. 604, 641. Since Fishlow estimates locomotive tractive power rose by 100 percent, and locomotive weight also rose by 100 percent, we assume the 60 percent rise in freight car weight reflects the rise in its effective cargo capacity.

17. Cornelius Vanderbilt of the New York Central was their greatest critic. But the classic analysis remains Charles and Henry Adams, *Chapters of Erie* (1871).

18. J. L. Ringwalt, *Development of Transportation Systems in the United States* (1888), p. 318.

19. In addition, it saved on repairs, oil, cleaning. William Cathcart, "The Compound Locomotive in the United States," *Cassier's Magazine* (November 1897), pp. 47, 49.

conclusion applied to automatic couplers, air brakes, improved journal boxes, and more. Because potential savings from these were so small their introduction was laggard. Indeed, it was only Congress that forced the introduction of some of these new technologies. Congress had been pressured by labor organizations protesting the deaths of brakemen (who fell from the tops of freight cars as they wrestled with old-fashioned hand brakes) and yard men (who were squeezed between cars as they were coupling them by hand).[20]

The high and steady profit rates earned by railroads during the 1860s inevitably lured dozens of new companies into the field. The major entries gravitated straight toward certain high profit routes. Thus the Pennsylvania Railroad had the sole rail route between Chicago and New York for many years. That was surely the most efficient mode for exporting the corn, wheat, and pork produced throughout the entire Midwest. Their monopoly was ended when the New York Central (through its affiliate, the Lake Shore Railroad) entered Chicago in 1869. This preliminary earth tremor was followed by a more overwhelming one in 1874 when both the Baltimore and Ohio and the Grand Trunk Railroad finally entered Chicago. Garrett (of the Baltimore and Ohio) had already forecast that when his line to Chicago was completed, "like another Samson he would pull down the temple of rates around the other trunk lines."[21] And so he did. It was no happenstance that one of the longest depressions in U.S. history began in late 1873 as the completion of these new lines became a certainty. Excess railroad capacity zoomed, eventually exposing farm and nonfarm producers to unbridled competition.

Of the many new lines established, particularly those Eastward from, and Westward to, Chicago, some were more efficiently located (or built) than others. As a result, these had a competitive advantage over others. To remain in business the less efficiently located lines began to carry goods at rates below those offered by the more efficient lines, which meant their profit rates were less than those earned on alternative investments. Indeed, as the competition between lines became harsh, some saw their profits run down to zero. Meanwhile, the efficient lines still enjoyed modest or even "average" profit rates.

Railroads constituted a special problem. Once the less efficient lines were completed, those who had invested in them could not simply close up shop and enter business someplace else, as a grocery store owner might do. A retailer going bankrupt might sacrifice 25 percent of his assets—for breaking a lease, abandoning store fixtures, and so on.[22] But abandoning a railroad meant abandoning far more. During 1865–75, when railroad competition

---

20. Fishlow, *Output, Employment*, pp. 635–38.

21. New York Assembly, *Proceedings of the Special Assembly . . . on Alleged Abuses . . . in Railroads* (Hepburn Committee) (1879), pp. 3171–72.

22. We have no data for the asset composition of grocery stores in the 1870s. As of 1960, active corporations in retail trade had 22 percent of their assets in depreciable assets or land. U.S. Internal Revenue Service, *Corporation Income Tax Returns, 1959–60*, Table 2.

reached its height, some 93 percent of railroad investment was solidly fixed in track and roadbed. A mere 7 percent was in the form of items which might be sold to some other railroad, such as locomotives and freight cars.[23]

Moving to some other location, then, would mean a sharp sacrifice for owners of a grocery store, but a total catastrophe for owners of an unused railroad. Railroads, therefore, simply kept operating in the hope of a future recovery or miracle. To do so they inevitably took every and any shipment that could at least pay a bit over variable costs. True, they were obligated to cover the fixed interest costs due on their bonds. But that obligation loomed over them whether or not they took the shipment, whether or not they made money, whether or not they closed down the business. The decision to take any given shipment, then, would be made provided *some* profit accrued above variable costs—that is, in economic terms, if marginal revenue exceeded marginal cost. For, in that event, they would be able to keep operating until conditions improved. Meanwhile, payment for that shipment (which they would not get if they charged any higher freight rate) would help cover the cost of keeping their work force intact. And it would help to pay a bit of those remorseless fixed costs. "Even without the Interstate [Commerce] Act . . . these new roads, with their inequalities in length and otherwise, would have reduced the revenues of the older lines. There were more to divide the business."[24]

Three predictable consequences of the new competition followed.

First, the prices charged by the railroads fell, and fell persistently. Symbolic were the rates from New York to Chicago. Garrett had indeed pulled "down the temple of rates." But, as the data indicate, competition even among the existing roads had already been destroying that temple. Declines in Southern rates were no less spectacular. The rate for shipping cotton across South Carolina fell 85 percent between 1870 and 1897 (by 25 percent alone from 1875 to 1879).[25] See Table 23.4.

Second, prices did more than fall precipitously over the long term. They varied sensitively and frequently with every short term increase in demand—for example, when spring crops came to market—and with every increase in competition. Perhaps peak variability in rates appeared when the New York Central finally began competing with the Pennsylvania for the New York to Chicago traffic. Rates for that service swooped and soared as fol-

23. We use Fishlow's estimate of real net capital stock in 1909 dollars, from *Output, Employment*, p. 606.

24. C. E. Perkins, in *Boston Daily Advertiser* (January 25 1889).

25. Rates from Columbia or Augusta to Charleston 1860 and 1897: quoted in James Watkins, *The Cost of Cotton Production*, U.S.D.A. Misc. Series, Bulletin 16 (1899), pp. 38–39. The rates fell from $6.25 to 95¢ a bale. The 1875–79 data are from J. L. Ringwalt, *Development of Transportation Systems in the United States* (1888), p. 249, and relate to shipments Atlanta to Charleston.

TABLE 23.4
FREIGHT RATES
(CLASS I SHIPMENTS PER 100 POUNDS)

	Actual (dollars)	Constant dollar index
1862	$1.59	100
1872	1.18	57
1882	.56	34

Source: Aldrich Report, *Wholesale Prices, Wages and Transportation,* S.R. 1394, I:435. Constant dollar index rates—deflated by wholesale price series from *Historical Statistics,* II:115, 117.

lows during a single year, shown in Figure 23.1. Price competition offered no finer example of its work.

In a world of risk aversion, such unsteadiness was, of course, quite abhorrent. As a leading newspaper man editorialized: "There is no steadiness, no system, no fixedness for anything, and the whole country is kept in a tremor of expectancy as to whether prices are going up or down from this unregulated course."[26] Predictably, a great exponent of railroad "cooperation" declared: "There is great uncertainty in the minds of people who have to invest money in commercial transactions how to operate for the future. The rates may be raised again tomorrow or the next day."[27]

And, third, as prices fell, profits fell. Net earnings of the New York Central per ton mile plummetted from 99 cents in 1869 to 64 cents in 1871, to 46 cents in 1872.[28] "Above normal" profit rates on the most fortunate routes vanished. "Normal" profit rates disappeared on other routes. Many roads found revenue barely covering costs. Others found it impossible even to cover variable costs. (Then came the depression of 1873–79, with nearly 25,000 more miles of competitive lines built, and the crash of 1893. By 1894 some 41,000 miles of bankrupt road were being operated by receivers.[29]

A universal panacea was offered to prevent such outcomes: cooperation. Joint price setting in a gentlemanlike manner was proposed. Perhaps the earliest lasting effort to establish fixed rates for all railroads was initiated in 1873 by those connecting Atlanta with the seaboard.[30] By 1875 that had ex-

26. Joseph Medill, editor of the *Chicago Tribune,* quoted in Edward Kirkland, *Industry Comes of Age* (1961), p. 81.
27. Albert Fink, *Why Railroad Tariffs Are Not Maintained* (1881), p. 5.
28. Ringwalt, *Development,* p. 244.
29. U.S. Census, *Historical Statistics . . . to 1970,* p. 732.
30. Ringwalt, *Development,* p. 274.

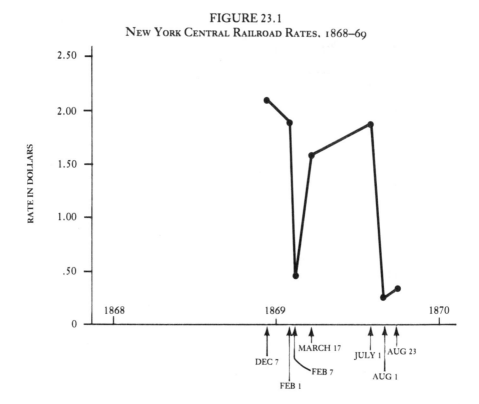

FIGURE 23.1
New York Central Railroad Rates, 1868–69

Source: Aldrich Report, *Wholesale Prices*, p. 432, for Class 1 shipments.

panded into the Southern Steamship and Railway Association.[31] That Association pegged the rates both for the railroad and for the steamships that took freight from the railroads. (For on some runs the ships competed directly with railroads.) The success of this cartel may have turned on the fact that it developed when many Southern railroad lines were being built, or rebuilt, after the Civil War. Their shared experience could well have assisted such cooperation. In any event, it was followed by many railroad pools in the North.

The prizes of cooperation were great indeed. The Southern roads were surely not atypical. Accordingly to their knowledgeable cartel manager, 15 percent of their gross revenue went back to customers in rebates, while 10

31. Its first meeting, ironically enough, was presided over by Joseph Brown (Albert Fink, *The Regulation of Railway Rates* (1905), p. 13.) Brown had been the recalcitrant, individualistic governor of Georgia who had given Jefferson Davis a minimum of cooperation all during the Civil War, reluctant to go along with any central government direction whatever.

percent additional revenue was spent on selling efforts.[32] The most splendid of these was surely the celebrated "Iowa Pool" of railroads operating westward from Chicago through Iowa. The most happily named, the "Chicago Eastbound Dead Freight Pool," controlled the market shares of member railroads by switching flour and pork shipments from one to the other. (Its Commissioner stationed himself on the floor of the Chicago Board of Trade. Price cuts quoted there for grain shipments tipped him off to which road was cheating on the pool.[33] Another pool switched immigrants headed west from Europe back and forth. The Interstate Commerce Commission (ICC) sympathetically described these "railroad associations"—cartels—as being "effectual in securing harmonious relations. . . . By this device the carriers are often enabled to restrain destructive competition."[34]

It had never been easy

> to maintain rates by mere agreements . . . among roads which are about equal in . . . distance, equipment and terminals; the difficulty is much greater when inferior roads become parties to the contest for business. . . . An old road with an established business, having pretty direct lines between commercial centers, can afford to maintain rates and let business go where it will, provided its competitors will do the same thing. But . . . a new road . . . or [one] with an indirect or long line between the same commercial centers cannot afford to . . . let business take its course. . . . [For] at equal rates business will . . . go mostly by the older and more direct lines.[35]

Hence, the wry observation by "an able railroad manager" that rate fixing agreements between railroads of unequal facilities "were generally made by the managers with the purpose merely of practicing deception upon each other."[36]

Cartels were formed, but then self-destructed. The process was immensely painful to the cartel leadership. "To secure business" the railroads made "secret agreements with shippers for reduced rates . . . this sort of process is generally called competition but . . . should not be practised by honorable men. When the officers of railroad companies . . . agree upon a joint

---

32. 44th Cong., 2d sess., H.D. 46, part 2, Joseph Nimmo, *First Annual Report on the Internal Commerce of the United States*, Appendix 21.

33. Thomas Ulen, *Cartels and Regulation* (unpublished paper, 1979). Its effectiveness in the decade after the Interstate Commerce Commission (ICC) seemed about as great as the decade before (1887–97). However, in the earlier period three new roads had been formed. Forcing their way into the business they inevitably tended to force rates down. With no roads formed in the later decade prices would have tended to be stable (or to rise) regardless of the ICC.

34. Interstate Commerce Commission, *Fourth Annual Report* (December 1, 1890), p. 22.

35. C. E. Perkins in *Boston Daily Advertiser* (January 25, 1889).

36. Insterstate Commerce Commission, *Fourth Annual Report*, p. 22.

tariff, each company should strictly adhere to it." Because they failed to do so, "the present [rate] war has arisen. While thus contending for a few hundred tons of freight the total revenues of the roads are decreased by millions. . . . When the people understand the subject better they will insist, either by the force of public opinion, or through legal enactments, to compel railroad managers to work . . . in harmony with each other."[37] Revenues to railroad stockholders, as noted, were "decreased by millions" under the process "called competition." Supporters of the railroad pools looked "to compel railroad managers to work . . . in harmony," if necessary by "legal enactment." And so the ICC was established in 1887. What was oddest about that result was that it was widely, almost universally, urged by opponents of the railroads.

The substantial clamor that eventually swayed Congress was generated by a host of railroad practices—from the fact that legislators got free passes to differences in rates per mile charged different shippers (rebates). Perhaps the most persistent and widespread complaints involved the pro-rata issue. Intrastate shipments were charged less per mile than shipments from out of state. As early as 1860 the New York State Assembly reported that "railroads of this state abuse their privileges and oppress our citizens, to wit:

1. Property of citizens of other states is allowed transportation on them for less—much less—proportionably than the products of our own citizens.
2. Citizens of given localities in this State are compelled to pay unequal rates of transportation as compared with other localities."

As proof of "the continuance and extent of discrimination," the Committee noted that in March 1859 the New York Central Railroad "carried flour, Sandusky to New York at 65¢ per bbl.," but only charged 70 cents from Buffalo to New York, though the latter stretch was longer.[38]

It has long been taken for granted that railroads set rates by a simple but harsh rule: "When it comes to setting transport rates, there is only one rational rule: it is to charge the merchandise all that it can pay."[39] That statement, by a French railway director, became, in American parlance: charge all the traffic will bear. But if the railroads, indeed, charged all the traffic will bear, why did they charge lower rates to traffic coming over long distances? Why not charge more and make still greater profits?

The missing factor is suggested by the fee schedule of the Erie Canal, the great artery run by the state of New York. Surely its rates should have re-

---

37. Fink, *Why Railroad Tariffs*, pp. 3, 4, 6.

38. State of New York Assembly Report 47, *Regulating Freights on Railroads* (February 1, 1860), p. 3.

39. M. Solacroup is quoted, and his principle rejected, in Edwin R. A. Seligman, *Essays in Economics* (1925), p. 187n.

sponded to the concerns expressed by the legislators. Yet the Canal charged 12 cents for the 415 miles from New York City to Syracuse and only 10 cents for the 514 miles from New York City to Buffalo. Moreover, canal rates for New York City to Lockport—448 miles within the state—were 16 cents, as compared to the 12 cents charged for 770 miles New York City to Cleveland. The freight agent of the Central concluded: "discriminations between long and short freights are general on all lines of transport."[40]

As Albert Fink wrote:

> A railroad connecting two commercial communities having the advantage of river transportation only improves the transportation facilities of the interior points. It does not change the relations [between them] and the river points in any other way. These discriminations—charging higher rates to the interior stations than to the river points, although the former are nearer—have [long] existed. . . . The construction of the railroad does not create, but . . . diminishes [them]. . . . The same influences . . . build up great centers of trade and manufacturing . . . and prevent the building up of interior places. . . . It seems to me to the interest of each railroad company to foster local enterprises . . . to build up business and population on its own line or road instead of concentrating it in a few great centers, where it is open to competition by many other lines.[41]

The reason why both the public canal and the private railroad charged less per ton mile for some long runs, then, turned on the facts of geography and enterprise: some locations had alternative transportation routes open to them. Rates from New York to Elmira were actually less than those from the much shorter distance New York to Susquehanna because Elmira was served by several competing railroads. Susquehanna had only the Erie railroad. The Erie, never noted as a charitable operation, knew well that if it charged a higher rate in Elmira, business would simply go to a competitor. Indeed, at a sufficiently low rate, goods would be shipped in the most tortuously circuitous fashion rather than directly. (Some twenty different routes were available for shipping goods from St. Louis to Atlanta.)[42] Illinois shippers, who assembled wheat from farmers throughout Illinois, sold directly to Liverpool importers. It mattered not at all to them whether the wheat went directly eastward to New York (via the New York Central), slightly to the south through Philadelphia (via the Pennsylvania Railroad), further south (via the Baltimore and Ohio), or far to the north (via Canada's Grand Trunk Railroad). What did matter was the total cost of getting wheat from Chicago to Liver-

40. State of New York, Assembly Report 70, *Pro Rata Freight Law* (February 1860), pp. 105–6. The canal data were for May (Buffalo, Syracuse) and June (Lockport, Cleveland) of 1859.

41. 44th Cong., 2d sess., H.D. 46, part 2, Joseph Nimmo, *First Annual Report on the Internal Commerce of the United States*, appendix pp. 44–45.

42. Ibid., pp. 55–57.

pool. They sought the lowest combined rate. Whenever a railroad arranged to guarantee a full load for a vessel leaving the East coast for Europe, or a steamship company sought the best offer from a railroad, it was the total shipping cost that decided the route. Hence, wheat from one Iowa farm might go via New York, while wheat from the adjoining farm left via Montreal.

But how did railroads manage with such a topsy-turvy method of pricing? Surely it cost more to ship per ton mile when the trip covered fewer miles than when it covered more. What counted, however, was not "total cost" but long-run marginal costs. Data for the 1870s are limited, but consistent with more precise data for recent years. They point to the decisive factors.

In the long run—and railroads are designed to last for many decades—most costs were marginal costs. Freight cars had to be replaced; rails had to be taken up as worn sections were replaced; and so on. A correct accounting of such costs in Table 23.5 shows that the long haul did cost less per ton mile.

Complaints about long haul-short haul "inequities" tended to reflect two underlying factors. First, thousands of small towns wished to protect their retailers, wholesalers, and manufacturers from competition by producers in great cities, who were brought closer to rural markets by the railroads.[43] In "the present railroad war . . . manufactured articles are brought from New York to Louisville for 21 cents per 100 [pounds]. The same articles manufactured in Syracuse . . . cost now 40 cents per 100 for transportation to Louisville. . . . The people of Syracuse lose the business."[44]

Of course taxpayers and producers in disadvantaged localities sought to protect their interests by putting cost walls around their cities. Thus in 1862 Maine forbid the railroad into Portland to change its track gauge.[45] For, if it shifted to the standard 4-foot 8-inch gauge, goods would have hurtled right through Portland on their way to Boston. The legislation ensured that shipments would still have to be unloaded in Portland from one railroad line to another. All of this generated incomes for Portland's laborers, truckers, and wholesalers. It also kept up the value of city lots and buildings. (Unfortunately it offered no long-run solution. Shippers began using cheaper, competing routes to market. Portland then failed to develop in its competition with Boston and Montreal as it might have but for that feat of policy, so shrewd in the short term.)

The primary complaint against the railroads may have been the long haul–short haul differential. But other complaints were not lacking. Chief

43. The role of small city and town merchants in putting through state regulations of railroad rates in the 1870s—the "Granger Laws"—is emphasized in George Miller, *Railroads and the Granger Laws* (1971).

44. 44th Cong., 2d sess., H.D. 46, part 2. *First Annual Report on Internal Commerce* (1877), appendix p. 36.

45. Edward Kirkland, *Men, Cities and Transport* (1948), pp. 214–15.

TABLE 23.5
RAILROAD COSTS (DOLLARS PER TON MILE)

Miles	Louisville and Nashville Railroad (1874)			U.S. railroads (average) (1950s)		
	Station	Line haul	Total	Station	Line haul	Total
10	0.10	1.00	1.10	6.56	0.32	6.88
400	0.01	1.00	1.01	0.83	0.32	1.15

Source: 1874 data from Louisville and Nashville Railroad Annual Report in The Railroads, Alfred Chandler, Jr., ed. (1965), pp. 111–13. Focussing on the difference between long and short haul marginal costs, we omit interest costs. 1950s data from John Meyer in Transportation Investment and Economic Development, Gary Fromm, ed. (1965), p. 46. The Louisville and Nashville Railroad figures are for runs of 9 and 377 miles while Meyers' are for 50 and 400.

among them, both in allocational impact and noisiness of protest, were rebates, the "free pass evil," and a lack of altruism.

Bargaining over price typified private markets from the most ancient times. The reduction of such bargaining in twentieth century American economic life has been a comfort to some and an advantage to others. But during the nineteenth century bargaining marked many, if not most, transactions between producers. However, given the multiplicity of people shipping freight and the cost advantage in billing and control, the railroads early established fixed—that is, "posted"—rates for classes of freight. Such standard rates failed to recognize the claims of those who shipped in large volume. Such shippers demanded discounts, as they still typically do in competitive markets. The roads yielded to their claims, albeit not always graciously, by returning part of the posted charge—that is, by "rebating." As Andrew Carnegie briefly put it: "Rebates were part of transportation in the early days, and railways fought each other as private manufacturers did."[46] Inevitably the largest shippers were the major cartels—the Standard Oil Trust, the Meat Packers Trust, the Steel Trust—and they received such rebates. But they were not alone. Various investigations of the Standard Oil Trust incidentally noted that many of their competitors likewise received rebates.[47] (At one point, half the entire business of the New York Central was apparently done at special rates.)[48] True, railroad costs of handling, billing, and collection were less per ton for such volume shippers. But the roads would also volun-

46. Quoted in Clara Clemens, My Father, Mark Twain (1931), p. 278. Carnegie was in a position to know, having worked for the Pennsylvania railroad before becoming a great steel tycoon, demanding his own rebates.

47. John McGee, "Predatory Price Cutting: The Standard Oil (N.J.) Case, Journal of Law and Economics (1958), p. 145, note 22.

48. Testimony before the Hepburn Committee in The Railroads, Alfred Chandler, ed. (1965), p. 171.

teer rebates to attract business whenever a shipper could threaten to use a competing route, by water or rail.

The railroads could hardly have looked on rebates with an indulgent eye. (The southern railroads had to give back in rebates some 15 percent of their revenues, according to the president of the Louisville and Nashville Railroad.[49] If competition had not forced such givebacks on the railroads their profits would have risen fifty percent or more.[50] However, the running against rebates was not made by the railroads. Their cartels kept breaking down as they fought for business. It was, instead, made by the smaller businessmen and towns throughout the nation. For every stockholder whose dividends were squeezed by rebates there were fifty shippers who received small rebate percentages, if any at all. That differential did more than cut into their profit rates. It menaced their ability to continue in business against rivals with such lower costs. Perturbed as well were city officials, taxpayers, and property owners (of city acreage and buildings). Their incomes and investment values were threatened whenever the smaller businesses lost in the competitive race. Land values fell, and other property owners had to make up the tax loss.[51] Consumers were not typically consulted in public inquiries. They could be expected to look for the lowest prices, giving little attention to whether the goods were supplied by honorable or ruthless competitors. Rebates to cartels—for example, the meat-packers' cartel—were not likely to find their way to consumers. However, most goods shipped under rebates appear to have been sent by firms in active competition. It is possible, therefore, that a goodly share of all rebates were typically transferred away from railroad stockholders to consumers. In any event, Congress sought to placate the aggrieved towns and smaller businesses by forbidding rebates, most notably in the Interstate Commerce Commission Act of 1887 and most explicitly by the Elkins Act of 1903.

The "free pass evil" reflected railroad attempts to buy good will, and recipient attempts to sell it. Such passes provided free transportation all year long to the fortunate recipients. Initially, numbers of governors and state legislators monetized their good will in return for such passes by sponsoring

---

49. 44th Cong., 2d sess., H.D. 46, *Internal Commerce*, part 2, Appendix 21.

50. Net receipts ran about one third of gross revenue on such major railroads as the New York Central, the Pennsylvania, and the Erie in the 1890s. Cf. data in Paul MacAvoy, *Economic Effects of Regulation* (1965), pp. 197–98. We assume that the ratio of 45 percent (i.e., 15 percent + 33 percent) would apply to major roads in general. Allowance for interest on debt would raise the percentage further. However, it did vary widely between roads.

51. Other businessmen did not object vociferously to the increase in surplus labor when workers were discharged by such failing firms. That workers would lose their jobs and have to look for other work was not primary among the complaints voiced in investigations of the "rebate evil."

legislation wanted by the railroads.[52] As the evil spread the railroads found themselves buying more and more good will, from both sides of the legislative aisles, and liking it less. (An analogy with competitive advertising is not forced.) Eventually, such unremunerative competitive behavior was sharply reduced by the ICC, thus reducing a minor but irritating cost to the railroads and an affront to the many who had to pay for their railroad tickets.

Uncouth and explicit utterances by key railroad leaders undoubtedly constituted more than an irritation, if less than a grievance. Commodore Vanderbilt, head of the New York Central, recurred to the vigor of his days as captain of a garbage scow when badgered by one reporter. The railroad, he said, wanted to abandon a special passenger express since it did not pay. His concern for the handful of wealthy passengers involved seemed nonexistent. "But don't you run it for the public benefit?" inquired the reporter provocatively. "The public be damned," responded Vanderbilt. "What does the public care for the railroads except to get as much out of them for as small a consideration as possible?"[53] To believe, as he did, that railroads were "not run on sentiment, but . . . to pay" was beginning to be anathema. And to declare "the public be damned" surely was.[54]

Farm, village, and city representatives combined pressures to establish the Interstate Commerce Commission in 1887. They struck a blow against out-of-state producers—as later attacks against multinational companies were heralded as blows for freedom. The ICC Act created a new harmony of railroads. Working together they created the long desired parity of long and short haul rates, required by the Act. They did so by raising long haul rates and reducing some short haul rates.

Two results followed. The move toward a more efficient allocation of resources was slowed. Put another way, the obsolescence of older factories, communities, and techniques was slowed down. These still had to adapt, for

52. The morality of such passes was not doubted by many for decades. For example, Ignatius Donnelly, soon to become a major populist crusader against monopoly, wrote to a railroad president asking for a free pass, as a member of the Wisconsin legislature. A few years later he declared passes an abomination. Cf. John D. Hicks, *The Populist Revolt* (1961), p. 71. Doubtless some political leaders, as the railroad presidents contended, volunteered their services: They offered *not* to sponsor legislation to which the railroads would object.

53. Interview in the *Chicago Daily News*, reprinted in Ray Billington et al., *The Making of American Democracy* (1963), p. 86.

54. Vanderbilt's forceful attempt to create a monopoly of railroad service from Albany to New York City was anathema to most consumers and nearly all economists. It was checked by the criminal activities of Gould, Fisk, and Drew in a wild struggle. Major losers in that fight were wealthy individuals such as Commodore Vanderbilt and August Belmont, as well as stockholders in the Erie railroad. The common reading of that experience was that railroads had excessive power. A brilliant, saturnine recounting of the episode appears in Charles Adams, Jr., and Henry Adams, *Chapters of Erie and Other Essays* (1886).

the forces of change bearing down on them were continental. But they no longer had to change as rapidly as railroad freight tariff changes had been forcing them to change.

The ICC also strengthened the hand of those railroad directors who were attempting to stabilize rates and keep them from being cut by energetic competitors. The 15 percent of rail revenues that Fink estimated were being given back to the strongest and largest shippers were no longer at risk. The ICC now protected railroad stockholders against the customers. Congress had decried rebates, demanding instead "reasonable and just" rates. The ICC followed that mandate. Thus it early, and openly, wrote to the chairman of the Western Freight Association—an industry group—objecting that "Complaints still reach us of alleged rate cutting from Missouri River points, though nothing definite or satisfactory as to the actual situation."[55] It was surely a striking advance in the art of managing the economy when a government agency complained about reductions in the price of railway services. For such prices were costs to farmers, to shippers, and eventually to the American consumer. Yet the new agency described these reductions in a chilling pejorative phrase as "rate cutting."

A broader view of the new world of railways under the first period of ICC regulation is given by contrasting the variability of freight rates before and after the ICC. In the decade before the ICC, rail rates from Chicago to New York for wheat changed two-thirds as often as lake and canal rates. In the decade after the ICC was set up they changed only one-third as often.[56] This heightened stability is consistent with Paul MacAvoy's conclusion that railroad stock prices were pushed above the trend—presumably by the ICC's "strong regulation" in 1887–93, by which it protected the roads against competitive rate cutting.[57]

Halcyon times for the railroads and their investors lasted until World War I. Shipment volumes rose, making more efficient use of existing facilities, while the ICC and intermittent cartel arrangements ensured a stability of

---

55. Interstate Commerce Commission, *Fourth Annual Report* (1890), p. 24.

56. Data computed from weekly rates for these years as cited in ICC, *Railways in the U.S. in 1902*, Appendix G, part II. Because rates are not cited with equal frequency for each mode, we computed periods in which rates changed as a percentage of the dates for which reports were given—i.e., actual as percentages of possible. These percentages were 82.4 for lake and canal, 54.7 for rail in 1878–86; and 63.5 and 22.1, respectively, in 1888–96—leading to ratios of 66 percent in the first, and 35 percent in the second period. Using the canal–lake rates as a norm permits an allowance for changing factors associated with general price trends.

57. Cf. Paul MacAvoy, *Economic Effects of Regulation* (1965), pp. 195, 202. MacAvoy's use of a simple time trend to extrapolate prices is clearly unsatisfactory. Yet it points the way to a more adequate procedure—and probably to similar conclusions. If one fits stock price data for 1880 to 1886, then compares the extrapolations to the post-ICC years with actual figures, more accurate indications appear. The conclusion remains the same.

TABLE 23.6
SHARE OF FREIGHT CARRIED BY TRANSPORT METHOD
(PERCENT OF TON MILES)

	Railroads	Waterways	Trucks	Total
1890	67	33	—	100
1936	49	40	4	100
1946	54	30	6	100
1976	34	30	19	100

Source: The share of ton miles of freight is computed from data in Harold Barger, The Transportation Industries, 1889–1946 (1951), pp. 183, 217, 242, 251, 254, 266, and 1978 Statistical Abstract, pp. 639, 675. For comparability we add the point difference from 1946 to 1976 in the Abstract data to Barger's 1946 percentages. We do not use Barger's total from pp. 34–36 because it includes international and noncontiguous water traffic activities in which railways never competed. His estimates show that the difference in trend between ton miles and revenue weighted ton miles was trivial. The "total" includes intercity pipe lines and air.

rates. Both factors enhanced profitability, inducing railroad consolidation. The top 10 railroad systems in 1880 controlled 20 percent of U.S. rail mileage. By 1900 the top 10 controlled 68 percent, and their share rose over the next decade.[58] Such consolidation gave the final stimulus to more substantial regulation of rates and procedures by the ICC. The end of the financial joyride for railroad investors came in the 1920s, with the development of the automobile. The price of trucks declined. Government provided free right-of-way for trucking.

From 1890 to 1936 the railroads hauled a declining share of total freight, gradually losing out to waterways, as shown in Table 23.6. They had a brief resurgence because of trucking's lack of parts, gasoline, and tires during World War II. They then began to lose to the new competitor. By extending its regulation, in 1936, to cover hired intercity trucking, the ICC imposed public controls of the new competitor of the railroads. But, in fact, the ICC worked toward an identity of rates charged by railroads and trucks for similar merchandise between similar points. By doing so, they automatically awarded the lead to trucks. For the latter provided faster delivery and through service at the same price. But probably more important in penalizing the railroads were other government actions. One was the immense road building program begun under a budget-conscious Republican administra-

58. 1880: Individual railroad data from 1880 Census, Transportation, II:16. 1900: Individual system data from U.S. Industrial Commission, Reports, XIX:308 and U.S. total from Statistical Abstract (1900) p. 374.

tion in the 1950s, with acclaim from both sides of the political aisle. That program cheapened the cost of operating trucks, giving them a greater margin of profit. A further political force was the ICC's predictable insistence on the railroads maintaining service to individual communities along their route. There embattled manufacturers, farmers, and occasional passengers insisted on retaining something like customary train service for those occasions when they decided not to use auto or truck transport. The consequent deterioration of rail service further diminished the rail market. Had the stockholders from the palmy days of railroading still owned the roads, something like poetic justice might have been at work. But the dead weight inefficiencies of keeping service going to locations that hardly used the railroads gradually brought a sequence of railroad bankruptcies, with no obvious gain to the nation. In time, farm state representatives and farm cooperatives began to help the bankrupt roads resume service. But before considering that much later experience it is desirable to look at how the nation's greatest industry was buffeted about during the great decades of railroad expansion.

They did break a little prairie that season, though it was too late to put in any crop. . . . They thought they could get it fenced before frost, but they couldn't. They hoped for a mild winter, but it proved a severe one . . . in bitter jest styled "the year eighteen-hundred-and-froze-to-death." . . . They resolved not to mortgage any of their land, but they were disappointed.

—JOSEPH KIRKLAND,
Zury, the Meanest Man in Spring County

24

Competition and Revolt

F OR fifty years after the Civil War American farmers played the lead in a gigantic mercantile drama. The scenes were laid in four continents. The story portrayed the destruction of ancient landed aristocracies, the creation of an odd assortment of nouveaux riches, with benefits almost incidentally flung to millions of urban workers. And it ended in one of the great protest movements of American history.

It began, for most observers, with a huge "outpouring of settlers onto the newly available lands of the Argentine, the United States, Canada and Australia," converting "the wheat market into a 'colossal bargain counter' for long periods of years."[1] "There was something inexplicable about the whole movement—especially since, the East being at that time in a very prosperous condition, no economic motive could be ascribed. . . . A Dr. Raphael Dubois of the University of Lyon, constructed an ingenious device to prove that man, like the squirrel in a cage, is irresistibly impelled to step westward by the fact of the earth's rotation eastward. Others . . . mentioned . . . 'mystic forces.' "[2]

Table 17.4 emphasized that food and fiber production in the United States had, in fact, been shifting westward for decades. The incentive behind

1. Wilfred Malenbaum, *The World Wheat Economy, 1885–1939* (1953), p. 30.
2. Robert M. Coates, *The Outlaw Years* (1930), pp. 11–12.

that migration was clear to agronomists. Every year from 1879 to 1885 North Dakota land yielded 20 bushels of wheat per acre, while Virginia farmers were harvesting less than half as much.[3] But of the 66,000 immigrants into the Dakota territory by 1880, many came from high-yield states. Why did 12,000 come from Wisconsin alone, 8,000 from Iowa?[4] William Graham Sumner provided an answer, acidulous, but precise: "There is no conception of enough when more can be had."[5]

Those thousands of farmers who sought "better" land in the Midwest and Southwest were following in the tracks of earlier immigrants. Trappers from the Hudson Bay Company pioneered in the eighteenth century. Avid men from all over the world invaded the West in their rush for gold—California in 1848, Nevada in 1859, the Black Hills of Dakota in 1876. Still others came with the great silver strikes. The cattlemen arrived, working north out of Mexico and westward from Kentucky. The Kiowa had been driven from Western lands by the Cheyenne, the Cheyenne then driven out by the Sioux. Now later immigrants arrived and drove the remaining Indians into an ever-dwindling area. Finally the "nester" came, seeking not merely his fortune but a nest in which to raise his family. His persistent, regular industry plus the corollary labors of his wife and children eventually converted the central states. They then grew food for most of the United States and much of Europe, and cotton for much of the world. (That history was recapitulated when European immigrants flooded into Australia, Canada, and the Argentine in the same decades, searching for homes and growing food or fiber.)

The economic success of the nester was apparent in the ever-rising volume of production and exports. That success, of course, required more than a deep desire for riches or a home on the land. It required persistent cost cutting. The mere move west should have brought some reduction in costs, and it did. Better land yielded more crops with the same effort. An ingenious analysis by William Parker has shown that the westward movement, with the consequent shift to growing wheat on better soils, plus the use of improved seed varieties, helped increase output per acre (by 18 percent). But output per acre in wheat growing actually rose by 317 percent over the same period. The massive productivity advance, then, reflects primarily (317 percent minus 18 percent) the use of new improved farm machinery.[6] From biblical times farmers strode across their fields, sowing handfuls of seed. Suddenly the new seed drill came into use. It not merely conserved seed but made plants come

3. U.S. Department of Agriculture, *Wheat, Acreage, Yield and Production*, Statistical Bulletin 158 (1955).

4. 1880 Census, *Population*, p. 483.

5. A. G. Keller and M. R. Davie, *Selected Essays of William Graham Sumner* (1924), p. 295.

6. National Bureau of Economic Research, *Output, Employment and Productivity in the United States after 1800* (1966), p. 533. Parker compares 1840–60 with 1900–10.

TABLE 24.1
TECHNICAL CHANGE ON FARMS, 1850–90

	Ratio of (horses plus mules) to oxen				
	1850	1860	1870	1880	1890
United States	2.9	3.3	6.3	12.2	15.4
Region:					
New England	0.7	1.0	1.3	2.4	3.3
Mid Atlantic	3.4	5.4	11.3	22.4	25.0
South Atlantic	3.4	3.6	3.8	4.9	4.9
East North Central	4.1	4.8	17.6	38.7	52.4
West North Central	2.3	2.3	8.3	32.7	49.7
East South Central	3.6	3.4	4.4	7.0	5.6
West South Central	2.1	2.4	3.7	8.6	9.2
Mountain	0.9	0.8	1.5	8.4	79.3
Pacific	2.5	5.7	26.1	42.9	104.2
State:					
Mississippi	2.0	2.2	3.0	3.9	3.2
Virginia	3.3	3.4	3.9	4.6	4.5
Iowa	1.8	3.2	20.8	333.9	571.9
Minnesota	1.3	0.6	2.2	7.3	14.5
North Dakota	—	0.3	1.3	3.9	6.5
Wisconsin	0.7	1.3	4.8	12.5	22.8
California	4.9	6.3	35.3	116.3	404.4

Source: Computed from state data in U.S. Census Office, *Compendium of the Eleventh Census: 1890* III (1897):619–22.

up in straight and simple lines that were far more readily plowed and weeded. From ancient days the grain crop had been harvested by workers slowly cutting handfuls of grain shoots as they moved across the fields. Now the harvester did the job automatically. And instead of horses treading the grain to separate out the kernels of ripe wheat, the thresher worked faster, wasting less grain in the process. To operate the new equipment farmers gradually substituted horses for oxen. The ratio of horses (plus mules) to oxen thus indexes the rate at which the new technology was introduced. Table 24.1 shows how vigorously the North Central and Pacific regions led that advance, and how laggard the South was, albeit still a major farming region. Though much of the new equipment was available in the 1850s, the gains, even in Iowa and California, were mild. The departure of farm laborers for the Union Army speeded the introduction in the North Central and Pacific states. The South's labor force was dimensioned to peak use in the cotton picking season; it hence had "surplus" labor in the other seasons and saw little advantage to buying seed drills, harrows, and more for use in other seasons.

Without the steady decline in the price of farm machinery farmers would never have been able to afford so many productive new machines. Mass production technology was reshaping the farm machinery industry in the 1850s and 1860s, from the manufacture of the basic plow and shovel to that of the new reapers and harvesters. Members of the British Parliament, visiting the United States in 1854, marveled at the use of "templates and labour-saving tools in the manufacture of ploughs, hay cutters and churns." In England all of these were still more or less whittled out of wood by skilled, and expensive, craftsmen. The Blanchard copying lathe, first developed to make the wooden stocks for rifles, had been adapted in the United States to turn out endless copies of the wooden parts in these farm implements.[7] Such new inventions made unbelievably great fortunes for McCormick and a few other early inventor–businessmen. But unless McCormick had also committed himself to mass production, price cutting, and mass distribution, he would not have made his own fortunes, nor that of hundreds of midwestern farmers. They could not have bought. He could not have sold. And he could not then have cut costs enough to penetrate vast export markets. As compared to the antique "cradle" the harvester reduced labor hours per acre by 40 percent.[8] That advantage boomed the sale of threshing machines. Some farmers covered their costs by threshing for their neighbors.[9] But custom harvesting did not really develop until the mid-twentieth century, when it dominated the wheat harvest from Kansas northward. For almost a century it had spread only slowly because another McCormick advance made outright purchase easy: installment selling. McCormick's low cost credit led many farmers to buy their own harvesters.

Adopting new technology plus new land cut the man-hours required to produce crops. Spectacular declines appeared from 1840 to 1880. But if this dramatic period is put in the context of other periods in United States experience (as in Table 24.2) two further inferences appear. The rate of decline had been equally dramatic during the first forty years of the century, when neither threshers not harvesters were being introduced. One sees as well the triviality of productivity advance in cotton growing between 1880 (and the end of slavery) and the 1930s. Only with the coming of the AAA and the incentives it gave did planters cease cultivating their worst lands, and cotton productivity resume its advance (at the price of pushing an increasing number

7. Joseph Whitworth and George Wallis, *The Industry of the United States in Machinery, Manufactures, and Useful and Ornamental Arts* (1854), pp. 19–20.

8. Paul David gives an elegant exposition of the cost advantage to the farmer of the harvester, based on the ratio of the wage the farmer paid for harvesting relative to the cost of the harvester, with the tipping point indicating when even those with small farms found it profitable to buy a harvester. Cf. his essay in *Industrialization in Two Systems*, H. Rosovsky, ed. (1966).

9. Cf. one example in Wayne Rasmussen, "The Civil War: A Catalyst of Agricultural Revolution," *Agricultural History* (October 1965), p. 190.

TABLE 24.2
FARM PRODUCTIVITY TRENDS, 1800–1980

	Man-hours per				
	(100 bushels) Wheat	(100 bushels) Corn	(1 bale) Cotton	(cwt.) Hogs	(cwt.) Turkeys
1800	373	344	601		
1840	233	276	439		
1880	152	180	304		
1900	108	147	283		
1910–14	106	135	276	3.6	31.4
1930–34	70	123	252	3.2	26.7
1960–64	12	11	47	1.9	2.4
1976–80	9	3	6	0.5	0.4

Source: U.S.D.A. Statistical Bulletin 346 Labor Used to Produce Field Crops (1964) Tables 1 & 2; and U.S. Statistical Abstract 1982–1983, p. 675.

of blacks off the farm). These productivity advances, combined with substantial increase in the number of farmers, inevitably tended to drive farm production up—and prices down. Farm protest followed almost as inevitably.

New land plus new technology cut man-hours per unit produced. Table 24.2 shows that trend, plus the resultant trend in the real price of wheat and cotton. In growing wheat the most basic cost was labor time, which fell at least as much as wheat prices. Still more substantial declines appeared in the price of farm machinery shown in Table 24.3. During the thirty year period major input costs fell roughly as much as final product prices, leaving unit returns largely unchanged. If one were to ignore capital gains it would be necessary to conclude that wheat farmers had neither gained nor lost much in their monetary returns from converting land into wheat.

The experience of farmers in the cotton South, however, was quite different. They cut their labor inputs only very slightly while final product prices collapsed. All over the world cotton growth expanded well beyond what buyers were willing to pay. And since U.S. cotton growers made only the slightest advance in man-hour productivity, adopting almost no machinery, the outcome was a steady pressure on land values, a steady sense of doom. In any other industry capital would have moved on to try other crops, and the labor force to try other locations. Some labor did move into the new cotton mills by the end of the century. But the bulk of black labor remained in the South, keeping down both its own incomes and prices of cotton and land. When the boll weevil came in 1892 it gradually decimated the cotton crops, and forced people to leave cotton for mixed farming (cattle and grain) or vegetable and fruit crops. Southern farming at that point began its late, slow

TABLE 24.3
FARM PRICES RECEIVED AND PAID (1870 = 100)

	Prices received for livestock and crops	Prices paid for farm machinery	Midwest interest rates	Freight and distribution cost for West North Central wheat
1870	100	100	100	100
1880	76	68	83	60
1890	64	48	68	45
1900	63	45	55	35
1910	95	45	52	24

Source: see Appendix A, this chapter.

advance. It was with good reason that Alabama later erected a monument to the boll weevil, inadvertent carrier of progress.

The evils of the South's "one crop" concentration on cotton have been attributed to madness, to ignorance, to tradition, and to the perversity of furnishing merchants who insisted on growing cotton to the total exclusion of food. DeCanio has shown, however, that the South concentrated on cotton much as the Midwest did on wheat.[10] Neither region was "locked in" to its primary product. Southern farmers adjusted the amount of their cotton plantings, and the mix between cotton and competing crops, even more speedily than did the wheat planters of the Midwest.

Annona, goddess of the corn supply, was worshipped by the ancient Romans. Americans, more secular, attended to Mary Lease, the "Kansas Pythoness," in the 1890s. Her recommendation to U.S. farmers was forceful, and unambiguous: "Raise less corn and more hell." Such practical advice was as shrewd as it was succinct. Had the farmers raised less corn they would indeed have gotten a higher price for every bushel they sold. The price for which they sold their hogs (fed largely on corn) would also have risen.[11] So would that for the wheat they grew (a partial substitute for corn). The precedent had been set by other small businessmen. The men who owned the steamboats on the Great Lakes in the 1840s had organized a cartel to reduce competition. And petroleum well owners repeatedly tried to restrict oil production in the 1870s and 1880s. But these were dismal precedents. They had largely failed. Nor did the farmers prove any more able to cooperate in reducing the food

10. Steven DeCanio, *Agriculture in the Postbellum South* (1974), pp. 257–61.
11. Her campaigning for prohibition tended, of course, the other way.

supply until a benevolent government organized that activity in the 1930s. Farmers in the 1870s were unable to work together for good reason. Every individual farmer matched the inevitable decline in his income if he sold fewer bushels of wheat against the promise of a rise in price per bushel if all his fellow farmers cooperated. If his fellows did not, or if venturesome speculators imported wheat from, say, Canada, the price per bushel need not have risen at all. He would then have ended up with a still lower income. That cogent, if depressing, train of logic made farmers in Kansas and elsewhere choose to "raise more hell."

Farmers were not obviously able to summon up a deeper sense of outrage than most other class or interest groups. But they did constitute the largest single group of voters in the nineteenth century. Beginning early in that century, and with intensified effort as time went on, American farmers began a protest movement that became a permanent element in American politics. Its initial targets were described as monopolies—the railroads, the farm machinery producers, "the money monopoly." "There are three great crops raised in Nebraska," declared the *Farmers' Alliance* newspaper. "One is a crop of corn, one a crop of freight rates, and one a crop of interest. One is produced by farmers who by sweat and toil farm the land. The other two are produced by men who sit in their offices and behind their bank counters and farm the farmers."[12] (One befuddled European intellectual added high tax rates as a further grievance.)[13]

The attack on the railroads began with the "Granger Laws," by which Iowa, Wisconsin, Nebraska, and other states tried to fix railroad rates. The evasive tactics of railroad presidents in buying up governors and legislators (at unreasonably low rates), their maladroit remarks, and their obvious dedication to the welfare of their stockholders, have obscured one central relationship of railroads to farm marketing. In the decade after the Civil War more farmers settled on land bought from railroads than on free homestead land from the federal government. Farmers evidently believed that they were getting a better deal from the railroads, even after paying for their land—because the land was richer, because it was closer to cheap transport, or for a combination of reasons. Nor were railroad rates in succeeding decades kept up by the local monopolies each railroad possessed. For new construction had multiplied the number of railroads. The intense competition in the railroad wars of

12. Quoted in John D. Hicks, *The Populist Revolt* (1931), p. 83.

13. A North Central farmer lived an Arcadian life "before the Civil War," but afterwards was "chronically in need of money, a lot of money, to pay his taxes," according to Rosa Luxemburg in *The Accumulation of Capital* (1951), pp. 389, 400. The typical farmer in the period about which she wrote could, however, pay his taxes with the output from only 4 of the 134 acres in his farm. (1903 Census, *Wealth Debt and Taxation*, p. 850 reports a 72-cent tax per $100 of true valuation.) The average value of farms was $3,038 and the average farm had 134 acres. (U.S. Census, *Agriculture* V, part I (1900):694.) The wheat yield per acre was about 13 bushels, and farm price about 40 cents per bushel.

the 1870s then drove railroad rates and related charges down in the 1880s. (See Table 24.3, Column 4.) The farmers' products were sent to market at ever lower rates with each passing decade. (Indeed, without such reduction farmers would have been far less able to invade foreign markets.) Farmers' protests about the machinery trust (i.e., International Harvester plus some follower firms formed a noted oligopoly) were similarly intense. But the price of farm machinery was also cut, falling faster than farm prices, thanks to efficient mass production. (See Table 24.3, Column 2.)

The great and central target of farmer protest from Kansas to Florida, however, was the "money monopoly." For they borrowed to buy farms and equipment, and to pay debts. It is, however, unlikely that a real money monopoly existed throughout any state, much less any region. Lenders in the rural Midwest competed as hard, and as much, in 1880 as a century later. From the earliest days affluent Midwesterners supplied capital by their cumulated savings. And still more originated in mortgage agencies of the East.[14] Eastern doctors, grocers, miners, and factory workers provided funds for investment via local agents in the farm states. An ever growing volume of funds was placed in the Midwest by eastern life insurance companies such as Aetna and Connecticut General. These were able to pay their policy holders only by investing millions in Western farms.

So extensive was the flow of funds that men from the East came to own 25 percent of the wealth in Kansas and Nebraska, 40 percent of that in Colorado and the Dakotas.[15] (That capital inflow then became a further, even if opposite, cause of complaint: "Our small farmers have had in large part to buy their farms on mortgage of men who live in cities to the east."[16]) Moreover, railroads in the growing Midwest, unlike those in the East, loaned money to farmers at well below market interest rates. Their goal, of course, was to induce farmers to settle along their line, thereby providing future revenue to their road. The railroad method provided an additional, and a significant, source of farm credit, helping to break up whatever local financial monopolies may have existed.

But there is a more direct test: the path of interest rates. A money monopoly would have extorted high profits by keeping interest rates up above competitive levels. What path did interest rates actually take 1866–96, that long period of "great hardship" for farmers as described by so many historians?[17] Table 24.3 shows that Midwestern interest rates were actually cut

14. The comprehensive and illuminating study by Allan Bogue, *Money at Interest* (1955), describes lending operations by the Davenport brothers of upper New York State.
15. Computed from 1880 Census, *Valuation, Taxation and Public Indebtedness* (1884), pp. 12–13.
16. Henry George, *Protection or Free Trade* (1886), p. 121.
17. Thus, the prevailing view was that the period 1864 to 1896 "was characterized on the whole by great hardship in agriculture." And for "cotton, grain and livestock producers the long

in half during these decades. That decline surely did not occur because demand weakened, for millions of new people were entering farming, borrowing for land or stock. Hence the actual decline must reflect supply forces. But what money monopolists in their right mind would have squeezed their profits by cutting the rates they charged? The record suggests that no money monopoly confronted the nation's farmers, or those of the Midwest.

Does it follow that populism, grangerism, reflected only the reactions of journalists and politicians? Not necessarily. To locate the origin of farm complaints one must first recognize that the typical U.S. farmer was a wealth-seeking businessman—a small entrepreneur to be sure, but a businessman nonetheless. He sought to increase his vested interest by adding profits from current income to capital gains from landholding. Unfortunately for the farmer if fortunately for nonfarm workers, U.S. society offered wide and democratic access to public land, permitted a multiplicity of lenders, and facilitated cheap transport of farm goods to markets. This social-political context drew millions of men into farming. The count rose from 3.1 million farmers in 1870, to 4.3 million in 1880, 4.9 million in 1890, and 5.8 million by 1900.[18]

Now, doubling the number of farmers, most of whom strove to increase their efficiency as producers, more than doubled the volume of farm products thrown onto the markets. That rising tide did more than keep farm prices from rising. It actually drove them down, slowing farm income growth. Those who farmed in 1866 or 1876 or 1886 could well have made handsome profits in the subsequent decade if only the government had forbidden anyone else to enter into competition with them. (Even as it was there were periods in which farmers had substantial increases in income, major capital gains. Farmers profited handsomely during the Civil War and immediate post-war years. In the 1880s, when they inundated Europe with their exports of food, they again profited largely.) But in a democratic, open society high profits were not perpetual. And the capital gains to which so many of them avidly looked forward eluded the group as a whole when periods as long as a working life (e.g., 30 years) are considered. European farmers, Asian farmers, had traditionally rented their land. But American farmers expected to own their farms. (As early as the Revolutionary War three-quarters of American farmers did. As of 1880, some 69 percent did.[19]) To do this they typically

run trend of farm prices—though not *necessarily* real farm income—was relentlessly downward . . . their declining real incomes relative to other sectors . . . impelled . . . the 'farm revolt.' " A more recent, judicious, review by a skilled economist appears in Robert Higgs, *The Transformation of the American Economy, 1865–1914* (1971).

18. Lebergott, *Manpower*, p. 511.

19. Ibid. Cf. Allan Bogue, *From Prairies to Cornbelt* (1963), p. 65, who gives data suggesting a slightly higher percentage 1850–70 for some Illinois counties.

borrowed money, hoping to pyramid their incomes and land value into substantial wealth.

An extensive study in the 1890 Census recorded the reasons why farmers throughout the United States had taken out mortgages. Few had borrowed because of family debts, or to eke out their consumption because incomes were low, their farms failing. (Indeed it was a rare banker who would loan money to the impoverished, needy, and bankrupt. The probability of getting such loans repaid was too small.) Well over 90 percent of farm mortgages had been taken out to buy land, or land, equipment, and farm animals. Table 24.4, derived from these Census data, reports the proportion of farm mortgages with relatively high interest rates (8 percent or more). The proportions are substantial, perhaps astounding, in the frontier states of the Midwest. It was there that farmers looked for capital gains on land so high as to warrant taking out mortgages at high interest rates. Such borrowers were few in New England, not because farmers there were prosperous, but because they were not. Thousands of New England farmers, in 1870–90 when such mortgages were being taken out, were abandoning their farms for a pittance. They then went West to better land or took jobs. Except for a few areas of expanding production, the proportions were likewise small in the South. Only in the West were such loans made. Both farmers and lenders there expected farming to be so successful, land values to rise so fast, that borrowing even at high rates would be profitable to the entrepreneurial borrower (and, of course, to the entrepreneurial lender).

While midwestern farmers managed to cope with a steady but mild decline in prices of their wheat and corn, the South's cotton farmers saw the price of their primary product collapsing. The century long escalation in world demand for cotton had slowed, as Gavin Wright reminds us. Moreover, their productivity, instead of advancing rapidly, changed little. The margin of profit left for Southern farmers, black and white, as for Southern land owners, was small, and it was diminishing.

Central to the farmer's feeling of doom was the nature of the mortgage contract that owners accepted. It was not that their farms were foreclosed when wheat and corn prices dropped.[20] (Lenders found few buyers then wanting to purchase foreclosed farms. They themselves had little desire to operate foreclosed farms.) Rather it was that the mortgage interest and repayment schedule did not change as the prices of their wheat and cotton changed. The inflation of the Civil War had worked out wonderfully well for farmers. Those who borrowed money when their wheat was selling for 50 cents a bushel, and repaid it when wheat sold for $1 a bushel, found it all a satisfying

20. Bogue, *Money*, p. 18, indicates that over the years 1868–1900 the Davenports foreclosed on only 19 out of 1,380 loans. The reasons they did not foreclose seem to be those noted above. At the same time there surely were hard-hearted local lenders described so effectively in Hamlin Garland's short story, "Under the Lion's Paw," *Main-Travelled Roads* (1899).

TABLE 24.4
PERCENT OF FARM MORTGAGES
PAYING OVER 8 PERCENT INTEREST, 1890

Region (state)	Percent
North Central	
South Dakota	84
North Dakota	81
Kansas	46
Nebraska	48
Wisconsin	11
Iowa	8
Illinois	2
New England and Mid Atlantic	
Connecticut	*
Massachusetts	*
New Jersey	*
New York	*
Pennsylvania	*
Rhode Island	*
South	
Mississippi	98
Florida	90
South Carolina	40
Missouri	40
Alabama	27
Georgia	24
Tennessee	7
Kentucky	4
Virginia	1
Maryland	*
North Carolina	*

*Under 1 percent.

Source: 1890 Census, *Farms and Homes,* p. 531.

and profitable exercise. (During the wartime inflation in the South, creditors ran away from their debtors, not wanting to transfer title to farms for a sum of money that would hardly buy a box of cigars.) But deflation eventually followed inflation. The secretary of the Treasury was bent on redeeming the greenbacks issued during the war, thereby cutting down the supply of money. Since the economy was expanding during the same years, the inevitable outcome was an overall decline in prices. Farmers found that the prices at which they sold fell sharply. (Wheat prices fell 20 percent from 1871 to 1876, and cotton, 43 percent.[21]) But the interest due on mortgages for the land they had bought went right on unchanged. In the words of the old song, the farmer worked hard, but "the mortgage worked hardest of all."

Farmers could have sought to cancel their debt by revolution, as had been done from Greece under Lycurgus to France under Robespierre. But that would have cancelled their titles to the land as well. Instead, they remembered the cheap money days of Connecticut in the 1740s, of Rhode Island in the 1780s. Let the government flood the nation with paper money, and economics would do the rest. Prices would rise, farmers could pay their debts (if not for a song, at least for a chorale), living happy as grigs on their own land ever after. Their analysis was correct. However, neither their creditors nor small savers around the nation were prepared to sacrifice their own interests. Farmers did form political parties after 1876 to advance these goals. Their Greenback Party did not, however, get a single electoral vote from 1876 through 1884. Having entered the Democratic party in force in 1892, they supported its plan urging "free silver"—to increase the money supply.[22] Lacking the support of urban workers and eastern farmers, however, they could not get the Democratic party to support their more darling plan, in which the Treasury would buy not merely silver to backing the currency, but wheat and cotton as well.[23] Farmer attempts to increase the money supply reached a crescendo of hope in the presidential election of 1896.

A memento of their political dreams appeared in 1898 at the Grand Exposition in Omaha—an immense pyramid of paper made up of farm mortgages from Nebraska and Kansas, paid off in the two prior years.[24] The price of wheat almost doubled between William Jennings Bryan's nomination and the election itself. The price of cotton likewise rose sharply.[25] These price gains soothed discontented farmers, kept them from actually voting for the "boy orator of the Platte." Observers noted once again the link between

21. Wheat: *Historical Statistics . . . to 1970*, p. 512. Cotton: Latham, Alexander and Company, *Cotton Movement and Fluctuation 1875 to 1882* (9th ed.) p. 93.

22. They sought support wherever they could. In 1912 the U.S. Socialist party limited its commitment to nationalizing private property to cases where that was "practicable." To attract the farm vote Oklahoma socialists declared they sought to make "much more secure ownership of private property by individuals." They actually got 41 percent of the vote in Marshall County, Oklahoma, in 1912. Cf. Garin Burbank, *When Farmers Voted Red* (1976).

23. Cf. the lively description in John Hicks, *The Populist Revolt* (1961), chap. 7.

24. Gerald White, "Economic Recovery and the Wheat Crop of 1897," *Agricultural History* (January 1939), pp. 20–21.

25. "Failure of the wheat crop in India with a shortage in Australia served to raise the price of American wheat from 53 cents per bushel in August to 94½ cents at the time of the election in November." A. P. Andrews, "The Influence of Crops Upon Business," *Quarterly Journal of Economics* (May 1906) p. 346. White notes a plague of locusts in Argentina, as well as a deficit of 5 million bushels in the Australian crop rather than the usual 12 million surplus.

the crop conditions and elections: The voters had responded to their perception of "good times."[26]

Sympathetic historians and novelists continue to treat the "farm problem" as one long descent into unrelieved misery.

If the prospects in farming were indeed as bleak as contemporary protest movements and later historians have described, what could have induced almost 3 million persons to become farmers by 1900, nearly doubling the 1870 count? One answer is implicit in the fact that farmers' income and net worth advanced faster than did those of the nonfarm population from 1896 to the mid-1920s. Indeed, the real value of farms rose spectacularly, as shown in Figure 24.1. These figures indicate that the stream of income to be expected from owning farms—which is, of course, what farm values embody—grew markedly over these decades of "despair and doubt." Of course farmers' real wealth did not increase in the 1890s at the wonderful rate they had enjoyed in the 1870s, while the burden of the debt that many had assumed became heavier. Such disappointments were inevitable in a society oriented to markets, and not prepared to force transfers of real income from urban workers to farm entrepreneurs.

Farm bloc leaders, like many historians, have made much of the great difference between farm and nonfarm money incomes. Since city workers, and their historians, have complained of their lot as well, the battle of adjectives and numbers has been somewhat confusing. However, simple comparisons between the money income—not real income—of farm and nonfarm populations mean little. First of all, city workers spent almost twice as much as farmers for any given budget of meat, milk, vegetables, eggs—to cover the cost of transport to the cities and retail markups in the cities.[27] And food took about one-third to one-half their income. Hence the higher cost of their (less fresh) food clearly eroded their "higher" money income. Second, city workers had to pay much higher ground rent to urban landlords for housing that offered no more space or amenity than the cheaper land in farm areas. Third, farmers collected a significant share of their wealth increases in the form of capital gains: The real value of farms rose steadily from 1870 onward (Figure

26. In 22 out of 25 elections, the quadrennial rainfall predicted the next president. J. D. Barnhart, "Rainfall and the Populist Party in Nebraska," *Political Science Review* (August 1925). Alexander Noyes, *Forty Years of American Finance* (1909), p. 20, matter of factly states: "They were about to receive in the Congressional elections, the usual chastisement experienced by a dominant party when the people vote in a period of hard times." Cf. Johann Akerman, "Political Economic Cycles," *Kyklos* (1947), vol. I. Ackerman uses the share price index as a measure of business conditions to forecast the vote from 1930 onward. Work by Rees, Tufte, and Fair on more recent elections is well known.

27. United States Department of Agriculture, Agricultural Economic Report No. 138, *Food*, Table 104, p. 177.

FIGURE 24.1
VALUE OF FARMS PER ACRE (IN 1870 PRICES)

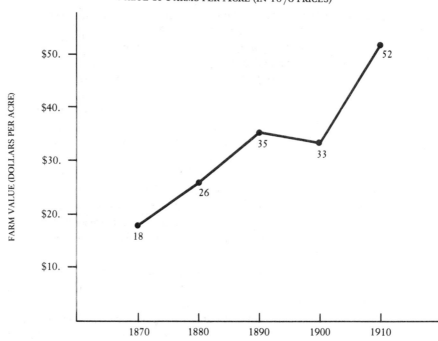

Source: Farm values in current prices deflated by the Warren-Pearson and Bureau of Labor Statistics Wholesale Price Series, *Historical Statistics . . . to 1970*, Series E40, E52, K15.

24.1).[28] Such wealth increases are all missed in the money income figures. It does not follow that the American farmer's lot was a happy one. But their real income and wealth gains 1866–96 compare favorably with those of nonfarm Americans (or the great world outside the United States).

In any event, the complaints of the 1890s could not be clearly heard as the farm income gains of the 1900–10 era began rolling in. Not to mention the still greater farm prosperity of the war years, with the vast exports of 1919–20. The subsequent story of American agriculture is best considered in the context of the New Deal farm program, to which it was a prelude.

The New Urban Competition: Industry and Distribution

The trend to corporate concentration has contributed to American life in various ways. Its most constructive achievement, and gayest, may well have

28. The current dollar value of farm land per acre, deflated either by the GNP deflator or the wholesale price index, reports such a rise.

been the marvelous prose it stimulated. The American Tin Plate Company, said Daniel Reid, its president, was formed "for the purpose of getting together to do away with foolishness in making prices."[29] The producers of cordage (i.e., ropes and hawsers), as one of them said, began meeting together monthly "to look each other in the face and maintain prices."[30] With soldierly bluntness General Alger declared that his firm, the Diamond Match Company, had bought up substantially all the U.S. match factories: "the price of matches was [then] kept up . . . to make large dividends above what could have been made had those factories been in the market to compete for the business."[31] Thorstein Veblen, great critic of capitalism, described it all with heavy irony. The "culminating achievement [of] West European culture, as well as of that dolicho-blond racial stock that bears this culture [is] dominion in business, and its most finished instrument is the quasi-voluntary coalition of forces known as a Trust."[32] "Its earlier, more elemental expression," he added, lay far back in the memorable raids of the Vikings.

An early American version was the 1840 arrangement made by owners of steamboats that ran between Buffalo and Chicago. By laying up some boats "during the dullest season of the year" they cut costs, kept prices from being bid down. They then collected the increased profits warranted by such ingenuity.[33] A host of contemporaries saw the U.S. trusts and mergers of the 1880s and 1890s as starting an inevitable trend. Kaiser William told a French journalist to warn the world of the

> future menace in these colossal trusts, so dear to the Yankee millionaire. . . . Suppose, he said . . . that a Morgan succeeds in combining under his flag several ocean lines. He occupies no official position in his country. . . . It would therefore be impossible to treat with him if an international incident or foreign Power were involved in the enterprise. . . . To guard against this danger the Kaiser forsees the necessity of forming . . . a European . . . customs league against the United States.[34]

(In his expert way the Kaiser went on to participate in a variety of "international incidents," such as World War I.) The hard-headed editor of *Engineering News* saw "the death of competition in the great proportion of industries as inevitable."[35] So, too, did Lenin, Rosa Luxemburg, and a long sequence of Marxist analysts.[36] And so did major American economists of the time. As

29. U.S. Industrial Commission, *Reports*, I:885.

30. Quoted by Chauncy Depew, *One Hundred Years of American Commerce*, 2 (1895):491.

31. Quoted in Hans Thorelli, *The Federal Antitrust Policy* (1954), p. 49.

32. "An Early Experiment in Trusts," *Journal of Political Economy* (March 1904), p. 271.

33. Ezra Seaman, *Essays on the Progress of Nations* (1846), p. 416.

34. Quoted from *The Literary Digest* (January 18, 1902), p. 90.

35. Charles Whiting Baker, *Monopolies and the People* (1889).

36. A more recent, astute, presentation of that view is Paul Baran's *The Age of Monopoly Capital* (1966).

George Stigler has wryly commented, only mavericks such as Henry George and Ida Tarbell, who were outside the tradition, whether classical or Marxist, asked the basic question: How was it that the giant firm had become so inevitable, so superbly efficient, in so many industries—all in such a brief period?

Mergers multiplied in the 1890s when promoters saw the possibility of capitalizing future monopoly profits in stock issues, and being paid from them. They continued when New Jersey and Delaware competed to offer a friendly spot in which to incorporate such businesses. They succeeded because a host of small savers found their way to the promised financial land of the New York Stock Exchange as capital markets improved.

Ralph Nelson reports that merging activity had little to do with technical innovation, or even the rate of industrial growth. It was more obviously linked to peaks "in industrial stock prices, stock trading and new business incorporation."[37] When, in Keynes's phrase, "animal spirits" were high, the public delighted in buying stock graciously made available by new and untried companies. It was then that merger makers were so successful in selling new stock, from which they provided profits both to promoters and to those who controlled the merging firms.

"Depend on it," said Dr. Johnson, "the prospect of hanging wonderfully concentrates the mind." For the magnates of steel their concentration on cartel possibilities was stimulated by the prospect of bankruptcy. Profit margins after the 1890s had declined sharply, and within a terribly brief period. For steel rails, the industry's key product, margins had fallen from $8 a ton (from 1890 to January 1897) to $2 (and even less) from March 1897 to February 1899. With speed, barely deliberate, they moved to protect their margins by cartel, merger, trustification. As a result, by December 1899 the margin rose to a hearty $14 a ton.[38] That improvement had been engineered by the fears of those who directed the individual companies and the skills of the investment banker. Andrew Carnegie, the leading steelmaker of the time, had driven his competitors wild by improving production processes. Making huge profits, he passed most of the savings along to customers in price cuts. (As prices fell from $65 to $20 a ton Carnegie produced about half the nation's steel.) One competitor petulantly remarked that such "unreasonable competition was childish and against public policy." Carnegie resisted joining a combination for many years, profitably going it alone. But in 1901 J. P. Morgan had worked out an arrangement, charging the confederates some $62.5 million for bringing them together and finally making Carnegie one of their number.

37. Ralph Nelson, *Merger Movements in American Industry, 1895–1956* (1959), pp. 5, 29. (A smaller boom appeared in the late 1920s, and a still smaller one in 1946–47 and 1954–55.)

38. Margin data: U.S. Industrial Commission, *Reports*, XII:771. The competitor, Willis King, of Jones and Laughlin, is quoted in W. Paul Strassman, *Risk and Technological Innovation* (1959), p. 46.

Creating a successful monopoly could be enormously profitable. Early attempts were made by collusion, mere working together. But collusion broke down because there were far too many ways by which individual members could cheat successfully. Moreover, after 1890 the Sherman Act made such conspiracies illegal.

Monopoly by merger was, however, still possible. It offered a signal advantage over mere collusion. Stock could be issued that immediately capitalized prospective monopoly profits, without the labor of remaining in the business for years in order to earn them. That surely was one important factor explaining Carnegie's agreement to sell to U.S. Steel after years of resisting a combination. He wanted to retire. Numbers of his partners did so at the same time, clutching their shares of U.S. Steel. But creating a solid merger of contentious businessmen required a strong spirit who could persuade all significant members of the industry to join. If even one stayed out, that spoiler could benefit from the cartel price, by selling an ever increasing volume at a price just a wee bit below the one his competitors were kindly keeping up for him.[39] Mergers during these years controlled an average of about three-quarters of the entire market.[40] Capitalizing monopoly profits also permitted the participants to compensate the master spirit from the monopoly potential which he himself had helped create. They did not even need to pay him a cent of their own money. Thus Morgan's $62 million for organizing U.S. Steel came from the monopoly value he had created solely by organizing the company.

Indeed the mode by which the organizational geniuses were paid off required that. The activity and stock watering of Judge Moore when he organized American Tin Plate provided a vignette of the procedure and interests. The new company issued $46 million in stock:[41] $18 in preferred stock to the 39 firms merged into the new company for the value of their plants; $18 in common stock to the same businesses, representing their share of the hoped-for increase from the new monopoly plus advances, if any in efficiency; $5 in

39. The temptations of that position were great. Geoffrey Cabot, leading maker of carbon black, describes repeated and generous offers by fellow producers in 1895: "Nine men representing four other carbon black interests . . . proposed 1. to buy my black for five years at 4¢ per lb. 2. to lease my factories. 3. to buy my factories for cash. 4. to buy my factories for 10% preferred stock on an appraisal. 5. to buy . . . for 10% preferred stock and secure me by a mortgage on the plant, all of which I declined. . . . I tried to persuade them to form a combine without me but this they absolutely refused to do." Leon Harris, *Only to God, the Life of Godfrey Lowell Cabot* (1967), pp. 151–52.

40. Estimated by George Stigler from U.S. Industrial Commission *Reports*. Cf. Stigler's *The Organization of Industry* (1968), p. 102.

41. U.S. Industrial Commission, *Hearings*, I:867, 885, 960. Mr. Griffith sold out to the new firm for preferred stock equal to the cash value of his plant, "and, as a bonus they gave you the same amount of common stock." It was surely an offer too good to refuse.

common stock to Judge Moore for $5 million working capital he put into the new concern; and $5 to Judge Moore for his services in creating a monopoly.

Some 39 firms, 15 of them headed for bankruptcy, were replaced by one spanking new firm, able to set tin plate prices.[42] The monopoly value embodied (i.e., "capitalized") in its stock equaled exactly half the total—or $23 million.[43] It was a classic example of "watered stock"—that is, stock for which no equivalent amount of plant and equipment were purchased. That fact mattered little to investors so long as the monopoly worked. Stigler has shown that investors in the heavily watered stock issued by U.S. Steel did very well indeed for many years, earning as much per dollar invested as those in other leading steel companies.[44] As Judge Moore noted, the stock in "all these companies I have organized" did not sell at mere par value. It actually sold "at a premium of 40 to 60 percent within a reasonable length of time" after its issuance.[45]

In return Moore was paid generously, but contingently. His credibility turned on the fact that he was willing, for example, to devote 1¼ years and put in $5 million[46] but be paid only in common stock of the new firm. That stock would be worthless if he failed to create a successful monopoly/oligopoly, but worth $5 million (or more) to him if he succeeded.

Stockholders were not entrapped into buying "overcapitalized" and "watered" stock that couldn't pay dividends. They counted on the prospect of effective monopolies, plus some vague expectation of greater "efficiency." U.S. Steel and other such novelties proved highly profitable. But a substantial number—perhaps one-third[47]—of the 156 trusts formed 1888–1905 proved abysmal failures. (Morgan's U.S. Steel was a great financial success. His International Marine Company was an equally great, international fiasco.) Cautious investors knew that stocks were inherently venturesome. They therefore put their money into U.S. government securities or blue chip bonds. Those who did venture into stocks, particularly of new firms, played to win unusual amounts. Not even Morgan's name always guaranteed them against the consequences of their greed.

The merger tide slowed sharply by 1905, after a twenty-year run. Political shifts had led the Justice Department to intervene, and two Supreme Court decisions marked the ebb of the tide. The Northern Pacific decision

42. The company controlled about 90 percent of tin plate output. U.S. Industrial Commission, *Reports*, I:867, 885, 960.

43. The total stock issue of $46 million represented $18 million preferred for the cash value of the existing firms plus $5 million in working capital Judge Moore put in.

44. Stigler, *Organization*, p. 110. From 1901 to the outbreak of World War I it did better than any leading steel company except Bethlehem Steel.

45. U.S. Industrial Commission, *Reports*, I:961.

46. Ibid., p. 960.

47. Shaw Livermore, "The Success of Industrial Mergers," *Quarterly Journal of Economics* (November 1935).

warned corporate executives of the dangers in that new political world.[48] But in 1911, when the Court broke up that most impressive and profitable of all trusts, Standard Oil, the knell rang for mergers to achieve monopoly.

Later collaborators therefore sought oligopoly. The tools they could use were weaker. The threats they could deploy were feebler. New techniques of price leadership had to be developed. They nonetheless pointed to a world well away from the old competitive norms.

What impact did all this have on the consumer? Did the trusts exact more from him because they were trying to cover payments on inflated stock totals? The argument has often been proposed: "The main objection to . . . stock watering is that it tends to raise or keep up passenger and freight rates."[49] The contemporary literature carries constant complaints about "overcapitalization" and "watered stock": time and again trusts issued more stock than warranted by the value of the physical assets they combined. Long preoccupied with that fact, Senator Robert LaFollette finally succeeded in getting the ICC to measure the "true" value of railroad mergers. Revealing their "true value" (i.e., historic) cost was somehow going to shame the giant corporations into charging the consumer less, or enable the ICC to force them to do so. But that analysis confronts an obvious question: What was the goal of monopoly or oligopoly? It is generally agreed that Standard Oil was capitalized with great caution. Its capitalization certainly did not far exceed the value of the plants it combined. Were its monopoly profits scanty? Why should one expect that they would be? After all, the purpose of any trust was to "do away with foolishness in making prices." No matter what the ratio of future value to acquisition cost, it surely charged as great a monopoly rent as it thought sensible for its long-run profits.

That some efficiency advances appeared shyly among the new trusts is unquestionable. (The Distillers and Cattle Feeders Company did discover how to squeeze 4.7 gallons of whiskey from each bushel of corn, rather than a mere 4.1 gallons.[50]) But the record is not peppered with advances. Unbridled productivity advances in steel during the competition by Carnegie in the 1880s and 1890s far exceeded those after the consolidation under U.S. Steel in 1901. The value of oligopolies was more often enhanced by increases in the efficiency of their finance, supplier rebates, plus their ability to fix prices.

The sheer drama of the robber barons, the titanic scale of some of the new cartels and corporations, the anguished cries of the smaller competitors,

48. By 1907, as George Stigler notes, U.S. Steel checked with President Theodore Roosevelt as to the acceptability of its buying up Tennessee Coal and Iron, although it had asked no one about buying Clairton Steel just 3 years earlier; Stigler, *Organization*, p. 101.

49. U.S. Industrial Commission, *Reports* (1900), XIX:405. Cf. Eliot Jones, *The Trust Problem in the United States* (1921), chap. 11.

50. U.S. Industrial Commission, *Reports* (1900), I:815.

have all shaped the imagination of novelists, social critics, historians. But what effect on the functioning of the economy? Both contemporary hearings by the Industrial Commission (published in many volumes) and behavior of those involved suggest that the process largely continued trends that were already apparent. Labor did not find the trusts or new giant firms notably different from their predecessors as employers; discipline, overbearing supervisors, hatred, conflicts were not obviously more common in the large than the small firms. Neither paid more than they had to in wages. Consumers paid monopoly profits to some large firms, but there is little basis for believing that the share of the consumer's dollar taken in monopoly profits differed for the host of small firms that had local monopolies, away from railroads and big cities, than the new giants. Indeed while the arrival of a new era in capitalism was widely described there is not even a clear indication that the concentration of resources was largely affected. Thus most mergers appeared in manufacturing—steel, farm machinery, leather, cans, sugar refining. Yet the concentration of resources within manufacturing did not change greatly. The percentage of factory employment in the largest firms, some 12 percent in 1832, was 9 percent in 1890, and 8 percent in 1900.[51] For even while the plug tobacco and cotton duck industries were being merged, new manufacturing industries were forming—autos, electrical machinery, tires. (Moreover, much of the "smart money" seeking high profits went into utilities, retail chain stores, and fields quite outside manufacturing.) The increased concentration in manufacturing developed decades later, and for reasons other than the surge of mergers.

Distribution

As the rail network expanded after the Civil War consumers faced a new reach of opportunity. They were increasingly offered products from all over the nation. Instead of buying from the local producer and supplier they now confronted wide product variety. But the cost of searching out the hidden disadvantages in a variety of products, then matching net advantage with cost, was a very real one.

Lance Davis and Douglass North have noted that "market failure engendered by very high information costs could be improved if some new arrangement can reduce the costs of that information."[52] By the same token, market success can offer such information at lower cost. This is precisely what the new competition did.

51. For method of estimation, see Appendix B, this chapter.
52. Lance Davis and Douglass North, "Institutional Change and American Economic Growth" *Journal of Economic History* (March 1970), p. 136. High information costs do not *per se* imply market failure, of course. Information has a cost, as do other valuable inputs. Those who produce information may be unable to monetize their product. But such private returns have lit-

The major breakthrough occurred when a set of fairly new authenticating institutions developed. They staked their reputation on reducing such risks to the consumer. They effectively guaranteed that any new brand or product they sold met a given standard. After they had sold the consumer one acceptable product they then built on that reputation to sell another, and another, however distant and unknown the product manufacturers might be. The first of these institutions was the department store. City markets had, of course, existed for centuries, their stalls ranged side by side in market areas. The department store became a natural extension, with individual distributors cheek by jowl under a common roof. The still elegant cast iron facades of Marshall Field and Wanamaker's call back the expansionary era of their growth, just after the Civil War. In time they took great and greater responsibilities for establishing common quality, conditions of credit, sale, and delivery of goods sold under their roof.

Another authenticating device was the mail order house. Montgomery Ward (founded in 1872) and Sears Roebuck (1886) also spread their brand name over the products they sold. To achieve low prices for each of their quality levels they did more than drive hard bargains with producers around the nation. Increasingly they specified the quality and characteristic details of every product they would purchase in the period ahead. After all it was their reputation that was at stake with the consumer. A badly printed calico dress could endanger next season's sale of a bicycle, and the later sale of a rock maple living room suite. Catalog shopping provided so great a boon to farmers that they successfully pressured Congress to begin rural free delivery (in 1896). Competition between the mail order houses then passed this federal subsidy along to the farmer, the taxpayer thus making catalog purchases still more attractive.

The third authenticating device was the chain store. The first great chain, the Atlantic and Pacific Tea Company, was founded in 1859. By 1870 it had added a full line of groceries to its specialties. The Woolworth 5- and 10-cent store chain ("nothing over 10 cents") began in 1879. By 1900 there were 60 large chains (of 11 or more stores each). Just as the department stores and the mail order houses, these too specified to the producer (farmer or manufacturer) the quality of the good they wished to buy, demanding prices consistent with the heavy volume they bought. Competition of chains with each other, and with the independent retailer, kept down the cost of distribution. At the same time the increasingly affluent consumers wanted new products and service outlets available within easy walking or driving distance, thus bringing up the costs of distribution.

tle to do with the social cost of information. Information is precisely what the new competition provided along with goods.

The net effect of these forces is suggested by the percentage share of the U.S. labor force devoted to trade:[53]

1840	6
1850	6
1860	8
1870	10
1880	11
1890	13
1900	14
1910	14
1920	14

This share rose markedly in the quarter-century after the Civil War, as the railroads expanded and cities burgeoned. It then pretty much leveled off for the next quarter-century.

Did that swiftly expanding network of retail stores drive up the costs of distribution? Such a conclusion has been widely drawn. ("While the proportion of prices which represented various distribution changes rose for most goods during this era, the tasks of distribution had grown much more complex.") Yet systematic study by Barger shows that the distribution mark up (which includes the entire retail margin, wholesaling plus freight costs) actually rose very little between the Civil War and 1949. The advent of these authenticating institutions, plus the new boxes and brands, had so thoroughly neutralized cost increases that productivity in distribution (output per man-hour) actually rose, by 1 percent per year, over these decades.[54]

Producers, however, were hardly happy about the hard bargains these "countervailing powers" drove. They therefore tried to reach consumers directly. Their earliest attempts to find a more profitable way to sell nationally involved door to door salesmen. Peddlers loaded up with tinware in Berlin, Connecticut, or books from Hartford, went south on horseback until they had sold their wares directly to farmers. Itinerant Bible salesmen appeared in America, as they had in Europe. Their tracks were followed by entrepreneurs such as Mark Twain, whose publishing company sold his own novels (and General Grant's memoirs) door to door. Insurance companies trained a huge

53. Lebergott, *Manpower*, p. 510.

54. Harold Barger's classic study, *Distribution's Place in the American Economy Since 1869* (1955), pp. 40, 47, finds that the gross trade margin for all consumables sold at retail rose from 59 percent to 71 percent of producers' value between 1869 and 1929. That increase was concentrated in two decades 1869–79 and 1919–1929. For 1869, however, his data rest on reports for a few individual food stores and Macy's. For 1879 it rests only on data for the state of Indiana, exclusive of food stores. Had he included Indiana food stores in 1879 the rise he discovers from 1869–1947 for this major group would have turned into a decline.

complement of their own salesmen to sell industrial insurance ("funeral insurance") door to door. Workers' families bought it for 5 cents and 10 cents a week. Singer's sewing machines, Colonel Pope's bicycles, were likewise sold house to house.

But such selling proved relatively expensive. Brand advertising promised lower selling costs. Producers escalated national advertising after the Civil War, providing information and seduction in mixed, if not in equal, measure. To cover advertising costs, commodities purchased by consumers carried a 2 percent higher price tag by 1870, an 8 percent higher tag by the eve of World War I.[55] The free introductory offer may have been pioneered by Eve, and the blandishments of salesmen, by Mephistopheles. But hitherto only the novelist had recorded events in the boudoir and bazaar. Now for the first time print and daguerreotype provided a veracious and tangible record. It has led many historians to regret these revelations of human weakness.

American patent medicine advertisements were no more misleading than the spiels of those who, in Donizetti's time, sold "The Elixir of Love," or those in Peiping who hawked New York's ginseng root as a rejuvenating medicine. However, they upset intellectuals and moralists who held that Americans should have transcended such simple-minded human illusions.

These new institutions—department stores, mail order houses, chain store, door to door salesmen, national advertising—kept down the prices consumers were charged by providing better information. Yet such market success was not widely commended. For it directly attacked monopolies possessed by thousands of small businesses throughout the land. These once had modest, but effective monopolies. Moreover, chains and large new stores relied on indifferent clerks to sell, rather than attentive owners. The result made at least one historian unhappy: they set "one price to all comers, and the old joy of higgling with a merchant over the price of the article was soon a thing of the past." (To the merchant, of course, the "joy of higgling" meant trying to extract the maximum rent from each buyer, charging the rich more than the middle class, charging the urgent buyer less than the barely interested shopper.)

55. We relate the volume of advertising to that for consumer purchases of goods, using data from *Historical Statistics . . . to 1957*, pp. 143, 526. The true percentages are surely lower. That is just as well given the widespread view that advertising took a huge chunk of spending. Cf. Paul Baran, "Theses on Advertising," in his *The Longer View* (1970). However, advertising widened markets, thereby expanding production runs and cutting costs. Without that sequence consumer costs would have been still greater. The net cost of advertising to consumers, therefore, has been less than 8 percent. No society, capitalist or noncapitalist, of course, need have advertising. However, the use of advertising in Soviet Russia suggests that at least one Communist nation would not fit into that alternative mold.

Retailers responded by getting legislatures to act against the import flood. States passed and enforced laws against peddling items from outside the state, even outside the municipality. Eventually the Supreme Court ruled in favor of the Singer sewing machine company (1876, 1880) and the Armour meat packing company (1890). Their shipments in interstate commerce, the court decided, could not be forbidden or restricted by state laws. (Not until retailers got the Robinson-Patman Act passed as part of New Deal reforms in 1936 did the federal government intervene effectively against interstate commerce and on behalf of small businesses.) The competition that then ensued even in the smallest town was far harsher, because more direct, than what tariffs were enacted to prevent. It brought down prices, aided consumers, made profits for what Theodore Roosevelt called "malefactors of great wealth." It also destroyed the profits of the benefactors, or malefactors, of small wealth. The legislatures and courts were concurrently widening interstate commerce to enable the small businessmen who ran farms to ship their products wherever they chose. Had that not been so, they might have taken a more sympathetic attitude toward small businessmen in towns and cities.

Appendix

Appendix A

Distribution margin for wheat: An average of the difference in wheat prices, New York-Iowa and New York-Wisconsin, from Jeffrey Williamson, *Late Nineteenth Century American Development* (1974), p. 259.

Farm sales prices and equipment prices: Marvin Towne and Wayne Rasmussen in Conference on Research in Income and Wealth, *Trends in the American Economy in the Nineteenth Century* (1960), pp. 266, 276. Farm equipment prices recorded by William H. Shaw, *Value of Product Since 1869* (1947), p. 294, linked to estimates of Dorothy Brady prior to 1890 show much the same change. Alvin Tostlebe, *Capital in Agriculture* (1957), p. 186, uses a more indirect method, and gets very different results.

Interest rates on farm mortgages for 1870–90: Average of rates for counties in Illinois, Nebraska, and Iowa, from R. F. Severson, Jr., et al., "Mortgage Borrowing as a Frontier Developed," *Journal of Economic History* (June 1966), p. 164; E. H. Hinman and J. O. Rankin, *Farm Mortgage History of Eleven Southeastern Nebraska Townships, 1870–1932.* University of Nebraska Research Bulletin 67 (1933):25; W. G. Murray, *An Economic Analysis of Farm Mortgages in Story County, Iowa, 1854–1931,* Iowa Agricultural Experiment Station. Iowa State College, Research Bulletin 156 (1933):396. For 1890–1910: Hinman and Rankin, *Farm Mortgage,* and Murray, *An Economic Analysis.*

Appendix B

CONCENTRATION OF MANUFACTURING EMPLOYMENT (000)

	1832	*1890*	*1900*
Total employment	375	4,000	5,124
In the 185 largest firms*	47	347	425
Percent in largest firms	12	9	8

*The data relate to the top 185 firms because the 1900 Census tabulation relates to that number of firms, a grouping which the Census used to mark out the set that contained the important trusts and monopolies of the time.

Source: 1832: The McLane Report, *Documents Relative to Manufactures* (1833), lists thousands of individual plants as of 1832, and we assume that its reports encompassed every large manufacturing plant in the nation. (It lacked coverage of Southern and Western states, but gave rather full coverage to New England and the Mid-Atlantic states.) Arraying the larger plants in the report and totaling employment in the 185 largest plants, we arrive at a figure of 46,475 employees. We relate this total to a manufacturing employment total of 375,000. This latter figure is derived from estimates of cotton and iron factory employment shown in Lebergott, *Manpower*, p. 510, on the assumption that the ratio of these groups to the total was 20 percent—the ratios in both 1810 and 1850 having been 20 percent.

    1890: The industrial combinations listed in 1900 averaged 2,297 employees per plant. (This figure can be compared with that of 1,876 for the plants with 1,000-plus employees in 1910—when the first size distribution of employment becomes available. (Cf. 13th Census, *Manufactures*, VIII, p. 207.) The date of organization given for combinations in 1900, and the value of their capital stock, suggest that virtually none of the resources included in them had been combined as of 1890. (12th Census, *Manufactures*, part 1, pp. lxxxii and lxxxvi.) We estimate an 1890 total as the product of 185 (for the largest plants) times the 1,876 figure. The resultant figure of 347,060 constitutes 8.7 percent of the 1890 total minus hand trades.

    1900: 1900 Census, *Manufactures*, part 1, pp. lxxxii, 3, 51–52. We exclude hand trades, and take the 185 organizations for which data are tabulated as equivalent to the 185 largest. Such an assumption is mildly in error: the Carnegie firm was omitted, as well as a few others who might supersede some of the smallest in that group.

"The world scouts at us whale hunters yet . . . unwittingly pays up the profoundest homage . . . almost all the tapes, lamps, and candles that burn around the globe, burn, as before so many shrines, to our glory!

—MELVILLE, *Moby Dick*

25

Oil

T HE U.S. petroleum industry was pioneered by itinerants who tossed blankets onto the oil seeping into Pennsylvania creeks, wringing that oil out into tiny bottles labeled "Seneca Oil." They then sold it as an Indian miracle cure for rheumatism, cholera, colds, corns, and neuralgia.[1] Petroleum which seeped into salt wells near Pittsburgh was also sent on to New York City to be sold for lamp oil.[2] The enormous petroleum industry that developed after 1860, however, was no patent medicine industry. Rather it substituted kerosene for tallow candles, lard, and whale oil—those older sources of light and lubrication.

The restless search by American mariners for the wandering whales had begun from Nantucket by 1715.[3] But its expansion was perpetuated by the rising demands of American industry for whale oil. Whale oil filled the lamps of the textile factories and lubricated their spindles. Whale oil brilliantly illuminated lighthouses from Cape Cod down along the coast, a subject for panegyric by Thoreau. And it proved invaluable for greasing railroad locomotives, mill wheels, machine tools. What shadowed the prospects for the whaling industry were the events of 1854.

British chemists had begun breaking coal down into heavy oils and lighter byproducts in the early 1850s. The Crimean War in 1854 boomed British demand for heavy oils, leaving an excess of lighter oils. By 1855 this

---

1. *The Derrick's Handbook of Petroleum* (1898), 1:1028, 1034.
2. Ibid., p. 1015.
3. *Collections of the Massachusetts Historical Society for 1794* 3(1810): 161.

excess supply was selling at only half the price of whale oil.[4] At such a price ratio even the newer, but smoky and odoriferous, product successfully began to compete with whale oil for lighting homes and greasing textile spindles. A U.S. "coal oil" industry sprang into existence. By 1860 nearly a million American homes relied for lighting on the coal oil produced by a handful of firms.[5] Most of these families had only begun to use coal oil within the prior two years.[6] The remaining 80 percent of American households still relied on tallow candles, lard oil in lamps, or whale oil (burned as oil or as sperm candles). But when the Civil War broke out, Confederate privateers seized many of the slow-sailing whalers. The number that were sent from Bedford and Nantucket to the South Seas then fell sharply. The price of whale oil rose just as sharply. As consumers predictably responded to that soaring (relative) price, its domain as a lighting source was reduced, and disappeared by the war's end.

The increase in demand led a host of entrepreneurs—from Yale professors to New York lawyers—to drill for oil.[7] Men had, of course, long drilled for salt springs in Pennsylvania and elsewhere. But in August 1859 "Uncle Billy Smith" drilled 69 feet into the earth and created, in effect, the first petroleum well.[8] His discovery immediately and dramatically broke the market price for coal oil.[9] Indeed these early wells brought such a flood of oil that prices fell to less than half a cent a gallon in 1861.[10] But that bargain price, plus very rapid development of techniques for refining kerosene, expanded demand rapidly. From 1 million families in 1860 who relied on petroleum oil for light, the number rose to about 7 million (two-thirds of all families) by 1880.[11]

Oil—and Standard Oil

When the U.S. Congress's Industrial Commission conducted an investigation of the entire U.S. economy in 1900, one key witness began his attack

4. John Butt, "Legends of the Coal-Oil Industry," *Explorations in Entrepreneurial History* (Fall 1964): 19, 23.

5. *Hunt's Merchants Magazine*, 42 (1860): 245, reported that "A coal oil lamp will consume about four gallons of oil during the year." at 70 cents a gallon. Data for the 1890s show families averaging 34 gallons and paying about 15 cents a gallon. (52d Cong., 1st sess., H.D. 232, part 2, Commissioner of Labor, *Seventh Report*, 1891, Table XVII, part E.) We assume that the average family consumed about 10 gallons a year at the higher price during the early stage of consumer adoption.

6. *Hunt's*, p. 246. *The Derrick's Handbook* I:16, reported consumption in 1858 at a mere 47,320 gallons. At a usage rate of 10 gallons a family, only 4,732 families then used coal oil.

7. *The Derrick's Handbook*, I: 16–17.

8. Ibid., p. 706. Uncle Billy was hired by the ex-railroad conductor Edwin Drake.

9. From the $.75–$1.00 range to 50 cents. Ibid.

10. Ibid., p. 712. The barrel of 42 gallons sold for 10 cents August 1861–January 1862.

11. 1880 Census, *The Technology and Uses of Petroleum and Its Products*, p. 266. The Census estimate of 13,000 barrels of home consumption a day for illumination, combined with the above estimate of 30 gallons per family, indicates 6,631,000 families relied on kerosene for light.

on combinations, and on Standard Oil, with the statement: "Robert Lockwood came from England with Winthrop in 1620. 147 of his descendants, one of whom was my great grandfather, participated in the Colonies on the side of the Revolution. The men who developed the oil regions of Pennsylvania were of the best families of the Republic."[12] Having made his breeding clear, he went on to describe how he had gone through the countryside of western Pennsylvania buying drilling rights from dozens of farmers. "It became evident that there was a 100 foot belt of oil extending from Butler County down into . . . Beaver County . . . I worked night and day and never stopped for anything. . . . I was interested in 1½ miles of this oil belt solid; I had it all. I thought I would make a million."[13]

The remarkable financial zeal that drove so many oil producers and refiners, both small and large, has never been better epitomized. But there was a difficulty: they got in each other's way. That multitude of would-be millionaires eventually proved most serviceable to the consumer, but hardly to each other. Between 1860 and 1900 they drilled about 100,000 wells in Pennsylvania alone, 20,000 in the single decade from 1870 to 1880.[14]

Crude oil sold for $12 to $16 a barrel in 1860, but for less than $1 in each year from 1879 to 1900.[15] The simple explanation of this immense depression in prices was that the industry, which had pumped less than 1 million barrels in 1860, was flooding the markets by 1900 with 63 million barrels annually.[16] It had expanded all over northwestern Pennsylvania, down into West Virginia, and over to Ohio.

Two forces drove that competitive surge. One force was geological, and legal. The first well in an area not merely drew oil from under the farm that had been leased, but from oil formations under adjoining farms. Whenever an oil strike advertised a new section of northwestern Pennsylvania (such as the great Bradford County strike of 1876), its farmers promptly welcomed the speculators who immediately descended on that region. They looked for royalties from "their" oil, by getting it out before neighboring farmers could tap into it. (In later decades Texas land owners, just as adjoining socialist republics in Soviet Russia, drilled slant wells from their side of the legal line, seeking to capture as much oil as they could reach.) Unitized drilling could have slowed the rush, enabled all land owners to share in a common royalty.

---

12. U.S. Industrial Commission, *Hearings*, 1:385.

13. L. M. Lockwood in Ibid., p. 395. "Competition," he observed, "was giving me all this oil was worth, as compared with what the consumer was paying for it, and I was getting rich." But once Standard Oil bought the competing pipe line in the area, the premium "of 20 or 30¢ a barrel" Standard Oil had been paying "came off from that oil. It was not better than any other oil. . . . The Standard Oil Company practically confiscated all that magnificent property."

14. Ibid., p. 434.

15. U.S. Census, *Historical Statistics . . . to 1970*, p. 594.

16. *The Derrick's Handbook*, I:19, 714–15.

But for many decades the farmers, individualistic and sanguine about huge profits, competitively rushed their land into production.

A second force must be noted. It cost relatively little to drill for oil. Generally, the land owner took a royalty (one eighth to one half of the oil lifted), and hence charged nothing if it turned out to be a dry hole. As of 1865, drilling a well cost less than $5,000, that cost rising little decade after decade.[17] Typically each well was financed by one or two entrepreneurs. The task these thousands of would-be millionaires set for themselves was twofold: first, to produce a product for which the consumers would pay, and second, to collaborate in keeping that price above free market levels.

The goal of keeping prices up by somehow restricting petroleum production was widely understood and just as widely accepted. Thus the notorious attempt at cartel formation by the South Improvement Company was an open and above-board proposition according to the Petroleum Producers Union, which had fought it to the death. "These persons," they declared, "accustomed to the crooked equivocal methods of railroad management and mismanagement, committed the error of openly avowing their purposes, and had not . . . sufficient moral perception to know that they were embarking on a criminal conspiracy."[18] The spectre they and their opponents feared was not any hidden conspiracy against consumer interests. It was instead a threat to their own entrepreneurial profits.

What first brought Standard Oil and John D. Rockefeller to national attention was undoubtedly the South Improvement Company. That company was an attempt, initiated by the railroads in 1872, to reduce the bitter competition to which they were exposed. For they competed in the transport of a hundred commodities, ranging from oil to wheat to immigrants. Railroads had tried a variety of cartel mechanisms—pools, agreements—on their routes through Iowa, New Jersey, and so on. Now, in the Pennsylvania oil regions, they were trying out a combination between the railroads and the refiners. They proposed to begin with the major refiners, to go on by including as many other refiners as would enable them to fix railroad rates at "reasonable" levels. They expected to combine "more than two-thirds [reckoning by their refining capacity] of the refiners of petroleum" together with the Erie, the Pennsylvania, and the New York Central railroads. This combination utilized a moldering Pennsylvania charter, taken out years before for a "South Improvement Company." In turn, (according to the leading spirit in the

---

17. An estimate of $4,290 for 1865 appears in the U.S. Industrial Commission, *Hearings*, I:411, 413. The cost of drilling the typical Pennsylvania well rose hardly at all from the late 1870s to the late 1890s, even though the wells went ever deeper. Cf. Harold Williamson's comprehensive review in the National Bureau of Economic Research, *Output, Employment and Productivity in the United States After 1800* (1966), p. 364.

18. Petroleum Producers Union Statement of 1880, in 50th Cong., 1st sess., H.R. 3112, *Trusts* (1888), p. 691.

Company, P. H. Watson), the refiners were to "secure the cooperation of the producers in carrying out plans for their mutual benefit."[19] The contract specified a rate of $2.92 for shipping a barrel of crude oil from the oil regions to New York City. The elegant centerpiece in the contract, however, was that $1.32 be rebated to the South Improvement Company, both for shipments by its own members and by those of other shippers.[20] If, therefore, the Company and a competitor each shipped a barrel of oil, the Company would pay 28 cents net, while its competitor paid $2.92. The incentive for all refiners to join the South Improvement Company was clearly overwhelming: no independent refiner could stand up against such a transportation differential. The explosion of wrath in the oil regions was instantaneous and widespread. It doomed the plan before it even began to operate. By April 1872 the charter to the South Improvement Company had been revoked. The incident had entered the history books.

But this hardly ended the affair, even apart from a long series of investigations. So far as the railroads were concerned, their enormous excess capacity and heavy fixed costs still continued. These still induced persistent attempts to develop other "pools," other cartel arrangements. Thus in December of that same year the railroads and mining companies formed the celebrated and long-lasting Anthracite coal combination—a similar attempt to moderate competition's harsh impact on profits. It was followed by the cattle owners pool, in which the roads paid selected shippers to police the allocation (as they had paid the South Improvement Company).

Nor was this the end so far as the oil regions were concerned. Cartelization remained their constant hope. A few months after the well owners had ended the South Improvement Company forever they formed the (Petroleum) Producers Association. Under the leadership of Captain William Hasson, they then proposed their own cartel. Rockefeller himself could not have put this view more forcefully: "There is . . . but one practicable way, and that is to sell through one agency . . . all the oil which the world requires, and through the same agency to retire and hold the remainder" (in inventory).[21] A new petroleum agency was to purchase enough oil, then stockpile it until they

19. *Testimony of P.H. Watson, given before the Committee on Commerce of the House of Representatives Containing A Full Account of the South Improvement Company* (1872), pp. 14–15, presents the rough draft of January 10, 1872, which specified inclusion of "more than two-thirds [reckoned by the actual production of crude petroleum at their wells] of the producers of petroleum in the valley of the Alleghany" and more than two-thirds of the refiners (by capacity). The actual contract of January 18, more realistically, did not specify inclusion of the producers, nor require two-thirds of the refiners (by capacity).

20. Ibid., p. 17.

21. "Address to Producers of Petroleum, Issued by the General Council of the Petroleum Producers Union," in *A History of the Organization, Purposes and Transactions of the General Council of the Petroleum Producers Unions and of the Suits, Prosecutions by it from 1878 to 1880* (February 1880), p. 12.

forced up the prices paid by the consumers. Stock in the new agency was subscribed by November 1872.

By December an agreement had been worked out with the giant enemy of the previous spring. For it was Rockefeller who signed the agreement—the "Treaty of Titusville"—on behalf of the Refiners Association. The heart of the scheme required the producers to suspend new drilling. Only thus could the multitude of small producers restrict supply enough to force up prices. But producers in Clarion County proved recalcitrant. They kept on drilling. In the words of the restrictionists, the "Pennsylvania Germans [were] greedy, narrow minded and stubborn."[22] In other words, they failed to see the virtue of squeezing more profits out of the consumer in the short run. They thereby broke the cartel. It did, however, temporarily restrict supply, and prices did indeed rise. But that very rise inevitably induced the "narrow minded" to drill new wells. Shipments then rose (by about 50 percent from October 1872 to January 1873). And prices responded by falling almost fifty percent.[23] The contract with the refiners had to be cancelled in January; the producers had proved unable to stand together.[24] The next producer attempt did not occur until 1887.

A Cautionary Tale

The Petroleum Producers Association was a trade association of oil well owners. A sympathetic congressman (himself a former oil well owner) asked during a public hearing: was it organized "to protect yourself against the monopoly in the purchase, refining, and transportation of your product?" Yes, of course, was the reply. Yet to achieve that goal the well owners proposed in 1887 to join with the great Standard Oil purchase and refining monopoly. (For they could not push up the price paid by the consumer to achieve their desired profit increase without the refiners' cooperation.) At this time some 31 million barrels of crude oil were filling the storage tanks, depressing the price of oil. Standard Oil agreed to set aside six million of the gallons it owned for the benefit of the oil well owners—provided they substantially reduced oil flow for three months. In that event the price of oil could be expected to rise, thereby increasing the value of the oil thus held for the oil well owners—and, of course, that retained by Standard Oil. The Association got enough producers to agree, achieving a "shrinkage" of 18,942 barrels in daily production between October 1887 and February 1888.[25]

---

22. Quoted in Allan Nevins, *Study in Power, John D. Rockefeller, Industrialist and Philanthropist* I (1955):166.

23. *The Derrick's Handbook*, I:713, 806.

24. Harold Williamson and Arnold Daum, *The American Petroleum Industry, The Age of Energy, 1899–1959* (1963), p. 359.

25. They agreed to cut production by 17,500 barrels for three months. In fact they did somewhat better: from 58,492 to 40,000 barrels between October 1887 and February 1888.

The market price did indeed stop falling. It actually rose by 29 cents.[26] In the immortal words of one happy oil well owner: "Somebody stood the difference" of 29 cents. That somebody, of course, was the consumer. And from him the oil well owners made approximately $1.7 million in profit on the oil Standard Oil had held on their account, and now sold.[27] (Standard Oil made its own profit of $1.2 million on its own holdings.)

But unhappily for all these would-be cartel operators the inevitable happened. The high price led to the drilling, and completion, of some 418 new wells in the same period. This new output thus cancelled part of the benefit of the "shrinkage" from the older wells. Moreover, the price rise continued to stimulate the drilling of still more new wells. These inevitably produced still more oil, and drove the price back down.

Unlike the years since the 1930s, there was no Department of Energy, no Texas Railroad Commission, ready to step in and fine violators. Nor were the maverick producers a handful of major firms which could be subjected to the pitiless force of newspaper and TV commentary on their lack of public spirit. Instead, they consisted of thousands of small entrepreneurs. These owned their own farms or leased a few drilling rights. They drilled at night, in obscure backwoods areas. They could not be disciplined to keep the price rising.

Two basic factors made cartel control or monopoly of oil production difficult, if not impossible in this period. The first was that entry into the industry proved incredibly easy. In 1865 it cost about $4,000 to drill an oil well; by 1867 it cost even less.[28] The second was the random element in oil discovery. Thus the great Bradford field (in northwest Pennsylvania) began to develop in 1874. Within five years, 9,000 wells had been drilled in that area, and the field was producing more than all the rest of America put together.[29] In later years the Lima field was discovered in Ohio, and the Gulf fields in California. These were drilled by thousands of individual entrepreneurs.

With this easy, random, and persistent entry into the producing end of the industry, one thing became crystal clear. If the oil industry were to achieve a "condition of harmony"[30]—a cartel or monopoly—it would obviously have to be at the manufacturing or distributing level, not in mining. The leaders of that effort formed the Standard Oil Company in 1872; John D. Rockefeller was the first among equals. These refiners had originally concen-

---

26. Ralph Hidy and Muriel Hidy, *Pioneering in Big Business* (1955), pp. 179, 739.

27. Six million barrels allocated to producers times 29 cents equals $1.7 million profit. 18,942 barrels a day shrinkage times 4 months = 2,273,040 times 29 cents equals 0.7 loss (0.659). This assumes that the profit was practically zero in October 1887. Standard Oil had 4 million barrels of its own in storage.

28. U.S. Industrial Commission, *Hearings*, I:413, 415.

29. 1880 Census, "Production, Technology and Uses of Petroleum and its Products," in *Report on the Mining Industries*, p. 263.

30. The phrase is from Patrick Boyle in Industrial Commission, *Hearings*, I:430.

trated in "the regions" where oil was pumped from the ground. But the center of refining soon shifted to Cleveland and New York City. Rockefeller and his associates led the move. In the struggle with the railroads Cleveland proved a better location for production. For in Cleveland refiners had a choice of transport: dozens of vessels (which traveled via the Great Lakes and the Erie Canal), as well as several competing railroads (through Canada as well as within the United States). Had the industry remained in the oil regions it would have been at the mercy of a railroad cartel, for there the only alternative (wagons) was inordinately expensive.

How did Rockefeller achieve a monopoly of refining? By refiner cooperation, as the Michigan Salt refiners did? A National Refiners Association was indeed tried from 1872 to 1873. But it failed, just as the Producers Association failed in the same period. Too many refiners were outside the group. These refiners simply stepped up production. And by 1873 the industry's capacity was about double that required for the year's output.[31] About half the capacity, therefore, was idle, earning nothing.[32] The industry had to reduce capacity, and/or to increase demand by cutting costs and thereby prices.

Rockefeller persuaded/bludgeoned other refiners into an association with him. Indeed the bulk of Standard Oil's management consisted of former business opponents. These shared proportionately in the profits. What induced them to join? Basically it was their share in four sources of profits. Profits from greater rebates—for the railroads had to pay larger rebates to the firms controlling a larger volume of shipments. Profits from specialization—with the firm members most expert in refining in charge of that activity, those more expert in sales in charge of watching competitors' every move and deploying their sales efforts. Profits from an approximation to monopoly in oil refining. Profits enabling them to cut prices—thereby violently expanding sales at the expense of coal oil and candles. They then gathered in the economics of (large) scale production.

The prospect of these four profit sources induced such tough competitors as Jacob Vandergrift and Jabez Bostwick to join the association relatively early. Others were bought out. To encompass all substantial competition (and leave no significant outsider who could cheat) the combine found it worthwhile to pay market prices, thus inducing firms to sell out.[33] These were, of course, often below the original construction costs, as many

31. Williamson and Daum, *American Petroleum*, p. 360.

32. Ibid.

33. Representative Thomas W. Phillips, who spoke for the opposition to Standard Oil, nonetheless declared it paid a "good price." U.S. Industrial Commission, *Hearings* I:362, 371, 673. Cf. John McGee's demonstration that Standard Oil made more money by buying out competitors, at market prices (or better) because it more promptly reached a monopoly. That policy made more financial dollars and sense for them than trying to cut prices against other producers. (Cf. his "Predatory Price Cutting," *The Journal of Law and Economics* (1958)).

witnesses complained in subsequent Congressional investigations. That fact is hardly surprising. For what industry with rapid technological advance—whether cotton textiles in the 1830s, railroads in the 1840s, or oil refining in the 1870s—did not find high depreciation on investment inevitable? In oil depreciation commonly ran 10 to 15 percent a year.[34] It was hardly to be expected, therefore, that oil refining properties would still be worth their original construction cost 5 or 10 years after they had been built, particularly by the depression years, 1873–79, when construction costs were falling. But for Standard Oil to pay market prices (or somewhat above) in order to achieve a monopoly made tough business sense.[35] Indeed, the answer by at least one of Standard Oil's opponents to a query by the U.S. Industrial Commission— "Has the Standard Oil Company been making attempts to secure control of the independent companies?"—was: "They offered more than the properties were worth."[36]

Inevitably, as in other industries, the small, inefficiently run, badly located firms kept failing. Lewis Emery, the great opponent of Standard Oil in many a public hearing, listed firms that had been "bankrupted, squeezed out, bought up, leased or dismantled" by Standard Oil.[37] His list is really composed of two groups. First, he rates twenty-one firms "squeezed out" in Erie County from 1864 (when Rockefeller was still in the grocery business) through 1876. These firms were tiny producers, with a median output of 500 gallons. Second, outside of Erie County, every firm with a capacity of 1,500 gallons or more of crude was either bought or leased by Standard Oil. As Emery declared in large type in his broadsheet: "Pennsylvania's Industry driven to New York." Pennsylvania had provided 97 percent of U.S. petroleum exports in 1863 but only 17 percent in 1878. Meanwhile, New York's output had risen from 9,000 to 177,000 gallons a day.[38] The destruction consisted of small refining firms, and those located in the "oil regions" of Pennsylvania. These badly located, high cost firms rarely blamed their fate on their high costs but pointed to Standard Oil and the new wave.[39] In 1872 "the regions" had refined 20 percent of all oil. By 1881 their share had fallen to 7 percent. It was hardly to be expected that the many producers, refiners, and retailers from those areas were ever resigned to that catastrophe.

34. According to Lewis Emery, a refiner and one of the Trusts' most determined opponents. McGee, "Predatory," p. 146.

35. Cf. McGee, "Predatory."

36. U.S. Industrial Commission, *Hearings*, I:270.

37. 50th Cong., 1st sess., H.R. 3112, *Trusts* (1888), p. 232.

38. *Petroleum Producers Addresses, 1878–79–80* (Baker Library Pamphlets).

39. As early as 1872 refining costs in the regions were 33 cents higher than Cleveland, and 41 cents above New York City. Cf. Jerome Bentley, *The Effects of Standard Oil's Vertical Integration . . . 1872–1884* (1979), pp. 134–35. Closer to the wells, they had some advantage in shipping costs: they did not have to ship one barrel of crude to Cleveland or New York City to get the usual 0.7 barrel of refined, the rest then being waste and low value product.

Mass Marketing

Standard Oil developed an industry based on mass production and mass marketing. From an output of 8,500 barrels of crude refined in 1859 the industry had increased to 26,245,571 barrels by 1880.[40] Its profits rested on high volume. It skimmed off a small amount on each sale, rather than relying on high unit profits from a small volume. Was that route a conscious choice? Perhaps not. But it proved admirably consistent with two basic facts, one ecological, the other political. If Standard Oil had chosen a high unit profit strategy, Knut Wicksell believed, consumption would have fallen and wells would have run to waste (storage being too expensive for the host of small producers). Public dissatisfaction would then have flourished, possibly leading to government intervention.[41]

Instead, the industry became a mass marketer. And oil prices fell decade after decade while oil consumption (in both U.S. and export markets) rose phenomenally. Standard Oil's profits rose no less phenomenally, and reached rates far above those for those firms that tried to nourish their monopolies by raising prices and cutting volume.

As with many innovating firms Standard Oil was not necessarily foremost in developing new procedures. Generous profits typically came from early adoption, not from basic development work. The great Lima oil field in Ohio was discovered in 1886, and Standard Oil established a refinery near it to process 30,000 barrels a day. The choice was a dubious one. After two years' work it failed to find any way to remove the sulfur from Lima oil. (The oil did sell, but for a mere 14 cents a barrel at a time when Pennsylvania oil was selling for 75¢ to $1.00 a barrel.)[42] Herman Frasch, an engineer who once worked for Standard Oil, went off to found his own company in Canada. There he eventually succeeded in finding a way to refine Lima oil. Standard Oil then bought out his plant and patents. The millions of gallons of oil that it had in storage rose in value; its stock jumped from $168 to $820 a share, and its dividends from 7 percent to 40 percent.[43]

There is, says Matthew Josephson, "a famous note to his [Rockefeller's] barrel factory . . . cited with amused contempt by his critics to show how at-

40. *The Derrick's Handbook*, I:805.

41. Knut Wicksell, *Lectures on Political Economy* (1901, 1935, reprint ed. 1967), p. 89.

42. *Standard Oil Company of New Jersey vs. United States of America*, U.S. Supreme Court (October term, 1909), Brief for Appellants, II:91 for price of Lima Oil. *The Derrick's Handbook*, 1:712 for price of Pennsylvania oil. For Standard's failure, Arthur Pound, *More They Told Barron* (1930), p. 90.

43. Supreme Court, Ibid., and Pound, Ibid. Barron declared that Standard Oil had contracted to sell its reserves at 14 cents, then bought them back at $1 after discovery of the Frasch process—still obviously making money on that decision. Frasch found that he could oxidize the sulphur by using black oxide of copper. Then by double refining he produced a competitive product. Cf. *1902 Census of Mines*, p. 755.

tention to small details absorbed his soul." It asked, "What has become of the other 500 bungs?" in a barrel inventory.[44] But the critics failed to recognize that this was no financially "small detail." Over a quarter century, Standard Oil was able to cut its refining costs by only 7 cents a barrel of oil despite its adoption of a host of technical advances.[45] But it reduced costs by $1.25 a barrel merely by making its own barrels and bungs (instead of buying them).[46] Since it used 3½ million barrels a year by 1888 it thereby achieved a prodigious saving.[47] Even if refining costs had been reduced to zero, then, the reduction in barrel costs would nonetheless have proved more advantageous.[48]

Other Standard Oil efficiency advances involved everything from producing its own cans for kerosene to better inventory control. Not least of these was its decision to fix its headquarters in New York, and its growth in size and reliability. Together these advances enabled it to borrow heavily in New York financial markets at rates well below available to it as a Cleveland firm.[49]

In the 1870s refineries chiefly produced illuminating oils and waste. About 20 percent of all petroleum production, benzine, and tar, was customarily "run into the creek at night, or run into holes in the ground and burned."[50] As late as 1880 illuminating oils still made up 84 percent of the value of refinery output. But by 1904 half the product was in the form of new and highly profitable items—lubricating oils, paraffin (for home canning and preserving), naphtha (for surfacing roads), and gasoline.[51] Standard Oil played an extremely active role in developing ways to convert petroleum fractions into such salable products.

Outcomes

The period from Drake's first well in 1859 to the breakup of Standard Oil by the Supreme Court in 1906 constitutes a natural stage in the expansion

---

44. Matthew Josephson, *The Robber Barons* (1934), pp. 270–71.

45. Cf. Table 25.2 *infra*.

46. Circuit Court of the United States, Judicial District of Missouri, *United States of America vs. Standard Oil Company* of New Jersey, Brief for the Defendants, I:21.

47. The number of barrels, and costs of $2.35 in 1872 and $1.25 in 1888, are reported in Samuel C. Dodd, *Trusts*, (1900), p. 67.

48. The cost of refining for a barrel of constant output had probably been cut more than shown in Table 25.2. But the utilization of previously wasted byproducts undoubtedly pushed costs up somewhat.

49. In Circuit Court, *Standard*. "They enjoyed high credit and were large borrowers, and the establishment of their branch house in New York enabled them to secure large sums of money at lower rates than could be obtained in the West."

50. Westgate, in U.S. Industrial Commission, *Hearings*, 1:371.

51. *Report of the Commissioner of Corporations on the Petroleum Industry* (1907), part I, p. 261. Cf. Archbold in U.S. Industrial Commission, *Hearings*, 1:570.

TABLE 25.1

STANDARD OIL ASSETS AND EARNINGS (AVERAGE PER TIME PERIOD)

	Assets ($000,000)	Earnings ($000,000)	Percent of Net Earnings to Mean Net Assets
1882–1891	87.5	13.2	15.1
1891–1899	148.5	31.3	21.1
1900–1906	258.5	65.1	25.2

Source: In the Circuit Court of the United States for the Eastern Division of the Eastern Judicial District of Missouri. United States of America, petitioner, v. Standard Oil company of New Jersey et al. defendants. Brief of Facts and Argument for Petitioner, 1:170–71.

of the petroleum industry. What was the outcome of its development in these decades? More particularly, what were the outcomes for each of the main parties at interest: Standard Oil investors, U.S. consumers, and other refiners and producers?

So far as Standard Oil investors were concerned, the results ranged from rosy to unbelievable. In its dissolution suit the government soberly reported the Trust's earnings, shown in Table 25.1.

What about U.S. consumers? Standard Oil, consciously or not, chose mass production as the path to high profits—not high profits per unit. Now mass consumption becomes most feasible at lower prices, not higher ones. The record to 1906 indicates persistent declines in major cost components paid by Standard Oil, and no less persistent declines in the prices they then charged the final consumer (see Table 25.2). Over the Trust's entire life, Standard Oil's net earnings averaged 1.4 cents per gallon of illuminating oil.[52] Now a competitive rate of return in such a risky, technologically fast-moving industry might have been about 10 percent. Had the Trust earned a competitive 10 percent instead of its actual monopoly rates, its earnings would have been only 46 percent of what they actually were. Hence consumers paid .0066 cents a gallon in monopoly profits.[53] During these years the average family bought about 30 gallons of illuminating oil a year.[54] Standard

52. The Circuit Court, United States, p. 205, reports data indicating an average of $.0192 per gallon of crude, reflecting Standard Oil's ability to utilize previously waste fractions and more. The Circuit Court, Brief for Defendants on the Facts III:561 shows an average $.0144 profit on illuminating oil 1895–1906.

53. To an average profit rate of $.0144 per gallon we apply a ratio of 46 percent. That ratio is the ratio of earnings on Standard Oil's assets at a 10 percent rate to its actual earnings.

54. 52d Cong., 1st sess., H.D. 232, part 2, Seventh Annual Report of the Commissioner of Labor, 1891. An average of 34 gallons was computed from reports for some 1,932 families on pp. 1094–143, relating to families of cotton textile workers in states throughout the United States.

TABLE 25.2

PETROLEUM COSTS AND CHARGES (IN DOLLARS)

Year	Price of crude (oil city, Pa.)	Cost of refining	Cost of wooden barrel (per barrel)	Transport	Price of refined oil
1865	6.50	$0.30[a]	$2.50	$4.59	$24.67
1872	3.75	0.42	1.25	1.50	9.66
1884	.83	0.46	1.25	.55[b]	3.36
		(0.22:Standard Oil)			

[a]1860.

[b]1888.

Source: Cost of refining: 1860: *The Derrick's Handbook of Petroleum* I (1889):19. 1872: Rice estimated "not over" 1 cent a gallon for 1871–80 in U.S. Industrial Commission, *Reports*, I:735. 1884: Williamson estimates $.00534 per gallon (a 42-gallon barrel) for Standard Oil in Conference on Research in Income and Wealth, *Output, Employment and Productivity in the United States after 1800* (1966), p. 378. 1884: Teagle in 50th Cong., 1st sess., H.R. 3112, *Trusts* (1888), p. 553.

Cost of wooden barrel: Testimony of John D. Rockefeller in the Circuit Court for the Eastern Division of the Eastern Judicial District of Missouri, *United States*, p. 21.

Price of refined oil (export): *The Derrick's Handbook . . .* , p. 783. We assume 42 gallons per barrel.

Price of crude: U.S. Industrial Commission, *Reports*, I:434.

Transport, (regions to New York City): 1865: U.S. Industrial Commission, *Reports* I:413. 1872: Joseph Dodd, *Trusts* (1900), p. 66. For March, Standard Oil's rate was $1.25 (*The Derrick's Handbook*, p. 175). 1888: Archbold in 50th Cong., 1st sess., H.R. 3112, *Trusts* (1888), p. 322.

Oil's monopoly profits from each consuming family thus came to 21 cents a year. (American workers at that time earned an average of $450 to $500 a year.[55]) Under mass consumption, it turned out, massive profits went hand in hand with low prices and low unit profits.

What of other refiners and producers—the Trust's competitors, who were gradually "Bankrupted, Squeezed out, Bought up, Leased or DISMANTLED by the great OIL MONOPOLY of Ohio and New York"?[56] Many of these firms were very small, used the earliest techniques, and were located in the oil regions of Pennsylvania, far from markets. They would eventually have been forced out of business by their limitations. As-

55. Lebergott, *Manpower*, p. 528.

56. The phrase is from a broadsheet by Lewis Emery, Jr., and appears in *Petroleum Producers Addresses, 1878–79–80*, a pamphlet collection in the Baker Library of the Harvard Business School.

sume, however, that all these firms would have survived if only Standard Oil had not existed. And assume, further, they would (as a group) have employed assets equal in amount to Standard Oil's and as efficiently, earning a competitive 10 percent. Dividing those profits among 135 firms[57] would have yielded each an annual income of $110,000—an extremely handsome figure, indeed, by the standards of the time. It is unlikely that the typical producer would then have spent so parsimoniously, reinvested so heavily, as Standard Oil did for many years, under Rockefeller's cautious eye. They surely would not have devoted such extreme sums to charities and family trusts.

They would clearly have been catapaulted into the nation's highest income group. That fact provided an acute grievance in a nation committed to capitalism, free markets, and extreme rewards to a limited set of successful entrepreneurs. Few players will hazard money on either the red or the black if the roulette wheel offers few prizes. The energizing element in classical capitalism has always included some magically great rewards. But Standard Oil snatched this chance away from a set of entrepreneurs. Each smarted under a sense of unfairness. Each was loudly certain that given "a fair chance" he would have been as efficient, as productive, as lucky and—therefore—as great a financial success. These aggrieved entrepreneurs spoke in terms readily understood by congressmen, by self-made newspaper proprietors, and intellectuals who shared their values and sympathized with their acute sense of monetary deprivation.[58]

But the U.S. economy was dynamic. Indeed, Standard Oil was one of the forces making it so. In such an economy not even the tightest, best-run monopoly can hope to have its profits guaranteed into the indefinite future. For Standard Oil that prospect was further darkened by the Supreme Court's decision of 1911, which broke it up into a gaggle of smaller companies. The rapid growth of electricity obviously doomed an industry so heavily committed to the old-fashioned kerosene lamp, smoky and unsafe as it tended to be. True, Standard Oil's ingenuity in expanding its export market, in creating

---

57. In Ibid., Emery listed some 58 refineries in Pittsburgh in 1867—of whom "twenty-eight refineries have been Crushed Out and Dismantled! No Record Left. Of the remaining Thirty, Twenty-nine have been bought up or leased by the great Monopoly." (Ibid.) For the oil regions and the rest of Pennsylvania he further provided a "Partial List of the Petroleum Refineries in Pennsylvania, Bankrupted, Squeezed out, Bought up, Leased or DISMANTLED by the great OIL MONOPOLY of Ohio and New York Known as The Standard Oil Company." (50th Cong., 1st sess., H.R. 3112, *Trusts*, pp. 232, 242.) The second list includes 77 refineries in existence at some date. Some were "squeezed out, 1864"—while others were "dismantled in 1877." Because of the overlapping of dates, his list is therefore longer than one applying to any given date. We add the two counts, however, and assume that 135 companies were forced out or bought out by Standard Oil.

58. Few interchanges in the U.S. Industrial Commission, *Hearings*, are more touching than those between Congressman Phillips (chairman of the commission, and ex-petroleum refiner) and the aggrieved entrepreneurs from the regions.

special lubricants, asphalt paving, all would have muted that decline. But they could hardly have prevented it. Yet Aladdin appeared (oddly disguised as Henry Ford). He and his competitors created a brand new market for petroleum products, and one that grew immensely. The refining industry turned, with great zest and little difficulty, to creating more gasoline fractions and fewer kerosene ones from the same old 42-gallon per oil barrel. It enjoyed an additional, profitable half-century in which it continued as a technological leader, paid high dividends, high wages, and was more discreet in its ways than its nineteenth century predecessor.

Some of us have chosen America as the land of our adoption; the rest have come from those who did the same.

—Learned Hand, "The Spirit of Liberty"

A man is of all sorts of luggage the most difficult to be transported.

—ADAM SMITH

26

Immigration

IMMIGRATION to the United States was inspired by the same force that stimulated westward migration within the nation—hope. Men left the known in Europe for the unknown in the United States. They left families, friends, and traditions. Their mixed feelings were summarized in an old Irish song, "There is plenty of wealth and wailing in the stranger's land." There may have been less of either than predicted. True, the richest Americans at many points in history were foreign-born—in 1774, Charles Carroll of Ireland; in the 1830s, John Astor of Germany; in the 1860s, A. T. Stewart of Ireland; in the 1890s, Andrew Carnegie of Scotland. But most immigrants did not become millionaires. And the seamiest slums in New York City were indeed immigrant centers (German immigrants in the 1860s populated shanties on the hills of Harlem, and Irish immigrants, the unspeakable slums of Five Points). But most immigrants moved fairly quickly from slums in New York City to better conditions.

Continuing immigration, decade after decade, was explicable by the immigrants' fairly clear vision of what may be termed a "prospect." Would-be immigrants contrasted the whole set of advantages to be expected from moving to the new land with those remaining in Europe, allowing for the costs (emotional and financial) of actual migration. Where the gain in prospect was marked, people immigrated, whether they were already well-to-do or impoverished. Thus the immigrant stream included well-to-do, skilled workmen from Britain as well as unskilled laborers from Rumania. Some indeed left countries where average incomes exceeded those in the United States. But most individual immigrants expected to earn still higher incomes by moving. Others came because of the beckoning opportunities to own land, to worship more freely, to flee an oppressive tsar, emperor, or local police chief.[1] Most Europeans, of course, did not leave their native land. Those who did were more optimistic, more driven, more able, or some combination of all these.[2] A further force stimulating the immigrant flow to the United States was the success, and the laborious saving, of those who had gone before. Men sent for their wives. Parents sent for children left behind in Europe. Brothers sent tickets for brothers. In 1901 about 20 million post office money orders were sent to Europe, averaging $16 apiece.[3] Most represented a significant share of the entire yearly income of a first-generation immigrant, earned as a railroad track walker, domestic servant, or miner. By 1900 about one-half of all steerage passengers arrived on steamship tickets prepaid by such sacrifices.[4]

Immigrants left European farms for two destinations. Some moved to the great cities of Europe—to London, Dublin, Budapest, Hamburg. Others continued on to foreign countries, notably the Argentine, Brazil, Australia, Canada, and the United States. Those who landed in New York, Boston, or New Orleans typically moved on to other U.S. cities.

The original push to immigration arose from the increasing births on European farms that were barely able to support the parents, much less more children. A further stimulus to move was provided by the jobs opening up in Europe's cities and small towns as industrialization increased. But a major stimulus came from the expanding growth of U.S. wheat and corn production. In the phrase of New York's Governor Seymour, the United States "bombarded Europe with casks and barrels" of food.[5] For U.S. food could be grown and shipped to Europe at lower production costs than European farmers could achieve.

European city workers therefore began to choose bread made from cheaper American flour, and hams from American pork, rather than more expensive European food. The landed nobility of Russia, Poland, Germany,

---

1. Current immigration examples reveal the same rich complexity. Immigrants from the highest income and status ranks in the Soviet Union—such as Solzenitsyn (who sought more freedom of thought and expression), Baryshnikov (who desired greater freedom in choice of choreography and dance)—came as well as low-income sailors.

2. E. A. Ross, the great liberal sociologist, however, argued that those from Eastern Europe were the "beaten members of beaten breeds." Quoted in Maldwyn Jones, *American Immigration* (1960), p. 267. Ross's *The Old World and the New* (1914) is a classic pejorative.

3. *Annual Reports of the Post Office Department* (1901), p. 1086.

4. Jones, *American Immigration*, pp. 186–87. In 1890 about 30 percent did. With perhaps 800,000 steerage passages, if half were prepaid in the United States 400,000 were bought overseas. The $250,000,000 in remittances could clearly have paid for the balance with a great deal left over for other purposes.

5. Horatio Seymour, *An Address Before the New York State Agricultural Society*, in *Transactions of the New York State Agricultural Society, 1877–1892* (1884), p. 115.

Rumania, whose economic interests anciently had been wrapped up in growing wheat, now had to look elsewhere for status and riches; and the peasants, for sustenance. The latter provided the central stream of immigrants out of Europe. Those who headed for the United States helped expand still further America's exports of food. Some grew wheat. Others built railroads that shipped the wheat. Still others worked as longshoremen, built roads, steamships, developed oil fields—all contributing to lower further the export price of wheat, corn, and pork.

After the Civil War migration to the United States burgeoned, largely because the costs and stresses of the ocean voyage were cut. The steamers took only one week rather than one to three months required by sailing ships. The migration pattern also changed after the Civil War. There was no decline in the attractiveness of the United States to those people from northwestern Europe. But there was a sharp rise for those from Russia and Italy, as shown in Table 26.1. The enormous 1890–1915 surge from these newer centers was created by the end of laws limiting migration out of Italian dukedoms, the Austro-Hungarian empire, and Slav nations once under Turkish control; and by religious persecution by the Russians (of Jews and Baptists) and the Turks (of Christians—Armenians and Syrians). The subsequent decline from 1915 to 1940 occurred because the United States closed its doors. Pressure to close those doors had, of course, been apparent long before the Civil War. But the opposition did not succeed until 1924, when Congress finally acted to establish the "racial preponderance [of] the basic strain of our people."[6] An enormous accumulation of people tried to flee Eastern Europe in later decades, as the Berlin wall testifies.[7] The size of that group, plus the steady flow of illegal immigration from Mexico, the Caribbean, and the Far East, indicates that millions of people around the world would have migrated to the United States after 1924 if that law had not been passed.[8]

Two powerful factors explain the immigrant trek across the land just after the Civil War.[9] First, those foreign-born moved to locations with a re-

6. As the first president of the United Mine Workers, John Mitchell, wrote in 1909, "The demand for the exclusion of Asiatics . . . is based solely on the fact that as a race their standard of living is extremely low, and the assimilation by Americans impossible." *Proceedings of the Asiatic Exclusion League* (San Francisco, January 1911).

7. Despite the dangers of admitting to a desire to immigrate, some 120,000 applications, some for whole families, had been filed at local police stations by those seeking to leave the German Democratic Republic by the end of 1976. *Encounter* (April 1979), p. 85.

8. Net migration would have increased about as much as gross migration. Thus despite the dissent about McCarthyism and Vietnam fewer than 5,000 persons in any year took up residence in foreign states, renounced U.S. nationality, etc. Cf. U.S. Immigration and Naturalization Service, *1976 Annual Report*, Table 51, and *1962 Report*, Table 51.

9. The percentage of foreign-born by state in 1870 correlates .984 with a set of explanatory variables. Those with the highest "t" ratios were the proportion of those foreign born in 1860, ten years earlier (t = 26.90), and whether the state was outside the South (t = 2.29).

TABLE 26.1

IMMIGRATION TO THE UNITED STATES BY PLACE OF ORIGIN (000)

	United Kingdom and Northwest Europe	Germany and Central Europe	Russia and East Europe	Italy and South Europe
1865–1890	5,532	3,304	262	409
1890–1915	8,010	4,692	3,258	4,141
1916–1940	1,121	1,047	216	976
1941–1965	935	1,028	24	481

Source: Historical Statistics of the U.S. . . . to 1970, pp. 105–6.

ception committee—that is, where others foreign-born were already concentrated. There they could hope to continue speaking their old language, could find ethnic grocery stores. Most importantly, they could work with workers and for employers who shared their old language and customs. Second, they stayed away from the South. (Maps of the United States distributed in Europe had "vast areas of the South printed in yellow, indicating 'yellow fever belt,' and other areas in black, indicating regions where white men do not and cannot live."[10]

But one may well ask, why then did earlier immigrants settle where they did? Was it all decided by the random choice of the very first immigrant? One clue to the deeper reasons for choices by the foreign-born is to be found in a paradox. Most Europeans necessarily came from farms and rural areas. Surely their skills would have led them to work on the land. There they could utilize such skills, realize higher incomes. But they did not. Over half of U.S.-born workers in 1870 were farmers or farm laborers, yet only about a quarter of the foreign-born were.[11]

One major reason turned on their choice of potential employers. In the U.S. countryside immigrants were limited to work on one of the half-dozen or so farms to which they could walk. (In Europe farmhouses were cheek by jowl. But in the United States the greater farm size spread them apart by a half-mile or more.) In the city a similar walk, or a 2 cent streetcar fare, enabled them to choose among hundreds of employers. Such urban freedom of choice gave them the chance to earn a higher wage, to work with fellow employees who spoke the same language or had the same background, plus the opportunity to work for an employer who would discriminate less (or not at

10. World's Work (May 1907), p. 8959. "A yellow fever outbreak in Brazil had carried off 9,000 Italian victims and had led the Italian government temporarily to ban emigration to that country." Jones, Immigration, p. 200.

11. 1870 Census, Industry and Wealth, pp. 832–33.

all) against their religion or background. Or it could involve a combination of all these.[12] A second reason was the earnest desire of some immigrants to stay away from the land, associated in their minds with lean living, or actual starvation, of the old country. (These primary tendencies, inevitably, had their exceptions. A large share of the Norwegians, Swedes, and even Germans headed straight for the Midwest.[13] And there they made highly successful careers in farming. Indeed, these were just the settlers Jim Hill sought out in the 1880s and 1890s for his Great Northern Railway line.)

"The steamers dumped their steerage passengers at the foot of Broadway. The commonest sight in the financial district [in 1910–14] was a convoy of greenhorns dressed in strange and usually tattered foreign clothes, carrying their possessions in bags and bundles, and gaping at the skyscrapers."[14] Once the immigrants had passed through this strange gauntlet, where Wall Street, the Waldorf's Peacock Alley, and Churchill's were the great landmarks, what did they do?

In percentage terms far fewer immigrants worked as common laborers than native Americans throughout much of the nineteenth century. For few were farm laborers. They constituted 22 percent of all workers, but a far greater percentage of certain crafts, and domestic service, a far smaller percentage of professional occupations (as shown in Table 26.2).

Similar differences appear in the records down to 1930. (After the national socialists came to power in Germany of the 1930s, immigrants were much more often professionals and craftsmen.)

Of the many changes that immigration made in the U.S. economy, three may be noted for special attention. The first was the effect of the heavy increase in labor supply on production and income. When the immigration flow was cut off in 1914 (first by the German submarines, then by legislation) wages rose markedly, as shown in Table 26.3. In the 15 years after 1914, workers' incomes rose as much as they had over the prior half-century. No speedup in entrepreneurial ingenuity or productive energies of workers was occurring at that dramatic rate. Congress, by shutting off the flow of workers from Europe, had helped push up workers' wages. (That outcome helped validate decades of union opposition to immigration even though many union leaders were themselves immigrants.)

---

12. Some writers apparently believe that employers discriminated in favor of immigrants. Thus Jay Mandle in "The Southern Plantation Economy After the Civil War," *Marxist Perspectives,* states: "In the North employer discrimination, favoring immigrants from Europe rather than Southern blacks, tended to shut this market off as a potential escape from plantation labor" (p. 19).

13. Milwaukee once had six newspapers published in German.

14. Will Irwin, *The Making of a Reporter* (1942), p. 119.

TABLE 26.2
IMMIGRANTS
AS PERCENTAGE OF
WORKERS IN SELECTED
OCCUPATIONS

All occupations	22
Bakers	60
Blacksmiths	28
Shoemakers	37
Brewers	76
Butchers	47
Cabinet makers	41
Tailors & furriers	41
Domestics	25
Lawyers	6
Physicians	10
Teachers	8

Source: 1870 Census, *The Statistics of the Population of the United States* (1871).

TABLE 26.3
AVERAGE EARNINGS OF
NONFARM WORKERS
(IN 1914 DOLLARS)

1860	457
1914	696
1929	898

Source: Computed from Lebergott, *Manpower,* pp. 428, 524.

The second change derived from the first. For many decades prior to 1914 open immigration kept down the price of labor, thereby slowing the substitution of capital for labor. After 1914, then, mechanization should have speeded up. And so it did, throughout manufacturing. Having risen about 15 percent in most prior decades, output per man-hour actually jumped by 72 percent from 1919 to 1929.[15]

A third change derives from the interaction between immigrant attitudes and the structure of the society into which the immigrants came. That society

15. U.S. Department of Commerce, *Long Term Economic Growth, 1860–1970* (1974), pp. 210–11.

was less class-ridden than most European and Asiatic societies of the time, and its labor market controlled less by law and tradition. As a result, the children of the immigrants moved up the class ladder faster than in Europe. (Which, of course, was one reason why their parents had moved in the first place. Their characteristic hope appeared in a host of letters and diaries: "To give the children a chance.")[16]

An early indication of the mobility rate for the children appears in the 1910 Census, taken just at the peak of immigration to the United States. E. P. Hutchinson took the proportion of foreign-born in the labor force as 100 percent, then computed the proportions for each occupation. Those occupations with relatively few foreign-born have ratios of 62 percent, 47 percent, and so on while those with relatively many have 173 percent, 208 percent, and so on. As shown in Table 26.4, the change in ratios from the first generation (the foreign-born) to the second (the foreign stock) is striking. Between the first generation and the second, significant increases occurred in the highest income occupations, and decreases in the lowest income occupations. Study of the full list of occupations shows the same homogenizing tendency. The first generation was notably absent from high status occupations and concentrated in low status ones. The second generation was far more evenly represented in all occupations. The foreign-born in 1900 made up 3.5 percent of professional occupations, but 10.5 percent of those in labor and service. By 1970 the proportions for their descendants, the foreign stock, were no longer so dissimilar: they composed 16 percent of professional and 13 percent of labor and service.[17] Such mobility between generations led many European observers to describe the United States as a "melting pot," for it contrasts so sharply with the persistence of class lines in Europe, Asia, and Africa over decades, even centuries.

Mass immigration ended in the 1910s. Immigrants then began to come from a sharply different group. Refugees from nazism and fascism in the 1930s concentrated in strikingly different occupations. So did those later, fleeing communism in Cambodia, Vietnam, China, Cuba, Russia, and dictatorship in Jamaica. The foreign-born immigrants of 1970 far more frequently had professional skills than did native whites. For example, the professional ratio for Chinese and Japanese immigrants was about twice that for native whites. Virtually all other nationalities also exceeded the ratio for native whites.[18]

16. They "tore themselves loose from an environment that was life itself—they served as drudges; and, finally, they were content if their children reaped the blessings that they had sought for themselves." Marcus Hansen, *The Immigrant in American History* (1948), p. 4.

17. 61st Cong. 3d sess, S.D. 747, U.S. Immigration Commission, *Reports*, pp. 780, 798; 1970 Census, *National Origins and Language*, Table 13.

18. *National Origins and Language*, Table 13. Needless to say, Russian Jews who were engineers drove taxis on their arrival, Vietnamese lawyers became cooks, etc.

TABLE 26.4
OCCUPATIONAL CONCENTRATION IN 1910
(OVERALL CONCENTRATION = 100)

	Foreign born	Foreign stock
All occupations	100	100
Accountants	62	131
Engineers	47	104
Lawyers	25	102
Physicians and dentists	45	86
Teachers	39	75
Domestics	173	87
Charwomen, porters	208	104
Janitors	168	102
Construction laborers	169	84
Transport laborers	224	58

Source: E. P. Hutchinson, *Immigrants and Their Children, 1850–1950* (1956), Table 39.

Always among the immigrants were those who came to the United States to make enough in a summer's work, or several year's work, for a dowry or a small farm in their native country. They accounted for a steady return flow. How many other immigrants were disillusioned returnees is difficult to determine. It certainly cannot be done on the basis of anecdotes, whether of great success or failure. Descriptions of slums in New York and Pennsylvania coal towns can all be matched with even more horrifying anecdotes of life in Calabria or Bohemia or Sheffield. It was the overall difference that mattered to the immigrants. A distant measurement of actual behavior is suggested by later data on the number of Americans who renounced their nationality and left the nation to reside in other lands during the 1960s and 1970s. Their number came to less than 5,000 persons a year—in a population of over 200,000,000.[19] Fairly persuasive evidence shows workers fleeing to the United States from many other nations, at the risk of their lives, and a continuous flow of men and women as illegal immigrants into the United States for half a century after legal immigration to the United States was drastically limited in the early 1920s.

19. Data for all persons expatriated ran about 5,000 a year in the 1950s. Despite the draft and the war in Vietnam it fell to 2,000 to 3,000 throughout the 1960s and 1970s. Cf. Table 51 in U.S. Immigration and Naturalization Services's *Annual Report* for 1962 and 1976, and unpublished material kindly provided by the State Department.

Science and the spirit of emulation, those are the forces
which have made us what we are.

—E. M. FORSTER
"The Other Side of the Hedge"

There are three roads to ruin, said the great Rothschild:
gaming, women, and . . . engineers. The first two are by
far the most agreeable . . . but the last is the most certain.

—DETOEUF

27

Technology and Innovation

A Deep Thinker, summing up the decade of the 1970s, asked:

What will happen to the long-held notion of progress in the American character? In the 19th century Alexis de Tocqueville remarked on the American
belief in 'indefinite perfectibility.' When he asked an American sailor why
American ships were not better made 'he answered offhand that the art of
navigation was making such quick progress that even the best of boats
would be almost useless if it lasted more than a few years'—one of the earliest affirmations of planned obsolescence.[1]

Who "planned" such obsolescence? What did the newer technology offer
beyond mere novelty? One contribution alone could explain why steamships
began to replace sailing vessels in de Tocqueville's time, then superseded
them after the Civil War. Steamships were speedier, giving cholera and
yellow fever less time to spread than did the longer sailing voyages. As a result deaths on steamships (from Europe in 1867–72) averaged only one-tenth
the rate on sailing vessels.[2]

---

1. Richard Eder, "Whatever Happened to the Idea of Progress?" *New York Times*, December
30, 1979.
2. 43d Cong., 1st sess., S.D. 23, *Letter from the Secretary of the Treasury . . . on Steerage-Im-
migrants* (1874), p. 46.

A second reason for "planned" obsolescence was the value of time. It took 31 days to travel from New York to New Orleans by sailing vessel but only 8 days by steamship.[3] True, a member of the nobility traveling for recreation might well enjoy the longer voyage. But an ordinary worker or farmer thereby lost an additional 23 days—days during which he earned no income. And days during which he also had to pay for food aboard ship. Planning for his own advantage, the faithless traveler increasingly turned from sailing ships to faster vessels. It was he who forced the obsolescence of sailing ships, and then each succeeding generation of steamships. He thereby guaranteed that the longer any vessel lasted the more surely it would fail to make money in its later years.

The margin of speed increased decade after decade, as shown in Table 27.1. A similar result appeared for machines, railroad tracks, bridges. There was, however, nothing peculiarly American about all this. Or at least not about the investment principle at work. Thus a British journal pointed out the principle in 1841: Americans built short-lived wooden bridges; the English built permanent stone bridges. But the capital that Americans saved by using cheaper materials could be invested (in, say, government securities) and the interest thus earned be used to replace the bridge. This thereby provided a new bridge at regular intervals, at no additional cost.[4] No less vital, Americans thus became able to adopt any advances in bridge safety and convenience discovered in the interim. And all for no more than the cost of the single long-lasting stone bridge.

Central to all this change, obviously, was the rate at which inventors, engineers, and entrepreneurs created new and more attractive products. The U.S. record suggests that indeed "progress was the great staple of the country." Traditions, class lines, embedded history—all these dominated technology in the United States far less than they did in those nations from which the immigrants came. Few Americans asked the status or heritage of anyone who proposed a new procedure, a new product. They asked, rather: will it work? That pragmatic attitude led to a persistent development of better items—from an apple corer to save work for the housewife, to a compound engine that drove steamships faster.

As a national market was created after the Civil War by the new rail links, the opportunity for selling such new items expanded. One of the best

---

3. Edward Smith, *Travels in Texas* (1849), p. 9. The steamer charged $60; the sailing vessel, $50.

4. *Athenaeum* (December 25, 1841), p. 987. The example given estimates a £2000 differences in costs. That yielded a further £6000 in interest at the end of 20 years—thus enabling the regular replacement of the entire wooden bridge indefinitely.

TABLE 27.1
TRAVEL TIME FROM NEW YORK
TO LONDON (IN DAYS)

1775	35
1818–27 (packet ship)	24
1850 (Clipper ship)	14
1901	8

Source: 1775: We average times indicated by the departure and arrival
dates in Walpole's letters. *Horace Walpole's Correspondence with Sir Horace
Mann,* W. S. Lewis, ed. VIII
(1970): 97, 119, 132, 204, 273, 331.
405, 410.

1818–27: Robert G. Albion,
Square Riggers on Schedule (1938), p.
322.

1850: 1880 Census, *Shipbuilding
Industry,* p. 74.

1901: 57th Cong., 1st sess.,
H.D. 14, *Annual Report of the Commissioner of Navigation* (1901), p. 499.

indexes of the startling growth in new products is the number of patents
granted, shown in Table 27.2.

In the decades after the Civil War technology was advanced by two quite
different groups. The first consisted of unskilled amateurs who experimented
in simple ways. Locomotive engineers used coal in their engines instead of the
traditional cord wood. They discovered that coal did as good a job, at one
third the cost.[5] In time other amateurs discovered that nature had not laid
minerals down uniformly: some coals proved better than others. Testing
began to discover which ones gave the best value. In 1869 the owners of San
Francisco's water works experimented for years, eventually finding that a ton
of Australian coal generated 50 percent more steam than a ton of Pittsburgh
coal, 28 percent more than a ton of Seattle coal.[6]

Such study and amateur experimentation may well have proved the most
fundamental force in the U.S. productive advance. But it was supplemented
by a newer force. The number of trained engineers, scientists, and tech-
nologists began to increase largely, as their worth became evident. New tech-

5. 34th Cong., 1st sess., H.R. 34, *Railroads in the Territories* (1856), pp. 23–24.
6. W. A. Goodyear, *The Coal Mines of the Western Coast of the United States* (1877), pp. 142–55.

TABLE 27.2
PATENTS ISSUED
PER DECADE (000)

1790–1860	5
1860–1870	72
1870–1880	125
1880–1890	195
1890–1900	222

Source: 1900 Census, vol.
X, Manufactures, p. 757.

nological institutes began to turn them out, far faster than the total labor force increased (Table 27.3).

Engineers had been hired for decades, in small numbers. Chemists had achieved notoriety in the United States as early as Liebig's work on fertilizers. But the new role of science probably began only in 1863, when Andrew Carnegie hired the first chemist to work in the U.S. iron and steel industry. From that beginning there developed a mountain range of knowledge, enabling industry to discover which ores, materials, could be worked most effectively.

In due time engineers went on to consider perhaps the most important and most refractory production input: human labor. Frederick Taylor, a Midvale Steel engineer specializing in raw materials, eventually asked the question: Is human work subject to the same physical laws as the material world? In time he developed what he termed, with little regard to public relations, "the science of shoveling." His vision was one in which workers became "efficient," the worker then getting a higher income while doing less exhausting work, and yielding his employer more output and more profits. Taylor's "scientific management" made its way because it did, indeed, yield both types of result. But it likewise generated a burning sense of outrage among those who felt that man was not to be confounded with material nature, and that to make a profit from human labor was essentially immoral.

New scientific techniques were applied in a variety of forms. One tactic to advance efficiency applied new knowledge more or less directly. Virtually no additional inputs were used, whether of land, labor, or capital. Jacob Reese described how blast furnaces increased their transformation of pig iron from 36 tons in 1868 to 75–100 tons by 1878. They did so "simply by adjusting the internal lines, increasing the temperature and volume of blast, according to scientific deductions but recently determined."[7] Making virtually no

7. National Export Convention, Proceedings of the National Convention of the United States Export Trade, held in Talmadge Hall, Washington, D.C., February 19 and 20, 1878 (1878), p. 52. Ten years previously it took 2½ hours of puddling to convert 500 pounds of pig to wrought iron; it "now" took only 20 minutes to convert 8 tons, and at half the labor cost. Similar results for a Scandinavian plant were later baptized "the Horndahl Effect" by economist Kenneth Arrow.

TABLE 27.3

ENGINEERS AND CHEMISTS IN THE
LABOR FORCE (1860 = 100)

	Total Labor Force	Engineers	Chemists
1860	100	100	100
1870	116	219	124
1880	157	245	315
1890	210	522	721
1900	262	803	1,422
1910	337	1,432	2,531

Source: Labor force: Lebergott, Manpower, p. 510. Engineers, chemists: data derived from Population Census reports.

changes in either capital or labor inputs, the "adjustments" cut the cost of production by a dazzling fifty percent or more.

Typically, however, technological advance was embodied in new products. These ranged from technically trivial items to ones requiring enormous feats of scientific and engineering skill. Their common denominator was that they cut costs. Changes in ocean shipping exemplify the range. For shipping wheat to Europe in the 1870s barrels were used. By the 1880s sacks had been substituted. The standard marine engine was replaced by the compound engine in the same decade. To develop the compound engine was a highly complex task. But it so expanded cargo space that a vessel could carry 2,200 tons of freight (and only 800 tons of coal for fuel) instead of 800 tons of freight (and 2,200 of coal). The change to sacks required very little production planning, and less engineering. Yet the simple substitution of sacks for barrels to transport wheat from Nebraska to Liverpool saved $25 for every $100 saved by switching to the new engine.[8]

Costs and expected profitability together determine the commercial wisdom of adopting any innovation. The innovation may be "socially" necessary. If so, the government, representative of that society, will have to make that decision. The investors in any firm have another goal: to increase the present value of the firm as far as possible. Doing so may interrupt the easy functioning of a given firm, may even destroy substantial investments recently made. Yet a firm serving the purposes of its stockholders will still go through that turmoil, will junk that investment, if the newer technology promises still

8. Cf. David A. Wells, Recent Economic Changes (1890), pp. 37, 168.

TABLE 27.4

INVESTMENT COST TRENDS,

1860–1900 (1860 = 100)

	Annual earnings of nonfarm workers	Average value of land per acre
1860	100	100
1871	103	117
1900	133	121

Source: Earnings: Lebergott, Manpower, p. 528. Land: Historical Statistics . . . to 1970, p. 457.

greater profits on its investment. The chase between costs of novelty and expected profitability dominates these decisions.

Central to the post-Civil War investment booms—in water supply systems, factory construction, railroad building, electric power plants—was the pervasive impact of a marked decline in costs. What were the elements of this change? Wage rates and land prices actually rose, as shown in Table 27.4. How is it possible, then, to say that costs fell? The answer turns on the declining cost of the third major input: capital. Its two major components were forgone interest (on the money locked up in machine or building) and depreciation (representing the using up of the machine over its useful life), both shown in Table 27.5. What happened to these two components of capital cost?

Both costs fell, heavily. We have already noted the reasons why interest rates declined: Savings (via insurance companies, savings banks) increased. Capital markets improved. Risk declined once the Civil War had demonstrated that the nation would not be split apart. Commercial credit agencies (Dun and Bradstreet) arose. Commercial information flashed across the nation (by telegraph) at incredible speed. Equipment prices also declined, thanks to innovations by the machine tool industry, blacksmiths, and makers of farm machinery and locomotives.

The declining user cost of capital in the face of rising labor and land costs induced producers to substitute machinery for direct labor. It also permitted sharp increases in the profitable use of longer lived capital. (The longer the life of a capital investment, the more decisive are interest costs in the decision to invest or not.)

Nations awash in political instability—Lebanon, Iran, Uganda, even today's Turkey—devote only a small proportion of GNP to long-lived capital investment. They are more apt to put capital into the inventory of street sellers, where returns are almost immediate—watches, cigarettes, transistor radios. Railroad lines, roads, factories will not pay off for years.

TABLE 27.5

User Cost of Capital, 1860–1900 (indexes)

Interest rates (index of railroad bond yields)		Depreciation of equipment (Producers durable equipment price index)	
1860	100	1869	100
1900	45	1900	55

Source: Interest rates: *Historical Statistics . . . to 1970*, p. 1,003. Depreciation of equipment: William H. Shaw, *Value of Commodity Output Since 1869* (1947), p. 294.

Until the Civil War the bulk of U.S. private investment was concentrated in land clearing, animals, flour mills, ships, farm machinery—all short lived. Indeed, the machinery and buildings of the first great growth factory industry, textiles, had only a 10-year life.[9] But the post-Civil War industrial era in the United States was marked by huge investments in very long-lived capital: Steel rails, locomotives, and freight cars, which replaced the shorter lived iron rails and locomotives of the first uncertain railroads;[10] street railways, whose normal life was about 24 years;[11] electric production and distribution, investments whose normal life (and pay-out period) was 50 years;[12] public investments in roads and water supply, again very long-lived investments of 25 and 50 years;[13] and subways, with a 100-year life.[14]

But new technology was rarely adopted as soon as it was created. The costs of changing from the older ways were rarely trivial. It took time before the expected benefits overcame the old. Electricity offered as good an example as any of the obstacles to the diffusion of new products. Electric motors had been developed in Italy back in the 1830s. Arc lights had come into use in the 1870s. Thomas Edison produced the first incandescent electric light in 1883. Yet by 1900 the proportion of American homes with electricity was still

9. Daniel Buffinton, David Anthony, and Nathaniel Burden in McLane Report, *Documents Relative to the Manufactures in the United States* I (1833):70, 72, 73. Cf. also pp. 138, 146, 150, which suggest still shorter lives, but which include insurance, etc. Bezaleel Taft on p. 80 estimates 4 percent for depreciation exclusive of wear and tear, and repairs.

10. Albert Fishlow, *American Railroads and the Transformation of the Antebellum Economy* (1965), pp. 398, 400. Iron rails lasted for perhaps 14 years, steel for 20 years—allowing for salvage value in both instances.

11. Melville Ulmer, *Capital in Transportation: Communications and Public Utilities* (1960), p. 342.

12. Raymond Goldsmith, *A Study of Saving* I (1955):602.

13. Ibid., p. 1052.

14. Ulmer, *Capital*, p. 422.

TABLE 27.6
EXPANDING MARKETS FOR ELECTRICITY

	Percent of U.S. homes with electricity	Percent of U.S. factory power produced by electricity
1899	3	4
1909	15	19
1919	35	50
1929	68	78

Source: Stanley Lebergott, *The American Economy* (1976), p. 280. Richard DuBoff, "Electrification and Capital Productivity," *The Review of Economics and Statistics* (November 1969), p. 427.

less than 5 percent. So was the proportion of power in American factories produced by electricity. Indeed, a quarter of a century after Edison's invention, only 15 percent of American families had electricity, as shown in Table 27.6.

Home owners hesitated to introduce the still developing, and potentially dangerous, new electric light. The gas companies spread the word about the dangers of this new competitor, creating fears similar to today's fears of explosions from nuclear power plants. (Gas companies made a particular point of the fact that New York State had recently instituted "the electric chair" for death sentences.) To meet such opposition the electric power companies in the 1910s staged "electrical circuses." There the public saw the new electrical lights, heaters, stoves, and coffeepots. Perhaps more persuasively, the companies offered a flat rate schedule in the early years. Without meters the new users could use all they wanted at no extra charge. They became accustomed to using more bulbs, trying new appliances. Their lighted homes were beacons at night, advertising the new utility.

In time the cost of both electricity and electric bulbs fell (Table 27.7). Such price declines produced their usual effect. More and more people came to rely on electricity. As they did, the production runs for electric bulbs, fixtures, and more grew still longer; costs and prices fell steadily. All of which initiated further acceptance.

Industry, however, was blocked by a much more potent deterrent. When a practical electric power supply appeared (in the 1890s), existing factories already had investments in power systems. For some it was the Lowell ponds, mill dam, water wheel, and gearing. For others it was the steam engine, belts, and shafting. Once the new and far better source of power was introduced, these ancient systems became largely obsolete. They then could be sold for not much more than junk. But what counted was expected profitabil-

TABLE 27.7

ELECTRICITY COSTS, 1880–1970

Year	Coal (pounds)	Central station total cost (cents)	Residential charge (cents)	Watts consumed per candle power	Incandescent Lamp		
					Life	Price (dollars)	Lumens
	(per kilowatt hour)				(hours)	(60-watt)	
1880[a]	30						
1883	10	3.1	24	6.5	550		
1890	8	2.4	20	3			
1900	5	1.7	16				
1910	4	1.5	9			$1.75	480
1920	3	1.2	7			0.40	580
1930	1.6	0.8	6.0	1	2,000+		
1940	1.3		3.8				
1950	1.2		2.9				
1960	0.9		2.5			0.26	840
1970	0.9		2.1			0.27	855

[a]Arc lighting.

Source: Coal and Central station total cost: 1883–1929: George Orrok, "Central Stations," Mechanical Engineering (April 1930), pp. 330–31. 1930–1970: Historical Statistics . . . to 1970, p. 826. 1880: Abram Foster, The Coming of the Electrical Age ot the United States (1969), p. 123.

Residential charge: Census, Historical Statistics, p. 827. 1902 data used for 1900, and 1912 for 1910.

Watts consumed and Incandescent lamp life: Orrok, "Central Stations," p. 333, and The Coming, Foster, p. 103.

Incandescent lamp price and lumens: James Bright, Automation and Management (1958), p. 30. 1908 data are used for 1910. For 1960 and 1970: unpublished data kindly provided by G. E.

ity of the new versus the old. And by a high irony, correct cost accounting indicated that it would cost the firm nothing in depreciation or interest to keep on using the obsolete power sources. True, a new power system could cut costs of operation. But to install one required charging interest for the money thus invested, and depreciation. Comparing the two streams of net returns, most firms continued to use the older technology. Indeed, they did so until breakdowns in the older power system, and/or mounting repair costs, eventually moved them on to electric power.[15]

15. The process was outlined in a classical study by W. E. G. Salter, Productivity and Technical Change (1960), chap. IV. Of course the owners of the obsolete investments had sustained a loss, once and for all. But they, or their successors, then still could choose to use, or not use, the new reduced price capital.

Was this sluggishness in adoption restricted to power generation? Or to the 1890s? A look at major technical innovations in manufacturing reveals the same process in many industries and in many decades. A plethora of new machine technologies became available in the decades after the Civil War. Had they instantly replaced the older hand methods, labor requirements per unit of factory output would have fallen by 82 percent. But requirements actually fell only 31 percent.[16] The new, the "best practice," technology was introduced first in newly built factories, then in some existing ones. The best-practice merchant blast furnace in 1911 turned out far more pig iron per man-hour than any other plant. The iron industry as a whole did not reach that level until about 1929. But by that time the new best practice plant was turning out nearly twice as much per man-hour as the industry as a whole (or even the one-time leader).[17] It generally took years for a novelty to penetrate a significant portion of the industry. By that time, of course, a newer technology had appeared, ready to compete in its turn. The occasional exception showed, by contrast, that it was indeed an exception. Perhaps the most famous was Andrew Carnegie's decision to scrap a brand new steel plant. By the time the plant had been built a still newer technology had appeared. Carnegie decided that it paid to scrap the new plant and start all over.[18] He followed Jevons' rule on sunk costs: bygones are bygones.

The new electrical era was the product of four separate revolutions. Any of them would have broken up the world of the nineteenth century. Together they destroyed it beyond recognition.

The first revolution was electrical power's replacement of water and steam power. In an era when we are rehabilitating old watermills and developing new windmills, one may well ask why electrical motors dislodged water power quite so overwhelmingly. Several factors conspired to that end.

In the first place, water power was neither steady nor reliable. In winter the windmills often froze up. Meanwhile their workers earned no wages, and capital investment earned no profits. In the spring freshets would flood through the mill race, damaging the water wheels and forcing the mill out of

16. Cf. the writer's estimates in Lance Davis et al., *American Economic Growth, An Economist's History of the United States* (1972), pp. 209–10.

17. U.S. Bureau of Labor Statistics, Bulletin 474, *Productivity of Labor in Merchant Blast Furnaces* (1929), pp. 27, 104–5. For over 3,000 years glass bottles were blown by human beings. The automatic machine of Michael Owens, introduced in 1904, produced over 100 times as many bottles per man-hour. But semi-automatic machines invented in the 1880s continued to be used well into the twentieth century. Cf. U.S. Bureau of Labor Statistics, Bulletin 441, *Productivity of Labor in the Glass Industry* (1927), pp. 1–8, 35.

18. The principle was, of course, the same in both general practice and in the exception: compare the two streams of expected costs and returns, allowing for the sales value of each set of assets at the decision point. The Carnegie decision is reported in Jonathan Hughes, *The Vital Few* (1973), pp. 259–60.

operation. In summer occasional droughts reduced the water power to a trickle. To prevent these mishaps required inordinately great investments, such as the Lowell mills' lengthy systems of canals and huge dams to impound a steady supply of water. (Had all New England factories built such reliable dams they would have flooded half the region.) Electric power needed only coal. That could be stocked in yards, quietly available in all weather, or it could be trundled in by trains quite regularly.

In the second place, electric power was cheaper in multiple ways. To operate an electric motor cost only one-fifth as much as to operate a steam engine.[19] Typically, one huge steam engine generated power, which was then transmitted by a maze of belting to individual machines throughout the factory. On average, two-thirds of the power so generated was wasted by friction in transmission.[20] When belting transmitted power from a central steam unit, "the whole plant must be run if a single man in the farthest end of the shop wishes to drill a half inch hole."[21] And whenever the main transmission belt had to be tightened the entire factory came to a halt. Such a concentrated waste of energy disappeared when individual electric motors were developed, attached to individual machines. Factories could be constructed at less expense once their walls did not have to stand up under the "strains of shafting and belting."[22] Fires were significantly reduced—and thereby fire insurance costs. Under the old system a single water wheel provided all power. The main transmission belt took power from that wheel, moved it to other transmission belts. The succession of belts rose from stream level up through the various factory floors. Sparks were thereby carried from the generator, or chafing belts, from one floor to another. When electric motors substituted for this incredible forest of wheels and belts, fires decreased markedly. Insurance rates fell. And costs thereby fell.

The second revolution was of city streets. In 1900 most cities had only occasional lighting. Some had areas lit by oil and gas lamps. But streets all over the nation now began to be lighted by electricity. First came the arc lights, dazzling residents in areas that had been dark at night for decades. These were soon replaced by incandescent lights. Cost was the incentive. Edison's first plant used only one-third as much coal to produce each kilowatt of electricity as the arc-lighting plants did.[23] That cost advantage, passed

19. Abram Foster, *The Coming of the Electrical Age to the United States* (1979), p. 295.

20. H. Lufkin, "The Economics of Electric Power," *Cassier's Magazine* (March 1894), p. 377–78.

21. E. H. Mullin, "Electric Power in the Machine Shop," *Cassier's Magazine* (January 1898), p. 244.

22. Lufkin, "The Economics," p. 369. The development of small motors made it possible to develop smaller central generating facilities, thereby reducing capital investment and costs. Cf. Richard DuBoff, "The Introduction of Electric Power in American Manufacturing," *Economic History Review* (December 1967).

23. Foster, *The Coming*, p. 123.

along in rate reductions, encouraged cities all over the nation to put in street lights. Some built their own plants and retained them for the next century. Others sold franchises to new corporations. These new beacons, of course, advertised the wonders of electric light to business and householders.

The third revolution took place in the home. It was not that any cost advantage of electricity over gas and kerosene for illumination induced householders to change rapidly: for Edison had priced electricity to equal the cost of gas (for equivalent illumination).[24] Moreover, the impediments were greater in households than in factories. That in 1881 William Vanderbilt's new New York City home required some five tons of copper indicates how primitive, and how expensive, the early installations were.[25] Moreover, bulbs often had to be taped to an existing gas fixture (or tied on with string). Wires (some of which were bare copper) were attached to wooden knobs, which served as insulators. The lights were usually attached in series: when one light on the line burned out, all the others promptly did the same.[26]

The fourth revolution changed workers' lives. Edison was committed to direct current. This meant that his Pearl Street station in lower Manhattan could deliver power no more than ten miles away. Factories were thus still tied to the source of power, though not as closely as they once were. After the industry adopted Westinghouse's alternating current, however, the range of transmission increased vastly. The improvement in conditions of work proved significant. As Charles Barnard wrote in 1889:

> The electric motor will produce as great a change as ever was seen before, because it is now possible to erect the motive power plant in one place, the manufacturing plant is an entirely separate one. . . . By our present system, the factory hands, men, women and little children must huddle together in a physical or moral swamp—near a canal or a noisy railroad yard in an unhealthy . . . district—in order to be near the motive power on which their work and wages depend. It is the same with the turbine. It must stand at the foot of its waterfall. . . . Perhaps not a thousand yards away cheap, dry, land is idle, simply because we have no mechanical means of transmitting power to such a distance. . . . Today we find sewing women crowded into a hot, stuffy room, close to the noise, smell, dust and terrible heat of some little steam engine at one end of the room.[27]

Power lines, alternating current, and the electric sewing machine eventually improved that world.

24. Ibid., p. 182.
25. Ibid., p. 108.
26. Ibid., pp. 103, 108.
27. Charles Barnard, "Something Electricity is Doing," in A. R. Foote, *Economic Value of Electric Light and Power* (1889), pp. 103–5.

The houses and stores seemed to have been set up in contemptuous haste, to provide shelter for the drab and unpleasant.
—SHIRLEY JACKSON, *We Have Always Lived in the Castle*

There have been civilizations without cities. But what about cities without civilizations? An inhuman thing, if possible, to have so many people together who begat nothing on one another.
—SAUL BELLOW, *The Adventures of Augie March*

28

Urban Growth

ARE cities inevitable? Desirable? Not necessarily. Jefferson believed that "those who labour in the earth are the chosen people of God."[1] A century later the Interstate Commerce Commission began its work of transport regulation by informing the nation that "in great cities great social and political evils always concentrate." One of the founders of American sociology held that "the extreme concentration of population at centers has . . . deplorable effects upon . . . health, intelligence and morals."[2] The farm bloc, potent in Congress for many decades, persistently emphasized the Jeffersonian ideal.

Other nations have also tried to hold on to, or return to, their ancient rural origins. Residents of Peking and Shanghai were dispersed to the countryside in the 1950s because socialist virtue was to be found there. Cambodia's Khmer Rouge forced a million people out of the sinful, and commercial, cities into the natural countryside—where they died. Cuba has

---

1. "If ever he had a chosen people," quoted Gilbert Fite in *American Farmers, The New Minority* (1981), p. 1. "The larger the cities . . . the more difficult it is to bring these evils under legal or moral restraints," in Interstate Commerce Commission, *First Annual Report* (1888).

2. *Sociological Theory and Social Research, Being Selected Papers of Charles Horton Cooley* (1969), pp. 65, 97. He added: "I share the common opinion that the concentration of population and wealth tends to excess."

sent thousands of students and other urban residents into rural areas for pro-longed periods of contact with pure nature, pure work, and pure people.[3] Russia has restricted housing construction in Moscow as a direct and effective way of limiting the inflow from the countryside. Other European socialist na-tions have likewise worked to restrain urban growth.[4] Conversely, nations that have allowed people to flock in from the countryside without providing "appropriate" housing, public services, and jobs have been persistently criticized for their "urban slums."[5]

Cities—from Kampala to Juneau—have steadily grown. Some 20 per-cent of the U.S. population lived in cities in 1860. By 1900 that figure had risen to 38 percent; and, by 1980, to 74 percent.[6] Cities have expanded despite government policy makers, specialists in nature and ecology, and a host of moralists around the world. Their growth must therefore have been driven by fairly powerful forces. These forces do not include high birth rates in cities. For city birth rates have been well below rural rates, below the level needed merely to regenerate their population from one generation to the next.

U.S. cities grew rather because of the in-migration of farm folk—Ameri-can and European. These immigrants persistently chose "A Hazard of New Fortunes" (in the words of William Dean Howells). Ex-farm boys included Jay Gould, the tanner's boy from upstate New York who rose with the Erie railroad to financial notoriety; Cyrus McCormick, the Virginian who estab-lished Chicago's greater post-Civil War industry, farm machinery; George Pullman; Henry Ford; and a hundred other leaders. Indeed, apart from a handful of city boys (J. P. Morgan, of Hartford; John D. Rockefeller, of Cleveland) the best-known industrial and legislative leaders between the Civil War and World War I came from farms or small villages.

What drew these immigrants to the cities? State or federal regulations? Hardly. A conspiracy of producers who sought cheap labor? Southern planters did insist that their loss of black labor to the North evidenced such a conspiracy. During World War I their claims became particularly strident. But the facts all point to voluntary out-migration. Did the immigrants senselessly fail to recognize that the cost of living was higher in the city, the

---

3. Fidel Castro declared: "The city is the cemetery of revolutionaries." While Regis Debray, theorist for Cuban revolt, urged "Abandon the city and go to the mountains." Both quoted in Melvin Lasky, *Utopia and Revolution* (1976), pp. 142–43.

4. Cf. Gur Ofer in Alan Brown and Egon Neuberger, *Internal Migration, A Comparative Per-spective* (1977), chap. 16.

5. The forthright solutions of the Cambodians have not found general acceptance. But neither have older models. Venice required 25 years' residence for full citizenship in the four-teenth century. In Genoa the homeless poor sold themselves as galley slaves. Adriatic peasants came down from the mountains to live in holes in the earth. Cf. Fernand Braudel, *Capitalism and Material Life* (1973), pp. 205, 403.

6. *Historical Statistics . . . to 1970*, pp. 11–12, *Statistical Abstract, 1982*, p. 15.

air dirtier, the slums deeper, the people less honest, sin more widespread, political machines more devious? Edmund Burke once wrote that it was difficult to "indict an entire nation." It is no less difficult to believe that millions of average people were so stupid, and that only later critics recognized such obvious facts.

What, then, were the reasons for migration? Much the same as those Seneca used to describe Rome, queen city of the ancient world: "Behold this concourse of men, for whom the houses of huge Rome scarcely suffice. . . . From their towns and colonies . . . have they flocked. Some have been brought by ambition, some by the desire for the higher studies [or] by the public spectacles . . . some have presented their beauty for sale, some their eloquence . . . and every class has swarmed into the city that offers high prizes for both virtues and vices."[7]

The freedom of worship offered by the city has long been known. To be a Muggletonian in the seventeenth century (or a Jehovah's Witness or Hare Krishna today) was surely easier under urban than rural conditions. The city also proffered the unmarried a wide choice of mates; and, to the married, a wide range of schooling for their children. The reach of opportunity presented to the consumer was even more noteworthy. Instead of being bound to a rural monopolist—whether doctor, grocer or carpenter—he found a host of services and tradesmen available.

Such advantages proved compelling attractions to the worker—who was believer, parent, and consumer as well as worker. But the city's attractions were multiplied many times over in the labor markets. Corporation president or janitor, the city worker benefitted richly from his wider choice of potential employers. The Arabian slave in our day (as the Scots slave in Boswell's) must serve a single employer. And the mutinous, bloody history of labor in mining towns and on shipboard reflects how workers reacted when—though free—freedom to quit one job and take another was restricted.

By contrast, the city offered freedom after feudalism—chiefly because it offered so great a host of employers. Given a nickel for trolley fare in 1900, a Chicago worker could reach anyone of almost 48,000 different employers.[8] Even an attempted employer cartel could not keep him out of work. Furthermore, the city offered immigrants many employers, some of whom spoke his own language, and who competed for workers' skills much as workers competed for jobs. By contrast, in downstate Illinois the same nickel, plus a walk, gave a worker access to at most a dozen employers during the course of a day.

But there were related reasons for the great influx to the cities. These lay on the demand side of labor. The innovations associated with electricity

7. John Basore (trans.) Seneca, *De Consolatione ad Helviam, Moral Essays* (1932), p. 429.
8. Data in the 1900 Census, *Manufactures*, part 1, p. 249; *Occupations*, pp. 516–17 indicates that count for manufacturing, hand trades, and trade alone.

ended the value of the ancient locations where industry had clustered. They created the modern urban network. No longer did factories have to locate along the rivers because they drew their power sources from the final river fall to the ocean. Hence, the historic manufacturing cities—Lowell, Lawrence, Naugatuck, Augusta—all began to lose their lead in the 1880s. And cities near the coal deposits—such as Pittsburgh—did well. In time, the older cities began to feel the competition of cities that drew electric power from distant sources. Buffalo began to get its power from Niagara Falls; Detroit, from huge new electrical generators; Denver, once condemned to remain small because it had no substantial river, no nearby coal resources, found it could import power from miles away through a power grid that tapped abundant coal resources.

Matching the slow, but remorseless, decline of many older urban centers whose power derived from rivers came the growth of the hinterland. This had begun as the interurban streetcar had steadily expanded its network in the 1890s. But it turned into a rout when the automobile replaced the streetcar. Shoppers went "to town" for a range of items; to the nearest village for groceries, farm tools, and gasoline; to the town for furniture; and to the big city for women's dresses, pianos, and entertainment.[9]

The growth of the new city required four major changes in the economy.

First, rail freight rates had to fall if increasing amounts of food were to be available in the new urban markets at prices workers could pay. Farmers from the immediate vicinity, trading in farmers' markets, no longer sufficed. That was well and good for a city of 1,000 or even 10,000. But it was sheer romanticism for a city of one million. A city of that size required the produce of 4,000 farms just for its daily bread.[10] And thousands more for meat, vegetables, and so on. The decline in freight rates, plus the rise in farm productivity, eventually made it possible for one farmer to feed 99 city people—at prices well within their budgets. This spectacular advance in farm and transport productivity eventually laid the basis for huge exports many decades later. Road paving within the city helped further (see Table 28.1).

Second, it required expanded disease control. Otherwise, immigration would have produced massive epidemics. In 1882 "half the children in Chicago died before reaching five years of age."[11] Prior to the Civil War each new wave of immigrants had forced up urban death rates. Thus doubling

9. Edmund deBrunner and R. Kolb, *Rural Social Trends*, p. 158.

10. Per capita consumption of wheat flour averaged 225 pounds 1880–1900. (M. K. Bennett and R. H. Pierce, *Food Research Studies* (May 1961), pp. 116–17.) Wheat averaged about 15 bushels per acre, each yielding about 40 pounds of flour. The average farm in 1880 had about 100 improved acres. Hence, 3,750 farms growing wheat were needed for a city of one million. Corn averaged about 100 pounds per capita.

11. Bessie L. Pierce, *A History of Chicago* 3 (1957):55.

TABLE 28.1
PUBLIC FACILITIES IN 1902

Population size group	Electric lights as percent of total lights	Lights per mile of road	Miles of road: Percent paved
Total U.S. cities	36	10	44
I. Over 200,000	25	15	57
New York, N.Y.	26	24	70
Chicago, Ill.	17	9	32
Philadelphia, Penn.	21	29	73
St. Louis, Mo.	11	18	51
Boston, Mass.	25	25	85
Baltimore, Md.	17	20	88
Cleveland, Ohio	11	16	35
Buffalo, N.Y.	31	13	53
San Francisco, Calif.	14	7	49
Cincinnati, Ohio	54	10	63
Pittsburgh, Penn.	45	15	66
New Orleans, La.	100	2	29
Detroit, Mich.	100	4	51
Milwaukee, Wisc.	35	9	59
Washington, D.C.	18	31	75
Newark, N.J.	47	17	18
Jersey City, N.J.	62	11	54
Louisville, Ky.	62	12	74
Minneapolis, Minn.	11	10	13
II. 110,000 to 200,000	43	11	44
III. 100,000 to 109,000	58	5	30
IV. 50,000 to 99,000	67	6	43
V. 35,000 to 49,000	69	4	29
VI. 30,000 to 34,000	73	5	26

Source: Computed from U.S. Department of Labor Bulletin #42 (September 1902), Tables X, XII Statistics of Cities.

migration into the United States from 1823–32 to 1845–49 had doubled New York City's death rates. But when immigration into New York City doubled from 1901 to 1905, and even when it quintupled from 1878 to 1882, it created only a slight increase in death rates. What, then, had saved hundreds of thousands of people from dying in New York City epidemics after the Civil War? And many more thousands in the other great port cities?

The key was the 1870–90 development of sewage systems, of piped water supply in those cities (though even by 1890 sewers were still lacking in dozens of other cities, from Newton, Gloucester, Waltham, Taunton, and

Quincy, Massachusetts, to New Orleans and Battle Creek).[12] The tremendous expansion of basic public facilities in so short a time had a heavy political price. It vastly expanded local and government spending—creating standard, almost inevitable, opportunities for corruption. The noteworthy "carnivals of crime" under Boss Tweed in New York and Boss Shepherd in Washington occurred in just this period. It turned out that democratically elected, non-profit city councils found financial opportunities when letting huge contracts for paving, sewage systems. Even the procurement of pipes—for water, sewers—led to a demand shift so powerful that firms throughout the eastern United States formed a cartel to fix prices. In turn their actions made legal history in the classic Supreme Court antitrust case: *United States vs Addystone Pipe.*

Third, it required improved fire protection. Squeezing more and more persons into the cities could not have been accomplished if the pre-Civil War fire probabilities had prevailed. The experience of Boston, one of the more densely settled cities in the eighteenth century, is suggestive. Boston had citywide fires in 1760, in 1775, in 1787, and again in 1794. Such destruction could only have intensified by the 1880s as the number of persons per square mile rose tenfold—each new person lighting fires, carrying candles or oil lamps, accidently spilling sparks and fire every month of the year. Citywide fires broke out throughout the nineteenth century. The most spectacular ones included property losses of $15 million in New York City in 1835; 10 million in Pittsburgh in 1845; 11 million in St. Louis in 1851; 10 million in San Francisco in 1851; 11 million in Portland in 1866; 75 million in Boston in 1872; 20 million in Seattle in 1889.[13]

Had the pre-Civil War fire frequency continued, cities could never have become the home of three-quarters of the nation's population—as they had by 1980. What changed? One element was the increased use of brick, stone, and other nonflammable materials instead of wood. When the Civil War ended, 79 percent of New York City dwellings were already made of brick and stone, but only 7 percent of the rest of New York State homes were as fireproof.[14] Our first data on new construction, for 1909, report that 99 percent of the buildings going up in Philadelphia were fireproof, and 74 percent of those in New York City. Nearly all other cities, however, were far behind. Only 13 percent in Cleveland were fireproof; 15 percent in Detroit; 8 percent in Providence.[15] And outside those major cities virtually all houses were still being built of wood.[16]

12. 1880 Census, *Report on the Social Statistics of Cities,* Parts I and II (1886), lists 55 cities with populations of 10,000 and more that had no sewers.

13. H. H. Bancroft, *Achievements of Civilisation, The Book of Wealth* Section 9 (1896):836.

14. *Census of the State of New York for 1865* (1867), p. 271. The proportions for Brooklyn were 41 percent, for Albany, 29 percent.

15. U.S. Geological Survey, *Mineral Resources of the United States,* Part 2 (1909):502–10.

16. Chauncey DePew, *One Hundred Years of American Commerce* 2 (1895):374.

Invaluable in reducing city fire storms were the expanding piped-water supply and the new city fire departments. Together these helped to halt fires that did break out. And the coming of electricity in the 1880s further reduced the menace that flaming candles, oil lamps, kerosene lamps, and gas jets posed to life in cities (see Table 28.1).

Fourth, city growth required cheaper transportation. As late as the 1880s most people walked to work. Owning a horse, much less a horse and carriage, was still impossibly expensive for most workers. And fortunately so. Eventually 3 million New Yorkers worked in the central city.[17] How 3 million horses could have been stabled near the factories and stores in which New Yorkers worked baffles the imagination. The burgeoning urban demand for workers, and the workers' demand for transportation between home and work, created an enormous transit market. The first way to reduce transport costs was somehow to use less than one horse per worker. That was tried (in the 1830s in New York) by simply stretching the ordinary carriage. That became a "horse car" accommodating 30 or 40 persons, yet requiring only two horses. But later there was more. Only about 8½ pounds of mechanical force were needed to move one ton on a railway compared to 200 pounds required on an earthen road.[18] That a horse railway thus required only one horse for every 24 required on a common road was enough to decide the issue. Trams took over in one big city after another. And with them came monopoly, since the streets had room for only one set of rails in each direction. Franchises for that monopoly began to raise the same issues as when the government disposed of public lands, of import licenses, contracts or any other item of great value. As Tom Johnson, millionaire reform mayor of Cleveland, remarked: "A street-railway franchise would corrupt the twelve Apostles if they were council-men."[19]

Cities, then, were able to grow because of the changing chances of death from disease and fire. And because improved transportation cheaply shuttled workers between home and work even at new, high densities. What was the special function of cities in the new era? Why workers wished to live in cities has already been suggested. But employers surely did not build stores, factories, and mills in cities just because workers wished to live there. A key is to be found in the list of major economic sectors. By 1900 cities had no more than their aliquot proportion of U.S. employment in factories, in construction, in entertainment services. They specialized largely in tertiary industry—trade, finance, and service. They had more than their proportionate

17. 1970 Census, *Population Detailed Characteristics*, Table 363.

18. Lewis Haupt, *The Relation of Common Roads to Railroads*, in the U.S. Department of Agriculture, Public Roads Inquiries, Bulletin 22, *Proceedings of the Third Annual Good Roads Convention* (1902), p. 63; Nicholas Wood, *A Practical Treatise on Railroads* (1838), pp. 451, 650, 678, 698.

19. Frederic C. Howe, *The Confessions of a Reformer* (1925), pp. 16–17. Cf. the lively discussion of franchises in Edward C. Kirkland, *Industry Comes of Age* (1961), chap. 12.

share of the U.S. labor force in finance, wholesale trade, transport, business and personal service, government, retail trade, and professional services.[20]

Within the great manufacturing sector the cities specialized in only a few subsectors. True, cities have actually turned out almost every kind of factory product we can imagine: the Gutenberg Bible, the hula hoop, the Rospigliosi Cup, and the first steamship. Yet the city does not possess an equal and universal set of advantages. On average, U.S. cities in 1900 employed about 55 percent of all factory workers. But they had a greater proportion of U.S. workers in apparel manufacture (91 percent), jewelry (75 percent), malt liquor (81 percent), and tobacco (65 percent).[21] Cities, then, specialized in producing articles of raiment and riot. A half-century later they still retained their special manufacturing advantage only in apparel and jewelry—fields where the quick continuous contact with fashion changes and a large supply of cheap assembly labor were important. Cities had advanced their share markedly in printing (today, almost completely an urban industry), in chemicals, and in instrument production. Most American production, then, was not concentrated in cities any more than American population was. The location of workers and consumers virtually decided the location of production. (The obvious exceptions for farming, forestry and mining—all resource-intensive—are taken for granted.)

The growing concentration of the nation's population in urban areas undoubtedly contributed to consequences well outside the domain of economics. Alienation has been described as developing whenever a worker does not both procure the materials for his work and produce a product or service by his unaided efforts. If so, it surely developed long before the dawn of agriculture. But if working for a foreman or boss produces more alienation than working for at most one of two buyers (as farmers did), or a hundred buyers (as artisans did), then the growth of cities massively contributed to alienation.

The breakup of traditional family control of children was also emphasized in the cities. When families lived on isolated farms the authority of the parents was more nearly unquestioned. But children were given multiple examples of how other families lived in the cities' multiple-dwelling units. As late as 1900 only a handful of families lived in dwellings in Detroit, Denver, Columbus, or Philadelphia that had three families or more. (Chicago already

20. Estimated in Stanley Lebergott, "Prospects for the Urban Labor Force," in *Planning for a Nation of Cities*, Sam Warner, ed. (1966), p. 229. Some of these were creations of the city. For example, the rise of insurance. The vast growth of "industrial insurance" turned on agents being able to make a living collecting 5 cents a week per family. Unless families were concentrated in cities it would have been impossible for agents to walk from door to door, hence no real growth in life insurance.

21. Ibid., p. 132.

had 20 percent such dwellings; New York and Fall River had 32 percent.)[22]
Eventually over half of all American families resided in such dwellings.[23]
With children persistently exposed to so many different family styles in their
immediate neighborhoods, the traditional authority of the family declined.
City public schools (and consolidated rural schools) intensified that result.
Country schoolhouses had mixed ages, so that each child was offered few peer
models of his own age.[24] The huge city schools, however, were partitioned by
grade. Each child saw many peers, many models.

Inevitably there were families not prepared to accept such consequences.
Their heads took city jobs, but the families moved into the suburbs. As a result the number living in the suburbs rose by 24 percent between 1900 and
1910. And much the same rate of gain appeared in every decade up to 1950.
But from 1950 to 1960, and again in 1960–70,[25] the suburban population rose
by 50 percent. Though often labeled "white flight," the increase reflected
chiefly a combination of federal programs that helped destroy central cities
(such as highway construction, housing loan insurance and subsidy, urban re-
newal) and higher incomes. The formation of cities and the elements of breakdown alike changed the prospects and returns for the American population.
Chiefly affected, necessarily, were those who labored for a living. We turn,
now, to the trends for that group.

22. 1900 Census, *Population*, II, part 2, p. clxxxiv.
23. 1970 Census, *Housing Characteristics by Household Composition*, p. 45. Some 57 percent of
two-or-more-person households and 51 percent of all households lived in them.
24. The consolidation of one-room rural schools into larger units had its greatest impact beginning in the 1890s.
25. 1960 Census, *Standard Metropolitan Statistical Areas*, Table 1, and 1970 Census, *General
Social and Economic Characteristics, U.S. Summary*, Table 108.

To play a social part [in the U.S.] you must either earn
your income or make believe you earn it.

      —HENRY JAMES, *Washington Square*

In America the working men are coming out into the
streets in readiness for the decisive struggle.

      —Lenin, 1919

29

Labor

A recent mission to China came back with some figures on labor productivity in that country.[1] Their results can be compared with U.S. data on the time required to produce a given quantity of cotton:[2]

United States	1 day
China	1 year

Did this spectacular difference arise because Chinese land was so much worse? Not obviously, for yield per acre in China was nearly half as great as that in the United States. Was it because U.S. labor worked harder? Even less probable: by all testimony the Chinese work at least as perseveringly. Was it because U.S. labor had more years of schooling in geography, music, arithmetic, and basketball—more "human capital"? It is very hard to see why efficiency in cultivating and picking cotton is affected much by time spent in school.

The difference primarily reflects two other factors. First, and most important, is the way labor has been allocated. The United States has largely allocated labor wherever the current market dictated. It did not long turn out a product because it could once be produced cheaply. Products in which the nation had a distinguished disadvantage—say, bananas—were simply not

1. Thomas Rawski, *Economic Growth and Employment in China* (1979), p. 99. We convert a yield of 0.6 kilograms per man-day into 1.32 pounds.
2. U.S. Department of Agriculture, *Agricultural Statistics* (1979), p. 443. These data indicate that the United States produced 480 pounds per day in 1974–78. (It took 30 days in 1915–19.)

366

produced. Instead, the United States has turned out those items for which the market reported it had a comparative advantage—wheat and steel in the nineteenth century; soybeans, blue jeans, computers in the twentieth. It then sold some of these items to countries that paid in bananas or themselves traded with banana producers. The second major factor is presumably its use of mechanical cotton pickers. However, even if China needed no labor at all for picking, it would still require 208 days compared to the 2 days for the United States.[3]

In this example, the productivity of labor turned out to be overwhelmingly determined by the efficiency of the system that decided what goods were worth producing and how they were to be produced; and the amount of capital equipment provided for each worker. Such factors have shaped the productivity of labor in hundreds of occupations throughout the American economy. For some—say, singing songs or practicing acupuncture—U.S.– foreign differences in productivity may have been very small. But for many they were highly significant. (And they account overwhelmingly for the huge difference in workers' incomes between the United States and China.) Before considering the sources of U.S. productivity it is desirable to look first at trends in the labor force itself.

"In the sweat of thy brow shalt thou labor" is one of the oldest descriptions of labor on record. It has long described the daily work of most of the world. The elements others share with the U.S. labor force are more powerful, probably, than the differences. But the differences are enough to induce millions of workers to have migrated to the United States ever since 1789, legally and illegally, while only a handful have moved the other way.[4]

Labor Force

Since 1800 over 90 percent of adult Americans have worked for a living—as in most nations. Close to 90 percent of the men were typically in the labor force. The small class of leisured men, present in some European nations, has been even less significant in the United States. Of adult women, at least 90 percent have worked. But the proportion "in the labor force" has been considerably smaller. Work in the home by adult women has been universal. The number so engaged did not rise during prosperity, decrease during depression, or change greatly over the decades. The percentage in the labor

3. Rawski's data show one third of all time devoted to harvesting. Since not all harvesting time is devoted to the actual picking China would presumably not be able to save a full third, as we here assume.

4. As noted elsewhere return migration in the nineteenth century may have averaged about 10 percent of migration. That figure included those returning for family reasons, those "industrial swallows" that had come only to earn a high summer's income, or the price of a farm. Hence the percent who changed their mind about U.S. conditions and returned was less.

TABLE 29.1
PERCENT OF WOMEN IN THE LABOR FORCE

	1900	1930	1950	1960	1970	1979
Married	6	12	23	32	40	50
Single	44	51	46	43	51	63
Widowed or divorced	32	34	33	36	37	40
Total	19	25	29	35	42	51

Source: See Appendix, this chapter.

force, however, did respond, as shown in Table 29.1. From 1900 to 1979 the gains for single women, for widows, and for divorced women were clear.[5] For married women, however, the gain (from 6 percent to 50 percent) was vastly greater.

The markedly greater gain for married women reflects three basic supply factors. First, the number of children born per married woman decreased markedly, by one-half from 1800 to 1900, and a further 33 percent by 1929.[6] The central responsibility that long kept married women working inside rather than outside the home was thereby reduced markedly.

Second, rising incomes enabled American workers to cut the housewife's workday by buying goods instead of making them. Prior to the Civil War the most important substitution was cotton yard goods. Housewives no longer spent endless hours carding wool or cotton, spinning fibers, weaving cloth. In the next few decades, moreover, many a family bought one of the new sewing machines. Isaac Singer pioneered that new mechanical device which required only foot power. He also pioneered installment selling, enabling many a lower income family to buy the machine. Sewing machines directly cut the hours housewives spent making family clothing. They also cut those hours indirectly, by lowering the price of ready-made clothing and thus expanding such purchase. (Primitive washing machines were also available, to rock the clothes back and forth by hand power, much as gold miners rocked the ore to get the precious flakes out. But these affected labor force participation little. They saved effort rather than hours.)

Major changes escalated in the twentieth century. Rising workers' incomes enabled families to buy appliances that cut the work day more substantially, and freed housewives to enter the labor force, as shown in Table 29.2.

5. Separate data for these three groups are noted in the Appendix, this chapter.

6. *Historical Statistics . . . Since 1970*, p. 49. The data are for the birth rate of women aged 15–44 (the child-bearing years).

TABLE 29.2
U.S. Families Owning Specific Items by Year (percent)

Item	1900	1920	1930	1970
washing machines	*	8	24	70
ice	18	48	40	*
mechanical refrigerators	*	*	8	99
vacuum cleaners	0	9	30	92
dishwashers	0	0	1	25

*Less than one percent.
Source: Lebergott, *The American Economy*, pp. 281, 286, 288.

Third, fewer families took in boarders and lodgers. In 1900 one urban family out of four shared its home with a boarder or lodger; by 1930, only 11 percent did so, and by 1970, a mere 2 percent did.[7]

Together such factors reduced housewives' meal preparation and cleaning time from 6 hours a day to 1½.[8] Time was thus freed for education, the pursuit of "culture," leisure. To a very great extent, however, it was used instead to work outside the home. By 1972 about 24 million women were employed, who would not have been at work if 1900 participation rates still prevailed. That number exceeded the total number of immigrants to the United States between 1920 and 1972. Such internal immigration helped keep down wage rates, employer costs, and prices.

Hidden amid this upward sweep was the difference in the trend for adult black females. Under slavery 90 percent of them had been in the labor force—the same proportion as all men. But after emancipation they reduced their participation rate to about 22 percent.[9] Despite the low level of family income, their obvious preference was for raising their children and keeping their own houses. (Cotton planters reported: "The women now seldom work in the fields; they all ambition 'keeping house.' ") Their rates remained at that lower level for many decades.

Two other aspects of labor force history warrant brief comment, particularly considering the attention novelists and photographers give to them.

First, American children aged 10–15 did work. As a host of novels and histories testify, saddened children broke slate in mines, carried bobbins in cotton mills, worked in factories, mines, or mechanical trades. As late as 1900, "less than a dozen states were seriously attempting to limit the labor of

7. Lebergott, *The American Economy*, p. 252.
8. Ibid., p. 106.
9. Cf. Lebergott's estimates in National Bureau of Economic Research, *Demographic and Economic Changes in Developed Countries* (1960), p. 391. The quotation is from F. W. Loring and C. F. Atkinson, *Cotton Culture and the South* (1869), pp. 14–15, 20, 106.

children in mills, mines factories," and other work places. Nor was there any federal legislation until 1916—and that was struck down by the Supreme Court.[10] How many children, then, did such work? Less than 5 percent from 1870 on. That tiny proportion probably fell below that for any other nation in world history. The proportion was, and had long been, so small not because of legislative intervention but because parents' attitudes and income kept them from sending their children to work.[11] Of the 13 percent of American children aged 10–15 who were "gainfully occupied," most typically worked on their parents' farms or in family stores. That percentage ranged between 13 percent and 18 percent from 1870 to 1910, falling to 5 percent by 1930.[12]

Second, city families did "gainful work" in their homes—sewing dresses, sorting rags. They were a particular favorite of some great photographers during the peak years of immigration, 1890–1914. But less than 5 percent of the immigrant families, and less than 4 percent of native white families vividly pictured were so engaged. (One of every three wives in black urban families, however, "took in washing" to supplement low incomes.)[13]

Two sharply different views have described how the labor force actually worked. One was the employer's. The other was the worker's. The employer was concerned with what Marx termed "labor power"—the efficiency and cost of man-hour input. The worker, however, was concerned with his work conditions and rewards from that work. We consider some aspects of each.

Training for Efficiency

One of the key differences between U.S. workers and those in the European countries from which so many immigrants came, and so much technical practice, was the contrast in class perspectives and training routines. European guild traditions reaching back to the Middle Ages had specified training routes by which workers were to accumulate experience. After years at each step some workers might, with great good luck, reach the higher grades. Many never had that choice. As early as 1388 England legislated that "he or she which used to labour at the Plough and Cart or other Labour or Service of Husbandry till they be of the Age of Twelve years . . . [must] abide at the

10. National Consumers' League, quoted in *Encyclopedia of the Social Sciences* 3 (1937):418.

11. Legislation became possible, in part, because so few parents wished to send their children to work and so few employers sought child workers.

12. 1940 Census, *Comparative Occupation Statistics for the United States, 1870 to 1940*, by Alba Edwards, p. 97. We estimate that children on family farms, stores, etc., accounted for three-quarters or more of the totals. A standard (1974) economic history, with a typical photograph of a "child tending spindles in a Carolina textile mill", states that "by 1910 nearly one-quarter of all children between the ages of ten and fourteen had full-time jobs." No source is given.

13. 61st Cong., 2nd Sess., S.D. 338, Reports of the Immigration Commission, *Immigrants in Cities* (1911), vol. I, Table 50.

same Labour." They were thereby forbidden to be trained for any trade "or handicraft."[14] Twelve-year olds, in other words, who worked as common field laborers could never achieve any higher skill. Such was practice in nearly every European nation for centuries. Most Asian and African nations didn't bother to legislate the inevitable. As late as the mid-nineteenth century so few workers moved up to skilled occupations, from low to higher pay, that classical economists described it as all but impossible. Few workers, they declared, could acquire "even the humble education of reading and writing." Few could break into occupations above their "social rank." So few that John Stuart Mill flatly declared in 1848: "So strongly marked . . . [a] line of demarcation [appears] between the different grades of laborers as to be almost equivalent to a hereditary distinction of caste; each employment being chiefly recruited from the children of those already employed in it."[15] Such was the European background. (Of course, Asian and African nations offered even less mobility than Europe did, caste, and tradition dominating.)

What of America? Even within the skilled crafts there was hardly a tradition of apprenticeship. Workers had little to fear from those who had gotten there first and sought to restrict entry. Even the American Medical Association, which began trying as early as 1840 to limit entry into the medical profession to those "properly qualified," failed to get anywhere before the 1910 Flexner report led to the closing of many "second class" medical schools. (Since these schools enrolled a disproportionate percentage of blacks and women, that change eventually redistributed opportunities, even if only slightly.) Indeed, as early as the 1840s many states acted to permit anyone to become a lawyer even if he had not gone to a law school or served a term in an attorney's office.

Significant was the minuscule ratio (as compared to Europe) of apprentices to total employees in factories and craft work: less than 2 apprentices per 1,000 workers in 1850 (when data first became available) and as late as in 1900.[16] Even in the building trades widespread unionization had only raised the ratio to 1 apprentice per 86 craftsmen by 1900.[17] Federal and state governments were increasingly pressed to support such apprentice programs. Yet even by the 1970s, no more than 1 in every 10 craftsmen was trained as an apprentice.[18] Most workers simply entered the skilled crafts whenever they

14. Quoted in Frederick J. Furnivall, *Early English Meals and Manners* (1868), p. xlvi.

15. John Stuart Mill, *Principles of Political Economy*, Book II, chap. XIV, part 2. A specialist in India, Mill used that as his reference when writing of "hereditary . . . caste," a phrase not irrelevant a century later.

16. 1900 Census, *Occupations*, pp. xl-xlviii, cvii.

17. Ibid., p. xl.

18. Robert E. Taylor, Howard Rosen, Frank Pratzner, eds., *Job Training for Youth* (1982), pp. 212–13. The data, from the National Longitudinal Survey, are for young men aged 24–34 who worked as craftsmen any time since leaving school. The percentage had apparently fallen since 1963 (p. 208).

found a willing employer. Surveys in the 1960s report less than 10 percent of U.S. workers received any training at all when they were put to work.[19]

Why did so striking a contrast develop between the United States and Europe, Latin America, Asia? The "career open to talents" characterized the United States far more than it did the stratified societies of France, Germany, Britain, Chile, Egypt, India. But how did that come about?

One cause was surely the speed and ubiquity with which productive techniques in the United States obsolesced. Both forces were reflected in the rate at which machinery was junked. For whenever machinery was rapidly replaced, the skills of workers who had worked with the machinery obsolesced correspondingly. (That was why most workers shrewdly "invested" very little in training.) A second powerful force was active, however. American workers usually remained on the job only a very short time. They kept wandering off to other employers offering higher wages. Nor were they prevented from doing so by laws and courts as in some European nations. They could head out to the frontier. They could attempt to farm on government or railroad land. They could try their hand at a business or craft of their own. And no one could forbid them to do so by alleging that they lacked training or had not remained on their prior job a suitably long time. (As late as 1978 half of all newly hired factory workers left their jobs before they had worked 12 months.[20])

Such incessant mobility made it thoroughly unwise for any employer to invest much in training his employees. Why train workers who could, and did, quit at any time, thus walking off with their employers' investment in training? Once slavery had ended, few U.S. employers could have much confidence in profiting by investing in worker training.

This typically American combination—rapid technological obsolescence, widening public education, and the opportunity to move to a frontier

19. A Department of Labor survey reported that 279,500 workers received orientation training in the spring of 1962. The number of new employees who received skill training could not be greater than that number. (U.S. Bureau of Apprenticeship and Training, *Training of Workers in American Industry . . . 1962* (n.d.), p. 22. If orientation averaged 1½ months, then 2.2 million workers at most received any kind of training in 1962. The net increase in wage earners from January 1962 to January 1963, plus 12 times the average monthly number of persons unemployed 1 to 4 weeks, gives 22.0 million jobs filled in 1962. (Bureau of Labor Statistics Special Labor Force Report 31, pp. A-38, A-18; and Report 23, p. A-20) Hence 2.2 of the 22.0 million new employees, or 10 percent received orientation training. Hardly as many as 5 percent could have received skill training.

20. The Bureau of Labor Statistics' new hire rate in manufacturing multiplied by the number employed in that industry in 1976 and 1977 (BLS Special Labor Force *Reports* 199, 212, 218) gives the number of new hires each year. Special Labor Force Report 235, *Job Tenure*, gives the number hired in each of those years still on the job in January 1978 (Tables D, E). About 27 percent of those hired in 1976, and 72 percent of those hired in 1977, were still employed in January 1978. Interpolating between those percentages indicates that 49.5 percent of those hired June 1976–June 1977 were still employed a year later, at the survey date.

or city—apparently produced greater upward mobility of labor than characterized most nations. In Europe the social classes were far more rigid. Children of the "lower classes" almost inevitably remained in their parents' occupations. But American workers moved up the ladder. The most reliable index is given by the contrasting experience of first- and second-generation immigrants—that is, the "foreign-born" versus the "foreign stock."[21] The first generation were anchored in unskilled work. Their children, the second generation, moved into higher skilled, better paid occupations (Table 29.3).[22] Thus foreign-born workers in 1910 provided more than twice as many miners, factory laborers, and almost twice as many domestic servants as their share in the overall population (100) would indicate. However, their descendants in 1950, that is, the "foreign stock," contributed less than their overall population share (100) to these occupations. No less predictably, the foreign-born in 1910 provided under half their population share to the professional occupations: teachers, physicians, lawyers. But their descendants appeared far more commonly in these and the other professional occupations.[23] And while the 1910 foreign-born found far fewer jobs in clerical work or sales or as craftsmen than their population share, their 1950 descendants achieved even more than their share.[24]

Supervision

An astute humorist once remarked that "it is more blessed to give than to receive—not more natural, but more blessed." For the worker to give "an honest day's work" as defined by the employer may be more blessed. It is certainly what employers and stockholders desire. But it is not more natural. Employers are therefore perpetually busy eliciting maximum effort from their workers. They have tried various tactics.

From 1860 to 1900 about one-third of the labor force consisted of farmers, craftsmen, and other self-employed workers. The economy had no

21. Many historical studies of great interest have been made of "occupational mobility" in individual cities or small groups. It is hard to conclude much from these. Many of these studies fail to locate in a second period, or generation, those studied originally. In addition, many relate to a single town or city. "If all the world were Philadelphia," to use Samuel Hay's magic phrase, that would present no sampling problem. But it is not. Samples with two major biasses give us no reliable guide.

22. E. P. Hutchinson, *Immigrants and Their Children, 1850–1950* (1956), Table 39.

23. Ibid. The rise for teachers was from 40 percent of their population share to 75 percent; for physicians from 45 percent to 86 percent; for lawyers, from 25 percent to 102 percent; for scientists, from 82 to 132 percent.

24. Gains for the smaller population groups cannot be ascertained from these same data. It appears, however, that gains for orientals and blacks were small prior to World War II. They became very marked for orientals after that date, but were only beginning to be apparent for blacks by the 1960s.

TABLE 29.3

OCCUPATIONAL CONCENTRATION INDEX, 1910–50
(MALE FOREIGN BORN AND FOREIGN STOCK)

	Foreign Born			Foreign Stock		
	1910	1920	1950	1910	1920	1950
All occupations (each year)	100	100	100	100	100	100
Professional, technical and kindred						
Welfare and religious workers, including clergymen	105	109	124	82	88	94
Nurses	105	102	103	108	107	88
Artists and literary workers	96	104	113	121	119	118
Scientists	82	67	77	132	122	114
Accountants and auditors	62	51	82	131	133	177
Health and medical workers	56	62	95	119	116	134
Engineers	47	52	68	104	108	103
Physicians and dentists	45	50	102	86	95	126
Teachers	39	39	56	75	78	87
Lawyers and judges	25	28	54	102	106	133
Farmers	52	49	45	71	76	68
Managers, officials and proprietors (nonfarmers)						
Trade (salaried)	132	152	163	109	99	116
Other industries (salaried)	91	85	112	114	113	109
Managers and officials	52	50	70	110	107	102
Clerical and kindred						
Bookkeepers	44	45	56	157	147	119
Stenos, typists, secretaries	27	29	51	167	174	126
Sales						
Salesmen (retail)	65	67	72	141	130	107
Insurance and real estate	64	71	73	107	108	100
Salesmen (not retail)	50	45	71	118	115	115
Craftsmen, foremen and kindred						
Mechanics and repairmen	113	65	76	117	113	101
Foremen	107	97	99	120	118	111
Cranemen, hoistmen and construction machine operators	85	87	74	115	106	89
Plumbers and pipefitters	74	73	79	195	169	114
Printing craftsmen	63	69	89	181	120	139
Electricians	54	51	48	146	135	95
Tailors	330	374	671	50	39	83
Bakers	235	258	296	96	84	123
Masons	169	181	203	109	106	107

TABLE 29.3 (CONTINUED)
OCCUPATIONAL CONCENTRATION INDEX. 1910–50
(MALE FOREIGN BORN AND FOREIGN STOCK)

	Foreign Born			Foreign Stock		
	1910	1920	1950	1910	1920	1950
Miscellaneous metal working craftsmen	129	137	117	120	107	114
Toolmakers, diemakers and setters	129	130	196	165	157	150
Other craftsmen and kindred workers	119	122	130	113	106	100
Machinists	112	109	132	144	130	123
Carpenters	109	116	108	87	86	78
Painters	99	116	138	112	104	93
Operatives and kindred						
Bus and taxi drivers	90	78	74	140	158	112
Truck drivers and deliverymen	86	85	44	158	132	95
Meat cutters	71	83	156	147	131	129
Mining	214	172	81	72	69	76
Apparel	211	232	431	113	106	145
Textiles	177	172	102	111	108	78
Food	170	164	130	135	118	102
Metal industries	140	143	119	147	130	132
Durable goods (except metal)	134	147	101	132	121	102
Laundry and dry cleaning	129	150	141	111	96	104
Nonmanufacturing	115	112	110	111	98	102
Service workers						
Charwomen and porters	208	237	339	104	94	100
Domestics	173	193	205	87	81	85
Waiters	169	237	204	132	85	136
Janitors	168	177	227	102	97	98
Guards and elevator operators	148	149	182	107	110	105
Barbers and beauticians	133	151	251	101	80	89
Firemen and policemen	69	62	43	193	178	134
Laborers						
Transportation and utilities	224	185	150	58	67	102
Manufacturing	208	192	148	73	75	102
Construction	169	149	108	84	86	93
Farm (except unpaid)	55	54	100	77	80	59

Source: E. P. Hutchinson, *Immigrants and Their Children, 1850–1950* (1956), Table 39.

problem in getting them to work hard. For they supervised themselves. But the proportion of the labor force who worked for employers had been slowly increasing for decades. It increased even faster in the twentieth century. The end result was the development of a "working class" in the United States. As one writer has put it: "The destruction and disappearance of small shopkeepers, small-scale family farms, independent professions and artisans continued unabated [after 1880] with the further advance of large-scale industry. . . . In short, the labor force has been undergoing a dramatic and continuing transformation over time from professional and independent owners of small capital into mere sellers of labor power—i.e., the process of proletarianization."[25] These wage earners had their effort elicited in one (or more) of three ways:

First, they were directly supervised by employers (in the smaller shops) or by foremen (in the larger). The ratio of foremen to employees rose slightly in 1910–40. It then rose substantially in 1940–70, as unions expanded and employers sought compensating control of costs.[26]

Second, where the cost of supervision proved too great, or too many opportunities for evasion remained, some producers began to pace workers by establishing a formal rhythm to the factory. The conveyor belt, now used in factories from Flint to Magnetogorsk, originated long before automobile assembly. In one form it appeared in Chicago slaughterhouses during the 1850s. (Hog carcasses were hung on hooks. These were then attached to standards and pushed along on "little trolleys.") Henry Ford developed the first auto conveyor belt to move chassis through his Highland Park plant. (He said he got the idea from flour mills he had seen in his youth.[27]) By 1810 Oliver Evans had indeed designed mills using belts that automatically moved the wheat to the top floor of the mill and then down floor by floor through processing that pushed barrels of flour out of the exit area.)

Third, U.S. employers elicited worker effort by paying workers piece rates or a share of the proceeds. Whalemen received a percentage of the oil from the whales they caught. Miners got a share of the coal or iron ore they hacked from the mine face. Lumberjacks were paid a portion of the sales proceeds. Even brickmakers were paid per brick.[28] American unions long fought piece rates. For they judged, correctly, that these were designed to make labor work as hard as possible, rewarding the ablest workers more than the majority of the union.

After the Civil War a smaller proportion of employees appears to have worked on piece rates than in earlier decades or in other nations. The first

25. Michael Reich in Richard Edwards et al., *The Capitalist System* (1972), p. 175.

26. The ratio moved from 2.4 foremen per 100 employees to 2.8—then to 4.8. Cf. the writer's estimates in Lance Davis, Ed., *American Economic Growth* (1972) P. 202 and 1970 Census, *Occupation by Industry*, Table 8, and *Industrial Characteristics*, Table 37.

27. Marc Connolly, *Voices Offstage* (1968), p. 210.

28. McLane Report, vol. 2, p. 739.

comprehensive census data, for 1890, show 18 percent of American factory workers paid on piece rates. (At that time 30 percent of workers in French industries, and still more in British, were on piece rates.) By 1958 the U.S. figure had risen to 27 percent, as laggard productivity industries (leather, apparel, knitting) increased their reliance on piece rates, as did some other industries that had not earlier routinized their work (stone, clay, transport equipment).[29] The U.S. figure of 27 percent may be compared with the 95 percent of Soviet factory and mine workers paid on piece rates to foster their "material self interest."[30] With so much less reliance on piece rates and performance criteria, how did U.S. employers keep their labor costs down? Or, more neutrally, how were U.S. wages determined?

U.S. wages depended more persistently on the working of two sets of skills: One was the ability of producers to hire and fire workers, and to motivate them, in ways that made their wages correspond to their productivity. And the second was the ability of workers to seek out jobs where their ability to produce was fully used and tangibly recognized. Figure 29.1 shows to what extent this interaction worked. It compares the trend of productivity for all workers with that for the earnings of nonfarm employees.[31] In every decade from 1870 to 1940 the two changed at much the same rate. After 1940, wages moved up far faster than productivity. The changed relation of government and unions to the labor market process in the 1930s may account for that new departure. However, the perception that an era of inflation had begun did not appear until several decades had passed.

The Returns to Work

The history of labor in the United States from the Civil War to the Great Depression is dotted with fascinating and dramatic events, and these have gotten due attention.[32] On the one hand, thousands of men rose to millionaire status from unskilled labor work and simple rural backgrounds, as the patri-

---

29. Data for the United States in 1890 and 1958 are from Lebergott, "The American Labor Force," in Lance Davis et al., *American Economic Growth* (1972), p. 201. The figure for France is from David Schloss, *Methods of Industrial Remuneration* (1898), p. 43. We infer a higher figure for Britain since unions with 57 percent of all trade union members in the 1890s "actually insist on piece work" and another 14 percent "willingly" accept them. Cf. Sidney and Beatrice Webb, *Industrial Democracy* (1897), p. 286.

30. Walter Galenson, "Wage Structure in Soviet Industry," in J. L. Meij, ed., *International Wage Structure* (1963) p. 319. Leonard Kirsch, *Soviet Wages* (1972), p. 25, indicates somewhat more than 95 percent by 1965, as a combination of time rates plus premiums for performance.

31. It would be conceptually more appropriate to report wages for all employees, which moved up even faster. However, the problems of measuring the earnings in kind (food, lodging) of farm workers makes the apparently more comprehensive measure not obviously superior.

32. A rich perspective is offered in Lloyd Ulman, *The Rise of the National Trade Union* (1955) and John R. Commons and Associates, *History of Labour in the United States* (1918, 1935 reprint ed.).

FIGURE 29.1
WORKER EARNINGS COMPARED TO NET PRODUCT
PER PERSON EMPLOYED, 1870–1940

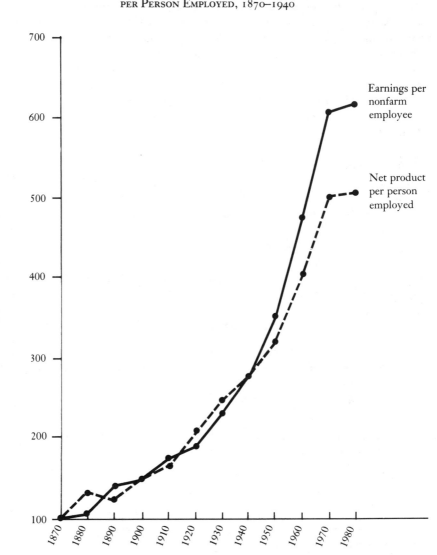

Source: See Appendix, this chapter.

otic historians observed.[33] On the other hand strikes broke out, from "turn-outs" of women factory workers in 1832 to southern tenant farmer strikes in the early 1930s as more dyspeptic writers iterated. Gross human suffering appeared in incidents from the Haymarket Riot of 1886 and the Triangle shirtwaist fire of 1910 to the Memorial Day Massacre of 1938.[34] Each of these contrasting aspects was real. But each had parallels in the contemporary world, from the coal mine catastrophes in nineteenth century France and the Polish strikes in the 1920s to the rise of new wealth in Hong Kong during the 1900s. What then most typified the labor market experience for American workers 1865–1929? Two vital aspects may be noted: their earnings, their working conditions. (Their chance to rise on the occupational and income ladder—no less vital—was briefly noted on page 373, Table 29.3, for those least likely to rise.)

Earnings

In market-type economies, workers' incomes are typically fixed or bounded by productivity on the job. Such productivity rarely yields the sum fixed by their needs, desires, or by someone's measure of "the just wage." (That outcome, of course, explains why so many persons reject the principles these economies use to fix wages and incomes.) The actual earnings trend for American nonfarm workers 1900–80 is shown in Table 29.4. Real earnings rose markedly over the lifetime of typical nonfarm workers, and in nearly every decade after the Civil War. (Since the labor force gradually shifted from farm to nonfarm jobs, wages of all employees rose even more markedly. Real earnings for all employees rose 78 percent from 1900 to 1929. Those for nonfarm employees rose by 63 percent.[35]) An "unrealistic" classical model of a competitive market economy would forecast that in the long run wages rose with worker productivity. But because we lack precise measures of the partial productivity of workers, we cannot test that model exactly for these decades. However, Figure 29.1 does show that worker earnings from 1870 to 1940 advanced as much as net product per person employed did.[36] Since few economic models presume employer generosity or worker supplication, such parallelism must reflect a fair amount of both employer competition and

33. Cf. the 1893 listing of names and backgrounds in W. Sidney Ratner, *New Light on the History of the Great American Fortunes* (1953). Some 84 percent of those with $1 million or more in that listing did not inherit wealth. The percentages for the top wealth groups in later years also show heavy recruitment from lower income groups. Cf. "The Nouveau Riche" in Stanley Lebergott, *The American Economy* (1976), p. 174.

34. The more dramatic episodes are vividly portrayed in Lewis Adamic, *Dynamite* (1934) and Graham Adams, *The Age of Industrial Violence* (1966).

35. Allowing for the imputed income of farm workers in the form of board, lodging, and washing is a more uncertain affair. Hence we do not focus on such figures here. However, estimates are available in Lebergott, *Manpower*, p. 523.

36. The 1880 discrepancy is a clear, but questionable, exception. Cf. ch. Appendix.

TABLE 29.4
NONFARM EMPLOYEES ANNUAL EARNINGS,
1900–80

Year	Money earnings when employed (dollars)	Real earnings (1914 dollars)		Consumer price index (1914 = 100)	Year	Money earnings when employed (dollars)	Real earnings (1914 dollars)		Consumer price index (1914 = 100)
		After deduction for unemployment (dollars)	When employed (dollars)				After deduction for unemployment (dollars)	When employed (dollars)	
1900	483	523	573	84.3	1941	1,593	931	1,088	146.4
1901	597	546	582	85.4	1942	1,877	1,080	1,159	162.0
1902	528	583	612	86.3	1943	2,190	1,239	1,273	172.0
1903	534	575	607	88.0	1944	2,370	1,331	1,354	175.0
1904	538	555	606	88.8	1945	2,460	1,338	1,375	179.0
1905	550	582	621	88.5	1946	2,575	1,253	1,326	194.2
1906	566	618	627	90.2	1947	2,802	1,194	1,262	222.1
1907	592	613	631	93.8	1948	3,067	1,216	1,281	239.4
1908	577	545	631	91.5	1949	3,088	1,190	1,303	237.0
1909	600	604	657	91.3					
					1950	3,276	1,272	1,368	239.4
1910	634	608	669	94.7	1951	3,560	1,317	1,378	258.3
1911	644	612	676	95.2	1952	3,777	1,375	1,431	263.9
1912	657	619	676	97.2	1953	3,986	1,442	1,499	265.9
1913	687	649	695	98.9	1954	4,110	1,427	1,538	267.3
1914	696	613	696	100.0	1955	4,318	1,529	1,621	266.3
1915	692	591	684	101.1	1956	4,557	1,597	1,686	270.3
1916	760	649	699	108.7	1957	4,764	1,608	1,702	279.9
1917	866	681	704	127.7	1958	4,956	1,574	1,724	287.5
1918	1,063	694	709	150.0	1959	5,217	1,674	1,800	289.8
1919	1,215	681	704	172.5					
					1960	5,402	1,706	1,834	294.5
1920	1,426	672	714	199.7	1961	5,584	1,719	1,877	297.5
1921	1,330	620	747	178.1	1962	5,829	1,804	1,938	300.8
1922	1,289	688	772	166.9	1963	6,045	1,847	1,986	304.4
1923	1,376	774	811	169.7	1964	6,327	1,921	2,052	308.4
1924	1,396	754	820	170.3	1965	6,535	1,968	2,083	313.7
1925	1,420	764	812	174.8	1966	6,860	2,028	2,126	322.7
1926	1,452	801	824	176.2	1967	7,156	2,058	2,155	332.0
1927	1,487	810	861	172.8	1968	7,675	2,126	2,219	345.9
1928	1,490	816	872	170.9	1969	8,277	2,165	2,257	364.5
1929	1,534	853	901	170.3					
					1970	8,821	2,155	2,285	386.1
1930	1,495	773	901	166.0	1971	9,423	2,181	2,340	402.7
1031	1,408	696	930	151.4	1972	10,066	2,265	2,420	416.0
1932	1,249	585	918	135.8	1973	10,767	2,303	2,437	441.9
1933	1,165	565	905	128.8	1974	11,632	2,521	2,372	490.4
1934	1,199	607	901	133.1	1975	12,702	2,148	2,373	535.2
1935	1,244	637	912	136.4	1976	13,727	2,216	2,425	566.1
1936	1,296	701	940	137.8	1977	14,743	2,256	2,447	602.6
1937	1,392	767	975	142.8	1978	15,847	2,279	2,443	648.7
1938	1,370	705	978	140.1	1979	17,183	2,229	2,381	721.8
1939	1,403	760	1,016	138.1	1980	18,861	2,114	2,300	820.0
1940	1,438	812	1,032	139.4					

Source: See Appendix, this chapter.

worker job quitting. All the evidence on U.S. mobility suggests that workers did a significant amount of job quitting. They frequently moved to other firms, even to other states, in their search for better jobs. About one in five workers actually moved to another state during their lifetime, according to the data for 1870 on.[37] In subsequent decades the mobility did not decline. The rootlessness of American workers has long "amazed" European observers.[38] But it was essential in eroding whatever monopsony powers small town and rural employers might otherwise have achieved.

One further force that increased real wages may be noted. More so than those in some other nations American employers saw quite early that when using expensive capital they achieved higher profits by using fewer, but better paid, workers. Alfred Marshall, Britain's leading economist from the 1880s to the 1920s, traveled in the United States in 1875. He judged that: "In all matters of this kind the leadership of the world lies with America, and it is a not uncommon saying there, that he is the best business man who contrives to pay the highest wages."[39]

Immigration mounted steadily after the Civil War, reaching new peaks in 1900–10. As Albert Rees has noted, "there undoubtedly were individual cases in which employers took advantage of the ignorance of immigrants to pay them less than their worth, but such cases could hardly drive a huge wedge between the movements of productivity and real wages for a large sector of the economy."[40] Indeed, real earnings of nonfarm workers did not slow during that decade. Table 29.1 reports that nonfarm earnings rose substantially in 1900–13. Moreover, as Figure 29.1 shows, they rose faster than net product per employee in the peak migration decade of 1900–10.

Working Conditions

What of working conditions? History, memoirs, and human experience are filled with stories of arduous and dangerous work, of harsh and ignorant superior authority. That is so whether the history is of individual families,

37. *Historical Statistics . . . to 1970*, series C-5, C-7. The earliest available quit rates, for manufacturing in 1919–20 show the equivalent of 70 percent of the employees quitting in a year. The rate in later years ran about 50 percent. *Historical Statistics . . . to 1970*, series D-1025.

38. The distinguished Swedish economist Bertil Ohlin noted that by contrast with the United States, "Most European workers appear to be reluctant to change their occupation or place of employment. . . . The extent to which the objective of full employment is interpreted as implying security of employment in the same job and in the same place has sometimes amazed outside observers." International Labour Office, *Social Aspects of European Economic Cooperation, Report by a Group of Experts* (1956), p. 99.

39. Alfred Marshall, *Principles of Economics*, 8th Ed. (1948), p. 550. Since Marshall revised his volume with care through the 1920 edition, we may assume the remark did not merely report his view of the United States in the 1880s.

Marshall's "American trip . . . coloured all his future work." J. M. Keynes, *Essays in Biography* (1963), p. 144.

40. Albert Rees, *Real Wages in Manufacturing, 1890–1914* (1961), p. 126.

ancient city states, peasant kingdoms, or modern industrial economies—Africa, Asia, Europe, or America. It is difficult to compare overall "working conditions" in one society with another, or to judge how any given economy changes over time. We do have some evidence, albeit suggestive, of how what the U.S. labor market offered 1790–1980 compared with that of many European nations. For year after year thousands of people from every continent on earth sought to move to the United States. Many entered illegally even though they ended up with "working conditions" worse than those of the typical U.S. citizen. Newspapers, letters, returning immigrants beamed these findings back to almost every nation. That the flow continued suggests how that comparison was seen by millions of actual workers.

Two more direct indicators of working conditions since the Civil War are, however, available. One is the persistent change in the U.S. occupational structure. The most arduous, dangerous, and distasteful work in any nation is typically done by common labor. But throughout the nineteenth century common labor jobs in the United States were steadily replaced by semi-skilled labor.[41] That switch meant the steady abolition of the worst jobs and working conditions. The endless harsh labor of ditch diggers gave way to steam shovel operators. The latter were typically better paid and well organized. Railroad track layers gave way to mechanical crane operators. Brick layers' helpers, accustomed to climbing unsteady ladders for ten hours a day with a hod full of bricks or mortar, were replaced by elevator and hoist operators. Pick and shovel miners, grimly accustomed to the ancient and extreme dangers of such work, gave way to operators of mechanical loaders and cutters. Glass blowers, used to working directly in front of the intense heat of molten glass, were replaced by operators of automatic glass bottle and window glass making machinery. All over the nation thousands of "firemen," who once shoveled coal into the intense heat of factory furnaces, exposed to pneumonia when they left work on winter days or heat prostration when they left in summer heat, gave way to operators of mechanical stokers. Most affected were millions of farm workers in the North and West. Their tasks had typically demanded hard, intense, extended labor—chopping, hoeing, weeding, digging, picking. But their lot was eased after the 1860s as mowing machines, threshers, reapers, hay rakes, were increasingly introduced. (When tractors and cotton pickers were introduced in the South, especially after World War II, they eventually changed the ancient practices in cotton growing.)

A second indicator of working conditions appears in occupational fatality rates. The only systematic comparisons can be made for coal mining. But that industry accounted for about half the occupational fatalities in 1900. Hence

41. Comparisons covering thousands of products can be made for the change from hand methods (using common labor in significant amounts) to machines (using little unskilled labor). Cf. U.S. Commissioner of Labor, *Thirteenth Annual Report, Hand and Machine Labor* (1899).

its trend is more than casually suggestive. Fatalities per 1,000 coal miners at work were cut about in half from 1870 to 1900.[42] Moreover, the number of miners needed to produce a given amount of coal was itself cut by the introduction of mechanical loaders. Hence the true social cost—deaths per million tons of coal produced—fell even more. The typical job, in sum, was distinctly less dangerous in 1900 than in 1870, because it was less likely to be in coal mining and because, if in mining, it was safer.

A third indicator was hours of work. These appear to have shortened somewhat after the Civil War and then fallen markedly from 58.5 in 1900 to 48.7 in 1929, for nonfarm wage earners as a whole. (A notable exception to that trend, prior to 1919, was the iron and steel industry, with its 12 hour workday. But that reflected both the technology of the industry and the opposition by the Amalgamated Association of Iron and Steel Workers. The latter feared the decline of income that a shorter workday would mean.)[43]

It may be taken for granted that much work, in the home and in the factory, continued to be arduous, difficult, boring. Such a view, however, applies to most known societies, whatever their ways of production. However, few American workers, in any decade since the Civil War, evidenced any desire to return to the working conditions of some halcyon period in the labor markets they knew.

Unions

"The first American Labor Movement," as Lloyd Ulman terms it, ended in the 1930s, when federal support of unions and reactions to the Great Depression began to reshape the entire labor market.[44] It began in 1648 when the Massachusetts Bay Colony granted charters to the shoemakers and the coopers of Boston.[45] These and earlier such organizations were, in fact, cartels of small businessmen who sought to keep up prices for the products or services they sold, and, thereby, their incomes. For many later decades their successors made up such American Federation of Labor (AFL) unions as the Barbers union, the Butcher Workman's union, and others.

Skilled wage earners began to organize against their employers somewhat later. Necessarily they held a somewhat stronger position in the labor market than semi-skilled or unskilled workers, the latter rarely being or-

42. *Historical Statistics . . . to 1970*, M-276.

43. Data for quarrying and metal and nonferrous mining begin in 1911 and show marked declines in subsequent years. *Historical Statistics . . . to 1970*, M-278, M-285. The twentieth-century experience with respect to occupational fatalities is considered below in Chapter 40. Hours trends: John D. Owen, *The Price of Leisure* (1969), p. 67. Iron and steel: John A. Fitch, *The Steel Workers* (1910), pp. 93–94.

44. Cf. Ulman's remarkably judicious and succinct historical review in *American Economic History*, Seymour Harris, ed. (1961).

45. John R. Commons, *Labor and Administration* (1913), p. 210.

ganized before "the second American Labor Movement" came along. If skilled workers went on strike they could not be replaced promptly. Hence they exercised some influence over their wages and working conditions. That influence, however, was modified when, as Marx noted, employers substituted machinery and new materials for skilled workers, freeing themselves from such threats.[46] Where union demands were not dramatically out of line with market prices, however, substitution against their members was slow. Skilled workers, in turn, provided leadership in some of the more dramatic strikes, such as the 1894 railway strike in Chicago, the strikes of electrical machinery workers in the 1930s and more.[47] Beyond the unions of skilled workers in a few occupations, two dramatic fringe groups appeared briefly. The first was the Knights of Labor, a combination of populist revolt, Masonic order, and union. The Knights had a brief growth spurt when they succeeded in organizing a railroad controlled by the notorious Jay Gould.[48] It seemed as though they could deliver on their commitment to the 8-hour day (with 10 hours pay), and their membership soared from 100,000 to 600,000 in a single year. Their immediate failure brought an almost equally precipitous decline and eventual disappearance of the order. With its members having no fall back in strike funds, savings accounts, or aid-to-dependent children, and with continuing immigration, it is, perhaps, no wonder that it failed.

Employers were equally fearful of the revolutionary program of the International Workers of the World. Centered among Western miners and lumbermen, it sought at once higher wages from business and the abolition of private business. Despite that seductive program its yearly membership never exceeded 6,000 (i.e., about 1 percent of the AFL membership.)[49] Its leadership of a textile strike in Lawrence, Massachusetts, and its dynamiting campaign, left images of great mythic importance, but improved the wages and working conditions of few American workers.[50]

46. Cf. Nathan Rosenberg, *Perspectives on Technology* (1976), pp. 117–20.

47. In the depression of 1893 the Pullman Company cut wages of shop employees in general by 11 percent—but cut highly skilled cabinet makers by 29 percent, and machinists by 21 percent. The result was the great Chicago strike of that year that stopped rail traffic throughout that city. It ended when federal troops were sent in to get the mails delivered. (*U.S. versus Pullman Company*, The Strike, Statements before the U.S. Strike Commission, p. 17) In a later era it may be impossible to believe that the federal government set such store on prompt delivery of mail, but President Cleveland was a Democrat, of unquestioned probity, and those were the reasons he reported. Skilled workers demoted to unskilled work because of a decline in General Electric orders led to the organization of the United Electrical Workers in a later era. Cf. Ronald Schaz, "Union Pioneers," *Journal of American History* (December 1979), p. 597.

48. Cf. Gerald Grob, "Knights of Labor versus American Federation of Labor," *Journal of Economic History* (June 1958), and the revealing autobiography of the great figure in the Knights, Terence V. Powderly, *The Way I Trod* (1940), who was given a consolation prize by Woodrow Wilson, being made Commissioner of Immigration.

49. Robert Hoxie, *Trade Unionism in the United States* (1924), p. 140.

50. The myths cherished by American novelists reached few workers, or even European revolutionaries. Of even Eugene Debs, the most famous socialist in America, Lenin asked Kollontai, "And what is Eugene Debs?" Bea Farnsworth, *Aleksandra Kollontai* (1980), p. 60.

The American Federation of Labor, organized in 1882, became the great holding company in which craft unions divided the terrain for organization and fought immigration, Contemptuously, but correctly, labeled as "business unionism" or "bread and butter unionism" by the radicals, the AFL held to a remarkably simple goal: "We have no ultimate ends. We are going from day to day. We are fighting only for immediate objects—objects that can be realized in a few years . . . we want to dress better and to live better and become better off."[51]

The dominating goal of a labor movement had to be to restrict entry into the labor force. In 1869 the first really national convention of labor unions, mostly white, proposed excluding Chinese contract labor. Four months later the first national convention of black unions likewise voted for exclusion.[52] Denis Kearney's Working Men's Party formed a "League of Deliverance," forced through a new California Constitution (1879) that forbid any corporation, or public work, to hire Chinese workers.[53] ("They are hiring all the Chinamen, and discharging you and me, But strife will be in every town . . . soon you'll hear the avenging cry, 'Drive out the China Man'."[54]) 1882 Congress did cut off Chinese immigration. But the real limitation of the supply of labor did not come until the 1920s. Over the intervening decades the AFL did indeed fight to restrict, and then to abolish, immigration.[55] That Kearney and Samuel Gompers (the first head of the AFL) and many other union leaders were themselves immigrants added irony. But it did not change the fact that by restricting immigration they would indeed help raise wages. The more astute AFL unions also called on the power of the state to restrict entry into their occupations. Public licensing requirements for electricians, plumbers, beauticians, and more then achieved what the unions could not achieve themselves.[56]

How attractive was union status to the American worker in the first century and a half of national existence? Table 29.5 indicates that before 1933 unions got almost no support from American workers. Unions in a few occupations exercised a powerful impact on wages and working conditions, as did city locals, here and there. But that impact was hidden amid the mass of nonunion workers. In Europe organized labor often became the major opposition. In time it dominated governments. What made for so extreme a difference?

51. Quoted in Leon Litwack, *The American Labor Movement* (1962), pp. 36–37.

52. John R. Commons, *History of Labour in the United States* (1921) vol. 2, pp. 137, 252–68. A National Labor Congress in 1866 had urged immigration restriction to "safeguard the living standards of native workers." Foster Dulles, *Labor in America* (1966), p. 100.

53. James Bryce, *The American Commonwealth* (1890), vol. 2, p. 399.

54. Philip S. Foner, *American Labor Songs of the Nineteenth Century* (1975), p. 135.

55. Isaac Hourwich, *Immigration and Labor* (1912).

56. Walter Gellhorn, *Individual Freedom and Governmental Restraints* (1956). Economists often treat the American Medical Association, which was first successful in restricting entry in 1910, as a quasi-union. Cf. Milton Friedman and Simon Kuznets, *Income from Independent Professional Practice* (1945).

TABLE 29.5
UNION MEMBERSHIP, 1830–1980

Year	Union members (000)	Workers in nonfarm enterprises[a]		Nonfarm labor force[b]	
		Number (000)	Percent in unions	Number (000)	Percent in unions
1830	26			1,235	2.1
1860	5			5,230	.1
1870	300			6,140	4.9
1880	50			8,470	.6
1890	325			13,360	2.4
1900	790	10,086	7.8	17,390	4.5
1905	1,891	13,270	14.3		
1910	2,052	16,391	12.5		
1915	2,454	18,275	13.4		
1920	4,795	22,536	21.3		
1925	3,255	25,509	12.8		
1930	3,401	26,195	12.0		
1935	3,584	24,550	14.6		
1940	8,717	29,990	29.1		
1945	14,322	37,210	38.5		
1950	14,300	43,982	32.5		
1955	16,802	47,837	35.1		
1960	17,049	51,487	33.1		
1965	17,299	58,222	29.7		
1970	19,381	67,691	28.6		
1975	19,553	73,951	26.4		
1980	20,000	85,539	23.4		

Source: See Appendix B, this chapter.

One theory argues that the leadership of the American working class was drawn off by opportunities in farming, management, business.[57] True, perhaps. But hardly an adequate explanation given the many able, tough, and determined people who remained in the working class. Instead of a theory of leadership (focused on the supply of union services) it is more useful to think of the workers themselves (the demand for union services). Millions of men and women in the labor force any year before the mid-1930s had migrated from Europe or Asia to a better life in America. It might have been hard to convince them that they were oppressed by grievously low American wages,

57. Selig Perlman, *A Theory of the Labor Movement* (1928, reprint ed. 1949), pp. 165–68.

given those they had left. Or that American employers and foremen were reactionary and unfair, given the quasi-feudal European farms that many had fled. Or that workers' housing in U.S. cities was ghastly, given the seamy urban slums from which they came. "Life was unfair." But they apparently judged the American labor market, compared with the one from which they had fled, not excessively unfair. (Of course, black workers may not have fully sympathized with the plaints of a generally white working class, nor women workers with those of a generally male working group.)

Appendix

Appendix A

Net Product: 1870–1929: Milton Friedman and Anna Schwartz, *Monetary Trends in the United States and United Kingdom* (1982), Table 4.8. *1930 and after:* Bureau of Economic Analysis, *National Income and Product Accounts of the United States 1929–1976*, Table 1.2 and *Survey of Current Business* (July 1982), Table 1.2.

Persons engaged: 1870–1947: Lebergott, *Manpower*, pp. 510, 512. 1948 and after: *Employment and Training Report of the President, 1981*, p. 155.

Earnings per nonfarm employee: 1870–1929: Lebergott, *Manpower*, pp. 524, 528. 1929 and after: Continued from 1929 by estimating procedures, given in Ibid., pp. 479–80, and in Stanley Lebergott, "Earnings of Nonfarm Employees," *Journal of the American Statistical Association* (March 1948), data from BEA Accounts cited above.

The major discrepancy in Figure 29.1 (for 1870–80) is noteworthy. It arises because real net product is improbably estimated to rise 80 percent 1870–80—faster than in any decade except 1940–50. The latter decade included World War II while 1870–80 included most of the 1873–82 depression—at least the second longest and deepest depression in U.S. history. The growing differences after 1930 reflects elements present in their source, primarily the *National Income Accounts.*

Appendix B

Union Membership: 1830–1890: From Stanley Lebergott's estimates in Lance Davis et al., *American Economic Growth* (1972), p. 220. 1900–20: From Leo Wolman, *Ebb and Flow in Trade Unionism* (1936), pp. 116, 192. For 1900 we exclude Canadian members from Wolman's total using his 1910 ratio of exclusion but allowing for the greater rate of growth in the transport unions which had most of the Canadian members. 1930–50: *Historical Statistics . . . to 1970*, p. 178. 1960 ff: Bureau of Labor Statistics Bulletin 2079, *Directory of National Unions and Employee Associations, 1979*, p. 59.

Nonfarm Employees: The Bureau of Labor Statistics figures on "employees in non-agricultural establishments," though used in Bulletin 2079 (*supra*), were not used here: They included twice those employees who move from job to job in the survey period, and also included domestic servants. Instead we used estimates from Lebergott, *Manpower*, p. 513, extended by Current Population Survey data appearing in Bureau of Labor Statistics, Special Labor Force Reports, no. 129 (p. A-21), no. 185 (p. A-18), no. 218 (p. A-24), no. 244 (p. A-24).

30

Cycles and Depressions

THE world has seen only two kinds of economies. One is subject to change. In the other resources are never reallocated. The latter is the stationary state, that heavenly (or boring?) alternative to the economy in which we live. The stationary state resembles Swinburne's *Garden of Prosperine:*

> Here where all the world is quiet
> Here, where all the trouble seems
> Dead winds' and spent waves' riot
> In doubtful dreams of dreams;
>
> . . . .
>
> Only the sleep eternal
> in an eternal night

But in the real world, change is central, omnipresent. Why? For the United States and other market economies one answer has been given by a distinguished Japanese economist: "The aggregate size of claims [on goods] emerges as a result of atomistic decision on the part of individual capitalists and thus cannot be controlled directly as an aggregate."[1] The count of such atomistic decisions is astronomical. Even the mere number of U.S. business decision makers has been huge: In 1870, there were 3.5 million U.S. businesses (3 million of them in farming); in 1900, 7 million U.S. businesses (6 million of which were in farming); and in 1929, there were 9 million U.S. businesses (6 million in farming).[2] Each businessman made his production decisions independently. Each did coordinate with the others, but only indirectly, by responding to the prices and costs they all faced.

1. Shigeto Tsuru, *Towards a New Political Economy* (1976), p. 131.
2. The number of farmers is from Lebergott, *Manpower*, p. 513. The number of entrepreneurs in manufacturing and the hand trades in 1870 and 1900 is reported in the 1870 Census, *The Statistics of Wealth and Industry* (1872), pp. 394, 583. Retail dealers from the 1870 Census, *The Statistics of the Population* (1873), p. 678 and 1900 Census, *Occupations*, p. 7. 1929 estimates of the nonfarm business population are from *Historical Statistics . . . Since 1970*, p. 911.

Was there any way to predict the decision rules they followed? One of the closest descriptions was given over a century ago by Karl Marx:

> The expansion or contraction of production . . . is determined by profit and by the proportion of this profit to the employed capital . . . instead of being determined by the relation of production to social wants. . . . The capitalist mode of production . . . comes to a standstill at a point determined by the production and realization of profit, not by the satisfaction of *social needs.*[3]

The extent and duration of the economy's expansion or contraction was fixed by the expected profit rate. How did that rate get defined? In a market economy it was necessarily established as the sum of expectations held by those millions of separate producers. To achieve his profit goal every producer in this multitude persistently sought to anticipate exactly what his consumers would want in the period ahead. For it was those consumers (inevitably and overwhelmingly) who bought the output of producers. It was therefore the needs and desires of the vast anonymous body of consumers that alone provided profits on outputs, and thereby drove the system.

A brilliant study by Steven Valavanis-Vail analyzed how business investment after 1870 responded to changes in profit expectations. Between 1870 and 1940 investment rose whenever profits rose, and slowed whenever the cost of investment rose.[4] Such relationships do reproduce the actual path of the business cycle, though not with precise fidelity. Study of a similar model (for a shorter portion of that historic record) shows that one key element must be added. That element is simply the constellation of odd events occurring in the real world: "shocks."[5] Shocks include economic events—the financial panics of 1884, of 1907, 1929; the discovery of Minnesota's huge iron reserves in the 1880s, California's gold in 1840, Nevada's silver in 1867, Alaska's gold in 1899. They include political events—the outbreak of war between Germany and France in 1870, 1914, 1939. They also include climatic events—the grasshopper invasions of North Dakota in 1874–76, the boll weevil migration from Mexico to Texas in 1892. These events all share one common characteristic: they were not anticipated by the participants in the economic process. Certainly no one foresaw them happening when they actually did. Such irregularities therefore broke any neat historic relationship be-

3. Karl Marx, *Capital*, III (1909):303. "Social needs" as defined by Marx are not necessarily expressed by mere consumers. They may be "needs" expressed by a group of wise men who certify to their own wisdom.

4. Stevan Valvanis-Vail, "Models of Economic Growth," *American Economic Review* (May 1955), p. 210. Investment was added to existing capital stock as a function of the rate of profit on existing capital and the interest rate. Actual profits were used as the rough-and-ready measure of expected profits, in anticipation of the rational expectations approach.

5. Irma and Frank Adelman, "Dynamic Properties of the Klein-Goldberger Model," *Econometrica* (October 1959).

tween investment on the one hand and such factors as past profits, and interest rates, on the other.[6]

Entrepreneurs in the U.S. market economy made their separate plans assuming that buyers would exercise large, if not limitless, freedom to act as they chose. The core of uncertainty that dominated entrepreneurial decisions came directly and overwhelmingly from that freedom. In April and May 1979 1.7 million cars were produced in the United States. A year later only 1.1 million were being produced—35 percent less.[7] Thousands of workers were laid off. The best-laid plans of General Motors, Ford, and Chrysler went awry. Extensive advertising to stabilize sales, their massive assets, their position in the structure of the U.S. economy, were all impressive. Nonetheless their sales plummeted. Their profit rates plummeted even faster.[8] That experience, of course, had happened before. And not merely with autos. Similar catastrophes during the depressions of the nineteenth century—for textiles, glass, iron, shoes—can be taken for granted. For firms were smaller, had less information on buyers' wants and less financial staying power in the depressions that began in 1817, 1837, 1857, 1873, and 1893.

U.S. customers were rarely prepared to wait months, much less years, to buy most consumer products. If the first store they tried didn't have a given item they tried the next. That option was unavailable in pioneer days and under frontier conditions. But as cities grew, and the distribution network expanded, such choice behavior multiplied. In response, the market increasingly inventoried thousands, perhaps millions, of items for the moment the consumer decided to drop in. When consumers changed their minds, then, producers were left holding excess inventories. They then cut purchases. In turn their suppliers cut production and employment.

In the planned economy of the U.S.S.R., on the other hand, consumers wait to buy many items. Automobiles, black olives, fresh lemons, are not normally in stock. Such items therefore have a ready market whenever they are imported or produced. Large numbers of people wait for new cars 4 to 6 years.[9] "Huge lines formed outside a major Moscow department store"—for a

6. It is only fair to add that theory stipulates that expected magnitudes—and not present ones (e.g., profits)—should determine investment. Shocks will indeed shift expectations. The practical measurement problem is that we have no systematic way of incorporating the value of random events into the expectations variables.

7. *Survey of Current Business* (June 1980), p. S-36.

8. That giant corporations try to stabilize sales was vigorously emphasized in John K. Galbraith's *The Affluent Society* (1958), pp. 152–60. Such attempts may have produced a more stable market than they would have faced without advertising. But actual market sales were nonetheless volatile. Numerous profit catastrophes within the auto industry italicize that fact—the Tucker, the Edsel, the Corvair, the Studebaker, Chrysler.

9. *New York Times* (June 29, 1975). By 1983 "At least two million people languish on the waiting list." But production was up to 1.4 million. *New York Times* (June 22, 1983), p. 2. Hence, a two year wait, allowing for those who did not sign up, seems more likely.

shipment of East German toilet paper.[10] East Germans waited—1 to 2 years for most furniture; 1 year for the services of a plumber or electrician; half a year for a pair of boots.[11] In Poland in 1980 "there was still a ten year wait for a new apartment."[12] Hence, producers in centrally planned economies need not face wild variations in consumer demand.

Such economies inventory consumers, not goods. Employment in industries that produce for such demands is stabilized, as are "profits." Such stability extends into the industries that supply steel, iron ore, coal, transport, electricity to these producers. Decisions by millions of individual consumers, to purchase or not to purchase, are precluded from determining production in the period ahead. "Social needs" instead determine that production. In practice a (necessarily) limited group of officials decide just what are "social needs." They do not consult every consumer in order to do so. They certainly do not consult the "needs," much less the desires, of every individual consumer every day.[13] They necessarily define "social needs" on the basis of past experience, giving due allowance to whatever priorities they wish to impose on behalf of the "needs" of the army, air force, the missile program. (If consumers are allowed to express their own "needs" they may decide that they wish spaghetti for lunch today. Yet salad may be the social need planned by officials, or by any given market producer. Consumers may decide to buy records made by a lively rock group rather than by a socially desirable symphony orchestra or a new novel rather than a classic. They may conclude that a brand-new instructive or expensive movie is a washout, and watch TV instead.)

A second, and related, force has made for instability in the U.S. economy. To provide a fast-food customer with a hamburger requires more than a year. Perhaps 5 minutes cooking time is needed. But 30 minutes are required to ship it from the warehouse. Plus 10 months to raise the cattle to slaughter weight. Plus 6 more months to raise the soybeans to feed the cattle, and so on. If customers decide to buy fish sandwiches instead, all that investment will prove mistaken. But whenever businesses make mistaken investments, their employees and investors are penalized by the market. They earn less than if they had the vision to foresee it all in advance.

10. *New York Times* (January 6, 1977).

11. Peter Kelman in the *New Yorker* (September 30, 1972), p. 90.

12. The "queues before the butcher shops still stretched around the corner on nearly every block." *New York Times* (September 28, 1980). The equivalent of a day a week standing in line in the U.S.S.R.—e.g., "an hour and 40 minutes in a store to buy oranges"—is reported in the *New York Times*(June 26, 1980), p. A12.

13. We are not referring to socialism, here, in which the use of the market (*a la* Taylor and Lange) would permit adjustments similar to those in capitalist markets. We refer to an economy in which "social needs," as described by Marx, decide. Actual planning in some command societies in fact resembles this process.

TABLE 30.1
ANNUAL GROWTH RATES OF INVESTMENT (IN PERCENT)

| Year | Soviet Union | | Poland | | Czechoslovakia | | United States |
	Total Capital	Fixed Capital in Industry	Total Capital	Fixed Capital in Industry	Total Capital	Fixed Capital in Industry	Capital in Industry
1950	18.7	—	38.0	63.6	20.8	—	11.8
1951	12.6	16.0	11.8	19.0	21.0	25.0	14.8
1952	11.9	10.3	19.0	44.1	18.1	21.2	0.2
1953	4.9	5.2	15.5	15.3	3.5	− 13.7	9.9
1954	17.8	17.8	6.5	2.7	− 2.0	− 1.5	− 0.9
1955	9.6	11.7	3.9	− 6.3	7.6	− 1.0	12.8
1956	16.2	14.3	4.4	6.0	13.6	22.5	14.1
1957	12.8	5.2	7.2	3.0	9.3	5.0	6.8
1958	13.6	13.7	9.8	8.3	13.1	31.0	− 10.8
1959	11.7	14.3	16.9	16.9	19.3	17.9	8.8
1960	12.4	8.2	6.0	2.9	12.4	8.8	5.3
1961	6.3	6.2	7.4	10.3	7.0	6.9	− 1.3
1962	6.4	6.7	10.9	15.7	− 2.7	8.8	8.8
1963	3.9	7.4	3.9	5.6	− 11.0	—	4.6

Source: Nikola Cobeljic and Radmila Stajanovic, *The Theory of Investment Cycles in a Socialist Economy* (1969), pp. 131, 135, 151, 158.

If, however, the economy had, say, a shoe commissariat whose plan simply says: "produce high-button shoes until 1984," they would be produced. None of those who work for the commissariat need fear unemployment. Nor the engineers who designed the factories. Nor the managers who run it. (True, other workers and farmers would have to lower their income somewhat to cover the waste of producing useless stocks of high-button shoes.) It is an empirical question how efficiently, how sensitively, any economy does actually achieve stability by its "plan." Table 30.1 suggests that significant production variations do take place in some centrally planned economies.[14] There must have then been corresponding swoops and slides in factory employment even under planning. Nonetheless, if consumers have to accept whatever goods are produced then the referred effects back on investment

14. An enormous theoretical literature has demonstrated that socialist economies could plan for stability, yet achieve much of the production advantages of "market" economies. The empirical record for "socialist" and "communist" economies is another topic. Investment data are available for prewar years for only one of the "planned" economies. The enormous variability of such investment in a period of mass starvation, however, must exaggerate the variability under planning per se, hence in Table 30.1 we use more recent data.

will be mild. (They will surely be milder than if the consumer is allowed to buy freely, change his mind whenever he chooses, and count on widespread inventories to suit his immediate desires.) The contrasting volatility of U.S. investment 1950–63 shown in Table 30.1 reflects that difference.

A third major force made for instability in the U.S. economy in the nineteenth century (as in the twentieth): Families were permitted to have babies whenever they chose. As a result, major swings in population developed. These brought multiple consequences to the demand for housing, schools, hospitals, sewage systems. Hence investment calm in one period was followed by a boom in the next. The Peoples Republic of China, on the other hand, adopted "a strict policy of delaying wedlock until the late 20's."[15] That policy set aside the decade from age 16 to 26, during which man and wife produced goods for the national economy. Thus they helped accumulate, in advance, the investment requirements (for example, housing, schools) needed to provide for the children they would eventually have. Figure 30.1 shows how the U.S. population varied after the Civil War, and the construction built to supply its housing demands. The population variability from 1870 to 1920 reflects not merely births and deaths, but also immigration. (China does not get millions of immigrants. The United States no longer welcomes immigrants. Hence immigration now contributes little instability to either country.) The variation in home construction, however, also reflects expanding private credit markets. These enabled Americans to command homes of their own (before they could buy them outright) instead of continuing to live with their parents. The variation likewise reflects the adoption of piped water, indoor toilets, central heating. These novelties induced departures from older structures, which had not depreciated.

A fourth source of disturbance appeared in the American economy. New technologies were introduced whenever capitalists found it profitable to do so. Sometimes these only arranged factory work stations differently, or crop rotations. But often they required new machinery—drills, harvesters, rolling mills, electric sewing machines. Such demands in turn raised employment in the production of steel, iron ore, shovels, and more. Canonized as "innovation" by Joseph Schumpeter, such production and distribution changes may well have been the great central force driving productivity advance. But they inevitably guaranteed the unpredictability of output and employment as well.

So much for the reasons why U.S. market capitalism revealed (and reveals) built-in tendencies toward instability. What has the cyclical record of the U.S. economy actually turned out to be? Over a century ago Marx saw all capitalist nations headed for economic collapse. More recently Robert

15. Fox Butterfield, *China Alive in the Bitter Sea* (1982), p. 141. "Legally women in the cities must wait till they are at least twenty-five years old, men till they are twenty-seven or eight."

FIGURE 30.1
CONSTRUCTION BUSINESS CYCLE CHANGES RELATED TO
POPULATION CHANGES

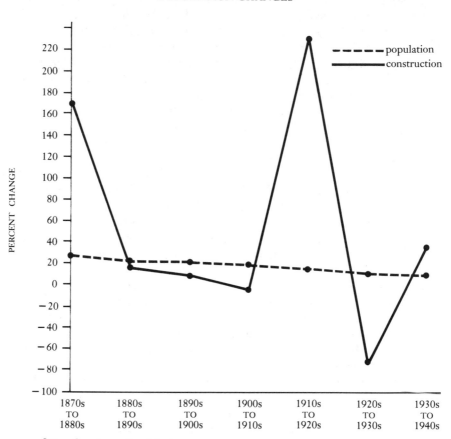

Source: See Appendix, this chapter.

Heilbroner has spoken of the "near catastrophic collapses suffered by the laissez-faire versions of capitalism characteristic of the late nineteenth and twentieth centuries."[16] Somewhat more mildly, Paul Baran observed that "the waste resulting from unemployment is neither an exclusively American phenomenon nor merely of historical interest . . . [it] has always depressed total output considerably below what it could have been in a rationally organized society."[17]

The typical review of U.S. cyclical experience focuses on "business conditions." These have generally relied on graphs and charts of somewhat mys-

16. Robert Heilbroner, An Inquiry into the Human Prospect (1974), p. 41.
17. Paul Baran, The Political Economy of Growth (1962), p. 41.

terious meaning, but all definitely showing "something" increasing and decreasing.[18] Other commentators, such as Engels and Marx, emphasized price changes and business failures under capitalism. Understandably, those whose incomes came directly from factory profits were deeply concerned with price declines and bankruptcies. Such events worried capitalists. But what about the rest of the nation? The most systematic measure used for the United States has been the classification of cyclical changes by the National Bureau of Economic Research. That measure somehow averages together data on variations in prices, the production of goods, bank clearings, inventories, and more.[19]

It reveals not 3 or 4 business downturns from 1854 to 1975, but 26. Which surely suggests much instability in the economy. True, it does not indicate that these downturns became any more severe as the decades passed—or more frequent. (Indeed their frequency has decreased since 1940. So has their severity.) But neither did it suggest that cycles in a capitalist market economy will cease.

There were, then, 26 cyclical declines in the U.S. economy 1854–1975. But there were also 26 recoveries. The cycle, by definition, had its declines and upturns. Such endemic instability did not mean systemic collapse.[20] For a great many policy concerns, however, neither the recovery nor the decline in "the cycle" was primary. What counted instead was how substantially resources were wasted, particularly human effort. Now "the business cycle" as usually measured relates to some "overall activity." Hence, for example, the official U.S. "business cycle" showed an economic decline from 1918 to 1919.[21] But unemployment did not rise from 1918 to 1919. And real incomes actually rose. At the other extreme the official cycle measure reported a "recovery" between 1933 and 1937. Yet 14 percent of the labor force remained unemployed. Table 30.2 therefore focuses not on cycles in the abstract but on unemployment, on production, output, and real wages. Unemployment increased in most cycle downturns, though not all. Industrial production actually rose in most nineteenth century recessions and in some recent ones. Farm production rose in almost every recession. Gross product rose in most, rather than falling. Real wages rose in many nineteenth-century recessions, declined

18. The Cleveland Trust Index of Business Conditions, for example, was popularized by Colonel Leonard Ayres, a well-known commentator on business conditions. The basis on which the measure was put together is not widely understood. But it is the most widely used measure of cycle changes before 1914.

19. Developed during decades of work by a distinguished group of economists, the designation of cyclical peaks and troughs, and their amplitude (i.e. severity) is intended to describe "a cycle"—which "consists of expansions occurring at about the same time in many economic activities, followed by similarly general recession, contractions, and revivals. . . . " Arthur Burns and Wesley Mitchell, *Measuring Business Cycles* (1946), p. 3.

20. As in other dynamic processes such as bicycle riding.

21. Cf. Geoffrey Moore, *Business Cycle Indicators* I (1961):670.

TABLE 30.2
BUSINESS CYCLE DECLINES, 1860–1975

Year	Change in percent unemployed	Percentage Change In			Change in real wage[a]	Real wage[a] at bottom of cycle (in dollars)
		Industrial production	Agricultural production	Gross national product		
1860–1900						
1860–61	*	—	—	—	− 18	$ 439
1865–67	*	+ 28.7	—	—	+ 10	338
1869–70	*	+ .9	—	—	− 5	375
1873–74	+ 10.0	+ 21.5	—	—	− 4	403
1882–85	+ 4.0	− 3.0	—	—	+ 62	492
1887–88	*	+ 3.7	—	—	− 4	505
1890–91	*	+ 2.9	+ 4.3	+ 4.5	+ 6	525
1893–94	+ 6.7	− 3.0	+ 3.6	− 3.2	− 21	484
1895–97	*	0	+ 15.6	+ 7.4	+ 9	529
1899–1900	*	+ 2.8	+ 1.4	+ 2.6	+ 10	573
1900–40						
1902–04	*	− 1.5	+ 6.2	+ 3.5	− 28	555
1907–08	+ 5.2	− 15.7	+ 1.9	− 8.8	− 68	545
1910–12	*	9.8	+ 11.7	+ 8.1	+ 11	619
1913–14	+ 3.6	− 5.9	+ 11.5	− 8.2	− 36	613
1918–19	*	− 12.2	+ 0.6	+ 4.1	− 13	681
1920–21	+ 6.5	− 19.3	− 6.1	− 2.3	− 52	620
1923–24	+ 2.6	− 4.6	− 5.2	+ 3.0	− 20	754
1926–27	*	+ 0.9	+ 2.8	+ 0.8	+ 9	810
1929–33	+ 22.0	− 36.3	+ 1.6	− 33.1	− 290	565
1937–38	+ 4.8	− 21.7	0	− 6.6	− 62	705
1940–75						
1948–49	+ 2.1	− 4.8	− 3.0	− 0.3	− 26	1190
1953–54	+ 2.7	− 5.8	+ 1.4	− 1.4	− 15	1427
1957–58	+ 2.5	− 7.2	+ 3.2	− 1.3	− 34	1574
1960–61	*	+ 0.8	—	+ 2.5	− 14	1719
1969–71	+ 2.4	+ 1.3	+ 7.8	+ 2.7	− 26	2181
1973–75	+ 3.6	− 9.2	+ 1.8	− 2.6	− 145	2148

[a]Of nonfarm employees (in 1914 dollars).

*Under two percentage points.

Source: See Appendix, this chapter.

in most twentieth-century recessions. But not since World War II. Over 95 percent of the labor force remained employed at the bottom of each cycle since then.

Output and prices undoubtedly varied during the centuries of Indian life in North America. But few people if any described such variation, although tradition may have handed down sharp descriptions of the famines and wars that surely brought about such variation. In the United States prior to the Civil War, variation continued to appear. Weather and insects continued to affect the production of the food, which then constituted the great bulk of national output. But before the great depression of the 1870s newer forces in cyclical changes were slight and had their greatest impact on the handful of people who were linked to nonfarm production and urban life. The classic studies of business cycles in the United States emphasize the great variation in prices from period to period, while searching for explanations of those changes. Many emphasize as fundamental the surge of innovations associated with the industrial revolution in England and the United States, with heavy investment in textile factories and steam engines from the 1780s to 1842, the subsequent intense investment in steel and railroads from 1842 to 1897, and electricity, chemical manufacturing, and automobiles from 1897 to 1920.[22] These long periods, referred to by Joseph Schumpeter as Kontratieffs (naming them in honor of a Russian economist who has written on the subject) came to an end when such investment weakened, and with it, prices, interest rates, and more. But while, as it were, only these giant mountain peaks and valleys can be seen at a great distance, if one comes closer there are other variations of importance. The Revolution, the Indian wars in Ohio and Florida, the Civil War, create fault lines across the economic landscape, associated with shorter term variations in production and prices that can hardly be ignored. And unpredictable, one-of-a-kind events, such as the discovery of gold in California in 1848, silver in Nevada in the 1860s, the opening of vast legal migration from Russia and Hungary in the last half of the century, add to such variation. Finally, very close up, such events as the bicycle craze of 1896–97 appear suddenly and then disappear as a sharp impulse to production, prices, and employment. Table 30.3 emphasizes the varying impulse to production growth and slow down for major investment items, and selected consumer goods.

What was the outcome of these rises and jolting declines on unemployment and income? One guide to an answer—the unemployment of the labor force—shows that over 85 percent of the entire labor force remained at work in every decade from 1789 on. Over 90 percent remained even during "depressions"; the single exception was the catastrophe of 1930–34.

That there is more to an economy than its cyclical behavior we know from the history of most developing nations. Thus millions of farmers in India, Ceylon, the Sudan, Chad, Egypt, are fully employed every day of the year—at an abysmally low level of income and output. It is important therefore to judge how much real incomes rose over the decades. How much did the

22. Joseph A. Schumpeter, *Business Cycles* (1939) 1:170. Standard reviews appear in Alvin Hansen, *Business Cycles and National Income* (1964), chap. 4; William Fellner, *Trends and Cycles in Economic Activity*, pp. 43–57, 81; James Duesenberry, *Business Cycles and Economic Growth* (1958), chap. 12.

TABLE 30.3
BUSINESS CYCLE CHANGES (PERCENT CHANGES BY DECADE)

	Population	Investments In					
		Railroads	Electric light and power	Telephones	Street railways	Gross residential construction	Output of producers equipment
1870s to 1880s	26	37			108	171	104
1880s to 1890s	22	−59	433	340	463	18	41
1890s to 1900s	22	106	206	116	14	13	104
1900s to 1910s	19	−13	−17	97	−101	−4	34
1910s to 1920s	16	−9	201	5800	10400	232	513
1920s to 1930s	11	158	−96	−88	−16	−75	−15
1930s to 1940s	9	114	981	1714	981	27	+234

Production (percent change year to year)

		Railroads	Electric light and power	Telephones	Street railways	Gross residential construction	
1895–96		6	3	−15	7	17	
1896–97		82	−1	16	−4	−1	
1897–98		27	5	43	9	−2	
1898–99		−32	4	54	−2	−10	
1899–1900		−44	2	−37	8	−11	
1900–01		−27	2	−23	3	−9	
1901–02		−17	1	119	10	4	
1902–03		−34	2	10	5	9	
1903–04		−41	−6	−7	3	5	
1904–05		118	1	−41	2	7	
1905–06		−9	4	55	11	23	

Source: See Appendix, this chapter.

great bulk of the labor force (who remained at work even during recessions) receive? It turns out that even in recessions their real incomes were as great as they had been during prosperous years a decade earlier. Or greater. During every recession except the catastrophe of 1930–34 persistent productivity advance and market performance yielded higher real incomes to the 90 percent of the labor force still employed than they had earned throughout most of their lives (column 6 of Table 30.2).

The 26 business cycle down-turns (in Table 30.2) fall into two categories. In one set, as Alfred Marshall put it, there is "a depression of prices, a depression of interest, and a depression of profits. . . . [But] I cannot see reason for believing that there is any considerable depression in any other respect."[23] The 1860–61 decline was just such a depression. In those years prices fell, as did the stock market. Businessmen, profit takers, and interest recipients became worse off. But the vast bulk of the community benefited insofar as businessmen were forced to sell their goods at bargain prices. Unemployment did not rise. Nor did the production of goods and services fall. So too in 1887–88, 1899–1900. Nor did unemployment rise in the business cycles declines of 1902–04, 1910–12, 1918–19, 1926–27, 1960–61.

Of more general concern were the other recessions, in which unemployment rose. The depression of 1893 and that of 1929–39 overwhelmingly affected the economic welfare of millions of families. The decades of stability and inflation since World War II point unmistakably to the political lesson learned from 1929–39—that the nation would no longer tolerate anything like such increases in unemployment.[24]

Appendix

Table 30.2 sources: To 1960: Unemployment: Lebergott, *Manpower*, pp. 178–79, 512, 527. Industrial production, agricultural production, gross national product: Census, *Long Term Economic Growth, 1960–70*, p. 184. Real wage: Lebergott, *Manpower*, pp. 524, 528.

After 1960: *Economic Report of the President, 1980*, pp. 204, 234, 248, 310, except real wage, which is derived from *National Income and Product Accounts of the United*

23. Quoted by D. H. Robertson, *Utility and All That* (1952), p. 195. Robertson quotes Giffen: "A general fall of prices . . . produces much of the gloom. The community need be none the poorer . . . somebody gets the benefit of the lower prices. But the leaders of industrial enterprise . . . are all poorer, and feel even poorer than they really are."

24. Had the milder declines, or the entire set of declines, reliably forecast the breakdown of the sytem, that fact would, of course, be of considerable concern. The data on unemployment rates and percent of capacity in use, however, show no such trend, unless observation is cut off at 1939. All recessions do presumably result in lower investment and hence a lower rate of future increase in real income. That conclusion, however, is one of comparative statics. It assumes that the businesses that fail, or cut back, are of the same productivity as those that replace them in bidding for the consumer's dollar.

States, 1929–1976 and *Employment and Training Report of the President* by methods described in Lebergott, *Manpower.*

    Table 30.3 sources: Decennial data: Population: Annual data averaged from *Historical Statistics . . . to 1970,* p. 8. Investment in regulated industries: Decennial data on net capital formation in 1929 dollars from Melville Ulmer, *Capital in Transportation, Communications and Public Utilities* (1960), p. 33. Residential, producers equipment, gross capital formation, 1929 dollars: Simon Kuznets, *Capital in the American Economy* (1961), pp. 576, 596.

    Annual data: *Historical Statistics . . . to 1970,* p. 690 quantity data. Bicycle data are current dollar estimates from William H. Shaw, *Value of Commodity Output Since 1969* (1947).

Part Four

THE
TWENTIETH
CENTURY

The opening proposition made by the Spirit of that Age involved the rectification of the Old World's hereditary wrongs.

—MELVILLE, *Billy Budd*

31

The Transition

T WO events in 1900 symbolize conflicting aspects of economic development in the new century.

One was the discovery of gold in the Klondike. Jack London, who made it a background for some novels, asked of it: "Who has profited? Who has lost? How much gold has been taken out of the ground? How much has gone into it?" He estimated that some 125,000 gold seekers had rushed into the "Northland Eldorado." Each gave "a year of his life. In view of the hardship and severity of their toil, $4 a day per man would indeed be a cheap purchase of their labor. One and all, they would refuse in a civilized country to do the work they did do at such a price." By adding to the $150 million for the value of their labor ($4 a day for 125,000 men) the $75 million that went for their transportation and food, London concluded: $220 million . . . [was] spent in extracting $22 million in gold from the ground."[1] Throughout the new century the vivid prospect of spectacular returns drew profit-seekers into new enterprises. Some did make millions in mining, in farm land, in the stock market. Others lost. Some made millions by developing the celluloid collar, the safety pin, the radio tube. Others lost millions in developing mechanical typesetters, direct electrical current, intercity trolley lines, jitneys, Piggly-Wiggly self-service grocery stores, the Reo, the Stutz (and almost 3,000 other vanished lines of automobiles).

But there was a second force. And that was the public attempt to restrain the zest of these entrepreneurs, to limit, tax, and penalize them. That attempt had been foreshadowed by outcry, and by occasional legislation in the

1. Jack London, "The Economics of the Klondike," *The American Monthly Review of Reviews* (January 1900), pp. 70–72.

403

nineteenth century. But it was pursued with far more pertinacity, and effect, in the twentieth century.

Less than a decade before the new century began Grover Cleveland vetoed an appropriation to provide free seeds to Texans whose crops had been destroyed by drought. That, he declared, was not the responsibility of the government. By contrast, Theodore Roosevelt acted as though the government carried the residual responsibility for almost anything. Roosevelt "had the will—the unappeasable will . . . to govern."[2] Discovering that Bob Maxwell, a great linesman, had been mangled in a football game he "issued an ultimatum that if rough play in football was not immediately ruled out, he would abolish it by executive decree."[3] Seeing that the Colombians had decided to double the payment they had agreed to accept from the United States for their land, Roosevelt, in his own words, "took the Canal" by sending naval forces to help the revolutionaries. Knowing that Congress was directly opposed, he took advantage of the last weeks of his term to issue an executive order arbitrarily putting thousands of acres of public land into national forests. Each of these acts represented a new and vigorous assertion of federal authority to bound the activity of the private sector.

The U.S. Industrial Commission, established by Congress and headed by Congressmen, began functioning in 1900. It sounded that note more expansively than ever before:

> It was the purpose of Congress in creating the Industrial Commission, to provide a national Tribunal, before which citizens engaged in industry . . . can obtain a hearing for the presentation of any injustice, inequality or discrimination, under which they labor, or think they labor, either as individuals, or communities, as wage earners or wage payers or as citizens . . . whether the same be due to existing laws, state or national, or lack of laws which might be enacted.[4]

The most popular book of the generation that began the nineteenth century was Tom Paine's *Common Sense*. It argued that government was at best a necessary evil. The Congress that began the twentieth century, however, invited the voters to present "any injustice . . . under which they . . . think they labor." The view of public responsibilities had shifted largely in the intervening years. It was to change even more drastically as the century went on.

2. John M. Blum, *The Progressive Presidents* (1980), p. 26. "More than any other man living within the range of notoriety "Roosevelt showed the singular primitive quality that belongs to ultimate matter . . . he was pure act." Henry Adams, *Education of Henry Adams* (1918), p. 417.

3. *Encyclopedia of Sports*, quoted in David Riesman, *Individualism Reconsidered* (1954), p. 251.

4. "Statement of the purpose of the Industrial Commission," in U.S. National Archives and Record Service Microfilm T-10-1, p. 40 (Papers of the Industrial Commission).

The Progressive Era

Three great economic issues were associated with this era of Presidents Roosevelt and Wilson, and those perpetual candidates, Bryan and Lafollette: imperialism, the fight for the income tax, and the fight against the "money monopoly."[5]

Imperialism

Economic imperialism often is, but not usefully, defined as military expansion and political intervention into the lives of others. That experience reaches back to the most primitive tribes, and forward to the invasion of Iran by Iraq, of Vietnam by the United States, and of Afghanistan by Soviet Russia. Nor is imperialism usefully defined as an attempt to merchandise goods abroad under the mantle of a dominant nation. The "essence of imperialism and imperialist parasitism," wrote Lenin, "is foreign investment on a new and immensely larger scale" in the era 1890–1914. "Under the old capitalism the export of goods was the most typical feature. Under modern capitalism, when monopolies prevail, the export of capital has become the typical feature."[6]

What, then, about the export of U.S. capital? Between the Civil War and 1897, American foreign investment rose from a mere $75 million to $685 million; it rose by nearly $20 billion from 1897 to 1929. Such an increase in U.S. foreign investment indeed seems impressive. But most numbers for such continental economies as the United States or China or Russia look big. How do they look when dimensioned against the entire flow of U.S. investment?

Of all U.S. investment from 1869 to 1897, the foreign share accounted for 1 percent; and from 1900 to 1929—the heyday of marine intervention—it accounted for only 6 percent. Put another way, from 1900 to 1929 the entire increase of U.S. foreign investment all over the globe did not equal the increased investment in California alone. And it "pushed the rate of return on U.S. capital from a bit over 4.8 percent to a bit under 4.9 percent."[7] Some individual companies made out very well indeed.[8] U.S. foreign policy, civilian and military, had important moral, political, and social consequences. But not because of the importance of its foreign investment component. In a later era still larger absolute dollar figures for U.S. foreign investment led to similar exaggeration of the importance of foreign investment. "Multinational corpo-

---

5. The tide of change moved no more swiftly under what John Blum calls "The Progressive Presidents" than under that sturdy reactionary, Taft.

6. Eugene Varga and L. Mendelsohn, *New Data for V.I. Lenin's Imperialism* (1949), pp. 138, 214.

7. Stanley Lebergott, "The Returns to U.S. Imperialism, 1890–1929," *Journal of Economic History* (June 1980), pp. 230–31.

8. Not to be overstated. Thus no less a financier than J. P. Morgan helped bankroll the giant Cerro de Pasco mine, which yielded no profits until after 15 years of investment and development.

rations at the end of the 1960's accounted for $180 billions a year. . . . U.S. multicorps accounted for over one half of all merchandise exports, and over one third of all merchandise imports in 1970." This statement is surely more dramatic, if no truer, than an equivalent statement: Such sales constituted less than 1 percent of all sales by American business in 1970. Infinite delight was undoubtedly derived by stockholders of Singer Sewing Machine and Carnegie Steel from their overseas sales in the 1880s and 1890s, and by General Motors, Fox Film, and United Fruit owners in later decades. But their importance for the general course of the nation's economy was limited.[9]

The Income Tax

The income tax offered a heady combination of arithmetic and romance. Tariffs had provided 90 percent of federal revenues in the nation's first century. The income tax offered a fresh alternative. The traditional distribution of income had been unequal. The income tax offered an improvement. Wealth accumulated increasingly after the Civil War in a new and unusual form, as symbolic capital (stocks and bonds) rather than its more ancient forms of land and luxurious homes. New York legislators, ever entrepreneurial, decided to impose a tax on such new types of property, expecting that it would be paid largely by the ineffably wealthy William Henry Vanderbilt (who owned most of the New York Central railroad—left him by his father). But the prey was wary. Vanderbilt promptly made J. P. Morgan's reputation by having the latter quietly sell his stock in England, thus baffling the avid legislators. Slow learners in other state legislatures (e.g., Virginia and Wisconsin) soon discovered the timidity and speed with which symbolic capital fled taxation. State income taxes proved an "iridescent dream," as a New York State Commission noted.[10] The national legislature recognized that the ability to flee from state to state mattered little for their purposes since most Americans wanted to remain domiciled in the United States. In 1894 they revived the transient Civil War income tax.[11]

The rich and their supporters were shocked, but not into silence. The

9. Explaining diplomatic policy declarations, and perhaps actions, is another matter. William Appleman Williams (*The Tragedy of American Diplomacy* (1972), p. 54) has proposed that "businessmen and other economic groups thought 10 percent [of "American overseas expansion"] made a crucial difference . . . the conviction of these groups would make the figure important . . . its relevance to foreign policy might be very high. Such was precisely the case with the American-China Development Company . . . Before it died it exerted an extensive influence on American policy in Asia."

10. Quoted in Edwin Seligman, *The Income Tax* (1914), p. 420. Thus in 1900 Pennsylvania collected one-third as much from income taxes as from liquor taxes, and Virginia one-fifth as much.

11. Tacked on to the Wilson-Gorman tariff of 1894, the tax was struck down by the Supreme Court as being a "direct tax," forbidden by the constitution. The sixteenth amendment then made its slow way through the state legislatures to permit income taxation.

Nation saw it as a tax that "exempts thirty nine men out of forty, offers a standing temptation to indefinite exploitation, indefinite extravagance."[12] Arguing against an income tax rate of 2 percent Rufus Choate, put forward the lurid case: it was the thin edge of the wedge; taxes on incomes over $50,000 might eventually rise to 20 percent.[13] (It is difficult to imagine what words Choate could summon up for an era when marginal tax rates on incomes of $50,000 ran to 49 percent.)

As a source of Federal revenues the tax proved a magnificent and ever increasing success. It had permitted naval armament increases when instituted by Britain in 1910, and Germany in 1913. In World War I it enabled the United States, Britain, and Germany to lavish incredible amounts of human and physical resources on producing ammunition for massive artillery barrages. After that war, public expenditure, for a variety of purposes, was increasingly financed by Americans as income recipients (via income taxation) rather than as consumers of that income (via tariffs). The substitution had one signal advantage. It efficiently conserved legislative energies. Life became simpler for Congress. For the battle against tariffs had always involved direct, urgent, and threatening lobbies. But the income tax, affected only a small group of widely censured individuals, from its earliest days until its expansion in 1936.

The second purpose of the income tax was to reduce income inequality. "In the half century following the Civil War . . . men accumulated fortunes of incredible size. Between 1892 and 1899 Rockefeller's personal dividends from Standard Oil amounted to between $30,000,000 and $40,000,000. In 1900 Andrew Carnegie had an income from his steel companies of $23,000,000. These revenues were not subject to tax."[14] The income tax was created in "response to the widespread demand to equalize tax burdens borne by the various classes . . . [It was to] be paid by the wealthier classes."[15]

As Congressman De Armond of Missouri declared, passage of the income tax would "mark the dawn of a brighter day, with more of sunshine, more of the songs of the birds, more of that sweetest music, the laughter of children well fed, well clothed, well housed . . . good, even-handed, wholesome Democracy shall be triumphant. God hasten the era of equality in taxa-

12. Quoted in Paul Angle, *Crossroads: 1913* (1963), p. 154. Petulantly it warned of "the habit, on the part of almost the entire population of the country, of regarding a small class as the sole bearers of the burden of any fresh governmental expenditure, they themselves being interested only in its benefits."

13. Noted in his Supreme Court argument against the 1894 tax. Cf. J. K. Beach, "The Income Tax Decision," *Yale Review* (May 1896), p. 62.

14. Galbraith, *The Affluent Society*, p. 38. Pedestrian economic analysis focuses not on who formally pays the tax (e.g., importer, corporation) but on who actually does (incidence).

15. Gerald Eggert, "Richard Olney and the Income Tax," *Mississippi Valley Historical Review* (June 1961), pp. 24–25. The tariff presumably "lay most heavily on the poorer classes."

tion and opportunity."[16] In time, income before tax was distributed more equally, but probably for reasons quite unrelated to the income tax (Table 39.2). Tax rates imposed on the very richest did escalate. But rates on the poor and lower income families likewise escalated. And the rich discovered means of converting income into nontaxable receipts. The net contribution of the income tax to inducing equality is not obvious. That later generations grumbled, complained, and feared does not demonstrate that the Congressman had mistaken the future. It may only mark the decline of faith in what such a secular gospel could offer.

The Money Monopoly

In 1913, Arsene Pujo, the senator from Louisiana, released his committee's long-awaited report. Preceded by years of Populist oratory, its theme was directly foreshadowed by President Woodrow Wilson in 1913: "The great monopoly in this country is the money monopoly." The Committee was explicit: "Far more dangerous than . . . the elimination of competition in industry is the control of credit through the domination of these groups over our banks and industries. . . . It is impossible there should be competition with all the facilities for raising money or selling large issues of bonds in the hands of these few bankers and their partners."[17]

Few reporters who rushed the story into print noticed who was in danger—namely, businesses selling "large issues of bonds." Such businesses, of course, were chiefly the firms busy putting together the gigantic cartels of the time. Few businessmen were thus endangered, and no farmers or workers. What about the concentration of "facilities for raising money"? J. P. Morgan did own many millions. So did his occasional allies, James Stillman (head of the giant National City Bank) and George Baker (head of the First National Bank). But Louis Brandeis also gives us the facts on their total resources, including the "huge deposits from their subjects." Altogether these totaled less than 5 percent of total bank deposits.[18] That would hardly enable them to fix interest rates in Maine, Nebraska, Georgia, or even in New York. For they competed with the giant life insurance companies in Connecticut, private capitalists (like Russell Sage), land investors (like the Davenport brothers), and others who lent money all over the United States wherever they could detect (or anticipate) a profit. Morgan et al. also had to compete with thousands of equally greedy bankers outside New York City, private mortgage lenders, and others. Monopoly powers could hardly be achieved in the face of such competition.

16. De Armond, quoted in Seligman, *Income Tax*, p. 502.
17. Quotations from Louis Brandeis, *Other People's Money* (1933), pp. 1–2.
18. Data for these three come from Ibid., pp. 16, 19–20. The total of $660 million deposits in their three banks is raised to $1 billion to include the private fortunes of these men. Deposits in all banks (some $20 billion) are reported in *Historical Statistics . . . to 1970*, p. 625.

A second theme of the period was cogently summarized by the Pujo Committee: "These banker-barons levy, through their excessive exactions, a heavy toll upon the whole community . . . upon consumers"—specifically by charging the railroads above-market interest rates on their bond issues.[19] Some back of the envelope calculating, however, shows how heavy that toll was: excessive banker exactions would have cost consumers at most, one extra dime for every $100 they spent.[20]

A third theme Brandeis urged was the gross mismanagement of the New Haven Railroad system under Morgan management. Not only did that system expand in a futile attempt to impose a transport monopoly on New England. Morgan also collected commissions on stock which the New Haven issued while he sat on its Board. (That stock was sold to raise money for buying up the other New England railroads and steamship companies.) Brandeis opposed such practices with an ancient maxim: No man can serve two masters. "A complete detachment of the banker from the corporation is necessary in order to secure for the railroad the benefit of the clearest financial judgment. . . . Soundness of judgment is easily obscured by self-interest."[21] Unfortunately, that lesson was not learned by the 1920s. Though bankers were not the only actors in those years, they played their part in overselling securities. They thus helped to bring on the 1929 stock market crash, which did more to destroy capitalism than the combined efforts of all the radicals in American history.

19. Brandeis, *Other People's*, p. 32.

20. Railroad freight charges on consumer goods shipped from producer to initial distributor in 1909 ran $565 million or, say, $570 million inclusive of rail freight from wholesaler to retailer: Harold Barger, *Distribution's Place in the American Economy Since 1869* (1955), p. 130. Total freight revenues of railroads ran $1,678 million. *Historical Statistics . . . to 1970*, p. 733. The implicit ratio of 34 percent was applied to total railroad interest charges of $0.4 billion. *Historical Statistics . . . to 1970*, p. 428. Hence, $136 million were passed on to consumers. Now railroad bonds in 1890 yielded 1.93 percent more than U.S. governments. That margin rose to 2.33 percent in 1910, after the bankers became prominent in financing. Had that margin not risen, the actual interest paid on railroad bonds would have been 14 percent lower, reducing the $15.20 billion actually spent for PCE goods to $15.19 billion.

21. Barger, *Distribution's*, p. 135.

Conservation is humanity caring for the future.
—NANCY NEWHALL

32

Conservation

IN "the first years of [Indiana] gas development, 100,000,000 cubic feet of this inestimable fuel was wasted every day . . . 60,000,000 feet per day were burning from waste pipes connected with the Pittsburgh supply alone."[1] For five years a single well (Haymaker No. 1) wasted 30,000,000 cubic feet of natural gas a day, while the McGuigan well "was not used for over a year after it was struck."[2] Gas came gushing out before markets had developed, or technology for its use. Its price was so low that producers did not even meter its sale. Without metering, further waste was inevitable. "Consumers have been slow to adopt improved mixers and burners. This is largely owing to the method of paying for the gas by the month or year, instead of by meter measure."[3] Consumers left lamps burning all day and night "to save matches and avoid the trouble of relighting."[4]

The same sequence—huge discoveries, low prices, waste—appeared in the early years of petroleum drilling. "The advent of the immense flowing wells [near] . . . Oil Creek [in 1861] caused such a sudden increase in the production that . . . prices went down to almost nothing. Thousands of barrels of the product were allowed to go to waste."[5] With crude oil cheap, manufacturers in turn treated it casually. Some 20 percent of the oil produced in the

1. Indiana Department of Geology and Natural Resources, *Eighteenth Annual Report, 1893* (1894), pp. 203, 211, 217. The "Wainwright Wonder . . . was a monster among gas wells, and was visited by thousands of people . . . to see the wonderful exhibition of its power . . . for months it was allowed to stand open, belching forth its millions of cubic feet of valuable fuel. When first drilled . . . [wells stood] open for days and weeks."

2. 1890 Census, *Report on Mineral Industries in the United States* (1890), pp. 507, 513.

3. Indiana Department of Geology, *Eighteenth Annual Report*, pp. 203, 211, 217.

4. Hosea Webster, "Natural Gas in the United States," *Cassier's Magazine* (January 1898), p. 302.

5. *The Derrick's Handbook of Petroleum* I (1898):706.

first factories was in the form of benzine and tar. These were useless for many years until Standard Oil eventually developed techniques for converting them into marketable products. They were therefore not saved, but "run into the creek at night [or] into holes in the ground, and burned."[6]

The increase in sheer waste, like the prospect of resource exhaustion, did not go on without notice or rebuke. Warnings were uttered. And from the most impressive sources. For decades official experts kept forecasting only a 20-year supply of lumber remaining. In 1864 the Department of Agriculture observed that "at the present rate of [timber] consumption . . . the whole region east of the Mississippi will be stripped . . . within the next twenty or thirty years."[7] Over a decade later a new Secretary of the Interior still warned: "only 20 years" of timber was left.[8] A third of a century later, Gifford Pinchot (head of the Forest Service and great conservation leader) reported less than a 30-year supply left.[9] Yet half a century later the Forest Service itself reported more saw timber available than at the time of Pinchot's warning.[10]

The exhaustion of other reserves was also foreseen. In 1920, the U.S. Geological Survey forecast that the nation's oil supply would "be exhausted in 14 years."[11] In the next half-century the auto industry grew phenomenally yet proved that oil resources after that growth were four times as great as when the forecast was made.[12]

In 1909 the Forest Service forecast that the United States would starve by 1950 unless it added a billion acres to the crop acreage then in use.[13] Three-quarters of a century later the United States had added only 5 percent

6. Westgate, in U.S. Industrial Commission, *Hearings* (1901), I:371.

7. U.S. Department of Agriculture, *Report of the Commissioner of Agriculture* (1864), p. 49. "The rapid disappearance of our forests should excite the serious attention of land owners generally. . . . A land owner pointed out to me over one hundred acres of land, once densely covered with timber, but now entirely cleared for the sole purpose of supplying his own family with firewood . . . where the timber has been cut for . . . towns, factories, steamboats, and railways, the devastation has been more rapid."

8. Quoted in Harold Barnett and Chandler Morse, *Scarcity and Growth* (1963), p. 86.

9. Ibid, p. 76. Cf. R. S. Kellogg, "The Drain Upon the Forests," U.S.D.A. Forest Service Circular No. 129 (1907), pp. 15–16.

10. Kellogg in "The Drain Upon the Forests" estimated "a stumpage of 1,400 billion feet, an annual use of 100 billion feet" with exhaustion due in 14 years. The "net volume of saw timber" available in 1970 was 2,421 billion feet. *U.S. Statistical Abstract* (1978), p. 731. Stuart Chase's celebrated *Men and Machines* (1929), p. 305, warned: "We are now cutting our timber four times as fast as it is growing. The end promises to come in thirty years."

11. U.S. Geological Survey *Annals* (May 1920) quoted in Hans Landsberg et al., *Resources in America's Future* (1963), p. 396.

12. *U.S. Statistical Abstract*, (1981), p. 735. Cf. American Petroleum Institute, *Petroleum Facts and Figures* (1959).

13. Raphael Zon, "The Future Use of Land in the United States," United States Department of Agriculture Forest Service Circular No. 159, p. 6.

of that amount. But it fed a far greater population than the Service had assumed, and devoted 100 million acres to feeding significant portions of Russia and China, exporting cotton, and more.[14]

What made these repeated predictions of doom incorrect? Mere luck? If so the odds of catastrophe may still be high. For what is wasted (or consumed) by one generation is surely unavailable to future generations. Today's use of scarce fossil fuels raises vital questions—but questions that should be asked about all intergenerational choices. How is it that French vineyards were laboriously conserved—for five centuries? How were Saxony's forests maintained so they yield as much wood in the twentieth century as in the eighteenth? How does an essential stock of capital equipment get left for each successive generation, instead of simply being used up by its predecessor? Is there a mechanism at work deciding these intertemporal choices? If so it should be evident in reactions by two economic groups to the changing prices they faced: owners and buyers of resources. What motives guided each? What were the resource consequences of their actions in the U.S. experience?

Owners of Resources

Attacks by reformers and federal officials provide unusually relevant and close evidence on the behavior of owners of forest lands. Henry George, the great opponent of "land monopoly," and sponsor of the single tax (on land), wrote: "There is in Marin County . . . a fine belt of redwood timber. . . . But it remains uncut, and lumber procured many miles beyond, is daily hauled past it . . . because its owner prefers to hold it for the greater price it will bring in the future." Moreover, "In the thickly settled parts of the United States there is enough land to maintain three or four times our population, lying unused, because its owners are holding it for higher prices, and immigrants are forced past this unused land to seek homes where their labor will be far less productive. . . . Mineral land . . . is frequently withheld from use while poorer deposits are worked . . . ."[15]

Some years later the U.S. Commissioner of Corporations attacked "tendencies toward greater concentration." Article I in his case against them was blunt: "Some large [forest] holders who are large lumber manufacturers as well, hold their timber and supply their mills from other sources. One manufacturing company, which owns over 5 billion feet [in standing timber] has felled no timber for nearly 20 years, but has bought its logs on the open market. . . . On many of the largest holdings no cutting at all is done."[16]

14. The increase in cropland from 1900 to 1950 appears in *Historical Statistics* (1957), J-52; the change from 1950 to 1965, in *Historical Statistics* (1970), p. 457; and from 1965 to 1978 in *Agricultural Statistics* (1979), p. 438. The variety of sources is needed to account for changes from cropland in the lower 48 states to 50 states, from cropland to acreage harvested.

15. Henry George, *Progress and Poverty* (1881), pp. 232, 361.

16. U.S. Bureau of Corporations, *The Lumber Industry* (1913):14.

Why did owners of valuable timber land, of minerals (coal, oil, iron) engage in this very odd behavior? George's answer is crystalline: They held the natural resource "for the greater price it will bring in the future." (The behavior of OPEC countries holding their oil during the early 1970s was equally clear, their motivation equally comprehensible.) Holders of large resource reserves knew that they could make money by selling their timber or minerals at once. But they expected to make still more money by holding out for future sale.[17]

Resource owners differed fundamentally from all other producers. That difference made them the earliest guardians of the nation's resources, and perhaps the most effective. Other producers made their profits by producing—horse carriages or bicycles, magazines or pig iron. In so doing they typically served consumer desires by running down the nation's resources. But those who actually owned those resources had a second way of making money—by *not* producing. The explanation was simple. Everyone knew that eventually—even if it took a million years—mankind was likely to exhaust the supply of iron ore or petroleum or coal. As long as any given resource deposit was being consumed, then, the value of the remaining resource deposits tended to rise. Businesses owning similar mines or forests were thereby guaranteed that they could charge increased scarcity rents. In equilibrium, their resource values had to increase along with "the common rate of return . . . for that risk class" of assets.[18] That increase raised the price, thereby slowing consumption of the scarce resources.

The powerful motivation of resource owners to conserve their resources derived from their desire for profits. Investors in mines (or timberlands) could alternatively hold their wealth in reproducible capital, such as factories, stores, inventories. Hence such investors would expect the value of their natural resource wealth to grow at a rate equal to the marginal product of reproducible capital. Why lock money up in timber unless it earned at least as much as it could earn in business?

Owners, in fact, would try to charge not merely the usual scarcity rent but whatever higher price monetized those fears that the end of the resource meant the end of civilization as we know it. Resource owners, then, were strongly motivated to charge as full a scarcity rent for their resources as anyone in society could measure that rent. History notes that when they

17. As long ago as the end of the eighteenth century the still feudal Scots landowners preserved their woods for financial reasons. They cut their woods "down in equal portions, in a rotation of sixteen years, and raise regular revenues out of them." Thomas Pennant, *Second Tour*, in John Pinkerton, *General Collection . . . of Voyages and Travels* (1805), p. 187.

18. The phrase comes from the characteristically witty and analytically close discussion by Robert Solow, "The Economics of Resources or the Resources of Economics," *American Economic Review* (May 1974). Cf. too the excellent study by Richard L. Gordon, "A Reinterpretation of the Theory of Exhaustion," *Journal of Political Economy* (June 1967).

shrewdly foresaw increasing demands for those resources they promptly raised their price. In the 1880s the French Secretan group foresaw the immense increase in world copper demand that was coming with the spread of electricity and telephone lines. They formed a cartel to drive up the price of copper. Their failure, after a few short years, warned future cartelists that they needed the power of government behind them to run an effective international cartel. (That lesson was reinforced when Joseph Leiter of Chicago cornered the world wheat market in 1898, but so briefly that he lost $9.8 million doing so.) However, the cartel did work for a while, driving up the scarcity rents accruing to those who owned the giant Anaconda Copper company in Montana, the Climax Mine in Arizona. By so doing, however, it induced J. P. Morgan and the Guggenheims to begin vast copper mine developments in Chile and Mexico, thus increasing the effective supply of copper.[19] Theodore Roosevelt set up the National Conservation Commission in 1908. Together they alarmed the citizenry with a doomsday scenario of how the nation's stock of timber, coal, range land, and copper would abruptly end in 20 or 30 years. Their warning helped drive up returns to mine owners still further.

Given the rapidity with which the ancient first growth forests were decimated, and well aware of such helpful warnings, tree owners also raised their scarcity rents. A clear index of that change appears on Table 32.1. As urbanization accelerated in 1866–86 wood was called for to build the houses springing up in Chicago and Brooklyn, in Denver and Atlanta. Pine prices rose by 9 percent (the general price level changing very little). But owners increased the price of standing trees ("stumpage") by 391 percent. By doing so, of course, they slowed the rate at which existing forests were cut down. They discouraged some of the least essential current uses (as judged by willingness to pay), thereby saving trees for future generations. From 1900 to 1950 douglas fir lumber prices rose by 415 percent. Stumpage then rose by 2,030 percent. (Interest rates, which marked the trend in equilibrium rates of return on many assets, rose hardly at all. Still later, owners of stumpage foresaw the increasing scarcity of trees as the post-World war II construction boom got underway. Noting the ever expanding federal housing programs (mortgage insurance, public housing, loans for veterans) they demanded higher and higher scarcity rents. They thereby slowed the cutting down of forests, and all but banned low-priority uses (e.g., apple crates).

Owners likewise acted in other ways to save resources—that is, conserve their assets. One way was by reducing waste. In 1880 fire destroyed

---

19. Copper mine owners did not merely collect scarcity rents, of course. With increased rents they began to work the lower and lower grades of ore that alone remained. Before 1870 copper ores in the United States yielded from 20 to 50 percent; by 1906 the ones being worked yielded only 2.5 percent; and by 1928, 1.4 percent. Cf., F. E. Richter, "The Copper Mining Industry in the United States, 1845–1925," *Quarterly Journal of Economics* 41 (February 1927):236–91.

TABLE 32.1
CONSERVATION INVESTMENT

	Price per 1,000 board feet (in dollars)		Interest rates on bonds (in percent)
	lumber	stumpage	
White pine:			
1866	11.75	1.12	8.0
1876	9.25	2.50	6.7
1886	12.75	5.50	4.6
1896	NA	5.20	4.3
1905	NA	15.00	3.9
Douglas fir:			
1900	8.67	0.77	3.1
1940	22.20	2.30	2.5
1950	73.30	16.40	2.0
1960	75.00	32.00	3.7
1970	92.00	41.90	6.5
1980	298.00	379.80	8.5

Source: White pine (Michigan): For 1866–1887, Chauncey Depew, *One Hundred Years of American Commerce* I (1895):201. For other years, 60th Cong., 2d sess., S.D. 676, Report of the National Conservation Commission, II:749, 751.

Douglas fir: For 1900, Conservation Commission, p. 749. For 1940–70, *Historical Statistics Since 1970*, p. 547. For 1980 *U.S. Statistical Abstract for 1981*, p. 706.

Bond yields: *Historical Statistics*, p. 1003; *U.S. Statistical Abstract, 1981*, p. 523. For 1896–1905, Railroad bonds; for 1900–1980, municipals.

10.3 million acres of timber. Then came advancing civilization, urbanization, carelessness, and the ubiquitous cigarette discards. Surely timber fires increased. Yet a century later fire destroyed less acreage—in fact, two thirds less—than in 1880. For increased fire prevention each year, mostly private, was saving the timber equivalent of 7 million forest acres.[20]

Similarly, producers of natural gas learned how to conserve gas once lost by leakage or accident and sell it for cold cash. They cut the proportion of total output wasted. Rough estimates are shown in Table 32.2. Persistent effort had cut waste. The neighborhoods around the giant "gas works" of Chicago and New York became less noisome. And profits greater. Natural gas had once been a dangerous byproduct to the early oil drillers. (Louisiana producers "set fire to the gas for an advertisement to the region."[21]) Producers

20. 1880 Census, Vol. IX, *Report on the Forests of North America* (1884) P. 491. *U.S. Statistical Abstract 1981*, P. 704.

21. U.S. Geological Survey, Bulletin 394 (1909), p. 59.

TABLE 32.2
WASTE GAS AS A
PERCENTAGE OF PRODUCTION

Year	Manufactured gas	Natural gas
1864	16	
1898	8	
1902	6	
1908		47
1950		11
1972		1

Source: Manufactured gas: *Congressional Globe* (June 10, 1864), p. 2817. U.S. Commissioner of Labor, *Fourteenth Annual Report*, (1899), pp. 484 ff. U.S. Geological Survey, *Mineral Resources of the U.S., 1902* (1904), p. 522.

  Natural gas: U.S. Geological Survey, Bulletin 394 (1909), pp. 59–60. American Gas Association, *Gas Facts* (1973), p. 29.

gradually laid pipelines to the wells, creating a product to compete profitably with manufactured gas. Such systematic reduction in waste yielded huge profits.

Buyers of Resources

  America's scarce mineral resources and timber were almost all bought by private businesses. These, however, were notoriously interested in keeping down their costs, whether for labor, taxes, or resource materials. They evidenced scant loyalty to the vested interests of their suppliers, even those in the resource industries.

  In 1849 the president of one railroad "got up a locomotive for burning coal." He concluded "that if railroads multiplied in the future as they had in the past, our beautiful and green hillsides would be stripped of their foliage . . . unless some other fuel than wood could be found for locomotives." (And wood would become impossibly expensive.) His first coal burner became "a scarecrow to those who furnished wood."[22] But locomotives eventually did substitute coal for wood, saving millions of trees.

  Lead mining provided a classic example. As soon as the Louisiana Territory was purchased by Jefferson, the United States took over its well-known lead mines, near Dubuque. It leased them on a royalty basis to individual miners and companies. As the decades passed the price of lead rose. Gradu-

22. S. M. Felton, quoted in John L. Ringwalt, *Development of Transportation Systems in the United States* (1888), p. 161.

ally buyers substituted other materials for it. Lead had been used for casket linings, and bathtubs. Galvanized iron was eventually substituted. Lead had been used for water pipes. Cast iron was eventually substituted by the pipe manufacturers. And toothpaste manufacturers gradually substituted plastic for lead in tubes. These various buyers conserved lead for future generations by substituting materials whose prices did not proclaim any equal scarcity.

The steel industry conserved iron ore by other means. In 1828 it used only ore. By 1870 it still stocked its furnaces chiefly with ore, but did rely on scrap for 14 percent of its iron input. In 1900 U.S. Steel, the industry's giant leader was organized. It owned an immense supply of cheap high-grade Minnesota ore. Yet the scrap share in the industry rose to 36 percent by 1910. By 1960 it reached 42 percent, and by 1977, 74 percent.[23] (Why the steady substitutions, saving ore? Cheap as ore was, scrap was cheaper.) Its use incidentally removed immense amounts from the urban landscape.

Lumber factories had long taken for granted cheap, and apparently endless, supplies of timber. In 1871 U.S. manufacture was "characterized by a waste that can be truly called criminal . . . timber has formerly been so cheap . . . that there has really been no time to . . . develop economic plans of cutting and handling timber . . . one fifth of all timber sawed is converted into sawdust . . . it might even be set down at one fourth, after the stock is squared. Circular and muley saw mills . . . give us five eighths lumber and three eighths sawdust."[24] Then came a gradual switch from circular to hand saws, reducing much of this waste.

Rising wood prices stimulated buyers to still more conservation. They kept switching from the highest price resources to ones that were less scarce and cheaper. Once they had accepted only the choicest hardwoods, and only the finest trees, free of knots. Such selective logging yielded only about 2,000 feet per acre of forest. By 1918, however, 8,000 to 10,000 feet were being taken off each acre. No longer were 6,000 to 8,000 feet wasted by crude cutting. Moreover, final consumers began accepting furniture made of field pine, gum, and older trees as the price of better lumber spiraled upward.[25] In time even these "inferior woods" rose in price. Buyers then substituted still further. Production of lumber fell somewhat from 1900 to 1980. But produc-

23. 20th Cong., 1st sess., H.R. 115, *Duties on Imports* (1828), pp. 22, 33. Three tons of iron ore were used to 1 ton of bar iron produced. 1870 Census, *Wealth and Industry*, vol. III, p. 625. U.S. Bureau of Mines and Works Progress Administration, *Technology, Employment and Output per Man in Iron Mining* (1940), p. 244. H. Landsberg, *Natural Resources for U.S. Growth* (1964), p. 8. 1977 Census of Manufactures, *Blast Furnaces*, MC77-1-33A, pp. 33A-40. We use the ratio of purchased scrap to scrap plus ore.

24. J. Richards, *A Treatise on the Construction and Operation of Wood-Working Machines* (1872), pp. 141, 143. "Allowing for shrinkage and warping, one eighth more" is wasted in shavings. These, at best, were used for fuel.

25. U.S. Bureau of Corporations, *The Lumber Industry* (January 1913), part 1, p. 189.

tion of plywoods and veneer rose over 2,000 percent.[26] When plywoods eventually rose in price buyers again shifted—to pressboard and chipboard. These were all created from rubbish once abandoned in the field or burned in donkey engines. The trend was not universal. Prudent reuse did not increase where rising costs failed to stimulate it. Thus newspapers actually began to use a smaller proportion of old paper and rags, but a greater proportion of pulp wood.[27] The reason, of course, was that Canada had its own interests. Feeling a shortage not of timber but of current income, it began to monetize its enormous forests by exporting pulp.

Producers intent on saving other resources increased the use of paper and pulp. For example, refiners discovered that so much sugar was wasted in scooping sugar from barrels in grocery stores that consumers could get cleaner sugar, at no extra cost, in cardboard packages.[28] (And fewer would become ill from contaminants.)

One long-term view of how the incentives of market competition shaped conservation is suggested by data for coal consumption. Figure 32.1 reveals how persistently technologies were changed over the decades. The newer steamships used less and less coal than prior designs. Electric power stations no less persistently cut their usage of coal, the key exhaustible energy source in the century from 1850 to 1950.

In the long term, as Barnett and Morse have shown, the price of minerals and other extractive resource products has not risen faster than the general price level.[29] This outcome, they indicate, was chiefly attributable to the steady decline in the quantity of labor used to extract these resources. Now, from one social point of view—human life and suffering—that surely marks an advance. Fewer man-hours in lumbering meant less employment in the most dangerous of industries as judged in terms of occupational fatality rates. Similar reductions occurred when coal mining substituted machinery for men.

But if society were less interested in saving the lives of human beings today than in laying up stocks of resources for future generations—to build houses and boxes from wood, or to convey ever more shoppers by gasoline automobiles—that outcome will not be sufficient. Society will then have a keener interest in keeping down the use of such products, and such restraint will not be induced merely by stable relative mineral prices. One would want to know to what extent private owners of resources were charging higher rent

26. *Historical Statistics . . . to 1970*, pp. 539, 541, and *Statistical Abstract* (1982), pp. 697, 699. Plywood output rose from 5 million to 1,395 million.

27. 1880 Census, p. 456, showed more than half the tonnage from waste. The 1963 Census, MC-63 (2)-26A, p. 26a-27 showed less than a tenth.

28. Earl Bobst, President of American Sugar Refining, quoted in Arthur Moore, *More They Told Barron* (1931), p. 239.

29. Harold Barnett and Chandler Morse, *Scarcity and Growth* (1963), chap. 8.

FIGURE 32.1
ENERGY UTILIZATION OVER THE LONG TERM, 1830–1930
(POUNDS OF COAL REQUIRED PER HORSEPOWER GENERATED ON STEAMSHIPS AND PER
KILOWATT HOUR GENERATED IN CENTRAL ELECTRICITY STATIONS)

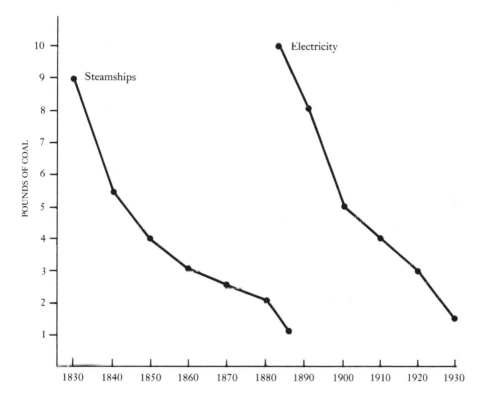

Source: Steamships: J. L. Ringwalt, *Development of Transportation Systems in the United States* (1888), p. 288. Electricity: George Orrok, "Central Stations," *Mechanical Engineering* (April 1930), p. 330.

for these resources. The stumpage prices noted above do report higher scarcity rent for trees. But what about non-renewable resources? It has recently become clear that even petroleum can be produced, or adequately substituted for, in a scenario of gene splicing that produces bacteria which yield energy indefinitely as they consume alfalfa. But assuming that petroleum, for example, is indeed non-renewable in finite time, what about the trend of real prices for such resources? The records indicate that a proxy for the scarcity rent of petroleum did more than double from the period 1946 to 1971, and surely rose markedly thereafter.[30]

The preceding discussion has dealt with privately owned resources. It was to be expected that their owners extracted as great a price as possible. To achieve that goal they chose not to sell their timber, minerals, or land at any given time. And as it became more obvious that exhaustible resources were in strong demand they kept them off the market, to bring still higher prices in the future.

What, however, about resources owned by government, by "society," by no one in particular? How they were conserved, if at all, depended on how much "the people" or government officials concerned themselves with any particular type of conservation. U.S. experience pointed in differing directions.

One of the most basic resources was the land itself. Private ownership of U.S. land developed in the seventeenth century. Before that the land was used by the various Indian tribes in an area and whatever other tribes they permitted to hunt or fish in that area. The conservation consequences varied. For example, prairie Indians "were in the habit, through carelessness or design, of firing the prairie grasses every spring . . . in pine woods such fires would destroy all the vegetation with which they came in contact." Thus, when the very first white men arrived in the Louisville area they found no trees for miles around. And fire scars marked the trees that edged that huge open area. Some 50 years passed between the time the Indians were driven away (at the end of the eighteenth century) and general settlement by white farmers. During that time the trees gradually reseeded themselves and spread over the area.[31] (One theory actually explains the extreme fertility of mid-western prairies by that succession of fires, triggered both by design and by lightning.)

As with the land, so with the water. The contrast between the whale and the trout is instructive. Once caught off Long Island, the whales retreated to the Antarctic during the nineteenth century. Other nations joined the bold Nantucket whalemen, and by 1928–38 men were taking almost twice the

30. The gene-splicing scenario has been outlined in talks by the editor of *Science*, the journal of the American Association for the Advancement of Science. The rent proxy is discussed by Santayan Devarajan and Anthony Fisher, "Exploration and Scarcity," *Journal of Political Economy* (December 1982). They show that the real exploration costs per barrel of U.S. oil and gas (in constant prices) rose markedly. That substantial percentage rise suggests, though it does not prove, the upward trend in scarcity rents. For firms tend to treat marginal discovery cost as an upper bound for rent; why pay more to add new reserves than the expected profits on them?

31. N. S. Shaler in 52d Cong., 1st sess., H.D. 1, part 5, *Report of the Secretary of the Interior* (1982), pp. 323–24. A long look at the broad topic appears in Stephen Pyne, *Fire in America* (1982).

maximum sustainable catch of blue whales. By 1945 the basic population had become too small and the catch fell.[32] American and Canadian self-restraint in later decades provided a better supply for Russian and Japanese factory ships.

Trout, too, were subject to the rule of capture. But they inhabited streams, not oceans. Fishing rights to streams in Scotland and England were long privately owned. Their noble owners, and fishing clubs, could and did sue to keep away outsiders, thereby preserving clean waters. Their fishing remained superb.[33] The value of such rights was then sold from generation to generation. But American streams were public property. The most ignorant American, paying at most a democratically priced license, could take any kind of fish in thousands of streams and lakes. Eventually, specialist fishermen increased, seeking only one kind of trout or salmon, or wanting to fish within easy reach of their homes. Finding almost no private rights they could buy, they turned to the government to stock streams and lakes suitably.

As public property, American lakes and streams had also been universally used for waste disposal. Aside from human and animal wastes, there were those connected with the provision of clothes, food, and fuel. In the eighteenth and nineteenth centuries, many households kept sheep. Others bought wool for clothing. Farm households, and the thousands of primitive fulling mills on which they relied, extracted the grease that naturally clings to raw wool. Close to half the weight of raw wool consisted of grease and potash.) Well before the industrialization of the nation, farmers were scattered throughout the wilderness. At each farm they cleaned the wool from their sheep, dumping the waste into streams and lakes. (In 1840 the 2.6 thousand fulling mills scattered throughout the nation poured close to 36 million pounds of grease into streams and lakes.[34]) By 1900 over a hundred thousand tons of wool grease and salts were annually being thrown into streams throughout the land—plus an equal quantity of sheep dirt.[35] The production of shoes and clothing cast another 250,000 tons or so of alum and dyes into rivers, lakes, and streams in every part of the nation.[36] And some

32. Partha Dasgupta and Geoffrey Heal, *Economic Theory and Exhaustible Resources* (1979), pp. 145–47.

33. Douglas Clarke in R. Dorfman and N. Dorfman, *Economics of the Environment* (1977), pp. 180–81.

34. In 1840 there were 2,585 fulling mills scattered around the nation to which nearly farmers brought their wool to be cleaned and processed. 1840 Census, *Compendium*, p. 360. In that same year 36 million pounds of wool entered the gross product. (An equal amount of grease was deposited in streams and on the land.) Cf. NBER, *Trends in the American Economy in the Nineteenth Century* (1960), p. 289.

35. By 1900 the number of establishments had dropped sharply, but output has risen. Cf. 1900 Census, *Manufactures*, part III, p. 76 and—for the loss in weight—part IV, pp. 736, 738, 545. Together with the grease perhaps a hundred tons of oil, sulfuric acid, soft soap, and chamber lye used in cleaning and coloring the wool were likewise dumped.

36. 1900 Census, *Manufactures*, part IV, p. 526. We assume all alum and dyes were used in tanneries, textile, or clothing production.

1.6 million tons of sulphuric acid alone dumped into rivers and lakes, together with great quantities of soap, lye, pickling liquor, and more.[37] Those simple pre-industrial handicrafts, cleaning wool and tanning leather, may have been as quaint and fascinating as travelers have long found the washing out of silk dyes into the river near Kyoto, in Japan, to be. Such pollution was rarely if ever described by John Bartram or Henry Thoreau. But such primitive activity nonetheless "polluted" the waters throughout the land.

Air, too, another common property resource, was treated as a universal dump. The more specialized sources may not have contributed most to pollution and illness. But they were concentrated, subject to objection and litigation. Neighbors targeted them as responsible for specific damages or threats. Information on the overall dimensions of the problem is limited, but graphic examples appear throughout U.S. history, as well as of other nations. One well-documented example involved copper refining. The Anaconda Copper Company smelter in Montana cast its emissions far and wide. In 1907 it poured some 30 tons of arsenic trioxide into the air each day. Farmers found their cattle killed, and sued. The firm spent a million dollars putting up a still higher exhaust stack, which only displaced the problem to the next range of hills. After years of research, engineers finally perfected an electrical precipitator in 1907.[38] Such precipitators were installed around the nation as time passed, and were improved. The federal government decided to intervene in the 1970s. The EPA found the Anaconda firm still emitting arsenic. The firm closed rather than accept the cost of making still further process adjustments. But it should be added, perhaps, that by that time the advance of technology, litigation, and public spirit had together reduced the Anaconda arsenic effluent by more than 95 percent.[39] Political judgments with respect to what was feasible and acceptable had changed even faster.

A far more pervasive source of air pollution, more generally menacing to animal and human health, was the burning of wood, coal, and other fuels.

Long before modern industry developed humans burned wood and coal to keep warm, cook their food, and make scythes or plow points. In so doing they inevitably, and persistently, polluted the air. London was so choked by household coal fires two centuries before the industrial revolution that Queen Elizabeth I forbid burning coal whenever Parliament was in session.

In 1796 a scientist wrote: "I never view from a distance . . . this black cloud which hangs over London without wishing to be able to compute the

37. Ibid.
38. The 1907 figures, from the U.S. Geological Survey reports, are from *Frank Cameron Cottrell, Samaritan of Science* (1952), pp. 118–24, 146–48.
39. The level of the Anaconda effluent in the late 1970s is reported in an unpublished EPA report. The EPA publicly stated, however, that the remaining largest plant, of ASARCO, put 0.85 tons of arsenic into the air, providing "nearly one-fourth of all arsenic emissions in the country," causing "about four deaths a year from lung cancer." *New York Times* (July 17, 1983), p. 8E.

immense numbers of chaldrons of coals of which it is composed."[40] And a century later Paul Valery declared, "Once, in London, I thought of hanging myself. The day was yellow, sulfurous. The smoke fell from the low roofs into the street where it curled."[41]

City families overwhelmingly relied on coal from the beginning of the nineteenth century. They found it cheaper than wood, and much more convenient. That it blackened the city and created a health hazard did not deter them. Factory owners, shopkeepers, did the same. The efficiency of coal conversion into heat, using open fireplaces, was low. As a result, coal shot up into the air unburned, and hung there as soot. One nineteenth-century authority estimated that "the actual quantity of smoke hanging any day over London is the fourth part of the fuel consumed on that day."[42] One in every four tons of coal ended up in the air, unburned—virtually all from home fireplaces. By the century's end, fireplaces had improved very little.

During the nineteenth century U.S. householders, too, came to rely on coal, for both cooking and heating. It was immensely more convenient for the housewife than kindling and cord wood. And it was usually cheaper. Factory owners, too, turned almost wholly from wood to coal after the Civil War. Unlike householder's chimneys, however, factory owners' smoking chimneys were subject to action by municipal "smoke inspectors."[43] Perhaps more important in terms of results, they sought to increase their profits by cutting costs. They, therefore, installed mechanical stokers to cut costs. They wasted less coal to the air. They cut labor costs. And they ended the backbreaking, blisteringly hot, task of shoveling thousands of tons of coal into factory furnaces each year. Factories tested dozens of competing systems for mechanical stoking.[44] Users could expect to save 10 percent of the fuel normally burned. And they could likewise keep from "deluging the neighborhood with soot."[45]

40. Count Rumford, quoted in Arthur Helps, *The Claims of Labour* (1845), p. 127. Almost a century earlier, of course, John Evelyn wrote his *Fumifugium*, an attack on "the smoky nuisance."

41. Paul Valery, *Cahiers* I (1973):100.

42. Helps, *The Claims*, quotes this "on scientific authority." Systematic studies of household fires in the United Kingdom in the 1880s and 1890s, when results may have differed for other reasons, show between 5 percent and 6 percent as the weight of soot passing up chimneys. Cf. Julius Cohen and Arthur Ruston, *Smoke, A Study of Town Air* (1912).

43. Cf. the Report of the Smoke Inspector in *Report of the Department of Health, City of Chicago for the Year 1886* (1887), p. 81. Of an estimated 7,500 steam boilers in use 438 were served notice to "abate smoke nuisances"—typically by installing burners that "prevent the emission of dense smoke."

44. Cf. W. C. Popplewell, *The Prevention of Smoke* (1901), p. 140.

45. C. H. Benjamin, *Smoke Abatement*, Purdue University, Publications of the Engineering Departments (October 1915), p. 11. Benjamin estimates that a saving of even 5 percent would cover the interest of 7 percent to 10 percent on investment in "a high priced stoker," while "a saving of two or three times this is not unusual." "A smokey chimney is evidence . . . that the owner of that particular plant does not realize that he is wasting fuel at the same time he is deluging the neighborhood with soot. No individual in a community has a right to . . . throw objectionable refuse over his neighbor's property."

TABLE 32.3
U.S. BITUMINOUS COAL AND SOOT, 1869–1969

Source	Percent coal burned	Percent of total coal burned	Vented as soot		
			Millions of tons		
			1869	1919	1969
Private homes	100	9	0.2	4.6	0.3
Factories					
Hand fired	100	8	14.4		
Mechanically stoked	100	4		23.0	

Source: Percentages vented are taken from data for Britain in William Bone, *Coal, Its Constitution and Uses* (1936), p. 221. For 1919 we arbitrarily estimate 5 percent for factories, assuming mechanical stoking was common for the major U.S. users. The volume of coal consumption by ultimate consumers is taken from William H. Shaw, *Value of Product Since 1869* (1947), p. 262 for 1869, 1919; and, for 1970, from *Mineral Yearbook, 1972*, vol. II, table 9. Industrial consumption is measured as the balance of production (minus exports plus imports) using data from Census, *Historical Statistics to 1970*, p. 590.

The contribution of the various U.S. sources to air pollution ran approximately as shown in Table 32.3. From the Civil War to World War I the shift to mechanical stoking saved coal and back-breaking labor. It also sharply cut the rate of factory pollution. But the tonnage of soot still increased as total production rose to serve an ever increasing population. The rate of air pollution from household fires was not cut. Moreover, more households, and higher income, meant even more household coal burned.

World War I marked a turning point for households. Though only 2 percent of American households enjoyed central heating in 1920, some 58 percent had adopted it by 1940.[46] That staggering change took place almost completely during the boom of the 1920s.[47] The coming of central heating rapidly cut down the inefficiency of heating through individual fireplaces and stoves. It thereby cut down the 5 million or so tons of coal dust and acids that households were venting annually into the common air.

Rising incomes in the 1940s, and government regulations that kept down the price of natural gas, brought a further shift after the Depression. In a mere twenty years oil and gas ended coal's long reign as the primary household fuel, as shown in Figure 32.2. Householders no longer faced their winter task of shoveling tons of coal into the furnace, and hauling out coal ash and clinkers. (Indeed, so inferior was coal considered as a fuel that by 1970 only 1 percent

46. Lebergott, *The American Economy*, p. 278.
47. Since residential construction during the 1930s was trivial we assume most of the 1920–40 rise had to occur during the 1920s.

FIGURE 32.2
PERCENT OF Homes HEATING WITH Coal, 1940–80

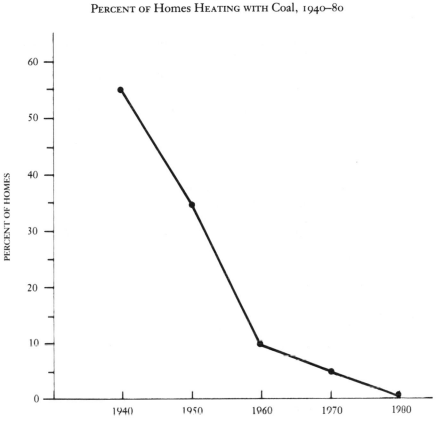

Source: 1960 Census, Housing, vol. 1, part 1, p. XL; 1982 Statistical Abstract, p. 758.

of even the poorest families used it.[48]) That switch, almost incidentally, about ended the wood and coal dust and other pollution that householders had been pouring into the common American air for two centuries.

As families cut air pollution created by their fireplaces they increased that from their automobiles. In 1800 few American families had any means of transport. Even by 1900 only 20 percent of all urban families owned a horse.

48. Of families using coal for cooking some 54 percent were in the Census "low-income" classification. These constituted only 1 percent of all families in poverty. Data derived by tabulating the 1970 Population Census sample tapes, using the 15 percent sample returns.

But by 1935, 44 percent, and by 1977, 84 percent, owned a car.[49] By 1980, indeed, there was one car per family—plus 45 million additional cars.[50]

Two overwhelming shifts had taken place. Rising incomes enabled most American families to buy their own means of transport. Not just those who were "well off," but also the middle and lower classes. (Indeed the government officially stipulated that families fell below a "minimum" standard of living if they lacked a car.) Rising incomes and changing social values likewise enabled many wives, many teenagers, to own their own vehicles. Millions did so by the 1980s. Had the 1900 ownership ratio not so changed, the politically acute "air pollution" problem of the 1970s might never have surfaced. For few families, fewer 20 to 30-year olds, and almost no wives, would have owned cars. Some 100 million automobiles would therefore have been absent from the auto stock. The rich had created little air pollution; there were so few of them. The masses changed all that. (Had hundreds of thousands of horses been used in cities, half of their number would have fallen dead in the streets each year.[51] They would also have littered the streets with offal and urine, as in "the good old days.")

In addition to common resources in land, air, and water there exists a critical subset. These are the "one-of-a-kind" resources. China closed four plants in 1979. Its drive for industry in recent years "had badly polluted the town [of Kweilin] whose dramatic, craggy landscape, carved out by water erosion, is depicted in countless traditional Chinese paintings."[52] The Soviet paper industry began massively polluting Lake Baikal, the largest fresh water lake in the world, in the 1960s and continued for decades.[53] Such destruction was therefore not peculiar to industrialized, western, or capitalist nations. It was the outcome of two forces: a drive for material goods and services (whether coal to keep children from freezing or gold to highlight replicas of Louis XIV marquetry); and the failure of society to put a "high enough" price

49. 1900: 1900 Census, *Statistics of Agriculture*, vol. V, part 1, Table 41. Ratios of horses to population in each city size group were computed from this source, applied to population counts for each size group from 1900, *Supplementary Analysis*, p. 25. The resultant figure is 1,438,487. There were 16 million households, of which 38 percent were urban, (*Historical Statistics to 1970*, pp. 11, 43) or, say, 6 million. Allowing for urban horses owned by livery stables and businesses we reduce the implicit 25 percent ratio to 20 percent. 1935: Lebergott, *The American Economy*, p. 290. 1977: *1981 Statistical Abstract*, p. 628.

50. Auto registration data for 1980 totaled 124 million, while there were 79 million households. Survey data for 1977 show 84 percent of all U.S. households owning cars, 83 percent for metropolitan areas. *1981 Statistical Abstract*, pp. 46, 628.

51. Martin Melosi, *Garbage in the Cities* (1981), p. 25.

52. *New York Times* (February 8, 1979). The Chinese press agency said that the rivers had been polluted, rocks whitened, and trees withered.

53. M. I. Goldman, *The Spoils of Progress: Environmental Pollution in the Soviet Union* (1972). Donald R. Kelley et al., *The Economic Superpowers and the Environment* (1976).

on the using up of such common property resources. That combination evidenced itself in most known societies.[54]

The extinction of one-of-a-kind resources, however, could not be prevented even by a vast cut in GNP. It required, in addition, social agreement on which items qualified as critical, and specific action to protect them. The mix of success and failure in government policy suggests human values differed largely even in a given society.

Individual species, as defined by zoologists, are one of a kind. In the natural course of evolution presumably some become extinct and others appear for the first time. The nineteenth century devoted much attention to the role of creation in evolution. The twentieth century has devoted equally intense concern to extinction in evolution. In 1600, "there were approximately 8,184 living species of birds. Since then ninety-four [or 1.09 percent] doubtless became extinct."[55] (Of these species only six ever inhabited North America.[56]) Evolution had not, of course, stopped during this period. As some species disappeared in millions of year of evolution, new ones appeared. A recent estimate reports 400 more bird species now than the above figure for 1600.[57]

But it is clearly no consolation to those who mourn the loss of a given cricket species that the layman can still observe 108 other cricket species in the Eastern United States. Nor to those saddened by the disappearance of one fish species that there are 25,000 others, to which over 100 new species are added each year.[58] Still other aesthetic preferences (for species or modes of evolution) have been expressed.[59] Thus, when someone observed that as the number of whales declined, the number of another species, the kryll (con-

54 The prolonged struggle to preserve the snail darter was between conservationists and the board of the TVA, an agency set up in the New Deal to control and limit the impact of profit-making utility companies. A circuit court had enjoined dam construction by the TVA. *New York Times* (February 6, 1977).

55. James Fisher et al., *Wildlife in Danger* (1969), p. 11.

56. A listing of the species itemized by conservationists appears in Vincenz Ziswiler, *Extinct and Vanishing Animals* (1967). Not all of the six lost in North America were necessarily lost in the United States—e.g., one was the Labrador duck.

57. Phillip Altman and Dorothy Dittmer, *Biology Data Book* (1964), p. 561, estimates 8,590 species. Biologists do not state what species are new since any date, or are newly discovered. Hence the rate of extinction cannot be estimated as confidently. Biologists have "classified about a million and a half different species of organisms, and yet each year more than ten thousand previously unknown species are discovered." Phillip Handler, ed., *Biology and the Future of Man* (1970), pp. 518–19.

58. The number of species is from Handler, *Biology*.

59. A well-known basketball star commissioned a bedspread to be made from the nose furs of 17,000 arctic wolves. "Wilt bought up one season's total crop; says killing wolves is necessary to keep the wolf population in ecological balance." *Ebony* (January 1974).

sumed by the whales for food), had to increase, Jacques Cousteau responded that the whales "are more interesting."[60]

Similarly, many people found particular geographic locations more beautiful, or overwhelming, than others—Yosemite, Mount Rushmore, Jones Beach. As the Honorable Madison Grant remarked, when accepting an award for his leadership of the Bronx Parkway Commission; unless the Commission's example were followed, "the next generation will never know the beauties of the woodland which we inherited."[61] (Mr. Grant was no less well known for his efforts to preserve a country clean of immigrants, or at least immigrants from non Anglo-Saxon countries.[62])

The one-of-a-kind phenomenon—whether the Oregon Wapiti, the spectacular Vanderbilt mansion in Newport, a Charles Ives manuscript—elicits such varied desires and is subject to such costs that no general outcome can be predicted. We only know that the U.S. market has tended to conserve anything which interests even a moderate number of people, provided the item—whether it be a mansion or a manuscript—can become private property. Other items, however, will be preserved only if social values work through political and social processes to preserve them.

When the conservation movement became of public note in the 1870s, only the rich could travel to Yosemite. As time passed, the conflict between conservationists plus Theodore Roosevelt on the one hand, and Congress plus the variety of interests it represented on the other, gradually created the national park system.

The system served for a few decades. But two economic changes guaranteed it would fail to meet the desires of conservationists. One was the arrival of cheap automobiles. The other was the rise of worker incomes. If only one percent of the million households in 1980 who owned cars[63] tried to visit a given wilderness area or park during four summer weeks, a queuing problem would develop far beyond the capacity of the political and social process to solve. (A national survey indicated that some 86 percent of campers objected

60. Learning that weasels may save more poultry than they kill (by killing rats, which kill poultry) someone remarked, "different people like different kinds of animals." E. R. Hall, "The Graceful and Rapacious Weasel," *Natural History* (November 1974). A similar preference for one species over another is evident in the decision by the Massachusetts Audubon Society to approve poisoning 3,000 seagulls so that state residents could view instead a "small tern population." *New York Times* (May 20, 1980.)

61. "I would not care to live in a country such as this will be in the future, when the streams are polluted, the hillsides eroded by wasteful farming, the air destitute of birds." *Journal of the National Institute of Social Sciences* XIV (December 31, 1929): P. 129.

62. Cf. Madison Grant, *The Passing of the Great Race* (1918). In some ways one is reminded of Chancellor Eldon, who fought fiercely to prevent cruelty to horses at a time when such delicacy of feeling was unknown in England—and who also fought to retain the penal laws which condemned to hanging men who snared an illegal rabbit.

63. *Statistical Abstract* (1978), p. 649.

to having another party camped within sight or sound, while 65 percent said: "It is best if you meet no one.")[64]

The dilemma originated in economics. Rising incomes since 1900 made it possible for many people to attempt what once only the rich could. And the market economy made such a visit possible by providing them with inexpensive transport, food, backpacks, and shelter. Those millions understandably sought to use a "free" publicly owned facility.[65] And for such facilities a political answer was requisite. The solution could not be reached through the market.

Two general policy issues should be noted. Many believed that the market priced pollution too low. The price of labor before World War I was so low, relative to that of materials, that it paid city children to clean the streets; they collected paper, bottles, iron, and junk.[66] Wage rates and incomes increased greatly after 1920. And private collection of litter fell sharply. As litter mounted up, however, public payments for such clean up, and/or public penalties, did not take over. Legislatures failed to provide enough street cleaners or incentives to replace private collection.[67]

Auto exhaust offered another example. Pollution altruists were notably scarce. In 1970 Earth Day was celebrated, with some intensity, on hundreds of campuses and in an equal number of newspaper editorials. The next year Chrysler offered exhaust control kits to reduce air pollution. As with other products they pioneered they were ahead of the market. They sold 50, at $20 apiece, and sent the remaining 13,000 back to the manufacturer. The altruists who installed exhaust kits to protect the environment were few. If "the people" wanted pollutant-free air they did not want it $20 worth.[68]

---

64. Cf. Mordechai Shechter and Robert C. Lucas, *Simulation of Recreational Use for Park and Wilderness Management* (1978), pp. 70–71. The "acceptable" rationing of 7.5 million visitor days to national forest wildernesses becomes almost impossible.

65. There is, of course, some exaggeration. Charges by park concessionaires rise and service declines. The pricing of such complementary inputs tends to ration the park's use.

66. In Betty Smith's *A Tree Grows in Brooklyn* the rate of 1 cent for 10 pounds of paper and 4 cents for one pound of iron proved sufficient to keep the heroine and many of her friends busy collecting junk. Children could then (1910) earn perhaps 50 cents a day. The paper–wage ratio obviously has to change sharply in an era when baby-sitting pays $1 to $2 an hour and children's allowances are vastly greater.

67. Even in the high wage era of the 1970s a charge of 5 cents a bottle proved sufficient in Vermont, Oregon, and Connecticut to wipe out such litter. City councils and legislatures have not yet sought to price other litter—e.g., abandoned automobiles. It is not to be assumed that legislators were, or are, ignoring the wishes of most voters.

68. *New York Times* (August 13, 1971). Given the extensive recent literature in economics indicating the presence of altruism in the utility function of individuals it seems that this example indicates a qualified altruism: I will *if* you will. Consumers may have reckoned on a higher cost of gas, though that considerations seems to have been widely noted only with the EPA requirements for catalytic converters.

The second issue concerned how resources were saved for future generations. Groups in the 1910s as the 1970s ardently desired more saving than was taking place. Legislatures could have readily achieved this result by severance taxes on production from forests and mines. Many states did just that, and taxes paid whenever trees were cut or ores mined clearly slowed the process of exhaustion. That Congress rarely adopted such tactics may well have reflected two perceptions. First, the tenure of Congressmen was less certain even than that of resource owners in developing nations. How much they could safely penalize present voters on behalf of future generations was unclear. Mexico's state-owned petroleum industry subsidized exhaust by keeping the price of gasoline low. The ratio of the price of gas to that of an engine tune-up was therefore low, and Mexico City choked in exhaust. And at the height of the energy crisis in 1974, the U.S. Congress lowered the price of oil, thus increasing its use.[69] Second and more important, perhaps, was that each U.S. generation enjoyed higher incomes than previous ones. Each worked less, played more, consumed far more material goods. For each generation was handed a huge industrial plant by the prior generation, and an ever improving technological base. Its standard of living was higher. Moreover, as the productivity series testifies, every generation seemed to find new and easier modes of production. And worked a shorter workweek.

As Hubert Henderson wrote many years ago, of another nation: "We in the twentieth century owe much of the material wealth that we enjoy to the fact that over the last century men saved as largely as they did. But our natural gratitude should not restrain us from doubting whether they were really well-advised to do so. . . . England, a century or even half a century ago, was not really a rich community."[70] The upward path of real incomes in the United States was even more extreme. That fact helps explain why Congress did not often tax a poorer contemporary generation in favor of a future one likely to be richer.[71]

---

69. Responding to President Ford's proposal to tax imported oil and reduce usage, "Congress decided to lower the price of controlled domestic oil by 15 percent. This blatantly political step encouraged demand, suppressed supply." Ezra Solomon, *Beyond the Turning Point* (1982), p. 101.

70. Quoted in D. H. Robertson, *Utility and All That* (1952), p. 117.

71. It is impossible for one generation to constrain the pattern of resource use by the next generation, of course. One wonders how many persons believe that this generation should make fewer trips to rock concerts so the next could make more to symphony concerts. Or vice versa.

Rumor has it that one mountain state's governor lost an election because he raised the gas tax by one cent a gallon. Hence, congressional concern was hardly hypothetical.

33

The Technology of
Dreams: The 1920s

T HE decade of Jay Gatsby, Florenze Ziegfeld, Calvin Coolidge, and
other figures larger than life opened boldly. The War and Navy Departments had guided the War to Make the World Safe for Democracy. Newer
agencies stood ready to guide democracy in peacetime. Of the new Prohibition Administration, its head declared: "No trouble is expected in enforcing
the law. In most states our organization is perfect."[1] Of the Federal Reserve
System, the comptroller of the currency was equally sanguine: "Under the
operation of this law such financial crises or 'panics' as this country experienced in 1873, in 1893, and again in 1907, with their attendant misfortunes
and frustrations, seem to be mathematically impossible."[2] By the end of the
twenties neither forecaster seemed likely to get the Perspicacity of the Decade
award.

Casual models simply deny the central characteristic of that decade. It
was, they suggest, not really a period of mass consumption, but a long era of
"underconsumption." Those in the upper 5 percent of the income distribution increased their share of the national income.[3] Labor's share of the national income did not rise at all. And workers suffered from unemployment.
By implication, then, the decade differed little from earlier ones.

The share of national income received by labor, however, tells us very
little about the real level of living for the working class. Thus, labor's share of

1. Quoted in Marc Connelly, *Voices Offstage* (1968), p. 64.

2. Comptroller of the Currency, *Annual Report*, I (1914):10. The board had little scope for
operation from its founding until after the constraints of war financing were over.

3. Data showing that the "top 5 percent" of the population increased their share of U.S. income from 24 percent to 33 percent between 1920 and 1929 have been invoked for the underconsumption argument. *Historical Statistics . . . to 1970*, G-342.

The argument is best expounded by Charles Holt, "Who Benefitted from the Prosperity of
the Twenties?" *Explorations in Entrepreneurial History* (July 1977). Unfortunately, the argument
turns on the use of income-tax returns to indicate the income of the top 5 percent at the various
dates. However, tax rates were reduced in the early 1920s, enabling the rich to get out of tax-
exempt bonds. Their reported income was thereby increased, but not their real after-tax income.

U.S. national income reached an all-time peak in 1933. (Profits had been overwhelmed by a sea of red ink and negative profits necessarily increased labor's share—of a smaller pie.) But 38 percent of non-farm workers then had no jobs. What good was the workers' "share"?

Equally confused theories report "underconsumption" in the 1920s. "Relatively high profits and fairly stable wages tended to concentrate income in . . . the upper income group . . . increasing the funds available for investment . . . . In retrospect more funds in the hands of consumers and less [for] investors would have produced a more stable economy."[4] There is, however, no evidence that the proportion of personal income going to consumption fell below that of any prior decade. Indeed, it actually rose during the decade.[5] Moreover, 98 of the 100 categories into which consumption is classified (e.g., food, tobacco, rent) did not slow down before the crash. They gained quite as much from 1925 to 1929 as from 1920 to 1924.[6]

The simplest way to evaluate the "underconsumption" criticism is to consider the rising ownership of household facilities and durables in the 1920s, and the real income and unemployment experience for wage earners. The gain in the standard of living during the 1920s, shown in Tables 33.1 and 33.2, was without precedent in U.S. experience. And certainly in that of Britain, France, Germany, or Russia. The "prosperity" of the 1920s was as real as prosperity in the U.S. has ever been.

One tight coherent explanation of economic change in the 1920s was given by Lawrence Klein's pioneering econometric model.[7] It proposed that personal consumption in the 1920s was driven by incomes and trend forces, while business investment depended on output (offset by the impact of the price of capital goods and the size of the existing capital stock). The model offers many insights. But it was not designed to explain the decade's unprecedented prosperity. Nor did it track the cyclical recessions of 1921, 1924, 1927 (or the subsequent upturns).

For the economy it was par excellence the period of two markets—the mass market and the stock market. The central forces that drove those markets to new highs in the 1920s were productivity and credit. Productivity advances cut prices, thereby expanding the mass market. They concurrently increased profits, kiting up the stock market. Credit advances then intensified both effects.

4. This quotation, from a standard history, could be duplicated in many others. The best presentation of the underconsumption approach is Waddill Catchings and William Foster, *Business Without a Buyer* (1928).

5. Personal consumption accounted for 68 percent of the value of GNP in the prosperity of 1919–20 and 76 percent in 1928–29. Kendrick, *Productivity*, p. 297.

6. Data on consumer goods shown in William Shaw, *Value of Product Since 1869* (1947), Table 1-2. and on services in Lebergott, *The American Economy*. Table 2.

7. Lawrence Klein, *Economic Fluctuations in the United State, 1921–1941* (1950), pp. 109, 112.

TABLE 33.1

PERCENT OF HOUSEHOLDS WITH FACILITIES, 1900–30

| Year | Percent of households with | | | |
	Electric lights	Inside flush toilets	Washing machines	Autos
1900	3	15	*	0
1910	15	—	*	1
1920	35	20	8	26
1930	68	51	24	60

*Under 1%.

Source: Lebergott, *The American Economy*, pp. 272–90.

TABLE 33.2

EMPLOYEE INCOME AND UNEMPLOYMENT, 1900–29

Year	Earnings (1914 dollars)	Unemployment rate (percent)
1900	445	5.0
1910	546	5.9
1920	619	5.2
1929	793	3.2

Source: Lebergott, *Manpower*, pp. 512, 523.

"Most features of the period," Schumpeter observed, "find their chief explanation" in the rapid growth in output, and the "unparalleled [development] in industrial efficiency."[8] Later scholarship gave chapter and verse for this shrewd insight. Presumably the deepest explanation of these productivity advances attributes them to the persistent attempt by entrepreneurs to push costs down and profits up. But why was the gain so great in this single decade? One may speculate on the role of three factors, all special to the decade. First was the coming of the automobile, and its country cousin the truck. These did more than provide a more efficient horse and wagon. Their greater speed and lower cost (per shipment) expanded the area of competition, perhaps as much as the railroad had in earlier decades. Leland and Ford and Durant intensified business competition, and thereby productivity, more than all the free-market economists and antitrust legislators in human history.

8. Joseph Schumpeter, "The Decade of the Twenties," *American Economic Review* (May 1946), p. 7.

Second was the nationwide demonstration of mass production techniques forced upon producers by war production. In 1918 the War Shipping Board, for example, took over an industry that went back to the time of Ulysses. It changed the ancient and immemorial practice by which individual parts of the ship were fabricated in the shipyards, or even on the hull. It substituted the new practice of prefabrication, in distant factories, in large volume, with assemblies then shipped to Hog Island (outside Philadelphia). There they were combined into completed vessels at a speed without historic precedent. (Steel ships, typically built in 9 to 12 months previously now required only 4 months or less.[9] Such longer production runs cut costs dramatically, and thereby pushed up productivity.

A further cause may have been the historic turnaround in the labor market. Fearful of the flood of immigrants who would want to leave a devastated Europe for the United States, and vigorously pressed by the A.F.L., Congress substantially ended mass immigration into the United States. One member of Wilson's cabinet declared that the most important law on the statute books was the new "law restricting immigration . . . [it] has been responsible for our prosperity."[10] That restriction guaranteed that the supply of labor, at any given price, would be cut—which meant that corporate labor costs necessarily started to rise. Factory owners and managers reacted by hiring from new domestic labor sources. Women were increasingly hired. During World War I 40,000 Southern blacks had found jobs in munitions, Chicago meatpacking, Pittsburgh steel mills.[11] They continued to move north in the 1920s. Detroit auto plants began to fill with "hillbillies" from the Kentucky and Tennessee highlands. But these sources hardly held wages down as steadily as the old immigration flows. Congress had taken a hard position limiting the labor supply. Producers therefore pressed on with traditional substitutes for labor: machinery, time and motion studies, newer techniques. All were used. All sped the unprecedented productivity rise shown in Table 33.3. As that table indicates, productivity gained nearly as much in the 1920s as it had over the two prior decades. The gains in manufacturing exceeded those in earlier decades by an unbelievable amount. In turn they created lower prices, higher real incomes—and mass markets.

Mass Markets

At the 1930 premier of *Whoopee*, its star, "dressed in high hat and tails, pulled up . . . in front of the marquee in a broken-down Model T Ford" rescued from a junkyard earlier that day. When the stunned doorman asked if

9. William C. Mattox, *Building the Emergency Fleet* (1920), pp. 14, 44–45, 248–49.
10. Pound, *More They Told Barron*, p. 317. The year was 1927.
11. *Monthly Labor Review* (January 1922) P. 144.

TABLE 33.3

PRODUCTIVITY AND INCOME GAINS, 1889–1929 (IN PERCENT)

Decade	Productivity gains[a]		Income gains[b]	
	Total economy	Manufacturing	Per capita GNP	Earnings of nonfarm employees
1889–1899	17	15	26	10
1900–1909	12	12	29	23
1910–1919	12	8	9	11
1920–1929	22	72	19	26

[a]Real gross private domestic product per unit of total factor input, and manufacturing productivity per unit of labor.

[b]GNP in 1958 prices. Earnings in 1914 prices.

Source: Productivity: Kendrick, *Productivity*, Table A-XXII and D-11. Per capita GNP: *Historical Statistics . . . to 1970*, Series F4. Earnings: Lebergott, *Manpower*, pp. 523, 528.

he'd like his car parked, the answer was: "No thanks. Just sell it and keep the change."[12] A decade of automobile worship made the jest widely appreciated.

At the beginning of the twentieth century automobiles were a luxury for a handful of enthusiasts. In 1899 a mere 56 were produced—compared to 26,000 tricycles.[13] The typical car was a Cadillac, Stutz, or Winton, a toy for the rich. Even by 1907 only a third of those turned out could be termed "low price."[14] During the next half-century many would have preferred to keep it as a luxury. Thus a Nobel prize winner-declared the automobile caused "social-economic waste" by "stimulating the spreading of population over large areas, as in the United States, making life as a whole more expensive. Usually it is argued that individual freedom is worth this price; but it remains to be seen whether or not this freedom and other feelings involved are only imaginary."[15] Ford, however, was determined to produce a mass car. His price cuts made the running and other producers had to follow. They thereby created a mass market. By 1929, 90 percent of all autos coming off the assembly lines were "low priced."[16] The size of the market enabled long production runs, which cut costs further. Competition among the auto companies then cut prices still further. (The price of the typical Ford fell 80 percent from 1909 to 1929.[17] Its true price fell even more. For by 1929 Ford had added a self starter, windshield wiper, better brakes.)

12. Arthur Marx, *Goldwyn* (1976), p. 169.

13. 1900 Census, *Manufactures*, IV:328.

14. Ralph Epstein, in *Recent Economic Changes* (1929), p. 60.

15. Jan Tinbergen, *Lessons from the Past* (1963), p. 13.

16. Epstein, *Recent*, p. 60.

17. William Abernathy, *The Productivity Dilemma* (1978), p. 33. The figures are in 1958 dollars.

TABLE 33.4
CONSUMER DEBT AND PURCHASES, 1899–1939 (BILLIONS OF DOLLARS)

| | Personal consumption spending[a] | Consumer installment debt[b] | | New housing[a] | Mortgage debt[b] |
		Total	Auto		
1899–1909	+ $176	+ $0.8	*	+ $7.9	+ $1.3
1909–1919	+ 324	+ 1.3	*	+ 10.2	+ 3.6
1919–1929	+ 650	+ 4.5	+ 1.1	+ 33.9	+ 19.2
1929–1939	+ 669	+ 0.1	+ 0.1	+ 12.1	− 4.3

*Less than .01.

[a]Decade total.

[b]Net change in debt outstanding over decade.

Source: Consumption: 1899–1929, Kendrick, *Productivity*, pp. 296–97. 1929–39, *National Income 1929–76*, Table 1.1. Other: 1919–29, *Historical Statistics . . . to 1970*, X-551.

More than a "low price" resulted. Ford was invited by the U.S.S.R. to design and direct the building of a truck plant. (They wanted no cars.) When a delegation of visitors from the U.S.S.R. visited Ford's Rouge plant, and saw thousands of workers' cars parked in its lots, they declared it all a misleading show put on by management. Mere workers, they knew, obviously did not own cars. Certainly not in such vast numbers. The broad rise in incomes, however, had indeed expanded the set of buyers for many items. Yet it alone was not enough to explain the auto boom the Russians saw.

What made it all real was a related change: the growth of mass credit. In the late nineteenth century the Singer Sewing Machine Company had discovered that even the poorest American families could be trusted to repay loans for sewing machines. International Harvester made the same discovery for farm machinery. Ford and General Motors then applied that lesson. By the mid-1920s three cars in every four were sold on credit.[18] Industry performance was stimulated by decisions made by banks and finance companies, as shown in Table 33.4.

Without credit, particularly consumer credit, there need not have been any crash in 1929, much less in 1924 or 1927. That alternative scenario is suggested in Figure 33.1 by the simple linear trend line through 1919–39 production of automobiles. If production and sales had been limited to that rate of growth, there would, by definition, have been no booms, no "excess" expenditures, no crashes, no mass unemployment. The cycle with its attendant

18. Wilbur Plummer, "Social . . . Consequences," *Annals of the American Academy* supplement (January 1927).

FIGURE 33.1
AUTOMOBILE REGISTRATION, 1929–39 (000)

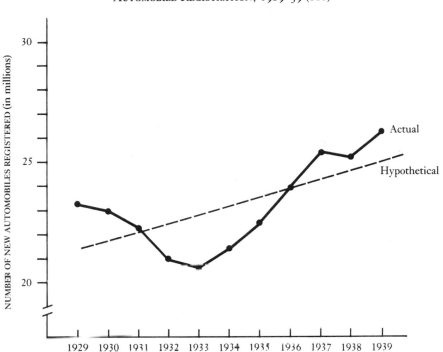

Source: U.S. Department of Commerce, Historical Statistics of the United States, p. 716.

misfortunes and human catastrophes would simply not have appeared. What permitted "over-expansion," inevitably followed by decline and recession, was credit.

Before 1920 consumers were accustomed to buy cars for cash. In the 1920s they began to buy ahead of their income, by borrowing. In the prewar decades consumers bought homes on the basis of mortgages to be paid off in 5 years. During the 1920s, however, the 20-year mortgage appeared. Millions of lower income workers and white collar employees could not, or would not, save up for a house or car. Before the 1920s they had rarely been offered credit to enjoy such goods in advance of saving. Few but the rich, therefore, did. By the late 1920s, however, banks, savings and loan associations, auto financing companies united to offer millions a chance to buy now and pay later, instead, perhaps, of never buying at all. In 1912 some 47 percent of expenditure for new homes was financed by credit. By 1920–22 the figure had risen to 55 percent. By 1925–29, to 66 percent.[19] The price for this anticipatory enjoyment became clear when the market crashed.

Farming

The long "depression" in farming during the 1920s reflected the deep disappointment of millions of small businessmen who had made a killing from 1916 to 1920, thanks to the war and government price guarantees. In 1920—1921 they had to return to the chilling reality of "normal profit" rates in competitive markets. True, farm labor, Southern sharecroppers, and sand-hill farmers fared slightly better in the 1920s than they had for the prior century. But the typical farmer was a small businessman. And a clamorous combination of patriotism, simple greed, and federal promises had led him into a speculative land buying spree during the war. An immense European market opened up as the invading German armies trampled over the farms of France and Belgium, and millions all over Europe were taken from farms and conscripted into uniform. Years of wartime prosperity followed for American farmers. After which they were given an additional stimulus. President Wilson, in September 1918, issued a proclamation guaranteeing $2.26 a bushel for all wheat marketed by June 1920.[20] Herbert Hoover had urged it—so that farmers would grow enough to feed the starving Belgians, and later, starving Austrians, Germans, Russians. (He obviously doubted that the private market foresaw European prospects the way he did.)

That unprecedented guarantee was sponsored by the archetypical reactionary. But it temporarily provided what the populists had been fighting for during many decades. It transformed market prospects. The stream of returns from using land was now guaranteed by Uncle Sam. Farmers, knowing that they had a sure thing, began to buy land, bidding its price up: The land values during 1870–1915 had gained 4.5 percent a year. In 1915–20 they gained 11.5 percent a year.[21] Increases in the value of existing farms were unbelievable. So too was the volume of borrowing to buy more land. When European soldiers returned to their farms, and the federal prop under prices was ended, prices of American land plummeted. The overhead charges for the farmers' bout of land speculation, however, remained. Mortgage payments for the additional land they bought continued on the terms as originally written. The land owners' cries of anguish echoed throughout the decade. (Others who speculated in food markets wrote off their losses. The National

19. Computed from data in Grebler, *Real Estate*, p. 454.

20. Frank Surface, *The Grain Trade During the War* (1928), pp. 147, 525. The base price (for Northern No. 1 at Chicago) had, of course, a set of related prices for other varieties, locations. That action was also supposed to restrain inflation.

21. Computed from *Historical Statistics . . . to 1970*, K-15 and Alvin Tostlebe, *Capital in Agriculture* (1957), Tables 7, 9.

City Bank, tempted by the world boom in sugar prices, speculatively opened not one but 16 branch offices in Cuba in the first half of 1919. When prices collapsed the bank's stockholders simply had to absorb the resulting losses.[22]) But farmers began a long campaign for federal subsidies to farm exports. A farm "debenture" scheme offered by Senators Charles McNary and Gilbert Haugen was the latest version of government support to farm prices and volume. Vetoed twice by President Coolidge it got a very cool reception in a period in which he and Hoover reflected the balance of voter attitudes on farm subsidies. The Democrats, with a larger farm base, mustered some support for these proposals. But they were searching for a political base that included more northern urban workers. Since the latter would have had to pay more for food under the debenture schemes, they too offered little real help to the farmers.

Farmers thus had to adopt the same two routes to rising profits as other businessmen. One was to increase their productivity, thereby cutting costs. The other was to expand their markets by selling more of their output. In their competition for the consumers' dollar, could they outwit all other producers, who had precisely the same tactics in mind? Could they hope to do better than the pack? As it turned out they did worse. Perhaps the most graphic indication contrasts their record with that of the industry symbolizing the boom of the 1920s, automobiles. Table 33.5 shows how productivity leaped in auto manufacturing but changed only trivially in farming. Thus farmers added little to their profits by advancing efficiency. What about market expansion resulting from price cuts? Farm prices fell far more than auto prices 1919–29. But that simple comparison was somewhat, perhaps largely, deceptive. For while the quality of wheat and veal and cotton changed little, that of autos rose markedly. (At the same list price autos began to include such valuable advances as self-starters in place of cranks, closed steel bodies instead of open ones, effective brakes in place of dubious ones.)

Most farmers were up against a basic fact by 1920–21: Americans were reasonably well-fed. They used their increasing incomes for other items, rather than more wheat, more corn, more lard. (Indeed, Americans actually cut their consumption of wheat, the great Midwestern crop, during the 1920s.[23]) Of those other items the car was foremost. The beacon was Ford's cutting the price of that incredible luxury, and then cutting it again—from $4,700 in 1909 to $1,000 by 1929.[24] With appropriate irony it was the farmers who led the pack in buying the Model T and the early trucks. (As early as

---

22. Cuban Economic Research Project, *A Study on Cuba* (1965), p. 236.

23. Per capita wheat flour consumption fell by 8 percent from 1919 to 1929. *Historical Statistics . . . to 1970*, G912. Since meat consumption did not rise only milk and vegetable producers achieved greater gains than those linked simply to population growth.

24. Abernathy, *The Productivity Dilemma*, p. 33.

TABLE 33.5
FARMING AND AUTOMOBILE INDUSTRY
PERFORMANCE, 1909–29

| | Farming | | | Automobile manufacturing | | |
	Productivity	Prices received	Volume of output	Productivity	Ford prices received	Volume of output
1909	100	100	100	100	100	100
1919	97	207	108	144	26	336
1929	110	141	121	500	21	935

Source: Agriculture: Kendrick, *Productivity,* p. 362, HS-3, K-344, K-414. Ford: William J. Abernathy, *The Productivity Dilemma* (1978), p. 33. Automobiles: Daniel Creamer et al., *Capital in Manufacturing and Mining* (1960), p. 40.

1920 some 29 percent had cars or trucks.)[25] Autos took the harvest to the nearest shipping point at half the cost of using old Dobbin.[26] And in due time farmers bought tractors, also from Ford, and from other producers. These, too, did a better job than horses, and far more cheaply.

One exception to the decline of agriculture after the fall of 1920 was cotton. Its market expanded worldwide, bringing high prices in 1922–24. Such prices again induced farmers to speculate in land. They expanded their cotton acreage by 20 percent to 1925–29. At that point nature provided a catastrophe: unprecedented bountiful growing conditions.[27] The resultant surge of cotton into world markets promptly forced down its price, and that of the land planters had rushed to buy. The value of bank portfolios in the South then fell, bank failures multiplied, and provided a beginning for the financial collapse of 1929–30.

The Stock Market

Legend describes "everybody" in the 1920s speculating in the market: head waiters, bootblacks, hairdressers. Was that so? Stock ownership had been rising since the Civil War. By 1900 about 15 percent of all families owned some stock. By 1929 the figure had risen to 28 percent.[28] Although significant that gain still left almost three-quarters of Americans out of the market, even at its peak.

25. Lebergott, *American Economy,* p. 290.
26. Joint Commission on Agricultural Inquiry, quoted in Ralph Epstein, *The Automobile Industry* (1929), p. 9.
27. Cf. James Stallings, "Weather Indexes," *Journal of Farm Economics* (February 1960), p. 183.
28. For derivation of these estimates, see Appendix, this chapter.

Stock investment did help raise capital for new investment. But such investment had never been a certain affair. Companies failed. Products missed their market. Costs went up unpredictably. The market therefore has always traded in hope—called speculation. Moralists had long been disturbed by this vulgar intrusion. Hope, they held, belonged to religion or to ethics. They therefore inferred that financial speculation, faintly immoral, inevitably led to financial collapse. "Everybody's head was full of such 'calculation' . . . such raving insanity. . . . Few people took *work* into their calculations . . . or outlay of money either; except the work and expenditure of other people."[29] That earnest view (of Mark Twain in the 1860s) was repeated decades later: "One thing in the twenties should have been visible even to Coolidge . . . Americans were displaying an inordinate desire to get rich quickly with a minimum of physical effort. The first striking manifestation of this personality trait was . . . the great Florida real estate boom."[30] Perhaps many civilizations evidenced only the desire to get rich slowly, deliberately. But such names as Midas, Nicias, Bernard, Fugger, Hatry suggest the contrary. And what of ten thousand other movers and shakers in Britain, France, India, Malaysia, and China of the 1920s?

U.S. productivity rose in that decade, and with it, profits. Not unreasonably, investing in the market for corporate securities seemed a sure thing. Speculation then fed on itself. Prices were steadily driven up, in anticipation of further price increases. But those very increases forced down the yield on stock investment. From 5.8 percent in 1921 industrial stocks declined to a 3.8 percent yield by 1928 (Table 33.6). That, of course, did not mark a clear danger limit beyond which capitalists would refuse to provide funds. The "euthanasia of the rentier" could continue to proceed on and on if many still to supply capital for 4 percent, 3 percent, even 2 percent.[31] (For long periods during the 1970s investors actually accepted zero real returns in the stock market.)

The financial authorities, however, concluded that the market had overreached itself. Roy Young, Chairman of the Federal Reserve Board, publicly insisted (in February 1929) that the market was too high. Paul Warburg, head of the great investment banking firm of Kuhn, Loeb, and Company, took a

29. Mark Twain, *Roughing It* I (1913):219. Twain was describing mining speculation during the 1860s.

30. J. K. Galbraith, *The Great Crash, 1929* (1961), pp. 8–9. Reference to "personality trait[s]" of Americans reveals the newer influence of psychology.

31. "Long before the multiplier and accelerator were dreamed of society suffered from self-fulfilling exponential price explosions of the form $P_t = (1 + k) P_{t-1} = P_0 (1 + k)^t \to \infty$ as $t \to \infty$. There is no reason why such a self-warranting tulip mania should end when it does end." Paul Samuelson, "Myths and Realities About the Crash and Depression," *Journal of Portfolio Management* (Fall 1979), p. 10.

TABLE 33.6
THE STOCK MARKET: 1900 TO THE CRASH OF 1929

| Year | Common Stock Prices (1900 = 100) | Yields (in percent) | | | Premium (in percent) | | Prime Rate minus call rate |
		Indus-trials	Util-ities	Muni-cipal bonds	Industrials over municipals	Utilities over municipals	
1900	100	5.74	5.38	3.12	2.62	2.26	
1910	152	5.33	5.04	3.97	1.36	1.07	
1920	130	5.54	8.06	4.98	.56	3.08	
1921	112	5.84	8.29	5.09	.75	3.20	.65
1922	137	5.37	7.62	4.23	1.14	3.39	.16
1923	139	5.40	7.59	4.25	1.15	3.34	.20
1924	147	5.25	7.35	4.20	1.05	3.15	.88
1925	181	4.75	6.13	4.09	.66	2.04	−.18
1926	205	5.24	5.57	4.08	1.16	1.49	−.18
1927	249	4.72	4.96	3.98	.74	.98	.06
1928	324	3.82	4.09	4.05	−.23	.04	−1.25
1929	423	3.65	2.29	4.27	−.62	−1.98	−1.89

Source: Computed from data in Census, *Historical Statistics . . . to 1970*, pp. 1001–4.

similar position.[32] On the other hand, Ivar Krueger, the great Swedish swindler, whose every word was treasured by speculators, assured the world that stocks had a long way to go.[33] And, of course, many (but not all) of those busy selling stocks to the public, and collecting their fees for so doing, did the same. (They included Richard Whitney—later to go from the New York Stock Exchange to prison—and Charles Mitchell of the National City Bank, whose affiliate was busy selling securities.)[34]

But these warnings and these assurances were ignored by those kiting up the Dow Jones average. The Federal Reserve System restricted the amount of call loans pouring into the market from the banking system. However, stock buyers offered higher and higher rates for such loans. Money was increasingly shipped in to them by Europeans, by other financial institutions.[35] And by American corporations whose treasures efficiently put their idle cash to work. Finally, in October 1929 there occurred that fatal accident in the New York Stock Exchange that stands as the proximate origin of the Great Depression.

32. Cf. Charles Kindleberger, *The World in Depression* (1973), p. 112. Bernard Baruch, speculator and advisor to presidents from Wilson to Roosevelt, also took this position.

33. Robert Shaplen's *Krueger* (1960) is a fast-paced classic.

34. Taking the same position was America's great economist, Irving Fisher of Yale University.

35. Kindleberger, *The World*, pp. 74, 75, 113.

Appendix

Some 15 percent of American families owned stock in 1900. We derive that figure as follows. George Blanchard, of the Erie Railway, studied stockholder lists and estimated that there were 950,000 stockholders in 1897 (U.S. Industrial Commission, *Reports*, vol. XIX, p. 403). At that time the value of railroad stock outstanding was $5,365 million (*Historical Statistics . . . to 1970*, p. 735). If so, the average holding was $5,647. Railroad stock outstanding then constituted about half of all stock (*Historical Statistics*, p. 253). Holdings by life insurance companies were small (Raymond Goldsmith, *A Study of Saving in the United States* I (1944):455). So were other institutional holdings. We therefore divided the average railroad holding into total stock outstanding to arrive at an estimate of 2,460,000 holders or 15 percent of the 16 million households.

In 1927, the Secretary of the Treasury estimated that there were some 3 million stockholders in the nation (*Annual Report of the Secretary of the Treasury* (1929), p. 280). Estimates of Bernheim and Schneider for 1929 indicate 7 to 9 million owners (Alfred Bernheim and Margaret Schneider, *The Securities Markets* (1953), p. 735; cf. also Edwin B. Cox, *Trends in the Distribution of Stock Ownership* (1963), pp. 28, 33. There were then about 30 million households—leading to a figure of 27 percent.

34

Crash and Depression

IN February, 1929, Eddie Condon's Hot Shots cut a record whose title was to keynote that year: "That's a very serious thing." Months later, on the night of October 29, 1929, "The usual crowd was wedged thickly into Jack and Charlie's. . . . Everyone sought to think through something that even the Yale businessmen could not explain, and a great deal of quite serious drinking was going on. Then one of those good-time Charlies, the life of every party . . . [was suddenly] hit over the head with a bottle. 'It wasn't a fun night,' Donald Ogden Stewart explained. 'I mean, everybody that afternoon had lost every shirt he had.' "[1] In time the bitter jokes proliferated. A passerby shook his fist at the closed branch of the United States Bank: "Even hanging is too good for such villains." Asked if he had lost any money in the bank he answered curtly, "None—if I had any money in there, would I be taking it so lightly?"[2]

In October of 1929 investors suddenly and massively recognized that the returns they could get from continuing to hold stocks were less than they had believed. Their revised expectations caused the greatest stock market collapse in American history, before or since. Why was the "shock of recognition" so enormous?

Table 33.6 reveals two basic reasons. First, ever since 1927 the premium for investing in industrials, rather than in far safer municipal bonds, had been falling sharply. As a result the typical investor in industrials really got nothing for his greater risk all through 1928 and 1929. And the premium for utilities investors, once generous, had dwindled to nearly nothing.

Second, in the early 1920s the call rates (paid by speculators to borrow money for buying stocks) ranged well above the prime rate (paid by corporations for money to be used in production). Beginning in 1928 the call rate rose sharply. Its new level actually exceeded the underlying rate of return from production in the firms whose stocks were being snapped up in the market.

1. John Keats, *You Might As Well Live* (1971), pp. 148–49.
2. Louis Nizer, *Reflections Without Mirrors* (1978).

Which meant that people were borrowing money at high rates to buy stock earning lower rates.

The recognition that for nearly two years stocks had been valued so much above their earning base could not be suppressed forever. The end of the long infatuation was catalyzed by a sequence of drastic events. When these hit the newspapers, the bears drove for a fall:

In February 1929 the Federal Reserve Board declared that the market was too high, stating that additional loans for buying stocks "constituted an improper use of federal reserve facilities."[3]

Beginning in June, employment in large factories fell.[4]

On August 9, the New York Federal Reserve raised its rediscount rate from 5 to 6 percent, thereby raising the cost of all loans.[5]

During August-September, the leading industry in the U.S. boom— autos—began to cut back production sharply.

On September 26 the Bank of England raised its rediscount rate by 1 percent, promptly pulling money that had been kiting the New York stock market to earn higher returns in London.[6]

From October 14 on, stock prices began to fall. October 24 proved to be an unprecedented 2 million share day.[7]

In 1929 a substantial share of all stocks were bought on margin: 10 cents on the dollar would "buy" stock, with later payment to come. Hence, when stock values collapsed, the typical investor was not about to throw 90 cents after the dime already down the drain. Why throw good money after bad? He simply abandoned the stock, which then sold for anything it could bring in a collapsing market. (After 1934, and the Securities and Exchange Act, stocks could only be bought on a 50 percent margin. When the market subsequently declined—for example, in 1962—investors often (and unreasonably) held on until the stock came back to the price at which they had bought it. No such motivation had been persuasive to margin buyers back in 1929.)

"From mid-1929 to the end of 1930 a somewhat 'normal' recession ensued," says one Nobel prize winner. "Until the fall of 1930," says another, "the contraction, though severe, had been a garden-variety recession, unmarred by banking difficulties, runs on the banks, or the like. . . . " There

3. *Annual Report of the Secretary of the Treasury* (1930), p. 19.

4. 72d Cong., 1st sess., Senate Committee on Manufactures, *Establishment of a National Economic Council* (1932), p. 19.

5. Since the Federal Reserve Board raised the rate at which banks could sell loans they had made, they in turn would charge more on loans they made with the money thus borrowed.

6. That action was opposed by the Labour Chancellor of the Exchequer. He feared it would hurt business. Kindleberger, *Depression*, p. 115.

7. *National Economic Council*, p. 722.

followed . . . a non-inevitable avalanche of bank failures, debt suspension . . . deflation and depression."[8]

As in prior panics owners rushed to close their bank accounts in 1929–1930. Before the Federal Reserve Act was passed banks handled such a flight to cash by refusing to pay—"restrictionism." Sometimes the more stable banks, grouped in "clearing houses" in major cities, provided temporary help to some of their weaker brethren. In time the immediate hysteria passed and most banks reopened. Most depositors then got their money, usually redepositing it. The Federal Reserve System, however, was designed to provide a better "lender of last resort"—offering small banks more even-handed treatment than clearing houses had, backed by the inexhaustible ability of the government to print money legally. It was thereby expected to prevent future financial panic and disaster. (In 1913 a leading Harvard professor advised his students not to study monetary problems; they had been solved by the creation of the Federal Reserve System.[9]) But, in late 1929–30 the supply of money was not expanded significantly. Indeed, it actually fell slightly. In late 1929 the Federal Reserve Bank of New York did move to expand by purchasing government securities. However, the central office of the Federal Reserve in Washington forcibly objected. And instead of expanding money supply over the next year or so to offset the contraction, the system allowed that supply to decline.

Lacking help, bankers' tactics for survival varied. One banker warned Chicago clearing-house members of what would happen if they failed to help him through a run on his bank by making a temporary loan: "You can force us to close the Foreman bank tomorrow . . . but that will make a run on every other bank in Illinois. We will be out of the banking business, but you will still be in it."[10] He got his help. But in New York City the much larger, symbolically named, United States Bank, was denied help by the local bankers. Despite earnest pleas by the state superintendent of banking, the Clearing House made the immortal judgment that the effects of its failure would be only "local."[11] They might have been correct if the Federal Reserve System were actively engaging in substantial open-market activities (providing greater bank liquidity, and inducing investment) and if bank deposits had been insured. But none of this was so. The Federal Reserve Board watched, though with keen interest, as the money supply fell by over one-third from August 1929 to March 1933—vastly more than its rate of fall in any prior depression. Banks jettisoned their bond portfolios, attempting to get enough liquidity to pay off their depositors. Each such move drove down the portfolio values of

---

8. The quotations are from Paul Samuelson and Milton Friedman in a remarkable set of articles in the *Journal of Portfolio Management* (Fall 1979), pp. 9, 18.

9. Seymour Harris, *American Economic History* (1961), p. 95.

10. John Gunther, *Taken at the Flood* (1961), p. 167.

11. The episode appears in the comprehensive chapter on "The Great Contraction 1929–33," in Milton Friedman and Anna Schwartz, *A Monetary History of the United States, 1867–1960* (1963).

TABLE 34.1
DEPOSITS IN SUSPENDED BANKS
(MILLIONS OF DOLLARS, AT ANNUAL RATE)

1928	141
1929	231
1930	
January–October	361
November	2,160
December	4,260
1931	1,690

the remaining banks. The destructive outcome was unprecedented, as shown in Table 34.1. Until October 1930 deposits locked in suspended banks increased, but not much more than they had in any previous recession. The "avalanche" of failures in November and December introduced the second stage of the recession. Oddly enough there seem to be no estimates of how many depositors lost their savings in the depression. But one can make a rough estimate: something close to 6 million depositors, or one family in every four, lost their savings (for many, their life savings) in the bank failures of 1929–33.[12]

Little of this need have occured if bank deposits had been insured. Five states had even tested out deposit insurance as early as 1907–1909.[13] But a concentrated effort to put such insurance into the Federal Reserve Act (of 1913) was solidly defeated by the Congressional majority, led by Carter Glass of Virginia. They were unwilling to do anything that might keep banks from failing, with bankers thereby being chastised by losing their own assets.[14] And they gave no evidence of any close thought about the depositors, who would inevitably be trapped in a common ruin with the bankers. (A later Congress belatedly forced through deposit insurance in 1933, over the opposition of both Herbert Hoover and Franklin Roosevelt.[15] Its value became so

12. See Appendix B, Chapter 35. Data in Table 34.1 are from Federal Reserve Board, *Banking and Monetary Statistics*, p. 285. The 1930 data are based on October 1, 1931 letter from Ogden Mills to President Hoover now in the Hoover Presidential Library, kindly made available by my colleague, William Barber.

13. T. Cooke, "The Insurance of Bank Deposits in the West," *Quarterly Journal of Economics* (1910).

14. A "solid Republican vote" for "insuring with government funds individual bank deposits," and "a solid Democratic vote against" are proudly reported in Carter Glass, *An Adventure in Constructive Finance* (1927), pp. 208–9. Glass, by then a Senator, was a leader in Congress under FDR. Presumably, populist reluctance to do anything that might help bankers, much less inefficient bankers, was at work.

15. Kindelberger, *Depression*, p. 201. Both feared that the "weak banks would pull down the strong"—about as relevant as a fear that life insurance must fail because the dying "would pull down" the living. If anything, such assurance would have kept many banks from depositor runs, enabling them to monetize their assets in orderly fashion, and thereby keep afloat.

obvious that later historians somehow began to describe it as one of the accomplishments of the New Deal.[16])

For more than a century Britain had provided a standard of financial security in world markets. In the fall of 1931 it abandoned the gold standard, no longer paying out gold to anyone presenting pound notes to the Bank of England. The U.S. Federal Reserve Board read this as requiring it to fight to protect the dollar's link to gold—by sharply increasing rediscount rates. Helping the Treasury keep a full stock of gold in its vaults was apparently going to cheer American investors, so much so that they would happily pay still higher interest rates to borrow money to invest and provide jobs for the unemployed.

While such advances in monetary policy were taking place what was fiscal policy up to? Inaction by government had characterized previous recessions, and the recessions had generally ended in a few years. Why change? The cities and states were obviously not doing so. But there was fierce objection to what little they did. Indeed, in 1932 Daniel Hoan, socialist mayor of Milwaukee, proudly described Milwaukee's advantage as a city without debt. Asked, "What is wrong with municipalities" and the federal government with "respect to their finances," he answered: "They are choking themselves to death by the borrowing habit."[17]

Other cities and states sought the same goal. True, want and unemployment stalked the land. But how could cities feed and clothe their own taxpayers? Even if they could borrow for such a program it would inevitably draw people into the city from areas that did not do so. And even if they were prepared to finance every new arrival their workers would object: competition for a handful of jobs would only increase. Between July and October 1935 alone some 30,500 people "in parties needing manual employment" had driven into California.[18] And, as one Californian remembered through the years, wages for packing fruit fell from $5 an hour to 50 cents a day.[19] Cities

16. "In the frenzied weeks from March to June 1933 Franklin D. Roosevelt . . . steered 15 major laws to enactment: among them . . . new regulations for banking. . . . The hundred days were only the start. . . . Who can now imagine a day when America offered . . . no Federal guarantee of bank deposits.?" Arthur Schlesinger in *New York Times* (April 10, 1983). On March 9, 1933, "the president signed the Emergency Banking Act. Between 1921 and 1932 more than 10,000 banks had failed—destroying faith in our most basic financial institutions." That Act "led to . . . the establishment of the Federal Deposit Insurance Corporation. It is this legislation which continues today to insure the deposits of our national banks and thrift institutions." Jennings Randolph in *New York Times* (April 10, 1983).

17. *The Literary Digest* (January 30, 1932), p. 13.

18. In automobiles "bearing out-of-state licenses." Reported by Paul Taylor in National Resources Committee, *The Problems of a Changing Population*, (1938), p. 228.

19. Quoted in V. S. Naipaul, *The Overcrowded Barracoon* (1973), p. 168. "You know what an Okie was? They moved here in hordes. . . . I was making five to six dollars an hour, packing fruit. When they came they worked for fifteen cents, twenty cents. Fifty cents a day."

TABLE 34.2
INCOME FLOWS, 1929–32
(MILLIONS OF DOLLARS)

Wages and salaries	– 51,034
Relief	
work	+ 132
direct	+ 266
Money raised by community chests	+ 25

therefore spent little more than their tax receipts—4 percent more in 1939, or virtually the same as the 3 percent more in 1929.[20] They cut highway construction by one-quarter, school construction by one-half.[21] And they stayed grimly within their budget constraint. Beyond this infinitesimal contribution by local governments, voluntary relief funds added a thin trickle. Their combined impact on the economic hurricane can be described very simply, as in Table 34.2.

Did the federal government compensate? It had not done so in past recessions. In 1893 Cleveland vetoed an appropriation to provide free seed to starving Texas farmers. No public works program was pursued in 1908 by Theodore Roosevelt, in 1921 by Harding, in 1924 or 1927 by Coolidge. It was not that other national governments had never done so. In 1819 Britain's prime minister was a classic reactionary, but Castelreagh provided money to build churches and public works so that the unemployed would have jobs.[22] Political acceptability, however, had apparently been changed by the age of mass unemployment. (In the late 1920s Britain found it preferable to provide a money dole. Some of its relief agencies required that unemployed workers be shut up in a closed room for 7 hours a day, doing nothing, in order to receive such benefits.[23] The United States adopted no such dole, set no such requirements.)

A policy of public works for depressions had been proposed by Arthur Bowley in 1909.[24] In 1923, Wesley Mitchell, leading U.S. economist and

20. U. S. Office of Business Economics *National Income and Product Accounts of the United States* (1929–1965), p. 54.

21. Lowell Chawner, *Construction Activity in the United States, 1915–37*, U.S. Department of Commerce, Domestic Commerce Series No. 99 (1938), pp. 51, 78.

22. Cf. C. J. Bartlett, *Castlereagh* (1966), p. 184. Castlereagh, however, asked of the proposal to "give the people food and employment": was it "possible for the legislature to do that . . . amidst all the fluctuations of commerce and manufactures? Upon what principles could government . . . take from one class merely . . . [to give] to another?"

23. Ronald C. Davison, *The Unemployed* (1929), p. 7.

24. *Royal Commission on the Poor Laws and the Relief of Distress, Report*, Command 4499 (1909), pp. 1195. 1237.

close associate of Hoover, had noted their potential.[25] Indeed, in the 1920s "the possible contribution of budget policy, particularly variation of public works expenditures, to short-run economic stabilization, was widely but not universally recognized."[26] In 1933 Arthur Gayer of Columbia argued that every job on public works, directly or in producing cement and steel for such buildings, would create still another job via succeeding demand for consumer goods.[27] In October 1931 William Randolph Hearst used his nationwide newspaper chain to campaign for a $5 billion bond issue to finance jobs via public works. His proposal was dramatically opposed by 50 leading economists, among others. They warned that such action would destroy U.S. credit, drive us from the gold standard, reduce private jobs as much as it increased public ones.[28]

In consequence, the accepted U.S. fiscal policy in 1929–32 proposed that "economic wounds would be healed by the action of the cells of the economic body"—not by physicians busying themselves with bandages and medicines.[29] Its results are best summarized by a single figure. In the spring of 1933 relief assistance averaged 80 cents a week per person—for those who qualified.[30] But a mere 12 percent of the population was receiving relief.[31] Divide the total of $317 million for relief in 1932 by the 12.1 million unemployed and one gets an average of $3.21 a week per unemployed person (in 1980 prices).

The slowdown from 1929 to 1932 could have been shortened, despite the Crash, despite the financial alarums, if only consumers and/or investors and/ or government had advanced real expenditure and employment. What in fact did each do?

Consumers cut their spending (in constant dollars) from 1929 to 1930, then to 1931, as unemployment rose from 3 percent to 9 percent to 16 percent. The unemployed accounted for little of that aggregate decline. Most workers were still employed. They nonetheless cut their purchases. Who could tell how long a job would last? Moreover, their workweek was shor-

25. Lionel Edie, ed., *The Stabilization of business* (1923), p. 44.

26. Herbert Stein, "Fiscal Policy," *International Encyclopedia of the Social Sciences*, 5:461.

27. Arthur Gayer, "Public Works," *Encyclopedia of the Social Sciences*, XII, p. 694.

28. Calvin Hoover, *Memoirs of Capitalism, Communism and Nazism* (1965), p. 150. Professor Hoover, in a private letter, indicate the proposed issue came to $5 billion. He quoted Alvin Hansen, one of those included, as explaining that we were still trying to stay on the gold standard and, besides, "This was before I believed what I do now"—i.e., before his conversion to Keynesianism.

29. Erving P. Hayes, *Activities of the Presidents Emergency Committee for Employment* (1936), p. 6.

30. Theodore Whiting, *Final Report of the Federal Emergency Relief Administration* (1942), pp. 23, 41 ($15 a month, and 4.4 persons per family).

31. Ann Geddes, *Trends in Relief Expenditures, 1910–1935*, WPA Research Monograph X (1937): 101.

tened, and their wage rates cut. They apparently responded more pessimistically to such fear and realities than had employed workers in prior recessions. A central force creating that pessimism was surely the unusually great decline in their wealth. About a quarter of all consumers had seen their stock market investments decline abruptly, often to near zero values. About a quarter (overlapping the first group) saw their bank deposits disappear in suspended banks. Many never got back a cent. Others waited years for partial payment. Perhaps half of all families owned homes, and saw the wealth imbedded in those homes turn into a phantom. By 1934 one-third of all home owners were delinquent in their mortgage payments.[32] (That the foreclosure rate was only about 3 percent was important.[33] But that fact led few to ignore the delinquency, to go out and expand their spending.)

Between the depressions of 1921 and 1929 a considerable number of American families had put together asset positions—in home ownership, stock ownership, savings and demand deposit ownership. They formed a new "establishment" group by 1929, just in time to be wiped out by the collapse of asset values. That their losses led them to slow their spending is not totally surprising. But in doing so they delayed recovery more than similar middle-income families did in older recessions. The rich had always had a cushion to permit increased spending. The poor always spent what they had. Only the newer groups varied their spending so consequentially as their economic circumstances varied.

So far as private domestic investment was concerned, two great deterrents developed in 1930–32, if not three. Because consumers were reluctant to keep up their real expenditure even at predepression rates the 1930 stock of plant and equipment continued to serve final markets quite adequately. Why, then, build any more?[34] Investment in new plant and equipment could only become warranted, as in many past recessions, if a marked cost advantage could be anticipated from it. And/or if investors foresaw new products so irresistible that consumers further reduced their savings, or borrowed. The

---

32. Computed from data for 233 individual cities as reported by David Wickens in U.S. Bureau of Foreign and Domestic Commerce, *Financial Survey of Urban Housing* (1937), Tables 16, 36. The cities were ranked by percentage of owners delinquent on mortgage payments, and the median figure used. Data relate to 1934. The percentage as of 1933 may have been somewhat greater. For some of those who hung on desperately would have abandoned their properties and/or been foreclosed, while few pecunious buyers would have been added to the owner total in 1933–34.

33. Foreclosure rate from *Historical Statistics . . . to 1970*, p. 65.

34. It is unnecessary to invoke "overproduction" and an "overhang" of plant and equipment in 1929 to explain the low level in 1930–32. The excess capacity argument is most cogently presented by E. Nourse et al., *America's Capacity to Produce* (1934), p. 416, who concludes that industry in 1929 was operating at only 80 percent of its "capacity" in 1929. Industrialists in later decades rarely operated at 100 percent. "Capacity" appeared to be an engineering concept applicable to brief periods, not achievable month in and month out.

cost advantage argument, however, was rarely attractive in the catastrophe years of 1930, 1931, and 1932. For relative prices of labor and capital were then declining, and so unpredictably that it was hardly clear what investment choices would best cut costs, or for how long. Some products would undoubtedly seduce consumers to take the last dollar out of the cookie jar. But who would finance their production? Six thousand banks, one in every four, had disappeared into the void between 1929 and 1932. Few of the surviving financiers would impassively finance the production of novel and unpredictable products in that world of disaster. Even the automobile companies were hesitant about financing the purchase of new cars. Plausible borrowers might be out of work the next week. The structure of production, however, guaranteed that if consumers didn't buy cars, employment in steel production fell. That cut production of iron ore, which generated a fall in employment in railroading, which then slowed grocery sales to railroad employees, and so on.

Government expenditure policy provided little more stimulus than the postal deficit. As for tax policy, the Congress in June of 1932 contributed to extend the depression by passing a new tax schedule—which did not cut rates to speed expenditure but actually raised them.[35]

---

35. It raised full-employment levels of federal tax by 1.5 billions. Cary Brown, "Fiscal Policy in the Thirties: A Reappraisal," *American Economic Review* (December 1956), p. 864.

[The Queen's Ministers in 1851] expressed 'confident hope' that the depression would pass away; that, said Disraeli, was 'the language of amiable despair.'
—MONEYPENNY AND BUCKLE, *The Life of Benjamin Disraeli*

35

The New Deal

THE New Deal provided a sense of hope. That may well have been its greatest contribution to society, and to whatever recovery took place after 1933. Year had followed hopeless year of economic catastrophe. Finally "somebody" was going to do something about the national ruin. That belief brought the huge vote for Franklin Roosevelt in 1932, and the still more overwhelming vote in 1936. (F.D.R. is still the only four-time president.) But the economic content of the New Deal was neither finely planned nor well dealt. Four major elements of its "recovery program" are of special note.

Reflation

The New Deal's first major program for recovery was "reflation": all prices were going to be raised.[1] Somehow that would increase jobs, real incomes, and profits. To achieve the reflation goal the Treasury was to begin buying silver (once again) and gold. The Agricultural Adjustment Administration (AAA) was organized to push up farm prices. And the National Recovery Administration (NRA) was created to increase the price of most other things, particularly nonfarm products and labor. "Reflating" the price of food and clothing would make a mockery of any wage increases workers got. But that did not appear to trouble the "Brain Trust" busily planning the improved

---

1. A minor program involved cutting federal spending by firing government employees. As F.D.R. declared in September 1932: "I accuse the present administration of being the greatest spending Administration in peacetime in all our history. . . . Reduction in Federal spending . . . is the most direct and effective contribution that Government can make to business." Quoted in Robert Lekachman, *The Age of Keynes* (1966), p. 114.

economic order. Nor did the fact that price increases for cotton, labor, steel, increased costs to producers in most nonfarm sectors. It thereby choked off their willingness to hire more workers to produce more goods. In time, however, the infatuation with forcing prices up gave way to concentration on a whole alphabet of new programs.

The NRA

The National (Industrial) Recovery Administration was planned to operate through governmentally sponsored cartels, one for each industry. Leading industrialists were invited to collaborate in preventing "destructive wage or price cutting" or similar activities. It was proposed to Congress as an "experiment of encouraging business organizations to get together to establish agreement that will promote fair competition, and primarily . . . fair competition in wages and working conditions."[2] "In a general way it encourages manufacturers to do the same things that the cartels are doing in Europe."[3] The president of the chamber of commerce saw the NRA assisting "industries to get back on their feet [because] they can fix a fair price for their products."[4]

The NRA was indeed effective, even before it had issued a regulation or set up an industry committee. From April to July of 1933 industrial production actually rose by 50 percent, though it never did anywhere near as well after the NRA began to operate. By early 1933 producers had seen that prices and wages were going to be raised by the NRA's industry committees. They therefore rushed to produce at the lower, pre-code, costs.[5] About a million people were added to factory payrolls January to July—no mean feat.[6] But because the employment spurt chiefly involved producers trying to beat the gun on price increases that the NRA would, and did, put in place, it failed to continue. In the last half of 1933 employment rose no more than it did in the last half of 1932. Equally important, as the NRA pushed hourly earnings up 10 percent June 1933–1934, that rise was immediately matched by a 10 percent rise in the cost of living.[7] Hence, the real gain in workers' wage rates was

2. Statement by Donald Richberg, the lawyer for the administration who presented the NRA's case to Congress. Cf. Leverett Lyon et al., *The National Recovery Administration* (1935), p. 98.

3. Ibid., p. 21.

4. Lyon, *Recovery*, p. 24. Herbert Hoover noted that the NRA's rationale closely resembled ideas urged by the president of General Electric for several years, declared "this stuff was sheer fascism." *The Memoirs of Herbert Hoover, 1929–1941, The Great Depression* (1952), p. 420. Clare Luce later claimed the credit for showing the NRA administrator—General Hugh ("Old Iron Pants") Johnson—a book written by "the economic think man for Mussolini," and Johnson "sketched NRA . . . right out of Fanfani's book." *New York Times* (April 22, 1973). Mrs. Luce was a New Dealer in 1933, ambassador to Italy under Eisenhower.

5. Lyon, *Recovery*, p. 797.

6. BLS Bulletin 610, *Revised Indexes of Factory Employment* (1935), p. 23.

7. Lyon, *Recovery*, p. 788.

zero. Keynes, who visited the United States, wrote in mid-1934 that during the year ahead he counted on U.S. recovery if there were "direct stimulus to production." But he had "no belief in the efficacy of the price and wage-raising activities of the N.R.A." for achieving U.S. economic recovery.[8]

By August 1934 basic "codes" had been worked out for 507 industries, not just the few originally envisaged—auto, steel, oil, lumber.[9] The codes regulated how many hours a day plants (and even individual machines) could operate. They limited production by quotas; restricted investment in new productive capacity. They limited production for inventory; protected producers in one region from competition by those in another region. They forbade selling below cost—without specifying what cost elements were to be included, or whose costs. (Industry wide? Average or marginal cost? Most efficient firm or median? Large firms or all? Which reference year or month?) And they rigorously forbade "destructive price cutting"—often by fixing minimum prices.[10] It was all a perfect gloss on Johnson's declaration that the NRA was to be "exactly what industry organized in trade associations makes it."[11] (As its Administrator General Johnson had a high claim to knowledge on that point.)

Of course, both restricting the operation of plants and machines and setting production quotas limited the number of jobs that opened up to the unemployed.[12] Forbidding price cuts, like fixing minimum prices, kept employed workers from benefiting by higher real incomes through cost of living declines. Such considerations were brushed aside. In the end the NRA collapsed. But not for such reasons.

8. It was reprinted, many years later, in the *New York Times* of April 10, 1983. There it was accompanied by an historian's assertion that "The First New Deal at least operated in terms of a realistic model of the market. If the N.R.A. and A.A.A. could stop prices from plummeting in the 1930's it is not beyond possibility that they may conceivably offer some clues as to how to stop prices from soaring in the 1980's." Whether the editor or makeup man for the newspaper provided this conjunction of columns is not clear.

9. Lyon, *Recovery*, p. 313. In attempting to prevent firms from going off on their own, such industries as "ashes, cinders, garbage and scavenger," "wet mop," "dry mop," and "mop stick" were defined (p. 98).

10. Ibid., chapter 24 describes these restraints at length (also p. 665). At the retail level the modes of evasion were unusually interesting. Thus an auto dealer was "accused of price cutting because he bought six suits of clothes from a tailor to whom he had sold a car." Kalman Cohen and Richard Cyert, *Theory of the Firm* (1965), p. 248.

11. Quoted in Barton J. Bernstein, ed., *Towards a New Past* (1968), p. 269. The heads of the Amalgamated Clothing Workers and the United Mine Workers urged suspending the antitrust laws to permit industry such collaboration. The NRA promise of an opportunity to organize unions presumably urged them on.

12. While the unemployed were kept out by restricting increases in production the employed were offered minimum wages as part of the codes. These adopted prevailing differentials—e.g., higher wages for North than South, men than women (p. 327). Construction and graphic arts had a 30-cent rate, cotton textiles and retail trade a 14-cent rate, Puerto Rican needlework, 12-cents (pp. 322–24).

First, the business community was too fragmented to cooperate. Large firms dominated the code-setting groups in many industries. When they insisted that the small ones fall into line, even if doing so thereby menaced their own continued existence, the small ones refused to comply. Moreover, new entrants tried to enter the industry on their own terms. The United States lacked both the toughness and the black-shirted bravos that Italy had used in the 1920s to force recalcitrants into line. Indeed, the industry malcontents generated so much protest that Roosevelt had to set up a special review board, under the leading civil rights lawyer, Clarence Darrow.[13] After lengthy review Darrow's board reached a harsh conclusion: the codes had encouraged "bold and aggressive monopolistic practices," had "permitted the most powerful interests to seize control of entire industries."[14] And in the end one contemptibly small firm, selling poultry in New York City, challenged the NRA—and brought it down. Every Supreme Court justice (including those who strongly favored federal intervention against the depression) found the grant of federal power to the major firms that operated the NRA cartels too irresponsible to approve.

Farm Policy: The AAA

The New Deal farm program had its origins in the Bland-Allison Act of 1879. By that act, Congress committed the Treasury to buying silver at prices above the market. (The silver was to be used as backing for U.S. currency.) Both silver producers and inflationists had their appetite whetted by that act, and pressed for still more purchases. Their efforts reached a peak in 1889—a year before their success with the Sherman Act—when C. E. Macune of the Southern Farmer's Alliance drew a logical conclusion. If the taxpayer could make gifts to the happy silver producers, why not to the producers of wheat? Or barley, rice, cotton, or tobacco? Why could these commodities not serve as backing for paper money?[15] Doing so would produce more inflation, and guarantee a market for farm products—both prospects dear to the farmers.

The government did, however, eventually make a market for farmers. In World War I it had guaranteed the price of wheat and pork, thus leading farmers to invest further in land. After that speculative boom collapsed, help from the taxpayer was again invoked. The president of the American Plow Company, George Peek, proposed an "equality for agriculture" scheme that

---

13. Darrow had been the lawyer for the McNamara brothers, the union leaders who had dynamited the *Los Angeles Times* building; for Tom Mooney, imprisoned because of opposition to World War I, and his radicalism; and for Clarence Scopes, prosecuted by the State of Tennessee and by William Jennings Bryan (leader of the populists in the 1890s and Secretary of State for Woodrow Wilson) for teaching evolution.

14. Charles B. Saunders, *The Brookings Institution* (1966), p. 55.

15. Cf. C. E. Macune's article, "The Populist Subtreasury Plan," in *American Farmer's Movements* Fred Shannon, ed. (1957), p. 146.

would "let the price of the domestically consumed portion [of farm output] rise behind a tariff wall."[16] City workers were thus invited to provide a double subsidy by paying a higher price for their bread and then by subsidizing bread and meat consumed by Europeans. Support for such schemes did not get far until in the 1930s, when Peek surfaced again, as effective adviser to the Secretary of Agriculture.

When the New Deal came to town in 1933 the idea that the government owed the farmer a living (though not the city worker) was more fully developed. The AAA was designed to raise prices for farm producers, as the NRA had been designed to raise prices of industrial products. In order to manipulate the price labels in farming, the supply was to be cut.[17]

In April 1932 F.D.R. had accurately declared: "The country . . . demands bold, persistent experimentation. . . . The millions who are in want will not stand by silent forever while the things to satisfy their needs are within easy reach."[18] How was that shrewd and sensitive judgment implemented when it came to agriculture? In August-September 1933 Henry Wallace initiated the Department of Agriculture's "emergency pig slaughter." That slaughter of 4 million hogs was not to provide meat for those who had none. 10 percent was turned into bacon and salt pork, while 90 percent was converted into fertilizer.[19] For a period of mass unemployment and inadequate diets that policy may seem less than humane or socially sensitive. But it was the program the farmers insisted upon.

"The program came from the farmers themselves, you betcha . . . we had twice too many pigs because corn'd been so cheap. And we set up what people called Wallace's Folly: killing the little pigs. Another farmer and I helped develop this. We couldn't afford to feed forty-five-cent corn to a three dollar hog. So we had to figure a way of getting rid of the surplus pigs. We went out and bought 'em and killed 'em. This is how desperate it was. It was the only way to raise the price of pigs. Most of 'em were dumped down the

16. Cf. the lively discussion in Gilbert Fite, *American Farmers, The New Minority* (1981), p. 42.

17. To Hoover, with his experience in feeding starving Europeans, the destruction of food was bad policy. He had long refused "proposals by which farmers would be forced to reduce production. . . . 'To him this meant sheer fascism.' " Richard Kirkendall, *Social Scientists and Farm Politics in the Age of Roosevelt* (1966), p. 41.

18. Cf. Wallace Davies and W. Goetsmann, eds., *The New Deal and Business Recovery* (1936), p. 4.

19. Data in E. G. Nourse et al., *Three Years of the Agricultural Adjustment Administration* (1937), pp. 134, 197, 204, indicate that the hog-kill weighed 1 billion pounds, yielded 100 million pounds of edible dry salt meat, and 7.7 million pounds of lard. (Another 15 million pounds of lard were made, but proved useless for human consumption because of the congestion at the packing plants while the huge slaughter took place.) The average hog weighed about 255 pounds. (Hog weight in 1934 from *Report of the Federal Trade Commission on Agricultural Income Inquiry* (1938), part I, p. 192). Hence the 1 billion pound estimate implies 3.9 million hogs slaughtered.

river."[20] As an economic policy the program involved a high irony. It increased, and cheapened, the supply of fertilizer. Thereby it stimulated the production of farm products so that next year's production would be even greater. (The tradition of destroying food continued: decades later newspapers showed Maine blueberry farmers, organized in a farmers "union," dumping blueberries in an abandoned slaughter yard to keep the price up.)[21]

Nor should this be viewed as a peculiar piece of American idiocy: "The best news on the European Agricultural front [in 1970] . . . is a somewhat lugubrious disclosure that 291,000 dairy cows had been slaughtered in the first community-wide program which the Common Market has undertaken to reduce milk and dairy production."[22]

An administration regularly supported by the solid South was naturally aware of the desolation of that region. In addition to the general AAA farm programs, it developed one for the great Southern farm product, cotton. In 1939 it initiated an export subsidy, which gave Europeans about $45 million from U.S. taxpayers in the form of lower prices for cotton than American consumers had to pay.[23] (No one proposed making such a gift to the American unemployed—possibly because the unemployed needed more than clothing.) One irony of this program arose because the subsidy exceeded the cost of shipping cotton to Europe. It thus became profitable to collect the subsidy, ship the cotton to Europe, and then return it to the United States.[24] The process thus transferred money from the Treasury mostly to Europeans, but to some alert Americans as well.

Fiscal Policy

The belief that fiscal policy and Keynesianism came in with the New Deal was held by the reactionary Liberty League during the 1930s and the more romantic historians of the Depression in later years. It can be evaluated no more rudely than by the administration's proud claim to the League of Nations in 1936. The administration asserted that its "reconstruction programme began in 1933," and had achieved "a considerable increase in both Federal and local revenue."[25] Incredible though it may seem by present standards of active fiscal policy, the administration and Congress had not cut the

20. Oscar Heline, former lobbyist for the state cooperative in Iowa, quoted by Studs Terkel in *The Atlantic* (March 1970), p. 82.

21. Portland, Maine, *Press Herald* (August 7, 1969).

22. *Washington Post* (April 19, 1970).

23. Geoffrey Shepherd, *Agricultural Price Control* (1945), p. 190.

24. U.S. Tariff Commission, *Cotton and Cotton Waste*, Report No. 137, second series (1939), pp. 18–19.

25. League of Nations, Organization for Communications and Transit, *National Public Works* (1936), p. 46. It also referred to reduced unemployment, increased purchasing power.

effective federal tax rate, but had raised it by 700 percent from 1932 to 1939.[26] State and local governments likewise increased their effective rates, proliferating sales taxes. Those increases increasingly burdened the lower and middle income groups. Fiscal policy in the 1930s was not an expansionary Keynesian device as some historians have it, but a fairly efficient system for keeping down expenditures and minimizing public debt.

New Deal expenditure policy was not starkly perverse. But it was very modest indeed. Though full-employment GNP rose by $35 billion from 1933 to 1939, federal spending rose by only $5 billion; very little contribution to recovery had been made by the federal expenditure programs.[27] The record of successive years suggests little "Keynesian" expenditure policy.

Between 1929 and 1931 GNP fell by some $27 billion while compensating federal expenditures rose by less than $2 billion. (Even that rise came chiefly because Congress voted a veteran's bonus payment over protests by Hoover.[28]) From 1932 to 1936 federal expenditures rose by about $5 billion, much of that going only to increase administrative employment in Washington. About $1.5 billion of that total was concentrated in 1936, when a further veteran's bonus was passed. (The bonus was vetoed by Roosevelt this time, not Hoover.)

The recession of 1937–38 simply added to the general depression still prevailing. One contributing cause was the beginning of the social security system. "A Good Thing," it probably energized investment and productivity in the long run. Unfortunately, it cut the paychecks of workers in the short run and slowed recovery.[29] Secondly, the administration began to tax undistributed profits, pursuing the rich and well born. The tax proved unworkable, politically and administratively.[30] It slowed business operations until it was repealed. (The Federal Reserve Board, ever fearful of inflation, also cut the rediscount rate and the money supply.) Although federal expenditures rose by $2 billion from 1931 to 1940, chiefly for ship construction and other defense, about 15 percent of the labor force was still unemployed in 1940. As Brown remarks, "fiscal policy . . . seems to have been an unsuccessful recovery device in the 'thirties—not because it did not work, but because it was not tried."[31]

26. By effective tax rates we refer to the yield of full-employment taxes (less transfers) in constant dollars. The figures are from Brown, "Fiscal Policy," p. 864.

27. Ibid. Potential GNP rose by 33 billion according to revisions by Larry Peppers, "Full Employment Surplus," *Explorations in Entrepreneurial History* (Winter 1973), p. 203.

28. Federal data from Bureau of Economic Analysis, *The National Income and Product Accounts of the United States, 1929–74*, Tables 3.2 and 3.12.

29. R. A. Gordon, *Economic Instability and Growth* (1974), p. 60, combined the federal deficit with the surplus on social security account to indicate a net deficit of $3.6 billion in 1936 and $0.4 billion in 1937.

30. The unworkability arose from the hard cases—widows and other lower income people who owned small amounts of stock. The tax reduced their dividends before they received them, even though they did not have incomes large enough to be liable to the tax.

31. Brown, "Fiscal Policy," pp. 865–66.

Monetary Policy

Monetary policy during this period, Friedman and Schwartz have emphasized, was largely passive.[32] In intent, however, it was not: the rediscount rate was progressively and repeatedly cut during late 1929 and later. But open-market purchases to provide liquidity, drive interest rates down further, and thereby induce new investment, were largely eschewed. In the international financial crisis of September 1931 (when England left the gold standard, other nations following) the Federal Reserve Board fought to protect the dollar's link to that standard. During the first two weeks of October it raised rediscount rates as much as it had cut them during the entire previous year.[33] Keeping a full stock of gold in the vaults was apparently more urgent than speeding loans, capital investment, and thereby jobs. The board tacitly held that confidence rested on the size of the gold stock held in the cellars of the Central Bank more than on the investment performance of the economy.

As loans and production fell, as more and more banks began failing all over the nation in 1932, "the monetary authorities stood by, apparently without any positive policy, in the final wave of liquidation."[34] In 1933 they believed that they had pursued "a policy of liberal open-market purchases."[35] But they reckoned by some recondite criterion, not by the immensity of the catastrophe all around them. Later judges have held that Federal Reserve purchases, made chiefly under pressure from Congress, were trivial. James Tobin, leading monetary scholar and Nobel prize winner, has written: "From today's vantage point no one will defend the passive acquiescence of the Fed in the monetary contraction and banking collapse [of 1929–33]. The Fed's failure to undertake an aggressive policy of open-market purchases seems incredible."[36] Incredible policy, unhappily, helped produce an all too credible result—four years of economic collapse. In an economy controlled and led by financial cues (prices, interest rates, expected profit rates) those four interminable years wrecked the old system irretrievably.

Almost as inexplicable as its 1929–33 failure was the Federal Reserve's action in 1937. In a year when 14 percent of the nation's labor was idle (and something close to the same percentage of other resources) the Fed was fearful of inflation and cut back on the money supply and thereby credit. It requires accepting no given theory of why the Depression began or developed, nor

32. Milton Friedman and Anna Schwartz, *A Monetary History of the United States 1867–1960* (1963), chaps. 8, 9.

33. While some Federal Reserve banks had reduced their rates less, the New York Federal Reserve rate, 3.5 percent in May 1930, was down to 1.5 percent on October 1, 1931. Federal Reserve Board, *Twentieth Annual Report of the Federal Reserve Board . . . for 1933*, p. 145.

34. Gordon, *Economic Instability*, p. 54.

35. Federal Reserve Board, *Report*, p. 20.

36. James Tobin, "The Monetary Interpretation of History," *American Economic Review* (June 1965), pp. 470, 483.

even why it lasted so interminably, to hold that the Fed failed to do what Congress had designed it to do. Nor even what the older route of bank suspension and banker's clearing house cooperation had provided, however insufficient that was by modern values. One of the most distinguished scholars of the subject, and long-time consultant to the Fed in later decades, has written: "In retrospect the Federal Reserve's monetary policy [in 1929–33], or lack of policy, was a disaster."[37] That characterization can be extended as well to policy over a longer period.

The New Deal

The New Deal consisted of two quite different sets of cards. One represented the combined economic wisdom of army generals, farm activists, business leaders, distinguished economists. The other represented the wisdom of ward politicians, social workers, and some economists.

The first set of policies hamstrung business by pushing prices and output around in such unpredictable ways, and by vague promises of "reform," that it delayed the new investment that would otherwise increase jobs and speed recovery. So contended Schumpeter, saturnine, shrewd supporter but critic of capitalism. And so agreed Robert Aaron Gordon, liberal and Keynesian though he was.[38]

The economy was still one in which private enterprise was expected to provide most jobs, and owners of private property were expected to invest and thereby stimulate the hiring of most of the unemployed. But the usual cues that private firms and investors used to guide their investment and employment decisions were now changed largely, frequently, and unpredictably. These changes were associated with the New Deal legislation and administration, much of which represented a long-delayed response to changes in the society. The problem for investors was in part the vagaries and irrelevancies of the early attempts to drive up prices as a recovery technique. In part it was the shifting advantage given to certain large firms and industries (via the NRA) and certain large planters and farms (via the AAA). In part it was the changing advantage given to one group of financial institutions as against others in the competition for funds. In part it was the passage of legislation that many considered due, and overdue, but which suddenly

37. George L. Bach, *Making Money and Fiscal Policy* (1971), p. 71. It is unnecessary to enter into the debate on the roles of monetary policy in general, or whether the Federal Reserve Board could have taken steps to reduce real interest rates further, thereby stimulating investment more. Two leading analyses are Peter Temin, *Did Monetary Forces Cause the Great Depression?* (1976), and Milton Friedman and Anna Schwartz, *Monetary Trends in the United States and the United Kingdom* (1982), pp. 32–33 and their *Monetary History*.

38. Cf. Joseph Schumpeter, *Business Cycles* 2 (1939):1038–50. Robert Gordon, *Economic Instability and Growth* (1974), p. 73, describes Schumpeter as "offering a persuasive argument that New Deal policies helped crystallize a 'climate of opinion' unfavorable to business and that this largely explains the disappointing nature of the recovery in the 1930s."

threatened to change costs of one industry or one product versus others in unpredictable ways.[39]

A radical might treat all this as one more example of the contradictions of capitalism. A New Deal liberal might consider it as the worthwhile price, in continued unemployment, of essential social advance. A reactionary might treat it as a set of ill-considered policies which could only delay helping the unemployed and poor. Regardless of such higher views, the impact of vast, irregular, frequent policy changes by the federal government in a private enterprise economy must have delayed action by the usually myopic investor and firm deciding whether to expand production or not.

In his stirring inaugural address F.D.R. committed himself to a New Deal for "The Forgotten Man."[40] It was only when the constitutionality of the new agencies was litigated up to the Supreme Court that the man's name became known. It was either Schechter or Filburn. The NRA, grand centerpiece of the first New Deal, proposed limiting how the Schecter brothers sold chickens in New York City. They, it appeared, were endangering the grand and national NRA effort to persuade U.S. Steel, General Motors, and other giants working together to raise their prices. The AAA was not equally indirect. The Department of Agriculture sought to raise prices by cutting down production. The entire power of the U.S. government then came down on one Filburn. The Court described Filburn as "raising a small acreage of winter wheat." His family baked most of that wheat into bread, or used it on the farm. But since he would "otherwise . . . purchase in the open market [his wheat] competed with the wheat in commerce." The Court agreed with the administration: Filburn had to be regulated. His few acres exercised a "substantial economic effect on interstate commerce."[41]

---

39. For example, the National Labor Relations (Wagner) Act of 1935 came after years in which the court system had denied workers elementary freedoms in the labor markets. It gave unions an organization charter from the federal government, and protection by it—"probably the most bluntly anticorporation legislation the United States has ever known." Quoted in Thomas Cochran, *The American Business System* (1957), p. 152. Similarly, the passage of the Social Security Act (unemployment and old-age insurance) and the Fair Labor Standards Act (minimum wages and maximum weekly hours) in 1936 and 1938, respectively, changed relative financial prospects in confusing ways, and private business expectation. They thereby held back new investment and the jobs it could create.

40. The phrase, as is perhaps appropriate in politics, was turned upside down. Earlier it had been used by William Graham Sumner, Yale's great reactionary sociologist-economist, to designate C, the man who would have to pay A if B decided that A needed a subsidy of some kind. F.D.R. irretrievably fixed it as designating A.

41. *Wickard v. Filburn*, 317 U.S. 111 (1942), 63 S. Ct. 82, 87. Most economists would have as readily agreed that Filburn had some effect on prices as that night club expenditures by millionaires had some effect on recovery. But they would hardly have attributed "substantial" economic effects to either one. In economics some elements are "de minimis".

Fortunately for the unemployed there were others around besides regulators and deep thinkers. A fruitful collaboration of ward politicians and social workers improved the federal contribution by offering welfare, and "make-work jobs" via the Works Progress Administration (WPA), the Civilian Conservation Corps (CCC), and the National Youth Administration (NYA). See Table 35.1. The number of families given relief under one or another program changed little from the last days of the Hoover administration to the beginning of war production for European markets in 1939. Federal public works jobs did expand briefly (from November 1933 to April 1934) with the short-lived Civil Works Administration. But a substantial and continuing public works program, the Works Projects Administration, did not begin until October 1935—almost six years after the Depression began. Economists noted that it provided about 15 additional off-site jobs (making shovels, bricks, etc.) for every 100 jobs on site.[42] That consideration led some leaders to press for more traditional public works—building post offices, government buildings, and thereby creating more private jobs. However, ex-social worker Harry Hopkins and a host of local politicians pressed hard and successfully for the WPA; it could employ the unemployed almost as soon as Congress made funds available, providing income and work. It was hardly sufficient to end unemployment. But it did provide a positive stimulus to increased private investment and consumption, and thereby to economic recovery, helping to cancel the worst impact of the first set of policies. More important still, these jobs helped keep the skills and attitudes of the unemployed from total deterioration. They provided money for family needs as well. Mass unemployment had declined, but by a depressingly small amount before war orders from Europe in 1939 began to alter market prospects (Table 35.1, Appendix A). That mass of suffering would have been far worse if the constriction of the economy by various New Deal policies had not been partially neutralized by these presumably simpleminded policies. Their contribution was direct, humane.

42. Cf. National Resources Planning Board, *The Economic Effects of the Federal Public Works Expenditures, 1933–1938* (1940), p. 46. The Public Works Administration created 100 off-site jobs while the WPA provided 15 for every 100 on site, according to this pioneering study by John Kenneth Galbraith. Moreover, the WPA programs that began in 1933 required about six months of preparation and negotiation before any one could be hired. By 1938 that delay had been reduced to about two months. Ibid., p. 86.

TABLE 35.1
UNEMPLOYMENT AND PUBLIC AID, 1933–40 (000)

Year	Unemployment	Public aid recipients		
		Total households	Relief recipients	WPA employment
January 1933	*	4,504	4,780	0
1933	12,830	5,014	4,747	0
1934	11,340	6,593	5,030	0
1935	10,610	6,320	5,376	482
1936	9,030	5,758	3,340	2,544
1937	7,700	5,202	3,531	1,792
1938	10,390	6,465	4,350	2,761
1939	9,480	6,285	4,623	2,407
March 1940	8,360	6,188	4,753	2,294

*Data not available.

Source: Relief includes: general relief, old age assistance, aid to dependent children and the blind. The National Youth Administration (work-study for college students) and the Civilian Conservation Corps (youth work building state parks under army supervision) are included in "total households." Data from National Resources Planning Board, Security, Work and Relief Policies (1942), Appendix 9 except for unemployment, which comes from Lebergott, Manpower, p. 512, and U.S. Census, Labor Force, Employment and Unemployment in the United States, 1940 to 1946, P-50, no. 2.

Appendix

Appendix A

The level of unemployment in the Depression was so appalling that some later commentators doubted the numbers. Some did so simply by assuming that labor supply functions must have had the same parameters in the 1930s as they did in the 1950s and 1960s.[1] However, two decades of political activism had intervened, unions had burgeoned, social insurance had become of major importance, women had entered the labor force in substantially greater numbers, legislation setting minimum wages, penalizing overtime hours, had been passed. Fiscal and monetary policy under Eisenhower and Kennedy was largely different than under F.D.R. It is difficult, then, to accept the arbitrary assumption that labor supply functions must nonetheless have remained unchanged from the 1930s to the 1950s and 1960s.

1. Cf. the interchange between Robert Coen, "Labor Force and Unemployment in the 1920s and 1930s," and Stanley Lebergott, "A New Technique for Time Series?," Review of Economics and Statistics (February 1973, November 1973).

Another view[2] challenges the assumption accepted by most contemporary political and economic leaders during the Depression, whether New Deal or Republican, and embodied in the 1940, end of depression, Census. These all included in the unemployment count workers with temporary incomes from the Works Progress Administration. (So did the NICB, leading employer economic research organization.[3]) That assumption cannot be rejected by a simple subsequent assertion that those workers were not really unemployed because they were not "seeking work." Since 1940, the Census Current Population Survey has in fact treated as unemployed those who have sought work by merely asking a friend, or reading advertisements. Moreover, in areas where no work was available (e.g., coal mining towns) the Census has included as unemployed workers who have not actually sought work. It has assumed that as soon as the mines opened up these workers would be expected to head for such jobs. Equivalently, those receiving WPA incomes during the Depression were typically ready to work as soon as mines and factories reopened.

It is useful to recognize that those unemployed with incomes from the WPA probably functioned differently in the labor market than those with no incomes at all. But those with incomes from unemployment insurance in the 1950s or 1980s likewise functioned differently than unemployed workers who lacked such income. Until, say, those on unemployment insurance are excluded from the later unemployment series for that reason, comparability requires accepting of the general judgment during the Depression that those on WPA were part of the unemployed.

Appendix B

Deposit totals for suspended banks are recorded in Federal Reserve Board, *Banking and Monetary Statistics* (1943), p. 285. The number of depositors affected does not appear to have been estimated. We estimate an average deposit of $500 on the basis of three reports. An excerpt from the 1955 Annual Report of the Federal Deposit Insurance Corporation entitled *Deposit Accounts and Insurance Coverage, September 21, 1955*, p. 55, gives the number and total for accounts in all insured banks. Those accounts averaged $723 in October 1934, and $785 in May 1936. The FDIC *Annual Report* (1939), p. 226, makes it possible to estimate the average deposit per insured depositor among the insured banks placed in receivership. As would be expected, failing banks were smaller. Their accounts averaged $68 in 1934, $189 in 1935, and $187 in 1936. Accounts in all 14,000 banks in 1934 probably exceeded the average for suspended banks, and banks suspending in 1929–33 were larger than those suspending in 1934–35. We therefore pick a $500 average for 1929–33. The *Annual Report of the Comptroller of the Currency for 1931*, p. 117, indicates that the average deposit in stock savings banks for 1930 was $528, with $772 for mutual savings banks. Those figures exceeded ones for the pre-Crash years, presumably because small depositors had disproportionately pulled their money out.

2. Michael R. Darby, "Three-and-a-Half Million U.S. Employees Have Been Mislaid," *Journal of Political Economy* (February 1976), and Jonathan Kesselman and N. E. Savin, "Three-and-a-Half Million Workers Were Never Lost," *Economic Inquiry* (April 1978).

3. Cf., for example, NICB, *Economic Almanac 1941–42* (1941), p. 123.

36

War and Postwar Transition

DURING World War II an immense battery of federal programs developed. Agencies were created; directives issued; resources moved around. To review the multitudinous and complex programs systematically would require substantial space. We emphasize a few key aspects.

The Congress gave the armed services absolute priority in the use of men. The draft, actually passed during peacetime (September 1940) gave the armed services the right to induct men between the ages of 18 and 27. Millions had their number chosen by lot and were then selected by a local "committee of your friends and neighbors." Patriotism and preference for an interesting berth generally filled up the places required by the Navy and the Air Force. The draft therefore chiefly supplied men to the infantry and other army units.

The War Manpower Commission supplemented this program, exempting from the draft those in certain selected occupations. Chiefly exempted were farmers and farm laborers. There was, however, no limit in principle as to which kind of farm products (and what quantities) were considered essential. Raspberries and wheat, oranges and lemons, any amount of cotton—all qualified. Exemptions were also given to copper miners and lumberjacks. (The commission likewise attempted to extend the workweek, thereby increasing war output. But neither its regulations nor its exhortations had much overall effect. Overtime pay rates induced whatever extra hours were provided.)

The Congress gave the armed services absolute priority in the use of men. The draft, actually passed during peacetime (September 1940), gave the plement that priority various programs were developed (notably the War Production Board's Controlled Materials Plan). These set aside portions of steel output, aluminum, copper, and rubber for the armed services. The balance was left for civilian markets. (The armed forces were also given priority in procuring coffee, cigarettes, etc.) Producers in the metal fabricating industries either had priority certificates (e.g., to buy the steel they needed to produce items for the armed services) or they scrambled for the remaining steel in the market.

Workers and investors together received some $97 billion to increase output from 1939 to 1945. If the economy had been functioning on a peacetime basis, approximately $97 billion in goods the income recipients wished to buy would have been produced—at existing prices. But the government had intervened. For it had also increased defense expenditures by $72 billion. If that $97 billion were allowed to enter the market and chase away only $46 billion worth of increased civilian supply, prices would have been bid up to dizzying heights.[1] And in the process, a steady supply to the military would have been out of the question. To restrain consumers, then, the government took $26 billion away from them by increasing taxes.[2] An enormous gap between increased demand and increased supply of specific products nonetheless still remained. The savings bond program drained off some of that income. But the primary tactic remained price control.

Both the administration and Congress sought to suppress this spurt in potential demand by repressing prices. (Dominated by those skilled in legislation and bureaucracies, they paid little heed to Keynes, Wallis, or other advocates of limiting total civilian expenditure.) The first target was wages, because wages constituted so large a fraction of costs. The War Labor Board (WLB) monitored (i.e., limited) wage increases by its unceasing review of wage settlements. In some disputes, for example, the United Mine Workers strike in 1942, a tough leader and a tough union simply ignored all rules. But in most cases patriotism, plus the threat of legal action by the government, induced companies to pay no more than "appropriate" wages, and induced unions to accept such settlements. Wage control, however, worked irregularly, and had sharply different impacts on different groups of workers. Lumber workers in the far West, nonferrous miners in the Mountain states, machinists in the Mid-Atlantic—these and other groups where labor was "scarce" were given increases far above those allowed other essential groups.

General price control was instituted in the spring of 1942. Wage control did not really bite until 1943; factory earnings rose 17 percent from 1941 to 1942, and then 12 percent to 1943.[3] Much of the second increase took place in the first half of 1943. By then, the WLB had "the Little Steel formula." According to that standard, a wage rise that merely compensated for the prior 15 percent rise in the cost of living (between January 1941 and May 1942) would be considered acceptable. But not a penny more. This fairly clear formula was whittled away in two directions. The board itself gave ground by allow-

1. Net national product rose $118 billions. Bureau of Economic Analysis, *The National Income and Product Accounts of the United States, 1929–76* (1981), Table 1.9. Deducting $72 billion of defense expenditure left $46 billion of goods and services for personal consumption. Incomes from production (less corporate retained earnings) rose by $97 billion.

2. Indirect business taxes—paid by eventual consumers—rose by $6 billion, while social insurance and personal taxes rose by $20 billion.

3. *Handbook of Labor Statistics* (1972), p. 220.

ing vacation pay, and other "adjustments" increasingly improvised outside the formula. But still more destructive to even-handed wage control, employers began transferring workers from a given job classification to a higher one. In that way the charge by the WLB was honored. For the wage in neither occupation was raised. But the worker's income was nonetheless upped. (These tactics were not properly labeled until Scandinavian employers in the 1950s used them to pay workers beyond the limits of "incomes policies." They were then baptized as "wage drift.")

The Office of Price Administration (OPA) sought to hold down prices for final products in parallel with the attempt to hold down wages. Its efforts did slow down price increases for final products. What was the nature, and outcome, of OPA price controls on the largest categories in the consumers' budget—food and clothing?

The OPA, by limiting the price of clothing along with the price for most other products at retail, instructed the nation in microeconomics by revealing the many dimensions of price. "The same rayon fabric could go into a dress wholesaling at $2.25 or $6.75. . . . Standards of tailoring were almost as flexible." A trade survey in December 1941 noted: "The $1 dress that was a 'good' value in the fall of 1940 . . . will have to retail at $1.98 for spring 1942." Shortages became "particularly serious in low-priced essential items, in men's shirts, underwear and work clothing."[4]

Low-priced lines of shirts, dresses, disappeared from the market, to be replaced by higher priced lines. The higher price lines yielded higher profits. Some categories of clothing whose prices, or margins, were effectively squeezed by the OPA disappeared altogether. The most celebrated example involved men's suits. Their production was cut in half during the war, while that of separate coats increased more than seven-fold.[5] It was not obvious that consumer preferences had forced that shift to higher margin categories. The impact of price control on producers' incentives may have done so. These and similar responses contributed to the fact that from the "hold-the-line" price order (April 1943) to the end of price control (June 1946) all clothing items in the cost of living index rose by 23 percent. That was six times as fast as the rise for other items. "Moreover, since the index did not take quality deterioration fully into account the effective rise in clothing prices was much higher. The great bulk of the [reported] rise in clothing prices was due to the disappearance of low-priced clothing."[6] The underlying increase in wages of low-income workers, of profits, like the host of disruptions caused by the war, were beyond the control of the OPA—or the consumer.

4. Wilfred Carsel in Office of Temporary Controls, Office of Price Administration, in Robert Armstrong, et al. *Problems in Price Control: Changing Production Patterns*, (1947) pp. 107–108.

5. Ibid., p. 109.

6. Ibid., p. 7. The clothing rise "accounting for over 40 percent of the total rise" of 7.5 percent, the balance rose by $7.5 - (.40 \times 7.5)$.

The largest component of the cost of living was that for food. The administration's goal for food prices, however, was not to keep them down. The Farm Bloc, and therefore the Congress, had insisted that farmers' prices be allowed to rise, price control or no price control. And so had others more sympathetic to the farmers than to the urban workers destined to finance these gains to farmers. In the fall of 1940, an administration economist, J. K. Galbraith, proposed to the National Defense Advisory Commission that farm prices be permitted to rise (until they reached "parity"). Meanwhile, nonfarm prices and wages were to be restrained. The first head of OPA, Leon Henderson, well aware of these massive political pressures, agreed. Almost as soon as he was appointed (in April 1941) he assured Representative Cannon, of the Farm bloc, that "prices of many commodities . . . have been too low to provide the farmer with a decent living wage."[7] Such a statement by the head of an agency set up to halt price increases was, of course, highly significant. Indeed, Henderson continued to favor farm prices rising to 110 percent of "parity" until Pearl Harbor. After December 7th he still urged that they rise, but now only to 100 percent of "parity."[8]

An ingenious political approach sought to reconcile rising prices for farmers with stable food prices paid by consumers. Taxes taken from workers' paychecks were to provide farm subsidies, so that when workers took their paychecks to the grocery store they would discover unchanged food prices. With taxation paid by workers increasing enormously during the war the transfer proved effective. Various government agencies provided subsidies to farmers. Some $1.7 billion went to meat producers, $643 million to wheat producers, and smaller amounts to producers of butter, peanuts, onions, and more.[9] When price control was nearing its end (in fiscal 1946), the OPA evaluated these food subsidies. They found they cost the taxpayer $1.7 billion a year, saving him $2.2 billion.[10] The administrative costs of OPA, CCC, RFC, and related agencies in the complex subsidy process, plus the costs that industry incurred (and charged consumers for) in coping with, and avoiding, regulation, were not included in that estimate. If they were it would not be clear by how much all this activity helped the typical urban taxpayer-consumer.[11]

7. Robert Armstrong, et al. *Problems in Price Control: Changing Production Pattern* (1947), pp. 377–78.

8. Ibid., p. 379.

9. Office of Price Administration, *Problems of Price Control: Stabilization Subsidies*, (Part II by Philip Ritz) (1947), pp. 235–38.

10. Ibid., p. 241.

11. A speculative but thoughtful view asserts that the reported price boom after the war merely "unveiled" price rises that had really taken place during the war—but been missed by the statistical agencies, prices in 1944 and 1945, being about 10 percent greater than reported. Cf. Milton Friedman and Anna Schwartz, *Monetary Trends in the United States of the United Kingdom* (1982) p. 102.

The Transition from War to Peace

Nearly every previous transition of the economy from war to peace ended in a depression—immediately in some cases, delayed in others. John Adams, second president of the United States, described the wars of 1745, 1755, and 1812: "Every one [was] followed by a general distress, embarrassments of commerce, destruction of manufactures."[12] World War II seemed even more certain to be followed by depression. For, in addition to these many precedents, there was a stark new fact. The war had followed a deep depression, the worst in American history. And the nation had not recovered from it before war production began.

The responses therefore were hardly surprising when a Gallup poll asked, in January 1945, "After the war, do you think that everyone who wants a job will be able to get one?" Some 68 percent of those interviewed answered: "No."[13] Wise men agreed with that majority. An official of the largest bank in Chicago declared: "We do not care to invest our money . . . in Southern California . . . because we are convinced that when the war is over Los Angeles is going to become a ghost town."[14] A leading economist of the Soviet Union likewise foresaw a crisis for American capitalism: "Only when millions of people were killing one another, and other millions were preparing weapons of murder, was capitalist society capable of giving work to all the workers. . . . The level of production today [1947] is one-third less than in 1943." Moreover, the short-term postwar boom "is creating the prerequisites for a crisis of overproduction."[15] The Federal Office of War Mobilization and Reconversion predicted (on September 8, 1945) "even under optimistic estimates of the speed of reconversion . . . unemployment of 6–8 millions . . . throughout 1946."[16] (A single optimist among leading economists was Vladimir Woytinsky, a Russian refugee, who had shrewdly noted certain significant economic changes during the war that led him to a more hopeful prospect.)

12. *The Works of John Adams*, Charles F. Adams, ed. (1856), vol. X, p. 384.

13. Bureau of Special Services, Office of War Information, *Current Opinions* (January 12, 1945). A *Fortune* survey in the same months found 49 percent of all Americans "expect we probably shall have a widespread depression within ten years or so after the war is over." At that time "depression" meant, inevitably, the 1929–40 depression from which the nation had only recently emerged.

14. J. Howard Edgerton, *The Story of California Federal Savings* (1969), p. 13.

15. Eugene Varga, in *Soviet Views on the Post-War World Economy, An Official Critique of Eugene Varga's 'Changes in the Economy of Capitalism Resulting from the Second World War'*, Leo Gruliow, trans. (1948), pp. 50, 125. V. K. Reikhardt stated that "the contemporary phase of the development of capitalism . . . is the stage of the decay and death of capitalism, beyond which no new phase of capitalism follows," p. 15.

16. Quoted in *Exhortation and Controls* Craufurd Goodwin, ed. (1975), p. 21. While not forecasting unemployment, Lebergott's "Shall We Guarantee Full Employment?" *Harper's* (February 1945) was no less pessimistic, deserving a rueful footnote.

TABLE 36.1
OUTPUT AND DEMAND 1945–47 (IN BILLIONS OF DOLLARS)

	First quarter[a]		
	1945	1946	1947
Government expenditure	99	36	28
Disposable income	152	153	166
Personal consumption	117	137	159
Domestic investment	8	21	27

[a]Annual rate

Source: U.S. Department of Commerce, The National Income and Product Accounts of the United States (1929–1974), Tables 1.1, 2.1, and National Income, (1954 edition), Tables 45, 47.

The pessimists were, of course, right in foreseeing that federal spending would fall tremendously. Table 36.1 shows such a drop did occur between 1945 and 1946. But it shows that they were wrong in fearing that a depression would follow. For Table 36.1 likewise reports the fact, however improbable, that disposable income did not decline. True, the munitions factories had closed down. True, millions of workers had been fired. But disposable income remained steady. Consumer spending rose by $18 billion. And investment by private business rose more than 200 percent.

Consumers had brought $55 billion in U.S. bonds during the war; other (nonbank) investors bought a further $80 billion.[17] As soon as the war ended many of these investors drew down those investments. Thus returning servicemen cashed their bonds to buy civilian suits, to make down payments on homes, to take well-earned vacations. Investors used their savings to finance new projects, buying equipment, erecting buildings and accumulating inventories. Because thousands of World War I soldiers (including President Truman) had seen their life savings go up in smoke when the value of Liberty Bonds plummeted during the 1919–21, the 1946 Treasury was firmly instructed to keep up the price of Treasury Bonds. The Federal Reserve Board was equally committed. It therefore became possible for soldiers, and other wartime buyers, to sell any amount of their savings bonds at full face value, without forcing down the price of their remaining holdings. They could readily take the cash, and make other purchases, other investments.

Further economic stimulus came from the ending of the "disequilibrium system"[18] of price and production controls that were maintained during the

17. June 30, 1939, to June 30, 1946. Estimates of Henry Murphy, quoted by R. A. Gordon, Economic Instability and Growth (1974), p. 86.

18. The title of a characteristically lively and well argued description of OPA, etc., by John K. Galbraith.

war. Wages were decontrolled in August 1945, and began escalating. Prices were decontrolled about a year later.

> The removal of controls . . . freed the economy for reaction to the accumulated demand pressures . . . contained previously by administrative devices. The result was a powerful inflationary shock. Partly because of the wartime heritage of financial liquidity and deferred demands which characterized alike the household, business and foreign sectors, aggregate demand was extraordinarily high at the time of decontrol. It was augmented also by the 'first round' of wage increases in early 1946.[19]

The armed forces fell from a high of 12 million in August 1945 (at the war's end) to 4 million by the next April—an extraordinarily swift demobilization considering how many men had been scattered throughout Asia and Europe. The return of eight million soldiers should have flooded the labor market, pushed down wages, and thereby forced down consumption, investment, and output. All this did not happen. And for several reasons.

First, about three million women quit the labor force between August 1945 and April 1946.[20] They had originally joined the labor force for patriotic reasons, as a way to cope with life while their boyfriends or husbands were overseas, and/or as a source of income. These reasons ceased to apply for many. Second, about one million soldiers entered college under the "G.I. Bill," with the taxpayers financing their education.[21] Third, still another one million utilized the Bill to help open their own businesses.[22]

These forces removed 5 million persons from competition in the job market. Meanwhile pent-up demand exploded. That combination tightened the labor market so sharply that unemployment hardly rose from August 1945 to 1946, 1947, or 1948. Wages rose persistently. Rising employment and rising wages stimulated consumer spending, and further energized the post-war boom.

After the Great Depression: 1948–62

Ten years of unprecedented depression had created deep and persistent doubts about the ability of the old economic ways to provide jobs and profits in adequate volume. Four years of unprecedented war then demonstrated a simple means to both: government spending. The spread of Keynesian ideas

19. Burt Hickman, *Growth and Stability of the Postwar Economy* (1960), p. 53.

20. Bureau of the Census, *Current Population Reports*, P-50, no. 2, Table 1.

21. Census, *Historical Statistics . . . to 1970*, p. 383. The enrollment data available are for 1944 and 1946. Given the downward enrollment trend during the war, the 1945–46 jump was greater than the 1944–46 change shown.

22. The total rise in male nonfarm self-employed from August 1945 to August 1946 was about 1 million.

helped to rationalize that conclusion, no doubt. The mere fact that the Republican party was kept out of the White House for thirty years after "Mr. Hoover's depression" offered further persuasion. The political conclusion appeared in bold type.

The theme of the new era was printed in the Employment Act of 1946, sponsored by loyal Democrats (Senator Murray of Montana) and progressive Republicans (Senator Flanders of Vermont). That Act declared it to be "the continuing policy and responsibility of the Federal Government to use all practical means . . . to promote maximum employment, production, and purchasing power."[23]

The extent to which Americans now believed that "maximum" employment and purchasing power were a public responsibility became obvious in 1953. The first Republican administration since Hoover then faced an economic downturn, created in siginificant measure by its ending the war in Korea, and its prompt cut in defense spending. How did the Republican party act after it returned to power? Contrary to prediction, to tradition, it initiated public works spending. It speeded the placement of defense purchase orders. It eased unemployment insurance. Such steps, till then, had seemed the monopoly of Democrats and "spenders." They now proved to be the common coin of political economy in a new era. Unemployment rose by 2 percent under the Democrats in 1948–49. They then acted to cut short the recession. It rose by 2.5 percent under the Republicans in 1953–54. They too acted, and similarly. In the recession of 1957–58 even greater reliance on the new structure of public spending and social insurance appeared. Though not as much as many sought. For the president saw it as only "a temporary emergency internally."[24]

How was the new policy to be implemented? Action rested, almost inevitably, on the two antique components of national policy: death and taxes. The market for defense items was infinitely wide and indefinitely expansible. (The military bought some 4,788,000 different products.)[25] Their purchases could be counted on to expand jobs in nearly every state, and almost any county. Directly (or indirectly through defense suppliers) the Department of Defense could drive up employment and profits in 469 of the nation's 485 industries.[26]

---

23. The origins of the Act are described in graphic detail by Stephen Bailey, *Congress Makes a Law* (1950). The rapid development of fiscal policy, pointing to public action as a solution, is comprehensively outlined in Herbert Stein, *The Fiscal Revolution in America* (1969).

24. Quoted in Stein, *Fiscal Revolution*, p. 344.

25. *Government Executive* (April 1976).

26. Cf. Bureau of Economic Analysis, *The Detailed Input-Output Structure of the U.S. Economy in 1972* (1979), vol. 1, Table 1. Defense bought from every industry except dolls and plated silverware.

War expenditures as a share of total output had risen only a few points during the century before 1942.[27] Once the 1945–46 transition to peace took place such spending escalated rapidly under Truman. It actually fell under Eisenhower. Perhaps ex-generals were less open to the inevitable professional fears of the Pentagon than ex-lieutenants or ensigns.

The means of destruction, however, had not merely to be bought. They had to be financed. The method of finance had already been discovered—the income tax.

What yielded revenue to the Pentagon was taxation imposed on payments to defense plant workers and rentiers.[28] An adjuvant was a brilliant administrative device initiated during the war—withholding taxes at the source.[29] After the 1940s workers never even saw most of the taxes being taken from their earnings. That regular cut in their standard of living was to become even less apparent than government's revenue from the inflation tax of the 1960s and 1970s. This spectacular innovation almost disproved Burke's remark that "to tax and to please, no more than to love and be wise, is not given to men.")[30]

Withholding became still more important after 1966 as inflation escalated. Increased wage rates increased the workers' nominal incomes and thereby their taxes. The quiet remorseless process of "bracket creep" yielded the federal government even more revenue but with never a need to petition Congress for a tax rate increase. The resultant yearly rise of income tax revenues was powerful and without precedent in American history.

An active policy against instability in employment and output triumphantly changed the duration of business contractions, shown in Table 36.2. Increased expenditure and active monetary policy by the Federal Reserve Board together shortened the recessions of 1949, 1953, 1957, 1972. Old-style

27. War expenditure here includes the budget item for "defense" plus three other items: veterans' pensions (i.e., delayed compensation to soldiers), interest on the national debt (virtually all of which prior to 1950 derived from bursts of wartime spending), and space expenditures. Excluding some reasonable portion of the final two items, and including some portion of State Department and foreign-aid expenditures—"Peace is the continuation of war by other means"—would change this conclusion very little.

Tax percentages relate the number of households (1914–36) and families plus unrelated individuals to the number of persons filing income tax returns. (*Historical Statistics . . . to 1970*, p. 41. *Statistical Abstract* (1981), pp. 42, 258.) While not precisely comparable, these data are quite sufficient to indicate a massive expansion of coverage. The first full year of the income tax was 1914.

28. Even if successive administrations had taxed away all incomes of rentiers and entrepreneurs, the sums thus realized could not remotely have sufficed. Most of the defense total inevitably came from workers' incomes.

29. One rationale presumed the average American was too incompetent to save money during the year to pay his taxes the coming April. Another argued that he would revolt against taxes and public expenditures if confronted by the entire bill at one time.

30. Speech on American Taxation in *American Archives*, Peter Force, ed., series IV (1846), vol. I, p. 159.

TABLE 36.2
ECONOMIC EXPANSIONS AND CONTRACTIONS, 1854–1980

| | Months of economic | | Percent |
	Expansion	Contraction	contraction
1854–1873	30	30	50
1879–1914	23	20	47
1921–1938	29	18	38
1945–1961	36	10	22
1961–1980	67	11	14

Source: Computed from U.S. Department of Commerce, Business Conditions Digest (June 1978), and unpublished NBER Reports.

capitalism had been ended. But there was a serpent in the garden. As early as 1945, when the new stability came into view, one economist rhetorically asked: "Prices and wages stop rising . . . when expansion ceases. . . . But would they stop if continued high demand were virtually guaranteed?"[31] The evidence accumulated. By the recession of 1957–58, Lee Bach shrewdly foresaw: "Inflation will continue as a persistent force over the decades ahead," for reasons ranging from the commitment to full employment to the gold standard.[32]

Trade union economists have praised unions for getting higher wages for their members, presumably higher wages than the market would have otherwise provided. Some conservative economists have inferred that such actions drove final prices up and generated inflation. But Milton Friedman, Nobel laureate and hardly radical, suggested a lack of cogent evidence that unions or monopolies had forced prices up significantly.[33] The experience of 1957–58 however, suggests that in some industries big unions and "big business" contributed to the inflationary spiral. In 1957 thousands of steel workers were unemployed. The union nonetheless struck for higher wage rates, and achieved them. That success was no mere matter of union muscle. It signaled a change in management attitudes and morale. When the nation's leading steel company was run by Andrew Carnegie, by Henry Frick, or even by Elbert Gary, it had fought through such major strikes as those in 1893 and 1919. Its version of corporate truth included low costs and high profits. By the late 1950s U.S. Steel's leaders were settling for stability and regular dividends. They had little desire for yet another U.S. president who would intervene in a steel strike on behalf of the workers. They settled for a wage increase. When in 1962 they tried to pass along cost increases by a price hike, the president set

31. Paul Homan and Fritz Machlup, Financing American Prosperity (1955), p. 117.
32. George Lee Bach, Inflation (1958), pp. 38–45.
33. Cf. Milton Friedman, Unemployment versus Inflation (1975), pp. 30–31.

the F.B.I. to inspecting their behavior.[34] That confirmed the arrival of a new order. New expectations became appropriate for shrewd corporate and union leaders.

Federal economic policy ratified these new expectations. It did so through an active fiscal policy that printed more money to validate the increased claims on final product.[35] The straightforward outcome of that immensely responsive fiscal and monetary policy was inflation. It should be added that voters throughout Europe were pressing their governments into similar action. And inflation appeared all over the third world, from Chad to Nigeria to Israel. Prices began escalating even in centrally planned economies that offered an opening for increased economic expectations, as Poland showed in the early 1980s. Claims there too outran supply. A new era had arrived not merely in the United States but in world economic history. U.S. policy was not constructed in isolation from the trend of attitude and expectation in scores of other nations, nor can it wholly be reviewed in isolation.

34. A president who had recently given the word for an armed invasion of Cuba was not to be trifled with. Cf. Roy Hoopes, *The Steel Crisis* (1963), chap. 5 on how FBI agents arrived at various steel company offices, and elsewhere, after the company had raised steel by $6 a ton. Steel rails rose far more every year in the 1970s without eliciting equal concern.

35. James Buchanan and Richard Wagner, *Democracy in Deficit; the Political Legacy of Lord Keynes* (1977) contend that the Federal Reserve Board inevitably bent to pressures by Congress and political instrumentalities, such pressures constituting the deeper cause.

37

The Greater Society

BY the mid-twentieth century Americans had reached a status rare in world history. They were "secure of bread and expectant of affluence."[1] Economic stability was being achieved. Surely affluence for all lay ahead. National policy became dominated, in Arthur Okun's succinct phrase, by the search for equity and efficiency.[2] The vast range of congressional and executive policy after 1962 testified, year after year, act after act, to a consensus in favor of a mixed economy. Trenchantly described by Moses Abramowitz, that consensus embodied

> a pragmatic compromise between the competing virtues and defects of decentralized market capitalism and encompassing socialism. Its goal is to obtain a measure of distributive justice, security and social guidance of economic life without losing too much of the allocative efficiency and dynamism of private enterprise and market organization. And it is a pragmatic compromise in another sense. It seeks to retain for most people that measure of personal protection *from* the state which private property and a private job market confer, while obtaining for the disadvantaged minority of people *through* the state that measure of support without which their lack of property or personal endowment would amount to a denial of individual freedom and capacity to function as full members of the community.[3]

The war had wiped out mass unemployment. The postwar boom had turned out a cornucopia of goods, new and old. Central economic policy had apparently reached a point where the chairman of the Council of Economic Advisers could sit at the console of his giant Wurlitzer and fine tune the economy.[4] The nation could now turn directly to the complex but morally ur-

1. The phrase is from George Saintsbury, *A History of Nineteenth Century Literature, 1789–1895* (1896), p. 72.
2. The economic issues are reviewed with unusual judiciousness and empathy in Arthur Okun, *Equity and Efficiency* (1975).
3. Cf. his Presidential address to the American Economic Association, "Welfare Quandries and Productivity Concerns," *American Economic Review* (March 1981), p. 13.
4. It was Robert Solow who first used the image of the giant theater organ, once present in every huge downtown movie theatre. The new view is judiciously presented in Walter Heller, *New Dimensions of Political Economy* (1966).

gent issues of equity. In reviewing those endeavors it is really impossible to dissociate action and consequence from U.S. involvement in the world, with its hydrogen bombs, Soviet bloc aggression, and U.S. response. It was a period when lesser characters had to register as foreign agents to forward the interests of a tiny Caribbean republic, but the president could proudly and publicly declare himself "a Berliner" in the capital of beleagured West Germany. Given that major qualification, however, one may consider U.S. economic experience *per se*.

The economic issues that claimed attention during the new era had typically been present in the American economy for decades. The outcome of some had been markedly changed by the working of agencies set up during the New Deal. Others had hardly been addressed by the federal government before the 1960s. We consider some of the major issues affected by the New Deal agencies in three sectors—labor, farming, and investment.

Labor

Competition in the labor markets was so largely altered as to be transformed by the New Deal programs. These programs grew, attracted new clients, then produced results not widely anticipated. Unemployment insurance was one of the most widely appreciated of the New Deal labor market programs. In 1936 the new Social Security system began requiring workers to set money aside for possible unemployment. (Formally, workers paid half and employers paid half, but the incidence of both taxes was on wages, so that one can appropriately speak of the workers having to set money aside.) In 1936, when the system began, less than 1 percent of all unemployed were covered by such insurance (all in private programs). By 1976, however, about two-thirds of all unemployed collected unemployment insurance.[5]

The goal of the program had been to offer financial support, making it unnecessary for the unemployed to take the first job that came along regardless of its rate of pay or working conditions. Expanding insurance coverage 1936–76, and raising its level, did just that. It achieved results by changing the pattern of job search. The agonized search hour after hour, from one employer to another, that had apparently marked the depression had been obviously transformed by Social Security and rising income levels. In the new era unemployed workers looked for work less than one hour a day, and "contacted" about one employer a week (by phone, mail or in person").[6]

5. The various data for 1976 referred to are derived from Bureau of Labor Statistics, Special Labor Force Report 222, *Job Search of Recipients of Unemployment Insurance*, particularly Tables 2, 3, 4. Sixty percent collected. Others did not bother because their unemployment was too short.

6. Unfortunately the Bureau of Labor Statistics study describes only those unemployed workers who failed to find work. It ignores those who were also unemployed in the preceding month but succeeded in finding work by the survey month. The latter group may also have had unemployment insurance coverage, but searched more persistently or differently.

To the assurance provided by the federal–state system a tough union added a supplement for its own members. The United Auto Workers faced companies in a booming market and gained "supplemental unemployment benefits." By the 1960s workers with such supplements received much the same disposable income for up to a year of unemployment as they did for a year of work.[7] These successes necessarily increased the level of unemployment even though the economy offered more and better jobs than an earlier era. The increasing number of students seeking part-time work did the same.

The second major change in the labor market bought about by New Deal reforms was the expansion of union membership. The "second American labor movement" took off in the mid-1930s. Suddenly a mass movement, it no longer belonged to some highly skilled workers or a tiny group more interested in revolution than paychecks. Its immediate origins lay in a tidal change in popular views evidenced by the sweep into office of a largely Democratic Congress. Union membership had varied together with the presence of such majorities since the beginning of the century. It had also risen whenever producers hired more labor. Both factors were at work from 1932 onward.[8] The passage of the Norris-LaGuardia Act of 1932 stopped local courts from continuing to provide the legal injunctions that had blocked union organizing campaigns. Two other acts stepped up the pace. The NRA (Section 7a) and the Wagner Act of 1935 enabled unions to mount successful campaigns in such bastions of industry as autos, steel, rubber, chemicals, glass. By establishing the federal National Labor Relations Board (NLRB), the Wagner Act led to an outburst of strikes in which unions implemented their new freedom. Now able to vote more freely in elections supervised by the NLRB, workers increasingly voted for union organization. In most instances they chose unions that were part of the Congress of Industrial Organizations (CIO), the AFL's new rival.

What impact did the spread of unions have on the labor market? Systematic data are lacking for early years. But recent comprehensive surveys probably rank the forces correctly. They indicate that the primary goal workers expected from unions was higher pay. Improved working conditions constituted a further (but distinctly secondary) goal.[9]

7. The complementary role of increased taxes was critical. Thus in one example after-tax income for a month of unemployment by a Massachusetts worker ran to 82 percent of his income when employed. Cf. Martin Feldstein, "The Economics of the New Unemployment," *The Public Interest* (Fall 1973), p. 31.

8. Orley Ashenfelter and John Pencavel, "American Trade Union Growth: 1900–1960," *Quarterly Journal of Economics* (August 1969), Table I. This study points, as well, to the importance of unemployment levels and increases in producers' prices.

9. Robert Quinn and Graham Staines, *The 1977 Quality of Employment Survey* (1979), p. 180. This survey was conducted for the U.S. Department of Labor. It is based on reports from an adequate national sample of American workers. Nineteenth- and twentieth-century statements by a handful of workers, or literate souls who talked to a few workers, may well be correct. But they may only reflect attitudes of a non-representative worker group.

How far did the new unions go in achieving such goals? Basic studies by Lewis and Mincer seem to agree that unions pushed up the wages of union workers about 10 percent above those paid to comparable nonunion workers.[10] A far more substantial effect appeared for unions of bituminous mine workers (organized as early as the late nineteenth century) and for airline pilots, while hardly any effect was apparent for those in cotton textiles, paints, footwear.[11]

Average wages in unionized and nonunion industries differ far more than 10 percent.[12] They do so, in part, because the giant auto, steel, electrical machinery firms employ more highly skilled workers, equip them with far more capital equipment, and sell their output in stronger, often oligopolistic, markets. But in part the difference reports how management responded to union wage pressures: it picked higher quality workers. Forced to pay higher wages, business found it advantageous to hire workers with more care, to supervise more attentively, and to retain those workers whose ability was sufficiently above average to warrant paying the high union wage rates. Jacob Mincer estimates that in recent years half the apparent union–nonunion wage difference was created by such selectivity, the remaining half representing union impact.[13] The greatest union wage impact appeared in the deep depression years of 1930–34, and the least in World War II when the War Labor Board set wages and compressed the union wage differential.[14]

Measures of union impact on working conditions are harder to come by. One indicator may be worker votes in NLRB elections. A large sample of such workers felt that unions would increase their chances of promotion, would reduce the extent to which supervisors played favorites.[15] It should be added that job benefits were narrowed by employers in an attempt to compensate for higher wage rates imposed on them by unions—by reducing

10. H. Gregg Lewis, *Unionism and Relative Wages* (1963), p. 191, summarizes the results of years of study by Lewis and able economists who worked with him. Jacob Mincer, "Union Effects," National Bureau of Economic Research Working Paper No. 808 (1981), p. 20. A figure of 12 percent for the United States (and of from 3.8 percent to 8.1 percent for Britain) appears in Charles Mulvey and John Abowd, "Estimating the Union/Nonunion Wage Differential," *Economica* (February 1980), p. 73.

11. Lewis, *Unionism*, pp. 86, 184–85, 280.

12. Daniel Mitchell, "Some Empirical Observations," *Journal of Labor Research* (Fall 1980), p. 197.

13. Mincer, "Effects," p. 18.

14. Lewis, *Unionism*, p. 222.

15. Henry Farber and Daniel Saks, "Why Workers Want Unions," *Journal of Political Economy* (April 1980), Table 2. Workers who felt that it was easy to find an equivalent job were also pro-union—consistent with the general finding that common labor has benefited proportionately more than semi-skilled labor from union organization.

workers' ability to take time off, workers' freedom of choice in the way the job is done, and in their job stability.[16]

Farming

The AAA began with the aim of helping farmers, who by definition were all either without income or with very low income. It evolved into something new and wonderful by the 1960s. Table 37.1 reports on federal spending for "stabilization of farm prices and income." Even ignoring other farm assistance (via subsidies on loans, electricity, etc.) expenditures per farmer mounted as the number of farm operators fell. By the 1950s the United States spent one-third as much per farm operator as he made from farming. During the 1930s the program had been overwhelmingly targeted for the South: cotton subsidies accounted for about half of total costs. By the 1950s, however, cotton farmers accounted for less than 1 percent of all costs. A plethora of producers of crops from wheat to figs, from almonds and filberts to potatoes and oranges, took their place.[17]

Men from all over the nation had discovered a rationale for increasing the price charged the urban consumer and for collecting funds from the taxes the consumer paid in addition. The farm group *per se* warranted assistance. It therefore did not have to pass a demeaning means test. In the acerbic judgment of one economist: "The proximate beneficiary of most farm programs is the landowner per se . . . migrant harvesters suffer from lower demand for their services [but] land owners who are not farmers, such as the matinee idols, senators, industrial executives . . . benefit hugely.[18] Assistance was given in proportion to "crops not grown", or to land diverted. Hence the bulk of the funds inevitably went to those operating large farms. As Table 37.2 indicates, the bottom 20 percent of farmers got a tiny percentage of federal payments whatever the crop. The top 5 percent of farmers, however, got 42 percent of all benefit payments.

Financial Regulation

The Great Crash inevitably generated a set of laws intended to put a leash on financial institutions, and to bring their markets into order. Of the new pieces of legislation the one establishing the Federal Deposit Insurance Corporation was perhaps most important in later decades. Although opposed

16. James Morgan, ed., *Five Thousand American Families—Patterns of Economic Progress* (1974), vol. II, chap. 6. The most obvious tightening up occurred for clerical and sales workers (p. 186). Unskilled workers, who presumably had few such freedoms before union organization, lost little in the process. Cf. Gregg Duncan and Frank Stafford, "Do Union Members receive Compensating Wage Differentials?," *American Economic Review* (June 1980).

17. 83d Cong., 2d sess., Senate Committee on Agriculture and Forestry, *General Farm Program* (1954), part I, pp. 79–84, 92.

18. Mason Gaffney, "The Benefits of Farm Programs," *Journal of Farm Economics* (December 1965), p. 1252.

TABLE 37.1
FARM INCOMES, 1940–80[a]

	Federal spending for stabilization of farm prices and incomes (millions of dollars)	Federal spending as percent of net income from farming	Net farm income per farm operator (dollars)
1940	749	16.7	706
1952	689	4.6	2,878
1953	3,665	28.2	2,604
1954	2,382	19.3	2,579
1955	2,348	20.8	2,429
1956	1,293	11.5	2,493
1957	896	8.1	2,536
1958	2,709	20.6	3,111
1959	1,932	18.0	2,615
1960	1,979	17.2	2,907
1961	2,769	23.2	3,126
1962	3,514	29.1	3,267
1963	2,810	23.9	3,295
1964	3,321	31.7	3,035
1965	3,326	25.8	3,843
1966	2,712	19.4	4,286
1967	3,008	24.4	3,903
1968	5,538	44.9	4,013
1969	5,620	39.3	4,764
1970	3,877	27.4	4,799
1971	4,371	29.9	5,042
1972	4,546	24.4	6,526
1973	2,647	7.9	11,813
1974	954	3.7	9,349
1975	1,726	7.1	8,845
1976	2,268	12.1	6,823
1977	6,024	32.8	7,506
1978	4,214	15.8	10,492
1979	1,861	5.8	13,312
1980	4,632	23.0	8,289

[a]Does not include federal spending for other farm programs.

Source: Expenditures: Bureau of Economic Analysis, *National Income and Product Accounts of the United States, 1929–1976, Survey of Current Business* (July 1982), Table 3.16; *and Historical Statistics . . . to 1970,* Y-625. Other: U.S. Department of Agriculture, Economic Research Service, Bulletin No. 674, *Economic Indicators of the Farm Sector* (1981), Tables 80, 81. For 1978 ff, *Statistical Abstract,* (1982), p. 663.

TABLE 37.2
DISTRIBUTION OF FARM PRICE SUPPORT PAYMENTS, 1964
(100 PERCENT OF TOTAL SUPPORT PAYMENTS)

| Federal Payments | *Share going to bottom or top percent group of farmer recipients* | |
	Lowest 20 percent	*Top 5 percent*
All	1	42
Wheat	3	31
Sugar Cane	1	63
Cotton	2	41
Feed Grains	1	24
Peanuts	4	28
Tobacco	4	25
Rice	1	35

Source: Bonnen in 91st Cong., 1st sess., Joint Economic Committee, *The Analysis and Evaluation of Public Expenditures: The PPB System* (1969), pp. 440, 446.

by F.D.R., and fought by the head of the Senate Finance Committee, that law stabilized the financial markets in 1933 and since. All members of the Federal Reserve System were required to join. Nine thousand other banks joined as well. The advantages to both were clear. Americans still feared to deposit their money in banks, which could fail. Banks offering deposit insurance had a marked competitive advantage. The value to society of that greater security became evident in the postwar decades. Scarcely a year passed without bleak headlines and TV stories of imminent financial collapse. One year it was the McKesson Robbins collapse; the next, the De Angelis oil receipts scandal; then, the bankruptcy of the New York Central Railroad, of the Penn Central; then the problems of financial recycling when OPEC drove oil prices upward, the failure of major brokerage houses, failure of New York City to pay its debts on time, and so on. Not one of those widely trumpeted disasters panicked depositors into withdrawing their money. Deposit insurance had brought an enduring component of security to financial markets.

Other banking regulations proved less clearly advantageous. It was, for example, legislated that banks should not pay any interest on demand deposits, or over given rates on savings deposits. Doing so would somehow "curb the excessive competition among banks that allegedly contributed to the 'unsoundness' of banking" in 1929. But it was the "banks which were the prime promoters of these measures," seeing them as a way "to limit interbank competition for funds."[19]

19. Lester Chandler and Dwight Jaffee, "Regulating the Regulators," *Journal of Money Credit and Banking* (November 1977), p. 622.

As the decades passed, market interest rates eventually soared (in the 1970s). Depositors proved reluctant to provide inadvertent subsidies of cheap money to banks and to saving and loan associations. Regulation did permit banks to offer nonmonetary supplements as a substitute for higher interest rates. But fuzzy animals, toasters, televisions were not enough. One leading bank did develop "variable rate notes" in the 1960s but was promptly halted by the Federal Reserve Board. The law was firm against such higher payments to investors. (The money funds then boomed, doing the job that banks could have done at lower social cost.) Meanwhile Congress spent years discussing but not revising the law.

The largest group of U.S. investors were, of course, American workers. Beginning in 1936 their wages were tapped to provide contributions toward their own retirement, via social security payments. (These contributions in fact constituted most of the saving currently put aside by the low-income groups.) The law required that such savings be loaned to the Treasury. By 1980 the Treasury was paying just over 7 percent interest on them—while paying about 14 percent to other lenders, who had a free choice about lending to the government.[20] Congress forbid workers to put their social security retirement money where it would yield them more. Investors in private savings banks and savings and loan associations, however, rocked them violently in the late 1970s when they moved their funds into new "money market funds," bank certificates of deposit (CDs), and other higher return sources.

In addition to regulating banking markets, legislators in the 1930s also attempted to shore up the stock market. Few people in 1933 were putting any money into stock issues. Brokerage houses saw little prospect of profit, and corporations had little hope for selling new stock issues. Here, too, the government provided a new kind of insurance whose outcome in the 1950s and 1970s was unanticipated. The insurance was awarded in the form of a federal guarantee: a new agency, the new Securities and Exchange Commission (SEC), now reviewed every stock issue offered to the public. Investors inferred that fly-by-night companies could no longer issue stock and that the stock would be indefinitely worth the price at which it was issued because "insiders" could no longer manipulate stock values in certain dubious ways. In fact the SEC did provide the public with more accounting information on companies that issued stock, led to more efficient markets, provided many more jobs for lawyers and accountants. Perhaps more importantly, it helped the securities industry in its competition for investors' dollars. For without such official "assurances" how promptly would the investing public have re-

20. In September 1980 the Treasury was borrowing money from investors in the open market at 11.3 percent. But it was then paying a mere 3.5 percent (or less) on $2 billion of its bonds held by the Old Age and Survivors Insurance System. Indeed it paid less than 9 percent on half the fund's assets. (*1982 Annual Report, Federal Old-Age and Survivors Insurance and Disability Insurance Trust Funds*, pp. 20–21, 49.) The market value of its $1 billion in 3.5 percent bonds due in 1990–1998 must have been trivial.

turned to stock investments? How probable would have been those long profitable Wall Street years of the 1950s and 1960s?

The prolonged depression of the '30s made savers cautious about providing funds for any new investments. (Declining prices alone made holding cash profitable.) Legislation in the 1930s induced savers to look more favorably on new stocks, a source for business investment. The New Deal also attempted to spur investment in housing more directly. Ownership was federally favored: "it gives people greater stability, closer ties in the community, more of a stake in law and order, and the like."[21] Thus the new Home Owners Loan Corporation began to supply mortgage money when the banking system was overwhelmingly reluctant to do so. In 1935 its successor, the Federal Housing Administration, guaranteed the security of mortgages on about a tenth of new housing starts. By the early 1970s the FHA (plus the Veterans Administration) were guaranteeing nearly 40 percent of housing starts. That share then fell to 20 percent or less through the 1970s, as FHA interest rates fell below market rates.[22]

The program stimulated construction activity, and led to higher earnings by construction firms, banks, and construction workers during the long upward swing of the 1950s and 1960s. It so underpinned the housing market that the proportion of all households owning their dwelling unit rose from 44 percent at the end of the Depression to an historic high of 65 percent by 1979. That unprecedent shift expanded housing in preference to other investments, induced greater social stability by expanding the group with landed property. That expansion in turn led up to the (homeowner) taxpayer revolt of the late 1970s.

21. Arthur Okun, *Prices and Quantities* (1981), p. 195.
22. Data from *Historical Statistics . . . to 1970*, pp. 639, 641, and *Statistical Abstract 1981*, p. 757.

Part Five

PAST AND
PRESENT

38

Effort and Return: The Content of Growth

W HERE has all the GNP gone? The primary accomplishment of any
    economy is to produce those goods and services sought by its consum-
ers for the least possible amount of human time and effort. Since humans keep
trading off between less effort and more goods, it is necessary to note the
record both for hours worked and for goods produced when assessing the
performance of the economy.

Working Housewives

For a thousand years the greatest share of labor in most societies has been
supplied by adult women. They produced and raised children. They also
produced much if not most of the goods and services essential to human existence and comfort. To do all this they typically worked from dawn to dusk,
and even later once artificial light permitted it.

In the past 75 years, however, major changes have taken place in the pattern of women's work in the United States. Between 1900 and 1975 the workday of U.S. housewives was cut in half, as shown in Table 38.1. It is difficult
to compare degrees of work effort. A poet has argued that "there is no harder
prison than writing poetry."[1] Yet few men took jobs as domestics. And few
housewives ever described their work as easier than that of poets. Their workday has also been longer. Cutting it in half, therefore, presumably amelio-
rated their working conditions. How was that change accomplished?

One major factor was that a typical woman in 1975 had 50 percent fewer
children than a woman in 1900.[2] In consequence her period of child care, and
therefore her workday, were both reduced. No less powerful in shortening
the housewife's workday was increased productivity in the market economy.
For as productivity rose the incomes of husbands—who constituted most of

1. Derek Wolcott on radio station WFCR, May 2, 1976.
2. From 133 births per 1,000 women aged 15-44 to 67 births. *Historical Statistics . . . to 1970*,
p. 49, and *1979 Statistical Abstract*, p. 61.

TABLE 38.1

HOMEMAKERS' TIME USE 1900–75 (HOURS PER WEEK)

	1900	1922	1975
Work	84	75	45
Free time		20	44

Source: For 1900, see Lebergott, *The American Economy*, p. 92. The only comprehensive sampling report prior to recent years comes from a survey of over 2,078 farm families in 11 states conducted by the U.S. Department of Agriculture, Bulletin 1466, *The Farmers Standard of Living* (November 1926), pp. 48, 50. We assume that work time on Sunday was half that of week days. The workday for urban housewives could not have been much shorter. For 1975 we use the Michigan Survey data as reported in John P. Robinson, "Massification and Democratization of the Leisure Class," in *Annals of the American Academy* (January 1978), p. 217.

the labor force—likewise rose. Indeed incomes quadrupled over these decades.[3]

Did husbands plan to use much of their increased income to shorten their wive's workday? Perhaps not, yet that was what happened. The purchase of washing machines, vacuum cleaners, canned goods, ready-made clothing all worked to that end. And so did the marked reduction in the percent of families that took in boarders and lodgers. Both increased spending and reduced income from lodgers, however, were only made possible by husband's increased labor productivity and wages.

Work: Labor Force Members

The typical labor force member until the 1940s was a prime-age male. His workweek, too, fell, by 30 percent between 1900 and 1975.[4] The reductions after 1900 in work effort by U.S. housewives and by U.S. wage earners undoubtedly exceeded those achieved over previous centuries of human history. They required the sacrifice of a significant number of goods and services that workers could have earned had they continued at the good old 60- or 70-hour workweek. The actual rise in workers' real incomes, however, was still substantial. As already noted in Table 29.4, real income per employee rose markedly.

---

3. Average employee income rose from $496 to $2,336 (in 1914 prices) between 1900 to 1975. Data from Lebergott, *Manpower*, p. 523, and computed for 1975 by similar procedures, using data from *Survey of Current Business* (July 1978), Tables 6.5 and 6.8.

4. From 66.8 hours a week to 45.0 hours.

Food, Housing, and Tobacco

For what was it used? Table 38.2 suggests some of the major changes. Consumption of inferior foods—lard, salt pork, potatoes,—declined steadily. In these decades Casimir Funk discovered the critical dietary role of meat, and Joseph Goldberger demonstrated that adding meat to Southern diets could end the age-old scourge of pellagra. But the rising consumption of meat, like that of sugar, is more probably explained by man's ancient hungers. Rising incomes now gave these a chance to work. Bread, processed vegetables, and entire meals were increasingly bought outside the home instead of being prepared by the housewife. (The 1900 housewife typically baked half a ton of flour a year into bread, rolls, etc.) Substantial expenditures for the installation of electricity, and the purchase of washing machines, refrigerators, and vacuum cleaners reduced the housewife's task. The refrigerator cut food spoilage, reduced waste. It thereby changed the diet: leftovers could be kept longer. (It also reduced required trips to the grocery.) Together with the improvement in transport it further changed the diet. A broad range of fresh and frozen vegetables are now consumed 12 months a year, instead of (almost solely) during the summer months.[5]

Rising expenditures changed the average dwelling in two ways. First, they increased its privacy. That was not achieved by increasing the size of the dwelling. (Indeed, the number of rooms occupied by the average family declined steadily.)[6] Rather the households themselves changed, and changed greatly. They reduced the number of strangers in the household, the percentage of families with boarders and lodgers 1900–1979 falling from 25 percent to 2 percent. And they reduced the number of children. Second, they added one facility after another: running water, then flush toilets; gas, then electric light; central heating. Coal was substituted for wood and then oil and gas for coal.[7] It was these installations by plumbers and electricians that largely increased the value of the average dwelling.[8] (The features added since 1900 account for perhaps one-quarter of present-day dwelling costs.)[9]

The enormous rise in cigarette consumption was accompanied, not coincidentally, by a tripling of the death rate from cancer. But cigarettes are produced around the world—and by governments themselves in the Soviet

---

5. Data largely from Lebergott, *The American Economy*, p. 294, and U.S. Department of Agriculture, Agricultural Economic Report No. 138, and 1977 Supplement.

6. Leo Grebler, *Capital Formation in Residential Real Estate* (1956), pp. 119–20, 427.

7. The housing data are from Lebergott, *The American Economy*, p. 252–80. For 1970 data on persons per sleeping room, estimates were derived from 1970 Census of Housing, *Space Utilization of the Housing Inventory*, HC (7)-3, Table A-4.

8. Since the number of rooms declined, it is possible that they accounted for more than the actual increase for a room-equivalent unit. However, the value of ground rent may have changed.

9. Grebler, *Capital*, p. 118.

TABLE 38.2
Consumption Changes, 1900 to 1979

	1900	1979
Food: Percent of families consuming		
Lard	95	9
Salt pork	83	4
Molasses	69	2
Corn meal	90	22
Food: Per capita consumption (pounds)		
"Inferior" foods		
Flour and meal	300	140
Potatoes	212	83
Milk	274	187
Preferred foods		
Sugar	86	132
Meat	148	222
Food preparation		
Flour: percent baked at home	92	22
Expenditures on raw vegetables as percent for all		
vegetables	96	30
Expenditures on food at home as percent for all food	99	82
Housing: Value of average dwelling (1958 dollars)	4,727	7,000
Housing: Percent of families		
With: boarders and lodgers	25	2
over 1 person per room	49	8
over 3½ persons per sleeping room	23	7
Without: running water	76	2
flush toilets	87	4
central heat	99+	22
gas or electric light	88	0
Heating with: wood	50	1
coal	50	3
Owning: refrigerator	18	99
washing machine	5[a]	70
vacuum cleaner	0	92
Tobacco: Cigarettes produced (millions)	5	673
Transport: Percent of urban families		
Owning a horse	20	
Owning a car		80
Recreation: Percent of families with		
Radio	0	96
TV	0	99
Phone	5	91

TABLE 38.2 (CONT.)
CONSUMPTION CHANGES, 1900 TO 1979

	1900	1979
Health: Death rate from		
Pneumonia	153	33
Diarrhea	116	0
Typhoid	31	0
Health: Physicians per 1,000 population	1.72	1.86
Service expenditures per capita (1972 dollars) (rent, health, transport, recreation, personal care, education, etc.)	37	340

ᵃRough approximation.

Source: See footnotes 5 and 7, this chapter.

Union, China, and France. And given rising consumption in nations around the world, it was clear that hundreds of millions of people, in all kinds of societies, felt that the satisfactions from smoking outweighed its costs in money and health. (Even where the health impacts over a lifetime were largely unknown, as in marijuana smoking, that conclusion holds.)

Transportation

The consumer shift from walking, using horses, or relying on public transportation, to buying and using cars marked a near universal American preference. (The number of years would-be buyers wait to purchase cars in Russia and East Germany, their proliferation in Western Europe suggests an even wider preference for them.) When car ownership in the nation went from 1 percent to 80 percent, the nation's way of life inevitably changed. That change forced the massive growth of cities and suburbs; broke up thousands of local monopolies once held by physicians, grocers, saloon keepers, furniture stores,; ended large numbers of monopsonies, in which one employer had provided the only place of work for hundreds, sometimes thousands, of workers who could get to work only by walking; substantially reduced parental control over behavior of their teenagers (in a simpler world the latter tended to live far more commonly in the physical presence of their parents); increased energy consumption as much as all other household uses put together; and generated impressively large spending programs by highway departments—city, state, and federal.

Without attempting to review the host of other changes in consumption it is possible to suggest their impact by an abrupt question: How many Americans today would prefer the set of goods and services available in 1900 to the wider set available today?

39

Problems of the 1930s
and Their Outcomes

THREE economic problems dominated existence in the 1930s, according to one leading economist: stagnation of the economic process, instability of the economy, and inequality of the income distribution.[1] What has been the subsequent record for each?

Stagnation

The weaker the economy became in the 1930s the more vigorous did theorizing about it become. One theory held that long-run investment opportunities had all been exhausted. Alvin Hansen (as many others) saw the end of the frontier and of immigration together forcing a long slowdown in the rate of population growth.[2] From that slowdown followed a weak market for housing and thereby for investment—in making steel, building materials, furniture, pipe for more water and sewage systems, telephones, and more. Permanent stagnation loomed ahead.

What in fact happened after 1939? Did the annual percentage rate of growth in GNP slow down? Comparison for selected periods shows the following:[3]

1900–29	3.0
1929–39	0.3
1939–46	5.9
1946–70	2.9
1970–80	3.2

The rates of gain for 1946–70 and 1970–80 were at or above the long-term pre-Depression rate—rather than far below it. Hansen and others had

1. Sumner Slichter, *Economic Growth in the United States* (1961), p. 197.
2. Alvin Hansen, "Economic Progress and Declining Population Growth," *American Economic Review* (March 1939). The dismal investment forecast was reminiscent of the similar pessimism of another great economist. Cf. Joseph Schumpeter, *Business Cycles* 2 (1939):1037.
3. Bureau of Economic Analysis, *Long Term Economic Growth, 1860–1970*, part V, and *1981 Statistical Abstract*, p. 423. Data relate to constant-dollar GNP.

concentrated on the experience of the 1930s. But a half-century of experience reports a return to the almost magical three percent growth rate. That experience hardly warrants their prediction of stagnation in output and employment growth for decades to come.

Instability

The expectation that the business cycle would persist after the 1930s was, however, confirmed by later experience. In the 1950s the International Economic Association turned out a volume entitled *Is the Business Cycle Obsolete?*. Yet, even in those palmy (economic) days none of the participants was sanguine enough to declare that it was. Production had not kept to any steady trend line.

In 1967 a well-known (conservative) commentator noted: "We have been enjoying for the last 6 years the biggest and largest economic boom in history. So when is the bubble going to burst?" For answer he referred to " 'a 1929 in 1969' warning by 'a confidential economic analyst for a number of blue chip corporations.' "[4] In September 1971 another (radical) commentator warned that "the entire capitalist world is barely inches away from that general collapse of world trade and production which will represent a Second Great Depression."[5] Over the next few years speculators did lose on arbitrage. With no increase in unemployment appearing that warning was intensified in March 1973: "A complete collapse of all world credit is now only months away."[6] Fear, then, did not provide a particularly good guide to forecasting. What did? What direction does the past sequence of U.S. business cycles forecast? Three historical aspects are relevant to an answer.

First, over 85 percent of all workers remained employed in every nineteenth century U.S. depression except that of 1894.[7] And were at work in even the worst days of twentieth-century declines. The Great Depression was the signal and massive exception: In 1934 over a quarter of all workers were unemployed. In the half-century since, over 90 percent of all workers have been employed, even during recessions.

Second, steady employment does not necessarily point to adequate achievement by any economy. For it does not measure a very deep economic concern with how much output society creates from its resources. In parts of Asia and Africa, for example, women sit all day in the hot sun to earn a few

---

4. Stewart Alsop, "When Will the Bubble Burst?" *Saturday Evening Post*, (December 30, 1967).

5. He added a word of qualified cheer: "If the Nixon regime abruptly turns toward a more sensible world monetary policy the depression might be delayed into early or middle 1972." The National Caucus of Labor Committees, *Socialism or Fascism?* (September 1971), p. 2, reprinting an earlier article from *New Solidarity*.

6. National Caucus of Labor Committees, *New Solidarity* (March 12–16, 1973).

7. Lebergott, *Manpower*, pp. 187, 512, 522.

pennies selling goods to passersby. They are, by most measures, fully employed. But they reap pitifully small reward for their full and arduous employment. Table 30.2 reported the well-known fact that workers in the United States increasingly reaped a greater return for their work. But it revealed something more: Even in the trough of each business cycle workers still earned more than they did in the peak prosperity year of the previous business cycle.

Third, is the system slowly winding down? Are its inefficiencies, its contradictions, beginning to overwhelm it? Such questions have motivated much invocation of business cycle history. The "first stage of the general crisis of capitalism" occurred "in the first decade of the twentieth century," according to leading Russian economists.[8] Half a century later a well-known American economist noted that the "rate of exploitation" fell from 29 percent to 23 percent in the years 1967–75, ominously marking "the predicament of the U.S. capitalists."[9] One way of evaluating the seriousness of that predicament is to refer back to the experience in the depression. By 1933 the "exploitation" rate had fallen not to 23 percent but all the way to 5 percent. Corporate profits vanished completely.[10] Yet the system lumbered on and even expanded.

A better insight into the prospects for system collapse is given by the actual long-run performance of the economy. Table 39.1 suggests that the average long-run unemployment performance of the economy has not changed for the worse over the past century. (If the analysis of cycles had stopped in 1933, a quite different conclusion could well have been drawn. The severity of the Great Depression still stands out. But the record for the next half-century emphasizes the lack of any long-term trend, up or down.)

Income Inequality

Income has been distributed unequally in the United States throughout its entire history,[11] as it was in nearly all, if not all, 200 members of the United Nations.[12]

8. The quotation is from Varga, and appears in *Soviet Views on the Post-War World Economy* Leo Gruliow, ed. (1948), p. 125. On p. 15 another Russian economist describes it as "the stage of the decay and death of capitalism."

9. John G. Gurley, *Challengers to Capitalism, Marx, Lenin and Mao* (1976), p. 154.

10. Data for making this estimate were derived from U.S. Bureau of Economic Analysis, *The National Income and Product Accounts of the United States, 1929–1974*, Table 1.14. Corporate profits in 1933 were, in fact, negative.

11. Cf. among others, Stanley Lebergott, *Wealth and Want* (1975); Lee Soltow, *Men and Wealth in the United States, 1850–1870* (1975); Jeffrey Williamson and Peter Lindert, *American Inequality* (1980); Stephen Thernstrom, *The Other Bostonians* (1973); Robert Gallman, "Trends in the Size Distribution of Wealth in the Nineteenth Century," in *Six papers on the size distribution of income and wealth* Lee Soltow, ed. (1969); Edward Pessen, *Riches, Class and Power Before the Civil War* (1973).

12. Income distribution data, available for perhaps a quarter of all members, are reviewed in United Nations, *A Survey of National Sources of Income Distribution Statistics* (1981).

TABLE 39.1
UNEMPLOYMENT AS A PERCENT
OF THE LABOR FORCE, 1870–1980
(DECADE AVERAGES)

1870–79[a]	10
1880–89[b]	4
1890–99	10
1900–09	4
1910–19	5
1920–29	5
1930–39	18
1940–49	5
1950–59	5
1960–69	5
1970–80	7

[a]The figures for 1870–89 are rough approximations.

Source: 1870–1960: Lebergott, *Manpower*, p. 189. 1960 ff: Bureau of Labor Statistics, Special Labor Force Report 218, *Employment and Unemployment During 1978*, Table 1, and *Statistical Abstract*, 1982, p. 375.

Interest in income distribution derives in part from concern with human suffering. In Anatole France's bitter phrase, the poor have liberty—the same liberty as the rich—to sleep under the public bridges. But do they have sufficient food to prevent malnutrition, decent clothing, medical care? Trends in the real income of the poor are considered in the section on poverty in Chapter 40.

Interest in income inequality derives also from an interest in inequality *per se.* It involves envy of the rich, distaste for their ways, their values, and/or their power. Though the changing inequality of income and wealth has been estimated for parts of the past two centuries, the record remains obscure. Tolerably reliable data begin with 1900 (Table 39.2).[13] They show a sharp decline in the share of personal income going to the top 5 percent, with the share of the upper income groups falling most swiftly after 1929. The lower fifth did not increase its share, a fact that may not have mattered to those whose primary concern with inequality was to cut the portion going to the

13. Major studies are as cited in footnote 11.

TABLE 39.2

PERCENT DISTRIBUTION OF FAMILIES—BY FAMILY INCOME, 1900–81

Family units by income level	1900	1929	1935–36	1941	1951	1961	1971	1981
Total families	100.0	100.0	100.0	100.0	100.0	100.0	100.0	100.0
Lowest 20 percent	4.8	3.5	4.1	4.1	5.0	4.6	4.8	4.4
Second lowest 20 percent	9.2	9.0	9.2	9.5	11.3	10.9	10.8	10.2
Third lowest 20 percent	13.0	13.8	14.1	15.3	16.5	16.3	16.4	16.3
Fourth lowest 20 percent	17.0	19.3	20.9	22.3	22.3	22.7	23.3	23.8
Highest 20 percent	56.0	54.4	51.7	48.8	44.9	45.5	44.6	45.3
(Top 5 percent)	35.7	30.0	26.5	24.0	20.7	19.6	19.1	18.8

Source: See Appendix, this chapter.

rich.[14] In any event it was the middle 60 percent who increased their share of personal income. Including many small businessmen, trade union members, professors, editorial writers, the group included many of those who most forthrightly favored redistribution away from the rich.

Just who was in the bottom of the income distribution? In 1900 that group included virtually all farm laborers, nearly all black families, many farmers,[15] common laborers. By 1979 very few farmers and farm laborers were around. Quite different types of family units appeared there. One group included college students, many from well-off families, who lived at college. Few tried to earn income all year. A second group included many old people. After 1936, social security enabled many of them to leave the higher income families of their relatives, and live apart. They thereby entered the lower income group. Neither the greater freedom it gave them and/or their children appears in these measures. Nor does the fact that 7 out of 10 owned their own homes.[16] A third group consisted of those rarely present in the 1900 count—women, often with children, whose husbands had deserted them. The surge of these three groups into the lowest income categories between

14. It was not likely to be the share of the rich *per se*. For example, in 1973–76 the top 20 percent of households in Sweden, a nation widely admired for its redistribution policies, apparently collected more of that nation's income than did the top 20 percent in the United States. Cf. United Nations, *Survey,* p. 314. An earlier comparison shows the U.S. share at about the median for a group including Canada, France, Australia, the United Kingdom, and Japan. Cf. A. B. Atkinson, *Economics of Inequality* (1975), p. 248.

15. Farmers, in part, because income measures fail to include freight and retail margins. They did *not* have to pay on the food they consumed; nor did their housing costs include urban levels of ground rent.

16. 1970 Census, *Housing of Senior Citizens,* Table A-4.

1900 and 1970 reported very little about the ability of the economic system to provide work for the unskilled, the unemployed, the less competent. If anything, the increase in one-person families (e.g., the aged living apart from their children, and college students living apart from their parents) pointed to real income increases.

These data ignore taxes, as do most of those used in discussing inequality. But surely taxing money away from the rich cuts income inequality. What, then, about income *after* taxes? Table 39.3 reports that taxes escalate, from 26 percent in the lowest fifth of the income distribution to 43 percent in the highest interval. That escalation was almost completely created by the income tax rates, which about doubled (19 percent to 35 percent). Nonetheless, the gain from the bottom to top quintile (22 percent to 27 percent) proved far milder than early and persistent proponents of the income tax desired. Congress proved reluctant to do more, ultimately because of the huge increase in federal spending since 1913. For there simply was not enough money in the top income group to finance so great an increase. Even if, for example, in 1970, the government confiscated all incomes above $25,000 a year, that would only have added $7 billion to the $193 billion the Treasury was already collecting.[17] To spend at the rate Congress and the administration did, therefore, it became increasingly necessary to tax the bulk of the population.

By the 1980s Congress was understandably reluctant to escalate the tax rate for its own members and the $20,000-to-$50,000 lawyers, teachers, small businessmen, editorial writers, physicians, skilled union members who (together with Congressman) made up most of the top fifth. By 1970 there were far more truck drivers than financiers in the $20,000-plus group; far more mechanics and construction craftsmen than heads of major corporations.[18] (The new administration in 1981 cut tax rates most—by 10 percent—for millionaires. But about half the total reduction in Treasury tax collections benefited one income group—those with incomes of $20,000 to $50,000.[19])

Property tax rates in 1970 rose from 6 percent in the lowest quintile to 8 percent in the top. This mild rise reflects the presence of two relatively sizable groups of property owners at the bottom of the income distribution.[20] One included older persons, who commonly owned their own homes

17. Cf. Lebergott, *The American Economy*, p. 30.

18. Over 90 percent of those in the top quintile had incomes of $20,000 to $50,000. Family income data for occupations from 1970 Census, *Occupational Characteristics*, Table 26. The number of corporations with receipts of $1 million and over in 1970 was 182,000.

19. Joseph Pechman, *Setting National Priorities, the 1983 Budget* (1982), Table A-4. And in 1983 the Democratic opposition tried to "cap" the administration tax cuts not for all those above, say, the median, but only for those above $50,000. Cf. *New York Times* (June 25, 1983).

20. Families with incomes under $1,000 had ten times as much wealth per dollar of income as the average American family. Cf. Lebergott, *The American Economy*, pp. 245–46, and data underlying those tables.

TABLE 39.3

TAX RATES: 1970 SHARE OF INCOME TAKEN BY TAXES (PERCENT)

Family units (by income level)	All taxes	Property taxes	Income and other taxes
Lowest fifth	26.1	6.1	19.0
Second lowest fifth	23.6	3.9	19.8
Third lowest fifth	25.2	3.2	22.0
Fourth lowest fifth	25.4	3.2	22.2
Top fifth	28.0	4.0	24.0
$20,000–$100,000	26.9	3.5	23.4
$100,000–$500,000	34.9	6.9	28.0
$500,000–$1,000,000	44.3	7.7	36.6
$1,000,000 and over	42.8	7.8	35.1

Source: We use unpublished data kindly provided by Joseph Pechman. They underly the figures in Henry Aaron and Michael Boskin, eds., *The Economics of Taxation* (1980), pp. 74–75. We average the most and least progressive incidence variants. If the social security taxes largely redistribute income from working to retirement years the progressivity of taxes would be greater than shown here. In the same study (pp. 386–87) Musgrave estimates that from 1902 on taxes took about half of all income increases for the top fifth of the distribution.

and farms.[21] The other included thousands of would-be entrepreneurs, farm and nonfarm, who sustained income losses in any given year. Both groups owned property, taxed by counties and towns at the same rate per dollar as the property of "the rich."[22]

What, then, of the 1900–81 change in the income distribution once one allows for taxes? Briefly put, the changes for the top and bottom income quintiles were probably much the same as shown in Table 39.2. The income tax did, indeed, substantially erode the incomes of the top group. But because entrepreneurs and retired people with property came to populate the bottom group, replacing farm laborers and sharecroppers, the property taxes of the bottom group likewise increased.

21. Of all households with heads aged 60 years and older and low income (under $3000), 58 percent owned their own housing units in 1970. 1970 Census, *Housing of Senior Citizens*, Table A-8. Ninety percent of older farmers owned their own home (Ibid., Table 1-1) and would have paid property taxes on the value of their farms even if their current incomes were low.

22. Not unrelated to such an approach was the wide Congressional support of a law exempting the first $100,000 profits by the elderly selling the family home, though "more than half will go to people earning $30,000 and more." *New York Times* (April 10, 1979), p. B-2. Since capital gains substitutes for income the progressivity of the income tax is undermined by such provisions.

Appendix

Data are for families plus unrelated individuals.

1929–71: *Survey of Current Business* (April 1958), p. 17; (April 1964), p. 8; (October 1974), p. 27.

1900: Approximately comparable figures from Lebergott, *The American Economy: Income, Wealth and Want* (1966), p. 321. Cumulative income and family counts from this source were interpolated to give quintile figures. For the top 5 percent the average income of the "$1,300 and over" income group was estimated as $6,083. That figure was a weighted average for farm families, based on the underlying distribution of farms by value of product sold, traded, or used; and, for nonfarm families, derived from the distribution of families by income class in 1914, with some interpolation by 1917 data, as shown in Edward White, "Income Fluctuation of a Selected Group of Personal Returns," *Journal of the American Statistical Association* (March 1922), p. 68.

1981: The estimates for earlier years are anchored to the BEA concept of family personal income, and adjusted by BEA for non-reporting in field surveys. No BEA estimate is available for 1981. To derive a comparable distribution we compute the percentage distributions for families and unrelated individuals from the Census P-60 report series for 1971 and 1981 (No. 97, *Money Income in 1973*, Table 22; No. 134, *Money Income and Poverty . . . 1981*, Table 4). The absolute differences between those distributions were then added on to the above BEA distribution for 1971 to arrive at one for 1981. This procedure roughly adjusts to the BEA concept and procedure.

The past is never dead.
It's not even past.

—WILLIAM FAULKNER, *Requiem for a Nun*

40

Present and Past:
The Costs of Growth

EVERY year since 1776, urgent issues confronted the workers and capitalists of the American economy. As soon as one problem was "solved" another took its place. Resources were limited; goals ceaselessly multiplied. The costs of real income growth turned out to generate an ever-present agenda of urgent, unsolved, perceived issues. By the end of the nation's second century, however, economic success seemed so inevitable, the technology of economic control so simple, that hard choices could be avoided, or at least redefined.

Voters urged the mixed economy of the 1970s and early 1980s toward government action, or guidance, to attack the most recent agenda: inflation, declining productivity, poverty, energy shortages, pollution, occupational fatalities. The historic origins of these problems cast a fascinating light on the solutions proposed and fought.

Inflation

The "progressive deterioration in the value of money through history is not an accident, and has behind it two great driving forces," wrote Keynes in 1924.[1] One was the "superior political influence of the debtor class." That force has only been mildly effective in the United States. Connecticut and Massachusetts experimented by printing paper money in the 1740s and Rhode Island by printing it in the 1790s. These represented the high point of debtor influence. Populism's failure in the 1890s, and the limited "reflation" of the 1930s, showed that such forces have been weak in the United States.

The second force, said Keynes, was "the impecuniosity of governments."[2] What is "raised by printing notes [i.e., money] is just as much taken from the public as is a beer duty or an income-tax. . . . In some countries it

1. J. M. Keynes, *Monetary Reform* (1924), p. 12.
2. Ibid.

seems possible to please and content the public . . . by giving them, in return for the taxes they pay, finely engraved acknowledgements on water-marked paper."[3] Inflation as a "potent instrument of government exaction" surfaced in 1968–69 when the federal government rapidly increased expenditure for both a war in Vietnam and a "war on poverty" at home. Over the next decade the voters revealed their desire for ever more programs of expenditure, welfare and/or defense, and an almost equal desire to pay no increased taxes for such programs. Inflation proved a way to reconcile these conflicting desires, as shown in Figure 40.1. Of course increased real expenditure could only be achieved at the expense of the vested interests. These included older people who held Treasury savings bonds (bought during World War II) and a host of workers with life insurance policies and payments into pension funds. On average the government gained $38 billion every year from 1965 to 1977 via the reduced value of its obligations[4] (Figure 40.1).

The war years proved that it was easy to reduce unemployment—by massive government spending, tight controls, the draft, patriotism, and war production. The political lesson drawn from that complex experience was that federal fiscal and monetary policy could stabilize the economy. Its first implementation came after the immediate postwar restocking boom, in 1949. The rise in unemployment was slowed by increased spending, then canceled out by military intervention in Korea.

But a far more significant implementation took place in 1954, when quite the opposite military sequence occurred. For in 1953 a new president (ironically, a general of the Armies) ended the war in Korea, and sharply cut Defense Department spending. Inevitably, unemployment began to rise. At that point the first Republican administration in thirty years (with its cabinet composed of "twelve millionaires and a plumber") took steps that would have appalled the preceding Republican president. It immediately increased federal spending and put pressure on the Federal Reserve Board to increase the money supply. Similar steps were taken in each subsequent economic downturn, under Republican or Democratic presidents.[5]

The tilt in federal economic policy had become far more predictable. No longer would presidents stand aside when aggregate demand began to falter, as they did in 1893, 1914, 1921, 1924, 1927, and 1930. Now they acted to pump up demand. This basic fact became a central element in the plans of every economic actor—institutional investor, labor union, farm group, or congressional committee. Business monopolies, labor unions, and farmers' associations previously had to consider that the market might fail to validate an

3. Ibid., pp. 68–69.
4. Estimates of net revaluation of government liabilities, in 1972 dollars, by Robert Eisner, in *The Measurement of Capital* Dan Usher, ed. (1980), p. 321. The liabilities were primarily public securities, but included currency, etc.
5. It can be argued that actions in 1957–58 were minimal.

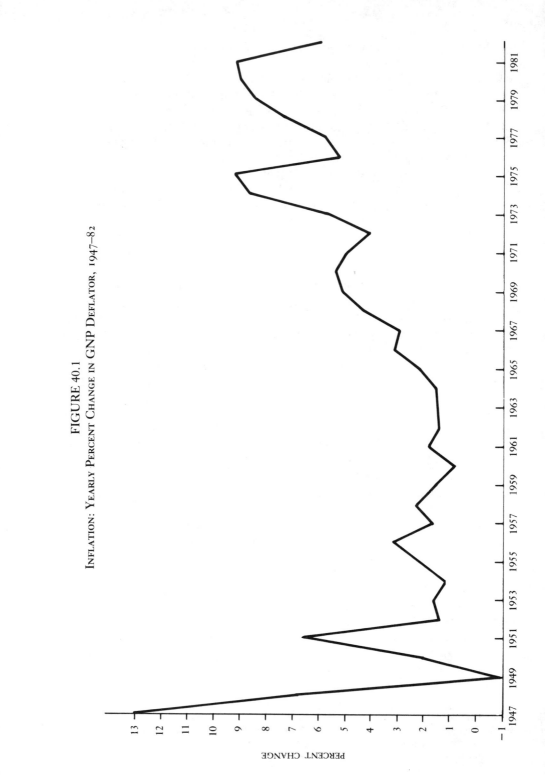

FIGURE 40.1

INFLATION: YEARLY PERCENT CHANGE IN GNP DEFLATOR, 1947–82

504

arbitrary price rise. If so the goods or services they were offering would go unsold. In the new era, however, prices forced on the market stood a far better chance of holding. Since "the" government is not "one and indivisible," it is necessary to note the possible contribution of government to accelerating the very inflation that it proposed to halt. As a major purchaser of goods and services the federal Government may have helped set the pace for inflation, by stepping smartly out in front. For example, in the Arab oil crisis of the fourth quarter of 1973 to the first quarter of 1974 while airlines paid 23 percent more for jet fuel, the Defense Department volunteered to pay 72 percent more.[6]

In any event, the post-1953 administrations, with wide political support, sped demand by both expenditure-tax and monetary policies. In 1981 a leading economist acknowledged that energy shocks and productivity declines added to the core inflation rate of the 1970s. But, he added, "We are now talking of getting the inflation rate down from 8 or 9 percent rather than . . . [from] 4 or 5 percent . . . [because] we have chosen, when there has been a choice, not to try to get the inflation rate down at the expense of employment."[7] One did not need to be a Keynesian or monetarist to predict an inflationary outcome. For the government was pursuing both routes. It was unnecessary to invoke the further sour explanation by one economist in 1947: of full employment, price stability, and strong trade unions, we might have two "but not all three." Or to quote Joan Robinson, England's leading, and radical, economist: After the 1930s "it was obvious that if we ever reached and maintained a low level of unemployment with the same institutions of free wage bargaining and the same code of proper behavior for trade unions . . . a vicious spiral of rising prices, wages, prices, would become chronic."[8]

Productivity

In recent decades, kindly administrations have tempered the wind to the shorn lamb—and, incidentally, to the mangy wolf. As already noted, the desire for economic stability and minimal unemployment brought an unpre-

6. Richard Ziemer and Karl Galbraith, "Deflation of Defense Purchases," in *The U.S. National Income and Product Accounts* Murray Foss, ed. (1983), p. 185. By the end of two years that gap had been removed.

7. Stanley Fischer in *Macroeconomics, Prices and Quantities* James Tobin, ed. (1983), p. 273.

8. C. O. Hardy in Federal Reserve Board, Postwar Economic Studies, No. 4, *Prices, Wages and Employment* (May 1946), p. 24. Joan Robinson, *Economic Philosophy* (1963), p. 93. Her insight goes back at least to 1943, when she noted that "No national plan . . . can guarantee everyone work in his own trade . . . it would be highly undesirable to allow the distribution of labour which happened to exist at the outset of planning to exercise a permanent influence in distorting the pattern of production." Joan Robinson, *Collected Economic Papers* (1960) I:86. The evolution of unemployment insurance administration, the development of supplemental benefits provided by firms in the United States, as the extension of home ownership, etc., however, induced expectations of just such stability in work prospects.

cedented program of federal intervention by expenditure-tax and monetary policies. Inevitably such a policy slowed down the rate at which businesses would otherwise have failed. (quite apart from specific intervention to save firms which villains had tied to the railroad track—such as Penn Central and Chrysler). The economy thus retained a growing set of inefficient firms. Each year thousands entered the business world seeking to imitate Andrew Carnegie, Ray Kroc, or Colonel Sanders. And each year, in the past, the vagaries of the business cycle forced out thousands of these aspirants. Many did well on the straightaways, but collapsed when the wave began to curl. The economy thus wiped out firms whose efficiency fell distinctly below average. It is hardly likely that the quality of new entrepreneurs suddenly improved in recent decades. No such presumption can account for declining failures after 1962, and particularly after 1966.[9] What can is the new economic stability.

TABLE 40.1
SOURCES OF GROWTH, 1909–81
(CONTRIBUTIONS TO GROWTH RATE IN PERCENTAGE POINTS)

	1909–29	1929–48	1948–73	1973–81[a]
National income	2.82	2.49	3.65	−1.86
Total factor input	2.26	1.52	2.13	1.60
Output per unit of input	.56	.97	1.52	−.80
Advances in knowledge and unknowns	.28	.46	1.10	−.58
Improved resource allocation	.00	.28	.29	−.62
Legal and human environment	.00	.00	−.04	−.21
Economies of scale and other	.28	.23	.17	.03

[a]Preliminary.

Source: Edward Denison: *The Sources of Economic Growth in the United States* (1962), p. 266; *Accounting for Slower Economic Growth* (1979), p. 104; "The Interruption of Productivity Growth in the United States," The *Economic Journal* (March 1983), p. 60. Denison shows the change for the nonresidential business sector from 1948–73, which we apply to his overall 1948–73 figures to arrive at rough preliminary figures for the latter period. Denison surmised (*Sources*, p. 192) that resale price maintenance laws, aided by the Miller-Tydings Amendment to the Sherman Act, had doubled gross margins for covered products. The result was to keep "inefficient retailers in business." From his margin estimates one may infer that over 100,000 excess retailers were kept in business as of 1957.

9. The failure rate per 100,000 firms fell to 24 in 1978 from 50–60 in the years 1957–67.

Is that outcome related to the rather dramatic decline in national productivity beginning in the late 1960s? After World War II productivity (i.e., factor output per unit of input) rose faster than it had in the generally depressed years from 1929 to 1948. But sometime around 1973, according to Edward Denison, a dramatic turnaround halted the growth, as shown in Table 40.1. In part, the growth of capital input slowed. And in some small part, increased regulation (pollution abatement, OSHA stipulations, etc.) slowed productivity, as did the rising cost of private police (in stores, airports). But only in part. More substantial factors were at work; the ongoing advance of "knowledge" and other unknown contributors to productivity likewise slowed decisively. The resulting drag on productive efficiency accentuated inflation after 1973.[10]

Poverty

Poverty declined in the twentieth century via the untidy working of unplanned economic growth. Incomes rose as investment created jobs. Firms competed for workers. Workers competed with each other. Unions fought management. Poverty fell. To simplify long-term estimation we take the basic official poverty cutoff level for 1979: $7,412 for a family of four. Adjusted for price changes that figure in 1967 prices is $3,000. Hence, the data in Table 40.2 for 1900–1947 and 1947–1979.

The percent of low-income families fell from 56 percent to 12 percent between 1900 and 1929. War production and full employment then cut the percentage dramatically from the low point in the depression. The decline continued after the war, with the greatest gains coming from peacetime prosperity.

In the 1960s the "War on Poverty" began. Federal spending for food stamps, school lunches, medicaid and medicare, social security and other transfer payments rose from $38 billion to $240 billion between 1965 and 1979—but the ratio of families with low incomes to all families fell by a mere 4 percent.[11] In reality the decline was somewhat greater since the usual income distribution figures simply ignored the fact that the "War" provided goods and services in kind (food stamps, medicaid), not in money. If one reck-

10. The issues are illuminated by Moses Abramowitz in his presidential address to the American Economic Association, "Welfare Quandries and Productivity Concerns," *The American Economic Review* (March 1981).

11. "Most economists would be taken aback by [the fact that] the incidence of pretransfer poverty fell minimally from 26 to 25 percent" from 1965 to 1972 even though "governmental social welfare expenditures" on that group rose from $31 billion to $52 billion in constant dollars. Glen Cain, "The Challenge of Segmented Labor Market Theories," *Journal of Economic Literature* (December 1976), p. 1218.

TABLE 40.2

PERCENT OF FAMILIES (HUSBAND-WIFE) WITH LOW INCOMES, 1900–79[a]

	Total	White	Black	Transfer payments as percent of personal income
Under $3,000 (in 1967 dollars)				
1900	56	51	91	0.6
1929	42			1.8
1935–36	51	47	91	4.6
1945	25	22	51	3.6
1947	27	24	62	6.2
1957	20	18	47	6.2
1967	13	11	27	8.3
Under $7,500 (in 1979 dollars)				
1967	16	14	33	8.3
1972	14	12	30	11.0
1977	14	12	31	13.5
1979	14 (8)[b]	11	30	12.8

[a]Low income: under $3,000 in 1967 prices or under $7,500 in 1979 prices.

[b]8 percent if allowance is made for income in kind, such as food stamps and medicaid.

Source: See Appendix B, this chapter.

ons in the market value of these items to the recipients, the percent with low incomes fell to 8 percent.

The above discussion relates to families with both husband and wife present.[12] Women who were deserted by their husbands typically lacked the experience and the time (often because children were present), required to earn an adequate income.[13] For that reason data inclusive of such families— for example, for all "consumer units," or "families and unrelated individuals," or "householders"—decline less. For they include the income experience of this special group, prevented though it be from earning more adequate incomes.

Productivity and economic growth lift the constraints that keep incomes down, thereby revealing more clearly an under-class, the permanent poor.

12. A contrary view, with no reference to the actual record, has been succinctly put: "In the United States, as is now sadly evident, economic growth does little for those at the bottom of the economic pyramid. . . . Growth only helps those who have a foothold in the system and it helps those who have the most." J. K. Galbraith, quoted in C. Lynn Munro, *The Galbraithian System* (1977), p. 164.

13. Desertion and lack of labor-force experience may each represent the outcome of rules in a "male-dominated society." But such issues are far broader than those that can be illuminated by a discussion of economic change *per se.*

TABLE 40.3
PERCENT IN THE LOWER TENTH, 1910–70—HUSBAND-WIFE
FAMILIES

	1910 (Under $440)	1970 (Under $4,000)
Native stock		
White	10	10
Negro	40	22
Foreign stock		
	Foreign born	Native born
Irish	9	9
German	11	17
Italian-North	28 ⎫ 36	⎱ 6
Italian-South	40 ⎭	⎰
Russian	43	5
All other	26	9
Total	26	9

Source: See Note 15, this chapter.

Present in most (or all?) economies their existence became more obvious when rising U.S. incomes removed more remediable types of poverty.

How large has this group been in the United States since World War II? Some "problem families," as they were termed in nineteenth-century Britain, had problem children, and they, problem grandchildren. It was even possible that generations of those with mental deficiencies—the Jukes and Kallikaks—actually existed. But the presence of a sizable "problem" group would point well beyond economics to issues in psychology and genetics. Oddly enough, despite all the concern expressed for such families, little attention has been paid to how large the "permanent poverty" group may be.[14] Lacking any extensive studies the answer to a corollary question may cast light on it.

That question is whether particular racial and ethnic groups remain at the bottom of the occupational and income pyramid generation after generation. For if there were a large group permanently poor, certain ethnic and nationality groups would bulk largely in it. On this question something more can be said. We consider here husband-wife families of the major foreign-born ethnic groups (as of 1910, peak period of immigration) and then their grandchildren (in 1970). The immigrants, of course, disproportionately crowded into the bottom tenth of the income distribution (Table 40.3). Only 10 percent of the native white population were in that low income group. But

14. U.S. agencies and scholars are not unusually remiss in this respect, however. It is not apparent that nations committed to communism or to complete free enterprise are more informed on this subject.

36 percent of the Italians were, 43 percent of the Russians, and 26 percent of the foreign-born group as a whole. And 40 percent of the Negroes were.[15]

Now, given any substantial inheritance of poverty—that is, given "permanent poverty"—one would expect the grandchildren to be similarly crowded into the low income group in 1970. Their inheritance of discrimination, contempt, and restricted access has been widely described. But, in fact, the foreign stock in 1970 shows about the same share in the lower decile as native whites. So do the separate figures for Irish, Italian, Russian, and others. For black families the figure, though down markedly, was still 22 percent. (However, poverty far more typically plagues all households, white or black, native or foreign born, in which the husband has deserted his wife and children. A greater percentage of such broken families appears among blacks than among the general population, substantially increasing the percentage of all black family units in poverty.)

Income comparisons over still longer periods might cast light on "permanent poverty" among the entire U.S. population. Such data are lacking. However, data on occupational mobility are suggestive. Comparison between the occupation of all sons in recent decades and their fathers'—something close to 30 years previously—appears in Table 40.4. Data reporting that 75 percent to 93 percent of the sons whose fathers worked in the lowest occupational groups rose out of them would seem to show substantial advance. (Particularly since not all of those remaining in low status occupations also remained in poverty.)

Is there any way of comparing these numbers against some standard from the real world? Mobility from blue- to white-collar jobs has been assessed for 24 free-market economies. The U.S. rate exceeds that for 20 of these 24, falling below only Israel, Canada, and Australia.[16] (Roughly comparable data for Great Britain indicate that some 73 percent of its laborers' sons rose to higher status jobs, compared to 60 percent in the U.S.[17] In the decades after World War II, then, the chance to exit from the bottom of the economic pyramid appeared as great, or greater, in the United States than in many "western" economies. Data for communist or third-world nations seem unavailable.[18]) For a shorter, but very recent, period one may refer to the

15. Actually we use the figure that separates the bottom decile not of the total but of the native white population—$440. Data here and in Table 40.3 are from Lebergott, *The American Economy*, p. 46, as corrected. The higher 1970 German stock rate reflects their greater concentration in rural areas. Their imputed income in food and rent was important, but is omitted in these—and other—money income measures.

16. Andrea Tyree et al., "Gaps and Glissandos: Inequality, Economic Development and Social Mobility in 24 Countries," *American Sociological Review* (June 1979), p. 416.

17. David Glass, *Social Mobility in Great Britain* (1954, reprint ed. 1963), pp. 182–83. A 1972 survey is reported in John Goldthorpe, *Social Mobility and Class Structure in Modern Britain* (1980), p. 41 and Table 2.2.

18. Reports on the occupational and educational concentration of children of Communist Party or military leaders in Russia or China are far too thin for comparison here.

TABLE 40.4
SONS' OCCUPATIONAL STATUS IN THE 1970S AS COMPARED TO
FATHERS' OCCUPATION (PERCENT IN HIGHER, SAME, OR
LOWER STATUS OCCUPATIONS)

| | | Son by level of occupation | | |
Father's Occupation	All	Higher status	Same status	Lower status
Operative	100	60	24	16
Service worker	100	75	19	9
Laborer	100	86	12	2
Farm laborer	100	93	7	—

Source: Tabulations from the National Research Corporation, General Social Survey tapes for 1970–78. For the first three groups combined Census data show about 60 percent moving to higher status. Cf. David Featherman, "Opportunities Are Expanding," Society (March–April 1979), p. 7.

families formed in 1968–74 by children who left households that were in poverty. About 4 of every 5 such children formed their own households—with incomes above the poverty line.[19]

Energy

Few owners of coal mines, natural gas and petroleum wells in 1900 were inclined to philanthropy in business. When they charged the U.S. population 2 percent of the national income, that surely covered the full scarcity payment, plus all costs of mining.[20] That tiny percentage, of course, inevitably rose over the next three-quarters of a century. For the auto was developed, and 125 million cars and trucks put on the roads. Moreover, electricity output rose from virtually nothing to 2 trillion kilowatts a year.[21] Homes installed central heating for the first time in history. So vast an increase in the demand for energy had to increase claims by producers of energy. It did. Their share rose from 2 percent—to 3 percent.[22] That slight rise did not exactly demon-

19. Frank Levy, How Big is the American Underclass?, Working Paper No. 0090–1, Urban Institute (1977).

20. The value of fuel production, plus imports minus exports, is derived from data in Historical Statistics . . . to 1970, pp. 582, 585. This is computed as a ratio to personal income. The author's unpublished estimates of personal consumption expenditures in 1900, comparable with the present Department of Commerce figures, were used. To these Goldsmith's total for personal saving (exclusive of consumer durables) from Historical Statistics, p. 262 was added, then rounded up to allow for personal taxes. The resultant figure is 1.8 percent.

21. U.S. Statistical Abstract (1978), pp. 612, 649. Historical Statistics . . . to 1970, p. 821. The rise was from 4 to 1,965 billion kilowatt-hours.

22. Fuel production plus net imports are derived from U.S. Statistical Abstract (1979), p. 746, and personal income from p. 440, giving a figure of 2.7 percent for 1973.

TABLE 40.5
OIL CONSUMPTION (PERCENT CHANGE)

	1965–73	1973–76
Japan	+ 14.3	− 5.0
France	+ 10.2	− 6.5
West Germany	+ 7.7	− 7.6
United Kingdom	+ 5.6	− 17.0
United States	+ 5.5	+ 1.0

Source: George P. Shultz and Kenneth Dam, Economic Policy Beyond the Headlines (1977), p. 188.

strate that priceless resources were being exhausted with mad speed. (Nor was the exiguous size of that increase attributable to the otherworldliness of oil well and coal mine owners.)

After 1973 two events occurred. OPEC price controls pushed up the price of petroleum and gas charged by Canada, Mexico, Saudi Arabia, Britain, and Venezuela. Owners of other fuels immediately jacked their prices up. By 1979 that cartel action had raised the share of income spent for energy at the wellhead from 3 percent of GNP—to 6 percent.[23] One supporting reason for even that much of a rise, however, was federal policy. The United States was the only major nation that continued to increase its oil consumption (Table 40.5), instead of cutting it markedly. Tight monopolies and cartels proved to be the conservationist's best friend. The International Bauxite Association, for example, sold the raw material for aluminum at something close to 60 percent above a competitive price. The OPEC cartel of the late 1970s extracted oil for a bit over $1 a barrel, sold it for $15.[24] With prices forced so far above competitive levels buyers cut down on natural resource use. They substituted other materials. Producers developed ways to use less per unit of output.

Government worked in the opposite direction. After 1960 the Federal Power Commission (FPC) kept down the price of natural gas. Producers were thereby attracted to the cheap supplies in the midwest, and set up plants to utilize natural gas instead of coal. (Gas consumption rose 100 percent from 1960 to 70; the number of exploration wells fell by 50 percent.) After OPEC turned the screws in 1973 Japan closed down its aluminum industry; it was too energy-intensive. The U.S. industry expanded, however. For by 1973 the FPC was ruling that gas equivalent in energy value to one barrel of oil (then selling in world markets for $12) had to be sold in the United States for

23. U.S. Statistical Abstract (1979), p. 746, and personal income from p. 440, giving a 5.6 percent figure.

24. These figures are from Partha Dasgupta and Geoffrey Heal, Economic Theory and Exhaustible Resources (1979), pp. 344, 351.

FIGURE 40.2
FUEL IMPORTS (QUANTUM 1970 = 100)

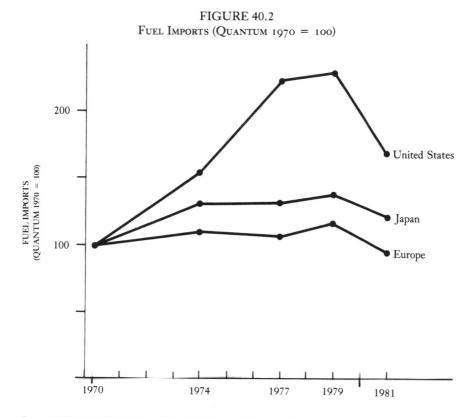

Source: *U.N. Monthly Bulletin of Statistics* (June 1982), p. xxvi.

$1.30. A boom of energy-intensive production in the United States was guaranteed. Meanwhile, competitive markets in Japan and Europe drove up their retail gasoline prices from 1974 on (see Figure 40.2.). Europeans and Japanese then drove their automobiles less, tuned their motors more often, produced less plastics from petroleum feedstock. The U.S. Congress was more euphoric. President Ford did propose a tax on imported oil, which would have decreased consumption. Congress instead legislated a 15 percent cut in gasoline prices. It thereby spurred consumption by OPEC's biggest single customer, validating OPEC's power. Not surprisingly, oil imports, less than 10 percent of consumption for decades, rose wildly, as shown in Table 40.6.

Pollution and Health

Almost as fast as the risk of death declined after the 1930s the remaining gap between an expectation of life of, say, 70 years and immortality increas-

TABLE 40.6
U.S. PETROLEUM CONSUMPTION
(PERCENT IMPORTED)

1940	3
1950	8
1960	11
1970	9
1979	44

Source: Shultz and Dam, *Economic Policy,* p. 188.

ingly became a political issue. The magic of human action was demonstrated by World War II production programs, expanded federal social programs in the 1960s, and the science fiction reality of sending men to the moon. Moreover, aggressive research led to pharmaceutical discoveries that abruptly ended the centuries-old reality of death from poliomyelitis, malaria, scarlet fever, smallpox, whooping cough. It became accepted that the material world could be manipulated at will.

It was only logical that possible deaths from nuclear explosions, and from air and water pollution, were next on the list for abolition. Proposals to do so induced much legislation. Given widespread agreement in the 1980s on the undesirability of pollution, one preliminary historical question must be raised. Where was everyone before *Silent Spring* appeared in 1962, before Earth Day in 1970? Were there no Americans with sensitive souls or endangered lungs? Was industrialism, or the pursuit of the dollar, so myopic that no one could be heard objecting to pollution? Whatever the truth of the implied answers, a set of historic facts must be noted for a realistic answer.

Prior to the 1930s Americans were attempting to reduce forces in the environment and workplace that were far more unpleasant, more widespread, and more deadly than recent threats. Instead of trying to preserve the Houston toad, or the snail darter, they were busy trying to save members of their own species. In 1850 some 31,506 Americans died from cholera.[25] By 1900 only 800 did. Between those two dates there occurred a massive expenditure on public sewage systems, and expansion of public garbage collection. In 1900 13,478 Americans died from typhoid. Even by 1930 9,013 did. By 1977 none did. Between those dates public water supply expanded further and water supplies all over the nation began to be chlorinated. In 1900 some 2,300,000 horses, pigs, and cattle littered the streets. (They also died there. In New York City alone 10,613 tons of dead animals were removed from the streets in 1903.) By the 1970s the number of such animals had not increased

25. Sources for the following data are from the Appendix C, this chapter.

with the increase in urban families. They had instead been reduced by at least 99 percent, thanks to huge investments all over the nation in trucks, meat packing plants, railroad refrigerator cars, retail store refrigerators and freezers. Figure 40.3 shows the spectacular long-term decline in U.S. death rates and the related fall in fertility rates).

Compared to such advances the number of lives to be saved in the 1970s, and illness to be reduced by striking at air pollution, at illness in the workplace, may seem slight indeed. But that task was clearly high on the social agenda of the 1970s. Legislated investments to improve health in the environment accelerated remarkably during the Nixon, Ford, and Carter administrations. From $18 billion in 1972 they reached $60 billion by 1981.[26]

Two policy problems surfaced almost at once. Both had major economic implications. The first was posed by the Environmental Protection Agency (EPA): "As the sensitivity of analytical methods [in chemistry] has improved, greater numbers of organic compounds" were found in water and air.[27] Chemists could once discover only 1 part of a chemical in 10 of water, then 1 in a thousand, then 1 in a million, then 1 in a billion. With each advance more chemicals were inevitably discovered in any body of air or water.

The economic consequences of the new view of health became most evident in the Clean Drinking Water Act. Since around 1910, water supplies have generally had chlorine added to them, at the urging of public health officials and others. Doing so from 1900 to 1970 saved thousands of people from dying of typhoid and other water-borne diseases. As late as 1965 a Nobel Prize winning biologist, writing about water pollution, described that accomplishment glowingly. It was one of which we can "be justly proud."[28] Yet less than a decade later newer analytic techniques became available. They revealed that chlorination produced trihalomethanes in drinking water. One analyst then speculated that chlorination might be causing some 36,000 deaths a year.[29] Optimizing "public health" could then require removing individual molecules from the billion-trillion molecules in each glass of water.[30] It might also require that individual molecules of benzene, and a thousand

26. *Survey of Current Business* (February 1983), pp. 16–17.

27. *Federal Register* (February 9, 1978), part 2, p. 5760.

28. Rene Dubos, *Man Adapting* (1965), pp. 200, 471.

29. Talbot Page, quoted in Richard Crandall and Lester Lave, *The Scientific Basis of Health and Safety Legislation* (1981), pp. 173, 215. Page estimates a low risk figure of only 3,650 deaths, and a high risk one of 65,700.

30. "A part per billion is clearly a very small number, but it still means roughly 100 million trillion molecules of the carcinogen per liter of water. There is evidence that cancers start from single cells and it is believed that a single molecule may be enough to start a cancer." Talbot Page, "A Generic View of Toxic Chemicals and Similar Risks," *Ecology Law Quarterly* (1978), no. 2, p. 222.

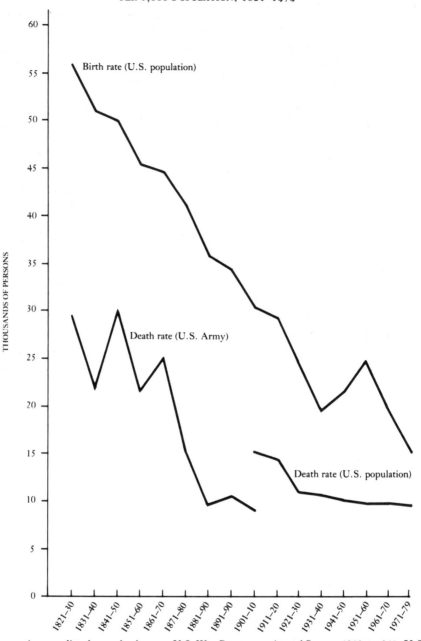

FIGURE 40.3
LIFE AND DEATH: LONG-TERM TRENDS IN U.S. BIRTH AND DEATH RATES
PER 1,000 POPULATION, 1821–1970

Birth rate (U.S. population)

Death rate (U.S. Army)

Death rate (U.S. population)

THOUSANDS OF PERSONS

1821-30 1831-40 1841-50 1851-60 1861-70 1871-80 1881-90 1891-90 1901-10 1911-20 1921-30 1931-40 1941-50 1951-60 1961-70 1971-79

Source: Army enlisted men death rates: *U.S. War Department Annual Reports, 1918,* p. 341. U.S. population death rates: Census, *Historical Statistics . . . to 1970,* p. 59; *1982 Statistical Abstract,* p. 60. Birth rates: 1820–1900, Mid-decade figures, from Irene Taeuber and Conrad Taeuber, *People of the United States in the Twentieth Century* (1971), p. 357; after 1900, Census, *Historical Statistics . . . to 1970,* p. 49, and *1982 Statistical Abstract,* p. 60.

516

other chemicals, be removed from the air.[31] The potentialities for increasing public investment to lower such risks were just short of infinite.

A second element was the increasing conflict between expenditure goals of different governmental agencies. To avoid deaths that may arise from drinking water did not require challenging half a dozen profit-making firms, but thousands of towns and cities who provided public water supplies. Faced by the immensity of the task, in 1978 the EPA settled for regulating less then 1 percent of the nation's water systems (serving half the nation's population), thereby preventing less than 1 percent of the deaths it forecast.[32] The other 99 percent of American cities and towns had been clearly put on notice of possible danger. Few of them, however, acted in the next half-dozen years. When it came to spending their own taxpayers' money some 40,000 cities and town councils apparently agreed that the threats seen by the EPA were courageously to be faced or were, indeed, trivial.

The Clean Air Acts (of 1963, 1965, 1967, 1969, 1970, 1971, 1973, 1974, 1977, 1980, 1981) created similar problems. Violators predictably included refineries, power plants, aluminum and steel companies. But they also turned out to include the U.S. government's national medical center, the Naval Ordnance Laboratory, the Puerto Rico Water Resources Authority, the cities of Boston, Marblehead, Lowell, Lawrence, Salem, the town of Eden in Vermont, and more. Plus four separate power stations of the federal Tennessee Valley Authority, the great nonprofit accomplishment of the New Deal.[33] Initial accomplishments in the private sector were noteworthy. EPA emission standards first applied to 1966 autos. By the 1970 models, "the industry had reduced hydrocarbon emissions by almost three-quarters and carbon monoxide emissions by about two-thirds."[34] Further reductions and other goals were then sought.

The beginning of economic choice models was becoming apparent. Data in reports by the Environmental Protection Agency and the Occupational Health and Safety Administration (OSHA) can be used to infer the expected count of lives to be saved, and money to be spent for compliance with each regulation; as shown in Table 40.7. If such differences in expenditure per life

31. From "the testimony of numerous scientists, the Secretary of Labor . . . concluded that a safe level of exposure to benzene had not been demonstrated. . . . "The testimony of . . . one of the world's leading experts was typical: 'Even one [part per million] . . . causes leukemia.'" *Industrial Union Department v. American Petroleum Institute*, 448 U.S. Sup. Ct. 700.

32. *Federal Register* (February 9, 1978), pp. 5764, 5775, statement of EPA Administrator Kimm. The regulation applied to 390 out of 40,000 water supply systems. Of those only 121 were expected to incur costs of change to exclude trihalomethanes or synthetic organics from the water they actually supplied to their users. A reduction of 322 cases was anticipated by the agency, according to Kimm in Crandall and Lave, *Scientific*, p. 239.

By 1983 the EPA had extended its coverage to a somewhat larger group.

33. Environmental Protection Agency, *Progress in the Prevention and Control of Air Pollution in 1974*, Appendix.

34. Environmental Protection Agency, *Annual Report to the Congress of the United States* (July 1971), pp. 2–3. That June, the EPA issued standards for nitrogen oxide emissions.

TABLE 40.7
LIVES SAVED AND COSTS (IMPLICIT AGENCY ESTIMATES)

	Lives saved annually	Expenditure per life affected (dollars)
EPA: drinking water	322	112,000
coke ovens	0.4	70,700,000
OSHA: benzene	211[a]	1,000,000+
hearing impairment[b]		1,500,000

[a]After 45 years.

[b]Persons affected.

Source: See Appendix B, this chapter.

affected were estimated by academics, such variation might be brushed aside as speculative. But these figures underly federal agency action. The agencies have stated how many lives their regulations are expected to save, and how much it was worth spending to do so. They required society to spend $70 million to save a life of Americans in one group, but only $112,000 in another. By reordering their criteria the agencies could very clearly have saved far more American lives for the same total expenditure.[35]

Social values are to be located "in the actions taken by society through its rules for making social decisions."[36] Was this indeed the new value system of the nation as it began its third century?

Worker Fatalities

The health of voters or consumers proved to be one major political concern of the 1970s. Another was their health as workers. To produce food, clothing, and delicacies all economies have sacrificed workers via occupational hazards. Few modern economies still kill many workers in the pursuit of wild animals for food, or by cholera in handling clothing taken from the dead. But industrial deaths, from such notable sources as coal mining accidents, still constitute a ghastly cost.

What can be said of trends in this human cost of production? When Congress passed the 1970 Occupational Health and Safety Act it saw a "grim his-

35. W. Kip Vicusi, "Labor Market Valuations of Life and Limb," *Public Policy* (Summer 1978), p. 379, notes that "additional lives could be saved if funds were reallocated so that the cost per life saved would be the same across different programs," but adds, "however [that] policy might not be optimal. . . ." We here take for granted the adequacy of agency figures. If one preferred data from the Federal Council on Price and Wage Stability, or industry, etc., the waters would be even murkier.

36. Kenneth Arrow, *Social Choice and Individual Values* (1963), p. 106.

TABLE 40.8
WORKER FATALITIES, 1900–79

	Coal mining	Railroads	All industries	
	(per million tons of coal mined)	(per hundred billion ton-miles of freight)	(per billion dollars of GNP— 1958 dollars)	Total fatalities
1900	5.5	4.4	182	14,000
1912	4.5	3.5	150	19,500
1979	0.2	0.1	7	6,300
Percent change, 1900–79	−97	−97	−96	−55

Source: Appendix D this chapter. Data on occupational injuries are ignored because they cover "any injury such as a cut, fracture . . . which results from a work accident or from exposure involving a single incident in the work environment." The precision with which records are kept for every cut, fall, has varied largely from decade to decade. Hence, there is little point in trying to measure trends 1900–1979, whatever the meaning of the data at any point.

Former Secretary of Labor Marshall stated that "over 33,000 were killed [in 1907] in all industrial accidents." F. Ray Marshall et al., *Labor Economics* (1980), p. 467. The decline to 1979 would, of course, have been still greater from that level.

tory of . . . failure to heed the occupational health needs of our workers."[37] Reviewing that legislation, the Supreme Court declared that "the failure of voluntary action and legislation at the state level had resulted in a 'bleak' and 'worsening' situation."[38] What in fact had occurred under "voluntary action and legislation at the state level"? Neither the Congress, nor the Court, referred to the facts on the "grim history" or "worsening situation." It may be serviceable to consider them.

We have data on the trend of fatalities in industries that accounted for about half of all industrial deaths in 1900—coal mining and railroads—and estimates can be made for workers in all industries. These are shown in Table 40.8.

With due respect to eminent justices and political leaders, the record does not reveal a "worsening" situation. It shows instead marked, even spectacular declines in fatalities. Americans sacrificed 5.5 workers in 1900 to extract each million tons of coal they consumed. Safety advances reduced that number by 97 percent by 1979. (Rates for Britain's coal industry ran slightly higher at both dates, and fell slightly less.) The number of railroad workers who died to carry each hundred billion ton-miles of freight was also reduced by 97 percent.

37. 92nd Cong., 1st sess., *Legislative History of the Occupational Safety and Health Act of 1970*, p. iii.

38. Justice Marshall in *Industrial Union Department v. American Petroleum Institute*, 448 U.S. Sup. Ct. at 691.

Two primary factors were at work. One was the advance in labor productivity: Fewer miners, fewer railroad workers were used to produce each additional unit of output. A second factor was also important: State workmen's compensation began to supplement tort law. In the single decade 1909–1919 most industrial states passed such laws under pressure from workers, unions, and such public interest groups as the National Consumers League. These laws imposed costs on firms for deaths linked to production. Firms were now obligated to carry insurance. Paid on a "no-fault" basis, that insurance typically gave the victims (or survivors) some compensation for industrial accidents, injuries, and disease. Firms then began to reduce their insurance premium costs—by installing machinery guards, by boiler inspections, care in training and supervising workers. That financial incentive helped bring a substantial and long-term decline in deaths. The pressure of unions in some industries provided a further force. But occupational injury and illness still occurred, defining a further important goal for workers, unions and a new participant, the Federal Occupational Health and Safety Administration, set up in 1970. The first five years of OSHA activity were concurrent with rises in premiums that insurance companies charged employers for workmen's compensation. As a result it is not clear how much OSHA cut industrial accident rates, if at all.[39] But the social concern was clearly expressed by both higher court awards for injuries (hence eventually higher insurance premiums on employers) and by the very formation of OSHA. Together these worked to change the environment in which injuries and death accompanied work.

Health

By 1970 the total number of deaths at issue was small. Among 2,000,000 U.S. deaths a year, not one known death had occurred from DDT exposure; not over two from nuclear power; and less than 1 percent (20,000), from all types of air pollution. But these became the center of public attention in the late 1960s, and the center of federal programs in the 1970s. By contrast, such major killers as cigarette smoking, alcohol, and fast motor vehicle usage were left untouched (see Table 40.9). Other nations did not follow a different policy. When was the failure of the tobacco crop cheered in Cuba, Nigeria, because lives would be saved? Or cigarette prices jacked up in Bulgaria, China,

39. One of the more extended studies arbitrarily attributes the entire decline to OSHA. It then finds that OSHA may have reduced the U.S. injury rate by 2 percent from 1970 to 1975. (John Mendeloff, *Regulating Safety* (1979), p. 117.) The total of "social losses" may have been less than the costs of additional investment in safety equipment, etc. (pp. 117–18). However, the estimated 40,000 workers not injured, and the social and political interests concerned with reducing rates, may well have found that comparison irrelevant.

A more developed study, by Ann Bartel, found that conformity to OSHA standards for equipment had little effect on injury rates. (Unpublished paper, National Bureau of Economic Research, 1982.)

TABLE 40.9
DEATHS IN 1967 LINKED TO SPECIFIED FACTORS

Cigarette smoking	300,000
Alcohol	56,000
Motor vehicles	55,000
Air pollution	18,000
Nuclear reactors	2
DDT	0

Source: Panel on Chemicals and Health, President's Science Advisory Committee, *Chemicals and Health* (1973), p. 35, and *Statistical Abstract of the United States*, (1978), p. 75. As of 1979 the smoking estimate was 346,000 deaths, according to the Department of Health, Education, and Welfare, *Smoking and Health, A Report of the Surgeon General* (1979), p. 11.

William Lowrance, *Of Acceptable Risk* (1976), p. 172, reported that "exposure to DDT [has] not produced any observable effect in controlled studies of volunteers." He adds: "Nor have massive occupational exposures or accidental ingestions, even by children, been known to cause a single death anywhere in the world in the thirty five years of DDT's history." A more accurate figure for DDT would be negative, reflecting the deaths from malaria that it prevented.

The nuclear reactor total relates to a later period, with somewhat more nuclear plants than 1967. Cf. U.S. Nuclear Regulatory Commission, *Reactor Safety Study* (October 1975), p. A-9.

Poland, or the Soviet Union to achieve that goal? What nation did not increase its use of motor vehicles as fast as was feasible? Moreover, effective speed limits in other countries generally exceeded those in the United States. It was hardly alone among world states, then, in hesitating to act on such major "controllable" causes of death.

At the same time, Congress initiated a program that spent billions to build better highways. By making higher speeds possible it increased highway fatalities. Doing so implicitly put a negative value on the lives of drivers. Congress then moved to advance safety by requiring cars to wear seat belts— but not drivers. In 1969 it required that miners who had developed pneumoconiosis had to be offered jobs in the safer, less dusty, area in the mines. Such jobs were paid less, for just those reasons, and fewer than 10 percent of the miners offered such jobs in the 1970s actually took them.[40] Congress did not act further. Even absolute political power has its limits. In practice, of course, no master plan guided Congress in its "health related" legislation. It was merely responding, as democratic practice required, to insistent demands by newswriters and constituent groups who urged particular policies.

40. Ronald G. Ehrenberg and Robert Smith, *Modern Labor Economics* (1982), p. 219.

While both public programs and private spending on health escalated, what of the trend in health—at least as crudely indexed by the death rate? (See Table 40.10.) The ten-fold spending increase from 1950 to 1975, a tripling in real dollars, did not obviously cut the death rate. New medications, procedures, surely accounted for most of the 1970–75 decline, rather than federal programs or private spending. Rising health expenditures and expanding programs are best seen, then, along with consumer expenditures in general as means to create desired psychic results. These they may indeed have helped to bring about.

As the nation began its first century the Reverend Abiel Holmes (grandfather of Oliver Wendell Holmes, Jr.) completed his history of the United States with the pious hope: "Under the same divine patronage may the prosperity of the United States be protracted until TIME SHALL BE NO LONGER." As the nation ended its second century prosperity had been protracted. But hopes had multiplied even faster, producing cross purposes, oddities, in the functioning of the economy.

Manufacturing production was more concentrated than ever before in dominant corporations.[41] Many a book had described how the wealthy, the "technostructure," controlled these corporations, and, through them, the economy. Yet for nearly a decade, from 1970 to 1980, these controllers accepted a falling rate of return on stocks representing the market value of those powers and those corporations. That return fell from its long-run level of 9 percent to almost precisely zero (0.001).[42] Meanwhile the world's most powerful communist nation paid its own capitalists a steady 3 percent rate of return.[43] In the same decade the Soviet Union was frequently unable to grow its own food, as required by its central plan. But the U.S. family farm—odd combination of individualism and federal support—produced enough to feed the United States, and ship millions of tons to the communist nations.[44]

41. With 8 percent of value added in 1900 (judging from employment data), the top 150 manufacturing corporations had 27 percent by 1947, 39 percent by 1977. (1977 Census of Manufacture, *Concentration Ratios in Manufacturing*, p. 9–7.) The smart money was moving into other fields; Kroc into Kentucky fried chicken, Ludwig into sand and gravel, Getty into oil. Concentration increased meteorically among those remaining in manufacturing: creamery butter (18 to 49 percent), chewing tobacco (56 to 81 percent), handbags (7 to 21 percent), etc., in various periods '935 to 1963. (*Concentration*, Table 7.)

42. Lawrence Summers, *Inflation and the Valuation of Corporate Equities* (NBER Working Paper 824). Summers finds that the tax treatment of inventories and depreciation accounted for "about half the underperformance of the stock market during the 1970's."

43. Soviet state bonds paid close to 3 percent while the inflation rate in the U.S.S.R. during 1965–76 was mild to nonexistent. *U.N. Yearbook of National Accounts Statistics, 1980* (1982), p. 1478. U.S. Joint Economic Committee, *Soviet Economies in a Time of Change* (1979) 1:787.

44. In 1979–80 the United States shipped 4 million tons of wheat to the U.S.S.R., 5 million to Eastern Europe, and 7 million to "other Asia"—chiefly China. U.S. Department of Agriculture, *Agricultural Statistics*, (1981), pp. 13–14.

TABLE 40.10

HEALTH EXPENDITURES AND DEATH RATE, 1950–80

	1950	1960	1970	1975	1980
Health expenditures (billions of dollars)	24	34	62	79	94
Death rate (per 1,000 persons)	9.6	9.5	9.5	8.9	8.9

Source: 1982 Statistical Abstract, pp. 73, 101. Expenditures are in 1967 prices.

From 1973 onward the United States worried about its dependence on foreign sources of energy, perhaps excessively. But it reduced its energy options (for fear of nuclear accidents). Meanwhile China planned for half a dozen giant nuclear plants in the 1980s.[45] And Russia operated an increasing number. (A single plant within the city of Leningrad generated 2 million kilowatts.[46])

Increasingly the American political process used economic resources to seek new types of goals, sometimes reaching unanticipated outcomes. After World War II the United States helped finance recovery in Europe. It also subsidized steel and auto production by its wartime enemies. In time such production by Germany, Japan, Britain cut into U.S. export markets. Moreover, Americans, as consumers, bought the cheaper foreign steel, and better autos. As voters Americans then became alarmed, voting to offset such gains — thus legislating for investors and workers in certain U.S. industries (at the cost of investors and workers in others).

Urging passage of the Constitution, James Madison declared: "The powers delegated . . . to the Federal Government are few and defined. . . . [They] will be exercised principally on external objects, as war, peace negotiations and foreign commerce, with which the last power of taxation will, for the most part, be connected." His list was far too parsimonious for a generation

---

Of total U.S. farm output in 1978, some 93% came from family farms or partnerships (15% from family-held corporations with ten or fewer stockholders). *U.S. Statistical Abstract (1982),* p. 653.

In 1921 Kamenev, about to sign the Anglo-Soviet trade agreement, declared: "With every additional shovel of coal . . . that we in Russia obtain through the help of foreign technique, capital will be digging its own grave." Quoted in George F. Kennan, *Russia and the West under Lenin and Stalin* (1961), p. 187. I. U. Annenkov has quoted Lenin to similar effect: capitalists, "by supplying us materials and technical equipment . . . will restore our military industry necessary for our future attacks against our suppliers." New York's *Novyi Zhurnal* (1961). I am indebted to Senator Daniel P. Moynihan for these quotations.

45. Rudi Volti, *Technology, Politics and Society in China* (1982), p. 172. In 1983 it was negotiating the construction of an 1.8 million kilowatt plant. *New York Times,* (April 12, 1983).

46. K. Roubal, "Congresses of Economic Parties about the Economic Theory of Socialism," *Czechoslovak Economic Papers* 18 (1982):10.

that sought to multiply public endeavors. Thus in 1980 over 750 distinct federal expenditure programs sought to achieve their separate purposes in the typical state. They ranged from dairy and beekeeper indemnity payments to ship operating differential subsidies. About 38,000 federal programs functioned in the fifty states.[47] Competing with one another for personnel, space, public support, what were their impacts on prices, wages, production? Who knew how well they achieved the 38,000 distinct congressional and executive goals? Or how many of those thousands of purposes conflicted with one another?

The complexities induced by high economic performance and ever multiplying public goals made it difficult to say where the American economy was headed. Those who saw it moving in a world committed to "the contrivance of havoc" could ask Figaro's question instead: "Who knows whether the world will last three weeks longer?" More confident Americans, looking back to two centuries of tough American achievement, could quote Yogi Berra: "It ain't over till it's over."

Appendix

Appendix A

Census poverty level: U.S. Census, *Characteristics of the Population Below the Poverty Level* (1979), Appendix A. Because the Census estimates not 1, but 124, threshold income levels (for families of different composition) it estimates 9 percent of families in poverty in 1979, which compares with our figures of 14 percent for "families below $7,500." The broad conclusions about the trend shown since 1900 probably would not differ significantly had more detail been available.

Income data, 1900, 1935–36: Lebergott, *The American Economy*, pp. 300, 321. 1929: *Survey of Current Business* (April 1958), p. 17. 1945ff: U.S. Bureau of the Census, *Current Population Reports*, Series P–60, No. 59 (Table 2), No. 129 (Table 12).

1979 Allowance for income in kind: Expenditure data from Timothy Smeeding, Bureau of the Census Technical Paper 50, *Alternative Methods for Valuing in-kind Transfer Benefits and Measuring Their Effect on Poverty* (1982), p. 3. Smeeding (p. 143) shows a poverty rate of 9.1 percent for family households in 1979 based on money income, reduced to 5.3 percent when allowance is made for the market value of in-kind items specified. We apply the ratio (9.1 percent ÷ 5.3 percent) to the 13.5 percent under $7,500 to adjust that percentage similarly. Some extension of benefits to the 28 percent of the poor persons who got none of them (Smeeding, p. 92) might cut the rate a further 1 percent or so.

Transfers, 1929ff: *The National Income and Product Accounts of the United States, 1929–76* and *Survey of Current Business* (July 1981), Table 2.1. 1900: Extrapolated from 1929 by data in Wesley Mitchell, ed., *Income in the United States* II (1922):216, 331.

---

47. U.S. Community Services Administration, *Geographic Distribution of Federal Funds in 1980* (1981).

Appendix B

EPA drinking water: *Federal Register* (February 9, 1978) statement indicated a $36 million cost per year in 1981. The assistant administrator who issued that statement later reported that the EPA estimated "the number of cancer cases avoided as a result of the promulgated regulation [was] 322 cases per year." Kimm in Crandall and Lave, *Scientific*, p. 239.

OSHA Coke Ovens: *Federal Register* (October 22, 1976), pp. 46742, 46749. OSHA estimated annual costs of $200 million, reducing excess mortality by 211 after 45 years. One can see how Administrator Kimm could refer seriously to an estimated cost of $158 million per life saved. Kimm in Crandall and Lave, p. 248.

OSHA Hearing Losses: The cost of removing a 25-decibel hearing loss accumulated over a 20-year span by affected workers. Cf. John Morrall in James Miller and Bruce Yandle, *Benefit Cost Analyses of Social Regulation* (1979), p. 50. If Congress were to decide that such hearing loss is in fact less of a catastrophe than the loss of a life, the expenditure per life implied in the OSHA regulation would have to be greater than $1.5 million.

EPA Benzene: EPA data summarized by Albert Nichols in D. Harrison et al, *Incentive Arrangements for Environmental Protection*, unpublished report to U.S. EPA (Jan. 19, 1981), pp. 238, 260.

Appendix C

Cholera, typhoid deaths: U.S. Census, *Mortality Statistics of the Seventh Census, 1850* (1855), U.S. Department of Commerce, *1930 Mortality Statistics* (1934); U.S. Department of Commerce and Labor, *Mortality Statistics, 1900 to 1904;* U.S. Department of Health and Human Services, *Vital Statistics of the United States* (1977), vol. II, "Mortality," part A, pp. 1–88.

Death rate in the U.S. Army: U.S. War Department, *Annual Reports* I (1918):341.

New York City animals: U.S. Census, *Bulletin 20* (1903).

Urban animals: Estimates for cities by population size group appear in 1900 Census, *Statistics of Agriculture*, vol. V, part I, Table 41. From these, and population data, rates were computed by type of animal and size of city. From these, extrapolations were made for the smaller city size groups.

U.S. population: Richard Easterlin, "American Population Since 1940," in *The American Economy in Transition*, Martin Feldstein, ed. (1980), p. 313. Fertility rates, white population: Ansley Coale and Melvin Zelnick, *New Estimates of Fertility and Population in the United States* (1963), p. 36.

Appendix D

Accident data: Fatalities and production data for coal and railroad transport appear in U.S. Census, *Historical Statistics . . . to 1970*, pp. 589–92, 607, 733, 740, and the *1981 Statistical Abstract*, pp. 613, 634, 728, 730.

Total fatalities in 1900 were estimated on the basis of data from the U.S. Bureau of Labor, Bulletin No. 8 (1908), p. 418. In that study, F. L. Hoffman, a leading actuary, states that "it is probably safe to estimate that half of the accidents" to gainfully occupied males in 1900 were "the direct result of [their] employment." His reference is to a rate of 1.13 for 1,000 in the registration states of 1900 as reported in the Census for that year. He increased that figure by 10 percent to allow for the limitation of the data to the "registration area" rather than the entire United States. We increased his estimate, for male deaths, to include those for females, by using data from the 1890 Census, *Vital Statistics*, part I, pp. 1007–9, 1025. From these one can compute a female ratio that is 10 percent of the male rate. Population weights are from the 1900 Census, *Occupations*, p. 1. Total fatalities in 1912 are estimated at 18,000 to 21,000, and at 14,300 in 1968 by the National Safety Council in 91st Cong., Senate Committee on Labor and Public Welfare, *Occupational Safety and Health Act, 1970 Hearings*, part 1, p. 573.

Total occupational fatalities and illness in industry in 1979 are reported by the Bureau of Labor Statistics in its Bulletin 2097, *Occupational Injuries and Illnesses in 1979: Summary*, Table 8. Its total—4,950—relates to all private employers with 11 or more employees. This was adjusted upwards by 1,010 to include the smaller employers, using unpublished BLS estimates based on the 1974–78 ratio of total fatalities to those for the 11-or-more groups. It was, however, necessary to include government employees as well. Since over 90 percent of government employees in 1980 were in public administration, education, or hospital employment (Cf. Bureau of Labor Statistics, *Employment and Unemployment* (1980), Table 26), this was done by applying the BLS fatality rate for finance, insurance, and real estate to the total for such employment. An alternative figure, for 1978, *(Statistical Abstract* (1981), p. 78) from the National Health Survey reported "industrial type accident" deaths of 5,168. That total includes deaths that were not job related—for example, home use of a chain saw—but excludes deaths related to occupational disease.

A largely different figure was used by the Secretary of Labor in testimony for the Occupational Safety and Health Act of 1970 (92nd Cong. 1st sess., Senate Committee on Labor and Public Welfare, *Legislative History of the Occupational Safety and Health Act of 1970*, p. 142). His source was the National Safety Council. (Letter from Secretary of State George Schultz., October 13, 1982.) Their estimates were derived before the probability survey of the BLS was initiated. The sharp difference in levels apparently testifies to claimants under workmen's compensation laws reporting a significant number of heart disease and motor vehicle accident victims as occupational fatalities, though the deaths were not occupationally related.

Gross national product figures (in 1958 dollars) for 1900 are from *Historical Statistics . . . to 1970*, p. 224, extrapolated to 1979 using data from the *1981 Statistical Abstract*, p. 421.

British coal mining data appear in Phyllis Deane and Brian Mitchell, *Abstract of British Historical Statistics* (1962), and U.K. Central Statistical Office, *Annual Abstract of Statistics in the United Kingdom, 1982*, pp. 205, 208.

Index

Aandahl, Andrew R., 22
Abramowitz, Moses, 60–61, 477, 507n
Adams, Donald, 73
Adams, John, 30, 33n, 49, 199, 470
   on Constitution, 54
Adams, John Quincy, 18, 94, 103
Adams, Samuel, 40, 50
Adams, Stephen, 228
Adelman, Irma, 65, 389n
advertising, brand, 319
Agricultural Adjustment Administration, 36n, 300,
   453, 456–58, 462
   export subsidy of, 458
   surplus reduction by, 457–58
agriculture, 411–12
   cooperation in, 302–5
   farm machinery and, 299–300, 320
   income levels and, 65, 69–70, 72, 305, 309–10
   incomes stabilized in, 481–83
   iron industry and, 131, 137–38
   labor inputs in, 268, 300–301
   manufacturing vs., 136–37
   money monopoly and, 304–5
   New Deal and, 456–58
   in 1920s, 438–40
   in Northeast, 202–3
   Northern vs. Southern, 65
   prices in, 301–2, 306–8, 320, 469, 481–83
   productivity trends in, 300–302, 439–40
   railroads and, 270–71, 275–76, 303–4
   regional differences in, 205–7, 298
   seed quality in, 165–68
   surplus reduction in, 457–58
   tariffs and, 140–41, 145–47, 149–50
   technology and, 165–68, 298–300
   in West, 205
   westward shift of, 297–98
   see also farmers; farms; sharecroppers
Agriculture Department, 411, 462
air pollution, 422–26, 429, 513–18
Akin, Warren, 242–43
Alexander VI, Pope, 9
Alger, General, 311
Allston, Robert, 145, 153
Almy and Brown, 130, 174
Amalgamated Association of Iron and Steel Workers,
   383

American Federation of Labor, 383, 385
American Medical Association, 371
American Tin Plate, 313–14
Ampsivarri, 17
Anaconda Copper Company, 414, 422
anaesthetics, 163
Anthony, David, 136
Appleton, Nathan, 130
Army, U.S., 261
Army Engineers, 91–92, 94, 102, 104, 109
Athenaeus, 139
Atlantic and Pacific Tea Company, 317
Austin, A., 22
Automobiles, 360, 433–37
   cities and, 360
   low prices for, 434–35, 439–40
   manufacturing productivity for, 435–36, 439–40
   pollution from, 425–26, 429

Bach, Lee, 475
Bacon, Francis, 9–10
Baker, George, 408
Baldwin, Loammi, 85–86, 178
Ball, Duane E., 24
Baltimore, Md., 104, 106
Baltimore and Ohio Railroad, 104, 106, 283
Bank of the United States, 116–17
Bank of the United States, second, 116–17
banks and banking, 121–23
   deposit insurance and, 447–48
   in Great Depression, 446–47, 460–61, 465
   local, 116–17
   as "money monopoly," 304–5, 408–9
   power of, 408–9
   regulation of, 481–84
   restrictionism by, 446
   state, 118–19
Baran, Paul, 311n, 319n, 394n
Barger, Harold, 318, 319n, 409n
Barnard, Charles, 356
Barnett, Harold, 418
Beard, Charles, 54, 251
Beard, Mary, 251
Bellow, Saul, 357
Birkbeck, Morris, 86
births and birth rates, see children

blacks, freed, *see* freedmen
Bland-Allison Act, 456
Bogue, Allan, 84*n*, 122*n*, 304*n*, 305*n*, 306*n*
bonds, 120, 458
Boone, Daniel, 40
Borah, Woodrow, 13*n*, 20*n*
Borel, Emile, 201
Boston Manufacturing Company, 130, 135
Bostwick, Jabez, 329
Bowley, Arthur, 449
Brady, Dorothy, 69
Bragg, Braxton, 233, 236
Braidwood, R. J., 21–22
Brandeis, Louis, 408–9
bridge construction, 346
British Board of Trade and Plantations, 32
Brougham, Lord, 126–29
Bryan, William Jennings, 269, 308
Buchanan, James, 69
Burke, Edmund, 24, 359
Burlington Railroad, 278–79
Butler, Pierce, 145

Cabot, George, 130
Calhoun, John C., 94, 228
  on tariffs, 146–47
California, settlement of, 227
Canada, 40, 418
canals, 98
  cost of, 102
  early, 101
  losses from, 108
  railroads vs., 107–12
  social cost of, 114–15
  speed on, 109–11
Capitalist Guide for 1859, The, 102
Caribbean, 45
  post-emancipation production in, 249
  slavery in, 201
Carnegie, Andrew, 291, 312–13, 348, 354, 407
cartels, 310–13, 362
  oil industry and, 325–29
  railroad, 285–88, 292, 325–26
  shipping rebates for, 291, 325–26
  see also Standard Oil Trust; trusts and monopolies
Catholics, Quebec Act and, 40
Central Pacific Railroad, 107
chain stores, 317
Charles II, king of England, 33, 39
Cherokee Nation, 20
Chevalier, Michael, 179, 181
children, 191–92, 368, 489
  cities and, 364–65
  family control over, 364–65
  of immigrants, 343
  in labor force, 369–70
  life expectancy of, 193–94
  as "producer's goods," 194
  quality of life for, 193
China, 100, 393, 426
Choate, Rufus, 407
cities, 357–65
  alienation in, 364
  automobiles and, 360
  children in, 364–65

construction materials in, 362
  countryside vs., 357–58
  disease control in, 360–62
  economic sectors in, 363–64
  electricity and, 359–60, 363
  expanding municipal facilities in, 360–62
  fire protection in, 362–63
  growth, 357–65
  immigration and, 186, 340–41
  labor opportunities in, 359
  rail freight rates and, 360
  reasons for migration to, 358–60
  regional growth and, 205–7
  social diversity in, 359
  suburbs of, 365
  transportation in, 363
Civil War, 89, 233–48
  aftermath of, 246–48
  destruction in, 243–45
  groups benefiting from, 245
  groups hurt by, 246
  incomes in, 246
  inflation during, 306–7
  manpower in, 239
  Northern vs. Southern economies in, 240–43
  prices in, 246
  see also Confederate States of America; Southern
    secession
Clark, George, 19
Clay, Henry, 94, 98, 99
  tariffs and, 147, 148
Clean Air Acts, 517
Clean Drinking Water Act, 515
Cleveland, Grover, 404
clothing, prices for, 468
coal:
  central heating and, 424
  conservation of, 418
  mechanical stokers for, 423–24
  natural gas vs., 424–25
  pollution from, 422–25
Coale, Ansley, 191*n*, 195*n*
coal oil, 322–23
Colombia, agrarian reform in, 18
colonies, American, 21, 30–38
  administration of, 32*n*
  British policy toward, 74
  development in, 31–32
  exports from, 32–38
  fur trading in, 31
  military protection of, 33–34
  Molasses Acts and, 33*n*
  Navigation Acts and, 33–34
  net burden on, 33–35
  planned societies in, 31
  population density of, 30
  representative assemblies in, 30–31
  subsidies to, 33–35
  taxation of, 39–40
  total income of, 35
  see also Revolution, American
colonists, American:
  European culture of, 25–27
  farm ownership by, 30–32
  independent characteristics, 30–31

land purchase available to, 27
livelihoods of, 30, 32
origins of, 25–27
Columbus, Christopher, 8
Common Sense (Paine), 404
communism, 88
Communist Manifesto, The (Marx and Engels), 88
Confederate States of America (CSA), 233
clothing supplies of, 241–42
food supplies of, 241
imports of, 242
impressment in, 243
military experience in, 239
monetary goals in, 243
munitions sources of, 240–41
physical capital destroyed in, 243–45
railroads in, 245
real estate values in, 244
slavery and, 234, 242–43
see also Southern secession
Confederation, 48–54
debt to soldiers of, 49–51, 54–56
financial power lacking for, 53–54
frontier security and, 51–52
private debts and, 52–53
states' revenue sought by, 48–49
taxing policy of, 48
Congress, U.S., 106–7, 339, 341, 452, 513, 518–19
bounty warrants from, 226, 269
under Confederation, 49–51
conservation and, 430
freedmen's property and, 251–52
immigration ended by, 434
Industrial Commission of, 316, 323–24, 330, 404
land sold by, 27, 77–81, 116
national transportation plan and, 104, 106–7
Pujo committee of, 408–9
safety legislation in, 283, 518–19, 521
state debts and, 120
veterans' commutation certificates issued by, 50–51, 54–56
World War II and, 466
Congress of Industrial Organizations (CIO), 479
Conrad, Alfred, 216–17
conservation, 410–30
of animal species, 427–28
by resource buyers, 416–20
incomes and, 428–30
methods of, 430
national park system and, 428–29
of non-privately owned resources, 420–30
of "one-of-a-kind" resources, 426–29
prices and, 412–15, 419–20
reserves, 411–12
waste reduction, 414–16
Conservation Commission, 273
Constitution, U.S., 54–56
slavery in, 211
Constitutional Convention, 54–56, 212
consumers, 69, 390–93
authenticating institutions for, 317
credit for, 436–38
distribution network and, 317–20
freedom of, 390–93
in Great Depression, 450

information for, 316–17, 319
money monopoly and, 409
new transport modes and, 100
in post-World War II transition, 471
rising incomes and, 490–93
slaves as, 101
Standard Oil and, 333–34
tariffs and, 148–50
trusts and, 315–16
Continental Congress, 39, 41–43, 49–50
land distribution and, 77
Revolutionary inflation and, 41–42
Cook, Sherburne, 13n, 20n
cooking, trends in, 67–68
Coolidge, Calvin, 439
Cooper, William, 24
copper, 414
corn, 166, 267
immigration and, 338–39
regional differences in, 206
corporations,
concentration, 310–16, 321
new, 1800–30, 126–31
cotton, 63–64, 201–2
baling of, 170–71, 177
boll weevils and, 301–2
British market for, 63, 201
export subsidy for, 458
in 1920s, 440
production of, after emancipation, 249–50, 300
raw, tariff on, 145–47, 152–54, 158, 160
regional differences in, 205–7
seed quality and, 167–68, 176
sharecroppers and, 262, 264–65, 267
slaves and, 63, 167–68, 170, 176–77
U.S. market for, 63–64
cotton gin, 168–70, 173, 177
Coulter, E. M., 235n, 236n, 237n, 239n, 241n
Cousteau, Jacques, 427–28
cows, milk yield of, 167
crashes and crises, financial:
of 1779–80, 46
of 1819, 80
of 1839, 119
crash of 1929, 409, 436–38, 442, 444–45
call rates and, 444–45
events preceding, 445
risk premium and, 444
see also Depression, Great; recessions and depressions
credit:
consumer, 436–38
in 1920s, 432, 436–38
outside banking system, 121–22
from railroads, 270, 275
see also interest rates
Cree Indians (Quebec), 15
Crèvecoeur, Hector St. John de, 11
crime, 115–16
Cross, Robert, 23
crown lands, 75–76
cycles, economic, 393–99, 474–75
income and, 397–99
overall activity and, 395–96
production growth and, 397–98

cycles, economic (*continued*)
    unemployment and, 397–99, 495–97
Czechoslovakia, 26

Danhof, Clarence, 86
Danton, George, 45
Darrow, Clarence, 456
Daum Arnold, 327*n*, 329*n*
David, Paul, 60–61, 62*n*
Davis, Jefferson, 164, 235, 241, 277
Davis, Lance, 28*n*, 125*n*, 191*n*, 208*n*, 273*n*, 316,
    354*n*, 377*n*
death rates, 382–83, 518–26
De Bow, James, 22–23, 158
DeCanio, Stephen, 302
Defense Department, 473–74, 503–5
defense spending, 19–20, 473–74
    tariffs and, 143
    in World War II, 467
Denevan, William, 23
Denison, Edward, 507
department stores, 317
deposit insurance, 447–48, 481
Depression, Great, 442, 444–63
    banks in, 446–47, 460–61, 465
    beginning of, 445–46
    consumers in, 450
    fiscal policy in, 448–50, 452, 458–59
    GNP in, 459
    investment in, 451–52
    monetary policy in, 446–48, 460–61
    money supply in, 446, 459–61
    public works programs in, 449–50, 463
    savings lost in, 447, 451, 465
    taxes in, 458–59
    unemployment in, 448–50, 463–65
    wages in, 448–51
depressions, *see* recessions and depressions
de Stael, Mme., 17
DeVore, Irven, 8*n*, 12*n*, 21*n*
distribution, retail, 316–20
    local laws concerning, 320
    retail stores and, 317–18
door to door salesmen, 318–19
Douglas Democrats, 229
Douglass, Frederick, 259
Drew, Daniel, 282
Dubois, Raphael, 178, 297
DuBois, W. E. B., 255, 261, 263
Dunbar, Paul Laurence, 249
DuPont, E. I., 166, 174
Durand, John, 10

Early, Jubal, 196, 233
Earth Day, 429
Easterlin, Richard, 28*n*, 190, 208, 209*n*
East Germany, 391
economic decisions, 388
economic growth, 60–63, 434–35, 441
    capital input in, 61–62
    costs of, 61–63
    Indians and, 8, 59
    investment and, 64
    labor input in, 60–61

outlook needed for, 8
    rate of, 59
    social matrix and, 63
    staple theory of, 63–64
    see also productivity
economic shocks, 389–90
Edison, Thomas A., 173, 351, 356
Eisenhower administration, 473
electricity, 335, 351–56
    cities and, 359–60, 363
    costs reduced by, 352–53, 355
    home use of, 351–52, 356
    resistance to, 351–53
    street lighting with, 355–56
    water and steam power replaced by, 354–55
Eliot, T. S., 85
Elkins Act (1903), 292
Ellsworth, Oliver, 49
Emery, Lewis, 330
Employment Act (1946), 473
energy, 511–13
    see also specific sources
Engels, Friedrich, 88, 227–28, 395
Engerman, Stanley, 125*n*, 131*n*, 132*n*, 208*n*, 209*n*,
    218*n*, 220*n*, 225*n*, 247*n*, 254*n*
Engineering News, 311
England, *see* Great Britain
entrepreneurs, 63, 125, 403–4
    consumer freedom and, 390–93
    public restraint of, 403–4
Environmental Protection Agency (EPA), 422,
    515–17, 525
Erie Canal, 104–8, 111, 114, 119
    competition to, 105, 288–89
    North Central States and, 203
Erie Railroad, 278, 282, 289
Europe:
    birth rate in, 19
    1848 revolutions in, 88, 227
    eighteenth-century life in, 25–27
    farm size in, 13–15, 180
    opportunity lacking in, 181–82
    U.S. railroads and, 280–81
Evans, Oliver, 173, 376
Evans, Robert, 216*n*, 219*n*
executions, 25–26
exports, 125–26, 201–2, 458
    British market for, 32–35, 45, 63, 146–47
    to France and Netherlands, 33, 45
export tariffs, 49

families:
    boarders/lodgers and, 369, 490
    debt of, 436–38
    gainful work done in, 370
    income gains and, 490–91
    size of, 191–93
    see also children; housewives
farmers, 12, 305
    capital savings of, 61
    Civil War and, 245
    complete land use sought by, 17–19
    freed blacks as, 253–60
    hunters vs., 12–17, 20–21
    Indians as, 15, 17

as land speculators, 17
net worth of, 309–10
political parties of, 308–9
transport availability and, 93, 270–71, 275–76, 303–4
see also agriculture
Farmers' Alliance, 303
farms:
average size of, 17
of colonists, 30–32
exports from 44–45
hauling crops and, 270–71, 275 76
mortgages on, 305–8, 320
real value of, 309–10
see also agriculture
Faulkner, William, 238
Federal Deposit Insurance Corporation, 481
Federal Gazette, 125
Federal Housing Administration (FHA), 485
Federal Power Commission (FPC), 512
Federal Reserve Act, 446–47
Federal Reserve System, 431, 442, 445–47, 459, 474, 483–84
panics and, 446
Field, James, 192–93
finance system, 115–23
railroads and, 112–13, 279
see also banks and banking; investment
financial regulation, 481–85
Fink, Albert, 289
fiscal policy, 448–50, 452, 458–59
responsiveness in, 476
fishing industry, 199
conservation in, 420–21
Fishlow, Albert, 64n, 99n, 109n, 112n, 273n, 278n, 282n, 283n, 284n, 351n
Fisk, Jim, 282
Floyd, James, 240
Fogel, Robert, 64n, 99n, 107n, 109n, 111n, 125n, 131n, 132n, 208n, 209n, 218n, 220n, 225n, 247n, 254n, 278n
food:
cost of, 69, 469
in Revolution, 41
see also specific foods
Ford, Gerald R., 513, 515
Ford, Henry, 358, 376, 435–36
Forest Service, 411
Forstall, Edmund, 153
Forster, E. M., 345
France, 179
American colonies of, 21
American exports to, 33, 45
eighteenth-century, 26
pirates and, 37
Revolution in, 45–46
Frasch, Herman, 331
Freedman's Bureau, 261
freedmen, 249–67
borrowing by, 253–54, 262–63, 266–67
ex-slave holders and, 258–61
as farmers, 253–60
Freedman's Bureau and, 261
as homesteaders, 254–55
income of, 260–61

as laborers, 253, 260
land ownership choices, 253–55
merchant monopolies and, 261–67
plantations divided among, 250
post-war production levels and, 249–50
property expected by, 250–53
renting by, 255
as sharecroppers, 252–53, 255–67
whites as competitors to, 260
see also slaves, slavery
French and Indian War, 21, 37, 74
Friedman, Milton, 446n, 460n, 461n, 469n, 475
Fulkerson, H. S., 241
Fulton, Robert, 107, 172, 175

Galbraith, John K., 390n, 407n, 441n, 463n, 471n, 508n
Gallatin, Albert, 85, 94–97, 103–4, 116, 125
Garden of Proserpine (Swinburne), 388
Gates, Paul, 74n, 78n, 80n, 81n, 83n, 165n, 199n, 207n, 263n, 272, 274n
Gayer, Arthur, 450
Genovese, Eugene, 224–25
George, Henry, 312, 412
George III, king of England, 46, 75
Georgia, 20, 31, 144, 259
crop lien law in (1867), 263
crown lands and, 76
Germany, 18–19, 391, 407
Gibbs, Willard, 163
Gipson, Lawrence, 36n, 40n
gold and silver, 203–4, 403
Goldin, C., 243–44, 246n
gold standard, 448, 460
Gompers, Samuel, 385
goods in transit, interest on, 98–99
Goodyear, Charles, 135–36
Gordon, Robert Aaron, 461
Gould, Jay, 358
government:
authority asserted for, 404
in Great Depression, 448–50, 452
investment and, 115–17, 120
public works programs of, 449–50, 463, 473
Grand Banks, fishing rights in, 199
Grand Trunk Railroad, 283
Granger Laws, 303
Grant, Madison, 428
Grant, Ulysses S., 251
Great Britain, 21, 179–80, 407
Civil War in, 33
class in, 370–71
colonial administration in, 32n,
colonial debts to, 36
colonial exports sought by, 32–35
colonies subsidized by, 33–35
cotton exports to, 63, 146–47
eighteenth-century, 25–26
Enumeration Acts of, 35
gold standard abandoned by, 448
Indians and, 40
Merchants in, 36
Navigation Acts of, 33–34
post-Revolutionary trade with, 45
slavery and, 201

Great Britain (continued)
    textile industry in, 126–29
    U.S. exports ordered seized by, 125–26
    U.S. frontier and, 51
    U.S. tariffs and, 112, 149–50, 156
    wheat tariff of, 112
    see also colonies, American; England; Revolution,
        American; Scotland
Great Western Territory, 74
Greeley, Horace, 238
Greenback Party, 308
Greenville, Treaty of, 85
Gross National Product (GNP):
    in Great Depression, 459
    railroads and, 281
    stagnation in, 494–95
Guadeloupe Hidalgo, Treaty of, 227

Hacker, Louis, 268
Hamilton, Alexander, 55, 76, 117, 125 on tariffs,
    140, 143, 145
Hancock, John, 33
Hand, Learned, 336
Hansen, Alvin, 494
Hansen, Marcus, 184n, 185n, 343n
Hardin, John J., 85
Harper, Robert, 77
Hartford, Conn., 106
Hasson, William, 326
Haugen, Gilbert, 439
Hawkins, Hiram, 263
health, 513–18, 520–23
    chlorinated water and, 515
    death rate and, 514–15, 522–23
    government expenditures and, 515–18, 520–23
    occupational fatalities, 502–26
    pollution and, 515–18
Hearst, William Randolph, 450
heating, household, 65–67
Heilbroner, Robert, 393–94
Henderson, Hubert, 430
Henderson, Leon, 469
Henderson, Richard, 40
Henry, Patrick, 36, 40, 78
Herbert, Victor, 114
highway development, 97–98, 101, 104, 521
Hill, Benjamin, 235
Hoan, Daniel, 448
Hodgson, Adam, 218
Holland Land Company, 78
Holmes, Abiel, 522
Holmes, Oliver Wendell, 55
Home Owners Loan Corporation, 483
Homestead Act (1862), 79, 251–52, 268–74
    defects of, 272–73
    fraud and, 273–74
    generosity of, 272
    specifications of, 269
    supervision of, 273–74
homesteading, 269–71
    by freedmen, 254
Hoover, Herbert, 438–39, 447
Hopkins, Harry, 463
House of Representatives, 106–7

housewives:
    appliances and, 368–69
    rising incomes and, 368
    time use by, 489–90
    working, 489–90
housing,
    investment in, 485
Howells, William Dean, 358
Hughes, Jonathan, 41n, 42n, 63n
hunters and fishers, 12, 20–22, 199
    farmers vs., 12–17, 20–21
Hutchinson, E. P., 189n, 343

Illinois Central Railroad, 93, 102–3
immigrants and immigration, 15–19, 78–90, 337–44
    children of, 343
    children as motive for, 182
    cities and, 186, 340–41
    destinations of, 185–86, 339–41
    diseases brought by, 183
    economic instability from, 188
    economic opportunity and, 89, 178, 181–82
    European prospects and, 178–80, 337–38
    food as motive for, 180–81
    incomes and, 188–89
    indentures and, 184–85, 190
    in labor force, 373–75
    labor union opposition to, 341, 385, 434
    limitations on, 189–90, 339
    market expansion and, 64, 190
    mechanization and, 342
    numbers, 187–88, 190
    occupations of, 189, 340–44, 373–75
    origins of, 338–40
    as percent of population, 190
    permanence of, 179, 344, 367
    post-Civil War, 339–40
    reasons for, 10–11, 178–82, 337–39, 509
    regional growth and, 209
    religious freedom and, 182
    repression and, 343
    shipboard deaths and, 182–83
    slavery and, 185
    South avoided by, 185–86, 227–28, 340
    transfer costs in, 184, 187–88, 339
    U.S. wheat and corn production and, 338–39
    wages and, 188–89, 341, 381
imperialism, 405–6
imports, 126–29, 131–33
    of petroleum, 512–14
    see also tariffs
income, national:
    of colonies, 35
    labor share of, 431–32
    railroads and, 111–12
income distribution, 71–73, 496–501
    bottom of, 498
    inequality in, 407–8, 496–500
    post-1900 (table), 498
    taxes and, 407–8, 499–500
incomes:
    in agriculture, 65, 69–70, 72, 305, 309–10
    in Civil War, 246
    conservation and, 428–30

economic cycles and, 397–99
farm vs. nonfarm, 309
of freedman, 260–61
growth of, 60, 434–35
housewives and, 368
immigration and, 188–89
increases in, 489–90
per capita, 28–29
productivity increases and, 489–90
in Reconstruction period, 260
regional differences in, 208–9
of sharecroppers, 258–59
tariffs and, 148, 157–58
see also wages
income tax, 406–8, 474
income inequality and, 407–8, 499–500
origins of, 406
as revenue source, 407
withholding of, 474
indentured servants, 184–85, 190
Indians, 7–9, 12–16, 19–20
British promises to, 40
conservation and, 420
economic growth and, 8, 59
family income of, 7–8
as farmers, 16, 17
land requirements of, 13–16, 22
population decline of, 13, 59n
public domain settlement and, 82–83
slaves of, 210
societies created by, 7
indigo, 201–2
Industrial Commission, 316, 323–24, 330, 404
industrialization:
Civil War and, 247
population growth and, 195–96
see also technology
inflation, 377, 476, 502–5
during Civil War, 306–7
government policies and, 503–5
during Revolution, 41–42
innovation, economic, 61–63
cost of, 62–63
receptiveness to, 61–63
instability, economic, 188, 390–93, 495–96
interest rates, 114–17, 120, 135, 350, 484
call rate as, 444–45
crime and, 115–16
on farm mortgages, 306–8
on goods in transit, 98–99
manufacturing and, 135
money monopoly and, 304–5
in Reconstruction, 252
sharecropping and, 262–63, 266–67
on slave sales, 214–15
Western migration and, 84
International Economic Association, 495
International Marine Company, 314
International Workers of the World (IWW), 88, 384
Interstate Commerce Commission (ICC), 282, 287–88, 293–96, 315, 357
Interstate Commerce Commission Act (1887), 292–93
Intolerable Acts, 40

investment, 64, 114–23
consumption vs., 114–15
costs of, 350–51
crime and, 115–16
depreciation in, 350
early immigrant view of, 8–9
equity and, 477–78
by Europeans, 117–20
Federal government and, 115–17, 120
foreign, 278–79, 405–6
in Great Depression, 451–52
in housing, 485
in inventories, 115
life expectancy of, 350–51
in manufacturing, 125–26, 130
New Deal and, 461–62
in oil industry, 330
planned obsolescence and, 346
in planned vs. free economies, 390–92
in post-World War II transition, 471
private, 121–23
productivity of, 114–15
profit expectations and, 389–90
regional attractions of, 205
regulation and, 484
in slavery, 213–18, 220–21, 237
in South, 117–19, 213–18, 220–21, 237
by state governments, 117–20
in stock market, see stock market
technology and, 346, 349–51
in transcontinental railroads, 277–78
Iowa Railroad, 271
Iredell, James, 55–56
Irish potato famine (1845–47), 111, 227
iron industry, 111, 115
domestic market for, 130–31
farming and, 131, 137–38
tariffs and, 147–50, 158
Isaac, Glynn, 23
Is the Business Cycle Obsolete? (International Economic
Association), 495
Italy, 339

Jackson, Andrew, 20, 83, 94, 117, 122
on slavery, 211
Jackson, Shirley, 357
James, Henry, 163, 366
James River and Kanawha Company, 106
Japan, 61–63
Jarvis, William, 166
Jay, John, 94
Jefferson, Thomas, 19, 32, 56, 76, 97, 122, 125, 357
on tariffs, 143
Johnson, Andrew, 250–51, 252n
Johnson, Herschel, 235
Johnson, Hugh, 455
Johnson, Samuel, 312
Johnson, Tom, 363
Jones, Alice, 30n, 32n, 71, 73, 93n
Josephson, Matthew, 331–32
Justice Department, 314

Kaldor, Lord, 155
Kearney, Denis, 385

Keith, Sir Arthur, 22
Keynes, John Maynard, 381n, 455, 502–3
Keynesianism, 458, 472–73
Kindleberger, Charles, 442n, 445n, 447n
King, Thomas, 98
Kirkland, Edward, 285n, 290n
Kirkland, Joseph, 297
Klein, Judith, 208n, 264n
Klein, Lawrence, 432
Klondike, 403
Knights of Labor, 384
Knights of the Golden Circle, 258, 260
Koopmans, Tjalling, 62
Korean War, 473
Krueger, Ivar, 442
Ku Klux Klan, 254, 258, 260

labor force, 63, 134–35, 366–87
    allocation of, 366–67
    apprentices in, 371–72
    capital equipment and, 367
    children in, 369–70
    class perspectives and, 370–73
    distribution of, 65–66
    earnings of, see wages
    hours of work for, 68–69, 383
    immigrants in, 373–75
    in manufacturing, 134–35, 321
    mobility of, 372, 377, 379–81
    national income share for, 431–32
    as percentage of total population, 367–68
    in post-World War II transition, 472
    productivity of, 366–67, 377–79, 387
    strikes by, 282, 379, 384
    supervision of, 373–76
    technological obsolescence and, 372–73
    in trade, 318
    training of, 370–72
    unemployment insurance and, 473, 478–79
    unskilled vs. skilled, 382
    women in, 195, 249, 367–69, 489–90
    working conditions of, 373–77, 381–83
labor unions, 88, 282–83, 383–87
    history of, 383–85
    immigration opposed by, 341, 385, 434
    impact, 479–81
    membership expansion, 479
    popularity of, 385–87
    prices and, 475
    skilled workers in, 383–84
    wages and, 480
LaFollette, Robert, 315
land, 118, 268–74
    auctions of, 273
    Congressional sale of, 27, 77–81, 116
    conservation of, 420
    food yield of, 22–24
    idleness rejected for, 17–19
    as payment for soldiers, 19
    railroad revenues and, 270–71, 275
    rents for, in Reconstruction, 252–53
    Revolutionary confiscation of, 46–47
    sale of, vs. homesteading, 269–71
    see also Homestead Act; public domain
land offices, 77, 79

land requirements, 13–16, 22–24
land speculation, 17
land value, 16–17, 35–36, 77–78, 350
    in CSA, 244
    post-Revolutionary deflation and, 52–53
    public domain settlement and, 84, 87
    railroads and, 93, 270–71, 274
    transport availability and, 93
    after World War I, 438–39
La Salle, Réné Robert, 21
Lawrence, D. H., 85
lawyers, Stamp Act opposed by, 39
lead mining, 416–17
Leake, Richard, 169–70
Lease, Mary, 268, 302
Lee, Arthur, 54
Lee, Richard, 8n, 12n, 21n
Lee, Robert E., 235–36
Leiter, Joseph, 414
Lemon, James T., 24
Lenin, V. I., 311, 366, 405
Lewis, F., 243–44, 246n
Lewis, H. Gregg, 480
Liberty Bonds, 471
Liberty League, 458
life expectancy, 193–94
lighting, household, 67
Lincoln, Abraham, 93, 233, 235, 238
living conditions, 65–72
Livingstone, Robert, 173
London, Jack, 403
Louisiana Territory, 21, 76, 203
Lowell, Francis, 146
lumber and timber:
    buyer conservation of, 417–18
    paper and pulp use and, 418
    quality decline in, 417–18
    scarcity rents for, 414–15
    shortage forecast for, 411
    waste reduction for, 414–15, 417–18
    withholding of, from market, 412–15
Luxemburg, Rosa, 303n, 311

MacAvoy, Paul, 275n, 292n, 294
McCormick, Cyrus, 91, 300, 358
McDonough, John, 219
McDougall, James, 98–99
McDuffie, George, 185
machinery industry, 136
Maclay, William, 142–43
McNary, Charles, 439
Macune, C. E., 456
Madison, James, 50, 55, 523
mail order houses, 317
Main, Jackson T., 46–47, 71n
Maine, land purchases by, 78
manifest destiny, 18
manufacturing, 64–65, 124–37
    agriculture vs., 136–37
    economic linkages and, 136
    foreign competition and, 126–29, 131–33
    home production vs., 132–35
    import/export interruptions and, 125–26
    interest rates and, 135
    investment in, 125–26, 130

labor in, 134–35, 321
markets and, 130–31
new products in, 135–36
obsolescence and, 136
quality of, 136
rise of, 130–37
tariffs and, 140–41, 147–48
transport costs and, 134–35
trusts in, 316
workday in, 68–69
markets:
    growth of, 63–64, 130–31
    immigration and, 64
    manufacturing and, 130–31
    Revolution and, 44–45
Marshall, Alfred, 277, 381
Marshall, John, 20
Martineau, Harriet, 86, 189
Marx, Karl, 88, 227–28, 370, 384, 389, 393, 395
Maryland, 31–32, 75
Mason, George, 36, 41
Massachusetts, 30–31
    Erie Canal and, 105
    land values in, 78
    Maine split from, 78
    trade vs. manufacturing in, 126–27
Massachusetts Railway, 105
mass marketing, 331–34, 432, 434–38
mass production, 300, 304, 311–34, 434–36
Maxim, Hudson, 193
Meade, Richard, 236
Melville, Herman, 322, 403
Memminger, G. G., 233
Mennonites, 31
Mercer, George, 198
merchants:
    British, 33–39
    colonial, 42–43, 52
    distribution, 316–20
    monopolies, 262–67
    transport and, 92, 107–8, 288–90
Mexican War, 226–27
Mexico, 430
Meyer, John, 216–17
Middle Atlantic states, 84
migration, 84–90, 298
    Indians and, 82–83, 85
    interest rates and, 84
    land values and, 84, 87
    land warrants and, 227–28
    of production, 44–45
    rates of, regional, 82–83
    reasons for, 87–88
    in recessions and depressions, 88–89
    as safety valve, 88
    transport costs and, 90
    wages and, 84, 87–89
    work done during, 86
Mill, John Stuart, 181–82, 238, 371
Mincer, Jacob, 480
mining, 64, 416–17, 521
    coal, fatalities in, 519–20
    prices and, 418
    safety in, 418
Mississippi, secession of, 234

Mississippi river system, 90, 93, 94
Mitchell, Charles, 442
Mitchell, Wesley, 449–50, 246n
mobility:
    to cities, 357–60
    conflict with Indians, 82–83
    Depression, 448
    freedmen, 254, 258–59
    geographic, 78–90, 203–9, 226–29, 297–99
    occupational, 371, 382
    slave, 212, 237
    social, 342–44, 370–73, 509–11
    see also immigrants and immigration
monetary policy, 446–48, 460–61
    responsiveness in, 476
money monopoly, 304–5, 408–9
money supply:
    in Great Depression, 446, 459–61
    state banks and, 118
monopolies, see trusts and monopolies
Monroe, James, 94
Montaigne, Pierre Eyquem de, 12
Montgomery, Benjamin, 254
Montgomery Ward, 317
Moore, Judge, 313–14
Morgan, Edmund S., 31n, 32n
Morgan, J. P., 312, 314, 358, 406, 408–9, 414
Morison, Samuel Eliot, 39n, 40n
Morris, Cynthia, 65
Morris, Richard, 32n, 42n, 53n
Morris, Robert, 77
Morse, Chandler, 418
Morse, Jedediah, 202–3
multinational corporations, 406
Myrdal, Gunnar, 208

Napoleonic Wars, 125
Nation, 406
National Bureau of Economic Research, 395
National Conservation Commission, 414
National Defense Advisory Commission, 469
National Labor Relations (Wagner) Act (1935), 462n, 479
National Labor Relations Board (NLRB), 479–80
national park system, 428–29
National Recovery Administration (NRA), 453–56, 462, 479
    codes of, 454–56
    failure of, 456
National Road, The, 104
natural gas, 512–13
    home heating with, 424–25
    waste of, 410
    waste reduction for, 415–16
Navy, U.S., 143
Nebraska, banking regulation in, 121
Nelson, Ralph, 312
Netherlands, American exports to, 33, 45
Nettels, Curtis, 33n, 48n, 75n, 76n, 77, 97n
Nevins, Allan, 169n, 327n
New Deal, 36n, 320, 453–63, 478–79, 485
    constitutionality of, 462
    investment and, 461–62
    labor and, 478–79
    reflation in, 453–58

New Deal (*continued*)
  relief from, 463
  vagueness of, 461
  see also specific programs
New England, tariffs and, 153–55
Newhall, Nancy, 410
New Haven Railroad, 409
New Jersey, crown lands sought by, 75
New Orleans, 93–94
New York, 49
  Erie Canal and, 104–5, 108
  land values in, 78
  railroad rates in, 288–89
  Standard Oil and, 332
New York, N.Y., 105–6
  natural harbor at, 199
New York Central Railroad, 284–86, 288–89, 291
Norris-LaGuardia Act (1932), 479
North, Douglass, 36*n*, 60*n*, 63, 200*n*, 316
North American Land Company, 77
North Carolina, 31, 239
North Central states:
  agricultural technology in, 299
  growth of, 203
  land use in, 269–70
  railroad construction in, 278
  wheat farms in, 203
Northeastern states, 84
  farming in, 202–3
  growth of, 202–3
  slavery and, 200–201
Northern states:
  post-Civil War production in, 246–47
  shipping industry and, 199–200
  South conflicts with, 233
  tariffs and, 144
  transport and, 117, 119–20
  see also Civil War

Occupational Safety and Health Administration (OSHA), 517–20, 525–26
O'Fallon, James, 19
Office of Price Administration (OPA), 468–69
Office of War Mobilization and Reconversion, 470
Oglethorpe, General, 31
oil industry, 322–36
  cartels and, 325–29
  coal oils and, 322–23
  competitive surge in, 324
  crude oil prices in, 324–28, 331, 419–20
  depreciation in, 330
  drilling costs and, 325, 328
  electricity and, 335
  geological conditions and, 324–25
  investment in, 330
  kerosene in, 323
  OPEC and, 413, 512–13
  product development in, 332
  railroads and, 325–26
  slant drilling in, 324
  small entrepreneurs in, 328
  "Treaty of Titusville" in, 327
  waste in, 410–11
  whale oil and, 322–23
  see also Standard Oil Trust

Okun, Arthur, 477, 485*n*
oligopolies, 315
Organization of Petroleum Exporting Countries (OPEC), 413, 512–13
Oswalt, Wendell, 7*n*, 20*n*
Otken, Charles, 263

Pacific region, agricultural technology in, 299
Paine, Tom, 404
Panama Canal, 404
Parker, William, 22, 28*n*, 69*n*, 208, 264*n*, 273, 280*n*, 298
Peckham, Howard, 41*n*, 48*n*
Peek, George, 456–57
Penn, William, 82
Pennsylvania, 19, 31
  canals and railroads built by, 106–9
  oil industry in, 322–27, 330
  tariff of, 142–43
Pennsylvania Railroad, 104
Pennsylvania Society for the Encouragement of American Manufacturing, 142
Perkins, D. W., 23
Pessen, Edward, 71*n*, 72*n*, 496*n*
petroleum:
  imports of, 512–14
  see also oil industry
Petroleum Producers Union, 325–27
Philadelphia, Pa., 104, 142
Phillips, Wendell, 238
Pilgrims, 31
Pinchot, Gifford, 411
pirates and piracy, 37
  from Algiers and Morocco, 51–52, 142
planned economies, 392–93
  consumer choice limited in, 390–93
plumbing, household, 67
Plymouth plantation, 13
Polk, James K., 158
pollution, 421–29, 513–18
  air, 422–26, 426, 513–18
  chemical technology and, 515
  health and, 515–18
  water, 421–22, 517
population density, 27–28, 195–96
  fertility rates and, 194
population growth, 191–97
  colonial, 44
  construction industry and, 393–94
  European emigration and, 10–11
  family size and, 191–93
  fertility rate and, 191–92
  industrialization and, 195–96
  life expectancy and, 193–94
  population density and, 194
  productivity and, 196–97
  social structure and, 197
  variability of, 393
  for whites vs. nonwhites, 196
  working women and, 195
populism, 282
pork:
  immigration and, 338–39
  price guarantees for, 456
  surplus of, 457–58

Portugal, 8–9, 25
potatoes, land required for, 14
poverty, 507–11, 524
  immigrants and, 509
  inheritance of, 510
  occupational mobility and, 510
  permanent, 508–11
  of racial and ethnic groups, 509–11
  War on, 507–8
Preemption Acts, 81, 83
Price, Jacob, 36n, 38n
price controls, 41–42
prices:
  in Civil War, 246
  conservation and, 412–15, 419–20
  of minerals and extractive resources, 418
  in New Deal, 453–58
  for nonrenewable resources, 419–20
  in post-World War II transition, 471–72
  regional differences in, 205
  tariffs and, 148–50
  unions and, 475
  World War II and, 467–69
Proclamation Line of 1764, 40, 74
productivity, 60–63, 434–35, 441
  decline in, 505–6
  economic cycles and, 397–99
  income resulting from, 489–90
  innovation and, 61–63
  labor market and, 434
  mass production and, 434
  in 1920s, 432–35
  NRA and, 454–56
  population growth and, 196–97
  sources of, 506–7
  trucks and, 433
  World War II and, 466–67
progressive era, 405–9
Prohibition Administration, 431
protectionism, see tariffs
Protestants, Quebec Act and, 40
public domain, 74–84
  credit terms for, 80–81
  crown lands and, 75–76
  Indians and, 82–83
  land offices for, 77
  Louisiana Purchase and, 76, 203
  minimum purchase of, 79
  new states created from, 83–84
  price for, 78–80
  Proclamation Line and, 40, 74
  settlement of, 79, 81–83
  speculators and, 77, 80–81
  squatters, 81–83
public works programs, 449–50, 463, 473
publishers, 39
Pujo, Arsene, 408–9
Pullman, George, 358

Quakers, 31
Quebec Act (1774), 40

railroads, 64, 98, 268, 277–96
  agriculture and, 270–71, 275–76, 303–4
  alternatives to, 278

canals vs., 107–12
capital mobility and, 283–84
cartels for, 285–88, 292, 325–26
cities and, 360
competition among, 282–85, 287–93, 325
competition resulting from, 281–82, 290
cost of, 102, 290
in CSA, 245
decline of, 295–96
early, 101
economic advantage from, 280–81
financing of, 112–13, 279
foreign investment in, 278–79
free passes from, 292–93
GNP and, 281
Granger Laws and, 303
ICC and, 282, 287–88, 293–96, 315, 357
land settlement encouraged by, 270–71
land value and, 93, 270–71, 274
loans from, 270, 275
locations of, 283
locomotive power increased on, 282
long vs. short hauls on, 288–91, 293
marginal costs in, 290
military needs and, 277
monetary motive behind, 277, 283
national income and, 111–12
oil industry and, 325–26
postwar expansion of, 277–96
profits of, 282–85, 292, 294
rebates from, 291–92, 294, 329
resistance to, 172, 175
safety of, 283, 519–20
shipping costs on, 278, 280, 282–94, 303–4, 360
speed of, 109–11
stability of rates on, 284–88, 294–95
steel rails and, 282
technological advances in, 282–83
transcontinental, 277–78
trucking vs., 295–96
wheat exports and, 112
wood to coal conversion of, 416
Randolph, John, tariffs and, 139, 145–46, 148
Ransom, Roger, 35, 64n, 109n, 245n, 250n, 251,
    253n, 254n, 255n, 260, 262–67, 275n
recessions and depressions:
  migration and, 88–89
  in post-World War II era, 474–75
  see also crashes and crises, financial; Depression,
    Great
Reconstruction period, 249–67
  criminality in, 258
  incomes in, 260
  interstate competition for labor in, 258–59
  land rents in, 252–53
  merchant "monopolies" in, 262–67
Reed, C. A., 21–22
Rees, Albert, 381
Reese, Jacob, 348
reflation, New Deal, 453–58
Refiners Association, 327, 329
regional growth, 198–209, 226–29
  immigrants in, 209
  natural resources and, 198–99
  in real income, 208–9

regional growth (*continued*)
  reasons for, 199–200
  specialization in, 207
  see also specific regions
Reid, Daniel, 311
Reid, Joseph, 256
religion, as motive for European expansion, 9
Report on Roads and Canals (Gallatin), 103–4
resources, natural, 198–99
  animal species as, 427–28
  buyers of, 416–20
  nonrenewable, price for, 419–20
  one-of-a-kind, 426–29
  owners of, 412–16
  publicly owned, 420–30
  regional growth and, 198–99
  scarcity rents for, 413–15
  withholding of, 412–15
  see also conservation
Revere, Paul, 150
Revolt of the Masses (Ortega y Gasset), 197
Revolution, American, 21, 39–47
  economic burden of, 40–43
  economic consequences of, 44–47
  food supplies in, 41
  inflation during, 41–42
  Loyalists in, 45
  price controls during, 41–42
  property confiscated during, 46–47
  reasons for, 39–40
  shortages during, 41–42
  slaves and, 47
  soldiers' pay in, 43, 49–51, 54–56
Rhode Island, 49
  tariffs and, 143, 144
rice, 34–36, 201–2
  commissions paid on, 35
  regional differences in, 206
Rice, Samuel, 119
Richardson, Boyce, 23
Rillieux, Norbert, 132
Robinson, Joan, 505
Robinson, Solon, 87
Robinson-Patman Act, 320
Rockefeller, John D., 325–32, 335, 358, 407
Rogers, Edward, 23
Romans, 17
Roosevelt, Franklin D., 447, 453, 456–57, 462, 483
Roosevelt, Theodore, 320, 404, 414
Ross, John, 124
Rumford, Benjamin Count of, 22
Rush, Benjamin, 15
Russia, 33, 179–80, 196, 339, 390–91, 426

salt, 131–32
Samuelson, Paul, 441*n*, 446*n*
savings:
  lost, in Great Depression, 447, 451, 465
  rates for, 72–73
Schumpeter, Joseph, 62, 136, 139–40, 393, 397, 433, 461
Schwartz, Anna, 460*n*, 461*n*, 469*n*
Scotland:
  eighteenth-century, 25–26
  factors in, 36, 38

Sears, John, 172
Sears Roebuck, 317
Secretan group, 414
Securities and Exchange Act, 445
Securities and Exchange Commission (SEC), 484–85
Seddon, James, 239
Seneca, Lucius Annaeus, 359
sewing machines, 368
Seymour, Horatio, 338
Shannon, Fred, 88*n*, 89, 272
sharecroppers, 255–67
  borrowing by, 262–63, 266–67
  crops of, 262, 264–65, 267
  farming risks and, 257
  hired labor vs., 257
  history of, 256
  incomes of, 258–59
  landlords of, 256–67
  merchant monopolies and, 261–67
  reasons for, 256–57
  rents and, 262, 264–66
  self-sufficiency of, 262, 264
  shares given by, 256
Shaw, George Bernard, 124
Shays Rebellion, 52
sheep, 166
Shepherd, Boss, 362
Shepherd, James, 32*n*, 35*n*, 36–37, 38*n*, 45*n*
Sherman, William, 250–51
Sherman Act, 313
shipbuilding industry, tariffs and, 153–54, 158–59
shipping, 28, 349
  costs for, 36–38
  idle time in port and, 38
  in Mediterranean, 51–52
  northeastern ports favored by, 199–200
  piracy and, 37, 51–52, 142
  steam vs. sailing vessels in, 280, 345–46
  tariffs and, 142, 154–55
  time element in, 346–47
Shreve, Henry, 91
Shumacher, Max, 24
Sibley, John, 198
Simms, William Gilmore, 196
Singapore, 61–62
Singer, Isaac, 368
Slater, Samuel 174
slaves and slavery, 31–32, 47, 118, 201, 210–25, 245, 247–48
  alternative investments vs., 216–17, 220–21
  American exports and, 32
  arguments over, 211–13
  in the Caribbean, 201
  in Constitution, 211
  costs of keeping, 217–18
  cotton yield and, 63, 167–68, 170, 176–77
  deaths in transit of, 182–83
  free labor vs., 220
  hiring out of, 215–16
  immigration and, 185
  importation ended for, 211–12
  of Indians, 210
  as an investment, 213–18, 220–21, 237
  labor efficiency of, 218–20, 224–25
  as a market, 101

"Marxist" view of, 217–18
Northeast and, 200–201
population growth of, 196
potential rebellion of, 237–38
prices for, 218–20
profitability of, 213–18
profits on labor of, 218
Revolution and, 47
sales of, interest rates on, 214–15
seigneurial returns from, 214
Southern secession and, 234–38
subsistence cost of, 217–23
see also freedmen
Smith, Adam, 337
Smith, Alfred G., 84n, 200n
Smith, "Uncle Billy," 323
Snyder, Carl, 163
Social Security system, 459, 478, 484, 498
Society for the Encouragement of Faithful Domestic
    Servants, 189
Soltow, Lee, 73
South, 200–202
    agriculture technology in, 299, 301
    Caribbean and, 201
    colonial debt of, 36
    crops exported by, 63, 201–2, 458
    Great Britain and, 63, 201
    growth of, 200–202
    immigration and, 185 86, 227–28, 340
    Indian conflicts in, 235
    investment in, 117–19, 213–18, 220–21, 237
    North conflicts with, 233
    post-Revolutionary exports of, 45
    postwar land use in, 269–70
    secession of, see Southern secession
    servile rebellion feared in, 237–38
    tariffs and, 144–47, 153–54
    transport lacking in, 101–2
    see also Civil War; Reconstruction period
South Carolina, 19
    Reconstruction spending in, 252
    secession of (1833), 84, 144, 153, 202
    secession of (1860), 233
    tariffs and, 144–45
Southern secession, 84, 233–38
    belligerence and, 235–36
    local loyalty and, 236
    slavery and, 234–38
    see also Civil War; Confederate States of America
Southern Steamship and Railway Associations, 285–
    86
South Improvement Company, 325–26
Soviet Union, 426
    consumers in, 390–91
    see also Russia
Spain, 8–9, 12, 21
    Mississippi River controlled by, 51, 93–94
stagnation, economic, 494–95
Stamp Act, 39
standard of living, 192–93
Standard Oil Trust, 291, 315, 325, 327–36
    assets and earnings of, 333–34
    competition of, 329–30, 334–35
    consumers and, 333–34
    costs and charges of, 333–34

efficiency of, 331–32
    mass production and marketing by, 331–34
    New York headquarters of, 332
    profit sources of, 329
    refining and distributing as focus of, 328
    technological advances and, 331–32
staple theory of economic growth, 63–64
states:
    debt of, 117
    debt certificates bought by, 54
    investment by, 117–20
    Loyalist land confiscated by, 46–47, 75
    public domain settlement and, 83–84
    public land sold by, 78
    tariffs of, 142–43
    see also specific states and regions
states' rights, 229
steamboats, 101–2, 172–73, 175, 280, 345–46
steel industry, 136
    domestic market for, 130–31
    ore conservation by, 417
steel trusts, 312–13
Stephens, Alexander, 235, 238
Stewart, Donald Ogden, 443
Stigler, George, 311–12, 313n, 314, 315n
Stillman, James, 408
stock market, 432, 440–45
    call rate in, 444–45
    margin buying in, 445
    regulation of, 484–85
Story, Joseph, 53
stoves, 71
Strickland, William, 107
strikes, 282, 379, 384
Suffolk Resolves, 40
sugar, 201 2, 418
Sumner, William Graham, 298
Supreme Court, 314–15, 332, 335, 370, 456, 462,
    519
Sutch, Richard, 225n, 245n, 250n, 251, 252n, 253n,
    254n, 255n, 260, 262 67, 275n
Swanton, John R., 22
Switzerland, eighteenth-century life in, 26
Symmes, John, 77

Taft, Bezaleel, 136
Taiwan, 61–63
Talleyrand-Perigord, Charles M. de, 124
Tarbell, Ida, 312
tariffs, 139–61
    agriculture and, 140–41, 145–47, 149–50
    as artificial ocean, 140–41
    consumer interests and, 148–50
    costs of, 153–55
    defense and, 143
    effective vs. nominal rates of, 150–52, 158–61
    effects of, 139–40
    on exports, 49
    incomes and, 148, 157–58
    industries aided by, 140–41, 143–44, 147–50, 155–
        56, 158
    iron industry and, 147–50, 158
    manufacturing interests and, 140–41, 147–48
    monopolies from, 155–56
    nationalism and, 143–44

tariffs (*continued*)
  ocean freight rates and, 149–51, 156
  potential interests and, 143–44
  prices and, 148–50
  on raw cotton, 145–47, 152–54, 158, 160
  raw materials vs. manufactured products, 150–52
  regional interests and, 144–45
  as revenue source, 140
  shipbuilding industry and, 153–54, 158–59
  shipping interests and, 142, 154–55
  South and, 144–47, 153–54
  for specific products, 141
  state, 142–43
  technology and, 147–50
taxes and taxation, 182
  in Great Depression, 458–59
  immigration and, 182
  property, 499–500
  war expenditures and, 474
  see also income tax
Taylor, Frederick, 348
Taylor, George R., 154*n*, 158*n*
Taylor, John, 124
technology, 12, 156, 162–77, 345–56, 393
  acceptance of, 170–73
  agriculture and, 165–68, 298–300
  direct application of, 348–49
  emotional reactions to, 172
  empiricism and, 164–65, 347
  financial interests and, 172–73
  foreign expertise and, 173–74
  imitation in, 173–74
  inventors and, 347–48
  investment and, 346, 349–51
  market expansion and, 346
  new production methods resulting from, 165–70, 348–49
  new products resulting from, 349
  obsolescence and, 172, 345–46, 372–73
  products improved by, 165–67
  profitability expected from, 351–53
  rate of development of, 346–48
  rental vs. sale of, 173
  resistance to, 351–54
  science and, 163–64
  tariffs and, 147–50
Temin, Peter, 244, 461*n*
Texas, 20, 226, 244
textiles:
  British competition for, 126–29
  factories established for, 126–30
  home vs. factory production of, 132–35
  investment in, 115
  tariffs and, 147–50, 157, 160–61
Thomas, Robert, 33–35
Timber and Stone Act (1878), 273
Titusville, Treaty of, 327
tobacco, 34–38
  costs and commissions, 35–37
  health and, 520–21
  packing improved for, 37–38
  regional production, 206
  rising consumption of, 491–93
Tobin, James, 460, 505*n*
Tocqueville, Alexis de, 17, 72, 345

Toombs, Robert, 148–49, 213, 236–37
trade, *see* exports; imports; tariffs
transport, 28, 90–113, 118, 134
  commercial reasons for, 92–93
  consumer benefits from, 100
  economic value of, 98–100
  farmers and, 93, 270–71, 275–76, 303–4
  federal spending on, 94–97, 104, 106–7
  improvements opposed for, 100
  land value and, 93
  local public investment in, 104–9
  migration and, 90
  military interest, 91, 92
  national plan for, 94–97, 103–4
  political (nationalistic) motive behind, 93–94
  political order as aid to, 102–3
  potential traffic for, 101
  private investment in, 97–98, 100–102, 111–13
  in South, 101–2
  state investment in, 117, 119–20
  technological competition in, 100
Treasury Department, 116–17, 471
trout, conservation and, 421
trucking, 295–96, 433
True American Society, 78–79
trusts and monopolies, 310–16
  capitalization of, 314–15
  cheating in, 313
  consumers and, 315–16
  economy and, 316
  efficiency advances of, 315
  investors in, 312, 314
  labor and, 316
  manufacturing as focus of, 316
  organization of, 313–14
  payoffs for organization of, 313–14
  profitability of, 312–13
  after Sherman Act, 313
  stock speculation as motive for, 312
  from tariffs, 155–56
  watered stock of, 314
  see also cartels; Standard Oil Trust
Tucker, Josiah, 181
Turner, Frederick Jackson, 88
turnpikes, 97–98, 101
Twain, Mark, 318–19, 441
Tweed, Boss, 362
twenties, the (1920s), 431–43
  agriculture in, 438–40
  underconsumption in, 431–32
  credit in, 432, 436–38
  household facilities and durables in, 432–33
  land values in, 438–39
  mass market in, 432, 434–38
  productivity in, 432–35
  unemployment in, 431–33
  worker income in, 431–32
Tyler, John, 226

Ulman, Lloyd, 377*n*, 383
unemployment:
  economic cycles and, 397–99, 495–97
  government policy and, 503
  in Great Depression, 448–50, 463–65
  after Korean War, 473

in 1920s, 431–33
supplemental benefits for, 479
unemployment insurance, 473, 478
Union Pacific Railroad, 107, 278
unions, labor, *see* labor union movement
United Auto Workers, 479
United Nations, 496
urban, *see* cities
U.S. Steel, 312–14, 475–76

Valavanis-Vail, Stephen, 389
Valery, Paul, 7, 423
Vanderbilt, Cornelius, 293
Vanderbilt, William, 356, 406
Vandergrift, Jacob, 329
Varga, Eugene, 405n, 470n, 496n
Veblen, Thorstein, 311
Victoria, queen of England, 11
Vietnam war, 41
Viner, Jacob, 98
Virginia, 19, 234
    British debts rejected by, 51
    Cohabitation Act of, 30
    colonial debts in, 36
    crown lands and, 75–76
    secession of (1861), 233, 235–36
    slavery in, 32
Volney, C. F., 13, 17

wage drift, 467–68
wages, 350, 378–81, 387
    in Great Depression, 448–51
    immigration and, 188–89, 341, 381
    labor mobility and, 377, 379–81
    labor productivity and, 377–79
    NRA and, 454–56
    piece rates and percentages, 376–77
    in post-World War II transition, 472
    regional differences in, 205, 208–9
    union vs. nonunion, 480
    Western migration and, 84, 87–89
    World War II and, 467–68
Wallace, Henry, 457
Walsh, Margaret, 277
Walton, Gary, 32n, 35n, 36–37, 38n, 45n
Warburg, Paul, 441–42
War Department, 143
War Labor Board (WLB), 467–68
War Manpower Commission, 467
War of 1812, 116, 126–29, 142, 143, 146
War on Poverty, 507–8
War Shipping Board, 434
Washington, George, 45, 49–50, 82–83, 93, 104–5
water:
    conservation and, 420–22
    pollution of, 421–22, 517
Watson, Elkanah, 23, 104–5
Watson, P. H., 325–26
wealth, distribution of, 71–73
    post-Revolutionary, 45–47
wealth, symbolic capital as, 406
Webster, Daniel, 117
    on tariffs, 153–54, 158
Weed, Thurlow, 117
Wellington, Duke of, 26–27, 87

West, 268
    agriculture in, 205
    beaver and, 203
    Civil War and, 268
    gold discovered in, 203–4, 227
    growth of, 203–4
    railroad construction in, 278
    soil fertility of, 204
Western Exchange Fire and Marine Insurance Company, 121
West Indies, 45
West North Carolina railroad, 93
West Virginia, 240
whale oil, 322–23
whales, 420–21, 427–28
wheat, 115, 165, 203–4
    immigration and, 338–39
    price guaranteed for, 438, 456
    railroads and, 112
    regional differences in, 205–7
    yield, average per acre, 275
White, K. D., 23
Whitefield, George, 31
Whitehead, Alfred North, 233
Whitney, Eli, 168–69, 173
Whitney, Richard, 442
Wicksell, Knut, 331
Wiener, Jonathan, 256n, 258n
William II, kaiser of Germany, 311
Williamson, Harold, 325n, 327n, 329n
Wilson, James, 42
Wilson, Woodrow, 408, 438
Wise, Henry, 228
women:
    black, 369
    black, percentage working, 249
    "deserted," 508
    fertility rates for, 191–95
    in labor force, 195, 249, 367–69, 489–90
Woodbury, Levi, 157
Woolf, Virginia, 178
Woolworth stores, 317
workday, 68–69, 383
workers, *see* labor force
Working Men's Party, 385
workmen's compensation, 520
World War I, 407
World War II, 41, 466–69
    draft and, 466
    prices in, 467–69
    recovery aid after, 523
    transition after, 470–76
    wages in, 467–68
Woytinsky, Vladimir, 470
Wright, Gavin, 255, 257n, 306

Yasuba, Yasukichi, 194, 217
Yeats, W. B., 162
Young, Roy, 441

Zelnik, Marvin, 191n, 195n